THE METROPOLITAN OPERA® BOOK
OF MOZART OPERAS

THE METROPOLITAN OPERA® BOOK OF *M*OZART OPERAS

Translations by JUDYTH SCHAUBHUT SMITH
DAVID STIVENDER
SUSAN WEBB

Executive Editor PAUL GRUBER

THE METROPOLITAN OPERA GUILD

HarperCollins*Publishers*

Library of Congress Cataloging-in-Publication Data

Mozart, Wolfgang Amadeus, 1756–1791.
   [Operas. Librettos. Polyglot. Selections]
   The Metropolitan Opera book of Mozart operas / the Metropolitan Opera.
     p. cm.
   Librettos in Italian or German with English translations and commentary.
   Contents: Introduction—Idomeneo—The abduction from the
seraglio—The marriage of Figaro—Don Giovanni—Così fan tutte
—La clemenza di Tito—The magic flute.
   ISBN 0-06-271519-4—ISBN 0-06-273051-7 (pbk.)
   1. Operas—Librettos. 2. Mozart, Wolfgang Amadeus, 1756–1791.
Operas. 3. Opera—18th century. I. Metropolitan Opera (New York,
N.Y.) II. Title. III. Title: Book of Mozart operas.
ML 49.M83M42   1991
782.1'026'8–dc20   91-55003

In memory of David Stivender

CONTENTS

INTRODUCTION

A century ago, at the centennial of Mozart's death, a collection of librettos for the Mozart operas in the Metropolitan Opera's repertory would have included just one: *Don Giovanni*. By the bicentennial of his birth, in 1956, *Le Nozze di Figaro* and *Die Zauberflöte* had become firm fixtures on the company's bills, a successful production had recently restored *Così Fan Tutte* to public attention, and a decade earlier there had even been four performances of *Die Entführung aus dem Serail*. Today, after thirty-five more years (corresponding to the composer's too-brief lifespan), that canon has grown to seven operas, encompassing Mozart's first undoubted masterwork for the theater, *Idomeneo*, and his final *opera seria, La Clemenza di Tito*.

This expanding appreciation reflects many influences—among them, changes in musical taste, a broadening of cultural sympathies to include different theatrical styles, the power of recordings to disseminate unfamiliar music, and, not least, the pioneering work of scholars and interpreters. And with the rediscovery of each opera, we have been further amazed by the incredible versatility of Mozart's genius, for each is *sui generis*, uniquely itself. Most recently, after learning to appreciate the prodigality and grandeur of *Idomeneo*, we encountered *La Clemenza di Tito*, which achieves comparable power and density of expression with an extraordinary economy of means.

How varied, too, are the sources of these seven operas—and their librettists, whose work, rather than Mozart's, actually makes up this book. Three are by Lorenzo da Ponte, one of the genius theatrical artificers of all time, a Venetian Jew who took Catholic orders and whose picaresque life ended in New York City. Whether working from a contemporary French comedy (*Figaro*), an earlier libretto drawing on one of Western European culture's most enduring archetypal figures (*Don Giovanni*), or a modern transformation of a classical theme (*Così*), da Ponte produced characters and situations that stimulated Mozart's inventiveness beyond all others. Abbé Giambattista Varesco, who drew *Idomeneo* from a 1712 French libretto, was a chaplain in Mozart's native Salzburg, while Caterino Mazzolà, who condensed *Clemenza* from a classic libretto by Pietro Metastasio, the dominant literary figure of eighteenth-century Italian opera, was court poet in Dresden and a friend of da Ponte. Alongside these Italians ensconced in the culture of Germany and Austria, we also find two German actor-playwrights, Gottlob Stephanie and Emanuel Schikaneder, whose respective texts for *Entführung* and *Zauberflöte* also derive from earlier works.

These considerations may suggest how welcome this collection of librettos is, including fresh, accurate translations and authoritative historical introductions, for the seven Mozart operas now in the Met's repertory. Conceived for study and listening rather than for singing, these English versions are intended to convey as precisely as possible the meaning and nuances of the originals. Indeed, the late David Stivender, who translated the two *opera serie* (and began *Don Giovanni* before his untimely death), took the greatest pleasure in watching how those librettos, in their initial separate publications, enhanced the understanding of singers in the Met productions—and thus, also enhanced the impact of their performances—for they had worked from scores lacking any English, even a singing version. And how good, too, to have in one place these careful explications of the classical references, these full explorations of the background to the dramas.

If is, of course, a sadness to recognize that in this book we have the last of David's literary contributions to the Metropolitan Opera; fortunately, the wisdom, dedication, and sheer musicianship he gave to the company, and especially to the Met Chorus, live on in our memories and inform our music-making every day. But it is also a happy event that his translations and notes, along with the work of Susan Webb and Judyth Schaubhut Smith, should become part of a volume that all lovers of Mozart will find a constant object of reference and study in our quest for better understanding of these endlessly fascinating operas.

JAMES LEVINE

IDOMENEO

WORLD PREMIERE: *Munich, Hoftheater, January 29, 1781*

UNITED STATES PREMIERE: *Lenox, Mass., Tanglewood, August 4, 1947*

METROPOLITAN OPERA PREMIERE: *October 14, 1982*

IDOMENEO

Drama for Music in Three Acts

Libretto: Giambattista Varesco
(after Antoine Danchet)

English Translation and Notes: David Stivender

Music: Wolfgang Amadeus Mozart

In memoriam
Jean-Pierre Ponnelle
1932–1988

IDOMENEO

CHARACTERS

IDOMENEO (Idomeneus), *King of Crete*   Tenor

IDAMANTE (Idamantes), *his son*   Mezzo-soprano

ILIA, *Trojan princess, daughter of Priam*   Soprano

ELETTRA (Electra), *princess and daughter of Agamemnon,*
    King of Argos   Soprano

ARBACE (Arbaces), *confidant of the King*   Tenor

HIGH PRIEST OF NEPTUNE   Tenor

SILENT CHARACTERS AND CHORISTERS: *Priests, Trojan Prisoners,*
    Men and Women of Crete, Argive Sailors.

The action takes place in Cydonia, capital of Crete.

IDOMENEO

SYNOPSIS

Idomeneus, King of Crete, after the siege of Troy, has wandered a long way from his home, where his son, Idamantes, grown to man's estate during his absence, awaits him in filial love. Electra, daughter of Agamemnon, banished by the people of Argos on account of the matricide of Orestes, has taken refuge with Idamantes, and becomes deeply enamoured of him. But Ilia, daughter of Priam, who, with other Trojan captives, has been sent to Crete by Idomeneus, has conceived a passion for Idamantes, which he returns. At the opening of the opera Ilia is struggling with her love for the enemy of her fatherland. Idamantes approaches her joyfully. He has received tidings that his father's fleet is in sight, and has sent his old confidant, Arbaces, to bring more exact intelligence. On this joyful day he gives freedom to all the Trojan captives, and declares his love for Ilia, which she reluctantly rejects. The captive Trojans are led in and loosed from their fetters. Electra comes and expresses dissatisfaction at the liberation of so many enemies. Then follows Arbaces with news (which is mistaken) of the shipwreck of Idomeneus. Idamantes departs overwhelmed with grief. Electra remains behind and gives vent to her jealousy and despair. The scene changes to the seacoast, and the fleet of Idomeneus is seen threatened by a storm, and driven on to the rocks, the mariners lamenting and beseeching aid. Neptune appears and commands the winds to depart. Idomeneus prays for his help, but the god casts threatening glances on him, and disappears. The sea being calmed, Idomeneus lands and declares that, during the storm, he has vowed to sacrifice to Neptune the first person who shall meet him on shore. He trembles at the rashness of his vow, and anxiously looks for the sacrifice he is to make. Idamantes enters, having sought solitude as ease to his grief. He offers shelter to the stranger, whom he fails to recognize. In the course of conversation it transpires that he is mourning for his father Idomeneus. Whereupon Idomeneus makes himself known, but overcome by the horror of his situation, he departs, forbidding Idamantes to follow him. The latter, ignorant of the cause, is inconsolable at his father's rejection of his proferred love and services. The warriors of Idomeneus disembark, are welcomed by their wives and children, and express their joy in a chorus.

At the beginning of the second act Idomeneus is in conversation with Arbaces. He communicates to him his fearful vow, from the fulfillment of which he wishes to escape. Arbaces insists that this is impossible. But when he hears that Idamantes is to be the sacrifice, he counsels his being sent to a distant country, and that during his banishment they should seek to appease the wrath of Neptune. Idomeneus decides upon commanding Idamantes to accompany Electra to Argos, and there ascend the throne, and commissions Arbaces to bid him prepare for the journey. Arbaces promises obedience, and departs. Ilia now appears, expresses delight at Idomeneus' safety, and, while extolling Idamantes' goodness, declares her own gratitude and submission. Her warmth causes Idomeneus to suspect their love, and his grief and confusion are thereby augmented. Electra, entering, thanks him for his care. He leaves her alone, and she expresses her joy at the fulfillment of her dearest wishes. The warriors assemble in the harbor to the sound of a march. Electra appears with her followers, the sea is calm, and all look forward to a fortunate voyage. Idomeneus dismisses Idamantes, who sees in this command a fresh proof of his father's inexplicable displeasure. They express their opposing sentiments in a trio. As they prepare to embark, a terrific storm arises, and a huge sea-monster rises from the waves. This convinces Idomeneus that his disobedience has offended Neptune, and he determines to die himself, and not to sacrifice the innocent. The storm continues to rage and the Cretans fly.

Ilia opens the third act, bewailing her unhappy love. Idamantes surprises her, and declares his resolve to seek death in combat with the monster who is laying waste the land; this leads to a disclosure of her love, and the two express their happiness in a duet. Idomeneus, entering with Electra, discovers them; he cannot bring himself to acknowledge to Idamantes the true cause of his mysterious behaviour, but commands him anew to leave Crete at once, and seek asylum in a distant land. The various emotions of those present are expressed in a quartet. Idamantes having departed, Arbaces enters and announces that the people are hurrying with the High Priest at their head to demand deliverance from the monster; Idomeneus goes to meet them, and Arbaces expresses his earnest wish for the happiness of his ruler. On an open space in front of the royal palace the High Priest appears with the multitude; he describes the ravages of the monster, which can only be terminated by the fulfillment of Idomeneus' vow, and demands to know the name of the promised victim. When Idomeneus names his son as the sacrifice, horror seizes the people. During a march Idomeneus with his subjects enters the temple of Neptune, and while the priests prepare for the sacrifice they offer their solemn prayers to the god; cries of joy are heard from afar, and Arbaces hastens in and announces that Idamantes has slain the monster in heroic combat. Idamantes is presently borne in by priests and warriors, crowned and in white robes; he now knows his father's vow, and satisfied as to his feelings towards him, he is ready to fall a joyful sacrifice to the angry god. As Idomeneus is in the act of striking the fatal blow, Ilia hastens in and restrains him; she insists upon taking the place of her lover, and a tender strife arises between them, which Idomeneus listens to with emotion, Electra with rage and jealousy. As Ilia kneels before the altar, a great subterranean disturbance is heard, the statue of Neptune totters, the high priest stands entranced before the altar, all are amazed and motionless from fear, while a deep and majestic voice declares the will of the gods: Idomeneus is to renounce the throne, which Idamantes is to ascend and be united to Ilia. At this unexpected issue, Electra breaks into violent anger, and goes off raging; Idomeneus arranges everything according to the divine will and expresses his grateful joy; Idamantes is crowned while the chorus sing a joyful conclusion to the opera.

MOZART AND *IDOMENEO*

Idomeneo stands at the beginning of the seven great operas that Mozart was to compose in the last ten years of his life. It is an important composition on at least two counts: it is his first large-scale work for the theater, in terms of length, orchestration and scope; and it is a watershed in his musical output, looking both backward in order to use and refine all that was best in his earlier works and forward to introduce and adumbrate those qualities in musical drama that we now qualify as "Mozartean." Indeed, Vincent Novello on his 1829 Mozartean pilgrimage quotes Constanze, Mozart's widow, as saying "he was fond of *Don Giovanni, Figaro* and perhaps most of all *Idomeneo,* as he had some delightful associations with the time and circumstances under which it was composed." This statement is borne out in even the most casual reading of his letters between 8 November 1780, after he had just arrived in Munich for final work on the opera, and 18 January of the following year as he waited for his father and sister to arrive and witness the opera's premiere. These letters are not only full of the excitement of composing an important commission but of the day to day happiness of meeting new friends, reviving old friendships, and music-making. It was in Munich that he saw again his friend Christian Cannabich, leader of the famous Mannheim orchestra (since 1778 resident in Munich). Here also he saw his friends from the orchestra, Franz and Johann Wendling, husbands of the two singers Elizabeth and Dorothea who were to sing the roles of Electra and Ilia. Since he knew the two women's voices, it is probable that he brought to Munich some of their music already written. He made contact again with the eminent tenor Anton Raaf, whom he had first met in Mannheim in 1777, and who was to create the role of Idomeneo as a farewell to a long and illustrious career. Surrounded by these old friends who were to help him perform his new opera, it is no wonder that Mozart looked back in later years on these four months as one of the happiest periods of his life.

The commission to compose *Idomeneo* had come to Mozart in the autumn of 1780. His previous opera, *Il Rè pastore*, had been performed four years earlier and he was naturally excited about working in the theater again. The Abbate Varesco, since 1766 the Court Chaplain of Salzburg, was chosen as librettist because he could work closely there with Mozart on the text. The subject chosen, based on an old French libretto, *Idoménée*, by Antoine Danchet set to music in 1712 by Campra, was Idomeneus and his vow. Danchet's piece is a *tragédie lyrique,* consisting of the usual prologue with mythological deities and the remainder of the drama cast in five acts, the deities occasionally descending to aid or confound the principal actors; all this including a wealth of dancing and choral singing. Varesco was charged with turning it into a three act *dramma per musica* in the Metastasian mold, but a few of the French characteristics were retained, principally the use of the chorus. It is now known that Mozart collaborated with all his librettists on his mature operas and it is probable that his practice began with Varesco. It is certain that Mozart took the completed libretto with him when he went to Munich, but exactly how great a hand he had in fashioning the actual work before he left we will never know. Judging from his letters to his father after he arrived (the librettist remained in Salzburg) we can imagine that he made his views known to Varesco from the very beginning of their work together. Danchet's Acts I and II became Mozart's I; III became II; and IV and V Mozart's III. With the exception of the deities appearing in Danchet (Eolus, Venus, Neptune, Proteus and Nemesis), Varesco follows the French outline fairly closely, in many cases making straightforward translations of the French text into Italian.

There is, however, one important difference in the two libretti. In Danchet, Idomeneus has fallen in love with Ilia and it is this which leads to the tragic denouement. Idomeneus decides to renounce his throne in favor of Idamantes and Ilia, but Nemesis appears and strikes him mad. He kills Idamantes, thinking him to be a sacrifice, and when he returns to sanity and realizes what he has done, attempts to kill himself but is held back. At which point Ilia says, "Let him live as punishment:/It is for me only to die." No further stage directions are provided, but presumably Ilia kills herself. All this was discarded in the Italian version in favor of the *lieto fine* in the contemporary Metastasio tradition.

This has the advantage that Idomeneus can be preoccupied throughout the opera with the vow he has made—how it rebounds on him when the first person he meets is his own son, and how he reacts to his son's love for a Trojan slave, Ilia. Throughout the opera, Idomeneus is constantly excoriating the gods: it is seldom that he will utter a *Numi!* or *Nettuno!* without an accompanying *ingiusti, barbari* ("unjust," "barbarous") or *spietato* ("pitiless"). He is seen trying to rationalize the making of this vow in any way he can—in his great recitative (II/3) before *Fuor del mar* he says, thinking of his son, "You were too precipitate, Idamantes, in/Loosening those chains . . . here is the crime/For which Heaven punishes you." When he describes to Arbaces how the vow was made (II/1) he is very clear that it basically was not his fault: Neptune "extorted from me/A human sacrifice as a vow." He cannot even be honest with his son in the supreme moment of his son's willingness to die in fulfillment of the terrible oath: "Pardon: this cruel office/Is not chosen by me, it is a punishment by Fate" (III/9). The King achieves truly tragic status through this concentration on his rash vow and his attempts to avoid its consequences. It is left for his son, in fourteen splendid lines of poetry (III/9), to point out that Idomeneus is indeed fortunate in his dilemma: since he gave his son life it is only right that he take it away and return it to the gods in exchange for his own and the lives of his people. Once he has done this, "Then sacred and true is the love of the gods." From this point on, Idomeneus will no longer use pejorative adjectives in connection with the gods, instead cautiously condemning that great abstraction, Fate. The moment of truth and acceptance comes for the King in III/10 after the Voice of Neptune has spoken: Idomeneus can only murmur quietly, *Oh Ciel pietoso!* ("Oh merciful heaven!").

It is noteworthy that he is able to arrive at this acceptance through the understanding and charity of his son, whose own conflict is two-fold: love for his father and for Ilia. Because the first performer of this role, the castrato dal Prato, was a neophyte in both singing and acting, the commentators over the years have tended to feel that Idamantes' character is somewhat pale. But careful and extended study of both his text and music belies this concept. It has already been seen how he leads his father to an awareness of the basic justice of Heaven; this quality of leadership has grown through his having had to govern the people of Crete in his father's stead. Notice the ease with which he gives orders in the second and third scenes of Act I and how after Electra's public rebuke in the latter he is able to retain his poise. Only Arbaces' news of Idomeneus' supposed death unnerves him. His exchanges with Ilia and III/10 show the depth of maturity which he has attained since the beginning of the opera.

Ilia, the only other developing character in the drama, is Mozart's first great heroine to be drawn in the musical round (it is a common-place of Mozart criticism to call her a study for Pamina). Her conflict is simpler and at the same time deeper than the two men's: finding herself an exile in enemy land, she has fallen in love with the son of the murderer of her own people. She is very aware of being the daughter of Priam and Hecuba (although the ancient writers do not list her name among their children, nor even among the names of Priam's children by his concubines) and by her own words (II/2) witnessed the bloody death of her father, the destruction of Troy, and her deportation in chains to Crete as a slave. It is no wonder she resists her love for the son of an enthusiastic participant in all this (just how enthusiastic Idomeneus was in battle can be read in the *Iliad*). Ilia matures during Mozart's opera, primarily through the music, but not without some help from Danchet/Varesco. One of the prime wonders of this opera is to watch her growth from "When will my bitter misfortunes/Ever have an end?" to her placing her head on the sacrificial block with the wonderful words (not in Danchet by the way), "I wish to cross the ultimate ford alone./I am yours, sacred minister." Both Idomeneus and Arbaces offer to take Idamantes' place on the scaffold, but only Ilia actually places herself there.

The only other major character, Electra, remains outside the drama. She is very much occupied with herself and her concerns. It is remarkable that after her interview with the King in II/4 (when he tells her Idamantes will escort her back to Argos) nearly all of her words are addressed *to herself*. When Ilia in III/3 asks her for comfort, Electra can only bitterly spit out, "I comfort you? and how?" before returning to her eternal dialogue with herself, "the base girl/Insults me again." By the time she reaches her great recitative and aria at the end of Act III she is completely in her own world (and that of her brother Orestes) and oblivious to anyone around her. But she is Mozart's most passionate character: only the Queen of the Night can equal her in this respect, although Electra is far more fully developed both dramatically and musically. Her arias in I and III which deal with the Furies are somewhat similar in their agitated, heated manner, but one should be aware that only when she is mad, in the third act aria, does Mozart allow her coloratura, and that obviously characterizing demonic laughter. A significant phrase, however, in the oboes and bassoons (bar 47 of the first aria) quotes the exact notes of a portion of her coloratura in the third aria. Her second act aria is striking in being completely opposite in musical characterization to the other two: it is accompanied by strings only and its phrases seem to question and answer one another, almost as if Electra in her reverie is holding a dialogue with herself. Here her coloratura is reflective, pastoral. Tamiri's A major aria in the second act of *Il Rè pastore, Se tu di me fai dono,* has much the same quality.

Danchet has three confidants in his libretto: one each for Idomeneus (Arcas), Idamantes (Arbas) and Ilia (Dirce). Varesco wisely cuts these down to one, Arbaces, who is described as the "confidant of the King." Varesco has made him a typically Metastasian character with his self-abnegating nature carried to extremes: "The vassal has no merit/In fidelity: virtue is not a duty./Here my life, my blood . . . ," and Idomeneus cuts him off with the abrupt, "Only one piece of advice is necessary/For me now." The character of Arbaces is consistent throughout, and his kind of character is necessary in this kind of opera: it is he who brings the news of Idomeneus' supposed death and also of Idamantes' victory over the monster sent by Neptune. His two arias are in the traditional counsellor mode, but he is given one great piece of declamatory singing, the accompanied recitative *Sventurata Sidon* (III/5). The text for this was expanded at Mozart's request for the elderly singer Panzacchi whom Mozart considered "a good actor" and felt the new lines would have "a capital effect."

On a par in importance with the four main characters, there is one other: the people of Crete. Varesco gave them nine major choruses; of these, four are integrated into the action, bringing the people to life much in the manner of those in *Boris Godunov* and *Peter Grimes.* This kind of chorus was a part of the French tradition, and had been fostered by Gluck in his mature operas. Such Italian composers as Jommelli in Stuttgart and Traetta in Parma had also been experimenting with integrated choruses in their operas, but unfortunately Mozart never again had a chance to write for chorus on this scale for the theater.

Varesco's libretto for *Idomeneo* has been much maligned over the years, and it is not difficult to see why. His use of language tends to be verbose and obscure, and often a good bit of time and thought are necessary to figure out exactly how his sentences are constructed, let alone what they mean. Idomeneus' command to his son in II/7 to leave Crete (*Parti, e non dubbia fama*) is a good case in point. The actual sounds of his verse can sometimes be grating: *Il cor mi si divide* (III/3) with its string of "ee" sounds is hardly mellifluous. In his grammatical constructions he favors attaching the pronoun to the future and remote past tenses, coming up with *stillommi, sdegnossi,* and, ugliest of all, *squammosi.* A little of this kind of thing goes a long way, and if the listener notices the usage there is already too much of it.

Though it is easy to criticize these quirks, there are positive features of the libretto which should be remarked. Being a churchman, the Abbate is fond of Latinisms and they occur throughout. In the seventh line of the opera Ilia refers to the *vittime generose* and here Varesco does not use the adjective in the sense of "generous," but rather "high-born," the meaning of the Latin *generosus.* The same use of the word can also be found in Danchet's libretto where Idamantes, meeting Idomeneus on the beach, refers to him as *Généreux Inconnu.* This meaning of the word in Italian, however, was by no means unusual in the literature of the period. There are echoes of Latin literature throughout Varesco's libretto: Idomeneus' *aura vitale* (I/9) is an echo from the *Aeneid* (I/38), *auris vitalis carpis;* Ilia's apostrophe to her father and brothers (I/1), *voi foste* (lit., "you were," meaning "dead") surely echoes the celebrated words in the *Aeneid* (II/325), *fuimus Troes, fuit Ilium* ("we Trojans are not, Ilium is not"); and an echo of

Dido's *Non ignara mali miseris succurrere disco* ("Not ignorant of ill do I learn to befriend the unhappy," I/630) lingers in Idamantes' gentle, "Very well, my friend,/Was I taught by my own miseries/To be moved by the miseries of others" (I/10). Though this line has its antecedent in Danchet, its lineage is nonetheless noble.

Whether he did it by design or not, Varesco has certain words attached to certain characters; thus Electra uses *smania* (frenzy) each time she calls on the Furies, and Idamantes uses the word *colpa* (fault) enough times so that attention is called to it. A good touch of irony is provided when Idomeneus' *Eccoci salvi al fin* ("We are saved at last") at his safe arrival on shore after the shipwreck (I/9) is repeated back to him unconsciously by Arbaces (III/8) on delivering the news that Idamantes has slain the monster. Even more telling is the return of Idamantes' "tyrannous gods." In his first encounter with Ilia (I/2) she rebuffs his declaration of love, whereupon in an aria he declares, *Colpa è vostra, o Dei tiranni* ("The fault is yours, oh tyrannous gods"). Ilia makes no response to this until the end of Act III when in Scene 10 she rushes in to stay the knife with which Idomeneus is about to sacrifice his son. Her words are explicit: "Idamantes is innocent, he is your son./He is the hope of the kingdom./The gods are not tyrants; you are all/Fallacious interpreters/Of the divine will." Here it is possible to see the Christian spirit of the churchman Varesco, an overlay of sentiment that occurs neither in Danchet or, needless to say, the ancient sources. These echoes in the libretto are of enormous aid to the singer. Not only are they guides to interpretation, action and reaction, but they are also clues to the temperament of the character the singer is impersonating. Ilia's patience is understood by her being able to wait and not react immediately to Idamantes' "tyrannous gods," but she remembers all of his words and is resolute in turning them to his and her own advantage.

Electra's text is shaped with particular care. She never refers to Ilia by name, always using epithets: "Trojan slave," "cowardly slave," and "base girl." She refers to Idamantes by name only twice, although thoughts of him obsess her throughout the opera. Only once (II/4) does she refer to something else, and then briefly, when she mentions to the King how her "hope grows green . . ./To see the foolish pride/Of the rebels humbled" back in Argos where she thinks she is returning with Idamantes. Even more striking is the fact that in all three references to Ilia and Idamantes as a pair she eschews any mention of their names: she can bring herself only to use pronouns. Thus *Chi* (Idamantes) *mi rubò quel core,/Quel* (Ilia) *che tradito ha il mio* (I/6); *quel foco* (of Idamantes) and *quei lumi* (of Ilia) in II/5; and, most telling of all, when she imagines in her great Act III accompanied recitative being pointed at in the streets *dall'uno* (Idamantes) *e dall'altra* (Ilia). Though Varesco can under no circumstances be called a great dramatist or poet, he nonetheless shaped the text of his dramatic poem with as much care as his gifts allowed him to.

Varesco's general layout of the plan of the opera is also good: the two central themes, Idomeneus' vow (with its corollary of the father/son relationship) and the love between Ilia and Idamantes, are clear and always easy to follow. The earlier part of each act is roughly taken up with the young lovers, the later part with Idomeneus' tragedy. The actual construction of the opera is also well planned and in this instance is certainly due to Varesco.

The whole work begins with Ilia's question "When will my bitter misfortunes/Ever have an end?" We can watch various answers being propounded: when she is freed of her chains; when she has forgiven her conquerors; when she has declared and accepted her love for Idamantes; when she is willing to sacrifice herself not only for him but for his people. But it is only at the very end that the final answer, made up of all the foregoing, is given: when she has become Queen of Crete. Varesco is here thoroughly Metastasian: a ruler must know how to serve his subjects and even sacrifice himself for them.

We know that Mozart had been familiar with the story of Idomeneus since at least 1770, for we find him writing to his sister from Bologna on 8 September of that year: "I am this moment reading *Télémaque* and have already got to the second part" (in Book V Fénelon tells the story of Idomeneus and the sacrifice of his son). So the Court's choice of subject must have been not only gratifying but also familiar to Mozart when it was proposed to him. Its strong father/son theme has not been lost on commentators but it is easy to make too much of this. Nonetheless, one cannot read Mozart's letters to his father without wondering what he must have thought when he came to set a line such as Idamantes' "Now I understand that your confusion/Was not wrath but paternal love." One of the strongest themes running through the letters is parental authority and how both parties came to terms with it. It must have taken all Leopold's love and understanding over the years to deal with the fact that his son was daily superseding him as a musician. It cannot have been easy for him to keep a sense of balance between Wolfgang the musician and the Wolfgang who did things Leopold felt were not commensurate with his musical genius.

Mozart wrote *Idomeneo* between October 1780 and January 1781, an incredibly short period of four months. It is one of his richest scores, using a large orchestra including piccolo and four horns. The piccolo is used in only one number and the full complement of horns in only four, yet by their very presence they give an idea of the spaciousness of the opera's layout. Mozart was writing for the most famous orchestra in Europe, one he knew well. It was originally based in Mannheim but became merged with the Munich musical establishment in that city in August 1778, after Carl Theodor had become Elector on the death of his predecessor on 31 December 1777. It was Carl Theodor who commissioned *Idomeneo* for the 1780–1 carnival season in Munich.

The score that Mozart produced for this commission is one of the wonders of his inspiration. One can do no better than quote Alfred Einstein: "Thus we find in this score, which one never tires of studying, and which will always remain a source of delight to every true musician, a veritable explosion of musical invention—not only of musical, but of musico-dramatic as well." An explosion it is, but a highly controlled one, all the more miraculous to contemplate when one realizes the dress rehearsal took place on 27 January 1781, Mozart's 25th birthday. To achieve this control Mozart employs a number of motives to bind his score together. These are not *Leitmotiven* in the Wagnerian sense, neither are they reminiscence-motives, but rather small melodic cells that occur throughout the score and serve to hold it together. There are three that are most conspicuous, the first being asserted in the very first bars of the Overture: a rising arpeggio of four notes beginning with the root of the chord. Far from being "conventional signals of pomp" (William Mann), this arpeggio seems to be connected with the will of the gods, usually Neptune, and, by extension, Idomeneus' vow. It rings out pompously in Act III when the High Priest says "To the temple;" it sounds in the orchestra (the preceding scene has been conducted entirely in *secco* recitative) at Idomeneus' words, "Most pitiless gods!" as he recognizes whom he will have to sacrifice as a result of his vow; it is sung in a minor key when the people flee the monster at the end of Act II, "Let us run, let us flee/That pitiless monster." There are many more appearances of it. A second, more chromatic turn of phrase, based on the leading tones and notes themselves of a descending arpeggio, is first heard in the last seven bars of the Overture. It will be combined with the arpeggio figure in minor to form the accompaniment to the chorus of shipwrecked sailors in I/7, a brilliant stroke, and also when Idamantes first recognizes his father, "Oh what transport." The third is a descending figure, presented in the ninth and tenth bars of the Overture, which consists of a beginning longer note, a quick, nervous descent (usually in a triplet) and then several repeated notes at the end. This motive is played in many guises: Ilia even sings a slow version of it at the words *Ilia infelice* in her opening recitative. Its most poignant appearance occurs in III/6, at Idomeneus' words, "The victim is Idamantes," played four times and then combined with the second motive to describe the King's overwhelming despair at being forced to execute his own son. Though the two examples given of it are played in a slow tempo, the motive usually appears *allegro*—for example in the lovers' duet in III/2 at Ilia's surprised words, "You will be/My husband?" It must be emphasized that these motives (and there are others) are in no way part of a system elaborated by Mozart for this opera. It was probably something of an experiment since he never repeated it to this extent in his later works. But it is an intrinsic part of the musico-dramatic invention referred to by Einstein earlier.

An important facet of this score is the wealth of accompanied recitatives. There are approximately twenty of them, all of varying lengths, an incredible amount for an opera of this period. Gluck, in his famous Preface to *Alceste,* advocated the banishment of harpsichord-accompanied recitative (so-called *secco,* "dry") and in his mature operas used no *secco* whatsoever. But this usage could have a disadvantage: since it must of necessity move at a slower pace than the simple recitative, it gave a heavy and sometimes solemn tone when used throughout. Mozart, as is clear from his letters, wanted musical theater to move at a natural pace, hence his combination of *secco* and *accompagnato.* He uses the orchestra in a sort of dialogue with the voice in his *accompagnati,* now referring to something the singer has just expressed, then commenting afterwards, or merely sustaining a note under the declamation. These orchestrally accompanied recitatives are usually played by the strings alone, although he will add woodwinds or even brass for dramatically important moments, such as the *accompagnati* of the recognition scene (I/10) or the King's defiance of Neptune between the last two choruses of Act II. Sometimes the orchestra will make an actual quote from an aria. In Idomeneus' contemplative recitative following Ilia's *Se il padre perdei,* for example, the orchestra recalls three phases from her aria, two of them transformed melodically and harmonically, the third exactly as it was first heard. In Electra's *accompagnato* which follows

Idomeneus' *Fuor del mar,* the orchestra quotes a theme from her aria which will follow the recitative. Throughout these *accompagnati* little tone poems abound. One of the most beautiful occurs in Ilia's opening recitative at the words, *o dolce morte,* when the strings paint the most comforting picture possible (in only two bars) of "sweet death." But Mozart reserves his greatest music in these *accompagnati* for the extraordinary ninth and tenth scenes of Act III, as Idamantes, now knowing the terms of his father's vow prepares both himself and his father for his execution. The scene is in three musical sections: *accompagnato* (Idomeneus and Idamantes finally come to terms as father and son), *aria* (Idamantes does not fear to die), *accompagnato* (Ilia is ready to sacrifice herself). At the beginning of the first section the strings play a warm melody in A flat major; this will return, transformed into E minor, at Idamante's words, "Ah, hear a son favorably,/Who at the point of death entreats and advises." Surely another of those lines that makes the listener wonder what Mozart was thinking as he composed it. All of the orchestra's music throughout the two *accompagnati* mirrors with a heartbreaking fidelity what the characters say. The melodic material that flickers by and is gone in an instant would serve as material for a dozen operas by a minor composer of the period—Mozart spreads it all before the listener with breathtaking prodigality. It is true that Mozart himself cut Idamantes' aria, *No, la morte,* and that it is usually omitted in modern performances. This is a great pity, since it not only breaks up the long stretch of string sound in the two *accompagnati* (the aria adds oboes and horns), but allows the spectator to see a side of Idamantes that has hitherto gone unnoticed: tenderness unmixed with melancholy. And then, too, his picture of Elysium is one of Mozart's most moving little tone pictures.

In the original version, as written before the premiere took place, a long *accompagnato* and aria for Electra followed soon after (the voice of Neptune intervenes), but due to the great length of the third act, Mozart first composed a shorter version of the recitative, then cut both recitative and aria, substituting a third, shorter *accompagnato* for them both. Needless to say, the original version of the recitative is the more interesting and is often restored in modern performances along with the aria. The opera is crowned by Idomeneus' long *accompagnato* where he abdicates in favor of Idamantes. Varesco's verse here almost attains the level of true poetry. Even Daniel Heartz, the editor of *Idomeneo* for the New Mozart Edition, and no great admirer of the Abbate, is moved to remark, "This speech is one of the most felicitous in the poem . . . Varesco . . . is able to sustain an elevated tone to the final lines, where he no longer has Danchet to guide him." This is the most spacious of all Mozart *accompagnati,* drawn on a large scale as befits the conclusion of a large-scale work, and is designed to move at a stately, not to say kingly, pace. Listening to it is somewhat like listening to a Bruckner symphony: the listener must simply yield to it and any attempt to hurry it along destroys its purpose. It is introduced by a prelude of eight bars which is made up of a fantasia on the three motives that have gone through the opera, surely a conscious design on Mozart's part.

Mention has already been made of the important part the chorus plays in the opera. Fewer in number, but equally important, are the three ensembles: duet, trio and quartet. The latter is justly famous and one of the great reflective ensembles in all opera. We know from Mary Novello's conversation with Constanze in 1829 that Mozart himself was much attached to this piece: ". . . after their marriage they paid a visit to Salzburg and were singing the Quartet of *Andrò ramingo* when he was so overcome that he burst into tears and quitted the chamber and it was some time before she could console him." Before the premiere of the opera he wrote his father (27 December 1780) that he had told Raaf, ". . . so far there is nothing in my opera with which I am so pleased as with this quartet." An extraordinary feature of the ensemble is that Mozart seems to have changed it from a piece of continuous action into a moment of arrested time. Though Varesco did not do so, Mozart repeats Idamantes' first words *Andró ramingo e solo* ("I shall go wandering and alone") and the exact same notes to which they are set, after the *a quattro* at the end of the piece. Can it be that Mozart is implying the two occurrences are the same, and all that happens between is but an instant in the minds of the four characters? Since this quartet occurs at an important moment in the drama, it is naturally the longest of the three and has the most dramatic, expressive and musical weight. Whereas it is composed in a single large unit, in one tempo, the trio and duet are both written in two sections, two tempi. They are both shorter and have less sense of finality to them; after all, they precede more important matters, both dramatic and musical. Again, Mozart's uncanny sense of balance is felt throughout.

The premiere of the opera, on 29 January 1781, was presumably a success, "presumably" because the one newspaper account of it only mentioned the scenic designs. There were two repetitions, and the opera disappeared from the public stages during Mozart's lifetime. He wished to present it in Vienna, saying that he would like to rewrite the part of Idomeneus for a bass and that of Idamantes for a tenor, but the closest he came to this realization was a performance, "probably a concert one" (Stanley Sadie) with severely curtailed recitatives on 13 March 1786 in Prince Auersperg's private theater behind his palace. For this performance he rewrote Idamantes' music for tenor voice (but left Idomeneus a tenor, merely shortening the coloratura in *Fuor del mar*), added a concerted aria with violin and a new duet for Ilia and Idamantes, but he never saw it again in an opera house. It is only in recent years that the opera has been revived with any frequency. For years it was felt that the *opera seria* form (even in the hands of Mozart) was stiff and devoid of propulsive dramatic interest and that it could only be produced in a version by another musician. Several of these were performed, the most famous being one by Richard Strauss, which has all but sunk into oblivion. It is only Mozart's "version" that is performed today.

But which version to perform? Mozart wrote a great deal of music for *Idomeneo* which he either recomposed at various times or omitted from the 1781 and 1786 performances. The most conspicuous pieces he cut from the Munich premiere were the three final arias in Act III. He also made further curtailments in the *secco* recitatives, most notably omitting Idomeneus' narration of the details of his vow as he arrives safely on shore (I/9). For this abridgement Mozart composed a short *accompagnato* based on a continuo figure in the *secco*. Withholding the terms of his bargain with Neptune heightens the interest of his meeting with Idamantes (the audience supposedly doesn't know what Idamantes doesn't know) and increases the interest in his opening Act II *secco* with Arbaces when he reveals the particulars of the vow to his confidant. Two cuts which Mozart made for the premiere are now never made, nor could they be: only the first halves of the great chorus, *O voto tremendo,* and Idomeneus' prayer to Neptune, *Accogli, o Re del mar,* were performed. This was surely pushing Mozart's making "a virtue of necessity" (18 January 1781) too far. In modern performances each conductor, in conjunction with the stage director, must make a version that seems musically and dramatically right to him, based not only on his previous knowledge of the work in the theater, but, perhaps what is closest to Mozart's criteria, also on the individual capabilities of the singers in his cast. By allowing everyone to perform at his optimum ability, only then will Mozart's interests be served.

When he completed *Idomeneo,* Mozart did not return to Salzburg. His years of apprenticeship were over. He was summoned to Vienna by the Archbishop of Salzburg, from whose service Mozart soon released himself. He had only ten years of life left to him, which were to be the richest of all. Yet *Idomeneo,* the work that stands at the crossroads of Salzburg and Vienna, apprenticeship and maturity, was never forgotten or abandoned by its composer. It is only right that today's audiences should now begin to understand its true greatness.

DAVID STIVENDER

A NOTE ON THE TRANSLATION

I have tried to make this translation as literal as possible within rational bounds. As I have pointed out, Varesco's convoluted sentences are not always easy to decipher. Though I try to keep the Italian word order in the English translation, no matter how stiffly it might read, it would be mere pedantry to insist on it if the sense was obscured. Varesco peppers his text with innumerable exclamations (*O Ciel! O Numi!*, etc.) and I have tried to leave them in the middle of sentences when they occur there. For words like *tempesta* and *acquisto* I have usually used the obvious English equivalent. Indeed, for the latter I tried many substitutes for "acquisition" but was always left with the feeling that that word is exactly what Electra means, and she is not a character to be trifled with. The libretto used as a basis for this translation was the first, long one printed before the 1781 premiere and thus before the last minute cuts were made. I have included any words that Mozart ever set to music, omitting only those that he himself omitted in the *secchi*. The lineation is that of Varesco. I have been a fervent devotee, not to say worshipper, of *Idomeneo* since a vocal score became easily available in 1952. For all the years since I have been puzzling over Varesco's convolutions and now welcome the opportunity to put them into some kind of concrete realization. I owe a debt of gratitude to Fabrizio Melano for combing through the entire libretto, word by word, with me and helping me solve the remaining problems.

The solid black lines to the left of the text indicate cuts that Mozart made in the *secchi* and the Voce for the 1791 premiere. The broken lines indicate those *secco* cuts generally used at the Metropolitan Opera. A short glossary of names and terms is given following the translation. The synopsis is adapted from the 1882 English translation of Otto Jahn's *Life of Mozart*.

D.S.

IDOMENEO

ACT ONE

SCENE I

*Gallery in the Royal Palace, giving on
to several apartments reserved for Ilia.*

ILIA (*alone*)

Quando avran fine omai
L'aspre sventure mie? Ilia infelice!
Di tempesta crudel misero avanzo,
Del genitor, e de' germani priva
Del barbaro nemico
Misto col sangue il sangue
Vittime generose,
A qual sorte più rea
Ti riserbano i Numi? . . .
Pur vendicaste voi
Di Priamo, e di Troia i danni, e l'onte?

Perì la flotta Argiva, e Idomeneo
Pasto forse sarà d'orca vorace . . .

Ma, che mi giova, o Ciel! se al primo
    aspetto
Di quel prode Idamante,
Che all'onde mi rapì, l'odio deposi,

E pria fu schiavo il cor, che m'accorgessi

When will my bitter misfortunes
Ever have an end? Unhappy Ilia,
Wretched remnant of a cruel tempest,
Deprived of father and brothers,
High born victims—
Their blood mixed with the blood
Of the barbarous enemy—
For what harsher fate
Are the gods reserving you? . . .
Did you indeed avenge
The losses and shame of Priam and of
    Troy?
The Argive fleet perished, and Idomeneus
Will perhaps be the meal of a voracious
    sea-monster . . .
But what good does it do me, oh Heaven!
    if at the first sight
Of that valiant Idamantes,
Who snatched me from the waves, I laid
    aside my hate,
And my heart became a slave before I
    realized

21

D'essere prigioniera.

Ah qual contrasto, oh Dio! d'opposti affetti

Mi destate nel sen odio, ed amore!

Vendetta deggio a chi mi diè la vita,

Gratitudine a chi vita mi rende . . .

O Ilia! o genitor! o prence! o sorte!
O vita sventurata! o dolce morte!
Ma che? m'ama Idamante? . . . ah no; l'ingrato
Per Elettra sospira, e quella Elettra,
Meschina principessa, esule d'Argo,
D'Oreste alle sciagure a queste arene
Fuggitiva, raminga, è mia rivale.
Quanti mi siete intorno
Carnefici spietati? . . . orsù sbranate
Vendetta, gelosia, odio, ed amore,
Sbranate sì, quest'infelice core!

> Padre, germani, addio!
> Voi foste, io vi perdei.
> Grecia, cagion tu sei,
> E un Greco adorerò?
> D'ingrata al sangue mio
> So che la colpa avrei;
> Ma quel sembiante, oh Dei!
> Odiare ancor non so.

Ecco, Idamante, ahimè!
Se'n vien; misero core
Tu palpiti, e paventi.
Deh cessate per poco, o miei tormenti!

That I was a prisoner.

Ah what conflict, oh god! of contrary feelings

Do you, hate and love, awaken in my breast!

I owe vengeance to the one who gave me life,

Gratitude to the one who restores life to me . . .

Oh Ilia! oh father! oh prince! oh Destiny!
Oh unfortunate life! oh sweet death!
Is it possible? does Idamantes love me?
. . . ah no; the ingrate
Sighs for Electra; and that Electra,
Wretched princess, exile from Argos,
Fleeing at the misfortunes of Orestes,
Wandering to these shores, is my rival.
How many of you are there around me,
Pitiless executioners? . . . come then:
Vengeance, jealousy, hate, and love; rend,
Yes, rend this unhappy heart!

> Father, brothers, farewell!
> You died, I lost you.
> Greece, you are the reason,
> And shall I adore a Greek?
> For being an ingrate to my blood
> I know that I would be guilty:
> But that countenance, oh gods!
> I still am unable to hate.

Alas! Idamantes, here
He comes; wretched heart,
You throb, and are afraid.
Ah, cease for a little, oh my torments!

Scene II

Idamantes, Ilia. Idamantes' suite.

IDAMANTES (*to his suite*)

Radunate i Troiani, ite, e la Corte

Sia pronta questo giorno a celebrar.

Assemble the Trojans, go, and let the Court

Be ready to celebrate this day.

Idomeneo

(to Ilia)

Di dolce speme a un raggio	With one ray of sweet hope
Scema il mio duol. Minerva della Grecia	My sorrow lessens. Minerva, the protectress
Protettrice involò al furor dell'onde	Of Greece, snatched my father
Il padre mio; in mar di qui non lunge	From the fury of the waves; at sea, not far from here,
Comparser le sue navi; indaga Arbace	His ships appeared; Arbaces is investigating
Il sito, che a noi toglie	The site, which is depriving us
L'augusto aspetto.	Of the royal countenance.

ILIA *(ironically)*

Non temer: difesa	Do not fear: Greece
Da Minerva è la Grecia, e tutta ormai	Is defended by Minerva, and by now all
Scoppiò sovra i Troian l'ira de' Numi.	The anger of the gods has burst on the Trojans.

IDAMANTES

Del fato de' Troian più non dolerti.	Do not be unhappy over the fate of the Trojans any longer.
Farà il figlio per lor quanto farebbe	The son will do for them as much as would
Il genitor, e ogn'altro	The father, and every other
Vincitor generoso. Ecco: abbian fine,	Generous victor. Look: let there be an end,
Principessa, i lor guai:	Princess, to their woes:
Rendo lor libertade, e omai fra noi	I am restoring their liberty, and now among us
Sol prigioniero fia, sol fia, che porte	There will be only one prisoner, only one, that bears
Che tua beltà legò care ritorte.	The dear chains that your beauty bound.

ILIA

Signor, che ascolto? non saziaron ancora	My lord, what do I hear? have not the hate and wrath
D'implacabili Dei l'odio, lo sdegno	Of the implacable gods been satiated
D'Ilio le gloriose	By the glorious, now ruined,
Or diroccate mura, ah, non più mura,	Walls of Ilium, ah, no longer walls,
Ma vasto, e piano suol? a eterno pianto	But a vast and level ground? Are our infirm eyes
Dannate son le nostre egre pupille?	Damned to eternal weeping?

23

IDAMANTES

Venere noi punì, di noi trionfa.	Venus punished us, and triumphs over us.
Quanto il mio genitor, ahi rimembranza!	How much did my father, ah memory!
Soffrì de' flutti in sen? Agamemnone	Suffer in his breast from the waves? Agamemnon
Vittima in Argo al fin, a caro prezzo	A victim in Argos at the end, at a dear price
Comprò que' suoi trofei, e non contenta	Bought these trophies of his; and not content
Di tante stragi ancor la Dea nemica,	With such destruction, what more did the enemy goddess
Che fè? il mio cor trafisse,	Do? she pierced my heart,
Ilia, co' tuoi bei lumi	Ilia, with your beautiful eyes,
Più possenti de' suoi,	More powerful than hers,
E in me vendica adesso i danni tuoi.	And now avenges your losses through me.

ILIA

Che dici?	What are you saying?

IDAMANTES

Sì, di Citerea il figlio	Yes, the son of Cytheraea
Incogniti tormenti	Drips unknown torments
Stillommi in petto. A te pianto, e scompiglio	Into my breast. To you Mars brought
Marte portò, cercò vendetta Amore	Weeping and confusion, Love sought vengeance
In me de' mali tuoi, quei vaghi rai,	For your wrongs through me, he employed
Que' tuoi vezzi adoprò . . . ma all'amor mio	Those enchanting eyes, those charms of yours . . . but because of my love
D'ira, e rossor tu avvampi?	Are you burning with anger and shame?

ILIA

In questi accenti	At these words
Mal soffro un temerario ardir; deh pensa,	I painfully suffer an audacious boldness; ah, think,
Pensa Idamante, oh Dio!	Think, Idamantes, oh god!
Il padre tuo qual è, qual era il mio.	Who your father is, who mine was.

IDAMANTES

Non ho colpa, e mi condanni,	The fault is not mine, and you condemn me,

Idol mio, perchè t'adoro.
Colpa è vostra, o Dei tiranni,

E di pena afflitto io moro
D'un error, che mio non è.
Se tu il brami, al tuo impero
Aprirommi questo seno.
Ne' tuoi lumi il leggo, è vero,
Ma me'l dica il labbro almeno,
E non chiedo altra mercè.

My idol, because I adore you.
The fault is yours, oh tyrannous gods,

And I die afflicted with the pain
Of a mistake that is not mine.
If you wish it, at your command
I shall open this breast of mine.
In your eyes I read it, it is true,
But at least let your lips say it,
And I will not ask any other pity.

ILIA (*seeing the prisoners led in*)

Ecco il misero resto de' Troiani,

Dal nemico furor salvi.

Here is the wretched remainder of the Trojans,

Saved from the fury of the enemy.

IDAMANTES

Or quei ceppi
Io romperò, vuo' consolarli adesso.

Now I shall break
Those chains; I wish to console them now.

(*to himself*)

(Ahi! perchè tanto far non so a me stesso!)

(Ah! why am I unable to do that much for myself?)

SCENE III

Idamantes, Ilia. Trojan prisoners, men and women of Crete.

(*The chains of the prisoners are taken off; they show gratitude.*)

IDAMANTES

Scingete le catene, ed oggi il mondo,
O fedele Sidon suddita nostra,
Vegga que' gloriosi
Popoli in dolce nodo avvinti, e stretti

Di perfetta amistà.
Elena armò la Grecia, e l'Asia, ed ora
Disarma, e riunisce ed Asia, e Grecia
Eroina novella,

Principessa più amabile, e più bella.

Loosen the chains, and today let the world see,
Oh faithful Cydonia our vassal,
Those glorious
Peoples bound in a sweet knot, and tightly tied
In perfect friendship.
Helen armed Greece and Asia, and now
A new heroine,
A more amiable and more beautiful princess,
Appears and reunites both Asia and Greece.

ALL

Godiam la pace,	Let us enjoy peace,
Trionfi Amore:	Let Love triumph:
Ora ogni core	Now every heart
Giubilerà.	Will rejoice.

TWO CRETANS

Grazie a chi estinse	Thanks to the one who extinguished
Face di guerra:	The torch of war:
Or sì la terra	Now indeed will the earth
Riposo avrà.	Have rest.

ALL

Godiam la pace,	Let us enjoy peace,
Trionfi Amore:	Let Love triumph:
Ora ogni core	Now every heart
Giubilerà.	Will rejoice.

TWO TROJANS

A voi dobbiamo,	To you we owe,
Pietosi Numi,	Merciful gods,
E a quei bei lumi	And to those lovely eyes,
La libertà.	Liberty.

ALL

Godiam la pace,	Let us enjoy peace,
Trionfi Amore:	Let Love triumph:
Ora ogni core	Now every heart
Giubilerà	Will rejoice.

SCENE IV

Electra, and the former.

ELECTRA *(stirred by jealousy)*

Prence, Signor, tutta la Grecia oltraggi;	Prince, Lord, you insult all Greece;
Tu proteggi il nemico.	You are protecting the enemy.

IDAMANTES

Veder basti alla Grecia	It is enough for Greece to see
Vinto il nemico; opra di me più degna	The enemy conquered; let it prepare to see

A mirar s'apparecchi, o principessa:	An action more worthy of me, oh princess:
Vegga il vinto felice.	Let it look on the vanquished: happy.

(He sees Arbaces approach.)

SCENE V

Arbaces, and the former. Arbaces is downcast.

IDAMANTES

Arbace viene.	Arbaces is coming.

(fearful)

Ma quel pianto che annunzia?	But what does that weeping presage?

ARBACES

Mio Signore,	My Lord,
De' mali il più terribil . . .	The worst of evils . . .

IDAMANTES *(anxious)*

Più non vive	My father
Il genitor?	No longer lives?

ARBACES

Non vive: quel, che Marte	He does not live: that which Mars
Far non potè fin or, fece Nettuno,	Was unable to do until now, Neptune,
L'inesorabil Nume,	The inexorable god, accomplished,
E degl'eroi il più degno, ora il riseppi,	And the worthiest of heroes, I was told it just now,
Presso a straniera sponda	Close by a foreign shore
Affogato morì.	Died by drowning.

IDAMANTES

Ilia, de' viventi	Ilia, here before you
Eccoti il più meschin; or sì dal Cielo	Is the most miserable of the living; now indeed will you
Soddisfatta sarai . . . barbaro Fato! . . .	Be satisfied by Heaven . . . barbarous Fate! . . .
Corrasi al lido . . . ahimè! son disperato!	Let me run to the shore . . . alas! I am desperate!

(He leaves.)

ILIA

Dell'Asia i danni ancora	I still feel Asia's losses
Troppo risento, e pur d'un grand eroe	Too much, and yet at the name and fate
Al nome, al caso, il cor parmi commosso,	Of a great hero my heart seems moved,
E negargli i sospir, ah no, non posso.	And I cannot, ah no, deny him my sighs.

(*She leaves sighing.*)

SCENE VI

ELECTRA (*alone*)

Estinto è Idomeneo? . . . Tutto a' miei danni,	Idomeneus is dead? . . . Heaven conjures everything,
Tutto congiura il Ciel. Può a suo talento Idamante disporre	Everything to my harm. Can Idamantes At his inclination dispose
D'un impero, e del cor, e a me non resta	Of an empire and a heart, and not a shadow of hope
Ombra di speme? A mio dispetto, ahi lassa!	Remain to me? In contempt of me, alas!
Vedrò, vedrà la Grecia a suo gran scorno	Shall I see, will Greece see to its great shame
Una schiava Troiana di quel soglio,	A Trojan slave share that throne,
E del talamo a parte . . . In vano Elettra	And the marriage bed . . . In vain, Electra,
Ami l'ingrato . . . e soffre Una figlia d'un Re, che ha Re vassalli,	Do you love the ingrate . . . and can The daughter of a king who has kings for vassals
Che una vil schiava aspiri al grande acquisto? . . .	Suffer a cowardly slave to aspire to the great acquisition? . . .
Oh sdegno! oh smanie! oh duol! . . . più non resisto.	Oh wrath! oh frenzy! oh sorrow! . . . I can endure it no longer.

Tutte nel cor vi sento,	I feel you all in my heart,
Furie del crudo Averno.	Furies of cruel Avernus.
Lunge a sì gran tormento	Keep love, mercy, pity
Amor, mercè, pietà.	Away from such great torment.
Chi mi rubò quel core,	Let her who stole my heart,
Quel, che tradito ha il mio,	He who betrayed mine,
Provin' dal mio furore	Feel the vengeance and cruelty
Vendetta, e crudeltà.	Of my fury.

(*She leaves.*)

SCENE VII

The shores of a still agitated sea surrounded by
rocks. Fragments of ships on the shore.

CHORUS NEARBY (*strongly*)

Pietà, Numi, pietà!	Pity, gods, pity!
Aiuto, o giusti Numi!	Help, oh just gods!
A noi volgete i lumi . . .	Turn your eyes to us . . .

CHORUS IN THE DISTANCE (*less strongly*)

Pietà, Numi, pietà!	Pity, gods, pity!
Il Ciel, il mare, il vento	Heaven, sea and wind
Ci opprimon di spavento . . .	Weigh us down with fear . . .

CHORUS NEARBY (*softly*)

Pietà, Numi, pietà!	Pity, gods, pity!
In braccio a cruda morte	Inhuman destiny thrusts us
Ci spinge l'empia sorte . . .	Into the arms of cruel death . . .

ALL (*very softly*)

Pietà, Numi, pietà!	Pity, gods, pity!

SCENE VIII

PANTOMIME

(*Neptune appears on the sea. He signals to the winds to return to their caves. The sea gradually calms down. Idomeneus, seeing the god of the sea, implores his aid. Neptune, regarding him with a menacing scowl, plunges into the waters and disappears.*)

SCENE IX

Idomeneus with his suite.

IDOMENEUS (*to his suite*)

Eccoci salvi al fin; o voi, di Marte,	We are saved at last; oh you,
E di Nettuno all'ire,	My faithful followers
Alle vittorie, ai stenti	In the victories, the hardships
Fidi seguaci miei,	And wrath of Mars and Neptune,
Lasciatemi per poco	Leave me for a little
Qui solo respirar, e al Ciel natio	To breathe here alone, and to my native sky
Confidar il passato affanno mio.	Confide my past grief.

(*His suite goes off, and Idomeneus advances along the beach, contemplating it.*)

Tranquillo è il mar, aura soave spira

Di dolce calma, e le cerulee sponde
Il biondo Dio indora; ovunque io miro,
Tutto di pace in sen riposa, e gode.

Io sol, io sol su queste aride spiagge
D'affanno, e da disagio estenuato
Quella calma, o Nettuno, in me non
    provo,
Che al tuo regno impetrai.
In mezzo a' flutti, e scogli,
Dall'ira tua sedotto, a te lo scampo

Dal naufragio chiedei, e in olocausto

Il primo de' mortali, che qui intorno
Infelice s'aggiri, all'are tue
Pien di terror promisi. All'empio voto

Eccomi in salvo sì, ma non in pace . . .

Ma son pur quelle, o Dio! le care mura,

Dove la prima intrassi aura vitale? . . .
Lungi da sì gran tempo, ah con qual core

Ora vi rivedrò, se appena in seno

Da voi accolto, un misero innocente
Dovrò svenar! oh voto insano, atroce!

Giuramento crudel! ah qual de' Numi
Mi serba ancor in vita,
O qual di voi almen mi porge aita?

    Vedrommi intorno
      L'ombra dolente,
      Che notte, e giorno:
      Sono innocente
      M'accennerà.

The sea is tranquil, a pleasant breeze
    breathes
Sweet calm, and the blond god gilds
The cerulean shores; wherever I look,
Everything reposes in the bosom of
    peace, and takes pleasure.
I alone, I alone on these arid shores,
Exhausted by grief and discomfort,
Do not feel that calm, oh Neptune,

Which I asked of your realm.
In the midst of waves and rocks,
Led astray by your anger, I begged
    deliverance
From the shipwreck, and as an offering,
    full of terror,
I promised the first of the mortals,
That unhappily roamed around here,
For your altars. Because of the inhuman
    vow
Here I am saved indeed, but not at
    peace . . .
But are those really, oh god! the dear
    walls
Where I took my first breath? . . .
Gone for such a long time, ah, with what
    heart
Shall I now see you again, if barely
    welcomed
To your breast, I shall have to execute
An unhappy innocent! oh, insane,
    atrocious vow!
Cruel oath! ah, which of the gods
Is still keeping me alive,
Oh, which of you is at least giving me
    help?

    I shall see around me
      The sorrowing shade,
      That night and day
      Will mention to me:
      I am innocent.

Nel sen trafitto,
  Nel corpo esangue
Il mio delitto,
  Lo sparso sangue
M'additerà.
Qual spavento,
  Qual dolore!
Di tormento
Questo core
Quante volte morirà!

In his wounded breast,
  In his bloodless body
He will point out to me
My crime,
The shed blood.
What terror,
  What pain!
How many times
Will this heart die
Of torment!

(He sees a man approaching.)

Cieli! che veggo? ecco, la sventurata

Heavens! what do I see? here, the
  unfortunate

Vittima, ahimè! s'appressa . . . oh qual
  dolore
Mostra quel ciglio! mi si gela il sangue,
Fremo d'orror . . . E vi fia grata, o Numi,

Legittima vi sembra
Ostia umana innocente? . . . e queste
  mani
Le ministre saran? . . . mani esecrande!

Barbari, ingiusti Numi! Are nefande!

Victim, alas! approaches . . . oh, what
  pain
That face displays! my blood freezes,
I tremble with horror . . . And will this
  be pleasing to you, oh gods,
Does an innocent human victim
Seem just to you? . . . and these hands

Will be the ministers? . . . abhorrent
  hands!

Barbarous, unjust gods! Abominable
  altars!

SCENE X

Idamantes, Idomeneus (apart).

IDAMANTES

  Spiagge romite, e voi scoscese rupi,
Testimoni al mio duol siate, e cortesi

Di questo vostro albergo
A un agitato cor . . . quanto spiegate

Di mia sorte il rigor solinghi orrori! . . .

Vedo fra quegl'avanzi
Di fracassate navi su quel lido

  Solitary shores, and you steep cliffs,
Be testimony to my sorrow, and
  courteous
With this shelter of yours
To an agitated heart . . . how well you
  interpret
The severity of my fate, solitary
  horrors! . . .
I see among those remnants
Of smashed ships on that shore

31

Sconosciuto guerrier . . . voglio ascoltarlo,	An unknown warrior . . . I want to hear him,
Vuò confortarlo, e voglio	To comfort him, and I want
In letizia cangiar quel suo cordoglio.	To change his great sorrow into gladness.

(He approaches and speaks to Idomeneus.)

Sgombra, o guerrier, qual tu ti sia, il timore;	Drive off, oh warrior, whoever you may be, your fear;
Eccoti pronto a tuo soccorso quello,	Here ready for your assistance is the one
Che in questo clima offrir te'l può.	Who can offer it to you in this clime.

IDOMENEUS (*to himself*)

(Più il guardo,	(The more I watch him,
Più mi strugge il dolor.)	The more my pain consumes me.)

(*to Idamantes*)

De' giorni miei	I owe you
Il resto a te dovrò; tu quale avrai	The remainder of my days; you, what reward
Premio da me?	Will you have from me?

IDAMANTES

Premio al mio cor sarà	It will be a reward to my heart
L'esser pago d'averti	To be satisfied with having
Sollevato, difeso: ahi troppo, amico,	Raised you up, upheld you: ah, very well, my friend,
Dalle miserie mie instrutto io fui	Was I taught by my own miseries
A intenerirmi alle miserie altrui.	To be moved by the miseries of others.

IDOMENEUS (*to himself*)

(Qual voce, qual pietà il mio sen trafigge!)	(What voice, what pity pierces my breast!)

(*to Idamantes*)

Misero tu? che dici? ti son conte	You miserable? what are you saying? are your misfortunes
Le tue sventure appien?	Fully known to you?

IDAMANTES

Dell'amor mio,	The dearest object,
Cieli! il più caro oggetto,	Heavens! of my love,
In quelli abissi spinto	The hero Idomeneus,
Giace l'eroe Idomeneo estinto.	Plunged into these abysses, lies dead.

Ma tu sospiri, e piangi?	But you sigh and weep?
T'è noto Idomeneo?	Did you know Idomeneus?

IDOMENEUS

Uom più di questo	A more deplorable man
Deplorabil non v'è, non v'è chi plachi	Than he, who must appease his austere fate,
Il Fato suo austero.	Does not exist.

IDAMANTES

Che favelli?	What are you saying?
Vive egli ancor?	Does he still live?

(to himself)

(Oh Dei! torno a sperar!)	(Oh gods! I return to hope!)
Ah dimmi, amico, dimmi,	Ah, tell me, friend, tell me,
Dov'è? dove quel dolce aspetto	Where is he? where will that sweet countenance
Vita mi renderà?	Restore life to me?

IDOMENEUS

Ma d'onde nasce	But whence is born
Questa, che per lui nutri	This tenderness of love that you
Tenerezza d'amor?	Nourish for him?

IDAMANTES

Potessi almeno	Could I at least
A lui stesso gl'affetti miei spiegare!	Unfold my affections to him himself!

IDOMENEUS *(to himself)*

(Pur quel sembiante	(Yet this face
Non m'è tutto stranier, un non so che	Is not entirely strange to me, an unexplained something
Ravviso in quel . . .)	I recognize in that . . .)

IDAMANTES *(to himself)*

(Pensoso il mesto sguardo	(He fixes his sad look
In me egli fissa . . . e pur a quella voce,	Thoughtfully on me . . . and yet by his voice,
A quel ciglio, a quel gesto uom mi rassembra	His face, his gesture he resembles a man
O in Corte, o in campo a me noto, ed amico.)	Known to me either in court or on the battlefield.)

IDOMENEUS

Tu mediti.	You are reflecting.

IDAMANTES

Tu mi contempli, e taci.	You are contemplating me, and are silent.

IDOMENEUS

Perchè quel tuo parlar sì mi conturba?	Why does your speech so disturb me?

IDAMANTES

E qual mi sento anch'io Turbamento nell'alma? ah, più non posso Il pianto ritener.	And why do I also feel Disturbance in my soul? ah, I no longer Can hold back my weeping.

(*He weeps.*)

IDOMENEUS

Ma dì: qual fonte Sgorga quel pianto? e quel sì acerbo duol, Che per Idomeneo tanto t'affligge . . .	But say: what fount Disgorges those tears? and what harsh sorrow, That so afflicts you for Idomeneus . . .

IDAMANTES (*emphatically*)

Ah, ch'egli è il padre . . .	Ah, because he is the father . . .

IDOMENEUS (*impatiently interrupting him*)

(Oh Dio!) Parla: di chi è egli padre?	(Oh god!) Speak: whose father is he?

IDAMANTES (*in a weary voice*)

È il padre mio.	He is my father.

IDOMENEUS (*to himself*)

(Spietatissimi Dei!)	(Most pitiless gods!)

IDAMANTES

Meco compiangi Del padre mio il destin?	Are you bewailing the fate Of my father with me?

IDOMENEUS (*sorrowful*)

Ah figlio! . . .	Ah son! . . .

IDAMANTES (*joyfully*)

Ah, padre! . . . Ah Numi! . . . Dove son io? . . . oh qual trasporto! . . .	Ah, father . . . Ah, gods! . . . Where am I? . . . oh what transport! . . .

Idomeneo

(He wishes to embrace him, but his father draws back disturbed.)

soffri,   permit

Genitor adorato, che al tuo seno . . .	Adored father, that on your breast . . .
E che un amplesso . . . ahimè! perchè ti sdegni?	And that an embrace . . . alas! why are you offended?
Disperato mi fuggi? . . . ah dove, ah dove?	You desperately run from me? . . . ah, where, where?

IDOMENEUS

Non mi seguir, te'l vieto:	Do not follow me, I forbid it:
Meglio per te saria il non avermi	It would be better for you
Veduto or qui; paventa il rivedermi.	Not to have seen me here; be fearful of seeing me again.

(He leaves hurriedly.)

IDAMANTES

Ah qual gelido orror m'ingombra i sensi! . . .	Oh, what cold horror encumbers my senses!
Lo vedo appena, il riconosco, e a miei	I barely see him, I recognize him, and at my
Teneri accenti in un balen s'invola.	Tender words he disappears in a flash.
Misero! in che l'offesi, e come mai	Wretch! in what did I offend, and how
Quel sdegno io meritai, quelle minaccie? . . .	Did I ever merit that wrath, those threats? . . .
Vuo' seguirlo, e veder, oh sorte dura!	I wish to follow him and see, oh harsh fate!
Qual mi sovrasti ancor più rea sventura.	What harsher misfortune may threaten me.

Il padre adorato	I find my adored father
Ritrovo, e lo perdo.	Again, and I lose him.
Mi fugge sdegnato	He runs from me wrathfully
Fremendo d'orror.	Shuddering with horror.
Morire credei	I thought I was dying
Di gioia, e d'amore:	Of joy and of love!
Or, barbari Dei!	Now, barbarous gods!
M'uccide il dolor.	Sorrow is killing me.

(He leaves sorrowfully.)

INTERMEZZO

(The sea is completely tranquil. The Cretan troops that arrived with Idomeneus disembark. The warriors sing the following chorus in honor of Neptune. The Cretan women run to embrace their men so happily arrived, and express their mutual joy in a general dance which ends with a chorus.)

MARCH OF THE WARRIORS
DURING THE LANDING

CHORUS OF WARRIORS WHO HAVE DISEMBARKED
ALL

Nettuno s'onori,	Let Neptune be honored,
Quel nome risuoni,	Let that name resound,
Quel Nume s'adori,	That god be adored,
Sovrano del mar;	Sovereign of the sea.
Con danze e con suoni	With dances and sounds
Convien festeggiar.	It is necessary to celebrate.

A PART OF THE CHORUS

Da lunge ei mira	From far off he sees
Di Giove l'ira,	The anger of Jove,
E in un baleno	And in a flash
Va all'Eghe in seno.	He goes to Aegae's breast.
Da regal sede	From his royal seat
Tosto provvede,	He quickly provides,
Fa i generosi	Causes the scaly steeds
Destrier squammosi	Of noble bearing
Ratto accoppiar.	To be yoked together swiftly.
Dall'onde fuore	From out of the waves
Suonan sonore	Robust and bold
Tritoni araldi	Triton heralds
Robusti, e baldi	Sound sonorous
Buccine intorno.	Buccinas all around.
Già riede il giorno,	Already the day is returning,
Che il gran tridente	Since the great trident
Il mar furente	Was able to tame
Seppe domar.	The raging sea.

ALL

Nettuno s'onori,	Let Neptune be honored,
Quel nome risuoni	Let that name resound,
Quel Nume s'adori,	That god be adored,

Sovrano del mar;	Sovereign of the sea.
Con danze e con suoni	With dances and sounds
Convien festeggiar.	It is necessary to celebrate.

A Part of the Chorus

Su conca d'oro	On his golden conch
Regio decoro	Neptune inspires
Spira Nettuno.	Regal dignity.
Scherza Portuno,	Portumnus sports,
Ancor bambino,	Still a child,
Col suo delfino,	With his dolphin
Con Anfitrite.	And with Amphitrite.
Or noi di Dite	He caused us to triumph
Fè trionfar.	Over Dis now.
Nereide amabili,	Amiable nereids,
Ninfe adorabili,	Adorable nymphs,
Che alla gran Dea	Who pay court
Con Galatea	To the great goddess
Corteggio fate,	With Galatea,
Deh ringraziate	Ah, render thanks
Per noi quei Numi,	For us to those gods
Che i nostri lumi	Who were able
Fero asciugar.	To dry our eyes.

All

Nettuno s'onori,	Let Neptune be honored,
Quel nome risuoni,	Let that name resound,
Quel Nume s'adori,	That god be adored,
Sovrano del mar;	Sovereign of the sea.
Con danze e con suoni	With dances and sounds
Convien festeggiar.	It is necessary to celebrate.
Or suonin le trombe,	Now sound the trumpets,
Solenne ecatombe	Let us go to prepare
Andiam preparar.	Solemn hecatombs.

End of Act One

ACT TWO

Scene I

The royal apartments. Idomeneus, Arbaces.

IDOMENEUS

Siam soli; odimi Arbace, e il grand arcano	We are alone; hear me Arbaces, and the great secret
In sen racchiudi; assai	Enclose in your breast; through
Per lungo uso m'è nota	Long habit your fidelity to me
Tua fedeltà.	Is well known.

ARBACES

Di fedeltà il vassallo	The vassal has no merit
Merto non ha: virtù non è il dover.	In fidelity: virtue is not a duty.
Ecco la vita, il sangue . . .	Here my life, my blood . . .

IDOMENEUS

Un sol consiglio	Only one piece of advice is necessary
Or mi fa d'uopo; ascolta:	For me now; listen:
Tu sai quanto a' Troiani	You know how fatal to the Trojans
Fu il brando mio fatal.	Was my sword.

ARBACES

Tutto m'è noto.	All is known to me.

IDOMENEUS

Gonfio di tante imprese	At its end fierce Neptune lay in wait for me,
Al varco al fin m'attese il fier Nettuno.	Puffed up with so many exploits.

ARBACES

E so, che a' danni tuoi	And I know that he,
Ad Eolo unito, e a Giove	Together with Eolus and Jove,
Il suo regno sconvolse . . .	Turned his realm upside down, to your loss . . .

IDOMENEUS

Sì, che m'estorse in voto	Yes, so that he extortcd from me
Umana vittima.	A human victim as a vow.

ARBACES

Di chi?	Who?

IDOMENEUS

Del primo,	The first
Che sulla spiaggia incauto a me s'appressi.	Who unwarily approached me on the shore.

ARBACES

Or dimmi: Chi primo tu incontrasti?	Now tell me: Who did you meet first?

IDOMENEUS

Inorridisci:	You will be horrified:
Il mio figlio . . .	My son . . .

ARBACES (*losing his courage*)

Idamante! . . . io vengo meno . . .	Idamantes! . . . I feel faint . . .

(*recovering himself*)

Ti vide? . . . il conoscesti?	Did he see you? . . . did you recognize him?

IDOMENEUS

Mi vide, e a offrirmi ogni sollievo accorse,	He saw me, and hastened to offer me every relief,
Credendomi stranier, e il morto padre	Believing me a stranger, and bewailing his
Piangendo; al lungo ragionar l'un l'altro	Dead father; after a long discourse, at the end
Conobbe al fin, ahi conoscenza . . .	Each knew the other; ah! the knowledge . . .

ARBACES

A lui	Did you
Il suo destin svelasti?	Reveal his fate to him?

IDOMENEUS

No, chè da orror confuso io m'involai,	No, for I vanished because of confused horror,
Disperato il lasciai.	I left him desperate.

ARBACES

Povero padre!	Poor father!
Idamante infelice!	Unhappy Idamantes!

IDOMENEUS

Dammi, Arbace, il consiglio,	Arbaces, give me advice,
Salvami per pietà, salvami il figlio.	For pity's sake, save me, save my son.

ARBACES (*considering, then resolved*)

Trovisi in altro clima altro soggiorno.	Let him find another residence in another clime.

IDOMENEUS

Dura necessità! . . . ma dove mai,	Harsh necessity! . . . but where,
Dove ad occhio immortal potrà celarsi?	Where will he be able to hide himself from the immortal eye?

ARBACES

Purchè al popol si celi.	He only need be hidden from the people.
Per altra via intanto	Meanwhile Neptune will be placated
Nettun si placherà, qualche altro Nume	By other means; another god
Di lui cura n'avrà.	Will have the care of him.

IDOMENEUS

Ben dici, è vero . . .	Well said, it is true . . .

(*As he sees Ilia coming.*)

Ilia s'appressa, ahimè! . . .	Ilia approaches, alas! . . .

(*He remains thoughtful for a little and then decides.*)

In Argo ei vada, e sul paterno soglio	Let him go to Argos, and restore Electra
Rimetta Elettra . . . or vanne a lei, e al figlio,	To the paternal throne . . . now go to her, and to my son,
Fa, che sian pronti; il tutto	Get them ready; arrange everything
Sollecito disponi.	Quickly.
Custodisci l'arcano; a te mi fido.	Guard the secret; I trust you.
A te dovranno, o caro, o fido Arbace,	To you will be owed, oh dear, oh faithful Arbaces,
La vita il figlio, e il genitor la pace.	The life of the son and the peace of his father.

ARBACES

Se il tuo duol, se il mio disio Se'n volassero del pari,	If your sorrow, if my desire Were to take wing in like manner,
A ubbidirti qual son io,	Your sorrow would be ready to flee

40

Saria il duol pronto a fuggir.
Quali al trono sian compagni,

Chi l'ambisce or veda, e impari:

Stia lontan, o non si lagni

Se non trova che martir.

As obedient to you as I am.
Whoever covets the throne, let him
  see and learn
Who are the throne's
  companions:
Let him stay away; or not
  complain
If he only finds martyrdom.

(*He leaves.*)

SCENE II

Idomeneus, Ilia.

ILIA

Se mai pomposo apparse

Su l'Argivo orizzonte il Dio di Delo,
Eccolo in questo giorno, o Sire, in cui
L'augusta tua presenza i tuoi diletti
Sudditi torna in vita, e lor pupille,

Che ti piansero estinto, or rasserena.

If the magnificient god of Delos ever
  appeared
On the Argive horizon,
Here he is this day, oh Sire, in which
Your august presence restores
Your happy subjects to life, and renders
  serene
Their eyes, which wept for you as one
  dead.

IDOMENEUS

Principessa gentil, il bel sereno
Anche alle tue pupille omai ritorni,
Il lungo duol dilegua.

Gentle princess, may lovely serenity
Now return to your eyes also,
May your long sorrow disappear.

ILIA

Io piansi, è vero,
E in vano l'are tue,
O glauca Dea bagnai:
Ecuba genitrice, ah tu lo sai!

Piansi in veder l'antico
Priamo genitor dell'armi sotto
Al grave incarco, al suo partir, al tristo
Avviso di sua morte; e piansi poi
Al vedere nel tempio il ferro, il fuoco,
La patria distrutta, e me rapita

I wept, it is true,
And in vain did I bathe
Your altars, oh glaucous goddess:
For Hecuba, my mother, ah well you
  know it!
I wept seeing my old father
Priam under the heavy load
Of arms, at his departure, at the sad
News of his death; and then I wept
At seeing in the temple the sword, fire,
My homeland destroyed, and myself
  taken away

In questa acerba età,
Fra nemici, e tempeste, prigioniera
Sotto un polo stranier . . .

In this harsh age,
Among enemies and storms, a prisoner
Under a foreign pole . . .

IDOMENEUS

Assai soffristi . . .
Ma ogni trista memoria or si sbandisca.

You suffered greatly . . .
But now banish every sad memory.

ILIA

Poichè il tuo amabil figlio
Libertà mi donò, di grazie, e onori

Mi ricolmò, tutta de' tuoi la gioia
In me raccolta io sento; eccomi, accetta

L'omaggio, ed in tributo
Il mio, non più infelice,
Ma avventurato cor
Al figlio, al genitor grato, e divoto.

Signor, se umile è il don, sincero è il voto.

Since your amiable son
Gave me freedom, overwhelmed me
With favors and honors, I feel
All the joy
Of your people gathered in me; here I
     am, accept
My homage, and in tribute
My no longer unhappy
But fortunate heart,
Grateful and devoted to the son and
     father.
My Lord, though the gift be humble, the
     vow is sincere.

IDOMENEUS

Idamante mio figlio,
Allor, che libertà ti diè, non fu
Che interprete felice
Del paterno voler. S'ei mi prevenne,
Quanto ei fece a tuo pro, tutto io
     confermo.
Di me, de' miei tesori
Ilia, disponi, e mia cura sarà
Dartene chiare prove
Dell'amicizia mia.

So Idamantes, my son,
Who gave you freedom, was only
The happy interpreter
Of the paternal will. If he anticipated me
In what he did for your good, I confirm it
     all.
Ilia, make use of me,
Of my treasures, and my care shall be
To give you clear proofs
Of my friendship.

ILIA

Son certa, e un dubbio in me colpa
     saria.
Propizie stelle! qual benigno influsso
La sorte mia cangiò? dove temei
Strazio, e morte incontrar, lieta rinasco.

Colgo dove credei avverso il tutto
Delle amare mie pene il dolce frutto.

I am certain, and a doubt in me
     would be a fault.
Propitious stars! what benign influence
Changed my destiny? where I feared
Torment, and to meet death, I am born
     again happy.
Where I believed everything hostile,
I gather the sweet fruit of my bitter pain.

Se il padre perdei,
  La patria, il riposo,
Tu padre mi sei.
  Soggiorno amoroso
  È Creta per me.
Or più non rammento
  Le angoscie, gl'affanni.
  Or gioia, e contento,
  Compenso a' miei danni,
Il Cielo mi diè.
	Though I lost my father,
	  You are my homeland,
	  Rest, father.
	  Crete is a loving
	  Residence for me.
	Now I do not remember
	  Anxieties, griefs.
	  Now joy and contentment,
	  Compensation for my losses,
	  Heaven gave me.

(She leaves.)

SCENE III

IDOMENEUS (*alone*)

Qual mi conturba i sensi Equivoca favella? . . . ne' suoi casi	Why does her ambiguous speech Disturb my senses? . . . in her circumstances
Qual mostra a un tratto intempestiva gioia La Frigia principessa? . . . quei, ch'esprime Teneri sentimenti per il prence, Sarebber forse . . . ahimè . . . Sentimenti d'amor, gioia di speme? . . . Non m'inganno; reciproco è l'amore.	Why does the Phrygian princess suddenly show Unexpected joy? . . . those tender sentiments That she expressed for the prince, Could they be perhaps . . . alas . . . Sentiments of love, joy of hope? . . . I am not mistaken; their love is reciprocal.
Troppo, Idamante, a scior' quelle catene Sollecito tu fosti . . . ecco il delitto,	You were too precipate, Idamantes, in Loosening those chains . . . here is the crime
Che in te punisce il Ciel . . . Sì, sì, a Nettuno Il figlio, il padre, ed Ilia, Tre vittime saran su l'ara istessa Da egual dolor afflitte, Una dal ferro, e due dal duol trafitte.	For which Heaven punishes you . . . Yes, yes, for Neptune Son, father and Ilia Will be three victims on the same altar Afflicted by equal pain: One wounded by the sword, and two by sorrow.

Fuor del mar ho un mare in seno,
  Che del primo è più funesto,
	Away from the sea I have a sea in my breast,
	  Which is more deadly than the first one,

E Nettuno ancora in questo
Mai non cessa minacciar.
Fiero Nume! dimmi almeno:
    Se al naufragio è si vicino
    Il mio cor, qual rio destino
    Or gli vieta il naufragar?

Frettolosa, e giuliva
Elettra vien; s'ascolti.

And even in this Neptune
Never ceases menacing.
Fierce god! tell me at least:
    If my heart is so near being a
    Shipwreck, what harsh destiny
    Now denies it the shipwreck?

Electra is approaching
Hastily and joyously; let us listen.

SCENE IV

Idomeneus, Electra.

ELECTRA

Sire, da Arbace intesi
Quanto la tua clemenza
S'interessa per me; già all'infinito
Giunser le grazie tue, l'obbligo mio.

Or, tua mercè, verdeggia in me la speme

Di vedere ben tosto
Depresso de' ribelli il folle orgoglio.
E come a tanto amore
Corrisponder potrò?

Sire, from Arbaces I learned
How much your clemency
Is concerned for me; already your favors
And my obligation have reached to
    infinity.

Now, thanks to your help, hope grows
    green in me

To see the foolish pride
Of the rebels humbled soon.
And how shall I answer to
So much love?

IDOMENEUS

Di tua difesa
Ha l'impegno Idamante, a lui m'en vado;

Farò, che adempia or or l'intento mio,

Il suo dover, e appaghi il tuo disio.

Idamantes has the charge
Of your defense; I am going to him about
    it;

I shall see that he fulfills immediately my
    intention,

His duty, and that he satisfies your desire.

(*He leaves.*)

SCENE V

ELECTRA (*alone*)

Chi mai del mio provò piacer più
    dolce?
Parto, e l'unico oggetto,
Che amo, e adoro, oh Dei!

Whoever felt a sweeter pleasure
    than mine?
I leave, and the one thing
I love, and adore, oh gods!

Meco se'n vien? ah, troppo,	Is coming with me? ah, my heart
Troppo angusto è il mio cor a tanta gioia!	Is far too inadequate for so much joy!
Lunge dalla rivale	Far from my rival
Farò ben io con vezzi, e con lusinghe,	I shall certainly see that with
	endearments and adulation
Che quel fuoco, che pria	That that fire, which earlier
Spegnere non potei,	I was unable to extinguish,
A quei lumi s'estingua, e avvampi ai miei.	Be extinguished for her eyes, and blaze
	for mine.

Idol mio! se ritroso	My idol! though another lover
Altra amante a me ti rende,	Gives you, reluctant, to me;
Non m'offende	Harsh man,
Rigoroso,	It does not offend me;
Più m'alletta austero amor.	An austere love attracts me more.
Scaccierà vicino ardore	A love nearby will drive away
Dal tuo sen l'ardor lontano:	An ardor far from your breast:
Più la mano	The hand of love
Può d'amore,	Can do more
S'è vicin l'amante cor.	If a loving heart is nearby.

(A harmonious march is heard in the distance.)

Odo da lunge armonioso suono,	I hear a harmonious sound from afar,
Che all'imbarco mi chiama; orsù si vada.	Which calls me to the embarkation;
	come, I will go.

(She leaves hurriedly.)

(The march is heard coming nearer, as the scene is changed.)

SCENE VI

The harbor of Cydonia with ships along the shore.
Electra, Argive and Cretan troops and sailors.

ELECTRA

Sidonie sponde! o voi	Cydonian shores! oh you,
Per me di pianto, e duol, d'amor nemico	Cruel shelter for me of weeping, sorrow,
Crudo ricetto, or, che astro più clemente	And unfriendly love, now that a more
	clement star
A voi mi toglie, io vi perdono, e in pace	Takes me from you, I pardon you, and in
	peace
Al lieto partir mio	At my happy departure
Al fin vi lascio, e do l'estremo addio!	At last I leave you, and give you my last
	farewell!

CHORUS

Placido è il mar, andiamo;	The sea is placid, let us go;
Tutto ci rassicura.	Everything reassures us.
Felice avrem ventura,	We will have a happy venture,
Su, su partiamo or or.	Come, let us leave immediately.

ELECTRA

Soavi Zeffiri	Sweet Zephyrs,
Soli spirate,	Only blow gently,
Del freddo Borea	Calm the anger
L'ira calmate.	Of cold Boreas.
D'aura piacevole	Be courteous
Cortesi siate,	With your pleasant breeze,
Se da voi spargesi	Since love is scattered
Per tutto amor.	Everywhere by you.

CHORUS

Placido è il mar, andiamo;	The sea is placid, let us go;
Tutto ci rassicura.	Everything reassures us.
Felice avrem ventura,	We will have a happy venture,
Su su, partiamo or or.	Come, let us leave immediately.

SCENE VII

Idomeneus, Idamantes, Electra. The king's suite.

IDOMENEUS

Vatene, Prence.	Go, Prince.

IDAMANTES

Oh Ciel!	Oh Heaven!

IDOMENEUS

Troppo t'arresti.	You are staying too long.
Parti, e non dubbia fama	Depart, and may they not be doubtful tidings
Di mille eroiche imprese il tuo ritorno	Of a thousand heroic undertakings that precede
Prevenga. Di regnare	Your return. If you wish to learn
Se l'arte apprender vuoi, ora incomincia	The art of ruling, begin now
A renderti de' miseri il sostegno,	To make yourself the support of the unfortunate,
Del padre, e di te stesso ognor più degno.	Always more worthy of your father and of yourself.

IDAMANTES

Pria di partir, oh Dio!	Before leaving, oh god!
Soffri, che un bacio imprima	Allow me to imprint a kiss
Sulla paterna man.	On the paternal hand.

ELECTRA

Soffri, che un grato addio	Allow my heart to express
Sul labbro il cor esprima:	A grateful farewell on my lips:
Addio, degno sovran!	Farewell, worthy sovereign!

IDOMENEUS (*to Electra*)

Vanne, sarai felice;	Go, you will be happy;

(*to Idamantes*)

Figlio! tua sorte è questa.	Son! this is your destiny.

ALL THREE

Seconda i voti, o Ciel!	Favor these wishes, oh Heaven!

ELECTRA

Quanto sperar mi lice!	How much may I hope!

IDAMANTES

Vado!	I go!

(*to himself*)

(e il cor qui resta.)	(and my heart remains here.)

ALL THREE

Addio!	Farewell!

IDOMENEUS and IDAMANTES (*each to himself*)

(Destin crudel!)	(Cruel destiny!)

IDAMANTES (*to himself*)

(Oh Ilia!)	(Oh Ilia!)

IDOMENEUS (*to himself*)

(O figlio!)	(Oh son!)

IDAMANTES

Oh padre! oh partenza!	Oh father! oh departure!

ELECTRA

O Dei! che sarà?	Oh gods! what will happen?

ALL THREE

Deh cessi il scompiglio;	Ah, let all confusion cease;
Del Ciel la clemenza	The clemency of Heaven
Sua man porgerà.	Will stretch forth its hand.

(They go to the ships.)

(As they go to embark, a sudden storm rises. The people sing the following:)

CHORUS

Qual nuovo terrore!	What new terror!
Qual rauco mugito!	What raucous bellowing!
De' Numi il furore	The fury of the gods
Ha il mare infierito.	Made the sea cruel.
Nettuno, mercè!	Neptune, mercy!

(The storm increases, the sea swells up, the sky thunders and flashes and the frequent lightning sets the ships on fire. A formidable monster appears above the waves. The people sing the following:)

CHORUS

Qual odio, qual ira	What hate, what anger
Nettuno ci mostra!	Neptune shows to us!
Se il Cielo s'adira,	If heaven is quarreling,
Qual colpa è la nostra?	What is our fault?
Il reo qual è?	Who is the guilty one?

IDOMENEUS

Eccoti in me, barbaro Nume! il reo!	Here I am, barbarous god, the guilty one!
Io solo errai, me sol punisci, e cada	I alone erred, punish me only, and let your wrath
Sopra di me il tuo sdegno; la mia morte	Fall on me; let my death
Ti sazi al fin; ma s'altra aver pretendi	Finally satiate you; but if you expect to have
Vittima al fallo mio, una innocente	Another victim for my error, I cannot give you
Darti io non posso, e se pur tu la vuoi,	An innocent person, and if you still wish it,
Ingiusto sei, pretenderla non puoi.	You are unjust, you cannot expect it.

(The storm continues. Terrified, the Cretans flee and in the following chorus express with their singing and in pantomime their terror, all of which forms an analogous action, and the act closes with the usual divertimento.)

Idomeneo

Corriamo, fuggiamo	Let us run, let us flee
Quel mostro spietato,	That pitiless monster.
Ah, preda già siamo!	Ah, we are already his prey!
Chi, perfido Fato!	Who, perfidious fate!
Più crudo è di te?	Is more cruel than you?

End of Act Two

ACT THREE

SCENE 1

The royal garden.

ILIA (*alone*)

Solitudini amiche, aure amorose,	Friendly solitude, loving breezes,
Piante fiorite, e fiori vaghi! udite	Flowering plants, and enchanting flowers! hear
D'una infelice amante	The lament of an unhappy
I lamenti, che a voi lassa confido.	Lover that I, weary, confide to you.
Quanto il tacer presso al mio vincitore,	How much being silent near my conqueror,
Quanto il finger ti costa, afflitto core!	How much dissimulation costs you, afflicted heart!
Zeffiretti lusinghieri,	Little flattering zephyrs,
Deh volate al mio tesoro,	Ah, fly to my treasure,
E gli dite, ch'io l'adoro,	And tell him that I adore him,
Che mi serbi il cor fedel.	That he keep his heart faithful to me.
E voi piante, e fior sinceri,	And you plants, and candid flowers,
Che ora inaffia il pianto amaro,	That now my bitter weeping sprinkles,
Dite a lui, che amor più raro,	Tell him that a rarer love
Mai vedeste sotto al Ciel.	Was never seen under heaven.
Ei stesso vien . . . oh Dei! . . . mi spiego, o taccio?	He himself is coming . . . oh gods! . . . do I explain myself or be silent?

49

Resto? . . . parto? . . . o m'ascondo? . . .

Ah, risolver non posso; ah, mi confondo!

Do I stay? . . . leave? . . . or hide myself? . . .

Ah, I cannot decide, ah! I am becoming confused!

SCENE II

Ilia, Idamantes.

IDAMANTES

Principessa, a' tuoi sguardi
Se offrirmi ardisco ancor, più non mi
    guida
Un temerario affetto; altro or non cerco,
Che appagarti, e morir.

Princess, if I dare offer myself again
To your glances, no longer does an
    audacious love
Guide me; now I look for nothing else
But to please you, and to die.

ILIA

Morir? tu, prence?

Die? you, Prince?

IDAMANTES

Più teco io resto, più di te
    m'accendo,
E s'aggrava mia colpa, a che il castigo

Più a lungo differir?

The more I stay with you, the more
    enflamed with you I become,
And my fault is aggravated, so why
    postpone
Punishment any longer?

ILIA

Ma qual cagione
Morte a cercar t'induce?

But what reason
Induces you to seek death?

IDAMANTES

Il genitore
Pien di smania, e furore
Torvo mi guarda, e fugge,
E il motivo mi cela.
Da tue catene avvinto, il tuo rigore
A nuovi guai m'espone. Un fiero mostro

Fa dapertutto orrida strage; or questo

A combatter si vada,
E vincerlo si tenti,
O finisca la morte i miei tormenti.

My father,
Full of restlessness and fury
Looks at me scowling, and flees,
And conceals the reason from me.
Bound by your chains, your severity
Exposes me to new misfortunes. A fierce
    monster
Is causing horrible slaughter everywhere;
    now
I am going to fight him,
And attempt to conquer him,
Or let death end my torments.

ILIA

Calma, o prence, un trasporto sì funesto;	Calm, oh Prince, such a mournful passion;
Rammenta, che tu sei d'un grand' impero	Remember that you are the only hope
L'unica speme.	Of a great empire.

IDAMANTES

Privo del tuo amore,	Deprived of your love,
Privo, Ilia, di te, nulla mi cale.	Deprived, Ilia, of you I care about nothing.

ILIA

Misera me! . . . deh, serba i giorni tuoi.	Unhappy me! . . . ah, preserve your life.

IDAMANTES

Il mio Fato crudel seguir degg'io.	I must follow my cruel fate.

ILIA

Vivi. Ilia te'l chiede.	Live. Ilia asks it of you.

IDAMANTES

Oh Dei! che ascolto?	Oh gods! what do I hear?
Principessa adorata! . . .	Adored princess!

ILIA

Il cor turbato	Wrongly did my weakness
A te mal custodì	Consign my disturbed
La debolezza mia;	Heart to you;
Pur troppo amore, e tema	Unfortunately I have love
Indivisi ho nel sen.	And fear undivided in my breast.

IDAMANTES

Odo? o sol quel, che brama	Do I hear? or does hearing only simulate that which it desires;
Finge l'udito, o pure il grand ardore	Or else does a great ardor agitate
M'agita i sensi, e il cor lusinga oppresso	My senses and a sweet dream flatter
Un dolce sogno?	My oppressed heart?

ILIA

Ah! perchè pria non arsi	Ah! why did I not burn
Che scoprir la mia fiamma? mille io sento	Before discovering my passion? I feel a thousand
Rimorsi all'alma; il sacro mio dovere,	Pains of conscience in my soul; ah, how greatly will

La mia gloria, la patria, il sangue
De' miei ancor fumante, ah quanto al
    core
Rimproveranno il mio ribelle amore! . . .
Ma al fin, che fo? già che in periglio
    estremo
Ti vedo, o caro, e trarti sola io posso,

Odimi, io te'l ridico:
T'amo, t'adoro, e se morir tu vuoi,

Pria, che m'uccida il duol morir non
    puoi.

My sacred duty, my glory, my homeland,
The still smoking blood of my family
    reprove
My heart for my rebellious love! . . .
But after all, what am I doing? I already
    see you,
Oh dear one, in extreme peril, and only I
    can hold you back;
Hear me, I will say it to you again:
I love you, I adore you, and if you wish to
    die,
You cannot die before sorrow kills me.

IDAMANTES

S'io non moro a questi accenti,
    Non è ver, che Amor uccida,
    Che la gioia opprima un cor.

Since I do not die at these words
    It is not true that love kills,
    That joy oppresses a heart.

ILIA

Non più duol, non più lamenti;
    Io ti son costante, e fida,

    Tu sei il solo mio tesor.

No more sorrow, no more laments;
    I am constant, and faithful to
        you,
    You are my only treasure.

IDAMANTES

Tu sarai . . .

You will be . . .

ILIA

Qual tu mi vuoi.

What you wish me.

IDAMANTES

La mia sposa . . .

My wife . . .

ILIA

Lo sposo mio
    Sarai tu?

You will be
    My husband?

IDAMANTES and ILIA (together)

Lo dica Amor.
    Ah! il gioir sorpassa in noi
    Il sofferto affanno rio;
    Tutto vince il nostro ardor!

Let Love say it.
    Ah! the joy in us surpasses
    The harsh suffering endured;
    Our ardor conquers everything!

SCENE III

Idomeneus, Electra, and the former.

IDOMENEUS (*to himself*)

(Cieli! che vedo?)   (Heavens! what do I see?)

ILIA (*to Idamantes*)

Ah, siam scoperti, o caro.   Ah, we are discovered, oh dear one.

IDAMANTES (*to Ilia*)

Non temer, idol mio.   Have no fear, my idol.

ELECTRA (*to herself*)

(Ecco l'ingrato.)   (Here is the ingrate.)

IDOMENEUS (*to himself*)

(Io ben m'apposi al ver; ah, crudo   (Well did I guess the truth; ah cruel
    Fato!)   fate!)

IDAMANTES

Signor, già più non oso   Lord—for I no longer dare
Padre chiamarti, a un suddito infelice,   Call you father—to an unhappy subject,
Deh, questa almen concedi   Ah, at least grant this
Unica grazia.   One favor.

IDOMENEUS

Parla.   Speak.

ELECTRA (*to herself*)

(Che dirà?)   (What will he say?)

IDAMANTES

In che t'offesi mai? perchè mi fuggi,   In what did I ever offend you? why
                             do you flee me,
M'odi, e aborrisci?   Hate me, abhor me?

ILIA (*to herself*)

(Io tremo.)   (I tremble.)

ELECTRA (*to herself*)

(Io te'l direi.)   (I could tell you.)

IDOMENEUS

Figlio, contro di me Nettuno irato   Son, angry Neptune has frozen my
                             heart

Gelommi il cor, ogni tua tenerezza
L'affanno mio raddoppia, il tuo dolore
Tutto sul cor mi piomba, e rimirarti
Senza ribrezzo, e orror non posso.

Against myself, each tenderness of yours
Redoubles my grief, your pain
Falls entirely on my heart, and I cannot
Look on you without shuddering and
    horror.

ILIA (*to herself*)

(Oh Dio!)

(Oh god!)

IDAMANTES

Forse per colpa mia Nettun
    sdegnossi;
Ma la colpa qual è?

Perhaps Neptune became angry
    because of a fault of mine;
But what is my fault?

IDOMENEUS

Ah, placarlo potessi
Senza di te!

Ah, if I could placate him
Without you!

ELECTRA (*to herself*)

(Potessi i torti miei
Or vendicar!)

(If I could avenge
My wrongs now!)

IDOMENEUS (*to Idamantes*)

Parti, te lo comando,
Fuggi il paterno lido, e cerca altrove

Sicuro asilo.

Leave, I command it of you,
Flee the paternal shore, and seek
    elsewhere
A secure haven.

ILIA (*to Electra*)

Ahimè! . . .
Pietosa principessa, ah mi conforta!

Alas! . . .
Compassionate princess, ah comfort me!

ELECTRA

Ch'io ti conforti? e come?

I comfort you? and how?

(*to herself*)

(ancor m'insulta
L'indegna.)

(the base girl
Insults me again.)

IDAMANTES

Dunque io me n'andrò . . . ma
    dove? . . .
O Ilia! . . . o genitor!

So I shall have to go . . . but
    where? . . .
Oh Ilia! . . . oh father!

Idomeneo

ILIA (*resolute*)

O seguirti, o morir, mio ben, vogl'io.　　My beloved, I wish to follow you, or die.

IDAMANTES

Deh resta, o cara, e vivi in pace　　　　Ah, stay, oh dear one, and live in peace
　　. . . Addio!　　　　　　　　　　　　. . . Farewell!
　　Andrò ramingo, e solo　　　　　　　I shall go wandering, and alone
　　　Morte cercando altrove　　　　　　Searching for death elsewhere
　　　Fin che la incontrerò.　　　　　　Until I meet it.

ILIA

M'avrai compagna al duolo　　　　　　You will have me for a companion
　　　　　　　　　　　　　　　　　　　in your grief

　　Dove sarai, e　　　　　　　　　　　Wherever you shall be, and
　　　dove　　　　　　　　　　　　　　where
　　　　　　　　　　　　　　　　　　You may die, I shall die.

　Tu moia, io morirò.

IDAMANTES

Ah no . . .　　　　　　　　　　　　　Ah no . . .

IDOMENEUS

Nettun spietato!　　　　　　　　　　Pitiless Neptune!
Chi per pietà m'uccide?　　　　　　　Who will kill me out of pity?

ELECTRA (*to herself*)

(Quando vendetta avrò?)　　　　　　　(When shall I have vengeance?)

IDAMANTES and ILIA (*to Idomeneus*)

(Serena il ciglio irato.)　　　　　　　(Make your angry brow serene.)

IDOMENEUS and IDAMANTES, ILIA

(Ah, il cor mi si divide!)　　　　　　　(Ah, my heart is breaking!)

IDOMENEUS, IDAMANTES, ILIA and ELECTRA

(Soffrir più non si può,　　　　　　　(One can suffer no more than this,
　　Peggio è di morte　　　　　　　　Such great sorrow
　　Sì gran dolore:　　　　　　　　　Is worse than death:
　　Più fiera sorte,　　　　　　　　　No one has ever endured
　　Pena maggiore　　　　　　　　　A fiercer destiny,
　　Nissun provò.)　　　　　　　　　A greater pain.)

(*Idamantes leaves sorrowfully.*)

55

Scene IV

Arbaces, Idomeneus, Ilia, Electra.

ARBACES

Sire, alla reggia tua immensa turba	Sire, an immense throng of people crowded together
Di popolo affollato ad alta voce Parlarti chiede.	Asks in a loud voice to speak to you At the royal palace.

ILIA (*to herself*)

(A qualche nuovo affanno Preparati mio cor.)	(Prepare yourself, my heart, For some new grief.)

IDOMENEUS (*to himself*)

(Perduto è il figlio.)	(My son is lost.)

ARBACES

Del Dio de' mari il sommo Sacerdote Lo guida.	The High Priest of the god of the sea Is leading them.

IDOMENEUS (*to himself*)

(Ahi troppo disperato è il caso! . . . Intesi, Arbace.)	(Ah, the situation is too desperate! . . . I understood, Arbaces.)

ELECTRA

Qual nuovo disastro!	What new disaster!

ILIA

Il popol sollevato? . . .	The people rebelling? . . .

IDOMENEUS

Or vado ad ascoltarlo.	I will go now to hear them.

(*He leaves upset.*)

ELECTRA

Ti seguirò.	I will follow you.

(*She leaves.*)

ILIA

Voglio seguirti anch'io.	I, too, wish to follow you.

(*She leaves.*)

SCENE V

ARBACES (*alone*)

Sventurata Sidon! in te qual miro

Di morte, stragi, e orror lugubri aspetti?

Ah Sidon più non sei,
Sei la città del pianto, e questa reggia

Quella del duol! . . . Dunque è per noi dal
  Cielo
Sbandita ogni pietà? . . .
Chi sa? io spero ancora
Che qualche Nume amico
Si plachi a tanto sangue; un Nume solo

Basta tutti a piegar; alla clemenza

Il rigor cederà . . . ma ancor non scorgo

Qual ci miri pietoso . . . Ah, sordo è il
  Cielo!
Ah, Creta tutta io vedo
Finir sua gloria sotto alte rovine!
No, sue miserie pria non avran fine.

Se colà ne' Fati è scritto,

  Creta, o Dei, s'è rea, or cada.

Paghi il fio del suo delitto;
Ma salvate il Prence, il Re.
Deh d'un sol vi plachi il sangue!

Ecco il mio, se il mio v'aggrada,

E il bel regno, che già langue,

Giusti Dei! abbia mercè.

Unfortunate Cydonia! what
  mournful aspects
Of death, destruction, and horror do I
  see in you?
Ah, you are no longer Cydonia,
You are the City of Weeping, and this
  royal palace
That of Sorrow! . . . Is therefore all pity
  banished
From us by heaven?
Who knows? I still hope
That some friendly god
May be placated by so much blood; only
  one god
Is enough to bring everyone to their
  knees; severity
Will yield to clemency . . . but I do not
  yet perceive
The one who may look on us mercifully
  . . . Ah, heaven is deaf!
Ah, I see all of Crete
End its glory in total destruction!
No, its miseries will not have an end
  before then.

If on high among the Fates it is
  written,
  That Crete, oh gods, is guilty, let
    it fall now.

  Let it pay the price for its crime;
  But save the Prince, the King.
Ah, let the blood of an individual
  placate you!
  Here is mine, if mine may please
    you,
  And the beautiful kingdom,
    which already is growing
    weak,
  Just gods! may have mercy.

Scene VI

Large square, ornamented with statues, before the palace,
the facade of which can be seen from one side.

(Idomeneus arrives accompanied by Arbaces and the royal suite; the King escorted by Arbaces, sits on
the throne used for public audiences; the High Priest, and a number of people.)

High Priest

Volgi intorno lo sguardo, o Sire, e vedi	Cast your glance around, oh Sire, and see
Qual strage orrenda nel tuo nobil regno	What horrible destruction in your noble kingdom
Fa il crudo mostro; ah, mira	The cruel monster is causing; ah, behold
Allagate di sangue	Those public streets
Quelle pubbliche vie, ad ogni passo	Overflowing with blood, at every step
Vedrai chi geme, e l'alma	You will see someone mourning, and the soul
Gonfio d'atro velen dal corpo esala.	Breathes forth from the body swollen with black poison.
Mille, e mille in quell'ampio, e sozzo ventre	Thousands upon thousands in that vast and filthy belly
Pria sepolti, che morti	I myself have seen die,
Perire io stesso vidi.	Buried before they were dead.
Sempre di sangue lorde	Those jaws are
Son quelle fauci, e son sempre più ingorde.	Always soiled with blood, and are always greedy for more.
Da te solo dipende	On you alone depends
Il ripiego, da morte trar tu puoi	The remedy, you can pluck from death
Il resto del tuo popolo, ch'esclama	The rest of your people, that cries out
Sbigottito, e da te l'aiuto implora,	In terror, and implores help from you,
E indugi ancor? . . . Al tempio, Sire, al tempio.	And you still delay? . . . To the temple, Sire, to the temple.
Qual è, dov'è la vittima? . . . a Nettuno	Who is, where is the victim? . . . to Neptune
Rendi quello ch'è suo . . .	Render that which is his . . .

Idomeneus

Non più. Sacro Ministro,	No more. Holy Minister,
E voi popoli, udite:	And you people, listen:
La vittima è Idamante, e or or vedrete,	The victim is Idamantes, and very soon you will see,
Ah Numi! con qual ciglio	Oh gods! with what aspect
Svenar il genitor il proprio figlio.	A father executes his own son.

Idomeneo

(*He leaves disturbed.*)

PEOPLE

O voto tremendo!	Oh tremendous vow!
Spettacolo orrendo!	Horrendous spectacle!
Già regna la morte,	Death now reigns,
D'abisso le porte	And opens wide
Spalanca crudel.	The doors of the cruel abyss.

HIGH PRIEST

O Cielo clemente!	Oh clement heaven!
Il figlio è innocente,	The son is innocent,
Il voto è inumano;	The vow is inhuman;
Arresta la mano	Stop the hand
Del padre fedel!	Of the faithful father!

PEOPLE

O voto tremendo!	Oh tremendous vow!
Spettacolo orrendo!	Horrendous spectacle!
Già regna la morte,	Death now reigns,
D'abisso le porte	And opens wide
Spalanca crudel.	The doors of the cruel abyss.

(*All leave mournfully.*)

SCENE VII

Exterior view of the magnificent temple of Neptune with a vast portico which surrounds it, through which can be seen the seashore in the distance.

(*The portico and the galleries of the temple are filled with a multitude of people; the priests prepare the things pertaining to the sacrifice. Idomeneus arrives accompanied by a large and richly dressed suite.*)

IDOMENEUS

Accogli, o Re del mar, i nostri voti,	Accept, oh King of the Sea, our vows,
Placa lo sdegno tuo, il tuo rigor!	Placate your wrath, your severity!

PRIESTS

Accogli, o Re del mar, i nostri voti,	Accept, oh King of the Sea, our vows,
Placa lo sdegno tuo, il tuo rigor!	Placate your wrath, your severity!

IDOMENEUS

Tornino a lor spelonche gl'Euri, i Noti,	Let Euras, Notus return to their caves,
Torni zeffiro al mar, cessi il furor!	Let the zephyr return to the sea, let their fury cease!

Il pentimento, e il cor de' tuoi divoti	The repentance and the hearts of your devotees
Accetta, e a noi concedi il tuo favor.	Accept, and grant us your favor.

PRIESTS

Accogli, o Re del mar, i nostri voti,	Accept, oh King of the Sea, our vows,
Placa lo sdegno tuo, il tuo rigor!	Placate your wrath, your severity!

CHORUS (*behind the scenes*)

Stupenda vittoria!	Stupendous victory!
Eterna è tua gloria,	Your glory is eternal,
Trionfa o Signor.	Triumph, oh Lord.

IDOMENEUS

Qual risuona qui intorno	What noise of victory
Applauso di vittoria?	Resounds all around here?

SCENE VIII

Arbaces entering hastily, and the former.

ARBACES

Sire, il prence,	Sire, the prince,
Idamante l'eroe, di morte in traccia	The hero Idamantes, desperately running
Disperato correndo	After death
Il trionfo trovò; su l'empio mostro	Found triumph; he furiously hurled himself
Scagliossi furibondo, il vinse, e uccise;	On the inhuman monster, conquered it, and killed it;
Eccoci salvi al fin.	We are saved at last.

IDOMENEUS

Ahimè! Nettuno	Alas! Neptune,
Di nuovo sdegno acceso	Incensed with new wrath,
Sarà contro di noi . . . or or, Arbace,	Will be against us . . . very soon, Arbaces,
Con tuo dolor vedrai,	With your sorrow you will see
Che Idamante trovò quel che cercava,	That Idamantes found that which he looked for,
E di morte egli stesso	And that he himself will be
Il trionfo sarà.	The trophy of death.

ARBACES (*seeing Idamantes led in*)

Che vedo? oh Numi!	What do I see? oh gods!

SCENE IX

Idamantes in white garb with a wreath of flowers on his head, surrounded by guards and priests. A multitude of sorrowful people, and the former.

IDAMANTES

Padre, mio caro padre, ah dolce nome!	Father, my dear father, ah sweet name!
Eccomi a' piedi tuoi. In questo estremo	Here I am at your feet. In this last
Periodo fatal, su quella destra,	Fatal period, on your right hand,
Che il varco al sangue tuo nelle mie vene	Which must open the passage in my veins
Aprir dovrà, gl'ultimi baci accetta.	To your blood, accept my last kisses.
Ora comprendo, che il tuo turbamento	Now I understand that your confusion
Sdegno non era già, ma amor paterno.	Was not wrath, but paternal love.
O mille volte, e mille	Oh thousand upon thousand fold
Fortunato Idamante,	Fortunate Idamantes,
Se chi vita ti diè vita ti toglie,	If he who gave you life takes it from you,
E togliendola a te la rende al Cielo,	And taking it from you returns it to heaven,
E dal Cielo la sua in cambio impetra,	And in exchange begs for his own from heaven,
Ed impetra costante a' suoi la pace,	And begs enduring peace for his people,
È de' Numi l'amor sacro, e verace!	Then sacred and true is the love of the gods!

IDOMENEUS

O figlio, o caro figlio! . . .	Oh son, oh dear son! . . .
Perdona: il crudo uffizio	Pardon: this cruel office
In me scelta non è, pena è del Fato.	Is not chosen by me, it is a punishment by Fate.
Barbaro, iniquo Fato! . . . ah no, non posso	Barbarous, unjust Fate! . . . ah no, I cannot
Contro un figlio innocente	Raise the sharp labrys
Alzar l'aspra bipenne . . . da ogni fibra	Against an innocent son . . . from every fibre
Già se'n fuggon le forze, e gl'occhi miei	My strength now flees, and murky night
Torbida notte ingombra . . . oh figlio! . . .	Encumbers my eyes . . . oh son! . . .

IDAMANTES (*faint, then resolute*)

Oh padre! . . .	Oh father! . . .
Ah, non t'arresti inutile pietà,	Ah, do not let useless pity stop you,
Ne vana ti lusinghi	Nor vain tenderness of love
Tenerezza d'amor; deh, vibra un colpo,	Tempt you; ah, strike a blow
Che ambi tolga d'affanno.	That delivers both from sorrow.

IDOMENEUS

Ah, che natura	Ah, my nature
Me'l contrasta, e ripugna.	Opposes it, and resists.

IDAMANTES

Ceda natura al suo Autor: di Giove	Let nature give in to its Creator:
Questo è l'alto voler.	This is the high will of Jove.
Rammenta il tuo dover. Se un figlio perdi,	Remember your duty. Though you lose a son,
Cento avrai Numi amici. Figli tuoi	You will have a hundred gods for friends. Your children
I tuoi popoli sono . . .	Are your people . . .
Ma se in mia vece brami	But if in my place you desire
Chi t'ubbidisca, ed ami,	One who will obey you, and love you,
Chi ti sia accanto, e di tue cure il peso	Who will be at your side, and bear the weight
Teco ne porti, . . . Ilia ti raccomando . . .	Of your cares with you, . . . I commend Ilia to you . . .
Deh un figlio tu esaudisci,	Ah, hear a son favorably,
Che moribondo supplica, e consiglia:	Who at the point of death entreats and advises:
S'ella sposa non m'è, deh siati figlia.	If she cannot be a wife to me, ah, let her be a daughter to you.

No, la morte io non pavento,	No, I do not fear death,
Se alla patria, al genitore	If, oh gods, it produces
Frutta, o Numi, il vostro amore,	Your love and the lovely serenity of peace
E di pace il bel seren.	For my country and my father.
Agl'Elisi andrò contento,	I will go contented to Elysium,
E riposo avrà quest'alma,	And my soul will have rest,
Se in lasciare la mia salma	If in leaving my dead body
Vita, e pace avrà il mio ben.	My beloved will have life and peace.

Ma, che più tardi? eccomi pronto, adempi	But why do you still delay? here I am ready, fulfill
Il sacrifizio, il voto.	The sacrifice, the vow.

IDOMENEUS

Oh qual mi sento	Oh, why do I feel
In ogni vena insolito vigor? . . .	Unusual vigor in every vein? . . .
Or risoluto son . . . l'ultimo amplesso	Now I am resolute . . . receive
Ricevi . . . , e mori.	My last embrace . . . , and die.

IDAMANTES

O padre!   Oh father!

IDOMENEUS

Oh figlio!   Oh son!

IDOMENEUS and IDAMANTES

Oh Dio!   Oh god!

IDAMANTES (*to himself*)

(Oh Ilia, ahimè . . . Vivi felice.)   (Oh Ilia, alas . . . may you live happily.)

IDOMENEUS and IDAMANTES

Addio!   Farewell!

(*As he is about to strike the blow, Ilia
appears unexpectedly and impedes it.*)

SCENE X

Ilia hurriedly, Electra, and the former.

ILIA (*running to hold back Idomeneus' arm*)

Ferma, o Sire, che fai?   Stop, oh Sire, what are you doing?

IDOMENEUS

La vittima io sveno,   I am executing the victim
Che promisi a Nettun.   That I promised to Neptune.

IDAMANTES

Ilia, t'accheta.   Ilia, be silent.

HIGH PRIEST (*to Ilia*)

Deh, non turbar il sacrifizio.   Ah, do not disturb the sacrifice.

ILIA

In vano   In vain
Quella scure altro petto   Does that axe attempt to wound
Tenta ferir; eccoti, Sire, il mio,   Another breast; here for you, Sire, is
                                                mine,
La vittima io son.   I am the victim.

ELECTRA (*to herself*)

(Oh qual contrasto!)   (Oh what a battle of wills!)

ILIA (*to Idomeneus*)

Idamante è innocente, è figlio tuo,	Idamantes is innocent, he is your son,
E del regno è la speme.	He is the hope of the kingdom.
Tiranni i Dei non son; fallaci siete	The gods are not tyrants; you are all
Interpreti voi tutti	Fallacious interpreters
Del divino voler; vuol sgombra il Cielo	Of the divine will; Heaven wishes Greece
De' nemici la Grecia, e non de' figli.	Purged of its enemies and not of its children.
Benchè innocente anch'io, benchè ora amica,	Although I, too, am innocent, although I now am a friend,
Di Priamo son figlia, e Frigia io naqui,	I am a daughter of Priam, and born Phrygian,
Per natura nemica al Greco nome.	Enemy by nature to the Greek name.
Orsù mi svena . . .	Come, execute me . . .

IDAMANTES

Ah troppo,	Ah, Ilia,
Ilia, sei generosa;	You are too noble;
Vittima sì preziosa il genitore	My father did not promise
Non promise a Nettun, me scelse il Fato.	Such a precious victim to Neptune, Fate chose me.
La Frigia in te ancor vive:	Phrygia still lives through you:
Chi sa a qual fine il Ciel ti serba in vita,	Who knows to what end heaven keeps you alive
E della Grecia in sen?	And in the bosom of Greece?

ILIA

In van m'alletti.	In vain do you charm me.

IDAMANTES

In van morir presumi.	In vain do you presume to die.

IDOMENEUS

Ah ch'io son fuor di me. Soccorso, o Numi!	Ah, I am beside myself. Help, oh gods!

ARBACES

Oh Ciel! che fia? . . . mi scoppia il cor	Oh heaven! what will happen? . . . my heart is bursting . . .

ELECTRA (*to herself*)

(In petto	(What burning
Quai moti ardenti io sento	Impulses of rage and fury
Di rabbia, e di furor!)	Do I feel in my breast!)

Idomeneo

Sire, risolvi omai.   Sire, determine now.

IDOMENEUS

Ma quella tu non sei . . .   But you are not the one . . .

ILIA

Sempre più grata è a' Dei   A voluntary victim
Vittima volontaria.   Is even more welcome to the gods.

IDAMANTES

Idolo mio!   My idol!
Deh dammi del tuo amor l'ultimo pegno.   Ah, give me a last pledge of your love.

ILIA

Ecco il mio sangue.   Here is my blood.

IDAMANTES

Ah no; la gloria in pace   Ah, no; allow me the glory
Lasciami di morire   Of dying in peace
Per la mia patria.   For my country.

ILIA

A me s'aspetta.   This glory awaits me.

IDAMANTES

Oh Dio!   Oh god!

ILIA

Gratitudine è in me.   In me it is gratitude.

IDAMANTES

In me è dover.   In me it is duty.

ILIA

Ma ti dispensa Amore.   But Love exempts you.
Nettun! eccoti il mio.   Neptune! here for you is mine.

(*She runs to the altar and wishes to kneel;
Idamantes holds her back.*)

IDAMANTES

O vivi, e parti,   Either live, and depart,
O insiem noi moriremo.   Or we will die together.

65

ILIA

No, sola io vuò varcar il guado estremo.

A te, sacro ministro . . .

No, I wish to cross the ultimate ford alone.

I am yours, sacred minister . . .

(She kneels before the High Priest.)

(In the same moment that Ilia kneels, a loud subterranean noise is heard. The simulacrum of Neptune shakes. The High Priest is before the altar in ecstasy. All remain astonished and immobile through terror. A deep voice pronounces the following judgement of heaven:)

THE VOICE

Ha vinto Amore . . .

A Idomeneo perdona
Il gran trascorso il Ciel, . . . ma non al Re,
A cui mancar non lice a sue promesse . . .

Cessi esser Re . . . lo sia Idamante, . . . ed Ilia
A lui sia sposa, e fia pago Nettuno,
Contento il ciel, premiata l'innocenza.

La pace renderà di Creta al regno

Stabilito nel Ciel nodo sì degno.

Love has conquered . . .

Heaven pardons the great error
Of Idomeneus, . . . but not the King,

To whom it is not permitted to fail in his promises . . .

Let him cease being King . . . let it be Idamantes, . . . and let Ilia
Be his wife, and Neptune will be satisfied,
Heaven contented, and innocence rewarded.

This most worthy union established in heaven

Will give peace to the kingdom of Crete.

IDOMENEUS

Oh Ciel pietoso!

Oh merciful heaven!

IDAMANTES

Ilia . . .

Ilia . . .

ILIA

Idamante, udisti?

Idamantes, did you hear?

ARBACES

Oh gioia! oh Amor! oh Numi!

Oh joy! oh love! oh gods!

ELECTRA

Oh smania! oh Furie!
Oh disperata Elettra!

Oh frenzy! oh Furies!
Oh, desperate Electra!

Addio amor, addio speme! ah, il cor nel seno	Farewell love, farewell hope! Ah, already
Già m'ardono l'Eumenide spietate.	The pitiless Eumenides are burning my heart in my breast.
Misera! a che m'arresto?	Wretched woman! why do I restrain myself?
Sarò in queste contrade	Shall I be the sorrowful spectator
Della gioia, e trionfi	Of joy and triumph
Spettatrice dolente?	In these streets?
Vedrò Idamante alla rivale in braccio,	Shall I see Idamantes in the arms of my rival
E dall'uno, e dall'altra	And be pointed at
Mostrarmi a dito? ah no, il germano Oreste	By the one and the other? ah no, I want to join
Ne' cupi abissi io vuò seguir. Ombra infelice!	My brother Orestes in the deep abysses. Unhappy shade!
Lo spirto mio accogli, or or compagna	Receive my spirit, very soon you will have me
M'avrai là nell'Inferno	As a companion there in the infernal regions
A sempiterni guai, al pianto eterno.	In sempiternal wailing, in eternal weeping.

> D'Oreste, d'Ajace
>   Ho in seno i tormenti.
>   D'Aletto la face
>   Già morte mi dà.
> Squarciatemi il core
>   Ceraste, serpenti,
>   O un ferro il dolore
>   In me finirà.

> I have the torments of Orestes,
>   Of Ajax in my breast.
>   The torch of Alecto
>   Already gives me death.
> Rend my heart,
>   Cerastes, serpents,
>   Or a sword will put an end
>   To sorrow in me.

(*She leaves enraged.*)

FINAL SCENE

*Idomeneus, Idamantes, Ilia, Arbaces. The suites
of Idomeneus, Idamantes and Ilia. People.*

IDOMENEUS

Popoli, a voi l'ultima legge impone	People, Idomeneus imposes his last law
Idomeneo, qual Re. Pace v'annunzio.	As King on you. I announce peace to you.

Compiuto è il sacrifizio, e sciolto il voto.	The sacrifice is completed, and the vow fulfilled.
Nettuno, e tutti i Numi a questo regno Amici son. Resta che al cenno loro	Neptune and all the gods are friends Of this kingdom. It remains for Idomeneus now
Idomeneo ora ubbidisca; oh quanto, O sommi Dei, quanto m'è grato il cenno! Eccovi un altro Re, un altro me stesso.	To obey their command; oh great gods, How welcome is this command! Here is another king for you, another I myself.
A Idamante mio figlio, al caro figlio Cedo il soglio di Creta, e tutto insieme	To Idamantes my son, my dear son, I cede the throne of Crete, and all the sovereign
Il sovrano poter; i suoi comandi Rispettate, eseguite ubbidienti, Come i miei eseguiste, e rispettaste; Onde grato io vi son: questa è la legge. Eccovi la real sposa; mirate In questa bella coppia un don del Cielo	Power with it; respect His commands, execute them obediently, As you executed and respected mine; For which I am grateful: this is the law. Here for you is the royal bride; see In this handsome couple a gift from heaven
Serbato a voi. Quanto or sperar vi lice!	Reserved for you. How much hope is now permitted you!
Oh Creta fortunata; oh me felice!	Oh fortunate Crete; oh happy me!

Torna la pace al core, Torna lo spento ardore, Fiorisce in me l'età; Tal la stagion di Flora L'albero annoso infiora,	Peace returns to my heart, The spent ardor returns, Age flourishes in me; Just as the season of Flora Embellishes the aged tree with leaves,
Nuovo vigor gli dà.	And gives it new vigor.

(There follows the coronation of Idamantes, which is carried out in pantomime; the chorus, which is sung during the coronation, and the ballet.)

Chorus

Scenda Amor, scenda Imeneo, E Giunone ai regi sposi. D'alma pace omai li posi La Dea pronuba nel sen.	May Love, Hymen and Juno Descend to the royal couple. May the patroness of marriage Now place the peace of the soul in their breasts.

The End

A Short Glossary of Names and Terms

Rather than encumber the text with footnotes or use a definition for the name of the person or term in the translation, a short identification is given below of all words that might need defining. Since Varesco invariably uses the Latin forms of the deities in spite of the drama having a Greek provenance (Minerva for Athena, Jove for Zeus, etc.), the Latin forms are retained here with no mention of their Greek equivalents. Most of the definitions are based directly on Lempriere (1865 edition), still the most inclusive and readable of all classical dictionaries in English.

Aegae. An Amazonian queen who, according to one ancient writer, drowned in, and gave her name to, the Aegean Sea. Her name is also found as Aega.

Agamemnon. King of Mycenae and Argos, he was supreme commander of the Greek forces in the Trojan War. After he returned home he was murdered by his wife Clytemnestra and her paramour Aegisthus.

Ajax. The bravest of all Greek warriors after Achilles, he was the son of Telamon and came to the war in twelve ships. He was bested by Ulysses in the contest for Achilles' armor and in his disappointment went mad, later killing himself. Electra's "torments of Orestes,/Of Ajax" (III/10) refers to their madness and indicates her awareness of her own incipient insanity.

Alecto. See Eumenides.

Amphitrite. Wife of Neptune, mother of Triton.

Argive. Properly, the inhabitants of the city of Argos and the neighboring country, but the word is usually applied to all the inhabitants of Greece.

Argos. One of the most powerful of the ancient Greek cities in the northeast Peloponnesus.

Avernus. A lake whose waters were so unwholesome that it was considered by the ancients as the entrance to the underworld and also one of its rivers.

Blond God. Apollo, most widely known as a god of light; he was also revered in connection with all the fine arts, medicine, music, poetry and eloquence.

Boreas. The north wind.

Buccina. The conch used by tritons and other sea gods as trumpets.

Cerastes. The horned viper.

Cydonia. Present-day Khania. One of the oldest cities in Crete, it is situated in the northwestern part of the island. Its inhabitants were famous for their archery prowess. Varesco refers to it as the capital of Crete (following Danchet); this was actually Knossos, though Minos traditionally spent much time in Cydonia.

Dis. Supposed to be the same as Pluto, the god of the underworld.

Electra. Daughter of Agamemnon and Clytemnestra, sister of Orestes. In Varesco's libretto Electra is supposed to have fled Argos to Cydonia in order to escape "the foolish pride of the rebels," presumably her mother and her mother's paramour.

Elysium. A place or island in the infernal regions where the souls of the virtuous were placed after death.

Eolus. The west wind.

Eumenides. The ministers of vengeance of the gods. They were three in number: Tisiphone, Megara and Alecto. The latter was represented armed with flaming torches, her head covered with serpents.

Euras. The east wind.

Fates. Three in number, they presided over the birth and death of mankind. They spun (Clotho), measured (Lachesis) and cut off (Atropos) the thread of life.

Flora. The goddess of flowers and gardens.

Furies. See Eumenides.

Galatea. A sea-nymph. At the death of her lover, the shepherd Acis, she had him changed into a fountain.

Glaucous Goddess. See Minerva.

God of Delos. Apollo.

Hecatomb. A sacrifice of 100 oxen.

Hecuba. Wife of Priam and supposed mother of Ilia, though her name figures in none of the ancient sources. In Danchet's *Idoménée* she is called Ilione, which Varesco easily translated into Ilia. The name is obviously derived from Ilium.

Helen. Wife of Menelaus, Agamemnon's brother, she was carried off because of her beauty by Paris, son of Priam, thus precipitating the Trojan War. The libretto reference to her arming Greece and Asia indicates geographically the two warring forces and their allies.

Hymen. The god of marriage.

Idomeneus. Son of Deucalion, he succeeded his father on the throne of Crete. The number of ships he brought to the Trojan War is usually given as 100. Whereas all ancient authorities agree on his vow to Neptune, there are a number of different conclusions given to the legend, some having him kill his son and being expelled by his disgusted people, others having him entrust his kingdom to one Leucos who then had Idomeneus exiled.

Ilium. See Troy.

Jove. The most powerful of all gods of the ancients. When Idamantes tells Idomeneus, "Let nature give in to its Creator," he is saying that Jove is more powerful than Neptune and his will must not be disobeyed under any circumstances; therefore Idomeneus has no choice whatsoever but to sacrifice his son.

Juno. By her marriage to Jove she became queen of all the gods. The cause of the Trojan War is traced back to her resentment of Paris' awarding the apple "for the fairest" to Venus (q.v.). She naturally was pro-Greek in the conflict between Greece and Asia. In her guise as *dea pronuba* (final chorus, one of Varesco's Latinisms) she was the patroness of marriage.

Labrys. A double axe, frequently seen as a religious symbol in prehistoric Crete.

Mars. The god of war. He favored the Trojans in the war.

Minerva. The goddess of wisdom, war and all the liberal arts. She favored the Greeks in the war. Often referred to as the "glaucous" (gleaming) goddess in the Homeric epics, the epithet may mean "bright-eyed," "grey-green eyed," or "owl-eyed," but modern authorities feel that "bright-eyed" is the safest rendering.

Neptune. The god of the sea. He was pro-Greek in the war.

Notus. The south wind.

Orestes. Son of Agamemnon and Clytemnestra, brother of Electra. He was pursued by the Furies and struck mad for killing his mother and her paramour after they had murdered his father. See Ajax.

Phrygia. A country in Asia Minor whose most famous city was Troy (which is why Ilia refers to herself as a Phrygian).

Portumnus. The god of harbors.

Priam. King of Troy, father of Paris, whose abduction of Helen of Sparta precipitated the Trojan War. Hecuba was Priam's second wife by whom, according to Homer, he had nineteen children. After the betrayal of Troy, he buckled on his armor and was about to join battle against the Greeks but Hecuba detained him at the altar of Jove. He was cut down and decapitated by Neoptolemus, the son of Achilles, and his mutilated body left among the slain. It is to this pathetic scene that Ilia refers in her speech to Idomeneus (II/2).

Son of Cytheraea. Cupid, the son of Mars and Venus (Cytheraea is a surname of hers taken from the island of Cythera near which she rose from the sea). Cupid is, of course, the god of love.

Triton. A sea deity, son of Neptune and Amphitrite.

Troy. Ancient city, sometimes called Ilium, situated about four miles from the mouth of the Dardanelles. Paris brought Helen here after abducting her from her husband Menelaus.

Venus. The goddess of love. She favored the Trojans in the war due to Paris awarding her the apple designated "for the fairest." In Danchet's *Idoménée* Electra calls on Venus to aid her in her love for Idamantes, which Venus promises to do, telling her, "Your vengeance is one with that of the gods."

Zephyr. The west wind.

Die entführung aus dem serail

WORLD PREMIERE: *Vienna, Burgtheater, July 16, 1782*

UNITED STATES PREMIERE: *Brooklyn, NY, Athenaeum, February 16, 1860*

METROPOLITAN OPERA PREMIERE: *November 29, 1946*

DIE ENTFÜHRUNG AUS DEM SERAIL
(THE ABDUCTION FROM THE SERAGLIO)

Singspiel in Three Acts

Libretto: Johann Gottlieb Stephanie the Younger
(based on a libretto by
Christoph Friedrich Bretzner)

English Translation: Susan Webb

Music: Wolfgang Amadeus Mozart

DIE ENTFÜHRUNG AUS DEM SERAIL

CHARACTERS

SELIM, PASHA	Speaking Part
KONSTANZE, *beloved of Belmonte*	Soprano
BLONDE, *Konstanze's maid*	Soprano
BELMONTE	Tenor
PEDRILLO, *servant of Belmonte and overseer of the pasha's gardens*	Tenor
OSMIN, *overseer of the pasha's country house*	Bass
KLAAS, *a sailor*	Speaking Part
A Watchman	Mute Role

Chorus of Janissaries (see Notes to the Translation)

The action takes place on the pasha's country estate.

DIE ENTFÜHRUNG AUS DEM SERAIL

ACT I

Pasha Selim has bought three Europeans from Turkish pirates—Konstanze, a Spanish woman of good family; Blonde, her English maid; and Pedrillo, the servant of Konstanze's fiancé, Belmonte, a Spanish nobleman. Belmonte has traced them to the pasha's seaside palace, where Konstanze is the pasha's favorite and Pedrillo acts as the gardener. Blonde has been given as a gift by the pasha to Osmin, overseer of his harem. Outside the palace walls, Belmonte yearns for Konstanze ("Hier soll ich dich denn sehen"). His first encounter is with the cantankerous Osmin, who is on a ladder picking figs and singing about how to deal with sweethearts ("Wer ein Liebchen hat gefunden"). Osmin is polite until Belmonte mentions Pedrillo, the overseer's rival for Blonde. Osmin then scares Belmonte away and rails at Pedrillo ("Solche hergelauf'ne Laffen"), who has come in hopes of making peace with him. Belmonte returns to find his servant, who tells him the pasha is in love with Konstanze but will not force himself on her. This makes Belmonte long even more to see his beloved ("O wie ängstlich, o wie feurig"), who soon appears with Selim, heralded by Janissaries. When the pasha asks why she is always depressed by his attentions toward her, Konstanze replies she cannot forget her love for the man from whom she was separated ("Ach ich liebte"), then leaves. Pedrillo introduces Belmonte to the pasha as a gifted young architect. Selim welcomes him and, departing, promises a conference the next day. Osmin bars the way when Belmonte and Pedrillo try to enter the palace (trio: "Marsch! marsch!"), but the two succeed in getting past him.

ACT II

In the garden, Blonde confounds Osmin by telling how he *really* ought to treat women—with tenderness and flattery ("Durch Zärtlichkeit und Schmeicheln"), then easily faces him down when he threatens her (duet: "Ich gehe, doch rate ich dir"). Konstanze appears, mourning her separation from Belmonte ("Traurigkeit ward mir zum Lose"). Her sad state of mind does not improve when the pasha again asks her to marry him. She proudly repeats her refusal, preferring torture and death ("Martern aller Arten"). When they have gone, Blonde and Pedrillo meet in the garden to plan escape: they will get Osmin drunk, and all four lovers will sail away in Belmonte's ship, which lies offshore. Blonde looks forward to telling Konstanze of Belmonte's arrival ("Welche Wonne, welche Lust"). Pedrillo screws up his courage ("Frisch zum Kampfe!"), then goes about plying Osmin with wine, finding the Moslem surprisingly cooperative ("Vivat Bacchus!"). Inebriated, Osmin weaves off with his wineskin, leaving the coast clear. Belmonte at last meets Konstanze, who greets him with tears of joy ("Wenn der Freude Tränen fließen"). Their happy reunion, shared by Blonde and Pedrillo, darkens when Belmonte and Pedrillo jealously question the women's faithfulness, but misunderstandings melt (quartet: "Ach, Belmonte! Ach, mein Leben!") into relief and joy.

Act III

Standing beneath Konstanze's balcony later that night, Belmonte puts his faith in the power of love ("Ich baue ganz"). Just before midnight, Pedrillo places a ladder against the ladies' window and sings a serenade about a maiden held captive by the Moors and rescued by a foreign lover; it is the signal for escape ("Im Mohrenland gefangen war"). But when the women finally appear, the noise awakens Osmin, who is not too hung over to realize what is going on. He takes great delight in having all four captured and bound, savoring their imminent death by hanging ("O! wie will ich triumphieren"). They are summoned before the pasha. While Konstanze offers to die to save her beloved, Belmonte more realistically suggests the pasha might collect a handsome ransom from his wealthy family, the Lostados. At this the pasha realizes that Belmonte is the son of an old enemy, the man who exiled him from his own country. His wrath is doubled, and when he retires to give orders for the lovers' torture, Belmonte and Konstanze vow to welcome death together ("Meinetwegen sollst du sterben"). But the pasha eventually decides that rather than take blood for blood he will free Konstanze and Belmonte, even Blonde and Pedrillo. This magnanimous act confounds Osmin, who protests the loss of Blonde to no avail: the pasha declares that love cannot be won by force. Osmin storms off as everyone else praises the pasha's wisdom and clemency before the couples sail for home.

Opera News

PREFACE

Die Entführung aus dem Serail, a singspiel with music by Wolfgang Amadeus Mozart and libretto by Gottlieb Stephanie the Younger, was one of Mozart's earliest operatic successes, in spite of the mixed reviews of its premiere. In today's operatic repertory it is performed more frequently than *Idomeneo* and *La Clemenza di Tito* (although these have been catching up in recent years), but never as often as *Le Nozze di Figaro, Don Giovanni, Così Fan Tutte* or *Die Zauberflöte.*

The opera's libretto suffers in comparison with the Da Ponte masterpieces. Yet it is not without interest; for one thing, it is the subject of a series of letters by Mozart to his father which not only document the problems of creating *Entführung*, but give us a treasure trove of information on Mozart's creative process and the role he played in shaping the librettos of his operas.

In 1781 Mozart left his native Salzburg for Vienna, where he soon met Gottlieb Stephanie the Younger, an impresario with a reputation for being difficult. (He was known as "the Younger" to distinguish him from his brother, a well-known actor.) An ex-soldier and actor, Stephanie the Younger was the chief writer and adapter at Vienna's National Theatre, and by the end of 1781 would be in complete charge of the theater.

This new theater had recently been established by Vienna's Emperor, Joseph II, with whom Stephanie had established close ties. It was an attempt to encourage the production of German singspiel—an up-hill battle, since the Viennese preferred the more musically sophisticated Italian operas to these German plays, with dialogue and songs interspersed. The company consisted of more actors than singers, and therefore was limited in the quality of music it could present. In addition, very few German works existed; most often the theater presented German translations of Italian operas. But the emperor's desire for a national theater appealed to Mozart, and soon he was to express the desire to write a singspiel that would "lift the national German stage to recognition in music."

On July 30, 1781, Stephanie gave Mozart the first draft of the libretto, which the latter described to his father as "quite good. The subject is Turkish, and it's called *Bellmont und Konstanze, or Die Verführung aus dem Serail*" [sic]. (Mozart got the title wrong, calling it *The Seduction from the Seraglio*, which would have made an altogether different opera.) The two hoped to complete the piece by September of that year, when the Grand Duke Paul of Russia (the future Tsar Paul I) was to visit Vienna.

The libretto was an unauthorized adaptation of a libretto by Christoph Friedrich Bretzner, a Leipzig merchant who had written five singspiel librettos, of which *Belmonte und Constanze* was his most recent. It had already been set to music by Johann André, but the concept of copyright protection was nonexistent at that time, and plays were frequently adapted without permission. Indeed, when Bretzner protested the Mozart opera (see Appendix), it was because his work had been rewritten without his participation rather than that it had been pirated.

That Stephanie gave Mozart a libretto with a Turkish theme was no accident, as Mozart had already played him some music from his Turkish opera, now known as *Zaïde*. Indeed, the figure of the Turk was quite popular in Europe during the seventeen and eighteenth centuries, especially after the siege of Vienna in 1683. Turkish instruments were introduced into military music, people dressed as Turks at masked balls and in Vienna there was at least one Türkencafe.

Turks abounded in plays and operas. By the time *Entführung* premiered, Europe had seen productions of such Turkish operas as *L'Arabo Cortese* and *Dardane* by Paisiello, *La Caravanne du Caire* by Grétry, *L'Isle Sonnante* by Monsigny and Gluck's *Le Rencontre Imprévue*. Some had plots and characters similar to those in *Entführung; La Schiava Liberata,* a libretto used by both Jarnelli and Schuster, had two European women in Turkish custody by a character named Selim, who are freed by arbitration. A 1775 play by Isaac Bickerstaffe called *The Sultan, or A Peep into the Seraglio* had a character named "Osmyn, Chief of the Eunuchs," and one very much like Blonde who was "Roxalana, an English slave." It's interesting to note that in the seventeen and early eighteenth centuries, when the Turks were at war with various European countries, they were usually portrayed as villains. As their political power waned and they became less of a threat in the eighteenth century the public remained fascinated with Turks, but they could now be drawn more humorously.

Presented with the September deadline, Mozart and Stephanie worked quickly on Act I, making few changes in Bretzner's text or running order; however, when the opening night was postponed, composer and librettist began to modify Bretzner's ideas, and Stephanie was called on to supply original material. Many of these changes seem to have been requested by Mozart, as letters to his father show.

For instance, on September 26 he reported, "As the original text began with a monologue, I asked Herr Stephanie to make a little arietta out of it, and then to put in a duet instead of making the two men chatter together after Osmin's short song. As we have given the role of Osmin to Herr Fischer, who certainly has an excellent bass voice (though the Archbishop told me he sang too low for a bass, so I assured him he would sing higher in future!), we ought to take advantage of it, especially as he has the entire Viennese public on his side. But in the original libretto Osmin has only this short song and nothing else to sing, except in the trio and the finale; so we have given him an aria in Act I, and he will have another in Act II. I have explained to Stephanie the kind of words I need for this aria: indeed I have finished composing most of the music for it before Stephanie knew anything about it. I enclose only the beginning and the end, which is bound to be effective. Osmin's rage is made comical by the accompaniment of the Turkish music. In working out the aria I have given full scope to Fischer's beautiful low notes (in spite of the Salzburg Midas) . . . But here is the rub: I finished the first Act more than three weeks ago, as well as one aria in Act II and the drunken duet (especially for the Viennese gentry) . . . But I cannot compose any more, because the whole plot is being altered—to tell the truth, this is at my own request. At the beginning of Act III there is a charming quintet, really a finale ensemble, which I should prefer to have at the end of Act II. In order to make this practicable, great changes must be made: in fact an entirely new plot must be introduced . . . Everyone abuses Stephanie. It may be that, with me, he is friendly only to my face, but, after all, he is arranging the libretto for me, and, what is more, doing so exactly the way I want it, so I can't, in all honesty, ask more of him than that."

A letter written on October 13th gives a clear picture of Mozart's thoughts on the role of the libretto in opera. "Now, as to the libretto of the opera, you are quite right as far as Stephanie's work is concerned. Still, the poetry is perfectly in keeping with the character of the stupid, surly, malicious Osmin. I am well aware that the verse is not exactly first-rate, but it fitted in and agreed so well with the musical ideas which were already buzzing about in my head that it could hardly fail to please me. I'd like to bet that, when it is performed no one will find any fault with the verse . . . Besides, in my view, in an opera the poetry must be completely the obedient daughter of the music. Why do Italian comic operas please people everywhere, despite their miserable libretti, even in Paris where I myself witnessed their success? Precisely because in them the music reigns supreme, and when one listens to it one forgets everything else. An opera is certain of success if the plot is well worked out, the words written to suit the music and not shoved in here and there for the sake of some miserable rhyme—which, God knows, never enhances the value of any theatrical performance, whatever it is, but rather detracts from it. I am talking about words, or even entire verses, which ruin the composer's whole idea. Verses are certainly the most indispensable element for music, but rhymes solely for the sake of rhyming are the most detrimental . . . The best thing of all is when a good composer, who understands the theatre and is talented enough to make useful suggestions, meets that true phoenix, an able poet. When that happens, no fears need be entertained as to the applause even of the ignorant. Poets rather remind me of the trumpeters with their professional tricks! If we composers were always to stick so faithfully to our rules, simply because they were very sound at that time and no one knew any better, we should be concocting music as unpalatable as their libretti."

Work proceeded slowly, with each alteration creating the need for another, and by the end of 1781 the opera was still far from ready. (The Grand Duke's visit had been postponed until November, and he attended a performance of Gluck's *Alceste*. He returned in October, and at that time saw *Entführung*, conducted from the keyboard by the composer.) Finally at the end of May 1782, ten months from the day Stephanie had given Mozart the libretto, the work was complete, and rehearsals commenced on June 3.

The premiere was on July 16; playbills went up on the day of the performance, and while Mozart's name was billed in small type, Bretzner, now a famous playwright, was given prominent billing, and Stephanie's name was nowhere to be seen. In spite of Mozart's complaint of cabals against him the performance went well. (It inspired the famous complaint of the emperor, "Too beautiful for our ears, and an enormous number of notes, my dear Mozart," and his reply "Only as many as are needed.") The opera was repeated several times that season, and soon was presented at many other theaters. It was Mozart's most popular opera in his lifetime.

Most of the criticism received after the premiere was leveled at the libretto, which many thought unpoetic and even immoral. Today's audiences may find parts of it tiresome, (and

Osmin is not the easiest character with whom to spend an evening.) There are also unpleasant aspects to the repeated discussions of torture, which although intended as comic, to modern ears may sound more like an ugly obsession. Despite the uneven quality of the verses, the alchemy produced by fleshing out "stock" characters and by exploring diverse cultures side by side makes *Entführung* more than just a symbolic success as a German Singspiel, and Mozart was now in full possession of his powers as a comic as well as a serious dramatist.

The story is fairly simple: Konstanze, Blonde and Pedrillo have fallen into the hands of pirates and have been sold as slaves to the pasha. Belmonte, who is Konstanze's betrothed and Pedrillo's master, has come to save them, and finds that Blonde has been given to Osmin, the gardens' overseer, while Constanze has been singled out by Pasha Selim for his special attention. ("Pasha" is a title, from the Turkish word "bas" meaning "head" or "chief," given to a Turkish officer of high rank, like a military commander or the governor of a province. Pasha Selim is also a renegade, that is, he has foresworn his Christian heritage and become a Moslem. Therefore he has characteristics appropriate to both cultures and is doubly and dangerously unpredictable.)

The comic pairing of a fat old man (Osmin) and a beautiful young woman (Blonde) is a very old theatrical tradition. But this particular duo has cross-cultural quarrels about some surprisingly modern matters. Osmin is a Turk, through-and-through; as far as he's concerned, Blonde is to be his slave in all things and that is that. However, Blonde refuses to accept a status so unsuitable to a free-born English woman. It's in Blonde's best interests to teach Osmin what sort of gentle treatment European women of any class expect, and she successfully keeps his cruelty at bay by threatening a little of her own.

This is not the only time that the question of who is being enslaved by whom comes up. Blonde's power comes from her mistress's hold over the Pasha Selim, and Osmin has no choice but to back away from his belligerent position or risk sore feet. The pasha has limitless power of force over Konstanze but prefers that she come to him of her own accord, and is ever more captivated by her as she desperately tries to stall, hoping for the arrival of *her* master, Belmonte.

The Europeans never accept their status as slaves, and refuse to be intimidated by their captors. They all quite openly criticize Turkish customs and attitudes, especially with respect to the status of women. Private fears and misgivings are voiced only among themselves. Even though Pedrillo and Blonde are servants to Belmonte and Konstanze, they are all Europeans in this together; the assumption seems to be that the most practical heads in the group belong to Blonde and then to Pedrillo, and that Belmonte and Konstanze would be unable to escape the seraglio without them. (We are familiar with the use of the word "seraglio," from the Persian word for "palace," as a synonym for "harem," Arabic for "the women's quarters of a Moslem dwelling." In this case, "seraglio" refers to Pasha Selim's seaside compound. Historically, the term was applied to a Turkish palace, especially that of the Sultan at Constantinople. This "Grand Seraglio," begun in 1465, was designed as a complex of buildings contained within fortress walls: a paradise on earth filled with gardens and the sound of running water, flocks of birds and herds of animals.)

The most startling confrontation between Turkish and European attitudes occurs in the opera's finale. The four Christians have been captured during the attempted abduction. At this terrible point, when they are as far away from civilized European ways as can be imagined, facing sure death by horrible means, comes what one writer has called "La Clemenza di Selim," the merciful act, which in this case is itself an act of sublime revenge. Selim despises Belmonte's father so much for past acts of cruelty that he is incapable of imitating the elder Lostados' behavior; he releases Belmonte (and his companions) so that he can go back to Spain and tell his father of Selim's beneficence. (In the original libretto the four are set free when the pasha discovers Belmonte to be his long-lost son!)

The four Europeans can scarcely believe their good fortune, and with Selim's praises on their lips, they board ship, doubtless preferring the perils of the sea to those of the slippery ground they have just left.

A NOTE ON THE JANISSARIES

Sultan Murad I, who succeeded to the throne of the Ottoman Empire in 1359, recruited into his army from among Christians a picked force to serve him personally.

The "Yeni Cheri" (Turkish for "new troops"), or Janissaries, were created by what a horrified Europe called "The Law of Tribute Children": a conquered district would be forced to give up Christian boys of a certain age who would be taken from their families and brought up as Moslems.

As the Sultan's personal infantry, they were hand-picked for physique and intelligence, subjected to rigorous training and discipline and paid on a higher scale than other troops. Their lives were devoted to military service: they were not permitted to marry, to own property, or to do any work.

The conquest of Constantinople in 1453 and two assaults on Vienna, in 1529 and in 1683, brought Europe face to face with these formidable soldiers, and they found their way into Occidental story and legend (probably told to terrify little Viennese children into doing what they were supposed to!)

Accounts attest to their bravery in the forefront of battle; perhaps of more interest to us is how they were accompanied as they surged forward—by an ear-splitting cacophony of chants, pipes, cymbals and drums, designed to raise their spirits and lower those of their enemies.

The *Harvard Dictionary of Music* lists as Janissary instruments big drums, cymbals, triangles and the Turkish crescent, a percussion instrument consisting of a wooden stick surmounted by crescent-shaped cross-pieces, and topped by an ornament hung with small bells and bits of metal.

Mozart provides us with his idea of what this unholy din might have sounded like, using

German and Turkish drums, cymbals and triangles; especially in the overture and the choruses we hear echoes of the Janissaries' savage martial accompaniments.

The decline of the Janissaries after about 1600 is a story of lax discipline and rebelliousness, enforced periods of idleness confined to barracks, even regicide. (Tsar Peter the Great's childhood was terrorized by the "streltsy," a force of picked infantry whose rise and fall bears a striking resemblance to that of the Janissaries.)

In 1826, Sultan Mahmud annihilated the rebellious Janissaries by shelling them in their own barracks, and abolished the troops by official proclamation.

SUSAN WEBB AND PAUL GRUBER

Material for this article was taken from *The Ottoman Centuries* by Lord Kinross. Also consulted were *The Operas of Mozart* by William Mann, *The Complete Operas of Mozart* by Charles Osborne, and the *Cambridge Opera Handbook* on the opera by Thomas Bauman.

ACKNOWLEDGMENTS

New York Public Library at Lincoln Center
Dr. Irene Spiegelman
Walter Taussig

DIE ENTFÜHRUNG AUS DEM SERAIL

ACT ONE

SCENE I

Square in front of the palace of Pasha Selim at the seashore.
Belmonte alone

No. 1: Aria

BELMONTE

Hier soll ich dich denn sehen,
Konstanze! dich mein Glück!
Laß Himmel es geschehen!
Gib mir die Ruh' zurück!
Ich duldete der Leiden,
O Liebe! allzuviel!
Schenk mir dafür nun Freuden
Und bringe mich ans Ziel.

Finally I am to see you here,
Konstanze! You, my happiness!
Let it come about, oh heaven!
Restore my peace of mind to me!
I have endured too much
Suffering, oh love!
In return, now grant me joy
And bring me to my goal.

(He speaks.)

Spoken monologue

Aber wie soll ich in den Palast kommen,
wie sie sehen, wie sprechen?

But how am I to enter the palace, to see
her, to speak to her?

SCENE II

Belmonte. Osmin with a ladder, which he leans up against
a tree in front of the palace; he climbs it and picks figs.

No. 2: Song and Duet

OSMIN

Wer ein Liebchen hat gefunden,
Die es treu und redlich meint,

He who has found a sweetheart,
Who treats him honestly and truly,

87

Lohn' es ihr durch tausend Küsse,	Should reward her with a thousand kisses,
Mach' ihr all das Leben süße,	Make all her life sweet,
Sei ihr Tröster, sei ihr Freund.	Be her comfort, be her friend.
Trallalera, trallalera!	Trallalera, trallalera!

Spoken dialogue

BELMONTE (*speaks*)

Vielleicht, daß ich durch diesen Alten etwas erfahre.—He, Freund! ist das nicht das Landhaus des Bassa Selim?—	Perhaps I will learn something from this old man. Hey, friend! Isn't this the country house of the Pasha Selim?

Song

OSMIN (*sings as before while he works*)

Doch sie treu sich zu erhalten,	But in order to keep her true,
Schließ' er Liebchen sorglich ein:	He should carefully lock her up;
Denn die losen Dinger haschen	For the silly things chase
Jeden Schmetterling und naschen	Every butterfly, and partake
Gar zu gern von fremden Wein.	All too gladly of someone else's wine.
Trallalera, trallalera!	Trallalera, trallalera!

Spoken dialogue

BELMONTE (*speaks*)

He, Alter, he! Hört Ihr nicht?—Ist hier des Bassa Selim Palast?	Hey, old man, hey!—Don't you hear me? Is this the palace of the Pasha Selim?

Song

OSMIN (*looks at him, turns back and sings as before*)

Sonderlich beim Mondenscheine,	Pay particular attention,
Freunde, nehmt sie wohl in acht!	Friends, when the moon is shining!
Oft lauscht da ein junges Herrchen,	Often then a young man is listening, who
Kirrt und lockt das kleine Närrchen,	Tempts and traps the little fool.
Und dann Treue gute Nacht!	And then fidelity, good night!
Trallalera, trallalera!	Trallalera, trallalera!

Duet

BELMONTE

Verwünscht seist du samt deinem Liede!	Curse you along with your song!
Ich bin dein Singen nun schon müde;	I am tired of your singing now;
So hör doch nur ein einzig Wort!	Listen to just one single word!

OSMIN

Was Henker laßt Ihr Euch gelüsten,	Why the devil do you permit yourself
Euch zu ereifern, Euch zu brüsten?	To fly into a rage, to give yourself airs?
Was wollt Ihr? Hurtig! Ich muß fort.	What do you want? Quick! I have to go.

BELMONTE

Ist das des Bassa Selim Haus? Is that the Pasha Selim's house?

OSMIN

He? Eh?

BELMONTE

Ist das des Bassa Selim Haus? Is that the Pasha Selim's house?

OSMIN

Das ist des Bassa Selim Haus. That is the Pasha Selim's house.

(*He is about to leave.*)

BELMONTE

So wartet doch— Please wait—

OSMIN

Ich kann nicht weilen. I can't stay.

BELMONTE

Ein Wort— One word—

OSMIN

Geschwind, denn ich muß eilen. Quickly, because I have to hurry.

BELMONTE

Seid Ihr in seinen Diensten, Freund? Are you in his employ, friend?

OSMIN

He? Eh?

BELMONTE

Seid Ihr in seinen Diensten, Freund? Are you in his employ, friend?

OSMIN

He? Eh?

BELMONTE

Seid Ihr in seinen Diensten, Freund?— Are you in his employ, friend?

OSMIN

Ich bin in seinen Diensten, Freund.   I am in his employ, friend.

Recitative

BELMONTE

Wie kann ich den Pedrill' wohl sprechen,   How can I possibly speak to Pedrillo,
der hier in seinen Diensten steht?   who is here in his employ?

Duet

OSMIN

Den Schurken?—der den Hals soll   To the scoundrel? Whose neck should be
brechen?   broken?
Seht selber zu; wenn's anders geht.   Find out yourself, if you can manage to
do so.

(is about to leave)

BELMONTE (to himself)

Was für ein alter, grober Bengel!   What an old, rude lout!

OSMIN (inspecting him, to himself)

Das ist just so ein Galgenschwengel!   That's the same kind of good-for-nothing!

BELMONTE (to him)

Ihr irrt, es ist ein braver Mann.   You are wrong, he is a good fellow.

OSMIN

So brav, daß man ihn spießen kann.   Good enough to put on a spit.

BELMONTE

Ihr müßt ihn wahrlich nicht recht   You must not really know him well.
kennen.

OSMIN

Recht gut; ich ließ' ihn heut verbrennen.   Very well; I would have him burned to
death this very day.

BELMONTE

Er ist fürwahr ein guter Tropf.   In truth he is a good fellow.

OSMIN

Auf einen Pfahl gehört sein Kopf.   His head belongs on a stake.

(He is about to leave.)

BELMONTE

So bleibet doch!   Stay a little longer!

OSMIN

Was wollt Ihr noch?   What else do you want?

BELMONTE

Ich möchte gerne . . .   I would like very much . . .

OSMIN (*mockingly*)

. . . so hübsch von ferne   . . . Nicely from a distance,
Ums Haus rumschleichen   To creep around the house
Und Mädchen stehlen?—Fort,   And steal the girls?—Go away,
Euresgleichen braucht man hier nicht.   Your kind isn't needed here.

BELMONTE

Ihr seid besessen! sprecht voller Galle   You are possessed! Spewing bile so
Mir so vermessen ins Angesicht!   Impudently into my face!

OSMIN

Nur nicht in Eifer!   Don't outdo yourself!

BELMONTE

Schont Euren Geifer.   Spare me your venom.

OSMIN

Ich kenn' Euch schon.   I know you already.

BELMONTE

Laßt Euer Drohn.   Stop your threatening.

OSMIN

Schert Euch zum Teufel! Ihr kriegt, ich   Go to the devil! Or else, I swear, you will
    schwöre,
Sonst ohne Gnade die Bastonade;   Get a merciless beating*;
Noch habt Ihr Zeit! Noch habt Ihr Zeit!   You still have time!

(*pushes him away*)

BELMONTE

Es bleibt kein Zweifel, Ihr seid von   No doubt remains, you are out of your
    Sinnen.   mind.

* Bastonado, bastinado: punishment or torture by caning on the soles of the feet.

| Welch ein Betragen auf meine Fragen, | What behavior in response to my question, |
| Seid doch gescheit, seid doch gescheit. | Be reasonable. |

(leaves)

OSMIN

Schert Euch zum Teufel, Ihr kriegt, ich schwöre,	Go to the devil! Or else, I swear, you will
Sonst ohne Gnade die Bastonade;	Get a merciless beating;
Noch habt Ihr Zeit, noch habt Ihr Zeit!	You still have time!

SCENE III

Osmin, afterwards Pedrillo

Spoken dialogue

OSMIN *(alone)*

Könnt' ich mir doch noch so einen Schurken auf die Nase setzen wie den Pedrillo, so einen Gaudieb, der Tag und Nacht nichts tut, als nach meinen Weibern rumzuschleichen und zu schnobern, ob's nichts für seinen Schnabel setzt. Aber ich laure ihm sicher auf den Dienst, und wohl bekomm' dir die Prügelsuppe, wenn ich dich einmal beim Kanthaken krieg!—Hätt' er sich nur beim Bassa nicht so eingeschmeichelt, er sollte den Strick längst um den Hals haben.

Should I take in another scoundrel like Pedrillo, a good-for-nothing, who day and night does nothing else but creep around my women and sniff out whether there is anything to his taste. But I'll certainly lie in wait for him, and may the thrashing do you good if I ever collar you. If he hadn't ingratiated himself so with the Pasha, he would have had a rope** around his neck long since.

PEDRILLO *(enters)*

| Nun, wie steht's, Osmin? Ist der Bassa noch nicht zurück? | So, how are things, Osmin? Isn't the Pasha back yet? |

OSMIN

| Sieh darnach, wenn du's wissen willst. | Go look for yourself, if you want to know. |

** Rope around the neck: could refer to hanging, however, the Janissaries used their bowstrings for strangulation!

PEDRILLO

Schon wieder Sturm im Kalender? Hast du dies Gericht Feigen für mich gepflückt?

In a rage again? Have you picked this dish of figs for me?

OSMIN

Gift für dich, verwünschter Schmarotzer!

Poison for you, you damned parasite!

PEDRILLO

Was in aller Welt ich dir nur getan haben muß, daß du beständig mit mir zankst. Laß uns doch einmal Friede machen.

What in the world must I have done to you that you continually quarrel with me? Let's make peace for once.

OSMIN

Friede mit dir? Mit so einem schleichenden, spitzbübischen Paßauf, der nur spioniert, wie er mir eins versetzen kann? Erdrosseln möcht' ich dich!—

Peace, with you? With a sneaky scamp, a rascally little watchdog like you, who only spies out ways that he can put one over on me? I would rather throttle you!

PEDRILLO

Aber sag nur, warum? Warum?

But just tell me why? Why?

OSMIN

Warum?—Weil ich dich nicht leiden kann.

Why?—Because I can't stand you.

No. 3: Aria

Solche hergelauf'ne Laffen,
Die nur nach den Weibern gaffen,
Mag ich vor den Teufel nicht.
Denn ihr ganzes Tun und Lassen
Ist, uns auf den Dienst zu passen,
Doch mich trügt kein solch Gesicht.
Eure Tücken, eure Ränke,
Eure Finten, eure Schwänke
Sind mir ganz bekannt.
Mich zu hintergehen,
Müßt ihr früh aufstehen,

Ich hab' auch Verstand.
Drum, beim Barte des Propheten!
Ich studiere Tag und Nacht,
Ruh' nicht, bis ich dich seh' töten,
Nimm dich wie du willst in acht.

By the devil, I don't like
The kind of roving dandies who only
Gape at and run after the women.
For everything you do, and don't do,
Is to get out of serving for us,
But such a face doesn't deceive me.
Your tricks, your schemes,
Your pretenses, your pranks
Are all well-known to me.
To get around me
You would have to get up early in the
    morning,
I am pretty smart too.
So, by the beard of the Prophet,
I am studying day and night,
Won't rest, 'til I see you killed,
Take whatever precautions you will.

Spoken dialogue

PEDRILLO

Was bist du für ein grausamer Kerl—und ich hab' dir nichts getan—	What a cruel fellow you are—and I have done nothing to you—

OSMIN

Du hast ein Galgengesicht. Das ist genug.	You have an ugly mug. That's enough.

Aria

Erst geköpft, dann gehangen,	First beheaded, then hanged,
Dann gespießt auf heiße Stangen,	Then spitted on hot skewers,
Dann verbrannt, dann gebunden	Then burned, then bound
Und getaucht, zuletzt geschunden.	And drowned, and finally skinned.

(*goes into the house*)

SCENE IV

Pedrillo, afterward Belmonte

Spoken dialogue

PEDRILLO (*alone*)

Geh nur, verwünschter Aufpasser, es ist noch nicht aller Tage Abend. Wer weiß, wer den andern überlistet; und dir mißtrauischem, gehässigem Menschenfeinde eine Grube zu graben, sollte ein wahres Fest für mich sein.	Go then, you damned watchdog, and don't count your chickens before they're hatched. Who knows which one will outwit the other; to dig a pit for you, you mistrustful, malicious misanthrope, should be a real pleasure for me!

BELMONTE

Pedrillo, guter Pedrillo!	Pedrillo, good Pedrillo!

PEDRILLO

Ach, mein bester Herr! Ist's möglich? Sind Sie's wirklich? Bravo, Madam Fortuna, bravo, das heißt doch Wort gehalten! Schon verzweifelte ich, ob einer meiner Briefe Sie getroffen hätte.	Ah, my dear master! Is it possible? Is it really you? Bravo, Lady Luck, bravo, that means you've kept your word. I was already in doubt whether one of my letters had reached you.

BELMONTE

Sag, guter Pedrillo, lebt meine Konstanze noch?	Tell me, good Pedrillo, does my Konstanze still live?

PEDRILLO

Lebt, und noch, hoff' ich, für Sie. Seit dem schrecklichen Tage, an welchem das Glück uns einen so häßlichen Streich spielte und unser Schiff von den Seeräubern erobern ließ, haben wir mancherlei Drangsal erfahren. Glücklicherweise traf sich's noch, daß der Bassa Selim uns alle drei kaufte: Ihre Konstanze nämlich, meine Blonde und mich. Er ließ uns sogleich hier auf sein Landhaus bringen. Donna Konstanze ward seine auserwählte Geliebte.—

She lives, and still, I hope, for you. Since the terrible day, when luck played such a mean joke on us and allowed our ship to be seized by pirates, we have undergone all sorts of hardships. Fortunately, it happened that the Pasha Selim bought all three of us; namely, your Konstanze, my Blonde and me. He had us brought at once to his country house. Donna Konstanze became the woman of his choice.—

BELMONTE

Ah! Was sagst du?

Ah! What are you saying?

PEDRILLO

Nu, nur nicht so hitzig! Sie ist noch nicht in die schlimmsten Hände gefallen. Der Bassa ist ein Renegat und hat noch so viel Delikatesse, keine seiner Weiber zu seiner Liebe zu zwingen. Und soviel ich weiß, spielt er noch immer den unerhörten Liebhaber.

Now, not so hasty! She has not yet fallen into the worst hands. The pasha is a renegade, and still has sufficient delicacy not to force any of his women into loving him. And as far as I know, he is still playing the unrequited lover.

BELMONTE

Wär' es möglich? Wär' Konstanze noch treu?

Could it be true? Could Konstanze still be faithful?

PEDRILLO

Sicher noch, lieber Herr! Aber wie's mit meinem Blondchen steht, weiß der Himmel! Das arme Ding schmachtet bei einem alten, häßlichen Kerl, dem sie der Bassa geschenkt hat; und vielleicht—ach, ich darf gar nicht dran denken!

Certainly, dear master! But how things stand with my Blondchen, heaven only knows! The poor thing languishes in the house of an old, ugly fellow, to whom the pasha has given her; and perhaps—ah, I dare not even think about it!

BELMONTE

Doch nicht der alte Kerl, der soeben ins Haus ging?

Not the old fellow who just went into the house?

PEDRILLO

Eben der.

The very same one.

BELMONTE

Und dies ist der Liebling des Bassa?

And this is the minion of the pasha?

PEDRILLO

Liebling, Spion und Ausbund aller Spitzbuben, der mich mit den Augen vergiften möchte, wenn's möglich wäre.

Minion, spy and paragon of rogues, who would poison me with his eyes, if it were possible.

BELMONTE

O guter Pedrillo! Was sagst du?

Oh, good Pedrillo! What are you saying?

PEDRILLO

Nur nicht gleich verzagt! Unter uns gesagt: ich hab' auch einen Stein im Brette beim Bassa. Durch mein bißchen Geschick in der Gärtnerei hab' ich seine Gunst weggekriegt, und dadurch hab' ich so ziemlich Freiheit, die tausend andere nicht haben würden. Da sonst jede Mannsperson sich entfernen muß, wenn eine seiner Weiber in den Garten kommt, kann ich bleiben; sie reden sogar mit mir, und er sagt nichts darüber. Freilich mault der alte Osmin, besonders, wenn mein Blondchen ihrer Gebieterin folgen muß.

Don't despair quite yet! Just between us, I am also in the pasha's good graces. By my trifling skill in gardening, I have gotten into his favor, and thus I have considerable freedom which thousands of others wouldn't have. When every other male must leave if one of his women comes into the garden, I can stay; they even speak with me, and he says nothing about it. To be sure, old Osmin grumbles, especially if my Blondchen must follow her mistress.

BELMONTE

Ist's möglich? Du hast sie gesprochen?— O sag, sag: Liebt sie mich noch?

Is it possible? You have spoken to her?— Oh, tell me, tell me: does she still love me?

PEDRILLO

Hm, daß Sie daran zweifeln! Ich dächte, Sie kennten die gute Konstanze als zu gut, hätten Proben genug ihrer Liebe.— Doch damit dürfen wir uns gar nicht aufhalten. Hier ist bloß die Frage, wie's anzufangen ist hier wegzukommen?

Hm, how can you doubt it! I thought you knew the good Konstanze well enough, and had sufficient proofs of her love. But let's not waste any more time on that. It is a question of how to manage to get away from here.

BELMONTE

Oh, da hab' ich für alles gesorgt! Ich hab' hier ein Schiff in einiger Entfernung vom Hafen, das uns auf den ersten Wink einnimmt und—

Oh, I have provided for everything! I have a ship here, a little distance from the harbor, which at the first sign will take us aboard and—

PEDRILLO

Ah, sachte, sachte! Erst müssen wir die
Mädels haben, ehe wir zu Schiffe gehen,
und das geht nicht so husch, husch, wie
Sie meinen!

Ah, easy, easy! First, before we go to the
ship, we must get the girls, and that
doesn't go as quickly as you think!

BELMONTE

O lieber, guter Pedrillo, mach nur, daß
ich sie sehen, daß ich sie sprechen kann!
Das Herz schlägt mir vor Angst und
Freude!—

Oh dear, good Pedrillo, only arrange for
me to see her, for me to speak to her! My
heart is throbbing with anxiety and
joy!—

PEDRILLO

Pfiffig müssen wir das Ding anfangen,
und rasch müssen wir's ausführen, damit
wir den alten Aufpasser übertölpeln.
Bleiben Sie hier in der Nähe. Jetzt wird
der Bassa bald von einer Lustfahrt auf
dem Wasser zurückkommen. Ich will Sie
ihm als einen geschickten Baumeister
vorstellen, denn Bauen und Gärtnerei
sind seine Steckenpferde. Aber lieber,
goldner Herr, halten Sie sich in
Schranken: Konstanze ist
bei ihm—

We must begin the thing slyly, and carry
it out swiftly, so that we can dupe the old
spy. Stay close by here. The pasha will
soon be returning from a pleasure trip on
the water. I will introduce you as a skilled
architect, since architecture and
gardening are his passions. But dear,
golden master, keep yourself under
control: Konstanze is with him—

BELMONTE

Konstanze bei ihm? Was sagst du? Ich soll
sie sehen?

Konstanze with him? What are you
saying? I am to see her?

PEDRILLO

Gemach, gemach, um Himmels willen,
lieber Herr! Sonst stolpern wir.—Ah, ich
glaube, dort seh' ich sie schon angefahren
kommen. Gehn Sie nur, auf die Seite,
wenn er kommt; bleiben Sie hier, ich will
ihm entgegengehen.

Gently, gently, for heaven's sake, dear
master! Otherwise we stumble.—Ah, I
think I already see them being conveyed
here. When he arrives, just go off to the
side; stay here, I will go to meet him.

(He goes off.)

SCENE V

Belmonte alone

No. 4: Recitative and Aria

BELMONTE

Konstanze! dich wiederzusehen! dich!—	Konstanze! To see you again! You!—
O wie ängstlich, o wie feurig!	Oh how anxiously, how passionately!
Klopft mein liebevolles Herz!	Beats my loving heart!
Und des Wiedersehens Zähre	May the tears of reunion
Lohnt der Trennung bangen Schmerz.	Be recompense for the uneasy pain of separation.
Schon zittr' ich und wanke,	I am already trembling and wavering,
Schon zag' ich und schwanke;	I am already hesitating and faltering;
Es hebt sich die schwellende Brust.	My swelling bosom is heaving.
Ist das ihr Lispeln?	Is that her whispering?
Es wird mir so bange.	It makes me so uneasy.
War das ihr Seufzen?	Was that her sighing?
Es glüht mir die Wange.	My cheeks are flushed.
Täuscht mich die Liebe,	Does love deceive me,
War es ein Traum?	Was it a dream?
O wie ängstlich, o wie feurig!	Oh how anxiously, how passionately!
Klopft mein liebevolles Herz!	Beats my loving heart!
Ist das ihr Lispeln?	Is that her whispering?
War das ihr Seufzen?	Was that her sighing?
Es wird mir so bange,	It makes me so uneasy,
Es glüht mir die Wange.	My cheeks are flushed!
O wie ängstlich, o wie feurig!	Oh how anxiously, how passionately!
Klopft mein liebevolles Herz!	Beats my loving heart!
Schon zittr' ich und wanke!	I am already trembling and wavering!
Schon zag' ich und schwanke!	I am already hesitating and faltering!
O wie ängstlich, o wie feurig!	Oh how anxiously, how passionately!
Klopft mein liebevolles Herz!	Beats my loving heart!

Spoken dialogue

PEDRILLO (*comes at a run*)

Geschwind, geschwind auf die Seite und versteckt! Der Bassa kommt.	Quickly, quickly, to the side and hide! The pasha is coming.

(*Belmonte hides.*)

SCENE VI

(The Pasha Selim and Konstanze are conveyed in a pleasure boat, preceded to the landing by another boat filled with Janissary musicians. The Janissaries place themselves in ranks along the shore, sing the following chorus, and then withdraw.)

No. 5a: March
No. 5b: Chorus

CHORUS

Singt dem großen Bassa Lieder, töne,
  feuriger Gesang;
Und vom Ufer halle wider unsrer Lieder
  Jubelklang!

Sing songs to the great pasha, let the fiery
  hymn sound;
And from the shore, may the jubilant ring
  of our songs echo!

FOUR SOLOISTS

Weht ihm entgegen, kühlende Winde,
Ebne dich sanfter, wallende Flut!
Singt ihm entgegen, fliegende Chöre,
Singt ihm der Liebe Freuden ins Herz!

Blow towards him, cooling winds,
Make yourself smoother, boiling flood!
Sing towards him, flying choirs,
Sing love's joys into his heart!

CHORUS

Singt dem großen Bassa Lieder, töne,
  feuriger Gesang;
Und vom Ufer halle wider unsrer Lieder
  Jubelklang!

Sing songs to the great pasha, let the fiery
  hymn sound;
And from the shore, may the jubilant ring
  of our songs echo!

(The Janissaries leave.)

SCENE VII

Selim, Konstanze

Spoken dialogue

SELIM

Immer noch traurig, geliebte Konstanze?
Immer in Tränen?—Sieh, dieser schöne
Abend, diese reizende Gegend, diese
bezaubernde Musik, meine zärtliche Liebe
für dich—sag, kann nichts von allem
dich endlich beruhigen, endlich dein Herz
rühren?—Sieh, ich könnte befehlen,
könnte grausam mit dir verfahren, dich
zwingen.—

Still sad, beloved Konstanze? Still in
tears?—Behold this beautiful evening,
this charming locale, this enchanting
music, my tender love for you—tell me,
can none of these finally calm you, finally
move your heart?—Look, I could
command you, could deal cruelly with
you, force you—

(Konstanze sighs.)

Aber nein, Konstanze, dir selbst will ich dein Herz zu danken haben—dir selbst—	But no, Konstanze, for your heart, I want to have only you to thank—only you—

KONSTANZE

Großmütiger Mann! O daß ich es könnte! Daß ich's erwidern könnte—aber—	Most generous man! If only I could! If only I could respond—but—

SELIM

Sag, Konstanze, sag, was hält dich zurück?	Tell me, Konstanze, tell me what is holding you back?

KONSTANZE

Du wirst mich hassen.	You will hate me.

SELIM

Nein, ich schwöre dir's. Du weißt, wie sehr ich dich liebe, wieviel Freiheit ich dir vor allen meinen Weibern gestatte, dich wie meine Einzige schätze.—	No, I swear to you. You know how much I love you, how much freedom I allow you compared to my other women, that I treasure you as if you were my only one—

KONSTANZE

O so verzeih!	Oh, then forgive me!

No. 6: Aria

Ach ich liebte, war so glücklich, Kannte nicht der Liebe Schmerz; Schwur ihm Treue, dem Geliebten, Gab dahin mein ganzes Herz. Doch wie schnell schwand meine Freude. Trennung war mein banges Los; Und nun schwimmt mein Aug' in Tränen, Kummer ruht in meinem Schoß.	Ah, I loved, was so happy, Knew not the pain of love; Swore to my beloved to be faithful, Surrendered my whole heart. But how quickly my joy disappeared. Separation was my bitter fate; And now my eyes swim in tears, Grief rests within me.

(During the aria the pasha paces angrily back and forth.)

Spoken dialogue

Ach, ich sagt' es wohl, du würdest mich hassen. Aber verzeih, verzeih dem liebeskranken Mädchen!—Du bist ja so großmütig, so gut.—Ich will dir dienen,	Ah, I told you, you would hate me. But forgive, forgive the lovesick maiden!— You are so generous, so kind.—I will serve you, be your slave until the end of

deine Sklavin sein bis ans Ende meines Lebens, nur verlange nicht ein Herz von mir, das auf ewig versagt ist.—

SELIM

Ha, Undankbare! Was wagst du zu bitten?

KONSTANZE

Töte mich, Selim, töte mich! Nur zwinge mich nicht, meineidig zu werden.—Noch zuletzt, wie mich der Seeräuber aus den Armen meines Geliebten riß, schwur ich aufs feierlichste—

SELIM

Halt ein! Nicht ein Wort! Reize meinen Zorn nicht noch mehr. Bedenke, daß du in meiner Gewalt bist—

KONSTANZE

Ich bin es, aber du wirst dich ihrer nicht bedienen, ich kenne dein gutes, dein mitleidvolles Herz. Hätte ich's sonst wagen können, dir das meinige zu entdecken?—

SELIM

Wag es nicht, meine Güte zu mißbrauchen—

KONSTANZE

Nur Aufschub gönne mir, Herr, nur Zeit, meinen Schmerz zu vergessen!—

SELIM

Wie oft schon gewährt' ich dir diese Bitte—

KONSTANZE

Nur noch diesmal!

SELIM

Es sei! Zum letzten Male!—Geh, Konstanze, geh! Besinne dich eines Bessern, und morgen—

my life, only do not require a heart from me, which must forever be denied you—

SELIM

Ha, ungrateful one! What do you dare to ask?

KONSTANZE

Kill me, Selim, kill me! Only do not force me to perjure myself. At the last, when the pirate tore me from the arms of my beloved, I swore a solemn—

SELIM

Stop! Not a word! Do not provoke my anger still further. Consider that you are in my power—

KONSTANZE

I am, but you will not take advantage of it; I know your good, merciful heart. Could I otherwise have dared to reveal mine to you?—

SELIM

Do not dare to abuse my kindness—

KONSTANZE

Only grant me respite, my lord, only time in which to forget my pain!—

SELIM

How often have I already granted you this request.—

KONSTANZE

Only this one more time!

SELIM

So be it! For the last time!—Go, Konstanze, go! Change your mind for the better, and tomorrow—

KONSTANZE (*leaving*)

Unglückliches Mädchen! O Belmonte, Belmonte!

Unhappy maiden! Oh Belmonte, Belmonte!

SCENE VIII

Selim, Pedrillo, Belmonte

SELIM

Ihr Schmerz, ihre Tränen, ihre Standhaftigkeit bezaubern mein Herz immer mehr, machen mir ihre Liebe nur noch wünschenswerter. Ha! wer wollte gegen ein solches Herz Gewalt brauchen?—Nein, Konstanze, nein, auch Selim hat ein Herz, auch Selim kennt Liebe—

Her pain, her tears, her steadfastness bewitch my heart even more, make her love even more desirable to me. Ha! Who would want to use force against such a heart?—No, Konstanze, no, Selim also has a heart, Selim also knows love—

PEDRILLO

Herr! verzeih, daß ich es wage, dich in deinen Betrachtungen zu stören—

Sire! Forgive me for daring to disturb you in your thoughts.—

SELIM

Was willst du, Pedrillo?

What do you want, Pedrillo?

PEDRILLO

Dieser junge Mann, der sich in Italien mit vielem Fleiß anf die Baukunst gelegt hat, hat von deiner Macht, von deinem Reichtum gehört und kommt her, dir als Baumeister seine Dienste anzubieten.

This young man, who, in Italy, has applied himself very diligently to the study of architecture, has heard of your might, of your wealth, and has come to offer his services as architect.

BELMONTE

Herr, könnte ich so glücklich sein, durch meine geringen Fähigkeiten deinen Beifall zu verdienen!

Sire, could I be so fortunate, by means of my paltry talents, as to earn your approval!

SELIM

Hm! Du gefällst mir. Ich will sehen, was du kannst.—

Hm! You please me. I want to see what you are capable of.

(*to Pedrillo*)

Sorge für seinen Unterhalt. Morgen werde ich dich wieder rufen lassen.

See to his needs. Tomorrow I will have you summoned again.

(*goes out*)

SCENE IX

Belmonte, Pedrillo

PEDRILLO

Ha, Triumph, Triumph, Herr! Der erste Schritt wär' getan.

Ha, success, success, master! The first step has been taken.

BELMONTE

Ach, laß mich zu mir selbst kommen!— Ich habe sie gesehen, hab' das gute, treue, beste Mädchen gesehen!—O Konstanze, Konstanze! Was könnt' ich für dich tun, was für dich wagen?

Ah, let me return to my senses!—I have seen her, I have seen the good, true, best maiden!—Oh Konstanze, Konstanze! What could I do for you, dare for you?

PEDRILLO

Ha, gemach, gemach, bester Herr! Stimmen Sie den Ton ein bißchen herab; Verstellung wird uns weit bessere Dienste leisten. Wir sind nicht in unserem Vaterlande. Hier fragen sie den Henker darnach, ob's einen Kopf mehr oder weniger in der Welt gibt. Bastonade und Strick um den Hals sind hier wie ein Morgenbrot.

Ha, gently, gently, dear master! Lower your voice a little; pretense will serve us far better. We are not in our fatherland. Here they ask the executioner whether there is one head more or less in the world. Here beatings and hangings are as regular as breakfast.

BELMONTE

Ach, Pedrillo, wenn du die Liebe kenntest!—

Ah, Pedrillo, if you had experienced love!—

PEDRILLO

Hm, als wenn's mit unsereinem gar nichts wäre! Ich habe so gut meine zärtlichen Stunden als andere Leute. Und denken Sie denn, daß mir's nicht auch im Bauche grimmt, wenn ich mein Blondchen von so einem alten Spitzbuben, wie der Osmin ist, bewacht sehen muß?

Hm, as if with our sort there were no such thing! I have just as many tender hours as other people. And do you think that it doesn't gripe me in the belly when I have to see my Blondchen shadowed by an old rascal like Osmin?

BELMONTE

O wenn es möglich wäre, sie zu sprechen—

Oh if it were possible to speak to her—

PEDRILLO

Wir wollen sehen, was zu tun ist. Kommen Sie nur mit mir in den Garten: aber um alles in der Welt: vorsichtig und fein. Denn hier ist alles Aug' und Ohr.	We'll see what's to be done. Just come with me into the garden; but for heaven's sake: cautiously and quietly. For everything here has eyes and ears.

(*They are about to go into the palace. Osmin come to meet them in the doorway, and stops them.*)

SCENE X

The above, Osmin

OSMIN

Wohin?	Where are you going?

PEDRILLO

Hinein!	Inside!

OSMIN (*to Belmonte*)

Was will das Gesicht?—Zurück mit dir, zurück!	What does this fellow want? Stand back, you, stand back!

PEDRILLO

Ha, gemach, Meister Grobian, gemach! Er ist in des Bassa Diensten.	Ha, gently, Mister Roughneck, gently! He is in the pasha's service.

OSMIN

In des Henkers Diensten mag er sein! Er soll nicht herein!	He could be in the hangman's service! He is not coming in here.

PEDRILLO

Er soll aber herein!	But he is coming in!

OSMIN

Kommt mir nur einen Schritt über die Schwelle—	Just come one step over the threshold—

BELMONTE

Unverschämter! Hast du nicht mehr Achtung für einen Mann meines Standes?	Insolent fellow! Have you no respect for a man of my standing?

OSMIN

Ei, Ihr mögt mir vom Stande sein!—Fort, fort, oder ich will Euch Beine machen.	Huh! You may be of *standing!*—Be off, be off, or *I* will get you *moving*.

PEDRILLO

Alter Dummkopf! Es ist ja der Baumeister, den der Bassa angenommen hat.

You old fool! He is the master builder whom the pasha has taken into his employ.

OSMIN

Meinethalben sei er Stockmeister, nur komm' er mir hier nicht zu nahe. Ich müßte nicht sehen, daß es so ein Kumpan deines Gelichters ist und daß das so eine abgeredete Karte ist, uns zu überlisten. Der Bassa ist weich wie Butter, mit dem könnt ihr machen, was ihr wollt; aber ich habe eine feine Nase. Gaunerei ist's um den ganzen Kram mit euch fremdem Gesindel; und ihr abgefeimten Betrüger habt lange euer Plänchen angelegt, eure Pfiffe auszuführen. Aber wart't ein bißchen! Osmin schläft nicht. Wär' ich Bassa, ihr wärt längst gespießt.—Ja, schneid't nur Gesichter, lacht nur höhnisch in den Bart hinein!

He could be a master canesman for all I care, just don't let him come too near me. I wouldn't want to see that it's some crony from your gang, and that this is some kind of scheme to outsmart us. The pasha is as soft as butter, you can do with him what you want to; but I have a keen nose. Cheating is the chief business of you foreign trash; and you wily tricksters have long had your little plans for carrying out your tricks. But wait! Osmin doesn't sleep. If I were pasha you would have been spitted long since.—Go ahead, just make faces, laugh spitefully in your beards!

PEDRILLO

Ereifere dich nicht so, Alter, es hilft dir doch nichts. Sieh, soeben werden wir hineinspazieren.

Don't get yourself so worked up, old man, it won't do you any good. You see, this very moment we're going to walk in.

OSMIN

Ha, das will ich sehen!

Ha, that I'd like to see!

(positions himself in front of the door)

PEDRILLO

Mach keine Umstände.—

Don't make any trouble—

BELMONTE

Weg, Niederträchtiger!

Out of the way, wretch!

No. 7: Trio

OSMIN

Marsch! Marsch! Marsch! Trollt euch fort!
Sonst soll die Bastonade
Euch gleich zu Diensten stehn!

March! March! March! You trot off!
Otherwise the bastonado
Will immediately be at your service!

Belmonte and Pedrillo

Ei, ei, ei! Das wär' ja schade,	Oho! It would be a great shame
Mit uns so umzugehn!	To treat us that way!

Osmin

Kommt mir nicht näher,	Don't come any closer to me,

Belmonte and Pedrillo

Weg von der Türe,	Away from the door,

Osmin

Sonst schlag' ich drein.	Or else I will use force!

Belmonte and Pedrillo

Wir gehn hinein!	We are going in!

(They push him away from the door.)

Osmin

Sonst schlag' ich drein!	Or else I will use force!

Belmonte and Pedrillo

Wir gehn hinein.	We are going in.

Osmin

Marsch fort! Ich schlage drein!	March away! I'll use force.

Belmonte and Pedrillo

Platz, fort! Wir gehn hinein!	Make way! We are going in!

Osmin

Marsch! Marsch! Marsch! Trollt euch fort!	March! March! March! You trot off!
Sonst soll die Bastonade	Otherwise the bastonado
Euch gleich zu Diensten stehn!	Will immediately be at your service!
Marsch fort! Ich schlage drein!	Or else I will use force!

Belmonte and Pedrillo

Wir gehn hinein! ei, das wär' schade,	We are going in! It would be a great shame,
Mit uns so umzugehn!	To treat us this way!
Platz, fort! Wir gehn hinein!	Make way! We are going in!
Wir gehn hinein! Platz, fort!	We are going in! Make way!

(They shove him aside and go inside.)

End of Act One

ACT TWO

SCENE I

Garden of the palace of the Pasha Selim. On the side, Osmin's house
Osmin, Blonde

Spoken dialogue

BLONDE

O des Zankens, Befehlens und Murrens
wird auch kein Ende! Einmal für allemal;
das steht mir nicht an! Denkst du alter
Murrkopf etwa, eine türkische Sklavin
vor dir zu haben, die bei deinen Befehlen
zittert? Oh, da irrst du dich sehr! Mit
europäischen Mädchen springt man nicht
so herum; denen begegnet man ganz
anders.

Oh will there be no end to all these
squabbles, orders and grumblings! Once
and for all, I won't put up with it! Do
you somehow think, you old grouch, that
you have a Turkish slave in front of you,
who trembles at your commands? Oh, in
that you are very much mistaken!
European girls are not to be treated like
that; they are to be approached very
differently.

No. 8: Aria

Durch Zärtlichkeit und Schmeicheln,
Gefälligkeit und Scherzen
Erobert man die Herzen
Der guten Mädchen leicht.
Doch mürrisches Befehlen
Und Poltern, Zanken, Plagen
Macht, daß in wenig Tagen
So Lieb' als Treu' entweicht.

With tenderness and flattery,
Pleasantness and joking
One easily conquers the hearts
Of good maidens.
But surly commands
And blustering, squabbling, pestering
Ensure that, in just a few days
Faithful love takes flight.

Spoken dialogue

OSMIN

Ei seht doch mal, was das Mädchen
vorschreiben kann! Zärtlichkeit!
Schmeicheln!—Es ist mir wie pure
Zärtlichkeit! Wer Teufel hat dir das Zeug
in den Kopf gesetzt?—Hier sind wir in
der Türkei, und da geht's aus einem
andern Tone. Ich dein Herr, du meine
Sklavin; ich befehle, du mußt gehorchen!

Oho! See how the girl can tell me what
to do! Tenderness! Flattery! I'll show you
to use tenderness! Who the devil put that
stuff into your head? We are here in
Turkey, and things take on a different
tone. I am your master, you my slave; I
command, you must obey.

BLONDE

Deine Sklavin? Ich deine Sklavin!—Ha, ein Mädchen eine Sklavin! Noch einmal sag mir das, noch einmal!	Your slave? I your slave!—Ha, a young maiden be a slave! Say that once more to me, once more!

OSMIN (*to himself*)

Ich möchte toll werden, was das Mädchen für ein starrköpfiges Ding ist.	I must be going crazy; what a pigheaded thing the girl is.

(*aloud*)

Du hast doch wohl nicht vergessen, daß dich der Bassa mir zur Sklavin geschenkt hat?	Hopefully you have not forgotten that the pasha has given you to me as a slave?

BLONDE

Bassa hin, Bassa her! Mädchen sind keine Ware zum Verschenken! Ich bin eine Engländerin, zur Freiheit geboren, und trotz' jedem, der mich zu etwas zwingen will!	Pasha here, pasha there! Girls are not goods to give away! I am an Englishwoman, free-born, and I defy anyone who wants to force me to do anything!

OSMIN (*aside*)

Gift und Dolch über das Mädchen!— Beim Mahomet! sie macht mich rasend.—Und doch lieb' ich die Spitzbübin, trotz ihres tollen Kopfs!	Hellfire and damnation* on the girl! By Mohammed! She makes me frantic.— And still I love the little imp, in spite of her crazy head!

(*aloud*)

Ich befehle dir augenblicklich, mich zu lieben.	I order you this minute to love me.

BLONDE

Hahaha! Komm mir nur ein wenig näher, ich will dir fühlbare Beweise davon geben.	Ha ha ha! Just come a little closer to me, I will give you palpable demonstrations of that.

OSMIN

Tolles Ding! Weißt du, daß du mein bist und ich dich dafür züchtigen kann?	You crazy thing! Don't you know that you're mine and that I can punish you for saying that?

BLONDE

Wag's nicht, mich anzurühren, wenn dir deine Augen lieb sind.	Don't you dare lay a hand on me, if you value your eyes.

* Hellfire and Damnation!: "Gift und Dolch" literally means "Poison and Dagger" and is a classic example of something "lost in translation"!

Die Entführung aus dem Serail

OSMIN

Wie? Du unterstehst dich—

What? You have the impudence to—

BLONDE

Da ist was zu unterstehen? Du bist der
Unverschämte, der sich zu viel Freiheit
herausnimmt. So ein altes, häßliches
Gesicht untersteht sich, einem Mädchen
wie ich, jung, schön, zur Freude geboren,
wie einer Magd zu befehlen! Wahrhaftig,
das stünde mir an! Uns gehört das
Regiment! Ihr seid unsere Sklaven und
glücklich, wenn ihr Verstand genug habt,
euch die Ketten zu erleichtern.

Is there something to be impudent about?
You are the cheeky one who takes too
many liberties. Such an old, ugly fellow
has the nerve to order a girl like me,
young, beautiful, free-born, around like a
serving-maid. I won't go along with that!
We rule here! You are our slaves and
you're lucky if you have enough sense to
lighten your chains.

OSMIN

Bei meinem Bart, sie ist toll! Hier in der
Türkei?

By my beard, she is crazy! Here in
Turkey?

BLONDE

Türkei hin, Türkei her! Weib ist Weib, es
sei, wo es wolle! Sind eure Weiber solche
Närrinnen, sich von euch unterjochen zu
lassen, desto schlimmer für sie. In Europa
verstehen sie das Ding besser. Laß mich
nur einmal Fuß hier gefaßt haben, sie
sollen bald anders werden.

Turkey here, Turkey there! A woman is a
woman, wherever she is! If your women
are such fools as to allow themselves to
be subjugated by you, then so much the
worse for them. In Europe they
understand things much better. Let me
just find a firm foothold here, they would
soon be changed.

OSMIN

Beim Allah! Die wär' imstande, uns allen
die Weiber rebellisch zu machen—
aber—

By Allah! She would be capable of making
all the women rebellious against us—
but—

BLONDE

Aufs Bitten müßt ihr euch legen, wenn
ihr etwas von uns erhalten wollt,
besonders Liebhaber deines Gesichters.

You must resort to pleading if you want
to obtain something from us, particularly
lovers of your sort.

OSMIN

Freilich, wenn ich Pedrillo wär', so ein
Drahtpüppchen wie er, da wär' ich
vermutlich willkommen, denn euer
Mienenspiel hab' ich lange weg.

Of course if I was Pedrillo, a little
marionette like him, then I would
probably be welcome; I figured out your
pantomimes long since.

BLONDE

Erraten, guter Alter, erraten! Das kannst du dir wohl einbilden, daß mir der niedliche kleine Pedrillo lieber ist als dein Blasbalggesicht. Also wenn du klug wärst—

Quite right, good old man, quite right. You can well imagine that cute little Pedrillo is dearer to me than you, fat-face. So if you were smart—

OSMIN

Sollt' ich dir die Freiheit geben, zu tun und zu machen, was du wolltest? He?

I should give you the freedom to do whatever and act however you wanted? Eh?

BLONDE

Besser würdest du immer dabei fahren: denn so wirst du sicher betrogen.

You would certainly fare better by doing so; as it stands you will certainly be deceived.

OSMIN

Gift und Dolch! Nun reißt mir die Geduld! Den Augenblick hinein ins Haus! Und wo du's wagst—

Hellfire and damnation! Now I'm losing my patience! Into the house this minute! And if you dare to—

BLONDE

Mach mich nicht zu lachen.

Don't make me laugh.

OSMIN

Ins Haus, sag' ich!

Into the house, I say!

BLONDE

Nicht von der Stelle!

I'm not moving from this spot!

OSMIN

Mach nicht, daß ich Gewalt brauche.

Don't make me use force.

BLONDE

Gewalt werd' ich mit Gewalt vertreiben. Meine Gebieterin hat mich hier in den Garten bestellt; sie ist die Geliebte des Bassa, sein Augapfel, sein alles, und es kostet mir ein Wort, so hast du fünfzig auf den Fußsohlen. Also geh—

I will turn force away with force. My mistress has summoned me here to the garden; she is the beloved of the pasha, the apple of his eye, his everything, and at one word from me, you would have fifty blows on the soles of your feet. Now *you* go—

OSMIN (*to himself*)

Das ist ein Satan. Ich muß nachgeben, so wahr ich ein Muselmann bin; sonst könnte ihre Drohung eintreffen.	She is a fiend. I must give in, as I am a true Muslim; otherwise her threat might become real.

No. 9: Duet

Ich gehe, doch rate ich dir, Den Schurken Pedrillo zu meiden.	I am going, but I advise you, To stay away from that rascal Pedrillo.

BLONDE

O pack dich, befiehl nicht mit mir, Du weißt ja, ich kann es nicht leiden.	Oh be off, just don't order me around, You know very well that I can't stand it.

OSMIN

Versprich mir—	Promise me—

BLONDE

Was fällt dir da ein!	What has come over you!

OSMIN

Zum Henker!	Drat it all!

BLONDE

Fort, laß mich allein!	Away, leave me alone!

OSMIN

Wahrhaftig kein'n Schritt von der Stelle, Bis du zu gehorchen mir schwörst.	Not one single step from this spot Until you swear to obey me.

BLONDE

Nicht so viel, du armer Geselle, Und wenn du der Großmogul wärst.	Not an inch, you poor fellow, Even if you were the Great Mogul himself.

OSMIN

O Engländer, seid ihr nicht Toren, Ihr laßt euren Weibern den Willen!	Oh Englishmen, aren't you fools, You let your women have their way!

BLONDE

Ein Herz, so in Freiheit geboren, Läßt niemals sich sklavisch behandeln, Bleibt, wenn schon die Freiheit verloren, Noch stolz auf sie, lachet der Welt!	A heart which is born in freedom, Will never allow itself to be enslaved, Remains, if freedom be lost, Still proud of it, laughs at the world!

OSMIN

Wie ist man geplagt und geschoren, Wenn solch eine Zucht man erhält!	How one is tormented and troubled If one receives such a lecture!

BLONDE

Nun troll dich!

Now trot off!

OSMIN

So sprichst du mit mir?

You speak like that to me?

BLONDE

Nicht anders.

No other way.

OSMIN

Nun bleib' ich erst hier!

Now more than ever I am staying!

BLONDE

Ein andermal, jetzt mußt du gehen.

One more time, you must go now.

OSMIN

Wer hat solche Frechheit gesehen!

Who has ever seen such insolence!

BLONDE

(*pretends that she wants to scratch out his eyes*)

Es ist um die Augen geschehen,
Wofern du noch länger verweilst.

I'll have your eyes,
If you stay around here any longer.

OSMIN (*timidly retreating*)

Nur ruhig, ich will ja gern gehen,
Bevor du gar Schläge erteilst.

Just keep your temper, I will gladly go,
Before you start swinging.

(*goes out*)

SCENE II

Blonde, Konstanze

Spoken dialogue

BLONDE

Wie traurig das gute Mädchen
daherkommt! Freilich tut's weh, den
Geliebten zu verlieren und Sklavin zu
sein. Es geht mir wohl auch nicht viel
besser, aber ich habe doch noch das
Vergnügen, meinen Pedrillo manchmal zu
sehen, ob's gleich auch mager und
verstohlen genug geschehen muß, doch
wer kann wider den Strom schwimmen!

How sadly the good maiden approaches!
Of course it hurts to lose your beloved
and to be a slave. It's not really much
better for me either, but at least I still
have the pleasure of seeing my Pedrillo
now and then, although it occurs scarcely
often enough and on the sly, but who can
swim against the current!

No. 10: Recitative and Aria

KONSTANZE (*not noticing Blonde*)

Welcher Wechsel herrscht in meiner Seele	What change prevails in my soul
Seit dem Tag, da uns das Schicksal trennte!	Since the day that fate separated us!
O Belmont! hin sind die Freuden,	Oh Belmonte! Gone are the joys,
Die ich sonst an deiner Seite kannte;	Which I once knew at your side!
Banger Sehnsucht Leiden	Now the pangs of anxious longing
Wohnen nun dafür in der beklemmten Brust.	Dwell in my oppressed bosom.
Traurigkeit ward mir zum Lose,	Sorrow has become my fate,
Weil ich dir entrissen bin.	Because I was torn from you.
Gleich der wurmzernagten Rose,	Like the rose, gnawed by the worm,
Gleich dem Gras im Wintermoose	Like the grass among winter mosses
Welkt mein banges Leben hin.	My uneasy life withers away.
Selbst der Luft darf ich nicht sagen	I must not even speak to the breeze
Meiner Seele bittern Schmerz,	Of my soul's bitter suffering,
Denn, unwillig ihn zu tragen,	Since, unwilling to bear it,
Haucht sie alle meine Klagen	It would breathe all my lamentations
Wieder in mein armes Herz.	Back into my poor heart.

Spoken dialogue

BLONDE

Ach, mein bestes Fräulein, noch immer so traurig?	Ah, my dear lady, still so sad?

KONSTANZE

Kannst du fragen, die du meinen Kummer weißt?—Wieder ein Abend, und noch keine Nachricht, noch keine Hoffnung!—Und morgen—ach Gott! Ich darf nicht daran denken.	Can you ask, you who knows my grief? Evening again, and still no news, still no hope.—And tomorrow—oh, God! I must not think about it.

BLONDE

Heitern Sie sich wenigstens ein bißchen auf. Sehn Sie, wie schön der Abend ist, wie blühend uns alles entgegenlacht, wie freudig uns die Vögel zu ihrem Gesang einladen! Verbannen Sie die Grillen und fassen Sie Mut!	Cheer up just a little. See how beautiful the evening is, how everything around us blooms and laughs, how joyfully the birds invite us to hear their singing. Put away melancholy thoughts and have courage!

KONSTANZE

Wie glücklich du bist, Mädchen, bei deinem Schicksal so gelassen zu sein! Oh, daß ich es auch könnte!	How lucky you are, maiden, to be so calm about your fate! Oh could I also be like that!

BLONDE

Das steht nur bei Ihnen. Hoffen Sie—	That is up to you. Be hopeful—

KONSTANZE

Wo nicht der mindeste Schein von Hoffnung mehr zu erblicken ist?	Where not the slightest glimmer of hope is to be seen?

BLONDE

Hören Sie nur: ich verzage mein Lebtage nicht, es mag auch eine Sache noch so schlimm aussehen. Denn wer sich immer das Schlimmste vorstellt, ist auch wahrhaftig am schlimmsten dran.	Just listen: as long as I live I will not despair, no matter how bad things may look. For she who always imagines the worst, finds herself in the middle of it.

KONSTANZE

Und wer sich immer mit Hoffnung schmeichelt und zuletzt betrogen sieht, hat alsdann nichts mehr übrig als die Verzweiflung.	And she who lets herself be flattered and ultimately deceived by hope, has nothing then left but despair.

BLONDE

Jedes nach seiner Weise. Ich glaube bei der meinigen am besten zu fahren. Wie bald kann Ihr Belmonte mit Lösegeld erscheinen oder uns listigerweise entführen? Wären wir die ersten Frauenzimmer, die den türkischen Vielfraßen entkämen?—Dort seh' ich den Bassa.	Each to his own. As for me, I believe in hoping for the best. How soon can your Belmonte show up with ransom money, or cunningly abduct us? Would we be the first females ever to escape the Turkish gluttons?—I see the pasha coming.

KONSTANZE

Laß uns ihm aus den Augen gehn.	Let's get out of his sight.

BLONDE

Zu spät. Er hat Sie schon gesehen. Ich darf aber getrost aus dem Wege trollen, er schaffte mich ohnehin fort.	Too late. He's seen you already. But I'd better trot along out of his way; he'd just send me packing anyway.

(as she is leaving)

Courage! Wir kommen gewiß noch in unsere Heimat.

Have courage! We will certainly return to our homeland.

SCENE III

Konstanze, Selim

SELIM

Nun, Konstanze, denkst du meinem Begehren nach? Der Tag ist bald verstrichen, morgen mußt du mich lieben, oder—

Now, Konstanze, are you considering my request? The day is soon past, tomorrow you must love me, or—

KONSTANZE

Muß? Welch albernes Begehren! Als ob man die Liebe befehlen könnte, wie eine Tracht Schläge!—Aber freilich, wie ihr Türken zu Werke geht, läßt sich's auch allenfalls befehlen.—Aber ihr seid wirklich zu beklagen. Ihr kerkert die Gegenstände eurer Begierden ein und seid zufrieden eure Lüste zu büßen.

Must? What a ridiculous command! As if one could order up love, like a sound beating! But the way you Turks go about it, it can even be ordered. But you are really to be pitied. You imprison the objects of your desire and are content to indulge your pleasures.

SELIM

Und glaubst du etwa, unsre Weiber wären weniger glücklich als ihr in euren Ländern?

And do you really believe our women to be less happy than you are, in your countries?

KONSTANZE

Die nichts Besseres kennen!

They haven't known anything better!

SELIM

Auf diese Art wäre wohl keine Hoffnung, daß du je anders denken wirst.

Thus there would not be any hope that you would change your mind.

KONSTANZE

Herr, ich muß dir frei gestehn—denn was soll ich dich länger hinhalten, mich mit leerer Hoffnung schmeicheln, daß du dich durch mein Bitten erweichen ließest.—Ich werde stets so denken wie itzt: dich verehren, aber—lieben? Nie.

Sire, I must freely confess to you—for why should I put you off any longer, why flatter myself with empty hope that you would allow yourself to be moved by my entreaties. I will always think as I do now: to honor you, yes, but—to love you? Never.

115

SELIM

| Und du zitterst nicht vor der Gewalt, die ich über dich habe? | And you do not tremble before the power which I have over you? |

KONSTANZE

| Nicht im geringsten. Sterben ist alles, was ich zu erwarten habe, und je eher dies geschieht, je lieber wird es mir sein. | Not in the slightest. Death is all that I expect, and the sooner that occurs the better it will be for me. |

SELIM

| Elende! Nein! Nicht sterben, aber Martern von allen Arten— | Wretched woman! No! Not death, but tortures of all kinds— |

KONSTANZE

| Auch die will ich ertragen; du erschreckst mich nicht, ich erwarte alles. | These will I also endure; you do not terrify me, I await anything. |

No. 11: Aria

Martern aller Arten	Tortures of every kind
Mögen meiner warten,	May await me,
Ich verlache Qual und Pein.	I laugh at suffering and pain.
Nichts soll mich erschüttern.	Nothing will shake me.
Nur dann würd' ich zittern,	If I could be unfaithful,
Wenn ich untreu könnte sein.	Only then would I tremble.
Laß dich bewegen, verschone mich;	Let yourself be moved, spare me;
Des Himmels Segen belohne dich!—	Heaven's blessing may reward you!—
Doch du bist entschlossen.	But you are determined.
Willig, unverdrossen	Willingly, undaunted
Wähl' ich jede Pein und Not.	I choose every pain and hardship.
Ordne nur, gebiete,	Just order, command,
Lärme, tobe, wüte!	Roar, storm, rage!
Zuletzt befreit mich doch der Tod.	Death will finally free me.

(She goes out.)

SCENE IV

Selim alone

Spoken monologue

SELIM

| Ist das ein Traum? Wo hat sie auf einmal den Mut her, sich so gegen mich zu | Is that a dream? Where does she suddenly get the courage to behave that |

betragen? Hat sie vielleicht Hoffnung, mir zu entkommen? Ha, das will ich verwehren!

way toward me? Has she perhaps some hope of escaping from me? Ha, I will prevent that!

(*is about to leave*)

Doch das ist's nicht, dann würde sie sich eher verstellen, mich einzuschläfern versuchen.—Ja! es ist Verzweiflung! Mit Härte richt' ich nichts aus—mit Bitten auch nicht—also, was Drohen und Bitten nicht vermögen, soll die List zuwege bringen.

But that is not it, she would rather hide her feelings then, seek to put me off my guard.—Yes! It is despair! With cruelty I will accomplish nothing—nor with entreaties—so what threats and entreaties cannot achieve, cunning will bring about.

(*goes out*)

SCENE V

Blonde alone

BLONDE

Kein Bassa, keine Konstanze mehr da? Sind sie miteinander eins geworden?— Schwerlich, das gute Kind hängt zu sehr an ihrem Belmont! Ich bedaure sie von Grund meines Herzens. Sie ist zu empfindsam für ihre Lage. Freilich, hätt' ich meinen Pedrillo nicht an der Seite, wer weiß, wie mir's ginge! Doch würd' ich nicht zärteln wie sie. Die Männer verdienen's wahrlich nicht, daß man ihrethalben sich zu Tode grämt.— Vielleicht würd' ich muselmännisch denken.

No pasha, no Konstanze still here? Have they come to terms with each other?— Hardly, the good child is too fond of her Belmonte! I pity her from the bottom of my heart. She is too sensitive for her situation. Indeed, if I didn't have my Pedrillo by my side, who knows how it would go with me! But I wouldn't be as tender-hearted as she. Men really don't deserve women who grieve themselves to death over them.—Perhaps I would think like a Moslem.

SCENE VI

Blonde, Pedrillo

Spoken dialogue

PEDRILLO

Bst, bst! Blondchen! Ist der Weg rein?

Pst! Pst! Blondchen! Is the way clear?

117

BLONDE

Komm nur, komm! Der Bassa ist wieder zurück. Und meinem Alten habe ich eben den Kopf ein bißchen gewaschen. Was hast du denn?

Come then, come. The pasha has returned and I have just blown up a little at the old man. So, what do you have?

PEDRILLO

O Neuigkeiten, Neuigkeiten, die dich entzücken werden.

Oh, news, news that will delight you.

BLONDE

Nun? Hurtig heraus damit!

Well? Quick, out with it!

PEDRILLO

Erst, liebes Herzensblondchen, laß dir vor allen Dingen einen recht herzlichen Kuß geben. Du weißt ja, wie gestohlnes Gut schmeckt.

First, dear, darling Blondchen, before anything else, let me give you a great big kiss. You know very well how stolen goodies taste.

BLONDE

Pfui, pfui! Wenn das deine Neuigkeiten alle sind—

Humpf! If that is all your news—

PEDRILLO

Närrchen, mach darum keinen Lärm, der alte spitzbübische Osmin lauert uns sicher auf den Dienst.

Little fool, don't make any fuss, that old scoundrel Osmin is surely on the lookout for us.

BLONDE

Nun? Und die Neuigkeiten?—

Well? The news?

PEDRILLO

Sind, daß das Ende unsrer Sklaverei vor der Tür ist.

Is, that the end of our slavery is within our reach.

(*He looks carefully around.*)

Belmonte, Konstanzens Gebieter, ist angekommen, und ich hab' ihn unter dem Namen eines Baumeisters hier im Palast eingeführt.

Belmonte, Konstanze's master, has arrived, and I have brought him into the palace as an architect.

BLONDE

Ah, was sagst du? Belmonte da?

Ah, what are you saying? Belmonte here?

PEDRILLO

Mit Leib und Seele!

In body and soul!

BLONDE

Ha! Das muß Konstanze wissen!

Ha! Konstanze must know that!

(*She is about to leave.*)

PEDRILLO

Hör nur, Blondchen, hör nur erst: Er hat ein Schiff hier in der Nähe in Bereitschaft, und wir haben beschlossen, euch diese Nacht zu entführen.

Just listen, Blondchen, just listen first: he has a ship in readiness nearby, and we have decided to abduct you tonight.

BLONDE

O allerliebst, allerliebst! Herzenspedrillo! Das verdient einen Kuß. Geschwind, geschwind zu Konstanzen!

Oh dearest, dearest! Darling Pedrillo! That deserves a kiss! Quickly, quickly to Konstanze!

(*is about to leave*)

PEDRILLO

Halt nur, halt, und laß erst mit dir reden. Um Mitternacht kommt Belmonte mit einer Leiter zu Konstanzens Fenster, ich zu dem deinigen, und dann geht's, heidi davon!

Just wait, wait, first let me tell you. At midnight Belmonte will come with a ladder to Konstanze's window, I to yours, and then away we'll all go!

BLONDE

O vortrefflich! Aber Osmin?

Oh splendid! but what about Osmin?

PEDRILLO

Hier ist ein Schlaftrunk für den alten Schlaukopf, den misch' ihm fein manierlich ins Getränke, verstehst du? Ich habe dort auch schon ein Fläschchen angefüllt. Geht's hier nicht, wird's dort wohl gehen.

Here is a sleeping potion for the old sneak, which I will mix properly in his drink, do you understand? I have there a little bottle already filled. If this potion doesn't work I'll resort to that one.

BLONDE

Sorg night für mich! Aber kann Konstanze ihren Geliebten nicht sprechen?

Don't worry about me! But can't Konstanze speak to her beloved?

PEDRILLO

Sobald es vollends finster ist, kommt er hier in den Garten. Nun geh und bereite

As soon as it's completely dark, he'll come into the garden here. Now go and

Konstanzen vor; ich will hier Belmonten erwarten. Leb wohl, Herzchen, leb wohl!

prepare Konstanze; I will wait for Belmonte here. Farewell, darling, farewell!

BLONDE

Leb wohl, guter Pedrillo! Ach, was werd' ich für Freude anrichten!

Farewell, good Pedrillo! Ah what joy I will bring!

No. 12: Aria

Welche Wonne, welche Lust
Herrscht nunmehr in meiner Brust!
Ohne Aufschub will ich springen
Und ihr gleich die Nachricht bringen;
Und mit Lachen und mit Scherzen
Ihrem schwachen, kranken Herzen
Freud' und Jubel prophezeien.

What bliss, what pleasure
Will reign from now on in my bosom!
Without delay I will run
And bring her the news immediately;
And with laughing and with joking,
Predict delight and jubilation
To her weak, ailing heart.

(*goes out*)

SCENE VII

Pedrillo alone

Spoken monologue

PEDRILLO

Ah, daß es schon vorbei wäre! daß wir schon auf offner See wären, unsre Mädels im Arm und dies verwünschte Land im Rücken hätten! Doch sei's gewagt, entweder itzt oder niemals! Wer zagt, verliert!

Ah, if only it were already over! If we were already on the open sea, our girls in our arms and our backs to this cursed country. But let it be dared, either now or never! He who hesitates is lost!

No. 13: Aria

Frisch zum Kampfe! Frisch zum Streite!
Nur ein feiger Tropf verzagt.
Sollt' ich zittern, sollt' ich zagen?
Nicht mein Leben mutig wagen?—
Nein, ach nein, es sei gewagt!
Nur ein feiger Tropf verzagt.
Frisch zum Kampfe! Frisch zum Streite!

Ahead into battle! Ahead into strife!
Only a cowardly simpleton loses heart.
Should I tremble, should I hesitate?
Not bravely wager my life?—
No, oh no, let it be dared!
Only a cowardly simpleton loses heart.
Ahead into battle! Ahead into strife!

SCENE VIII

Pedrillo, Osmin

Spoken dialogue

OSMIN

Ha! Geht's hier so lustig zu? Es muß dir verteufelt wohl gehen.

Ah! What's so cheerful around here? You must be feeling damned good.

PEDRILLO

Ei, wer wird so ein Kopfhänger sein; es kommt beim Henker dabei nichts heraus! Das haben die Pedrillos von jeher in ihrer Familie gehabt. Fröhlichkeit und Wein versüßt die härteste Sklaverei. Freilich könnt ihr armen Schlucker das nicht begreifen, daß es so ein herrlich Ding um ein Gläschen guten, alten Lustigmacher ist. Wahrhaftig, da hat euer Vater Mahomet einen verzweifelten Bock geschossen, daß er euch den Wein verboten hat. Wenn das verwünschte Gesetz nicht wäre, du müßtest ein Gläschen mit mir trinken, du möchtest wollen oder nicht.

Oh, who wants to mope around; you get dratted little out of it! From time immemorial the Pedrillos have had cheerfulness as a family trait. Happiness and wine sweeten the cruelest slavery. Of course, you poor wretches can't understand that a glass of good, old merrymaker is such a great thing. Really, your father Mohammed made a terrible mistake when he forbade you to drink wine. If it weren't for that cursed law, you would have to drink a glass with me, whether you wanted to or not.

(to himself)

Vielleicht beißt er an: Er trinkt ihn gar zu gerne.

Maybe he'll bite: he'll drink it only too gladly.

OSMIN

Wein mit dir? Ja Gift—

Wine, with you? Hellfire—

PEDRILLO

Immer Gift und Dolch und Dolch und Gift! Laß doch den alten Groll einmal fahren und sei vernünftig. Sieh einmal, ein Paar Flaschen Zypernwein!—Ah!

Always hellfire and damnation and damnation and hellfire! Let your old resentment go for once and be sensible. Look here, two bottles of Cypriot wine!—Ah!—

(He shows him two bottles, one larger than the other.)

die sollen mir trefflich schmecken!

which will taste excellent to me!

OSMIN

Wenn ich ihm trauen dürfte?

If only I could trust him?

PEDRILLO

Das ist ein Wein! Das ist ein Wein! That's *some* wine! That's *some* wine!

(He sits down on the ground in Turkish fashion and drinks from the small bottle.)

OSMIN

Kost' einmal die große Flasche auch. Sample the big bottle also.

PEDRILLO

Denkst wohl gar, ich habe Gift Do you think that I have put poison in it?
hineingetan? Ha, laß dir keine grauen Ha, don't grow any grey hairs over it. It
Haare wachsen. Es verlohnte sich der isn't worth the trouble to go to the devil
Mühe, daß ich deinetwegen zum Teufel on your behalf. There, see if I drink.
führe. Da sieh, ob ich trinke.

(He drinks a little from the big bottle.)

Nun, hast du noch Bedenken? Traust mir Now, do you still have doubts? Still don't
noch nicht? Pfui, Osmin! soll'st dich trust me? Phooey, Osmin, you should be
schämen.—Da nimm! ashamed of yourself.—There, take it!

(He offers him the big bottle.)

Oder willst du die kleine? Or do you want the little one?

OSMIN

Nein, laß nur, laß nur! Aber wenn du No, it's all right, it's all right! But if you
mich verrätst— are deceiving me—

(looks carefully around)

PEDRILLO

Als wenn wir einander nicht weiter As if we didn't need each other anymore.
brauchten. Immer frisch! Mahomet liegt Go ahead! Mohammed has long been
längst auf'm Ohr und hat nötiger zu tun, napping, and has more urgent things to
als sich um deine Flasche Wein zu do, than to bother about your bottle of
kümmern. wine.

No. 14: Duet

Vivat Bacchus! Bacchus lebe! Vivat Bacchus! Long live Bacchus!
Bacchus war ein braver Mann! Bacchus was a good man!

OSMIN

Ob ich's wage?—Ob ich trinke?— Should I dare it?—Should I drink?—
Ob's wohl Allah sehen kann? Can Allah really see it?

PEDRILLO

Was hilft das Zaudern? hinunter! hinunter!	What good is hesitating? Drink it down, drink it down!
Nicht lange, nicht lange gefragt!	Don't deliberate so long!

OSMIN

Nun wär's geschehen, nun wär's hinunter!	Now it's happened, now it's down!
Das heiß' ich, das heiß' ich gewagt!	That's what I call daring!

BOTH

Es leben die Mädchen, die Blonden, die Braunen!	Long live the girls, the blonds, the brunettes!
Sie leben hoch!	Long may they live!

PEDRILLO

Das schmeckt trefflich!	That tastes excellent!

OSMIN

Das schmeckt herrlich!	That tastes great!

BOTH

Ah, das heiß' ich Göttertrank!	Ah, I call that fit for the gods!

OSMIN

Vivat Bacchus! Bacchus lebe!	Vivat Bacchus! Long live Bacchus!
Bacchus, der den Wein erfand!	Bacchus, who invented wine!

BOTH

Vivat Bacchus, Bacchus lebe,	Vivat Bacchus, long live Bacchus!
Bacchus, der den Wein erfand!	Bacchus, who invented wine!
Es leben die Mädchen, die Blonden, die Braunen!	Long live the girls, the blonds, the brunettes!
Sie leben hoch!	Long may they live!
Vivat Bacchus! Vivat, der den Wein erfand!	Vivat Bacchus! Vivat, he who invented wine!

Spoken dialogue

PEDRILLO

Wahrhaftig, das muß ich gestehen, es geht doch nichts über den Wein! Wein ist mir lieber als Geld und Mädchen. Bin ich verdrießlich, mürrisch, launisch: hurtig nehm' ich meine Zuflucht zur Flasche, und kaum seh' ich den ersten Boden: weg	Truthfully, I must confess, there is nothing better than wine! Wine is dearer to me than money and girls. If I am bad-tempered, grumpy, moody: quick, I resort to the bottle, and scarcely have I seen the bottom of the first one, when my

ist all mein Verdruß!—Meine Flasche macht mir kein schiefes Gesicht wie mein Mädchen, wenn ihr der Kopf nicht auf dem rechten Fleck steht. Und schwätzt mir von Süßigkeit der Liebe, des Ehestands, was ihr wollt: Wein auf der Zunge geht über alles!

annoyance is gone! My bottle doesn't make wry faces at me like a girl does, when her head is not in the right place. Nor prattle on to me about the sweetness of love, of marriage, whatever you can think of. Wine on the tongue is better than anything!

OSMIN

(begins to feel the effects of the wine and the sleeping potion already, and until the end of the scene gets sleepier and more sluggish, but the actor should not exaggerate; he must remain only half-dreaming and drunk with sleep.)

Das ist wahr—Wein—Wein—ist ein schönes Getränke, und unser großer— Prophet mag mir's nicht übel nehmen— Gift und Dolch! Es ist doch eine hübsche Sache um den Wein!—Nicht—Bruder Pedrillo?

That's true—wine—wine is a lovely drink, and our great prophet mustn't think ill of me for—Hellfire and damnation! Wine is such a wonderful thing! Isn't it—Brother Pedrillo?

PEDRILLO

Richtig, Bruder Osmin, richtig!

Right, Brother Osmin, right you are!

OSMIN

Man wird gleich so—munter—

One is—right away—so cheerful—

(He nods now and then.)

so vergnügt—so aufgeräumt!—Hast du nichts mehr, Bruder?

so jolly—so high-spirited!—Don't you have any more, Brother?

(He reaches in a ridiculous way for the second bottle, which Pedrillo hands him.)

PEDRILLO

Hör du, Alter, trink mir nicht zu viel; es kommt einem in den Kopf.

Listen, old man, don't drink too much; it goes to your head.

OSMIN

Trag doch keine—Sorge, ich bin so— so—nüchtern wie möglich.—Aber das ist wahr—

Don't have any—worries, I am as—as sober as possible. But it is true—

(He begins to stagger back and forth.)

es schmeckt—vortrefflich!—

it tastes—splendid!—

PEDRILLO (to himself)

Es wirkt, Alter, es wirkt!

It's working, old man, it's working!

OSMIN

Aber verraten mußt du mich nicht—
Brüderchen—verraten—denn—wenn's
Mahomet—nein, nein—der Bassa
wüßte—denn siehst du—liebes
Blondchen—ja oder nein!

But you mustn't betray me—little
brother—betray—because—if
Mohammed—no, no—the pasha
knew—then you see—dear
Blondchen—yes or no!

PEDRILLO (*to himself*)

Nun wird's Zeit, ihn fortzuschaffen!

Now it's time to get him away from here!

(*aloud*)

Nun komm, Alter, komm! Wir wollen
schlafen gehn!

Now come, old man, come! We will go to
sleep.

(*He raises him up.*)

OSMIN

Schlafen?—Schämst du dich nicht?—
Gift und Dolch! Wer wird denn so
schläfrig sein—es ist ja kaum Morgen—

To sleep?—Aren't you ashamed of
yourself?—Hellfire and Damnation!
Besides, who's sleepy now—it is scarcely
morning—

PEDRILLO

Ho ho, die Sonne ist schon hinunter!—
Komm, komm, daß uns der Bassa nicht
überrascht!

Ho ho, the sun is already down! Come,
come, so that the pasha won't catch us by
surprise!

OSMIN (*being led out*)

Ja, ja—eine Flasche—guter—Bassa—
geht über—alles! Gute Nacht —
Brüderchen—gute Nacht.

Yes, yes—a bottle—good—pasha—is
better than—anything! Good night—
little brother—good night.

(*Pedrillo leads him inside, but comes back right away.*)

SCENE IX

Pedrillo, later Belmonte, Konstanze, Blonde

PEDRILLO (*imitating Osmin*)

Gute Nacht—Brüderchen—gute Nacht!
Hahahaha, alter Eisenfresser! Erwischt
man dich so? Gift und Dolch!—Du hast
deine Ladung! Nur fürcht' ich, ist's noch
zu zeitig am Tage; bis Mitternacht sind
noch drei Stunden, und da könnt' er

Good night—little brother—good night!
Ha ha ha ha, old braggart! Can one catch
you out that easily? Hellfire and
damnation!—You have your cargo! Only
I'm afraid that it's too early in the day;
there are still three hours until midnight,

leicht wieder ausgeschlafen haben.—Ach, kommen Sie, kommen Sie, liebster Herr! Unser Argus ist blind, ich hab' ihn tüchtig zugedeckt.

and by then he could easily have slept it off. —Ah, come on, come on, dear master! Our Argus is blind, I have covered him up well.

BELMONTE

O daß wir glücklich wären! Aber sag: ist Konstanze noch nicht hier?

Oh, if only we were lucky! But tell me: is Konstanze not yet here?

PEDRILLO

Eben kommt sie da den Gang herauf. Reden Sie alles mit ihr ab, aber fassen Sie sich kurz, denn der Verräter schläft nicht immer.

She is just now coming up the walk. Arrange everything with her, but make it brief because the traitor won't sleep forever.

(During Belmonte's discussion with Konstanze, he converses softly with Blonde to whom he shows through pantomime the whole scene with Osmin, imitating him; finally he instructs her as well that at midnight he will be coming with a ladder to her window in order to abduct her.)

KONSTANZE AND BELMONTE
(in each other's arms)

O mein Belmonte! / Konstanze!

Oh my Belmonte! / Konstanze!

KONSTANZE

Ist's möglich!—Nach soviel Tagen der Angst, nach soviel ausgestandnen Leiden, dich wieder in meinen Armen—

Is it possible? After so many days filled with anxiety, after enduring so much suffering, you again in my arms—

BELMONTE

O, dieser Augenblick versüßt allen Kummer, macht mich all meinen Schmerz vergessen—

Oh, this moment sweetens all grief, makes me forget all my pain—

KONSTANZE

Hier will ich an deinem Busen liegen und weinen!—Ach, jetzt fühl' ich's,—die Freude hat auch ihre Tränen!

I want to lie here on your bosom and cry!—Ah, now I feel,—that joys also have their tears!

No. 15: Aria
BELMONTE

Wenn der Freude Tränen fließen, Lächelt Liebe dem Geliebten hold! Von den Wangen sie zu küssen, Ist der Liebe schönster, größter Sold.

When tears of joy are flowing, Love laughs sweetly at the beloved! To kiss them from her cheeks Is love's most beautiful, greatest payment.

Ach, Konstanze! dich zu sehen,	Ah, Konstanze! To see you;
Dich voll Wonne, voll Entzücken	Full of bliss, full of delight
An mein treues Herz zu drücken,	To press you to my faithful heart,
Lohnt fürwahr nicht Krösus' Pracht!	Croesus' wealth is not reward enough!
Daß wir uns niemals wiederfinden,	That we might never have found each other again,
So dürfen wir nicht erst empfinden,	Makes us finally realize
Welchen Schmerz die Trennung macht.	What pain separation causes.

Spoken dialogue

Ich hab' hier ein Schiff in Bereitschaft; um Mitternacht, wenn alles schläft, komm' ich an dein Fenster, und dann sei die Liebe unser Schutzengel!	I have a ship in readiness here; at midnight, when everyone is asleep, I will come to your window, and then may love be our guardian angel!

KONSTANZE

Mit tausend Freuden! Was wollt' ich nicht mit dir wagen? Ich erwarte dich—	With a thousand joys! What wouldn't I dare with you? I'll await you—

PEDRILLO

Also, liebes Blondchen, paß ja hübsch auf, hörst du's?	So listen, dear Blondchen, keep a good eye out.

BLONDE

Sorge für mich nicht. Das wär' das erste Abenteuer, das ein Mädchen verschlafen hätte.	Don't worry about me. That would be the first adventure that a girl ever slept through.

PEDRILLO

Du wirst's schon merken, wenn du so was Gesungenes hörst, wie's so meine Art des Abends immer ist; dann paß auf, und dann mit einem Sprung ins Schiff! Nur hübsch Mut gefaßt und nicht verzagt: Wer alles zu verlieren hat, muß alles wagen!	If you hear something sung, as is usually my way in the evening, you will be alerted; watch out and then with one leap, into the ship!—Just hang on to your courage and don't lose heart: he who has everything to lose must risk everything!

KONSTANZE

Wenn es aber nur glücklich abläuft!	If only it runs smoothly!

BELMONTE

Wir wollen's hoffen; die Liebe wird unsre Begleiterin sein.	We will hope for it: love will be our companion.

No. 16: Quartet

KONSTANZE

Ach, Belmonte! ach, mein Leben!   Ah, Belmonte! Ah, my life!

BELMONTE

Ach, Konstanze! ach, mein Leben!   Ah, Konstanze! Ah, my life!

KONSTANZE

Ist es möglich? Welch Entzüken!   Is it possible? What joy!
Dich an meine Brust zu drücken   To press you to my breast
Nach so vieler Tage Leid.   After so many days of sorrow.

BELMONTE

Welche Wonne, dich zu finden!   What bliss, to find you!
Nun muß aller Kummer schwinden!   Now must all grief vanish!
Oh, wie ist mein Herz erfreut!   Oh, how my heart is gladdened!

KONSTANZE

Sieh, die Freudentränen fließen.   See the tears of joy flowing.

BELMONTE

Holde, laß hinweg sie küssen!   Sweet one, let me kiss them away!

KONSTANZE

Daß es doch die letzten sein!   May they be the last ones!

BELMONTE

Ja, noch heute wirst du frei.   Yes, from today forth you will be free.

PEDRILLO

Also, Blondchen, hast's verstanden?   So, Blondchen, have you understood?
Alles ist zur Flucht vorhanden,   Everything is on hand for the escape,
Um Schlag Zwölfe sind wir da.   At the stroke of twelve we'll be there.

BLONDE

Unbesorgt, es wird nichts fehlen,   Don't worry, nothing will be lacking,
Die Minuten werd' ich zählen,   I will be counting the minutes.
Wär' der Augenblick schon da!   If only the moment were already here!

ALL FOUR

Endlich scheint die Hoffnungssonne   Finally the sun of hope shines
Hell durchs trübe Firmament.   Brightly through the clouded firmament!
Voll Entzücken, Freud' und Wonne   Full of delight, joy and rapture
Sehn wir unsrer Leiden End'!   We behold the end of our sorrows!

BELMONTE

Doch ach! bei aller Lust	But ah! With all this pleasure
Empfindet meine Brust	My breast is still filled with
Noch manch' geheime Sorgen!	Many a secret worry!

KONSTANZE

Was ist es, Liebster, sprich,	What is it, beloved, speak,
Geschwind, erkläre dich,	Quickly, explain yourself.
O halt mir nichts verborgen!	Oh keep nothing hidden from me!

BELMONTE

Man sagt—man sagt, du seist—	They say—they say, you were—

KONSTANZE

Nun weiter?	Well?

(Belmonte and Konstanze look at each other fearfully in silence.)

PEDRILLO

(shows that he risks being hanged)

Doch Blondchen, ach! die Leiter!	But Blondchen, ah! The ladder!
Bist du wohl soviel wert?	Are you really worth so much?

BELMONTE

Hans Narr! Schnappt's bei dir über?	Jack Fool! Have you gone crazy?
Ei, hättest du nur lieber	Ah, you should rather have turned
Die Frage umgekehrt.	The question around the other way.

PEDRILLO

Doch Herr Osmin—	But Mister Osmin—

BLONDE

Laß hören—	Let me hear it—

KONSTANZE

Willst du dich nicht erklären?—	Won't you explain yourself?—

BELMONTE

Man sagt—	They say—

PEDRILLO

Doch Herr Osmin—	But Mister Osmin—

BELMONTE

Du seist—	You were—

PEDRILLO

Doch Herr Osmin—   But Mister Osmin—

KONSTANZE

Nun weiter—   Well?—

BLONDE

Laß hören—   Let me hear it—

KONSTANZE

Willst du dich nicht erklären?—   Won't you explain yourself?—

BELMONTE

Ich will. Doch zürne nicht,   I will. But don't be angry,
Wenn ich nach dem Gerücht,   If I dare ask, trembling,
So ich gehört, es wage,   Shaking, whether, according
Dich zitternd, bebend frage,   To the rumor I have heard,
Ob du den Bassa liebst?   You love the pasha?

KONSTANZE

O wie du mich betrübst!   Oh how you distress me!

(She weeps.)

PEDRILLO

Hat nicht Osmin etwan,   Has not Osmin by chance,
Wie man fast glauben kann,   Which one can almost believe,
Sein Recht als Herr probiert,   His rights as lord tested,
Und bei dir exerzieret?   And exercised with you?
Dann wär's ein schlechter Kauf!   Then you would be a bad bargain!

BLONDE (*gives Pedrillo a slap*)

Da nimm die Antwort drauf!   There, take the answer to that!

PEDRILLO (*holds his cheek*)

Nun bin ich aufgeklärt!   Now I am enlightened!

BELMONTE (*kneeling*)

Konstanze, ach, vergib!   Konstanze, ah, forgive me!

BLONDE (*goes angrily away from Pedrillo*)

Du bist mich gar nicht wert.   You are just not worthy of me.

KONSTANZE (*sighing*)

Ob ich dir treu verblieb?—   Whether I remained faithful to you?

BLONDE (*to Konstanze*)

Der Schlingel fragt noch an,	The little brat even inquires
Ob ich ihm treu geblieben?	Whether I have remained faithful to him?

KONSTANZE (*to Blonde*)

Dem Belmont sagte man,	They told Belmonte that
Ich soll den Bassa lieben!	I am supposed to love the pasha!

PEDRILLO (*holds his cheek*)

Daß Blonde ehrlich sei,	That Blonde is honorable,
Schwör ich bei allen Teufeln.	I swear by all the devils.

BELMONTE (*to Pedrillo*)

Konstanze ist mir treu,	Konstanze is faithful to me,
Daran ist nicht zu zweifeln.	There can be no doubt about it.

KONSTANZE AND BLONDE

Wenn unsrer Ehre wegen	If with respect to our honor
Die Männer Argwohn hegen,	Men become mistrustful,
Verdächtig auf uns sehn,	Look on us suspiciously,
Das ist nicht auszustehn.	That is not to be endured.

BELMONTE AND PEDRILLO

Sobald sich Weiber kränken,	As soon as women feel aggrieved,
Wenn wir sie untreu denken,	That we think them to be unfaithful,
Dann sind sie wahrhaft treu,	Then are they truly faithful,
Von allem Vorwurf frei.	Free of all blame.

PEDRILLO

Liebstes Blondchen, ach! verzeihe!	Dearest Blondchen, ah! Pardon!
Sieh, ich bau' auf deine Treue	See, I rely more on your faithfulness now
Mehr itzt als auf meinen Kopf!	Than on my own head!

BLONDE

Nein, das kann ich dir nicht schenken,	No, I can't excuse you for it,
Mich mit so was zu verdenken,	To blame me for something like that
Mit dem alten, dummen Tropf!	With the stupid old simpleton!

BELMONTE

Ach, Konstanze, ach, mein Leben!	Ah, Konstanze, ah, my life!
Könntest du mir doch vergeben,	Could you ever forgive me,
Daß ich diese Frage tat.	For having asked that question.

KONSTANZE

Belmont! wie, du könntest glauben,	Belmonte! How could you believe,
Daß man dir dies Herz könnt' rauben,	That someone could rob this heart from you,
Das nur dir geschlagen hat?	That has only beat for you?

BELMONTE

Ach, verzeihe!	Ah, pardon me!

PEDRILLO

Ach, verzeihe!	Ah, pardon me!

BELMONTE

Ich bereue!	I am penitent!

PEDRILLO

Ich bereue!	I am penitent!

KONSTANZE AND BLONDE

Ich verzeihe deiner Reue.	I accept your repentance.

ALL FOUR

Wohl, es sei nun abgetan!	Well, let's put that all aside!
Es lebe die Liebe!	Long live love!
Nur sie sei uns teuer,	Let only love be dear to us,
Nichts fache das Feuer	Let nothing fan the flames
Der Eifersucht an.	Of jealousy.

End of Act Two

ACT THREE

SCENE I

Square in front of the Pasha Selim's palace; on one side the palace of the pasha; opposite it, Osmin's house; in the back, view of the sea. It is midnight. Pedrillo, Klaas, who is bringing a ladder

Spoken dialogue

PEDRILLO

Hier, lieber Klaas, hier leg sie indes nur nieder und hole die zwote vom Schiff.	Here, dear Klaas, lay it down here and get the second one from the ship. But be

132

Aber nur hübsch leise, daß nicht viel Lärm gemacht wird: es geht hier auf Tod und Leben.	good and quiet about it, so that there won't be much noise: it's a matter of life and death.

KLAAS

Laß mich nur machen, ich versteh' das Ding auch ein bißchen—Wenn wir sie nur erst an Bord haben!	Just leave it to me, I also understand a thing or two.—If only we had them finally on board!

PEDRILLO

Ach, lieber Klaas! Wenn wir mit unsrer Beute glücklich nach Spanien kommen; ich glaube, Don Belmonte läßte dich in Gold einfassen.	Ah, dear Klaas! If we arrive safely in Spain with our booty, I believe Don Belmonte will let you be set in gold.

KLAAS

Das möchete wohl ein bißchen zu warm aufs Fell gehen; doch das wird sich schon geben. Ich hole die Leiter.	That might be a little too warm a coat to wear; but I'll get used to it. I'll get the ladder.

(*goes out*)

PEDRILLO

Ach! wenn ich sagen sollte, daß mir's Herz nicht klopfte, so sagt' ich eine schreckliche Lüge. Die verzweifelten Türken verstehn nicht den mindesten Spaß, und ob der Bassa gleich ein Renegat ist, so ist er, wenn's aufs Kopfab ankommt, doch ein völliger Türke.	Ah! If I were to say that my heart wasn't pounding, then I would be telling an awful lie. The terrible Turks don't understand the most trifling joke, and while the pasha is certainly a renegade, he is also, when it comes to beheading, most definitely a Turk.

(*Klaas brings the second ladder.*)

So, guter Klaas, und nun lichte die Anker und spann alle Segel auf, denn eh' eine halbe Stund' vergeht, hast du deine völlige Ladung.	Well, good Klaas, now raise the anchor and set the sails because, before a half-hour has passed, you will have your full cargo.

KLAAS

Bring sie nur hurtig, und dann laß mich sorgen.	Just bring them quickly, and then let me take over.

(*goes out*)

SCENE II

Belmonte, Pedrillo

PEDRILLO

Ach!—Ich muß Atem holen.—Es zieht mir's Herz so eng zusammen, als wenn ich's größte Schelmenstück vorhätte!— Ach, wo mein Herr auch bleibt!—

Ah!—I must take a breath.—My heart is squeezed as tightly as if I had the worst mischief planned! Ah, where could my master be!—

BELMONTE (*calls softly*)

Pedrillo! Pedrillo!

Pedrillo! Pedrillo!

PEDRILLO

Wie gerufen!

Just at the right time!

BELMONTE

Ist alles fertig gemacht?

Is everything ready?

PEDRILLO

Alles! Jetzt will ich ein wenig um den Palast herum spionieren, wie's aussieht. Singen Sie indessen eins. Ich hab' das so alle Abende getan, und wenn Sie da auch jemand gewahr wird oder Ihnen begegnet—denn alle Stunden macht hier eine Janitscharenwache die Runde—so hat's nichts zu bedeuten, sie sind das von mir schon gewohnt; es ist fast besser; als wenn man Sie so still hier fände.

Everything! Now I will spy around the palace a little, to see how things look. In the meanwhile, you sing something. I have done so every evening, and if someone catches sight of you or meets you—since a Janissary watchman makes rounds here every hour—it won't mean anything, they are already used to that from me; it is almost better than if they found you here being quiet.

BELMONTE

Laß mich nur machen und komm bald wieder.

Let me take care of it and come back soon.

(*Pedrillo goes out.*)

SCENE III

(*Belmonte alone*)

BELMONTE

O Konstanze, Konstanze! Wie schlägt mir das Herz! Je näher der Augenblick kommt, desto ängstlicher zagt meine

Oh Konstanze, Konstanze! How my heart is beating! The nearer the moment comes the more anxiously my soul wavers; I fear

Seele; ich fürchte und wünsche, bebe und hoffe. O Liebe, sei du meine Leiterin!

and wish, tremble and hope. Oh love, be my guide!

No. 17: Aria

Ich baue ganz auf deine Stärke,
Vertrau', o Liebe, deiner Macht!
Denn ach! was wurden nicht für Werke
Schon oft durch dich zustand gebracht.

I rely completely on your strength,
Trust, oh love, in your power!
For, ah! What sorts of accomplishments
Have you already often succeeded in
    bringing about.

Was aller Welt unmöglich scheint,

Whatever to the whole world seems
    impossible,

Wird durch die Liebe doch vereint.

Will yet be brought about by love.

SCENE IV

Belmonte, Pedrillo

Spoken dialogue

PEDRILLO

Alles liegt auf dem Ohr; es ist alles so ruhig, so stille, als den Tag nach der Sündflut.

Everyone is asleep; everything is as calm, as quiet as on the day after the Deluge.

BELMONTE

Nun so laß uns sie befreien. Wo ist die Leiter?

Well, let's free them now. Where is the ladder?

PEDRILLO

Nicht so hitzig. Ich muß erst das Signal geben.

Not so hasty. First I have to give the signal.

BELMONTE

Was hindert dich denn, es nicht zu tun? Mach fort!

What is preventing you from doing it? Get on with it!

PEDRILLO (*looks at the clock*)

Eben recht, Schlag zwölfe. Gehen Sie dort an die Ecke und geben Sie wohl acht, daß wir nicht überrascht werden.

Just right, the stroke of twelve. Go over there to the corner and make sure that we are not taken by surprise.

BELMONTE

Zaudre nur nicht!

Just don't delay any longer!

(*He goes out.*)

PEDRILLO (*as he produces his mandolin*)

Es ist doch um die Herzhaftigkeit eine erzläppische Sache. Wer keine hat, schafft sich mit aller Mühe keine an! Was mein Herz schlägt! Mein Papa muß ein Erzpoltron gewesen sein.	It's the silliest thing about courage. He who doesn't have it, can't get it no matter how hard he tries. How my heart is beating! My father must have been an arch-coward.

(*begins to play*)

Nun, so sei es denn gewagt!	Well, let's dare it.

(*sings and accompanies himself.*)

No. 18: Romance

Im Mohrenland gefangen war Ein Mädel hübsch und fein; Sah rot und weiß, war schwarz von Haar,	In the land of the Moors a girl, Pretty and delicate, was imprisoned; Red-lipped, with white complexion and black hair,
Seufzt' Tag und Nacht und weinte gar, Wollt' gern erlöset sein. Da kam aus fernem Land daher Ein junger Rittersmann, Den jammerte das Mädchen sehr. «Jach», rief er, «wag ich Kopf und Ehr', Wenn ich sie retten kann.»	She sighed day and night, and even wept, She wanted so badly to be freed. Came there from a distant land A young knight, He felt extremely sorry for her. "Hah" he called "I'd bet my head and honor If only I could rescue her."

Spoken dialogue

Noch geht alles gut, es rührt sich noch nichts.	Everything is still going all right, nothing is stirring yet.

BELMONTE (*comes back*)

Mach ein Ende, Pedrillo.	Finish it off, Pedrillo.

PEDRILLO

An mir liegt es nicht, daß sie sich noch nicht zeigen. Entweder schlafen sie fester als jemals, oder der Bassa ist bei der Hand. Wir wollen's weiter versuchen. Bleiben Sie nur auf Ihrem Posten.	It's not my fault that they haven't shown themselves yet. Either they are sleeping more soundly than usual, or the pasha is close by. We need to keep trying. Just stay at your post.

(*Belmonte goes out again.*)

Romance

«Ich komm zu dir in finstrer Nacht,
Laß, Liebchen, husch mich ein!
Ich fürchte weder Schloß noch Wacht,
Holla! Horch auf! um Mitternacht
Sollst du erlöset sein.»

Gesagt, getan; Glock zwölfe stand
Der tapfre Ritter da;

Sanft reicht sie ihm die weiche Hand,
Früh man die leere Zelle fand;—

Fort war sie, hopsasa!

"I come to you in the dark of night,
Quickly, dearest, let me in!
I fear neither lock nor guard,
Ho! Listen! At midnight
You are to be freed."

No sooner said than done; at the stroke
Of twelve the valorous knight stood
  there;

She tenderly offered him her soft hand,
In the morning they found the cell
  empty;—

She was gone, hooray!"

(Pedrillo coughs several times. Konstanze opens the window.)

Spoken dialogue

Sie macht auf, Herr! Sie macht auf.

She is opening it, master! She is opening
it!

BELMONTE

Ich komme, ich komme!

I am coming, I am coming!

KONSTANZE *(above at the window)*

Belmonte!

Belmonte!

BELMONTE

Konstanze! hier bin ich! Hurtig die Leiter!

Konstanze! Here I am! Quick, the ladder!

*(Pedrillo positions the ladder under Konstanze's window,
Belmonte climbs up; Pedrillo holds the ladder.)*

PEDRILLO

Was das für ein abscheuliches Spektakel
macht.

What an awful noise that makes.

(holds his hand over his heart)

Es wird immer ärger, weil es nun Ernst
wird. Wenn sie mich hier erwischten, wie
schön würden sie mit mir abtrollen, zum
Kopfabschlagen, zum Spießen oder zum
Hängen. Je nu! Der Anfang ist einmal
gemacht, itzt ist's nicht mehr aufzuhalten;
es geht nun schon einmal aufs Leben oder
auf den Tod los.

It's becoming even worse since now it's
for real. If they caught me here, how
beautifully they would trot off with me to
my beheading, spitting or hanging. Oh,
well! Once we have begun, there is no
more holding back now; it's now become
a matter of life and death.

137

BELMONTE

(comes out of the door below with Konstanze)

Nun, holder Engel, nun hab' ich dich wieder, ganz wieder. Nichts soll uns mehr trennen.	Now, sweet angel, now I have you back again, finally back again. Nothing shall separate us any more.

KONSTANZE

Wie ängstlich schlägt mein Herz! Kaum bin ich imstande, mich aufrecht zu halten: wenn wir nur glücklich entkommen.	How anxiously my heart beats! I am scarcely capable of keeping myself upright; if only we get safely away.

PEDRILLO

Nur fort! nicht geplaudert! Sonst könnt' es freilich schief gehen, wenn wir da lange Rat halten und seufzen.	Just run! No chatter! Else things could really go awry if we deliberate and sigh.

(pushes Belmonte and Konstanze along)

Nur frisch nach dem Strande zu! Ich komme gleich nach.	Just go briskly to the beach! I am coming right behind you.

(Belmonte and Konstanze leave.)

Nun, Kupido, du mächtiger Herzensdieb, halte mir die Leiter und hülle mich samt meiner Gerätschaft in einen dicken Nebel ein!	Now, Cupid, you mighty thief of hearts, hold the ladder for me and wrap me together with my belongings in a thick fog!

(All the while he has been positioning the ladder beneath Blonde's window, and has been climbing up.)

Blondchen, Blondchen! Mach auf, ums Himmels willen, zaudre nicht! Es ist um Hals und Kragen zu tun.	Blondchen, Blondchen! Open up, for heaven's sake, don't delay! Our necks are on the line.

(The window is opened, he climbs inside.)

SCENE V

(Osmin and a black mute open the door of Osmin's house, into which Pedrillo has just climbed. Osmin, still half drunk with sleep, has a lantern. The mute tries to make Osmin understand through signs that something is not right, that he has heard people, etc.)

OSMIN

Lärmen hörtest du? Was kann's denn geben? Vielleicht Schwärmer? Geh, spioniere, bringe mir Antwort.	You have heard noises? What can be going on? Maybe night owls abroad? Go, spy out and bring me the answer.

*(The mute listens around a little; finally he catches sight
of the ladder beneath Osmin's window, is startled and shows
it to Osmin who, still groggy, is leaning against the door
to his house with the lantern in his hand and nodding.)*

Gift und Dolch! Was ist das? Wer kann
ins Haus steigen? Das sind Diebe oder
Mörder.

Hellfire and damnation! What is that?
Who can have climbed into the house?
They are thieves or murderers.

*(He rushes around, but since he is still half-drunk with sleep
he bumps himself here and there, etc.)*

Hurtig, hole die Wache! Ich will
unterdessen lauern.

Quick, get the guard! Meanwhile I will lie
in wait.

*(The mute leaves. Osmin sits on the ladder with the lantern in
his hand and nods off. Pedrillo climbs out the window again
backwards and is about to come back down the ladder.)*

BLONDE *(above, at the window, catches sight of Osmin, and calls to Pedrillo)*

O Himmel, Pedrillo! Wir sind verloren.

Oh heavens, Pedrillo! We are lost!

PEDRILLO

*(looks around, as soon as he catches sight of Osmin, stops short,
looks at him and climbs back in the window)*

Ah! welcher Teufel hat sich wider uns
verschworen!

Ah! What devil has conspired against us!

OSMIN

(up the ladder, after Pedrillo, calls)

Blondchen! Blondchen!

Blondchen! Blondchen!

PEDRILLO *(climbing inside, to Blonde)*

Zurück, nur zurück!

Stay back, just stay back!

OSMIN *(climbs back down)*

Wart, Spitzbube, du sollst mir nicht
entkommen. Hilfe! Hilfe! Wache, hurtig,
hier gibt's Räuber! Herbei, herbei!

Wait, you rascal, you are not going to get
away from me. Help! Help! Guard! Quick,
there are robbers here! Come here, come
here!

*(Pedrillo comes out the door below with Blonde, looks timidly
towards the ladder and sneaks away under it with Blonde.)*

PEDRILLO AND BLONDE
(as they are going off)

O Himmel, steh uns bei! sonst sind wir verloren.

Oh heaven, stay with us! Or else we're lost.

OSMIN

Zu Hilfe! zu Hilfe! Geschwind!

Help! Help! Quickly!

(He is about to go after them.)
(The guard with torches stops Osmin.)

GUARD

Halt, halt! Wohin?

Stop, stop! Where to?

OSMIN

Dorthin, dorthin.

There, there.

GUARD

Wer bist du?

Who are you?

OSMIN

Nur nicht lange gefragt, sonst entkommen die Spitzbuben. Seht ihr denn nicht? Hier ist noch die Leiter.

Just don't ask too many questions, or else the rascals will get away. Don't you see? The ladder is still here.

GUARD

Das sehn wir. Kannst nicht du sie angelegt haben?

We see that. Couldn't you have placed it there?

OSMIN

Gift und Dolch! Kennt ihr mich denn nicht? Ich bin Oberaufseher der Gärten beim Bassa. Wenn ihr noch lange fragt, so hilft euer Kommen nichts.

Hellfire and damnation! Don't you know me? I am the overseer of the pasha's gardens. If you deliberate much longer, then your coming was no help.

(Part of the guard brings Pedrillo and Blonde back.)

Ach endlich! Gift und Dolch! Seh' ich recht? Ihr beide? Warte, spitzbübischer Pedrillo, dein Kopf soll am längsten fest gestanden sein.

Ah finally! Hellfire and damnation! Am I seeing right? You two? Wait, Pedrillo, you rascal, your head is to be impaled at long last.

PEDRILLO

Brüderchen, Brüderchen! Wirst doch Spaß verstehn? Ich wollt' dir dein Weibchen nur ein wenig spazieren führen, weil du heute dazu nicht aufgelegt bist. Du weißt schon

Little brother, little brother! Don't you understand it's a joke? I just wanted to take your little lady out for a walk, since you weren't in the mood for it today. You know

(secretly to Osmin)

| wegen des Zypernweins. | because of the Cypriot wine. |

OSMIN

| Schurke, glaubtest du mich zu betäuben? Hier verstehe ich keinen Spaß. Dein Kopf muß herunter, so wahr ich ein Muselmann bin. | Scoundrel, did you think you could get me drunk? I don't consider it a joke! As sure as I am a Moslem, your head must fall. |

(Another part of the guard, also with torches, brings Belmonte and Konstanze.)

BELMONTE *(still putting up resistance)*

| Schändliche, laßt mich los! | Vile ones, let me go! |

GUARD

| Sachte, junger Herr, sachte! Uns entkommt man nicht so geschwinde. | Easy, young master, easy! One doesn't get away from us so quickly. |

OSMIN

| Sieh da! die Gesellschaft wird immer stärker. Hat der Herr Baumeister auch spazierengehen wollen? O ihr Spitzbuben! Hatte ich heute nicht recht, | Look there! The company is growing larger. Did the master architect also want to take a walk? Oh you scoundrels! Wasn't I right today, |

(to Belmonte)

| daß ich dich nicht ins Haus lassen wollte? Nun wird der Bassa sehen, was für sauberes Gelichter er um sich hat. | not to want to let you into the house? Now the pasha will see what a nice gang he has around him. |

BELMONTE

| Das beiseite! Laßt hören, ob mit Euch ein vernünftig Wort zu sprechen ist. Hier ist ein Beutel mit Zechinen, er ist Euer, und noch zweimal so viel; laßt mich los. | Put that aside! Let's hear if a reasonable word can be spoken with you. Here is a pouch filled with gold coins, it is yours, and twice again as much; let me go. |

KONSTANZE

| Laßt Euch bewegen! | Let yourself be moved! |

OSMIN

| Ich glaube, Ihr seid besessen. Euer Geld brauchen wir nicht, das bekommen wir ohnehin: eure Köpfe wollen wir. | I think you must be crazy. We don't need your money, we'll get that in any case. It's your heads we want. |

(to the guard)

| Schleppt sie fort, zum Bassa! | Drag them away to the pasha! |

KONSTANZE

Laßt Euch bewegen!	Let yourself be moved!

BELMONTE

Habt doch Erbarmen!	Have mercy!

OSMIN

Um nichts in der Welt! Ich habe mir längst so einen Augenblick gewünscht. Fort, fort!	Not for anything in the world! I have long wished for such a moment. Away with you, away!

(The guard leads Belmonte and Konstanze away, together with Pedrillo and Blonde.)

No. 19: Aria

O, wie will ich triumphieren, Wenn sie euch zum Richtplatz führen	Oh, how I will gloat, When they lead you to the place of execution
Und die Hälse schnüren zu! Hüpfen will ich, lachen, springen Und ein Freudenliedchen singen; Denn nun hab' ich vor euch Ruh'.	And tighten the ropes around your necks! I will hop, laugh, jump And sing a song of joy; Because now you'll leave me in peace.
O, wie will ich triumphieren, Wenn sie euch zum Richtplatz führen	Oh, how I will gloat, When they lead you to the place of execution
Und die Hälse schnüren zu! Schleicht nur säuberlich und leise,	And tighten the ropes around your necks! Even if you creep around carefully and quietly,
Ihr verdammten Haremsmäuse, Unser Ohr entdeckt euch schon. Und eh' ihr uns könnt entspringen, Seht ihr euch in unsern Schlingen Und erhaschet euren Lohn.	You damned harem-mice, Our ear will surely detect you. And before you can escape, You will see yourself in our snares And you'll get your reward.
Ha, wie will ich triumphieren, Wenn sie euch zum Richtplatz führen	Ha, how I will gloat, When they lead you to the place of execution
Und die Hälse schnüren zu!	And tighten the ropes around your necks!

(goes out)

SCENE VI

The pasha's room
Selim with attendants, afterwards Osmin, Belmonte, Konstanze and guards

Spoken dialogue

SELIM (*to an officer*)

Geht, unterrichtet Euch, was der Lärm im Palast bedeutet; er hat uns im Schlaf aufgeschreckt, und laßt mir Osmin kommen.	Go, learn what the noise in the palace means; it has roused us from our sleep; and have Osmin come to me.

(*The officer is about to go, just as Osmin comes in haste, but still a little sleepy.*)

OSMIN

Herr! Verzeih, daß ich es so früh wage— deine Ruhe zu stören.	Master! Pardon me for daring—to disturb your rest so early.

SELIM

Was gibt's, Osmin, was gibt's? Was bedeutet der Aufruhr?	What's the matter, Osmin, what's the matter? What does the uproar mean?

OSMIN

Herr, es ist die schändlichste Verräterei in deinem Palast—	Master, there is the most shameful treachery in your palace—

SELIM

Verräterei?	Treachery?

OSMIN

Die niederträchtigen Christensklaven entführen uns—die Weiber. Der große Baumeister, den du gestern auf Zureden des Veräters Pedrillo aufnahmst, hat deine—schöne Konstanze entführt.	The base Christian slaves are abducting— our women. The great architect you employed yesterday at Pedrillo's urging has abducted your—beautiful Konstanze.

SELIM

Konstanze? Entführt? Ah, setzt ihnen nach!	Konstanze? Abducted? Ah, after them!

OSMIN

O 's ist schon dafür gesorgt! Meiner Wachsamkeit—hast du es zu danken, daß ich sie wieder beim Schopfe gekriegt habe. Auch mir selbst hatte der—	Already taken care of! You can thank my vigilance—that I have them by the hair again. The roguish—Pedrillo had the same honor in store for me, and he

spitzbübische Pedrillo eine gleiche Ehre zugedacht und er hatte mein Blondchen schon beim Kopfe, um mit ihr—in alle Welt zu reisen.—Aber Gift und Dolch! Er soll mir's entgelten! Sieh, da bringen sie sie!

already had put in Blondchen's head to travel with him—into the wide world.— But hellfire and damnation! He'll pay me for that! Look, they're bringing them!

(Belmonte and Konstanze are led in by the guards.)

SELIM

Ah, Verräter! Ist's möglich?—Ha, du heuchlerische Sirene! War das der Aufschub, den du begehrtest? Mißbrauchtest du so die Nachsicht, die ich dir gab, um mich zu hintergehen?

Ah, traitor! Is it possible? Ha, you hypocritical siren! Was that the delay that you sought? Did you thus misuse the leniency I extended to you in order to trick me?

KONSTANZE

Ich bin strafbar in deinen Augen, Herr, es ist wahr. Aber es ist mein Geliebter, mein einziger Geliebter, dem lange schon dieses Herz gehört. O nur für ihn, nur um seinetwillen fleh' ich Aufschub. O laß mich sterben! Gern, gern will ich den Tod erdulden, aber schone nur sein Leben—

In your eyes I should be punished, Sire, it is true. But he is my beloved, my only beloved, to whom this heart has long since belonged. Oh only for him, only on his account did I beg for delay. Oh let me die! Gladly, gladly will I suffer death, only spare his life—

SELIM

Und du wagst's, Unverschämte, für ihn zu bitten?

And you dare, shameless woman, to plead for him?

KONSTANZE

Noch mehr: für ihn zu sterben!

Even more: to die for him!

BELMONTE

Ha, Bassa! Noch nie erniedrigte ich mich zu bitten, noch nie hat dieses Knie sich vor einem Menschen gebeugt. Aber sieh, hier lieg' ich zu deinen Füßen und flehe dein Mitleid an. Ich bin von einer großen spanischen Familie, man wird alles für mich zahlen. Laß dich bewegen, bestimme ein Lösegeld für mich und Konstanze so hoch du willst. Mein Name ist Lostados.

Ah, pasha! Never have I debased myself to beg, never has this knee bent before any man. But behold, here I lie at your feet and beg your mercy. I am from a great Spanish family; they will pay anything for me. Let yourself be moved; specify a ransom for me and Konstanze, as high as you please. My name is Lostados.

Die Entführung aus dem Serail

SELIM (*astonished*)

Was hör' ich! Der Kommandant von Oran, ist der dir bekannt?

What do I hear! The commandant of Oran, do you know him?

BELMONTE

Das ist mein Vater.

That is my father.

SELIM

Dein Vater? Welcher glückliche Tag! Den Sohn meines ärgsten Feindes in meiner Macht zu haben! Kann was Angenehmers sein? Wisse, Elender! Dein Vater, dieser Barbar, ist schuld, daß ich mein Vaterland verlassen mußte. Sein unbiegsamer Geiz entriß mir eine Geliebte, die ich höher als mein Leben schätzte. Er brachte mich um Ehrenstellen, Vermögen, um alles. Kurz, er zernichtete mein ganzes Glück. Und dieses Mannes einzigen Sohn habe ich nun in meiner Gewalt! Sage, er an meiner Stelle, was würde er tun?

Your father? What a lucky day! To have the son of my worst enemy in my power! Can anything be more pleasant? Know then, wretch! Your father, this barbarian, is responsible for my having to leave my fatherland. His relentless greed tore my beloved one from me, whom I cherished more than my life. He took away from me honorable standing, wealth, everything. In short, he completely destroyed all my happiness. And now I have this man's only son in my grasp. Tell me, if he were in my place, what would he do?

BELMONTE (*completely downhearted*)

Mein Schicksal würde zu beklagen sein.

My fate would be lamentable.

SELIM

Das soll es auch sein. Wie er mit mir verfahren ist, will ich mit dir verfahren. Folge mir, Osmin, ich will dir Befehle zu ihren Martern geben.

And so it shall be. As he dealt with me, so shall I deal with you. Follow me, Osmin, I will give you orders for their torture.

(*to the guards*)

Bewacht sie hier.

You stand guard here.

(*He goes off with his attendants and Osmin.*)

Scene VII

Belmonte and Konstanze

No. 20: Recitative and Duet

BELMONTE

Welch ein Geschick! O Qual der Seele!	What a fate! Oh anguish of soul!
Hat sich denn alles wider mich verschworen?	Has everything then conspired against me?
Ach! Konstanze! durch mich bist du verloren!	Ah! Konstanze! Because of me you are lost!
Welch eine Pein!	What agony!

KONSTANZE

Laß, ach, Geliebter! laß dich das nicht quälen.	Do not, ah, beloved! Do not let this torment you.
Was ist der Tod?—Ein Übergang zur Ruh'!	What is death? A passage to repose!
Und dann an deiner Seite	And then, at your side,
Ist er Vorgeschmack der Seligkeit.	It is a foretaste of eternal bliss.

BELMONTE

Engelsseele! Welch holde Güte!	Angel's soul! What sweet goodness!
Du flößest Trost in mein erschüttert Herz,	You lave my agitated heart with comfort,
Du linderst mir den Todesschmerz,	You relieve me of the pain of death.
Und ach! ich reiße dich ins Grab!	And, ah! I pull you down into the grave.
Meinetwegen sollst du sterben!	On my account you are to die!
Ach, Konstanze! kann ich's wagen,	Ah, Konstanze! Can I still dare to
Noch die Augen aufzuschlagen?	Raise my eyes to you?
Ich bereite dir den Tod!	I am causing your death!

KONSTANZE

Belmont! Du stirbst meinetwegen,	Belmonte! You are dying on my account,
Ich nur zog dich ins Verderben,	Only I drew you to your ruin,
Und ich soll nicht mit dir sterben?	And am I not then to die with you?
Wonne ist mir dies Gebot!	This requirement is bliss to me.

BOTH

Edle Seele, dir zu leben	Noble soul, to live for you
War mein Wunsch und all mein Streben;	Was my wish and my whole aspiration.

Ohne dich ist mir's nur Pein,	To be without you any longer
Länger auf der Welt zu sein.	In this world is only torment for me.

BELMONTE

Meinetwegen sollst du sterben!	On my account you are to die!

KONSTANZE

Belmont! Du stirbst meinetwegen!	Belmonte! You are dying on my account!

BELMONTE

Ach, Konstanze, kann ich's wagen,	Ah, Konstanze, can I dare to
Noch die Augen aufzuschlagen?	Raise my eyes to you?

KONSTANZE

Ich nur zog dich ins Verderben,	Only I drew you to your ruin,
Und ich soll nicht mit dir sterben!	And am I not then to die with you?

BELMONTE

Ich bereite dir den Tod!	I am causing your death!

KONSTANZE

Wonne ist mir dies Gebot!	This requirement is bliss to me!

BOTH

Edle Seele! Dir zu leben	Noble soul! To live for you
Ist mein Wunsch und all mein Streben;	Is my wish and my whole aspiration;
Ohne dich ist mir's nur Pein,	To be without you any longer
Länger auf der Welt zu sein!	In this world is only torment for me.

KONSTANZE

Ich will alles gerne leiden.	I will gladly suffer anything.

BELMONTE

Ruhig sterb' ich und mit Freuden—	I die peacefully and with joy—

BOTH

Weil ich dir zur Seite bin.	Since I am by your side.

BELMONTE

Um dich, Geliebte!	For you, beloved!

KONSTANZE

Um dich, Geliebter!	For you, beloved!

BOTH

Geb' ich gern mein Leben hin!	I gladly sacrifice my life!
O welche Seligkeit!	Oh what blessedness!

Mit $\frac{\text{dem Geliebten}}{\text{der Geliebten}}$ sterben	To die with one's beloved
Ist seliges Entzücken!	Is blessed delight!
Mit wonnevollen Blicken	With blissful gaze
Verläßt man da die Welt.	One then abandons the world.

SCENE VIII

(Pedrillo and Blonde are led on by another part of the guard; and the above.)

Spoken dialogue

PEDRILLO

Ach, Herr, wir sind hin! An Rettung ist nicht mehr zu denken. Man macht schon alle Zubereitungen, um uns aus der Welt zu schaffen. Es ist erschrecklich, was sie mit uns anfangen wollen! Ich, wie ich im Vorbeigehen gehört habe, soll in Öl gesotten und dann gespießt werden. Das ist ein sauber Traktament! Ach! Blondchen! Blondchen! Was werden sie wohl mit dir anfangen?	Ah, master, we are lost! There's no point in thinking about rescue anymore. They are already making all the preparations for sending us out of the world. It is terrifying what they want to do with us! I, as I have heard in passing, am to be boiled in oil and then spitted. That's nice treatment! Ah! Blondchen! Blondchen! What will they do to you?

BLONDE

Das gilt mir nun ganz gleich. Da es einmal gestorben sein muß, ist mir alles recht.	I don't care at all at this point; since we have to die now, it's all the same to me.

PEDRILLO

Welche Standhaftigkeit! Ich bin doch von gutem altchristlichem Geschlecht aus Spanien, aber so gleichgültig kann ich beim Tode nicht sein!—Weiß der Teufel . . . Gott sei bei mir! Wie kann mir auch itzt der Teufel auf die Zunge kommen?	What steadfastness! I am of good old Christian stock from Spain, but I can't be so indifferent about death! The devil knows—God be with me! Now how can the devil have come off my tongue?

FINAL SCENE

The above. Pasha Selim, Osmin (full of joy) and attendants

SELIM

Nun, Sklave! Elender Sklave! Zitterst du? Erwartest du dein Urteil?

Now, slave! Miserable slave! Are you trembling? Do you await your judgment?

BELMONTE

Ja, Bassa, mit so vieler Kaltblütigkeit, als Hitze du es aussprechen kannst. Kühle deine Rache an mir, tilge das Unrecht, so mein Vater dir angetan!—Ich erwarte alles und tadle dich nicht.

Yes, pasha, with as much cold-bloodedness as the heat with which you can pronounce it. Wreak your revenge on me, eradicate the injustice that my father did you!—I await anything and do not reproach you.

SELIM

Es muß also wohl deinem Geschlechte eigen sein, Ungerechtigkeiten zu begehen, weil du das für so ausgemacht annimmst? Du betrügst dich. Ich habe deinen Vater viel zu sehr verabscheut, als daß ich je in seine Fußstapfen treten könnte. Nimm deine Freiheit, nimm Konstanzen, segle in dein Vaterland, sage deinem Vater, daß du in meiner Gewalt warst, daß ich dich freigelassen, um ihm sagen zu können, es wäre ein weit größeres Vergnügen, eine erlittene Ungerechtigkeit durch Wohltaten zu vergelten, als Laster mit Lastern tilgen.

It must be unique to your family to perpetuate injustice, since you take it thus for granted? You are deceiving yourself. I loathed your father much too much, ever to be able to follow in his footsteps. Take your freedom, take Konstanze, sail to your fatherland, tell your father that you were in my grasp, that I let you go free to be able to tell him, that it is a far greater pleasure to repay a grievous injustice with beneficence, than to cancel out one vice with another.

BELMONTE

Herr! . . . Du setzest mich in Erstaunen . . .

Sire! You move me to amazement . . .

SELIM (*looking at him disdainfully*)

Das glaub' ich. Zieh damit hin, und werde du wenigstens menschlicher als dein Vater, so ist meine Handlung belohnt.

That I believe. Depart then, and if you will become more human than your father, then my action will be rewarded.

KONSTANZE

Herr, vergib! Ich schätzte bisher . . . deine edle Seele, aber nun bewundere ich . . .

Sire, forgive! I cherished until now . . . your noble soul, but now I admire . . .

SELIM

Still! Ich wünsche für die Falschheit, die Sie an mir begangen, daß Sie es nie bereuen möchten, mein Herz ausgeschlagen zu haben.

Silence! I wish that, for the deception you committed against me, you need never regret having rejected my heart.

(on the point of leaving)

PEDRILLO

(steps in his way and falls at his feet)

Herr! Dürfen wir beide Unglückliche es auch wagen, um Gnade zu flehen?—Ich war von Jugend auf ein treuer Diener meines Herrn . . .

Sire! May we two unfortunates also dare to plead for mercy?—Since my youth I have been a faithful servant of my master . . .

OSMIN

Herr! beim Allah! Laß dich ja nicht von dem verwünschten Schmarotzer hintergehen! Keine Gnade! Er hat schon hundertmal den Tod verdient.

Master! By Allah! Don't let yourself be deceived by the damned parasite! No mercy! He has earned death a hundred times over.

SELIM

Er mag ihn also in seinem Vaterlande suchen.

Then he may seek it in his fatherland.

(to the guard)

Man begleite alle viere an das Schiff.

Accompany all four to the ship.

(gives Belmonte a document)

Hier ist euer Paßport.

Here is your passport.

OSMIN

Wie! Meine Blonde soll er auch mitnehmen?

What! He is also to take my Blonde with him?

SELIM (jokingly)

Alter! sind dir deine Augen nicht lieb?— Ich sorge besser für dich, als du denkst.

Old fellow! Aren't your eyes dear to you?—I take better care of you than you realize.

OSMIN

Gift und Dolch! Ich möchte bersten!

Hellfire and damnation! I would like to burst!

SELIM

Beruhige dich. Wen man durch Wohltun nicht für sich gewinnen kann, den muß man sich vom Halse schaffen.

Calm yourself. Whomever you cannot win over with benevolence, you must get rid of.

No. 21A: Vaudeville

BELMONTE

Nie werd' ich deine Huld verkennen,
Mein Dank bleibt ewig dir geweiht;

An jedem Ort, zu jeder Zeit
Werd' ich dich groß und edel nennen.
Wer so viel Huld vergessen kann,

Den seh' man mit Verachtung an.

Never will I undervalue your kindness,
My thanks remain forever dedicated to you;

In every place, at any time
Shall I call you great and noble.
Anyone who can forget so much kindness.

Should be looked on with disdain.

KONSTANZE, BELMONTE,
PEDRILLO, BLONDE, OSMIN

Wer so viel Huld vergessen kann,

Den seh' man mit Verachtung an.

Anyone who can forget so much kindness,

Should be looked on with disdain.

KONSTANZE

Nie werd' ich im Genuß der Liebe
Vergessen, was der Dank gebeut;
Mein Herz, der Liebe nur geweiht,
Hegt auch dem Dank geweihte Triebe.

Wer so viel Huld vergessen kann,

Den seh' man mit Verachtung an.

Never will I, while enjoying love
Forget that which calls for thanks;
My heart, dedicated only to love,
Harbors also the blessed impulse toward thanks.

Anyone who can forget so much kindness,

Should be looked on with disdain.

KONSTANZE, BELMONTE,
PEDRILLO, BLONDE, OSMIN

Wer so viel Huld vergessen kann,

Den seh' man mit Verachtung an.

Anyone who can forget so much kindness,

Should be looked at with disdain.

PEDRILLO

Wenn ich es je vergessen könnte,
Wie nah ich dem Erdrosseln war,
Und all der anderen Gefahr:

As if I could ever forget
How near I was to being strangled,
And all the other dangers:

Ich lief als ob der Kopf mir brennte.	I ran as if my head were on fire.
Wer so viel Huld vergessen kann,	Anyone who can forget this,
Den seh' man mit Verachtung an.	Should be looked at with disdain.

KONSTANZE, BELMONTE,
PEDRILLO, BLONDE, OSMIN

Wer so viel Huld vergessen kann,	Anyone who can forget this,
Den seh' man mit Verachtung an.	Should be looked at with disdain.

BLONDE

Herr Bassa, ich sag' recht mit Freuden	Sir Pasha, I say plainly with joy
Viel Dank für Kost und Lagerstroh.	Thanks very much for food and bed-straw;
Doch bin ich recht von Herzen froh,	However I am very glad in my heart,
Daß man mich läßt von hinnen scheiden.	That I am being allowed to depart from here.

(*pointing at Osmin*)

Denn seh' er nur das Tier dort an,	For just look at the beast there;
Ob man so was ertragen kann.	How can anything like that be tolerated.

OSMIN

Verbrennen sollte man die Hunde,	The dogs should be burned to death
Die uns so schändlich hintergehn.	Who so disgracefully deceive us.
Es ist nicht länger auszusteh'n,	It is not to be endured any longer.
Mir starrt die Zunge fast im Munde,	My tongue almost stiffens in my mouth,
Um ihren Lohn zu ordnen an:	When it comes to ordering their reward.
Erst geköpft, dann gehangen,	First beheaded, then hanged,
Dann gespießt auf heiße Stangen,	Then spitted on hot skewers,
Dann verbrannt, dann gebunden	Then burned, then bound
Und getaucht; zuletzt geschunden.	And drowned; finally skinned.

(*runs away in a rage*)

KONSTANZE, BELMONTE,
BLONDE, PEDRILLO

Nichts ist so häßlich als die Rache.	Nothing is as ugly as vengeance.
Hingegen menschlich gütig sein	However to be humanly good
Und ohne Eigennutz verzeihn,	And to pardon without selfishness
Ist nur der großen Seelen Sache.	Is only a matter for the great souls.

KONSTANZE

Wer dieses nicht erkennen kann,	Anyone who can forget this,
Den seh' man mit Verachtung an.	Should be looked on with disdain.

KONSTANZE, BELMONTE,
BLONDE, PEDRILLO

Wer dieses nicht erkennen kann,	Anyone who can forget this,
Den seh' man mit Verachtung an.	Should be looked on with disdain.

No. 21B: Chorus

CHORUS OF THE JANISSARIES

Bassa Selim lebe lange!	Long live Pasha Selim!
Ehre sei sein Eigentum!	Honor be to his title!
Seine holde Scheitel prange	Let his sweet head be resplendent
Voll von Jubel, voll von Ruhm.	With rejoicing, with glory.
Bassa Selim lebe lange!	Long live Pasha Selim!
Ehre sei sein Eigentum!	Honor be to his title!

The End

APPENDIX

Christoph Friedrich Bretzner (1748–1807), German playwright and librettist, wrote in 1781 for the composer and publisher Johann André (1744–99) the singspiel libretto *Belmonte und Constanze,* which Gottlieb Stephanie the Younger revised for Mozart. (For more details, see the preface to this libretto.)

Bretzner's first public protest against this unauthorized use of his libretto is said to have been published in 1782, although it may not have been written by him. It reads, "A certain man by the name of Mozart has had the audacity to misuse my drama *Belmonte und Constanze* as an opera libretto. I hereby formally protest this infringement of my rights and reserve to myself further protests."

His "further protest" appeared in the "Litteratur-und-Theater Zeitung", Berlin, of June 21, 1783. In part, it reads: "Since the alterations in the dialogue are not substantial, I'll skip over those: however, at the same time, the adaptor has inserted a bunch of songs in which quite heartbreaking and uplifting little verses are to be found."

The offending musical numbers include Belmonte's arias "Hier soll ich denn dann sehen," "Wenn der Freude" and "Ich baue ganz", Osmin's two arias, Blonde's rondo "Welche Wonne," Konstanze's "Martern alle Arten", the Blonde-Osmin duet, the Belmonte-Osmin duet, the Belmonte-Konstanze duet, a piece of the Act II finale and the whole vaudeville.

According to Thomas Bauman, author of the Cambridge University Press book on *Die Entführung,* "Bretzner himself, or someone sharing his contempt for Stephanie's poetic contributions, seems to have [attempted] a laundering of the new verses."

This revised version of the text is found in scores, and can be heard in performances and on recordings; some singers find it easier to sing, and in some cases, it makes better sense. Many of these alterations are sung by artists in the current Met production.

Act One

No. 1: Aria

BELMONTE

Hier soll ich dich denn sehen,	Then I am to see you here,
Konstanze, dich mein Glück!	Konstanze! You, my happiness!
Laß Himmel hör mein Flehen . . .	May heaven hear my plea . . .
Gib mir dafür nun Freuden . . .	In return, now give me joy . . .

ACT TWO

No. 9: Duet

BLONDE

Ein Mädchen zur Freiheit geboren,	A free-born maiden,
Läßt nie sich als Sklavin befehlen,	Never lets herself be commanded like a slave,
Und ist auch die Freiheit verloren,	And even if freedom is lost,
Doch bleibt sie noch Fürstin der Welt!	She still remains sovereign of the world!

No. 10: Recitative and Aria

KONSTANZE

Welcher Kummer herrscht in meiner Seele	What grief prevails in my soul
Seit dem Tag, da ich mein Glück verloren!	Since the day that I lost my happiness!
Belmonte! hin sind die Freuden	Belmonte! Gone are the joys
Die ich einst an deiner Seite kannte;	Which I once knew at your side;
Banger Sehnsucht Leiden	Now the pangs of anxious longing
Wohnen nun dafür in der beklomm'nen Brust.	Dwell in my uneasy bosom.

No. 11: Aria

KONSTANZE

. . . .	. . . .
Doch dich rührt kein Flehen,	But no plea moves you,
Standhaft sollst du sehen,	You must see that
Duld' ich jede Qual und Not,	I steadfastly endure every pain and hardship,
Ordne nur, gebiete,	Just order, command,
Drohe, strafe, wüte . . .	Threaten, punish, rage . . .

No. 12: Aria

BLONDE

Welche Wonne, welche Lust	What bliss, what pleasure
Regt sich nun in meiner Brust!	Now stir in my bosom!
Voller Freuden will ich springen,	Full of joy I will jump up,

Ihr die frohe Nachricht bringen;	To bring her the glad news;
Und mit Lachen und mit Scherzen	And with laughing and with joking
Ihrem schwachen, kranken Herzen	Predict comfort and rescue
Trost und Rettung prophezeihn.	For her weak, sick heart.

No. 15: Aria

BELMONTE

. . . .	. . . .
Ach, Konstanze, dich zu sehen,	Ah, Konstanze, to see you,
Dich voll Wonne, voll Entzücken	Full of bliss, full of delight,
An dies treue Herz zu drücken,	To press you to my faithful heart,
Lohnet mir nicht Kron und Pracht.	Crown and luxury are no reward to me.
Ha dieses sel'ge Wiederfinden	Ha, this blessed reunion
Läßt innig erst mich ganz empfinden . . .	Allows me to feel very deeply . . .

ACT THREE

No. 20: Duet

BELMONTE

. . . .	. . . .
und ach, ich reiße dich ins Grab!	and, ah, I pull you down into the grave!
Ha, du solltest für mich sterben,	Ah, you are to die for me,
. . . .	. . . .

KONSTANZE

Ach, für mich gibst du dein Leben,	Ah, you give your life for me,
. . . .	. . . .

BOTH

Ach, Geliebte, dir zu leben war mein Wunsch . . .	Ah, beloved, to live for you was my wish . . .

No. 21: Vaudeville

KONSTANZE

Nie werd' ich selbst im Schoß der Liebe,	Never will I, even in the haven of love,
Vergessen, was der Dank gebeut,	Forget that which calls for thanks.

BLONDE

Nehmt meinen Dank mit tausend Freuden,	Take my thanks with a thousand joys,
Herr Bassa, lebt gesund und froh,	Sir Pasha, live healthy and happy,
Osmin, das Schicksal will es so,	Osmin, fate will have it so,
Ich muß von dir auf ewig scheiden;	I must part from you forever;
Wer so wie du nur zanken kann,	One looks with disdain on him
Den sieht man mit Verachtung an.	Who, like you, can only grumble.

ALL FOUR

Den edlen Mann entstellt die Rache,	Vengeance disfigures the nobleman,
Großmütig, menschlich, gütig sein,	To be generous, human, good,
. . . .	

LE NOZZE DI FIGARO

WORLD PREMIERE: *Vienna, Burgtheater, May 1, 1786*

UNITED STATES PREMIERE: *New York, Park Theatre, May 10, 1824*

METROPOLITAN OPERA PREMIERE: *January 31, 1894*

LE NOZZE DI FIGARO
(The Marriage of Figaro)

Comic Opera in Four Acts

Libretto: Lorenzo Da Ponte

English Translation: Judyth Schaubhut Smith

Music: Wolfgang Amadeus Mozart

PREFACE

On May 1, 1986, *Le Nozze di Figaro* was "200 years young." Beyond its playfulness of mood and complexity of plot, *Figaro* is especially noted for its characterizations. To each of the principals Mozart has given one or two arias that tell a great deal about his or her personality, and these traits are maintained in the ensembles and finales that he constructed with architectural skill. Small wonder that despite advanced age, *Figaro* remains as much fun as any opera in the repertory—entertaining, revealing musical theater, sparked by a mischievous sense of people's foibles, warmed by a sense of the humanity that transcends them.

Wolfgang Amadeus Mozart (1756–91), an Austrian-born natural genius who adapted readily to all forms of music, had a predilection for opera seria and German singspiel, both of which he worked to bring to a new level of flexibility and expression. That he understood and appreciated Italian opera buffa as well became evident during 1786–90, when he responded to the demand for Italian-style comedies in Vienna and Prague. From this brief period, just before his death, date the three collaborations with erstwhile court poet Lorenzo da Ponte— *Le Nozze di Figaro, Don Giovanni, Così Fan Tutte*—that mark the fullest flowering of this genre in musical history.

Figaro, most overtly comic of the three, also stems from the most distinguished source— *Le Mariage de Figaro, ou La Folle Journée*, second of a trilogy of plays by Pierre Augustin Caron de Beaumarchais, a lively satirist and theater-lover. Critical of the privileges of the nobility and looking toward a freer society, *Figaro* was judged controversial, and in fact Emanuel Schikaneder's troupe was banned by imperial order from presenting the comedy in Vienna in early 1785. By playing down the overt social criticism (though its message remains, from the very first scene onward), Da Ponte was able to placate opposition and make the subject acceptable in opera form. Incidentally, the other plays of Beaumarchais' trilogy were set to music too—*Le Barbier de Séville* by Paisiello and Rossini, *La Mère Coupable* by Darius Milhaud in the twentieth century. After the premiere of Mozart's *Figaro*, Beaumarchais tried his hand at writing an opera libretto—for *Tarare* (Paris 1787), the major work of Antonio Salieri—and prefaced it with pithy comments on the principles of opera, not included in the Henle Edition published in Munich in 1978.

Mention of Salieri conjures up thoughts of the play and film *Amadeus*, Peter Schaffer's fanciful evocation of the rivalry between Mozart and Salieri that culminated, according to beliefs once held, in Salieri's poisoning of his colleague. Though the poisoning theory is widely discounted today, there is no doubt about the rivalry. Here is a first-hand account of the *Figaro* premiere in Vienna, May 1, 1786, from the memoirs of the Irish singer Michael Kelly, the first Don Curzio:

There were three operas now on the tapis, one by Righini, another by Salieri (*The Grotto of Trophonius*) and one by Mozart, by special command of the Emperor [Joseph II]. . . . These three pieces were nearly ready for representation at the same time, and each composer claimed the right of producing his opera for this first. The contest raised much discord, and parties were formed. The characters of the three men were all very different. Mozart was as touchy as gunpowder and swore he would put the score of his opera into the fire if it was not produced first. . . . Righini was working like a mole in the dark to get precedence. The third candidate [Salieri] was Maestro di Cappella to the court, a clever shrewd man, possessed of what Bacon called "crooked wisdom"; and his claims were backed by three of the principal performers, who formed a cabal not easily put down. Every one of the opera company took part in the contest . . . [which] was put an end to by His Majesty issuing a mandate for Mozart's *Nozze di Figaro* to be instantly put into rehearsal. . . .

All the original performers had the advantage of the instruction of the composer, who transfused into their minds his inspired meaning. I never shall forget his little animated countenance, when lighted up with the glowing rays of genius. It is as impossible to describe it as it would be to paint sunbeams.

Kelly goes on to describe the enthusiasm of the audience at the first evening, which caused the emperor to lay down a rule against encores at subsequent performances. "Never was anything more complete than the triumph of Mozart and his *Nozze di Figaro*, to which numerous overflowing audiences bore witness." The success was repeated when the opera reached Prague, occasioning Mozart to visit there for four months and write *Don Giovanni* for that city.

Since Beaumarchais' play had been introduced in Paris only two years before, *Figaro* was a timely success, given nine times in its first season and revived for a longer run three years later. Meanwhile, it traveled to other German-speaking stages—usually in translation, which proved that its appeal reached past the aristocracy to the larger audience that Mozart had been hoping to lure with German singspiels. Though the composition of *Figaro* had kept him busy for some months, he did find time to write his Piano Concertos Nos. 22 in E-flat, 23 in A and 24 in C minor, which proved scarcely less popular. By later standards the composer was not well compensated, but he certainly did not lack appreciation.

Unlike *Don Giovanni* and *Così Fan Tutte, Le Nozze di Figaro* is not a problem opera, causing scholars and interpreters to probe for inner meanings. The backstairs shenanigans it depicts may have raised eyebrows, and indeed may still; the intricacies of the story remain hard to follow. But apart from the Countess' moments of sadness over her husband's wandering affections, there are few clouds dense enough to darken the prevailing sunshine of Beaumarchais' "day of madness." The sincerity of the count's plea for forgiveness at the end, and the gentle understatement with which his wife grants it, are moving examples of *comédie larmoyante* at its least sentimental; but because they are light touches, there is no need for tears. Only as an afterthought may we realize that the Almavivas are not necessarily destined to live happily ever after. As for the charming adolescent Cherubino, his descendants roam through many a later opera, notably Richard Strauss' *Der Rosenkavalier* and *Ariadne auf Naxos*.

In both *Don Giovanni* and *Così*, Mozart related his overture to the score of the opera proper—in *Don Giovanni* with the Commendatore's music, in *Così* with the motto sung by Don Alfonso from which the work takes its title. For *Figaro*, however, Mozart supplied a musical description of the *folle journée* itself, a distillation of the spirit of the work without quotations from it.

Not long after the premiere of *Così*, Da Ponte left Vienna—under a cloud, it was said, because of his intriguing, and perhaps more because of his romantic entanglements, not unlike those of his friend Casanova. In later life, a reformed man, the writer lived in New York and founded what is now the Italian Department at Columbia University. In 1824, the year after his memoirs were published, *Figaro* had its first American performance, at the Park Theatre, New York, in an English adaptation. In 1826 he fulfilled his dream of seeing *Don Giovanni* once again, though this was not a U.S. premiere—the work had been performed at the Park Theatre eight years before. The music of Mozart, Da Ponte realized, was too sophisticated for public tastes in America of that period, but the operas, occasional novelties at first, usually attracted praise and attention. The day would arrive, though not for another century, when they would be considered indispensable.

The history of Mozart's operas on the stage of the Metropolitan bears this out. *Don Giovanni* was given during the company's first season, 1883–84, to be followed by *Figaro* a decade later, after a fire had occasioned restoration of the old Opera House's interior. In the cast on January 1, 1894, were Emma Eames as the Countess, Lillian Nordica (whose other Mozart roles included both Donna Anna and the Queen of the Night!) as Susanna, Sigrid Arnoldson as Cherubino, Mario Ancona as Figaro and Édouard de Reszke as the Count, with Emilio Bevignani conducting. The letter duet was encored (shades of the world premiere in Vienna), and the press was favorable, but there were only three performances that season, with one the following. This pattern prevailed in subsequent revivals. In 1898–99, Marcella Sembrich (Susanna) and Giuseppe Campanari (Figaro) joined the cast, followed by Fritzi Scheff as Cherubino in 1902–03 and Antonio Scotti as the Count in 1902–03. The season after that, Heinrich Conried's first as general manager, saw a single performance with Johanna Gadski as the Countess. The next landmark date was 1908–09, when Gustav Mahler conducted a revival with Geraldine Farrar as Cherubino.

In spite of Mahler's efforts—he had led a production in Vienna for Mozart's 150th birth anniversary in Vienna in 1906—*Le Nozze di Figaro* was still considered occasional fare. It cropped up again in 1916–17 under Artur Bodanzky, with Farrar joined by Margarete Matzenauer (Countess), Frieda Hempel (Susanna), Giuseppe De Luca (Figaro) and Adamo Didur (Count) for five performances that and the next season, but Richard Aldrich noted in his review that only Hempel showed a grasp of Mozart style. *Figaro* finally had its redemption at the historic new production of February 20, 1940, under Ettore Panizza's energetic baton, with Herbert Graf as director and Jonel Jorgulescu as designer. This time the principals were unquestioned Mozarteans—Elisabeth Rethberg, Bidú Sayão, Risë Stevens, Irra Petina, Ezio

Pinza, John Brownlee—and the public, conditioned by records and reports from the Glyndebourne Festival performances of the mid-1930s, was ready.

Bruno Walter, Fritz Busch and Fritz Reiner conducted notable revivals in later seasons. For new productions *Figaro* had to await the managership of Rudolf Bing (1959–60 season—staged by Cyril Ritchard and designed by Oliver Messel) and the new Opera House at Lincoln Center (1975–76—staged by Günther Rennert and designed by Robert O'Hearn). For its 200th birthday, Mozart's liveliest comedy has a new investiture by designer-director Jean-Pierre Ponnelle, who already had overseen productions of *Figaro* for Salzburg, Vienna, Cologne, Paris, Chicago, Washington and television. Given the commitment of music director James Levine to Mozart's operas, their future has never looked brighter at the Met.

JOHN W. FREEMAN

LE NOZZE DI FIGARO

CHARACTERS

COUNT ALMAVIVA, a Spanish noble	Baritone
COUNTESS ALMAVIVA, his wife	Soprano
SUSANNA, the Countess' maid, fiancée of	Soprano
FIGARO, the Count's valet	Bass
CHERUBINO, the Count's page	Soprano
MARCELLINA, a governess	Soprano
BARTOLO, a doctor of Seville	Bass
BASILIO, a music teacher	Tenor
DON CURZIO, a judge	Tenor
BARBARINA, the daughter of	Soprano
ANTONIO, the Count's gardener and Susanna's uncle	Bass
CHORUS OF PEASANT MEN	
CHORUS OF PEASANT WOMEN	
CHORUS OF VARIOUS CLASSES OF PEOPLE	

The action takes place in the castle of Count Almaviva.

LE NOZZE DI FIGARO

SYNOPSIS

ACT I

Figaro, former barber of Seville, measures the room he will occupy after his marriage to Susanna. Both are in the service of Count Almaviva, and when Susanna warns Figaro that the Count has designs on her, he vows to outwit his master ("Se vuol ballare"). Into the now empty room comes Dr. Bartolo, the Countess' onetime guardian and suitor, eager for revenge on Figaro (who made him lose his ward to Almaviva), with his housekeeper, Marcellina. Since Figaro once gave Marcellina his promise of marriage as collateral on a loan, Bartolo persuades Marcellina to press charges ("La vendetta") and leaves; she then trades insults with Susanna ("Via resti servita"). Marcellina gone, the skirt-chasing page Cherubino steals in, begging Susanna's protection from the Count, who found him flirting with Barbarina, the gardener's daughter. After pouring out his amorous enthusiasm ("Non so più"), he hides as the Count enters to woo Susanna. When the gossiping music master Don Basilio appears, the Count in turn hides, stepping forward when Basilio hints that Cherubino has a crush on the Countess. Figaro brings in a group of fellow servants to salute the Count for abolishing the *droit du seigneur*, an old custom giving the local lord the first night with any bride among his retainers. The Count drafts Cherubino into his regiment and leaves Figaro to tease the boy unmercifully ("Non più andrai").

ACT II

In her boudoir, the Countess laments the waning of her husband's love ("Porgi, amor") but plots to chasten him, encouraged by Figaro and Susanna. Cherubino, disguised as Susanna, will meet with the Count. The page comes to serenade the Countess with a song of his own composition ("Voi che sapete"). While dressing the boy in girl's clothes, Susanna goes out for a ribbon, and the Count knocks, furious to find the door locked. The Countess locks Cherubino in a closet. The jealous Count hears a noise; the Countess insists it's Susanna, but he doesn't believe her. He takes her out to fetch some tools to force the lock, giving the eavesdropping Susanna a chance to help Cherubino from the closet and out a window, entering the closet herself and thus baffling the Count *and* Countess when they return. As the gardener, Antonio, appears with crushed carnations, Figaro, who has run in to say the wedding ceremony is ready, claims he jumped from window to flower bed, faking a twisted ankle. When the Count questions a paper found among the flowers, Figaro identifies it as Cherubino's commission, given him for sealing. Marcellina, Bartolo and Basilio burst in and show Figaro's loan contract to the Count, who is delighted to postpone the wedding.

ACT III

In the palace audience room, Susanna promises the Count a rendezvous ("Crudel! perchè finora") but fires his suspicions when he overhears her laughing with Figaro. Enraged, he vows revenge ("Vedrò mentr'io sospiro"). Marcellina now demands that Figaro pay his debt or marry her, but a birthmark proves he is her long-lost son by Bartolo, and the parents call off their suit, confounding the Count (sextet: "Riconosci in questo amplesso"). Alone, the Countess hopes to revive her husband's love ("Dove sono"). She dictates a note to Susanna, inviting the Count to the garden ("Che soave zeffiretto"). Peasants bring flowers to their lady; among them is the disguised Cherubino, whom Antonio spots. But the Count is distracted by the wedding, and Susanna slips him the note, which has been sealed with a pin.

ACT IV

The pin is meant to accompany the Count's reply, and Barbarina, his messenger, has lost it in the dusky garden ("L'ho perduta, me meschina"). Figaro is hurt to hear of Susanna's treachery but gives Barbarina another pin, planning to ambush his bride with the Count. He turns to Marcellina for comfort, and the mother tries to calm her son, but the crafty Basilio says it pays to play the fool. Figaro curses women ("Aprite un po' "), and Susanna rhapsodizes on her love for Figaro, without naming him ("Deh vieni"). The concealed Figaro is beside himself, assuming she means the Count. Susanna and the Countess secretly exchange dresses, and in the darkness both Cherubino and the Count woo the Countess, thinking her to be Susanna ("Pian, pianin le andrò più presso"). Figaro at last perceives the joke and gets even by wooing Susanna in her Countess disguise. Now the Count returns, seeing (or so he thinks) Figaro with his wife. He calls the whole company to witness his judgment but is silenced when the real Countess reveals the ruse. She grants the Count's pleas for forgiveness ("Contessa, perdono"), and everyone celebrates.

OPERA NEWS

LE NOZZE DI FIGARO

ACT ONE

A partly unfurnished room with an armchair in the middle.

SCENE I

Susanna and Figaro

No. I Duet

FIGARO (*measuring the room*)

Cinque . . . dieci . . . venti . . . trenta . . .	Five . . . ten . . . twenty . . . thirty . . .
Trentasei . . . quarantatré . . .	Thirty-six . . . forty-three . . .

SUSANNA

(aside, gazing at herself in the mirror, in front of which she is trying on a little hat trimmed with flowers)

Ora sì ch'io son contenta:	Yes, now I'm really happy:
Sembra fatto inver per me.	You'd think it was made just for me.

(to Figaro, as she continues gazing at herself)

Guarda un po', caro Figaro,	Come and see, my darling Figaro,
Guarda adesso il mio cappello.	Come and look at my hat.

FIGARO

Sì, mio core, or è più bello:	Yes, my dear, it's much prettier:
Sembra fatto inver per te.	You'd think it was made just for you.

SUSANNA and FIGARO

Ah, il mattino alle nozze vicino	Oh, on the morning of our wedding

171

Quanto è dolce al $\begin{cases} \text{mio} \\ \text{tuo} \end{cases}$ tenero

  sposo

Questo bel cappellino vezzoso

Che Susanna ella stessa si fe'.

How dear to $\begin{cases} \text{my} \\ \text{your} \end{cases}$ tender

  bridegroom

Is this charming little hat

That Susanna made all by herself.

Recitative

SUSANNA

Cosa stai misurando,
Caro il mio Figaretto?

But what are you measuring,
My dear Figaro?

FIGARO

Io guardo se quel letto
Che ci destina il Conte
Farà buona figura in questo loco.

I'm seeing if the bed
That the Count's giving to us
Will go all right in this spot.

SUSANNA

In questa stanza!

In this room!

FIGARO

Certo: a noi la cede

Generoso il padrone.

But of course: It's been
given to us
By our generous lord and master.

SUSANNA

Io per me te la dono.

As for me, you can have it.

FIGARO

E la ragione?

And your reason?

SUSANNA (*tapping her forehead*)

La ragione l'ho qui.

I've got my reasons up here.

FIGARO (*doing the same*)

Perché non puoi
Far che passi un po' qui?

And why can't you
Share them with me?

SUSANNA

Perché non voglio.
Sei tu mio servo, o no?

Because I don't want to.
Are you my humble servant, or not?

FIGARO

Ma non capisco
Perché tanto ti spiaccia
La più comoda stanza del palazzo.

But I don't understand
Why you're so unhappy with
The most convenient room in the palace.

SUSANNA

Perch'io son la Susanna, e tu sei pazzo.	Because I'm Susanna, and you're just crazy.

FIGARO

Grazie: non tanti elogi. Guarda un poco	Thank you: You're much too kind. But why don't you see
Se potria meglio stare in altro loco.	If we'd be better off in some other place.

No. 2 Duet

Se a caso Madama	If by chance my lady
La notte ti chiama:	Should call you at night:
Din din, in due passi	Ding dong, in two steps
Da quella puoi gir.	You can be at her door.
Vien poi l'occasione	And then when it happens
Che vuolmi il padrone:	That my master needs me:
Don, don, in tre salti	Ding dong, in three bounds
Lo vado a servir.	I can be at his service.

SUSANNA

Così se il mattino	And suppose some morning
Il caro Contino:	The dear little Count:
Din din, e ti manda	Ding, dong, should send you
Tre miglia lontan;	Three miles away;
Don don, e a mia porta	Ding dong, and the devil
Il diavol lo porta,	Should lead him to my door,
Ed ecco in tre salti . . .	And then in three bounds .

FIGARO

Susanna, pian pian.	Susanna, be quiet.

SUSANNA

Ascolta.	No, you listen to me.

FIGARO

Fa' presto.	Quick, tell me!

SUSANNA

Se udir brami il resto,	Well, if you want to hear the rest,
Discaccia i sospetti	Dismiss all those suspicions
Che torto mi fan.	That are so unfair to me.

FIGARO

Udir bramo il resto:
I dubbi, i sospetti
Gelare mi fan.

Yes, I must hear the rest:
My doubts and suspicions
Make my blood run cold.

Recitative

SUSANNA

Orbene, ascolta e taci.

Well then, just listen and keep quiet.

FIGARO (*anxiously*)

Parla, che c'è di nuovo?

Tell me, what's happened?

SUSANNA

Il signor Conte,
Stanco di andar cacciando le straniere
Bellezze forastiere,
Vuole ancor nel castello
Ritentar la sua sorte;
Né già di sua consorte, bada bene,
Appetito gli viene.

His lordship the Count,
Who's tired of pursuing fresh
Foreign beauties,
Wants to try his luck once again
In the castle;
But it's not his wife, mind you,
Who whets his appetite.

FIGARO

E di chi, dunque?

Who is it, then?

SUSANNA

Della tua Susannetta.

Your own little Susanna.

FIGARO (*surprised*)

Di te?

It's you?

SUSANNA

Di me medesma. Ed ha speranza
Che al nobil suo progetto
Utilissima sia tal vicinanza.

The very same. And he's hoping
That having us so near him
Will be most useful to his noble scheme.

FIGARO

Bravo! Tiriamo avanti.

Bravo! Now let's hear more.

SUSANNA

Queste le grazie son, questa la cura

Ch'egli prende di te, della tua sposa.

So these are the favors, and this is the
attention
That he's lavished on you and your bride.

FIGARO

Oh, guarda un po' che carità pelosa!   Oh, his kindness overwhelms me!

SUSANNA

Chétati: or viene il meglio. Don Basilio,   Just be quiet! Now comes the best part.
                                                       Don Basilio,

Mio maestro di canto e suo *factotum*,   My singing teacher and his go-between,
Nel darmi la lezione   Repeats the same old tune every day
Mi ripete ogni dì questa canzone.   While he's giving me my lesson.

FIGARO

Chi? Basilio? Oh, birbante!   Who? Basilio? That scoundrel!

SUSANNA

                              E tu credevi   And you thought
Che fosse la mia dote   That my dowry was
Merto del tuo bel muso?   A reward for your handsome mug?

FIGARO

Me n'era lusingato.   I'd flattered myself so.

SUSANNA

                          Ei la destina   He's given it to me
Per ottener da me certe mezz'ore   So he can claim those half-hours of
                                                       pleasure
Che il diritto feudale . . .   That feudal rights . . .

FIGARO

Come! ne' feudi suoi   What! On his own estates
Non l'ha il Conte abolito?   Hasn't the Count already abolished them?

SUSANNA

Ebben, ora è pentito; e par che tenti   Maybe so, but now he's sorry: And it
                                                       seems that he's trying
Riscattarlo da me.   To buy them back again from me.

FIGARO

                      Bravo! mi piace!   Bravo! Very nice!
Che caro signor Conte!   How kind of the Count!
Ci vogliam divertir: trovato avete . . .   So he's out for some fun: Well, he's
                                                       found . . .

(A bell rings.)

175

FIGARO

Chi suona? La Contessa.

Who's ringing? It's the Countess.

SUSANNA

Addio, addio, addio, Figaro bello.

Good-bye, good-bye, good-bye, Figaro darling.

FIGARO

Coraggio, mio tesoro.

Be brave, my treasure.

SUSANNA

E tu, cervello.

And you be careful.

(*She goes off.*)

SCENE II

Figaro alone

FIGARO (*pacing feverishly up and down the room and rubbing his hands*)

Bravo, signor padrone! Ora incomincio	Bravo, my lord and master! Now I'm beginning
A capir il mistero . . . e a veder schietto	To understand the mystery . . . and to see all too clearly
Tutto il vostro progetto: a Londra, è vero?	Your entire scheme: So we're off to London, are we?
Voi ministro, io corriero, e la Susanna	With you as the minister, me as your courier, and Susanna as
Segreta ambasciatrice . . .	Your secret ambassadress . . .
Non sarà, non sarà: Figaro il dice.	Well, that shall never be: Figaro has said so.

No. 3 Cavatina

Se vuol ballare,	If you want to dance,
Signor Contino,	My dear little Count,
Il chitarrino	I'll play the tune
Le suonerò.	On my guitar.
Se vuol venire	If you want to come
Nella mia scuola,	To my school,
La capriola	I'll teach you
Le insegnerò.	How to cut capers.
Saprò . . . Ma, piano:	I'll know how . . . But wait:
Meglio ogni arcano,	By dissembling
Dissimulando,	I can best discover

Scoprir potrò.	Every secret plan.
L'arte schermendo,	Outwitting your cunning
L'arte adoprando,	By using my cunning,
Di qua pugnendo,	Stinging here,
Di là scherzando,	And joking there,
Tutte le macchine	All your plots
Rovescerò.	I'll overthrow.
Se vuol ballare,	If you want to dance,
Signor Contino,	My dear little Count,
Il chitarrino	I'll play the tune
Le suonerò.	On my guitar.

(*He goes off.*)

SCENE III

Marcellina and Bartolo

Recitative

BARTOLO

Ed aspettaste il giorno	And you've waited for the day
Fissato per le nozze,	Fixed for the wedding
A parlarmi di questo?	To tell me all about this?

MARCELLINA (*holding a contract in her hand*)

Io non mi perdo,	My dear Doctor,
Dottor mio, di coraggio:	I've not yet lost heart:
Per romper de' sponsali	To break off engagements
Più avanzati di questo	More advanced than this one
Bastò spesso un pretesto; ed egli ha meco,	Often a mere pretext's sufficed: And he's got
Oltre a questo contratto, certi impegni . . .	Other obligations to me, besides this contract . . .
So io. Basta: conviene	I should know . . . But enough: We must
La Susanna atterrir; convien con arte	Frighten Susanna; we must cunningly
Impuntigliarla a rifiutare il Conte.	Persuade her to reject the Count.
Egli per vendicarsi	And he, out of revenge,
Prenderà il mio partito,	Will take my side,
E Figaro così fia mio marito.	And then Figaro will be my husband.

BARTOLO (*taking the contract from Marcellina*)

Bene, io tutto farò: senza riserve	Well then, I'll do all that I can: But tell me
Tutto a me palesate.	Everything without reserve.

(aside)

Avrei pur gusto	Oh, how I'd relish
Di dar in moglie la mia serva antica	Giving my old servant in marriage
A chi mi fece un dì rapir l'amica.	To the one who stole my sweetheart from me.

No. 4 Aria

La vendetta, oh, la vendetta	Vengeance, yes, vengeance,
È un piacer serbato ai saggi;	Is a pleasure reserved for the wise;
L'obliar l'onte, gli oltraggi,	To forget affronts and insults
È bassezza, è ognor viltà.	Is always baseness and cowardice.
Con l'astuzia, con l'arguzia,	With cunning and cleverness,
Col giudizio, col criterio	With judgment and discretion
Si potrebbe . . . Il fatto è serio;	I could . . . The case is serious,
Ma, credete, si farà.	But, believe me, it shall be done.
Se tutto il codice	If I have to pore over
Dovessi volgere,	The whole legal code,
Se tutto l'indice	If I have to read
Dovessi leggere,	The whole index through,
Con un equivoco,	With an ambiguity, or
Con un sinonimo	Maybe a synonym
Qualche garbuglio	I'll find some way
Si troverà.	To create confusion.
Tutta Siviglia	All of Seville
Conosce Bartolo:	Knows Doctor Bartolo;
Il birbo Figaro	That rascal Figaro
Vinto sarà!	Has met his match!

(He goes off.)

SCENE IV

Marcellina, then Susanna

Recitative

MARCELLINA

Tutto ancor non ho perso:	All's not yet lost:
Mi resta la speranza.	I still have hopes.

(*Susanna enters carrying a cap, a ribbon and a dress.*)

(aside)

Ma Susanna si avanza. Io vo' provarmi . . .	But Susanna's coming: Let's just try . . .
Fingiam di non vederla . . .	I'll pretend not to see her . . .

(*aloud*)

E quella buona perla	So that's the little gem
La vorrebbe sposar!	He's going to marry.

SUSANNA (*aside, remaining backstage*)

Di me favella.	She's talking about me.

MARCELLINA

Ma da Figaro, alfine,	But from Figaro, after all,
Non può meglio sperarsi: *l'argent fait tout.*	Nothing better can be expected: Money is everything.

SUSANNA (*as before*)

Che lingua! Manco male	What a tongue! Luckily
Che ognun sa quanto vale.	Everyone knows what it's worth.

MARCELLINA

Brava! questo è giudizio!	Well said! That's so sensible!
Con quegli occhi modesti,	With those modest eyes,
Con quell'aria pietosa,	And that pious look,
E poi . . .	And then . . .

SUSANNA (*as before*)

Meglio è partir.	I'd better go.

MARCELLINA

Che cara sposa!	What a lovely bride!

(*Both make as if to leave, and meet in the doorway.*)

No. 5 Duet

MARCELLINA (*curtsying*)

Via, resti servita,	After you,
Madama brillante.	My fine lady.

SUSANNA (*curtsying*)

Non sono sì ardita,	I'd not be so bold,
Madama piccante.	My pert lady.

MARCELLINA (*as before*)

No, prima a lei tocca.	No, you go first.

SUSANNA (*as before*)

No, no, tocca a lei.	No, no, after you.

SUSANNA and MARCELLINA

Io so i dover miei,	I know my position,
Non fo inciviltà.	I'd not be so rude.

MARCELLINA (*as before*)

La sposa novella!   The bride-to-be!

SUSANNA (*as before*)

La dama d'onore . . .   The matron of honor . . .

MARCELLINA (*as before*)

Del Conte la bella . . .   The Count's little favorite . . .

SUSANNA

Di Spagna l'amore . . .   The pride of all Spain . . .

MARCELLINA

I meriti . . .   Your qualities . . .

SUSANNA

L'abito . . .   Your dress . . .

MARCELLINA

Il posto . . .   Your position . . .

SUSANNA

L'età!   Your age!

MARCELLINA (*aside*)

Perbacco, precipito,	By God, I'll explode
Se ancor resto qua!	If I stay any longer!

SUSANNA (*aside*)

Sibilla decrepita!	Decrepit old hag,
Da rider mi fa.	You do make me laugh.

(*Marcellina goes off in a fury.*)

SCENE V

Susanna, then Cherubino

Recitative

SUSANNA

Va' là, vecchia pedante,	Go on, you old pedant,
Dottoressa arrogante!	You arrogant old school-marm!

Le Nozze di Figaro

| Perché hai letto due libri, | Just because you managed to read a couple of books, |
| E seccato Madama in gioventù . . . | And bored my lady to death when she was a girl . . . |

(She drapes the dress over the armchair.)

CHERUBINO *(entering hurriedly)*

| Susannetta, sei tu? . . . | My little Susanna, is that you? . . . |

SUSANNA

| Son io; cosa volete? | Yes, it's me: Now what do you want? |

CHERUBINO

| Ah, cor mio, che accidente! | Oh, my darling, what a disaster! |

SUSANNA

| Cor vostro? Cosa avvenne? | Your darling? What's happened? |

CHERUBINO

Il Conte, ieri,	Yesterday the Count
Perché trovommi sol con Barbarina,	Found me alone with Barbarina,
Il congedo mi diede;	And sent me packing for good;
E se la Contessina,	And if the Countess,
La mia bella comare,	My beautiful godmother,
Grazia non m'intercede, io vado via,	Doesn't intercede, I'll have to go away.

(anxiously)

| Io non ti vedo più, Susanna mia! | I'll never see you again, my Susanna! |

SUSANNA

Non vedete più me! Bravo! Ma dunque	Never see me again! Bravo! So then
Non più per la Contessa	It's no longer for the Countess
Segretamente il vostro cor sospira?	That your heart secretly sighs?

CHERUBINO

Ah, che troppo rispetto ella m'ispira!	Oh, I respect her too much for that!
Felice te che puoi	You're so lucky to be able
Vederla quando vuoi!	To see her whenever you want to!
Che la vesti il mattino,	You dress her each morning,
Che la sera la spogli, che le metti	And at night you undress her, and you put on
Gli spilloni, i merletti . . .	Her pins and lace . . .

(sighing)

181

Ah, se in tuo loco . . .   Oh, if I were in your place . . .

Cos'hai lì? dimmi un poco . . .   But what's that you've got there? Let me
see . . .

CHERUBINO

SUSANNA (*imitating him*)

Ah, il vago nastro, e la notturna cuffia   Oh, just a pretty ribbon, and a night-cap

Di comare sì bella . . .   For such a beautiful godmother . . .

CHERUBINO

Deh, dammelo, sorella,   Come on, give it to me, my sister,

Dammelo, per pietà.   Give it to me, for pity's sake.

(*He snatches the ribbon from her.*)

SUSANNA

Presto, quel nastro!   Quick, give me that ribbon!

(*Susanna tries to take it back, but he starts running around the armchair.*)

CHERUBINO

O caro, o bello, o fortunato nastro!   Oh, dearest, sweetest, luckiest of ribbons!

(*He kisses the ribbon again and again.*)

Io non tel renderò che con la vita.   I won't give it back to you except with
my life.

SUSANNA

(*She starts running after him, but then stops as if she were tired.*)

Cos'è quest'insolenza?   Just what is all this insolence?

CHERUBINO

Eh, via, sta' cheta!   Come on now, just calm down!

In ricompensa, poi,   And in exchange,

Questa mia canzonetta io ti vo' dare.   I'll give you this little song of mine.

(*He pulls a song out of his pocket.*)

SUSANNA

E che ne debbo fare?   And what am I supposed to do with this?

(*She takes it from him.*)

CHERUBINO

Leggila alla padrona,   Read it to my lady,

Leggila tu medesma,   Read it to yourself,

Leggila a Barbarina, a Marcellina,   Read it to Barbarina, and to Marcellina,

Idomeneo

ABOVE: *Ileana Cotrubas as Ilia, Luciano Pavarotti as Idomeneo and Frederica Von Stade as Idamante in the 1982 production, designed by Jean-Pierre Ponnelle (© Beth Bergman 1991)*

RIGHT: *Luciano Pavarotti and Frederica Von Stade (© Beth Bergman 1991)*

BOTTOM RIGHT: *John Alexander as Arbace, Hildegard Behrens as Elettra, Luciano Pavarotti, Ileana Cotrubas, and Frederica Von Stade (© Beth Bergman 1991)*

BELOW: *Hildegard Behrens (© Beth Bergman 1991)*

DIE ENTFÜHRUNG AUS DEM SERAIL

ABOVE: *Eleanor Steber as Konstanze and Hugh Thompson as Selim in the 1946 production, designed by Donald Oenslager (Opera News)*

RIGHT: *Eleanor Steber (Metropolitan Opera Archives)*

BELOW: *Werner Klemperer as Selim (left) and Edda Moser as Konstanze in the 1979 production, designed by Jocelyn Herbert (© Beth Bergman 1991)*

LE NOZZE DI FIGARO

TOP: *Frieda Hempel as Susanna, Margarete Matzenauer as the Countess, and Geraldine Farrar as Cherubino in the 1909 production, designed by Anton Brioschi and Burghart & Co. (Opera News)*

CENTER *Elisabeth Rethberg as the Countess, Ezio Pinza as Figaro, Bidú Sayão as Susanna, Alessio de Paolis as Don Basilio, John Brownlee as the Count, Irra Petina as Marzellina, and Virgilio Lazzari as Bartolo in the 1940 production, designed by Jonel Jorgulesco (Opera News)*

BOTTOM: *Bidú Sayão, John Brownlee, and Risë Stevens as Cherubino (Opera News)*

Le Nozze di Figaro

TOP: *Bidú Sayão and Ezio Pinza*
(Opera News)

CENTER: *Victoria De Los Angeles as*
the Countess, George London as the
Count, and Nadine Conner as
Susanna (Opera News)

BOTTOM: *Lisa Della Casa as the*
Countess and Frank Guarrera as the
Count (Opera News)

Le Nozze di Figaro

ABOVE: *Evelyn Lear as the Countess and Frederica Von Stade as Cherubino in the 1975 production, designed by Robert O'Hearn (© Beth Bergman 1991)*

RIGHT: *Kathleen Battle as Susanna and Ruggero Raimondi as Figaro in the 1985 production, designed by Jean-Pierre Ponnelle (© Beth Bergman 1991)*

BELOW: *Act I, 1985 production (© Beth Bergman 1991)*

DON GIOVANNI

RIGHT: *Antonio Scotti as Don Giovanni (Opera News)*

ABOVE: *Ezio Pinza as Don Giovanni (Opera News)*

BOTTOM: *James Melton as Don Ottavio, Zinka Milanov as Donna Anna, Bidú Sayão as Zerlina, Jarmila Novotna as Donna Elvira, Ezio Pinza and Salvatore Baccaloni as Leporello (Opera News)*

DON GIOVANNI

TOP: *Fernando Corena as Leporello and Cesare Siepi as Don Giovanni (Metropolitan Opera Archives)*

BOTTOM RIGHT: *Cesare Siepi and Roberta Peters as Zerlina in the 1957 production, designed by Eugene Berman (Metropolitan Opera Archives)*

BOTTOM LEFT: *George London as Don Giovanni (Metropolitan Opera Archives)*

DON GIOVANNI

TOP: *Joan Sutherland as Donna Anna (James Heffernan)*

CENTER: *Samuel Ramey as Don Giovanni in the 1990 production, designed by Franco Zeffirelli (© Beth Bergman 1991)*

BOTTOM: *Karita Mattila as Donna Elvira, Jerry Hadley as Don Ottavio, and Carol Vaness as Donna Anna (© Beth Bergman 1991)*

(transported with joy)

Leggila ad ogni donna del palazzo!	Read it to every woman in the palace!

SUSANNA

Povero Cherubin, siete voi pazzo?	My poor Cherubino, have you gone mad?

CHERUBINO

No. 6 Aria

Non so più cosa son, cosa faccio . . .	I don't know what I am anymore, or even what I'm doing . . .
Or di fuoco, ora sono di ghiaccio . . .	Sometimes I'm on fire, and then I'm all ice . . .
Ogni donna cangiar di colore,	Every woman makes me change color,
Ogni donna mi fa palpitar.	Every woman makes my heart throb.
Solo ai nomi d'amor, di diletto	The mere mention of love or delight
Mi si turba, mi s'altera il petto,	Upsets me, and unsettles my heart,
E a parlare mi sforza d'amore	And I find myself talking about love
Un desio ch'io non posso spiegar!	From a need I can't even explain!
Parlo d'amor vegliando,	I talk about love when I'm awake,
Parlo d'amor sognando:	I talk about love in my dreams:
All'acque, all'ombre, ai monti,	To the rivers, the shadows, the mountains,
Ai fiori, all'erbe, ai fonti,	The flowers, the grass, and the fountains,
All'eco, all'aria, ai venti,	To the echo, the air, and the winds,
Che il suon de' vani accenti	Which carry away with them
Portano via con sé . . .	The sound of my useless words . . .
E, se non ho chi m'oda,	And if there's no one to hear me,
Parlo d'amor con me.	I talk about love to myself.

(He starts to leave, but sees the Count in the distance, returns
in terror and hides behind the armchair.)

SCENE VI

Susanna and Cherubino, then the Count

Recitative

SUSANNA

Taci, vien gente . . . Il Conte! Oh, me meschina!	Be quiet, someone's coming . . . It's the Count! Oh, poor me!

(She tries to hide Cherubino.)

COUNT *(entering)*

Susanna, tu mi sembri	Susanna, you seem so
Agitata e confusa.	Upset and confused.

SUSANNA *(nervously)*

Signor . . . io chiedo scusa . . .	My lord . . . Excuse me . . .
Ma, se mai . . . qui sorpresa . . .	But if anyone . . . sees you here . . .
Per carità, partite.	For pity's sake, please go.

COUNT

Un momento, e ti lascio.	Just one moment, and I'll leave you.
Odi.	Now listen to me.

(He sits down in the armchair, and takes Susanna's hand; she tears it away.)

SUSANNA

Non odo nulla.   I'll hear nothing.

COUNT

Due parole. Tu sai	Just a couple of words. You know
Che ambasciatore a Londra	That the king's appointed me
Il re mi dichiarò; di condur meco	Ambassador to London; and I've decided
Figaro destinai . . .	To take Figaro with me . . .

SUSANNA *(timidly)*

Signor, se osassi . . .   My lord, if I only dared . . .

COUNT

Parla, parla, mia cara! E con quel dritto   Speak up, my dear! And by that right

(rising)

Ch'oggi prendi su me finché tu vivi,	That you'll claim from me today for as long as you live,

(tenderly, trying to take her hand again)

Chiedi, imponi, prescrivi.	You've only to ask, command, or decide.

SUSANNA *(in a frenzy)*

Lasciatemi, signor; dritti non prendo:	Leave me, my lord; I've claimed no rights:
Non ne vo', non ne intendo . . . Oh, me infelice!	Nor do I intend to . . . Oh, how unhappy I am!

COUNT

Ah, no, Susanna, io ti vo' far felice!
Tu ben sai quanto io t'amo: a te Basilio
Tutto già disse.

Oh no, Susanna, I want to make you
  happy!
You know how much I love you! Basilio's
  already
Told you everything.

(*as before*)

Or senti:
Se per pochi momenti
Meco in giardin, sull'imbrunir del
  giorno . . .
Ah, per questo favore io pagherei . . .

Now listen:
If you'll meet me in the garden
For a few moments at dusk . . .

Oh, for this favor I'd pay . . .

BASILIO (*off-stage*)

È uscito poco fa.

He's just gone out.

COUNT

Chi parla?

Who was that?

SUSANNA

Oh, Dei!

Oh, my God!

COUNT

Esci, e alcun non entri.

Go on out, and don't let anyone in.

SUSANNA (*extremely agitated*)

Ch'io vi lasci qui solo?

And leave you here alone?

BASILIO (*as before*)

Da Madama ei sarà: vado a cercarlo.

He'll be with my lady: I'll go and look for
  him.

COUNT (*pointing to the armchair*)

Qui dietro mi porrò.

I'll get behind here.

SUSANNA

Non vi celate.

Oh, please don't hide there.

COUNT

Taci, e cerca ch'ei parta.

Do be quiet, and make sure that he
  leaves.

SUSANNA

Ohimè! che fate?

Oh dear! What are you doing?

(The Count goes to hide behind the armchair, while Susanna stands between him and the page. The Count pushes her gently aside, and she retreats. Meanwhile, the page comes around to the front of the armchair, and throws himself into it, curling up as best he can. Susanna covers him with the dress which she had draped over the armchair.)

SCENE VII

Susanna, Cherubino, the Count and Basilio

BASILIO *(entering)*

Susanna, il ciel vi salvi; avreste a caso	God bless you, Susanna: Have you by any chance
Veduto il Conte?	Seen the Count?

SUSANNA

E cosa	And what
Deve far meco il Conte? Animo, uscite.	Would the Count be doing with me? For heaven's sake, go away.

BASILIO

Aspettate, sentite:	Wait just a moment, and listen to me:
Figaro di lui cerca.	Figaro's looking for him.

SUSANNA *(aside)*

Oh, cielo!   Oh, my God!

(to Basilio)

Ei cerca	. The Count's
Chi dopo voi più l'odia.	The very one who, after you, must hate him most.

COUNT *(aside)*

Veggiam come mi serve.	Now we'll see how well he serves me.

BASILIO

Io non ho mai nella moral sentito	I've never heard any law that states
Ch'uno ch'ama la moglie odii il marito.	That he who loves the wife must therefore hate the husband.
Per dir che il Conte v'ama . . .	Which is to say that the Count loves you . . .

SUSANNA *(resentfully)*

Sortite, vil ministro	Just get out, you vile agent
Dell'altrui sfrenatezza: io non ho d'uopo	For someone else's lechery: I've no use for

Della vostra morale,	Your laws,
Del Conte, del suo amor . . .	The Count, or his love . . .

BASILIO

Non c'è alcun male.	There's no harm done.
Ha ciascun i suoi gusti: io mi credea	Each to his own tastes, I always say: I only thought
Che preferir doveste per amante,	That you'd prefer as a lover,
Come fan tutte quante,	As all the other ladies do,
Un signor liberal, prudente e saggio;	A generous lord, who's prudent and wise,
A un giovinastro, a un paggio . . .	To a mere boy, a page . . .

SUSANNA (*anxiously*)

A Cherubino!	To Cherubino!

BASILIO

A Cherubino, Cherubin d'amore,	Yes, to Cherubino, that little cherub of love,
Ch'oggi, sul far del giorno,	Who was prowling around here
Passeggiava qui intorno	Today at dawn,
Per entrar . . .	Just trying to get in . . .

SUSANNA (*vehemently*)

Uom maligno!	You wicked man!
Un'impostura è questa!	That's a vicious lie!

BASILIO

È un maligno con voi chi ha gli occhi in testa.	Anyone who's got eyes in his head is bound to be wicked to you.
È quella canzonetta?	And what about that little song?
Ditemi in confidenza: io sono amico,	Now tell me confidentially: I'm your friend,
E ad altrui nulla dico:	And I'll say nothing to anyone else:
È per voi, per Madama?	Is it for you, or for my lady?

SUSANNA (*aside, and obviously upset*)

Chi diavol gliel'ha detto?	Who the devil told him that?

BASILIO

A proposito, figlia,	By the way, my dear daughter,
Istruitelo meglio: egli la guarda	You'd do well to warn him: He looks at her
A tavola sì spesso,	So often when he's waiting on table,
E con tale immodestia,	And with such indiscretion,

Che se il Conte s'accorge . . . ehi, su tal punto,	That if the Count should ever notice . . . Well, on that point,
Sapete, egli è una bestia.	You know, he's a beast.

SUSANNA

Scellerato!	Oh, you scoundrel!
E perché andate voi	And why do you go around
Tai menzogne spargendo?	Spreading such lies?

BASILIO

Io! che ingiustizia! Quel che compro io vendo.	Me! How unfair! I'm only repeating what I've heard.
A quel che tutti dicono	And I haven't added a thing
Io non aggiungo un pelo.	To what everyone else is saying.

COUNT (*stepping forward*)

Come! Che dicon tutti?	How's that? And just what is everyone saying?

BASILIO (*aside*)

Oh, bella!	Oh, how perfect!

SUSANNA

Oh, cielo!	Oh, my God!

No. 7 Trio

COUNT (*to Basilio*)

Cosa sento! Tosto andate,	What do I hear? Go at once,
E scacciate il seduttor.	And throw the seducer out.

BASILIO

In mal punto son qui giunto!	I'm afraid I've arrived at a very bad time!
Perdonate, o mio signor.	Do forgive me, my lord.

SUSANNA (*swooning*)

Che ruina, me meschina!	Oh, what a disaster, I'm ruined forever!
Son oppressa dal dolor.	And I'm overcome with grief!

COUNT and BASILIO (*supporting Susanna*)

Ah, già svien la poverina!	Oh, the poor girl's almost fainting!
Come, oddio, le batte il cor!	My God, how her heart's beating!

BASILIO

(leading her towards the armchair to get her to sit down)

Pian pianin: su questo seggio . . .	Easy now . . . right here in this chair . . .

SUSANNA

Dove sono?	Where am I?

(recovering)

Cosa veggio?	What am I seeing?
Che insolenza! Andate fuor!	Such insolence! Just go away!

(She pulls back from both of them.)

COUNT

Siamo qui per aiutarti,	We're only here to help you,
Non turbarti, o mio tesor.	Don't be so upset, my darling.

BASILIO *(maliciously)*

Siamo qui per aiutarvi:	We're only here to help you,
È sicuro il vostro onor.	Your honor's safe with us.

(to the Count)

Ah, del paggio quel ch'ho detto	Oh, what I said about the page
Era solo un mio sospetto!	Was just a suspicion of mine!

SUSANNA

È un'insidia, una perfidia:	It's all a plot, a vicious lie:
Non credete all'impostor.	Don't you believe this imposter.

COUNT

Parta! parta, il damerino!	No, he's got to go! That young rascal's got to go!

BASILIO and SUSANNA

Poverino!	The poor boy!

COUNT *(sarcastically)*

Poverino!	The poor boy!
Ma da me sorpreso ancor.	And I've caught him at it again.

SUSANNA

Come!	How's that?

BASILIO

Che!	What's this?

Recitative

COUNT

Da tua cugina	Yesterday at your cousin's
L'uscio ier trovai rinchiuso;	I found the door locked;
Picchio, m'apre Barbarina	So I knocked, and when Barbarina opened it,
Paurosa fuor dell'uso.	She looked more flustered than usual.
Io dal muso insospettito,	Her appearance made me so suspicious
Guardo, cerco in ogni sito,	That I looked and searched in every corner,
Ed alzando pian pianino	And when I very gently lifted
Il tappeto al tavolino,	The cover from the table,
Vedo il paggio!	Who should I see but the page!

(He imitates his gesture with the dress, and discovers the page. In amazement)

Ah, cosa veggio!	Oh, what am I seeing?

SUSANNA (*fearfully*)

Ah, crude stelle!	Oh, how cruel fate can be!

BASILIO (*laughing*)

Ah, meglio ancora.	Oh, this is even better!

COUNT

Onestissima signora,	Well, my virtuous lady,
Or capisco come va.	Now I finally understand.

SUSANNA

Accader non può di peggio:	Nothing worse than this could happen:
Giusti Dei! che mai sarà!	Good heavens, now what's going to be?

BASILIO

Così fan tutte le belle!	All pretty women are the same!
Non c'è alcuna novità.	It's nothing new to me!

Recitative

COUNT

Basilio, in traccia tosto	Basilio, go at once
Di Figaro volate:	In search of Figaro:
Io vo' ch'ei veda . . .	I want him to see . . .

190

(*He points at Cherubino, who does not move from the spot.*)

SUSANNA (*gaily*)

Ed io che senta: andate.	And I want him to hear: Go on.

COUNT (*to Basilio*)

Restate!	No, wait!

(*to Susanna*)

Che baldanza! E quale scusa,	You're so sure of yourself! And what excuse have you got,
Se la colpa è evidente?	If your guilt is more than clear?

SUSANNA

Non ha d'uopo di scusa un'innocente.	Innocence needs no excuses.

COUNT

Ma costui quando venne?	But when did he come in?

SUSANNA

Egli era meco	He was with me
Quando voi qui giungeste, e mi chiedea	When you got here, and he asked me
D'impegnar la padrona	To beg my lady
A intercedergli grazia: il vostro arrivo	To intercede for him: Your arrival
In scompiglio lo pose,	Alarmed him,
Ed allor in quel loco si nascose.	And that's when he hid in the chair.

COUNT

Ma s'io stesso m'assisi	But I sat down there myself
Quando in camera entrai!	When I entered the room!

CHERUBINO (*timidly*)

Ed allora di dietro io mi celai.	And that's when I hid behind it.

COUNT

E quando io là mi posi?	And when I went back there?

CHERUBINO

Allor io pian mi volsi, e qui m'ascosi.	I crept around quietly and hid in here.

COUNT (*to Susanna*)

Oh, ciel! Dunque ha sentito	Oh, God! Then he heard
Quello ch'io ti dicea?	What I was saying to you?

CHERUBINO

Feci per non sentir quanto potea.	I did all that I could not to listen.

COUNT

Oh, perfidia!   Oh, you traitor!

BASILIO

Frenatevi: vien gente.   Be careful: Someone's coming.

COUNT (*to Cherubino*)

E voi restate qui, picciol serpente!   And you stay right where you are, you
                                          little snake!

(*He drags him out of the armchair.*)

SCENE VIII

Susanna, Cherubino, the Count, Basilio, Figaro, and peasant men and women

(*Figaro is carrying a white dress in his hand: The peasant men and women—the latter dressed in white—are holding little baskets of flowers to scatter in front of the Count.*)

No. 8 Chorus

CHORUS

Giovani liete,	Come, happy young maidens,
Fiori spargete	And scatter your flowers
Davanti al nobile	Before our
Nostro signor.	Noble lord.
Il suo gran core	For his generous heart
Vi serba intatto	Has kept intact for you
D'un più bel fiore	The purity
L'almo candor.	Of a still fairer flower.

Recitative

COUNT (*to Figaro, in amazement*)

Cos'è questa commedia?   Just what's all this nonsense about?

FIGARO (*to Susanna, sottovoce*)

Eccoci in danza.   The fun's just now beginning:
Secondami, cor mio.   Bear with me, my darling.

SUSANNA (*aside*)

Non ci ho speranza.   Oh, I'm so discouraged.

FIGARO (*to the Count*)

Signor, non isdegnate   My lord, please don't reject

Questo del nostro affetto
Meritato tributo. Or che aboliste

Un diritto sì ingrato a chi ben ama . . .

This worthy token
Of our affection. Now that you've
   abolished

A privilege so painful to all true
   lovers . . .

COUNT

Quel diritto or non v'è più: cosa si
   brama?

That right doesn't exist anymore: So what
   is it you want?

FIGARO

Della vostra saggezza il primo frutto

Oggi noi coglierem: le nostre nozze
Si son già stabilite. Or a voi tocca

Costei, che un vostro dono
Illibata serbò, coprir di questa,
Simbolo d'onestà, candida vesta.

Today we're about to gather the first
   fruits
Of your wisdom, and our wedding
Is already arranged. Now we're asking
   you to place
This pure white veil
On the head of the maiden
Who owes her virtue to you.

COUNT (*aside*)

Diabolica astuzia!
Ma fingere convien.

How devilishly clever!
But I'll just play along.

(*aloud*)

      Son grato, amici,
Ad un senso sì onesto.
Ma non merto, per questo,
Né tributi né lodi: e un dritto ingiusto

Ne' miei feudi abolendo,
A natura, al dover lor dritti io rendo.

      I'm most grateful, my friends,
For such loyal devotion,
But for this I don't deserve
Either tributes or praise: It was an unjust
   privilege,
And by abolishing it on my own estates,
I've merely restored their rightful claims
   to both nature and duty.

ALL

Evviva, evviva, evviva!

Three cheers for the Count!

SUSANNA (*maliciously*)

Che virtù!

How virtuous!

FIGARO

    Che giustizia!

    And how just!

COUNT (*to Figaro and Susanna*)

A voi prometto	I promise you both
Compier la cerimonia.	That I'll perform the ceremony.
Chiedo sol breve indugio: io voglio, in faccia	I'm only asking for a brief delay: For I want to have
De' miei più fidi, e con più ricca pompa,	My most faithful subjects with me, and with all the pomp I can muster,
Rendervi appien felici.	I'll make your happiness complete.

(*aside*)

Marcellina si trovi.	We must find Marcellina.

(*aloud*)

Andate, amici.	Now go, my friends.

CHORUS (*scattering the rest of the flowers*)

Giovani liete,	Come, happy young maidens,
Fiori spargete	And scatter your flowers
Davanti al nobile	Before our
Nostro signor.	Noble lord.
Il suo gran core	For his generous heart
Vi serba intatto	Has kept intact for you
D'un più bel fiore	The purity
L'almo candor.	Of a still fairer flower.

(*The peasant men and women go off.*)

Recitative

FIGARO

Evviva!	Three cheers!

SUSANNA

Evviva!	Three cheers!

BASILIO

Evviva!	Three cheers!

FIGARO (*to Cherubino*)

E voi non applaudite?	And why aren't you applauding?

SUSANNA

È afflitto, poveretto,	He's miserable, poor boy,
Perché il padron lo scaccia dal castello.	Because my lord has thrown him out of the castle.

FIGARO

Ah, in un giorno sì bello!   Oh, and on such a happy day!

SUSANNA

In un giorno di nozze!   On the day of our wedding!

FIGARO (*to the Count*)

Quando ognuno v'ammira!   And just when everyone's singing your
                                                        praises!

CHERUBINO (*kneeling down*)

Perdono, mio signor . . .   Forgive me, my lord . . .

COUNT

       Nol meritate.   You don't deserve it.

SUSANNA

Egli è ancora fanciullo.   But he's only a child.

COUNT

Men di quel che tu credi.   Less so than you think.

CHERUBINO

È ver, mancai; ma dal mio labbro   It's true, I was wrong: But I'd never
  alfine . . .   tell . . .

COUNT (*raising him from his knees*)

Ben, ben; io vi perdono.   Well, then: I forgive you.
Anzi, farò di più: vacante è un posto   And I'll even do more: There's a place
                                                        free

D'uffizial nel reggimento mio;   For an officer just now in my regiment;
Io scelgo voi. Partite tosto; addio.   It's yours. Now leave at once; good-bye.

(*The Count starts to leave, but Susanna and Figaro stop him.*)

SUSANNA and FIGARO

Ah! fin domani sol . . .   Oh! Just until tomorrow . . .

COUNT

      No, parta tosto.   No! He's got to leave right away.

CHERUBINO (*sighing deeply*)

A ubbidirvi, signor, son già disposto.   I'm at your service, my lord.

COUNT

Via, per l'ultima volta   Come on now, and embrace your Susanna
La Susanna abbracciate.   One last time.

(aside)

Inaspettato è il colpo.   I've taken him by surprise.

(Cherubino embraces Susanna, who seems embarrassed.)

FIGARO

Ehi, capitano,   Well then, my captain,
A me pure la mano.   Shake hands with me, too.

(softly to Cherubino)

Io vo' parlarti   I want to speak to you
Pria che tu parta.   Before you leave.

(aloud, with assumed joy)

Addio,   Good-bye,
Picciolo Cherubino.   My little Cherubino.
Come cangia in un punto il tuo destino!   How your luck has changed in just one
                                           brief moment!

No. 9 Aria

Non più andrai, farfallone amoroso,   No more you'll wander, my
                                              amorous butterfly,

Notte e giorno d'intorno girando,   Flitting about both night and day,
Delle belle turbando il riposo,   Disturbing all those pretty girls,
Narcisetto, Adoncino d'amor.   My little Narcissus, Adonis of love.

Non più avrai questi bei   No more you'll wear those fancy
   pennacchini,   feathers,
Quel cappello, leggero e galante,   That smart jaunty cap,
Quella chioma, quell'aria brillante,   Those gorgeous curls, that lively
                                              look,

Quel vermiglio, donnesco color.   Those rosy girlish cheeks.

Tra guerrieri, poffarbacco!   You'll be among warriors, by Jove!
Gran mustacchi, stretto sacco,   With your bushy whiskers, and
                                              tightly held knapsack,

Schioppo in spalla, sciabla al fianco,   A gun on your shoulder, a saber at
                                              your side,

Collo dritto, muso franco,   With your head held high and bold
                                              of face,

Un gran casco, o un gran turbante,   And some great helmet, or maybe a
                                              turban,

Molto onor, poco contante,	Lots of honors, but not much money,
Ed invece del fandango,	And instead of the fandango,
Una marcia per il fango.	You'll be marching through the mud.
Per montagne, per valloni,	Over the mountains, through the valleys,
Con le nevi e i sollioni,	In the snow and scorching sun,
Al concerto di tromboni,	To the sound of trumpets blaring,
Di bombarde, di cannoni,	Shells and cannon-balls;
Che le palle in tutti i tuoni	And as they whistle by,
All'orecchio fan fischiar.	Your ears will surely ring.
Cherubino, alla vittoria!	Cherubino, on to victory!
Alla gloria militar!	And to military glory!

(They all leave in military style.)

End of Act One

ACT TWO

A magnificent room with an alcove. To the right is the entrance door, to the left a dressing-room. At the back is a door leading to the maids' quarters, on the side a window.

SCENE I

The Countess alone

COUNTESS
No. 10 Cavatina

Porgi, amor, qualche ristoro	Oh love, grant some relief
Al mio duolo, a' miei sospir.	To my sorrow and my sighs.
O mi rendi il mio tesoro,	And if you won't give me back my loved one,
O mi lascia almen morir.	At least, I beg you, let me die.

SCENE II

The Countess and Susanna, then Figaro
(Susanna enters.)

Recitative

COUNTESS (*sitting down*)

Vieni, cara Susanna:	Come in, my dear Susanna,
Finiscimi l'istoria.	And tell me the rest of your story.

SUSANNA

È già finita.	It's already finished.

COUNTESS

Dunque, volle sedurti?	So he tried to seduce you?

SUSANNA

Oh, il signor Conte	Oh, my lord the Count
Non fa tai complimenti	Doesn't waste any compliments
Con le donne mie pari:	On girls of my station:
Egli venne a contratto di danari.	To him it was just a matter of money.

COUNTESS

Ah, il crudel più non m'ama!	Oh, the cruel man doesn't love me anymore!

SUSANNA

E come, poi,	Then why is it
È geloso di voi?	He's so jealous of you?

COUNTESS

Come lo sono	He's just like all
I moderni mariti: per sistema	Modern husbands are: on principle
Infedeli, per genio capricciosi,	Unfaithful, by nature fickle,
E per orgoglio, poi, tutti gelosi.	And only jealous out of pride.
Ma se Figaro t'ama, ei sol potria . . .	But if Figaro loves you, he could surely . . .

FIGARO (*off-stage, humming*)

La, la la la, la la la, la la la,	La, la la la, la la la, la la la.
La, la la la, la la la, la.	La, la la la, la la la, la.

(He enters.)

SUSANNA

Eccolo. Vieni, amico:	Here he is now. Come on in, my darling:
Madama impaziente . . .	My lady's getting impatient . . .

FIGARO (*gay and self-possessed*)

A voi non tocca	You shouldn't
Stare in pena per questo.	Take all this to heart.
Alfin, di che si tratta? Al signor Conte	After all, just what does it come down to?
	· My lord the Count
Piace la sposa mia;	Is attracted to my bride,
Indi segretamente	And so secretly
Ricuperar vorria	He'd like to reclaim
Il diritto feudale:	His feudal right:
Possibile è la cosa, e naturale.	It's not only possible, it's natural.

COUNTESS

Possibil!	It's possible?

SUSANNA

Natural!	It's natural?

FIGARO

Naturalissima.	It's perfectly natural.
E, se Susanna vuol, possibilissima.	And if Susanna's willing, it's perfectly possible.

SUSANNA

Finiscila una volta.	Will you hurry up and finish?

FIGARO

Ho già finito.	I already have.
Quindi, prese il partito	So now he's decided
Di sceglier me corriero, e la Susanna	To name me as his courier, and Susanna
Consigliera segreta d'ambasciata:	His secret ambassadress:
E, perch'ella ostinata ognor rifiuta	And because she obstinately refuses
Il diploma d'onor ch'ei le destina,	The honorary title that he's offered to her,
Minaccia di protegger Marcellina.	He's threatening to take Marcellina's side.
Questo è tutto l'affare.	So now you know the whole story.

SUSANNA

Ed hai coraggio di trattar scherzando	And you have the nerve to joke about
Un negozio sì serio?	Such a serious matter?

FIGARO

Non vi basta
Che scherzando io ci pensi? Ecco il
　progetto.

Aren't you glad
That I can take it so lightly? Now listen
　to my plan.

(to the Countess)

Per Basilio un biglietto
Io gli fo capitar, che l'avvertisca
Di certo appuntamento
Che per l'ora del ballo
A un amante voi deste.

By way of Basilio I'll send him
A little note, warning him
About a certain assignation
That you've made with a lover
During the ball.

COUNTESS

O ciel! che sento!
Ad un uom sì geloso! . . .

Good heavens! What are you saying?
When he's such a jealous man? . . .

FIGARO

Ancora meglio:
Così potrem più presto imbarazzarlo,
Confonderlo, imbrogliarlo,
Rovesciargli i progetti,
Empierlo di sospetti, e porgli in testa

Che la moderna festa,
Ch'ei di fare a me tenta, altri a lui faccia;

Onde qua perda il tempo, ivi la traccia.

Così, quasi *ex abrupto*, e senza ch'abbia
Fatto per frastornarci alcun disegno,
Vien l'ora delle nozze,

So much the better:
Then we can embarrass him more easily,
And confuse him, embroil him,
And upset his schemes;
We'll fill him with suspicions, and make
　him understand
That these modern tricks,
Which he's trying to play on me, can also
　be played on him;
He'll waste his time on a wild-goose
　chase.
And all of a sudden, before he can
Interfere with our plans any further,
The hour will come for the wedding,

(to Susanna, pointing at the Countess)

e in faccia a lei
Non fia ch'osi d'opporsi ai voti miei.

and in front of her
He won't dare to prevent our vows.

SUSANNA

È ver; ma in di lui vece
S'opporrà Marcellina.

That's true; but instead of him
Marcellina will oppose us.

FIGARO (to Susanna)

Aspetta: al Conte
Farai subito dir che verso sera

Just a moment: You'll let
My lord know at once that towards
　evening

Attèndati in giardino:	He should wait for you in the garden:
Il picciol Cherubino,	Then we'll get our little Cherubino,
Per mio consiglio non ancor partito,	Who's agreed not to leave yet,
Da femmina vestito,	To dress up as a woman,
Faremo che in tua vece ivi sen vada.	And go there instead of you.
Questa è l'unica strada	This is the only way
Onde Monsù, sorpreso da Madama,	That my lord, who'll be caught in the act by my lady,
Sia costretto a far poi quel che si brama.	Can be forced to do what we want.

COUNTESS (*to Susanna*)

Che ti par?	What do you think?

SUSANNA

Non c'è mal.	It's not bad.

COUNTESS

Nel nostro caso . . .	In our situation . . .

SUSANNA

Quand'egli è persuaso . . . E dove è il tempo? . . .	If he's sure that . . . But is there enough time?

FIGARO

Ito è il Conte alla caccia, e per qualch'ora	The Count's gone hunting, and he won't be back
Non sarà di ritorno.	For a couple of hours.

(*leaving*)

Io vado, e tosto	I'm off now, and I'll send
Cherubino vi mando: lascio a voi	Cherubino at once: I'm leaving it to you
La cura di vestirlo.	To get him dressed.

COUNTESS

E poi?	And then?

FIGARO

E poi . . .	And then . . .

(Reprise of No. 3)

Se vuol ballare,	If you want to dance,
Signor Contino,	My dear little Count,
Il chitarrino	I'll play the tune
Le suonerò.	On my guitar.

(*He goes off.*)

SCENE III

The Countess and Susanna, then Cherubino

Recitative

COUNTESS

Quanto duolmi, Susanna,	How it hurts me, Susanna, to think
Che questo giovinetto abbia del Conte	That this young boy overheard
Le stravaganze udite, ah, tu non sai! . . .	The Count's foolish words. Oh, you can't imagine . . .
Ma per qual causa mai	But why in the world didn't he
Da me stessa ei non venne? . . .	Come right to me? . . .
Dov'è la canzonetta?	Just where did you put his little song?

SUSANNA

Eccola: appunto	Here it is: Yes,
Facciam che ce la canti.	Let's have him sing it for us.
Zitto, vien gente: è desso. Avanti, avanti,	Be quiet, someone's coming: It's him. Forward march,

(Cherubino enters.)

Signor uffiziale.	My fine young officer.

CHERUBINO

Ah, non chiamarmi	Oh, please don't call me
Con nome sì fatale! Ei mi rammenta	By that terrible name! It just reminds me
Che abbandonar degg'io	That I have to leave
Comare tanto buona.	Such a kind, sweet godmother.

SUSANNA

E tanto bella!	And so beautiful!

CHERUBINO *(sighing)*

Ah . . . sì . . . certo . . .	Oh . . . yes . . . of course . . .

SUSANNA *(imitating him)*

Ah . . . sì . . . certo . . .	Oh . . . yes . . . of course . . .

(aside)

Ipocritone!	You little hypocrite!

(aloud)

Via, presto! La canzone	Come on now, quickly! Just sing

| Che stamane a me deste | My lady the song |
| A Madama cantate. | That you gave me this morning. |

COUNTESS (unfolding it)

| Chi n'è l'autor? | Who wrote this? |

SUSANNA (pointing at Cherubino)

| Guardate: egli ha due braccia | Just look at him: He's blushing |
| Di rossor sulla faccia. | Like a school-girl. |

COUNTESS

| Prendi la mia chitarra e l'accompagna. | You take my guitar and accompany him. |

CHERUBINO

| Io sono sì tremante . . . | I'm trembling all over . . . |
| Ma se Madama vuole . . . | But if my lady insists . . . |

SUSANNA

| Lo vuole, sì, lo vuol . . . manco parole. | Yes, she insists, and so do I . . . Now no more talking. |

(Susanna plays the refrain on the guitar.)

CHERUBINO

No. 11 Canzone

Voi che sapete	Oh, you who know
Che cosa è amor,	What love's all about,
Donne, vedete	Tell me, my ladies,
S'io l'ho nel cor.	What's in my heart.
Quello ch'io provo	I'll try to describe
Vi ridirò;	My feelings for you,
È per me nuovo,	But they're so new
Capir nol so.	That I can't understand them.
Sento un affetto	Sometimes I feel
Pien di desir	A strange longing
Ch'ora è diletto,	That brings happiness
Ch'ora è martir.	Or despair.
Gelo, e poi sento	I freeze, and then
L'alma avvampar,	My soul's on fire,
E in un momento	And a moment later
Torno a gelar.	I'm freezing again.

Ricerco un bene
Fuori di me,
Non so chi'l tiene,
Non so cos'è.

Sospiro e gemo
Senza voler,
Palpito e tremo
Senza saper.

Non trovo pace
Notte né dì:
Ma pur mi piace
Languir così.

Voi che sapete
Che cosa è amor,
Donne, vedete
S'io l'ho nel cor.

I'm seeking a pleasure
That's beyond me,
I don't know where to find it,
Or even what it is.

I sigh and I moan
Without meaning to,
And I shake and tremble
Without knowing why.

I can find no peace
Either night or day,
Yet I've come to enjoy
My suffering.

Oh, you who know
What love's all about,
Tell me, my ladies,
What's in my heart.

Recitative

COUNTESS

Bravo! che bella voce! Io non sapea

Che cantaste sì bene.

Bravo! What a charming voice! I didn't know

You could sing so well.

SUSANNA

Oh, in verità
Egli fa tutto ben quello ch'ei fa.
Presto, a noi, bel soldato:

Figaro v'informò . . .

Oh, to tell you the truth,
He does everything well.
Now quickly, come here, my handsome soldier:

Figaro's already told you . . .

CHERUBINO

Tutto mi disse.

He's told me all about it.

SUSANNA

Lasciatemi veder.

Now let's see.

(*She measures Cherubino against herself.*)

Andrà benissimo:
Siam d'uguale statura . . . Giù quel manto.

This will do just fine:
We're the same height . . . Now off with your coat.

(*She takes off his coat.*)

Le Nozze di Figaro

COUNTESS (*to Susanna*)

Che fai?

What are you doing?

SUSANNA

Niente paura.

There's nothing to fear.

COUNTESS

E se qualcuno entrasse?

And what if someone should come in?

SUSANNA

Entri: che mal facciamo?

Let them come: We're not doing
anything wrong.

La porta chiuderò.

I think I'll lock the door.

(*She locks the door.*)

Ma come, poi,
Acconciargli i capelli?

But what am I going to
Do with his hair?

COUNTESS

Una mia cuffia
Prendi nel gabinetto.
Presto!

Go and get one of my caps
From the dressing-room.
Quickly now!

(*Susanna goes into the dressing-room to get a cap. Cherubino approaches the Countess and shows her his commission, which is in his breast pocket; the Countess takes it and unfolds it, and notices that the seal is missing.*)

Che carta è quella?

What is this document?

CHERUBINO

La patente.

It's my commission.

COUNTESS

Che sollecita gente!

They didn't waste any time!

CHERUBINO

L'ebbi or da Basilio.

I got it from Basilio.

COUNTESS

Dalla fretta obliato hanno il sigillo.

In all the hurry he forgot the seal.

(*She gives it back to him.*)

SUSANNA (*returning with the cap*)

Il sigillo di che?

The seal for what?

COUNTESS

Della patente.   For his commission.

SUSANNA

Cospetto! Che premura!   My goodness! How careless!
Ecco la cuffia.   But here's the cap.

COUNTESS (to Susanna)

Spicciati: va bene.   Hurry up now: That's just fine.
Miserabili noi, se il Conte viene.   I'd feel sorry for us if the Count should
                                       come in.

SUSANNA

(She takes Cherubino and makes him kneel down in front of her, a
little distance away from the Countess, who has seated herself.)

No. 12 Aria

Venite . . . inginocchiatevi . . .   Come here now . . . Kneel
Restate fermo lì . . .   down . . .
                                       And keep perfectly still . . .

(She combs his hair on one side; then she takes him by the chin
and turns his head as she wishes.)

Pian piano, or via, giratevi . . .   Now turn your head around
                                           slowly . . .
Bravo . . . va ben così.   Bravo . . . that's good.
La faccia ora volgetemi,   Now turn your face towards me.

(While Susanna is combing his hair, Cherubino gazes tenderly at the Countess.)

Olà! quegli occhi a me . . .   Hey! Look at me . . .
Drittissimo . . . guardatemi . . .   Right this way . . .
Madama qui non è.   Just pretend my lady's not here.

(She goes on combing his hair and then hands him the cap.)

Più alto quel colletto . . .   Put your collar up a little higher . . .
Quel ciglio un po' più basso . . .   And keep your eyes down lower . . .
Le mani sotto il petto . . .   Fold your hands across your
                                           chest . . .
Vedremo poscia il passo,   Now we'll see how you walk,
Quando sarete in piè.   When you're on your feet again.

(softly to the Countess)

206

Mirate il bricconcello,	Just look at the little rogue,
Mirate quanto è bello!	Look how pretty he is!
Che furba guardatura,	What a cunning air,
Che vezzo, che figura!	What charm, and what a figure!
Se l'amano le femmine,	If the ladies fall in love with him,
Han certo il lor perchè.	I can certainly understand why.

Recitative

COUNTESS

Quante buffonerie!	What utter nonsense!

SUSANNA

Ma se ne sono	I'm even
Io medesma gelosa!	Jealous of him myself!

(She takes Cherubino by the chin.)

Ehi, serpentello,	So, my little rascal,
Volete tralasciar d'esser sì bello?	Who gave you the right to be so pretty?

COUNTESS

Finiam le ragazzate. Or quelle maniche	Now that's enough of these childish pranks. Push those sleeves up
Oltre il gomito gli alza,	Above his elbows,
Onde più agiatamente	So that you can put on his dress
L'abito gli si adatti.	More easily.

SUSANNA *(carrying out her instructions)*

Ecco.	There now!

COUNTESS

Più indietro.	Even higher.
Così . . .	Like that . . .

(discovering a ribbon that he has tied around his arm)

Che nastro è quello?	But what's this ribbon here?

SUSANNA

È quel ch'esso involommi.	It's the one he stole from me.

COUNTESS *(She takes off the ribbon.)*

E questo sangue?	And where did this blood come from?

CHERUBINO *(agitated)*

Quel sangue . . . Io non so come . . .	That blood . . . I don't know how . . .
Poco pria, sdrucciolando	A little while ago, I stumbled over

In un sasso . . . la pelle io mi graffiai,   A rock . . . I scratched my arm,
E la piaga col nastro io mi fasciai.   And I bandaged myself with the ribbon.

SUSANNA

Mostrate: non c'è mal. Cospetto! Ha il braccio
    Let's see it: It's nothing much. Good heavens! His arm
Più candido del mio! Qualche ragazza . . .
    Is whiter than mine! Just like a girl's . . .

COUNTESS

E segui a far la pazza?   Are you still fooling around?
Va' nel mio gabinetto, e prendi un poco
    Go into the dressing-room, and get me a little
D'inglese taffetà, ch'è sullo scrigno.
    Piece of sticking-plaster; it's on my desk.

(*Susanna hurries off.*)

In quanto al nastro . . .   And as for this ribbon . . .

(*She looks at the ribbon a moment. Cherubino, kneeling, watches her carefully.*)

inver . . . per il colore . . .   To tell the truth . . . because of the color . . .
Mi spiacea di privarmene . . .   I'm sorry to let it go . . .

SUSANNA

(*Coming back in, she gives her the plaster and scissors.*)

Tenete: Here you are:
E da legargli il braccio?   And what should we use to bandage his arm?

COUNTESS

Un altro nastro   Go and get another ribbon
Prendi insiem col mio vestito.   Together with my dress.

(*Susanna leaves by the door at the back and takes Cherubino's coat with her.*)

CHERUBINO

Ah, più presto m'avria quello guarito!   Oh, that one would have healed me faster!

COUNTESS

Perché? Questo è migliore.   But why? This one's even better.

CHERUBINO

Allorché un nastro
Legò la chioma, ovver toccò la pelle . . .
D'oggetto . . .

Well, when a ribbon's
Bound the hair, or touched the skin . . .
Of someone . . .

COUNTESS (*interrupting him*)

. . . Forastiero,
È buon per le ferite; non è vero?
Guardate qualità ch'io non sapea!

. . . Who's a stranger,
It's good for your wounds, am I right?
Those are powers I've never heard of!

CHERUBINO

Madama scherza, ed io frattanto parto.

My lady's teasing me, and just when I
have to leave.

COUNTESS

Poverin, che sventura!

You poor thing, how unlucky!

CHERUBINO

Oh, me infelice!

Oh, how unhappy I am!

COUNTESS (*agitated and moved*)

Or piange!

Now he's crying!

CHERUBINO

O ciel! perché morir non lice!
Forse, vicino all'ultimo momento . . .

Questa bocca oseria . . .

God help me! Why can't I just die now!
Perhaps, when the final moment is
near . . .
These lips might dare . . .

COUNTESS

Siate saggio: cos'è questa follia?

Be good now: What is all this nonsense?

(*She dries his eyes with her handkerchief.*
Someone knocks at the door.)

Chi picchia alla mia porta?

Who's knocking at my door?

SCENE IV

The Countess and Cherubino; the Count outside the door

COUNT (*off-stage*)

Perché chiusa?

Why is it locked?

COUNTESS (*standing up*)

Il mio sposo! O Dei, son morta!

It's my husband! Oh God, I'm ruined!

(*to Cherubino*)

Voi qui senza mantello,	Here you are without your coat,
In questo stato! Un ricevuto foglio . . .	And in this condition! He received that note . . .
La sua gran gelosia!	And he's so horribly jealous!

COUNT (*louder*)

Cosa indugiate?	Why don't you open up?

COUNTESS (*confused*)

Son sola . . . ah, sì, son sola . . .	I'm alone . . . oh, yes, I'm all alone . . .

COUNT

E a chi parlate?	Then who were you talking to?

COUNTESS

A voi . . . certo . . . A voi stesso . . .	To you . . . of course . . . Just to you . . .

CHERUBINO

Dopo quel ch'è successo, il suo furore . . .	After everything that's happened, his fury . . .
Non trovo altro consiglio!	I've got no other choice!

(*He goes into the dressing-room, and closes the door.*)

COUNTESS

Ah, mi difenda il cielo, in tal periglio!	Oh, may heaven protect me, in this hour of danger!

(*She takes the key from the dressing-room door, and runs to open up for the Count.*)

SCENE V

The Countess, and the Count in hunting costume

COUNT (*entering*)

Che novità! Non fu mai vostra usanza	This is a new one! You never used
Di rinchiudervi in stanza!	To lock yourself up in your room!

COUNTESS

È ver; ma io . . .	You're right; but I . . .
Io stava qui mettendo . . .	I was trying on . . .

COUNT

Via: mettendo . . .	Go on: You were trying on . . .

COUNTESS

Certe robe . . . Era meco la Susanna . . .	Some of my things . . . And Susanna was here with me . . .
Che in sua camera è andata.	But she's gone off to her room.

COUNT (*looking closely at her*)

Ad ogni modo,	At any rate,
Voi non siete tranquilla.	You seem upset.
Guardate questo foglio.	And just take a look at this note.

COUNTESS (*aside*)

Numi! È il foglio	My God! It's the note
Che Figaro gli scrisse!	That Figaro wrote to him!

(*Cherubino knocks over a little table and a chair in the dressing-room, making a loud noise.*)

COUNT

Cos'è codesto strepito?	What's all this commotion?
In gabinetto	Something's fallen down
Qualche cosa è caduta.	In your dressing-room.

COUNTESS

Io non intesi niente.	I didn't hear anything.

COUNT

Convien che abbiate i gran pensieri in mente.	I guess you've got lots of weighty things on your mind.

COUNTESS

Di che?	What things?

COUNT

La v'è qualcuno.	I'm telling you, somebody's in there.

COUNTESS

Chi volete che sia?	But who could it possibly be?

COUNT

Lo chiedo a voi . . .	That's what I'm asking you . . .
Io vengo in questo punto.	I've only just come in.

COUNTESS

Ah, sì, Susanna . . . appunto . . .	Oh yes, it's Susanna . . . of course . . .

COUNT

Che passò, mi diceste, alla sua stanza!	But you told me she went to her room!

Countess

Alla sua stanza, o qui: non vidi bene . . .

To her room, or maybe she's still here: I really didn't notice . . .

Count

Susanna! E donde viene
Che siete sì turbata?

Susanna! Then just why
Are you so upset?

Countess (*forcing a little laugh*)

Per la mia cameriera?

You mean about my maid?

Count

Io non so nulla:
Ma turbata, senz'altro.

I'm not sure what I mean:
But I do know you're upset.

Countess

Ah! questa serva,
Più che non turba me, turba voi stesso.

Oh! This maid of mine
Upsets you a lot more than she does me.

Count

È vero, è vero; e lo vedrete adesso.

True, true; and now you'll see just why.

Scene VI

The Countess and the Count; Susanna on one side

(*Susanna enters through the door by which she left, and stops when she sees the Count, who is talking by the dressing-room door.*)

No. 13 Trio

Count

Susanna, or via, sortite,
Sortite! Così vo'.

Susanna, come on out now,
Come out of there, I say!

Countess (*distressed, to the Count*)

Fermatevi . . . Sentite . . .
Sortire ella non può.

No, stop . . . Just listen . . .
She can't come out right now.

Susanna (*aside*)

Cos'è codesta lite?
Il paggio dove andò?

But what's this fighting all about?
And where did the page go to?

Count

E chi vietarlo or osa?

And who dares to forbid it?

212

COUNTESS

Lo vieta l'onestà:	Decency forbids it:
Un abito da sposa	For she's trying on
Provando ella si sta.	Her wedding-dress.

COUNT (*aside*)

Chiarissima è la cosa:	The reason's all too clear:
L'amante qui sarà!	She's got her lover here!

COUNTESS (*aside*)

Bruttissima è la cosa:	The situation's really desperate:
Chi sa cosa sarà.	Who knows what'll happen next.

SUSANNA (*aside*)

Capisco qualche cosa:	I'm beginning to catch on:
Veggiamo come va.	Now let's see what'll happen next.

COUNT

Dunque, parlate almeno,	Well, at least say something,
Susanna, se qui siete . . .	Susanna, if you're really in there . . .

COUNTESS

Nemmen, nemmen, nemmeno!	No, no, don't answer him!

(*towards the door*)

Io v'ordino, tacete!	I order you, be quiet!

SUSANNA (*aside, as she hides in the alcove*)

O cielo! Un precipizio,	Oh heavens! A disaster,
Un scandalo, un disordine	A scandal, a catastrophe
Qui certo nascerà.	Will surely come out of all this.

COUNT and COUNTESS

Consorte {mia, / mio, giudizio!	And you, {my wife, / my husband, be careful
Un scandalo, un disordine	We've got to avoid
Schiviam, per carità.	Any scandals.

Recitative

COUNT

Dunque, voi non aprite?	So you still won't open up?

COUNTESS

E perché deggio   And just why should I

Le mie camere aprir?   Open up my rooms for you?

COUNT

Ebben, lasciate . . .   All right then, don't bother . . .

L'aprirem senza chiavi . . . Ehi gente! . . .   We'll open it without the key . . . Hey,
                                       servants! . . .

COUNTESS

Come?   You'll do what?

Porreste a repentaglio   You'd dare to compromise

D'una dama l'onore?   A lady's honor?

COUNT

È vero, io sbaglio.   You're right, and I'm wrong.

Posso, senza rumore,   Without the least bit of noise,

Senza scandalo alcun di nostra gente,   Or breath of a scandal among the
                                       servants,

Andar io stesso a prender l'occorrente: I myself can get all that's needed;

Attendete pur qui . . . Ma, perché in   Now wait right here . . . But just so my
   tutto

Sia il mio dubbio distrutto, anco le porte   Doubts are completely dispelled, I'm also

Io prima chiuderò.   Locking the doors.

(He locks the door that leads to the maids' quarters.)

COUNTESS *(aside)*

Che imprudenza!   Oh, how impulsive he is!

COUNT

Voi la condiscendenza   And now if you'd be good enough

Di venir meco avrete.   To come along with me.

(assuming an air of gaity)

Madama, eccovi il braccio. Andiamo.   My arm, my lady. And off we go.

COUNTESS *(trembling)*

Andiamo.   Yes, off we go.

COUNT *(aloud, as he points at the dressing-room)*

Susanna starà qui finché torniamo.   Susanna can just stay put until we return.

(They go off.)

Le Nozze di Figaro

SCENE VII

Susanna and Cherubino

No. 14 Duet

SUSANNA

(coming out of the alcove hurriedly and approaching the dressing-room door)

Aprite, presto, aprite!	Open up, oh, hurry, open up!
Aprite: è la Susanna.	Open up: It's me, Susanna.
Sortite, via, sortite ...	Come out now, come on out ...
Andate via di qua!	And get away from here as fast as you can!

CHERUBINO *(entering breathless and confused)*

Ahimè, che scena orribile!	Oh dear, what a horrible mess!
Che gran fatalità!	What a disaster this really is!

(They go first to one door and then another, and find them all locked.)

SUSANNA

Di qua, di qua, di là.	Over here, no there, no here.

SUSANNA and CHERUBINO

Le porte son serrate.	The doors are all locked tight.
Che mai, che mai sarà!	Who knows what'll happen next!

CHERUBINO

Qui perdersi non giova.	I've got to keep my wits about me.

SUSANNA

V'uccide, se vi trova.	He'll kill you if he finds you here.

CHERUBINO

Veggiamo un po' qui fuori.	Just let me look outside a moment.

(standing by the window that overlooks the garden)

Dà proprio nel giardino.	It looks right onto the garden.

(He makes as if to jump out; Susanna holds him back.)

SUSANNA

Fermate, Cherubino!	Cherubino, stop!

(She also looks out, and then draws back.)

Fermate, per pietà!	Stop, for pity's sake!

CHERUBINO

Qui perdersi non giova:	I've got to keep my wits about me:
M'uccide, se mi trova.	He'll kill me if he finds me here.

SUSANNA (*still holding him back*)

Tropp'alto, per un salto.	It's too high up to jump.
Fermate, per pietà!	Stop, for pity's sake!

CHERUBINO (*He breaks away from Susanna.*)

Lasciami: pria di nuocerle,	Let me go: Before I'd ever hurt her,
Nel foco volerei.	I'd leap right into the fire.
Abbraccio te per lei,	Give her this kiss for me.
Addio. Così si fa.	Good-bye forever. So be it.

SUSANNA

Ei va a perire, oh, Dei!	Oh God, he'll kill himself!
Fermate, per pietà.	Stop, for pity's sake.

(*Cherubino jumps out; Susanna utters a loud cry,*
sits down for a moment, and then goes to the window.)

Recitative

Oh, guarda il demonietto! Come fugge!	Oh, just look how that little rascal can run!
È già un miglio lontano!	He's already a mile away!
Ma non perdiamci invano.	But let's not waste any time.
Entriam nel gabinetto:	I'll just slip into the dressing-room:
Venga poi lo smargiasso, io qui l'aspetto.	Let the bully come back, I'm ready for him now.

(*She goes into the dressing-room and closes the door behind her.*)

SCENE VIII

The Countess and the Count
(*Re-enter the Count and Countess, the former holding a hammer and*
pliers. As soon as he arrives, he examines all the doors, etc.)

COUNT

Tutto è come il lasciai: volete dunque	Everything's just as I left it: Now will you
Aprir voi stessa,	Unlock the door yourself,

(*as he is about to force open the door*)

o deggio . . .	Or must I . . .

COUNTESS

Ahimè, fermate,   No, wait a moment,
E ascoltatemi un poco.   Just listen to me.

(The Count throws the hammer and pliers onto a chair.)

Mi credete capace   Do you really think I could
Di mancare al dover? . . .   Ever betray you? . . .

COUNT

Come vi piace.   As you please,
Entro quel gabinetto   But I mean to see who's
Chi v'è chiuso vedrò.   Inside your dressing-room.

COUNTESS *(in fear and trembling)*

Sì, lo vedrete . . .   Yes, of course you'll see . . .
Ma uditemi tranquillo.   But calm down for a moment and listen.

COUNT *(suddenly angry)*

Non è dunque Susanna!   So it's not Susanna after all!

COUNTESS *(as before)*

No, ma invece è un oggetto   No, it's not, but instead it's someone
Che ragion di sospetto   Who could never arouse your suspicions:
Non vi deve lasciar: per questa sera . . .   We were just preparing . . .
Una burla innocente   An innocent diversion
Di far si disponeva . . . ed io vi giuro . . .   For this evening . . . And I swear to
                                                you . . .
Che l'onor . . . l'onestà . . .   That my honor . . . your good name . . .

COUNT *(angrier still)*

Chi è dunque? Dite! . . .   Just who is it then? Tell me! . . .
L'ucciderò.   I'll kill him.

COUNTESS

Sentite.   Listen to me.
Ah, non ho cor.   No, I haven't got the courage.

COUNT

Parlate.   Well then, speak up!

COUNTESS

È un fanciullo . . .   It's a boy . . .

217

COUNT (*as before*)

Un fanciul . . .   A boy . . .

COUNTESS

Sì, Cherubino.   Yes, it's Cherubino.

COUNT (*aside*)

E mi farà il destino   And it seems I'm condemned
Ritrovar questo paggio in ogni loco!   To find that page every time I turn
                                              around!

(*to the Countess*)

Come? non è partito? Scellerati!   What's this? He hasn't gone yet? Oh,
                                              those scoundrels!

Ecco i dubbi spiegati, ecco l'imbroglio,   So this is the reason for all my doubts,
                                              and all your conniving;

Ecco il raggiro onde m'avverte il foglio.   This is the plot the note warned me
                                              about.

No. 15 Finale

COUNT (*at the dressing-room door, in a rage*)

Esci, omai, garzon malnato!   Come out of there, you low-life!
Sciagurato, non tardar.   You little wretch, be quick about it!

COUNTESS

Ah, signore, quel furore   Oh, my Lord, all this rage

(*dragging the Count back*)

Per lui fammi il cor tremar.   Makes my heart tremble for him.

COUNT

E d'opporvi ancor osate?   And you still have the nerve to
                                              interfere?

COUNTESS

No, sentite . . .   No, but listen . . .

COUNT

Via, parlate.   Go ahead and have your say.

COUNTESS (*trembling with fear*)

Giuro al ciel ch'ogni sospetto . . .   I swear to God that all your
                                              suspicions . . .

E lo stato in che il trovate . . .
Sciolto il collo . . . nudo il petto . . .

And the state you'll find him in . . .
With his collar off . . . and his chest
bare . . .

COUNT

Sciolto il collo . . .
Nudo il petto . . . Seguitate.

With his collar off . . .
And his chest bare . . . Well then,
do go on.

COUNTESS

Per vestir femminee spoglie . . .

So he could dress up as a
woman . . .

COUNT

Ah, comprendo, indegna moglie;

Mi vo' tosto vendicar!

Oh, now I understand, you
shameless creature;
But I'll soon get my revenge!

(He approaches the dressing-room, and then turns back.)

COUNTESS (*forcefully*)

Mi fa torto, quel trasporto;
M'oltraggiate, a dubitar.

When you carry on like this,
It's insulting and degrading.

COUNT

Qua la chiave.

Just give me the key.

COUNTESS

Egli è innocente,
Voi sapete . . .

But he's innocent,
And you know it . . .

(She gives the Count the key.)

COUNT

Non so niente.
Va' lontan dagli occhi miei.
Un'infida, un'empia sei . . .
E mi cerchi d'infamar.

I know nothing of the sort!
Now get out of my sight.
You're unfaithful and wicked,
And you've only tried to disgrace
me.

COUNTESS

Vado . . . sì . . . ma . . .

All right, I'm going . . . but . . .

COUNT

Non ascolto.

I'm not listening to you.

COUNTESS

Non son rea ...   But I'm not guilty ...

COUNT

Vel veggo in volto.   And I can see it on your face.

COUNT

Mora, mora, e più non sia   Let him die, and I'll finally get rid
Ria cagion del mio penar!   Of the source of all my suffering!

COUNTESS

Ah, la cieca gelosia   Oh, he's blinded by his jealousy,
Qualche eccesso gli fa far! ...   And he's going to do something
                                                          rash! ...

*(The Count opens the dressing-room door, and Susanna comes to the door
completely straight-faced, where she stops.)*

SCENE IX

The Countess, the Count and Susanna

COUNT (*astonished*)

Susanna!   Susanna!

COUNTESS (*astonished*)

Susanna!   Susanna!

SUSANNA

Signore!   My Lord!
Cos'è quel stupore?   But why do you look so amazed?

(*ironically*)

Il brando prendete,   So you'd take up your sword,
Il paggio uccidete;   And kill the page;
Quel paggio malnato   Well, that poor little low-life
Vedetelo qua.   Is standing right here.

COUNT (*aside*)

Che scuola! La testa   Just what is all this? My head
Girando mi va.   Has started to spin.

COUNTESS (*aside*)

Che storia è mai questa!   But what can have happened?
Susanna v'è là?   Susanna's in there?

220

SUSANNA (*aside*)

Confusa han la testa:	Their minds are all confused:
Non san come va.	They don't know what to think.

COUNT (*to Susanna*)

Sei sola? . . .	Are you all alone? . . .

SUSANNA (*to the Count*)

Guardate,	Well, why don't you just see
Qui ascoso sarà.	Who might be hiding in there.

COUNT

Guardiamo, guardiamo,	Yes, let's just look and see
Qui ascoso sarà.	Who might be hiding in there.

(*He goes into the dressing-room.*)

COUNTESS

Susanna, son morta:	Susanna, I'm fainting:
Il fiato mi manca.	I can't seem to catch my breath.

SUSANNA

(*gaily, showing the Countess the window from which Cherubino jumped*)

Più lieta, più franca!	Just stop worrying and be happy!
In salvo è di già.	He's already safe and sound!

COUNT

(*coming out of the dressing-room in confusion*)

Che sbaglio mai presi!	Oh, what a terrible mistake I've made!
Appena lo credo.	I can hardly believe it myself.
Se a torto v'offesi,	And if I've insulted you unjustly,
Perdono vi chiedo;	I'm asking your forgiveness;
Ma far burla simile	But playing jokes like that
È poi crudeltà.	Is really very cruel.

COUNTESS and SUSANNA

(*The Countess is holding a handkerchief to her mouth to hide her embarrassment.*)

Le vostre follie	Your outrageous behavior
Non mertan pietà.	Doesn't deserve any pity.

COUNT

Io v'amo!	But I love you!

COUNTESS (*gradually recovering from her confusion*)

Nol dite!   Don't say that to me!

COUNT

Vel giuro!   I swear it!

COUNTESS (*forcefully and angrily*)

Mentite!   You're lying!
Son l'empia, l'infida   I'm just wicked, and unfaithful,
Che ognora v'inganna.   And I'm always deceiving you.

COUNT

Quell'ira, Susanna,   Oh, help me, Susanna,
M'aita a calmar.   To calm her anger.

SUSANNA

Così si condanna   With all your wild suspicions
Chi può sospettar.   You've brought this on yourself.

COUNTESS (*resentfully*)

Adunque la fede   So this is the reward
D'un'anima amante   I should expect
Sì fiera mercede   For my years of
Doveva sperar?   Love and devotion?

COUNT

Quell'ira, Susanna,   Oh, help me, Susanna,
M'aita a calmar.   To calm her anger.

SUSANNA (*pleading*)

Signora!   My lady!

COUNT (*pleading*)

Rosina!   Rosina!

COUNTESS (*to the Count*)

Crudele!   Oh, you're so cruel!
Più quella non sono,   I'm not her anymore,
Ma il misero oggetto   I'm just the miserable object
Del vostro abbandono,   Of your neglect,
Che avete diletto   And you take pleasure
Di far disperar.   In making me suffer.

COUNT and SUSANNA

Confuso, pentito,	I'm⎫ He's⎭ so confused, and so sorry,
Son⎫ È ⎭ troppo punito:	And⎰I've⎱ been punished enough: ⎱he's⎰
Abbiate pietà.	I beg you, have pity on me. him.

COUNTESS

Crudele!	How cruel you are!
Soffrir sì gran torto	This heart of mine can never
Quest'alma non sa.	Forgive so terrible an insult.

COUNT

Ma il paggio rinchiuso? . . .	And what about the page who was locked up in there? . . .

COUNTESS

Fu sol per provarvi.	I was only trying to test you.

COUNT

Ma i tremiti, i palpiti? . . .	And your fears, and your trembling? . . .

COUNTESS

Fu sol per burlarvi.	I was only trying to tease you.

COUNT

E un foglio sì barbaro? . . .	And so nasty a note? . . .

COUNTESS and SUSANNA

Di Figaro è il foglio,	The note was from Figaro,
E a voi, per Basilio . . .	And he sent it by Basilio . . .

COUNT

Ah, perfidi! Io voglio . . .	Oh, those traitors! I'd like to . . .

COUNTESS and SUSANNA

Perdono non merta	He who can't forgive others
Chi agli altri nol dà.	Doesn't deserve to be forgiven himself.

COUNT (*tenderly*)

Ebben, se vi piace,	Well, if you like,
Comune è la pace:	Let's all make peace;

Rosina inflessibile
Con me non sarà.

And Rosina won't bear
Any resentment towards me.

Countess

Ah, quanto, Susanna,
Son dolce di core!
Di donna al furore
Chi più crederà?

Oh, how soft-hearted
I am, Susanna!
Who can ever take seriously
A woman's fury?

Susanna

Cogli uomin, signora,
Girate, volgete,
Vedrete che ognora
Si cade poi là.

When it comes to men, my lady,
No matter where you turn,
You'll see that you always
End up like that.

Count (*tenderly*)

Guardatemi . . .

Oh, just look at me! . . .

Countess

Ingrato!

For shame!

Count

Ho torto, e mi pento!

I was wrong, and I'm sorry!

(*He kisses the Countess' hand over and over again.*)

Count, Countess and Susanna

Da questo momento
Quest'alma a conoscer { vi / mi / la
Apprender potrà.

From this moment on
This heart will try to learn
To understand { you / me better. / her

Scene X

The Countess, the Count, Susanna and Figaro

Figaro (*entering*)

Signori, di fuori
Son già i suonatori:
Le trombe sentite,
I pifferi udite.
Tra canti, tra balli
De' vostri vassalli,
Corriamo, voliamo
Le nozze a compir!

My lord and lady,
The musicians are already outside:
Just listen to
The trumpets and the pipes.
While your vassals
Are singing and dancing,
Let's hasten
To celebrate our wedding!

(*He takes Susanna by the arm and makes as if to leave; the Count holds him back.*)

COUNT

Pian piano, men fretta.   Just a moment, not so fast.

FIGARO

La turba m'aspetta.   But the crowd's waiting for me.

COUNT

Un dubbio toglietemi   Before you go, I want you
In pria di partir.   To relieve a doubt of mine.

COUNT, COUNTESS, FIGARO and SUSANNA (*aside*)

La cosa è scabrosa;   The situation's difficult;
Com'ha da finir?   And how is it going to end?
Con arte le carte   I've got to play
Convien qui scoprir.   My cards just right.

COUNT

(*showing him the note he received from Basilio. Figaro pretends
to examine it.*)

Conoscete, signor Figaro,   Have you any idea, Master Figaro,
Questo foglio chi vergò?   Who might have written this note?

FIGARO

Nol conosco . . .   No, I don't . . .

SUSANNA (*to Figaro*)

Nol conosci?   You don't know?

FIGARO

No.   No, I don't.

COUNTESS (*to Figaro*)

Nol conosci?   You don't know?

FIGARO

No.   No, I don't.

COUNT (*to Figaro*)

Nol conosci?   You don't know?

FIGARO

No.   No, I don't.

COUNT, COUNTESS and SUSANNA

Nol conosci?   You don't know?

FIGARO

No, no, no!   No, no, no!

SUSANNA

E nol desti a Don Basilio . . .   And didn't you give it to Don
                                               Basilio . . .

COUNTESS

Per recarlo . . .   So he'd take it . . .

COUNT

Tu c'intendi . . .   And you know all about it . . .

FIGARO

Oibò, oibò.   Oh dear, oh dear!

SUSANNA

E non sai del damerino . . .   And what about the page . . .

COUNTESS

Che stasera, nel giardino . . .   Who this evening, in the garden . . .

COUNT

Già capisci . . .   But now you understand . . .

FIGARO

Non lo so.   Oh no, I don't.

COUNT

Cerchi invan difesa e scusa.   Don't bother to look for excuses.
Il tuo ceffo già t'accusa;   Your mug's already given you away;
Veggo ben che vuoi mentir.   I can see that you're lying.

FIGARO (*to the Count*)

Mente il ceffo, io già non mento.   Well then, my mug must be lying,
                                               not me!

COUNTESS and SUSANNA (*to Figaro*)

Il talento aguzzi invano.   You're wasting all your efforts.
Palesato abbiam l'arcano: We've already solved the mystery:
Non v'è nulla da ridir.   And there's nothing left to say.

COUNT

Che rispondi?   So what's your answer?

FIGARO

Niente, niente.   I haven't got one.

COUNT

Dunque, accordi?   Which means you admit it?

FIGARO

Non accordo.   No, I don't.

COUNTESS and SUSANNA (*to Figaro*)

Eh, via, chétati, balordo: Just keep quiet, you silly fool:
La burletta ha da finir.   It's time the comedy was over.

FIGARO

Per finirla lietamente   And so to have a happy ending
E all'usanza teatrale,   In theatrical tradition,

(*taking Susanna's arm*)

Un'azion matrimoniale   Let's finish it up
Le faremo ora seguir.   With a wedding celebration.

SUSANNA, FIGARO and COUNTESS (*to the Count*)

Deh, signor, nol contrastate: My lord, don't bar the way:

Consolate i$\begin{cases}\text{miei}\\\text{lor}\end{cases}$desir.   Just grant$\begin{cases}\text{my}\\\text{their}\end{cases}$fondest wish.

COUNT (*aside*)

Marcellina, Marcellina,   Marcellina, Marcellina,
Quanto tardi a comparir!   What's taking you so long?

SCENE XI

The Countess, the Count, Susanna, Figaro and Antonio
(*Enter Antonio, the gardener, half drunk, carrying a broken pot of carnations.*)

ANTONIO (*enraged*)

Ah! signore . . . signor . . .   Oh, my lord . . . my lord . . .

COUNT (*anxiously*)

Cosa è stato? . . .   What's the matter? . . .

ANTONIO

Che insolenza! Chi 'l fece, chi fu?   Oh, what nerve! Who did it? Who
                                                      was it?

COUNT, COUNTESS, FIGARO and SUSANNA (*anxiously*)

Cosa dici, cos'hai, cosa è nato?

What're you saying, what's the
matter, what happened?

ANTONIO

Ascoltate.

Well now, listen to this.

COUNT, COUNTESS, FIGARO and SUSANNA

Via, parla, di' su.

Just hurry up and tell us!

ANTONIO

Dal balcone che guarda in giardino
Mille cose ogni dì gittar veggio;

E poc'anzi, può darsi di peggio?

Vidi un uom, signor mio, gittar giù!

I see a thousand things a day
Thrown off the balcony that
overlooks the garden;
And a little while ago, can you
imagine anything worse?
Somebody actually threw down a
man!

COUNT (*animatedly*)

Dal balcone?

From the balcony?

ANTONIO (*showing him the broken flower-pot*)

Vedete i garofani?

Just look at these carnations!

COUNT

In giardino?

From the garden?

ANTONIO

Sì!

Oh, yes!

SUSANNA and COUNTESS (*sottovoce to Figaro*)

Figaro, all'erta!

Oh, Figaro, watch out!

COUNT

Cosa sento!

What's this I hear?

COUNTESS, FIGARO and SUSANNA (*aside*)

Costui ci sconcerta.

He's getting us very upset.

(*aloud*)

Quel briaco che viene a far qui?

What's this old drunkard doing in
here?

COUNT (*excitedly, to Antonio*)

Dunque un uom . . . Ma dov'è,
dov'è gito?

So you saw a man . . . But where is
he? Where did he go?

ANTONIO

Ratto ratto il birbone è fuggito,
E ad un tratto di vista m'uscì.

The rascal took to his heels,
And the next thing I knew, he was
out of sight.

SUSANNA (*sottovoce to Figaro*)

Sai che il paggio . . .

Did you know that the page . . .

FIGARO (*sottovoce to Susanna*)

So tutto, lo vidi.

I know everything. I saw him.

(*laughing loudly*)

Ah, ah, ah, ah!

Ha, ha, ha, ha!

COUNT (*to Figaro*)

Taci là.

You be quiet!

ANTONIO (*to Figaro*)

Cosa ridi?

What's so funny?

FIGARO (*to Antonio*)

Tu sei cotto dal sorger del dì!

And you're tipsy from morning 'till
night!

COUNT (*to Antonio*)

Or ripetimi: un uom dal balcone . . .

Now tell me again: A man fell off
the balcony . . .

ANTONIO

Dal balcone.

Off the balcony.

COUNT

In giardino . . .

And into the garden . . .

ANTONIO

In
giardino.

Into the garden.

SUSANNA, COUNTESS and FIGARO

Ma, signore, se in lui parla il vino!

But, my lord, he's drunk, can't you
see?

COUNT (*to Antonio*)

Segui pure. Né in volto il vedesti?

Just keep talking. And did you see
his face?

ANTONIO

No, nol vidi.   No, I didn't.

SUSANNA and COUNTESS (*sottovoce to Figaro*)

Olà, Figaro, ascolta.   Oh, Figaro, will you listen to him!

FIGARO (*to Antonio*)

Via, piangione, sta' zitto una volta: Come on, stop the whining, just be
                                 quiet for once:

(*touching the flowers contemptuously*)

Per tre soldi far tanto tumulto!   All this fuss over nothing!
Giacché il fatto non può stare   Well, if you must know the truth:
  occulto: I'm the one who jumped out of
Sono io stesso saltato di lì.   there.

COUNT

Chi? vio stesso?   Who? It was you?

COUNTESS and SUSANNA (*aside*)

Che testa! che ingegno!   How brilliant! How clever he is!

FIGARO (*to the Count*)

Che stupor?   Why are you so surprised?

COUNT

Già creder nol posso.   I just can't believe it.

ANTONIO (*to Figaro*)

Come mai diventaste sì grosso?   So how come you've gotten so big?
Dopo il salto non foste così.   When you jumped you weren't like
                                 that at all.

FIGARO

A chi salta succede così.   That's what happens when you
                                 jump.

ANTONIO

Chi 'l direbbe?   Who'd have thought such a thing?

SUSANNA and COUNTESS (*aside*)

Ed insiste, quel pazzo!   He just doesn't give up, that idiot!

COUNT (*to Antonio*)

Tu che dici?   And what have you got to say?

Le Nozze di Figaro

ANTONIO

A me parve il ragazzo.   It looked like that boy to me.

COUNT (*excitedly*)

Cherubin!   Cherubino!

SUSANNA and COUNTESS (*aside*)

Maledetto!   Oh, poor thing!

FIGARO (*sarcastically*)

Esso appunto.   Yes, of course it was him.

Da Siviglia a cavallo qui giunto,   He's come all the way back from
                                                   Seville on horseback,

Da Siviglia ov'ei forse sarà.   From Seville, where he's supposed
                                                   to be.

ANTONIO (*slow and stupid*)

Questo no, questo no: ché il cavallo   No, that's not the way it was: I
                                                   didn't see

Io non vidi saltare di là.   Any horse jump out of there.

COUNT

Che pazienza! Finiam questo ballo!   This is really too much! That's
                                                   enough of this nonsense!

COUNTESS and SUSANNA (*aside*)

Come mai, giusto ciel, finirà?   Heaven knows how it's going to
                                                   end!

COUNT (*to Figaro, excitedly*)

Dunque, tu . . .   So it was you who . . .

FIGARO (*nonchalantly*)

Saltai giù.   Jumped down.

COUNT

Ma perché?   But why?

FIGARO

Il timor . . .   I was scared.

COUNT

Che timor?   You were scared?

231

FIGARO (*pointing to the maids' quarters*)

Là rinchiuso,   I was in there,

Aspettando quel caro visetto . . .	Waiting for that sweet little face . . .
Tippe tappe, un susurro fuor d'uso . . .	When all of a sudden, I heard a lot of commotion . . .
Voi gridaste . . . lo scritto biglietto . . .	You were shouting . . . I thought about the note . . .
Saltai giù dal terrore confuso . . .	So I jumped down scared to death . . .

(*rubbing his foot, as if he had hurt himself*)

E stravolto m'ho un nervo del piè!	And I twisted my foot when I fell!

ANTONIO

Vostre, dunque, saran queste carte Che perdeste . . .	So these must be yours, And you lost them . . .

(*He hands several folded papers to Figaro; the Count takes them away from him.*)

COUNT

Olà, porgile a me.	Just give them to me.

FIGARO (*sottovoce to Susanna and the Countess*)

Sono in trappola.	I'm caught in a trap.

SUSANNA and COUNTESS (*sottovoce to Figaro*)

Figaro, all'erta!	Oh, Figaro, watch out!

COUNT

(*He opens the document, then immediately folds it up again.*)

Dite un po', questo foglio cos'è?	Now tell me, what's this paper?

FIGARO

Tosto . . . tosto . . . n'ho tanti, aspettate.	Right away . . . No, wait just a moment . . . I've got so many of them in here.

(*He pulls some papers out of his pocket and pretends to look at them.*)

ANTONIO

Sarà forse il sommario de' debiti.	It's probably a list of his debts.

FIGARO

No, la lista degli osti.	No, it's not, it's a list of the inn-keepers.

COUNT (*to Figaro*)

Parlate. Speak up, my man.

(*to Antonio*)

E tu, lascialo! And you, just let him be!

COUNTESS, SUSANNA and FIGARO (*to Antonio*)

Lascia$\begin{cases}\text{mi!}\\\text{lo!}\end{cases}$ E parti! Just leave$\begin{cases}\text{me}\\\text{him}\end{cases}$alone! And get out!

ANTONIO

Parto, sì, ma se torno a trovarti . . . All right, I'm going, but if I ever
find you again . . .

(*He goes off.*)

FIGARO

Vanne, vanne, non temo di te. Oh, go away, you can't scare me.

COUNT

(*He unfolds the paper and then folds it up again at once. To Figaro*)

Dunque? . . . Well then? . . .

COUNTESS (*to Susanna, sottovoce*)

O ciel! La patente del paggio! Good heavens! The page's commission!

SUSANNA (*sottovoce to Figaro*)

Giusti Dei! La patente! . . . Oh, my God! The commission! . . .

COUNT (*to Figaro, sarcastically*)

Coraggio! How about it?

FIGARO (*as if he suddenly remembered*)

Uh, che testa! Quest'è la patente Oh, how stupid of me! That's the
commission

Che poc'anzi il fanciullo mi diè. I just got from the boy.

COUNT

Per che fare? What for?

FIGARO (*in confusion*)

Vi manca . . . It's missing . . .

COUNT

Vi manca? It's missing?

COUNTESS (*sottovoce to Susanna*)

Il suggello . . . The seal . . .

SUSANNA (*sottovoce to Figaro*)

Il suggello! The seal!

COUNT (*to Figaro, who pretends to be thinking*)

Rispondi? What's your answer?

FIGARO

È l'usanza . . . Well, it's usual . . .

COUNT

Su via: ti confondi? Come on now: Are you getting confused?

FIGARO

È l'usanza di porvi il suggello. It's usual to seal a commission.

COUNT

(*He looks and sees that the seal is missing; then tears up the paper.*
Aside.)

Questo birbo mi toglie il cervello.	This rascal's driving me crazy.
Tutto, tutto è un mistero per me.	The whole thing's a mystery to me.

(*In an absolute fury he throws down the paper.*)

COUNTESS and SUSANNA (*aside*)

Se mi salvo da questa tempesta,	If I can just weather this storm,
Più non havvi naufragio per me.	I won't be shipwrecked after all.

FIGARO (*aside*)

Sbuffa invano, e la terra calpesta;	He can huff and puff, and stamp his feet:
Poverino, ne sa men di me.	Poor thing, he knows less about it than me.

SCENE XII

The Countess, the Count, Susanna, Figaro, Marcellina, Bartolo and Basilio

MARCELLINA, BARTOLO and BASILIO (*entering, to the Count*)

Voi, signor, che giusto siete,	Oh just and noble lord,
Ci dovete or ascoltar.	We beg you, hear our case.

COUNT (*aside*)

Son venuti a vendicarmi.	They've come to avenge me.
Io mi sento consolar.	I already feel some relief.

COUNTESS, FIGARO and SUSANNA (*aside*)

Son venuti a sconcertarmi.	They've come to thwart my plans.
Qual rimedio ritrovar?	What solution can I find?

FIGARO (*to the Count*)

Son tre stolidi, tre pazzi.	All three of them are stupid fools.
Cosa mai vengono a far?	What in the world are they up to now?

COUNT

Pian pianin, senza schiamazzi	That's enough of this commotion;
Dica ognun quel che gli par.	Let everyone have his say.

MARCELLINA

Un impegno nuziale	This fellow's promised
Ha costui con me contratto;	To marry me;
E pretendo che il contratto	And I contend that the contract
Deva meco effettuar.	Must be carried out.

COUNTESS, FIGARO and SUSANNA

Come! come!	What's all this?

COUNT

Olà, silenzio:	Quiet, everyone!
Io son qui per giudicar.	I'm the one who's judging this case.

BARTOLO

Io da lei scelto avvocato	As her appointed lawyer,
Vengo a far le sue difese,	I've come in her defense.
Le legittime pretese	I'm also here to prove
Io qui vengo a palesar.	The legitimacy of her claim.

COUNTESS, FIGARO and SUSANNA

È un birbante!	But he's a scoundrel!

COUNT

Olà, silenzio!	Quiet, everyone!
Io son qui per giudicar.	I'm the one who's judging this case.

BASILIO

Io, com'uom al mondo cognito,	As a man of the world,
Vengo qui per testimonio	I've come here to testify

Del promesso matrimonio	That he promised to marry her
Con prestanza di danar.	When she lent him some money.

COUNTESS, FIGARO and SUSANNA

Son tre matti!	All three of them are crazy!

COUNT

Lo vedremo:	Well, first we have to see:
Il contratto leggeremo.	We'll just read over the contract.
Tutto in ordin deve andar.	One thing at a time, I always say.

COUNT, MARCELLINA, BARTOLO and BASILIO (*aside*)

Che bel colpo, che bel caso:	What a stroke of luck:
È cresciuto a tutti il naso!	Just look at those long faces!
Qualche Nume a noi propizio	Some extraordinary power
Qui { li / ci } ha fatti capitar.	Must have brought { those / us } people here.

COUNTESS, FIGARO and SUSANNA (*aside*)

Son confus { a, / o, } son stordit { a, / o, }	I'm confused, I'm dazed,
Disperat { a, / o, } son sbalordit { a! / o! }	I'm desperate and dismayed!
Certo, un diavol dell'inferno	It was the devil himself, I'm sure,
Qui li ha fatti capitar.	Who brought those people here.

End of Act Two

ACT THREE

A richly decorated hall, with two thrones, prepared for the wedding festivities.

SCENE I

The Count alone

Recitative

COUNT (*aside, pacing back and forth*)

Che imbarazzo è mai questo! Un foglio anonimo . . .	What a terrible predicament this is! An anonymous letter . . .

La cameriera in gabinetto chiusa . . .	The maid locked in the dressing-room . . .
La padrona confusa . . . un uom che salta	Her mistress all in a dither . . . somebody jumps
Dal balcone in giardino . . . un altro, appresso,	Off the balcony into the garden . . . somebody else
Che dice esser quel desso . . .	Who claims it was him . . .
Non so cosa pensar: potrebbe forse	I don't know what to think: It might even have been
Qualcun de'miei vassalli . . . a simil razza	One of my servants . . . they're certainly the type
È comune l'ardir . . . Ma la Contessa . . .	That would take such a chance . . . But the Countess . . .
Ah, che un dubbio l'offende . . . ella rispetta	Oh, any doubt on my part would only insult her . . . she has
Troppo se stessa; e l'onor mio . . . l'onore . . .	Too much respect for herself; and what about my honor . . .
Dove diamin l'ha posto umano errore!	Just look what human frailty has done to it now!

SCENE II

The Count, the Countess and Susanna

(Enter the Countess and Susanna, who stop at the rear of the stage, unnoticed by the Count.)

COUNTESS

Via, fàtti core: digli	Come on now, just take heart: Tell him
Che ti attenda in giardino.	To wait for you in the garden.

COUNT (*still aside*)

Saprò se Cherubino	I've got to make sure that Cherubino
Era giunto a Siviglia: a tale oggetto	Really went to Seville: I've sent Basilio
Ho mandato Basilio . . .	To find out . . .

SUSANNA

Oh, cielo! e Figaro . . .	Good heavens! And if Figaro . . .

COUNTESS

A lui non dèi dir nulla: in vece tua	Don't say a word about it to him: I myself
Voglio andarci io medesma.	Intend to go in your place.

COUNT (*as before*)

Avanti sera   He should be back

Dovrebbe ritornar . . .   By this evening . . .

SUSANNA

Oddio! non oso.   Oh, my God! I don't dare to.

COUNTESS

Pensa ch'è in tua mano il mio riposo.   Just remember that my happiness is in
your hands.

(*She hides.*)

COUNT (*as before*)

E Susanna? Chi sa ch'ella tradito   And what about Susanna? Who knows if
she's betrayed

Abbia il segreto mio . . . Oh, se ha
parlato,   My secret . . . Oh, if she's talked,

Gli fo sposar la vecchia.   I'll make him marry that old woman.

SUSANNA (*aside*)

Marcellina!   Marcellina!

(*to the Count*)

Signor . . .   My lord . . .

COUNT (*in earnest*)

Cosa bramate?   What is it you want?

SUSANNA

Mi par che siate in collera!   You seem so angry!

COUNT

Volete qualche cosa?   Do you want something from me?

SUSANNA

Signor . . . la vostra sposa   My lord . . . my lady

Ha i soliti vapori,   Has the vapors, as usual,

E vi chiede il fiaschetto degli odori.   And needs your flask of smelling-salts.

COUNT

Prendete.   Just take it.

SUSANNA

Or vel riporto.   And I'll bring it right back.

COUNT

Eh, no: potete
Ritenerlo per voi.

Oh, no: You can
Keep it for yourself.

SUSANNA

Per me?
Questi non son mali
Da donne triviali.

For me?
But common girls
Don't have ailments like that.

COUNT

Un'amante che perde il caro sposo
Sul punto d'ottenerlo . . .

Even a girl who loses her bridegroom
Just before the wedding? . . .

SUSANNA

Pagando Marcellina
Con la dote che voi mi prometteste . . .

But if we pay back Marcellina
With the dowry you promised me . . .

COUNT

Ch'io vi promisi? Quando?

I promised you? When was that?

SUSANNA

Credea d'averlo inteso . . .

That's how I understood it . . .

COUNT

Sì, se voluto aveste
Intendermi voi stessa.

Well yes, if you'd cared
To understand me as well.

SUSANNA

È mio dovere;
E quel di sua Eccellenza è il mio volere.

It's my duty to do so;
And my lordship's wish is my command.

No. 16 Duet

COUNT

Crudel! Perché finora
Farmi languir così?

You cruel girl! Just why
Have you made me suffer like this?

SUSANNA

Signor, la donna ognora
Tempo ha di dir di sì.

My lord, there's always time
For a woman to say yes.

COUNT

Dunque, in giardin verrai?

So you'll come to the garden?

SUSANNA

Se piace a voi, verrò.

If that's what you want, I will.

COUNT

E non mi mancherai?

And you won't disappoint me?

SUSANNA

No, non vi mancherò.

No, I won't disappoint you.

COUNT (*aside*)

Mi sento dal contento
Pieno di gioia il cor.

I'm so happy I feel like
I'm bursting with joy.

SUSANNA (*aside*)

Scusatemi se mento,

Voi che intendete amor.

All those who know what true
love's about,
Forgive me for my lie.

Recitative

COUNT

E perché fosti meco
Stamattina sì austera?

But why were you so cold
To me this morning?

SUSANNA

Col paggio ch'ivi c'era . . .

With the page there and all . . .

COUNT

Ed a Basilio,
Che per me ti parlò . . .

And you were also mean to Basilio,
Who was speaking on my behalf . . .

SUSANNA

Ma qual bisogno
Abbiam noi che un Basilio . . .

But why do we need
Someone like Basilio . . .

COUNT

È vero, è vero.
E mi prometti, poi . . .
Se tu manchi, o cor mio . . . Ma la
Contessa
Attenderà il fiaschetto.

You're right, you're right.
So you promise me . . .
And if you disappoint me, my dear . . .
But the Countess
Is waiting for the flask.

SUSANNA

Eh, fu un pretesto:
Parlato io non avrei, senza di questo.

Oh, that was just an excuse:
I wouldn't have dared to speak to you
without one.

COUNT (*He takes her hand; she pulls back.*)

Carissima!   My darling!

SUSANNA

Vien gente.   Someone's coming.

COUNT (*aside*)

È mia senz'altro.   Now she's really mine.

SUSANNA (*aside*)

Forbitevi la bocca, o signor scaltro.   Wipe that smirk off your face, you sly old
                                        fox.

(*She tries to leave, and meets Figaro in the doorway.*)

SCENE III

The Count, Susanna and Figaro

FIGARO

Ehi, Susanna, ove vai?   Hey, Susanna, where are you going?

SUSANNA

Taci. Senza avvocato   Just keep quiet. Even without a lawyer
Hai già vinta la causa.   You've already won your case.

(*She goes off.*)

FIGARO

Cosa è nato?   Now what's happened?

(*He follows her.*)

SCENE IV

The Count alone

COUNT

No. 17 Recitative and Aria
Recitative

Hai già vinta la causa! Cosa sento!   You've already won your case? What's this
                                       I hear?

In qual laccio cadea! Perfidi! Io voglio   What trap did I fall into? Those traitors!
                                       They'll get

Di tal modo punirvi . . . A piacer mio   What they deserve . . . I'll decide

La sentenza sarà . . . Ma s'ei pagasse

La vecchia pretendente?

Pagarla! In qual maniera? . . . E poi v'è
Antonio

Che a un incognito Figaro ricusa

Di dare una nipote in matrimonio.

Coltivando l'orgoglio
Di questo mentecatto . . .

Tutto giova a un raggiro . . . Il colpo è
fatto!

The punishment myself . . . But what if
he pays off

The old woman?

Pay her off? But how could he? . . . And
then there's Antonio,

Who'll refuse to give his niece in
marriage

To someone like Figaro, whose past is a
mystery.

Now if I can just play up
To that moron . . .

Everything's falling into place . . . The die
is cast!

Aria

Vedrò, mentr'io sospiro,
Felice un servo mio?
E un ben che invan desio
Ei posseder dovrà?

Vedrò per man d'amore
Unita a un vile oggetto
Chi in me destò un affetto

Che per me poi non ha?
Ah, no! Lasciarti in pace

Non vo' questo contento!
Tu non nascesti, audace!
Per dare a me tormento!
E forse ancor per ridere
Di mia infelicità.
Già la speranza sola
Delle vendette mie
Quest'anima consola
E giubilar mi fa.

Shall I live to see a servant of mine
So happy, while I am left to sigh?
And possessing a treasure
That I desire in vain?

Shall I live to see the hand of love
Unite this good-for-nothing
To the one who arouses those
passions in me
That she doesn't feel herself?
Oh, no! I'll never give you the
satisfaction
Of getting what you want!
You weren't born, my bold one,
To cause me all this torment,
And maybe even to laugh
At my unhappiness.
The only hope I have left
Is my revenge,
Which consoles me
And makes me rejoice.

(He starts to leave, and meets Don Curzio.)

SCENE V

The Count, Marcellina, Figaro, Bartolo and Don Curzio; then Susanna

Recitative

DON CURZIO
(entering, to Marcellina, Bartolo and Figaro, who are following him)

È decisa la lite:	The case has just been settled:
«O pagarla, o sposarla». Ora ammutite.	"Either pay her, or marry her". Now everyone hold your peace.

MARCELLINA

Io respiro.	I can breathe again.

FIGARO

Ed io moro.	And I'm a goner.

MARCELLINA *(aside)*

Alfin sposa io sarò d'un uom che adoro.	I'm finally marrying the man I adore.

FIGARO *(to the Count)*

Eccellenza, m'appello . . .	My lord, I want to appeal . . .

COUNT

È giusta la sentenza:	The ruling is fair:
«O pagar, o sposar». Bravo Don Curzio.	"Either you pay up, or you marry her". Bravo, Don Curzio.

DON CURZIO

Bontà di sua Eccellenza.	Your lordship's much too kind!

BARTOLO

Che superba sentenza!	What a perfect ruling!

FIGARO

In che, superba?	And just why is it so perfect?

BARTOLO

Siam tutti vendicati.	Because we've all had our revenge.

FIGARO

Io non la sposerò.	Well, I'm not going to marry her.

BARTOLO

La sposerai.	Oh yes, you are.

243

Don Curzio

«O pagarla, o sposarla». Lei t'ha prestato

Duemila pezzi duri.

"Either you pay up, or you marry her".
She lent you

Two thousand crowns.

Figaro

Son gentiluomo, e senza
L'assenso de' miei nobili parenti . . .

But I'm a gentleman, and without
The consent of my noble parents . . .

Count

Dove sono? chi sono?

Where are they? Who are they?

Figaro

Lasciate ancor cercarli:
Dopo dieci anni io spero di trovarli.

I wish someone would find them:
For ten years now I've been looking for
them.

Bartolo

Qualche bambin trovato? . . .

So they left you on the doorstep? . . .

Figaro

No, perduto, dottor; anzi rubato.

No, my good doctor, I was lost; or rather,
I was kidnapped.

Count

Come?

How's that?

Marcellina

Cosa?

What's this?

Bartolo

La prova?

But where's the proof?

Don Curzio

Il testimonio?

And were there any witnesses?

Figaro

L'oro, le gemme e i ricamati panni,

Che ne' più teneri anni
Mi ritrovaro addosso i masnadieri,

Sono gl'indizi veri
Di mia nascita illustre; e sopra tutto
Questo al mio braccio impresso
   geroglifico.

The gold, the jewels and the embroidered
   clothes,
Which the robbers found on me
When they kidnapped me as a young
   child,
Are the real proof
Of my noble birth; and what's more,
There's this birthmark on my arm.

MARCELLINA

Una spatola impressa al braccio destro . . .

A strawberry birthmark on your right arm . . .

FIGARO

E a voi chi 'l disse?

And who told you about it?

MARCELLINA

Oddio!
È egli . . .

Oh, my God!
It's him . . .

FIGARO

È ver, son io.

You're right, it's me.

DON CURZIO

Chi?

Who?

COUNT

Chi?

Who?

BARTOLO

Chi?

Who?

MARCELLINA

Raffaello.

It's Raffaello.

BARTOLO

E i ladri ti rapir? . . .

And the robbers kidnapped you?

FIGARO

Presso un castello.

Near a castle.

BARTOLO

Ecco tua madre.

This is your mother.

FIGARO

Balia . . .

My nurse-maid . . .

BARTOLO

No, tua madre.

No, your mother.

COUNT and DON CURZIO

Sua madre?

His mother!

FIGARO

Cosa sento!

What's this I hear?

245

MARCELLINA

Ecco tuo padre.   And this is your father.

(She runs up to Figaro and embraces him.)

No. 18 Sextet

Riconosci in questo amplesso   My long-lost son, embrace me
Una madre, amato figlio.   As your adoring mother.

FIGARO (to Bartolo)

Padre mio, fate lo stesso: My father, you embrace me, too,
Non mi fate più arrossir.   And don't make me blush with
                                                             shame.

BARTOLO (embracing Figaro)

Resistenza la coscienza   My conscience won't let me
Far non lascia al tuo desir.   Refuse what you ask.

DON CURZIO (aside)

Ei suo padre, ella sua madre: If he's his father, and she's his
                                                             mother,
L'imeneo non può seguir.   The wedding can't take place.

COUNT (aside)

Son smarrito, son stordito: I'm astounded and bewildered:
Meglio è assai di qua partir.   And I think it's best to get out of
                                                             here.

MARCELLINA

Figlio amato!   My beloved son!

BARTOLO

Figlio amato!   My beloved son!

FIGARO

Parenti amati!   And my beloved parents!

(The Count goes to leave; Susanna stops him, as she enters with a purse in her hand.)

SUSANNA

Alto, alto, signor Conte: Just a moment, if you please, my
                                                             lord:

Mille doppie son qui pronte.   I've got a thousand double crowns
                                                             in here.

A pagar vengo per Figaro,   I've come to pay for Figaro,
Ed a porlo in libertà.   And set him free for good.

COUNT and DON CURZIO

Non sappiam com'è la cosa:	We're not sure what's going on:
Osservate un poco là.	And now look over there.

(Susanna turns around and sees Figaro embracing Marcellina. She makes as if to leave.)

SUSANNA

Già d'accordo colla sposa:	He's already made peace with his bride:
Giusto ciel, che infedeltà!	My God, how fickle he is!

(to Figaro)

Lascia, iniquo!	Leave her alone, you vile creature!

FIGARO *(He tries to hold her back; she struggles.)*

No, t'arresta.	No, wait.
Senti, o cara.	And hear me out, my darling.

SUSANNA *(slapping him)*

Senti questa.	And you hear this!

FIGARO, BARTOLO and MARCELLINA

È un effetto di buon core:	It's all because her heart's so full:
Tutto amore è quel che fa.	She did it out of love.

COUNT and DON CURZIO

Frem $\left\{{o \atop e}\right.$ smani $\left\{{o \atop a}\right.$ dal furore:	$\left.{I'm \atop He's}\right\}$ trembling and seething with rage:
Il destino $\left\{{\text{me la} \atop \text{gliela}}\right.$ fa.	$\left.{My \atop His}\right\}$ fate has done $\left\{{me \atop him}\right.$ in.

SUSANNA

Fremo, smanio dal furore,	I'm trembling and seething with rage:
Una vecchia me la fa.	That old woman has done me in.

MARCELLINA *(to Susanna)*

Lo sdegno calmate,	Now calm yourself,
Mia cara figliuola,	My darling daughter,
Sua madre abbracciate,	And come and embrace his mother,
Che vostra or sarà.	For I'll soon be yours as well.

(She runs to embrace Susanna.)

SUSANNA

Sua madre?   His mother?

ALL

Sua madre.   His mother.

FIGARO

E quello è mio padre,   And here's my father,
Che a te lo dirà.   He'll tell you so himself.

SUSANNA

Suo padre?   His father?

ALL

Suo padre.   His father.

FIGARO

E quella è mia madre,   And here's my mother,
Che a te lo dirà.   She'll tell you so herself.

(All four run to embrace each other.)

SUSANNA, FIGARO, MARCELLINA and BARTOLO

Al dolce contento   This heart of mine
Di questo momento,   Can hardly bear
Quest'anima appena   The sweet happiness
Resistere or sa.   Of this moment.

COUNT and DON CURZIO

Al fiero tormento   This heart of mine
Di questo momento,   Can hardly bear
Quest'anima appena   The fierce torment
Resistere or sa.   Of this moment.

(The Count and Don Curzio go off.)

SCENE VI

Susanna, Marcellina, Figaro and Bartolo

Recitative

MARCELLINA (*to Bartolo*)

Eccovi, o caro amico, il dolce frutto   And there, my dear friend, is the sweet
                                              fruit
Dell'antico amor nostro . . .   Of our young love . . .

248

BARTOLO

Or non parliamo
Di fatti sì remoti. Egli è mio figlio:

Mia consorte voi siete;
E le nozze farem quando volete.

Now let's not talk
About things that happened so long ago.
He's my son:

And you're my wife;
We'll be married as soon as you please.

MARCELLINA

Oggi, e doppie saranno.

Today, and it'll be a double wedding.

(to Figaro, giving him the contract)

Prendi, questo è il biglietto
Del danar che a me devi; ed è tua dote.

Take this, it's the contract
For the money you owe me; I want it to
be your dowry.

SUSANNA *(throwing down the purse of money)*

Prendi ancor questa borsa.

Take this purse, too.

BARTOLO *(doing the same)*

E questa ancora.

And this as well.

FIGARO

Bravi: gettate pur, ch'io piglio ognora.

Fine! I'll take as much of it as I can.

SUSANNA

Voliamo ad informar d'ogni avventura

Madama e nostro zio.
Chi al par di me contento?

Now let's run and tell my lady and my
uncle
About everything that's happened.
Who could be happier than I am?

FIGARO

Io.

Me!

BARTOLO

Io.

Me!

MARCELLINA

Io.

Me!

SUSANNA, FIGARO, MARCELLINA and BARTOLO

E schiatti il signor Conte al gusto mio!

And the Count can explode, for all I care!

(They go off arm in arm.)

Scene VII

Barbarina and Cherubino

Barbarina

Andiamo, andiam, bel paggio: in casa mia

Tutte ritroverai
Le più belle ragazze del castello.
Di tutte sarai tu certo più bello.

Come on now, my dear little page: At my house
You'll find
All the prettiest girls in the castle.
And you'll certainly be the prettiest of all.

Cherubino

Ah! Se il Conte mi trova,
Misero me! Tu sai
Che partito ei mi crede per Siviglia.

Oh! If the Count should ever find me,
I'll really be in trouble! You know
That he thinks I've left for Seville.

Barbarina

Oh, ve' che maraviglia! E se ti trova,

Non sarà cosa nuova.
Odi, vogliam vestirti come noi:

Tutte insieme andrem poi
A presentar de' fiori a Madamina.
Fidati, o Cherubin, di Barbarina.

How silly you are! Even if he does find you,
It won't be anything new.
Now listen, we want to dress you up like one of us:
And then we'll all go together
To present a bunch of flowers to my lady.
Just leave everything to your Barbarina.

(They go off.)

Scene VIII

The Countess alone

Countess

No. 19 Recitative and Aria
Recitative

E Susanna non vien! Son ansiosa

Di saper come il Conte
Accolse la proposta. Alquanto ardito

Il progetto mi par; e ad uno sposo
Sì vivace e geloso . . .
Ma che mal c'è? Cangiando i miei vestiti

And Susanna still hasn't come! I'm anxious
To know how the Count
Reacted to her proposal. The whole plan seems
A bit risky to me; and with a husband
So impulsive and jealous . . .
But what's the harm in it? I'm just changing clothes

Con quelli di Susanna, e i suoi co'
   miei . . .
Al favor della notte . . . O cielo! A quale

Umil stato fatale io son ridotta
Da un consorte crudel; che, dopo avermi,
Con un misto inaudito
D'infedeltà, di gelosie, di sdegni,
Prima amata, indi offesa, e alfin tradita,
Fammi or cercar da una mia serva aita!

With Susanna, and she's changing hers
   with me . . .
Under cover of night . . . Heavens!
   What a
Pathetic state I've been reduced to
By such a cruel husband;
With an unheard-of mixture
Of unfaithfulness, jealousy, and disdain,
First he loved me, then he insulted me,
And finally he betrayed me.
Now he's forcing me to get help from my
   maid!

Aria

Dove sono i bei momenti

Di dolcezza e di piacer,
Dove andaro i giuramenti
Di quel labbro menzogner?

Perchè mai, se in pianti e in pene

Per me tutto si cangiò,
La memoria di quel bene
Dal mio sen non trapassò?

Ah! se almen la mia costanza
Nel languire amando ognor
Mi portasse una speranza
Di cangiar l'ingrato cor.

Where are those cherished
   moments
Of sweetness and pleasure?
Where have they gone,
The vows he so deceitfully made?

Why then, when everything's
   changed
Into tears and pain for me,
Has the memory of that happiness
Never left my breast?

Ah! If only my devotion
In longing for his love
Could give me some hope
Of changing his ungrateful heart.

(She goes off.)

SCENE IX

The Count and Antonio

Recitative

ANTONIO *(with a hat in his hand)*

Io vi dico, signor, che Cherubino
È ancora nel castello:
E vedete per prova il suo cappello.

I'm telling you, my lord, Cherubino
Is still in the castle:
And here's his hat to prove it.

COUNT

Ma come, se a quest'ora
Esser giunto a Siviglia egli dovria?

But how could that be? By now
He should be in Seville.

ANTONIO

Scusate, oggi Siviglia è a casa mia.

Pardon me, but today Seville's at my
house.

Là vestissi da donna, e là lasciati
Ha gli altri abiti suoi.

He's been dressed up as girl there,
And he's left his own clothes, too.

COUNT

Perfidi!

Those traitors!

ANTONIO

Andiam, e li vedrete voi.

Just come and see for yourself.

(*They go off.*)

SCENE X

The Countess and Susanna

COUNTESS

Cosa mi narri! E che ne disse, il Conte?

What's this you're telling me! And what
did the Count have to say?

SUSANNA

Gli si leggeva in fronte
Il dispetto e la rabbia.

You could see by his face
How upset and angry he was.

COUNTESS

Piano: ché meglio or lo porremo in
gabbia.
Dov'è l'appuntamento
Che tu gli proponesti?

Wait though: It's much easier to catch
him now.
Where did you arrange
To meet him?

SUSANNA

In giardino.

In the garden.

COUNTESS

Fissiamgli un loco. Scrivi.

Let's decide on a definite place. You write
him a note.

SUSANNA

Ch'io scriva . . . Ma, signora . . .

Me write him a note . . . But, my lady . . .

COUNTESS

Eh, scrivi, dico; e tutto	Just write to him, I say;
Io prendo su me stessa.	And I'll take it all upon myself.

(Susanna sits down to write.)

Canzonetta sull'aria . . .	A little song on the air . . .

SUSANNA

Sull'aria . . .	On the air . . .

No. 20 Duet

COUNTESS (*dictating*)

«Che soave zeffiretto . . .»	"What a gentle breeze . . ."

SUSANNA (*repeating the Countess' words*)

Zeffiretto . . .	Breeze . . .

COUNTESS (*as before*)

«Questa sera spirerà . . .»	"There'll be this evening . . ."

SUSANNA (*as before*)

Questa sera spirerà . . .	There'll be this evening . . .

COUNTESS (*as before*)

«Sotto i pini del boschetto».	"Beneath the whispering pines".

SUSANNA (*asking her*)

Sotto i pini?	Beneath the pines?

(writing)

Sotto i pini del boschetto.	Beneath the whispering pines.

COUNTESS

Ei già il resto capirà.	And the rest he'll understand.

SUSANNA

Certo, certo: il capirà.	Of course: he'll understand.

(They read the letter over together.)

Recitative

SUSANNA

Piegato è il foglio . . . Or come si sigilla?	I've folded up the letter . . . Now how do we seal it?

COUNTESS (*She takes out a pin and gives it to her.*)

Ecco, prendi una spilla:	Here, take this pin:
Servirà di sigillo. Attendi . . . scrivi	It'll serve as a seal. No, wait . . . write
Sul riverso del foglio:	On the back of the letter:
«Rimandate il sigillo».	"Send back the seal".

SUSANNA

È più bizzarro	It's stranger
Di quel della patente.	Than the one on the commission.

COUNTESS

Presto, nascondi . . . Io sento venir gente.	Quick, hide it . . . I can hear some people coming.

(*Susanna puts the note in her bosom.*)

SCENE XI

The Countess, Susanna, Barbarina, Cherubino and peasant girls
(Enter several peasant girls with bunches of flowers, led
by Barbarina. Among them is Cherubino dressed like them.)

No. 21 Chorus

CHORUS

Ricevete, o padroncina,	My dear mistress, please accept
Queste rose e questi fior,	These roses and these flowers,
Che abbiam colto stamattina	Which we picked this very morning
Per mostrarvi il nostro amor.	To show you our affection.
Siamo tante contadine,	We're only simple peasant girls,
E siam tutte poverine:	And we're all so very poor;
Ma quel poco che rechiamo	But the little we possess
Ve lo diamo di buon cor.	We give you from our hearts.

Recitative

BARBARINA

Queste sono, Madama,	These, my lady, are
Le ragazze del loco,	The girls from the village,
Che il poco ch'han vi vengono ad offrire,	Who've come to offer what little they have,
E vi chiedon perdon del loro ardire.	And beg your pardon for being so bold.

COUNTESS

Oh, brave! Vi ringrazio.　　　　　　　Oh, how kind! I thank you.

SUSANNA

Come sono vezzose!　　　　　　　And how pretty they all are!

COUNTESS (*pointing to Cherubino*)

　　　　E chi è, narratemi,　　　　　　　　　　　Now tell me,
Quell'amabil fanciulla　　　　　　　Who's that sweet little girl
Ch'ha l'aria sì modesta?　　　　　　With such a modest air?

BARBARINA

Ell'è una mia cugina, e per le nozze　　　She's a cousin of mine who arrived
È venuta ier sera.　　　　　　　　Last night for the wedding.

COUNTESS

Onoriamo la bella forastiera.　　　　Well then, let's honor our pretty guest.

(*to Cherubino*)

Venite qui . . . datemi i vostri fiori.　　　Come over here . . . and let me have your
　　　　　　　　　　　　　　　flowers.

(*She takes the flowers from Cherubino, and kisses him on the forehead. Then, aside*)

Come arrossì!　　　　　　　　　How she blushes!

(*to Susanna*)

　　　Susanna, e non ti pare　　　　　　　　Susanna, doesn't she
Che somigli ad alcuno?　　　　　　Remind you of someone?

SUSANNA

　　Al naturale . . .　　　　　　　　　The spitting image . . .

SCENE XII

The Countess, Susanna, Barbarina, Cherubino, the Count and Antonio

(*Enter the Count and Antonio. The latter is carrying Cherubino's hat: He enters very quietly, pulls the
girl's cap off Cherubino's head, and puts the hat on him instead.*)

ANTONIO

Eh, cospettaccio! È questi l'uffiziale.　　　Well, I'll be . . . ! There's your officer.

COUNTESS (*aside*)

Oh, stelle!　　　　　　　　　　Oh, my heavens!

SUSANNA (*aside*)

Malandrino!

Oh, that rascal!

COUNT (*to the Countess*)

Ebben! Madama . . .

Well, madam? . . .

COUNTESS

Io sono, o signor mio,
Irritata e sorpresa al par di voi.

My lord, I'm just as
Annoyed and surprised as you are.

COUNT

Ma stamane?

But what about this morning?

COUNTESS

Stamane . . .
Per l'odierna festa
Volevam travestirlo al modo stesso
Che l'han vestito adesso.

This morning . . .
For today's festivities
We wanted to dress him up the same way
They've dressed him now.

COUNT (*to Cherubino*)

E perché non partiste?

And why didn't you leave?

CHERUBINO (*tearing his hat off his head*)

Signor . . .

My lord . . .

COUNT

Saprò punire
La sua disobbedienza.

You'll be punished
For not obeying your orders.

BARBARINA

Eccellenza, Eccellenza,
Voi mi dite sì spesso,
Qual volta m'abbracciate e mi baciate:
«Barbarina, se m'ami,
Ti darò quel che brami».

Oh, my lordship,
How often you've said,
When you're hugging and kissing me:
"Barbarina, if you'll just love me,
I'll give you whatever you want".

COUNT

Io, dissi questo?

I said that?

BARBARINA

Voi.
Or datemi, padrone,
In sposo Cherubino,
E v'amerò com'amo il mio gattino.

Yes, you did.
Oh master, if you give me
Cherubino for a husband,
I'll love you as much as my kitten.

COUNTESS (*to the Count*)

Ebbene: or tocca a voi . . .   Well then . . . now it's up to you . . .

ANTONIO (*to Barbarina*)

Brava figliuola!   Good girl!
Hai buon maestro che ti fa la scuola.   You've learned your lesson well.

COUNT (*aside*)

Non so qual uom, qual demone, qual Dio   I'd like to know what man or demon or god

Rivolga tutto quanto a torto mio.   Has turned everything against me.

SCENE XIII

The Countess, Susanna, Barbarina, Cherubino, peasant girls, the Count, Antonio and Figaro

FIGARO (*entering*)

Signor . . . se trattenete   My lord . . . if you keep
Tutte queste ragazze,   All these girls here,
Addio festa . . . addio danza . . .   That's the end of the feast . . . the end of the dancing . . .

COUNT

E che! Vorresti   What's this!
Ballar col piè stravolto?   So you think you can dance with a twisted ankle?

FIGARO

(*He pretends to stretch his leg, and then tries a few steps.*)

Eh, non mi duol più molto.   Oh, it really doesn't hurt much anymore.

(*He calls all the girls, and starts to leave; the Count calls him back.*)

Andiam, belle fanciulle . . .   Let's go, my pretty ones . . .

COUNTESS (*sottovoce to Susanna*)

Come si caverà dall'imbarazzo?   Now how's he going to get out of this?

SUSANNA (*sottovoce to the Countess*)

Lasciate fare a lui.   Just leave it to him.

COUNT

Per buona sorte   Luckily the flowerpots
I vasi eran di creta.   Were made of clay.

FIGARO

Senza fallo.　　　　　　　　　　　　That's right.
Andiamo, dunque, andiamo.　　　　　Come along now, let's get going.

(*He starts to leave; Antonio calls him back.*)

ANTONIO

E intanto, a cavallo,　　　　　　　And meanwhile the page
Di galoppo a Siviglia andava il paggio.　　　Was galloping off to Seville.

FIGARO

Di galoppo o di passo . . . buon viaggio.　　Galloping or trotting . . . well, good luck
　　　　　　　　　　　　　　　　　to him!

(*as he is about to leave*)

Venite, belle giovani.　　　　　　Come on then, girls.

COUNT (*bringing him back again*)

E a te la sua patente　　　　　　And his commission
Era in tasca rimasta . . .　　　　Somehow stayed in your pocket . . .

FIGARO

Certamente.　　　　　　　　　　　　　　But of course.
Che razza di domande!　　　　　　What a question!

ANTONIO (*to Susanna, who is making signs to Figaro*)

Via, non fargli più motti: ei non t'intende.　　Don't bother making signs to him: He
　　　　　　　　　　　　　　　　　can't understand what you mean.

(*He takes Cherubino by the hand and presents him to Figaro.*)

Ed ecco chi pretende　　　　　　And here's the fellow
Che sia un bugiardo, il mio signor nipote.　　Who'll make a liar out of you, my dear
　　　　　　　　　　　　　　　　　nephew.

FIGARO

Cherubino!　　　　　　　　　　　Cherubino!

ANTONIO

Or ci sei.　　　　　　　　　　　Now you're in for it.

FIGARO (*to the Count*)

Che diamin canta?　　　　　What the devil's he trying to say?

COUNT

Non canta, no, ma dice　　　　He's not trying to say anything, he's just
　　　　　　　　　　　　　　　told me

Ch'egli saltò stamane in sui garofani . . .	That the boy jumped out on his carnations this morning . . .

FIGARO

Ei lo dice! . . . Sarà . . . Se ho saltato io,	He says that! . . . Well, maybe so . . . If I jumped out,
Si può dare che anch'esso	It's just possible
Abbia fatto lo stesso.	He did the same.

COUNT

Anch'esso?	He, too?

FIGARO

Perché no?	Why not?
Io non impugno mai quel che non so.	I never dispute what I don't know.

No. 22 Finale

(A Spanish march is heard in the distance.)

Ecco la marcia . . . andiamo.	There's the march . . . now let's go.
A' vostri posti, o belle, a' vostri posti.	My pretty ones, take your places.
Susanna, dammi il braccio.	And Susanna, give me your arm.

SUSANNA

Eccolo.	Here I am.

(Figaro takes Antonio by one arm and Susanna by the other, and they all go off, except the Count and Countess.)

COUNT (aside)

Temerari!	They're just shameless!

COUNTESS (aside)

Io son di ghiaccio.	And I feel like I'm made of ice.

(The march gets gradually louder.)

COUNT

Contessa . . .	My lady . . .

COUNTESS

Or non parliamo.	Let's not say anything now.
Ecco qui le due nozze:	Here come the two happy couples:
Riceverle dobbiam; alfin si tratta	We've got to receive them well; and at least
D'una vostra protetta.	One of them's your ward.
Seggiamo.	Let's just go and sit down.

COUNT

Seggiamo.   Yes, let's just go and sit down.

(aside)

E meditiam vendetta.   And meditate on our revenge.

(They sit.)

SCENE XIV

The Count, the Countess, Figaro, Susanna, Bartolo, Marcellina,
Cherubino, Barbarina, peasant girls, villagers and hunters

(Enter hunters with rifles on their shoulders; lawyers; peasant men and women; two young girls
carrying a bridal head-dress with white feathers; two more with a white veil; two more with gloves and
a bouquet of flowers; two more girls carrying a similar head-dress for Susanna, etc.; Figaro with
Marcellina; Bartolo with Susanna; Antonio, Barbarina, etc.; Bartolo leads Susanna up to the Count,
and she kneels down to receive the head-dress from him, etc.; Figaro leads Marcellina up to the
Countess, and does the same.)

TWO PEASANT WOMEN

Amanti costanti,   Come, all faithful lovers,
Seguaci d'onor,   And those in honor bound,
Cantate, lodate   Join us in singing the praises
Sì saggio signor.   Of a wise and noble lord.

A un dritto cedendo   In renouncing a right
Che oltraggia, che offende,   That insults and offends,
Ei caste vi rende   He has kept you chaste
Ai vostri amator.   For the ones you adore.

CHORUS

Cantiamo, lodiamo   Join us in singing the praises
Sì saggio signor.   Of a wise and noble lord.

(Susanna, who remains kneeling during the duet, plucks the Count's sleeve, and shows him the note;
then she puts the hand nearest to the audience to her head, while the Count, who is pretending to
adjust her head-dress, takes the note from her. The Count puts it furtively in his breast. Susanna rises,
and curtsys to him: Figaro comes forward to receive her; and they begin to dance the fandango.
Marcellina rises a little later: Bartolo comes forward to receive her from the hands of the Countess.
The Count stands aside, takes out the note, and seems to prick his finger: He shakes it, and squeezes
it, and sucks it; then he sees that the note has been sealed with the pin, which he throws to the
ground as he speaks. Meanwhile the orchestra is playing very softly.)

COUNT

Eh, già, si sa; solita usanza: Oh yes, of course; as usual,

Le donne ficcan gli aghi in ogni loco . . .	Women have to stick their pins wherever possible . . .
Ah! Ah! Capisco il gioco.	Ha, ha! Now I get the point.

FIGARO (*who has seen it all, to Susanna*)

Un biglietto amoroso	It's just a love letter
Che gli diè nel passar qualche galante;	That some lady gave him in passing;
Ed era sigillato d'una spilla	It must've been sealed with a pin,
Ond'egli si punse il dito;	And now he's pricked his finger.

(*The Count reads the note and kisses it, looks for the pin, finds it, and puts it in the cuff of his sleeve.*)

Il narciso or la cerca. Oh, che stordito!	Our little Narcissus is trying to find it. Oh, how stupid he is!

COUNT

(*Recitative*)

Andate, amici! E sia per questa sera	Go now, my good friends! And let all the
Disposto l'apparato nuziale	Arrangements for the wedding this evening
Colla più ricca pompa. Io vo' che sia	Be made with the greatest of splendor. I want this celebration
Magnifica la festa; e canti e fochi,	To be magnificent; with songs and fireworks,
E gran cena e gran ballo. E ognuno impari	And a great banquet and ball. So each of you will know
Com'io tratto color che a me son cari.	How I treat those who are dear to me.

(*The chorus and march are repeated, and everyone goes off.*)

CHORUS

Amanti costanti,	Come, all faithful lovers,
Seguaci d'onor,	And those in honor bound,
Cantate, lodate	Join us in singing the praises
Sì saggio signor.	Of a wise and noble lord.
A un dritto cedendo	In renouncing a right
Che oltraggia, che offende,	That insults and offends,
Ei caste vi rende	He has kept you chaste
Ai vostri amator.	For the ones you adore.
Cantiamo, lodiamo	Join us in singing the praises
Sì saggio signor.	Of a wise and noble lord.

End of Act Three

ACT FOUR

A lush garden with two arbors to the right and left. Night.

SCENE I

Barbarina alone

BARBARINA
(carrying a paper lantern and looking for something on the ground)

No. 23 Cavatina

L'ho perduta . . . me meschina! . . .	I've lost it . . . oh, dear me! . . .
Ah, chi sa dove sarà?	Oh, wherever can it be?
Non la trovo . . . E mia cugina . . .	I can't find it . . . And my cousin . . .
E il padron, cosa dirà?	And the master, what will he say?

SCENE II

Barbarina, Figaro and Marcellina

Recitative

FIGARO *(entering with Marcellina)*

Barbarina, cos'hai?	Barbarina, what's the matter?

BARBARINA

L'ho perduta, cugino.	I've gone and lost it, cousin.

FIGARO

Cosa?	What?

MARCELLINA

Cosa?	What?

BARBARINA

La spilla	The pin
Che a me diede il padrone	The master gave me
Per recar a Susanna.	To take back to Susanna.

FIGARO

A Susanna? la spilla?	To Susanna? What pin?

(angrily)

E così tenerella . . .	And at such a tender age,
Il mestiere già sai . . .	You're already learning . . .

(quietly)

Di far tutto sì bien quel che tu fai?	To do everything as well as you do?

BARBARINA

Cos'è? vai meco in collera?	What's wrong? Are you angry with me?

FIGARO

E non vedi ch'io scherzo? osserva . . .	Can't you see that I'm joking? Look here . . .

(He searches the ground for a moment, after adroitly removing a pin from Marcellina's dress or cap, and gives it to Barbarina.)

Questa	This
È la spilla che il Conte	Is the pin that the Count
Da recare ti diede alla Susanna,	Gave you to take back to Susanna.
E servia di sigillo a un bigliettino.	And it was used to seal a little note.
Vedi s'io sono istrutto.	As you can see, I know all about it.

BARBARINA

E perché il chiedi a me, quando sai tutto?	So why are you asking me, if you already know everything?

FIGARO

Avea gusto d'udir come il padrone	I just wanted to hear my lord's
Ti diè la commissione.	Exact instructions.

BARBARINA

Che miracoli!	Oh, is that all?
«Tieni, fanciulla, reca questa spilla	"Come here, my girl, and take this pin
Alla bella Susanna, e dille: "Questo	To my pretty little Susanna, and tell her: 'This
È il sigillo de' pini"».	Is the seal of the pines' ".

FIGARO

Ah, Ah! de' pini!	Aha! The pines!

BARBARINA

È ver ch'ei mi soggiunse:	That's right, and then he added:
«Guarda che alcun non veda»;	"Make sure that no one sees you";
Ma tu, già, tacerai.	But you won't tell on me, will you?

FIGARO

Sicuramente.   No, of course I won't.

BARBARINA

A te, già, niente preme.   And it's no concern of yours.

FIGARO

Oh, niente, niente.   Of course not.

BARBARINA

Addio, mio bel cugino: Well, good-bye now, my dear cousin:
Vò da Susanna e poi da Cherubino.   I must find Susanna and then Cherubino.

(*She skips off.*)

SCENE III

Figaro and Marcellina

FIGARO (*dumbstruck*)

Madre.   Mother!

MARCELLINA

Figlio.   My dearest son!

FIGARO

Son morto.   I'm done for.

MARCELLINA

Càlmati, figlio mio.   Now just calm down, my son.

FIGARO

Son morto, dico.   I'm done for, I tell you.

MARCELLINA

Flemma, flemma, e poi flemma: il fatto è   Whatever you do, you must have
  serio,   patience: I know it's serious,
E pensarci convien. Ma guarda un poco   And requires a lot of thought. But do you
                                               realize
Che ancor non sai di chi si prenda gioco.   That you don't even know who the joke
                                               is really on?

FIGARO

Ah! quella spilla, o madre, è quella stessa   Oh no, my dearest mother, that's the very
                                               same pin
Che poc'anzi ei raccolse.   He was just looking for.

MARCELLINA

È ver . . . Ma questo
Al più ti porge un dritto
Di stare in guardia e vivere in sospetto:
Ma non sai se in effetto . . .

That's true . . . At most
This will keep you on your guard
And heighten your suspicions:
But you don't know if they actually . . .

FIGARO

All'erta, dunque: il loco del congresso
So dov'è stabilito.

On guard, then: At least I know
Where they've agreed to meet.

(*He starts to leave.*)

MARCELLINA

Dove vai, figlio mio?

But where are you going, my son?

FIGARO

A vendicar tutti i mariti. Addio.

To avenge all good husbands. Good-bye.

(*He goes off in a fury.*)

SCENE IV

Marcellina alone

MARCELLINA

Presto, avvertiam Susanna . . .
Io la credo innocente: quella faccia . . .
Quell'aria di modestia . . . È caso ancora
Ch'ella non fosse . . . Ah! quando il cor
   non ci arma
Personale interesse,
Ogni donna è portata alla difesa
Del suo povero sesso,

Da questi uomini ingrati a torto oppresso.

Quick, let me warn Susanna . . .
I'm sure she's innocent: That face . . .
That modest air . . . But then again,
Supposing she's not . . . Ah! when
   personal interest
Doesn't harden our hearts,
Every woman's inclined
To come to the defense of her own poor
   sex,
So wrongly oppressed by these ungrateful
   men.

No. 24 Aria

Il capro e la capretta
Son sempre in amistà;
L'agnello all'agnelletta
La guerra mai non fa;

The billy and the nanny-goat
Are always the best of friends:
And the ram would never wage war
On the helpless ewe.

Le più feroci belve	The most ferocious beasts
Per selve e per campagne	In the woods or on the plains
Lascian le lor compagne	Are content to leave their mates
In pace e libertà.	In peace and liberty.
Sol noi, povere femmine,	It's only us poor women,
Che tanto amiam questi uomini,	Though we dote so on our men,
Trattate siam dai perfidi	Who are treated so very cruelly
Ognor con crudeltà.	And betrayed by all of them.

(She goes off.)

SCENE V

Barbarina alone

Recitative

BARBARINA *(carrying fruit and cakes)*

«Nel padiglione a manca», ei così disse.	"In the arbor on the left", I think he said.
È questo, è questo . . . E poi, se non venisse?	Yes, this is it . . . But what if he doesn't come?
Ah, ah, che brava gente! A stento darmi	Oh, what a generous lot they are! I could hardly get them
Un arancio, una pera e una ciambella.	To give me an orange, a pear and a piece of cake.
«Per chi, madamigella?»	"And who's this for, my dear?"
«Oh, per qualcun, signore!»	"Oh, just for someone I know, kind sir!"
«Già lo sappiam». Ebbene:	"Yes, I know that". Oh well:
Il padron l'odia, ed io gli voglio bene!	My master hates him, and I love him so!
Però costommi un bacio . . . E cosa importa?	But it cost me a kiss . . . And what does it matter?
Forse qualcun mel renderà . . .	Maybe somebody will give me one back . . .

(She hears someone coming.)

Son morta!	I'm in for it now!

(She runs and hides in the arbor on the left.)

SCENE VI

Figaro; then Bartolo, Basilio and workers

FIGARO *(alone with a cape and a lantern)*

È Barbarina . . .	It's Barbarina . . .

266

(*He hears people coming.*)

Chi va là?	Who's there?

BASILIO (*entering with Bartolo and a group of workers*)

Son quelli	You asked us to come,
Che invitasti a venir.	And here we are.

BARTOLO

Che brutto ceffo!	What a frown you've got on your face!
Sembri un cospirator. Che diamin sono	You look like a conspirator. And why the devil
Quegli infausti apparati?	All these strange preparations?

FIGARO

Lo vedrete tra poco.	You'll find out soon enough.
In questo stesso loco	On this very spot
Celebrerem la festa	We're going to celebrate the union
Della mia sposa onesta	Of my virtuous bride
E del feudal signor . . .	And the lord of the manor . . .

BASILIO

Ah, buono, buono!	Oh, so that's what it is!
Capisco come egli è.	Now I see how things stand.

(*aside*)

Accordati si son senza di me.	They've worked it out by themselves.

FIGARO

Voi da questi contorni	You there, just stay
Non vi scostate. Intanto	Near at hand. Meanwhile
Io vado a dar certi ordini	I'm going to give some instructions
E torno in pochi istanti:	And I'll be back in just a few moments:
A un fischio mio correte tutti quanti.	And when I whistle, I want you all to come running.

(*They all go off, except for Bartolo and Basilio.*)

SCENE VII

Bartolo and Basilio

BASILIO

Ha i diavoli nel corpo.	He's out of his mind.

BARTOLO

Ma cosa nacque?	But what's going on?

BASILIO

Nulla:	Nothing.
Susanna piace al Conte. Ella, d'accordo,	The Count likes our Susanna. She's agreed
Gli diè un appuntamento	To meet him here,
Ch'a Figaro non piace.	And Figaro doesn't like it one bit.

BARTOLO

E che, dunque: dovria soffrirlo in pace?	And he's supposed to put up with it and not say a thing?

BASILIO

Quel che soffrono tanti	When so many others have put up with such nonsense,
Ei soffrir non potrebbe? E poi, sentite:	Why shouldn't he put up with it, too? And then, listen:
Che guadagno può far? Nel mondo, amico,	What would he stand to gain? In this world, my friend,
L'accozzarla co' grandi	It's always been dangerous
Fu pericolo ognora:	To clash with the powerful few:
Dàn novanta per cento, e han vinto ancora.	They give you ninety percent, and they've still won over you.

No. 25 Aria

In quegli anni in cui val poco	In those years when inexperienced reason
La mal pratica ragion,	Is of little or no avail,
Ebbi anch'io lo stesso fuoco:	I too was impulsive and headstrong:
Fui quel pazzo ch'or non son.	I was just as big a fool.
Ma col tempo e coi perigli	But with time no less than dangers,
Donna flemma capitò;	Mistress Mindful at last appeared,
E i capricci ed i puntigli	And drove all fancies and spite
Dalla testa mi cavò.	Right out of my silly head.
Presso un picciolo abituro	One day she led me
Seco lei mi trasse un giorno;	To a little hut;
E, togliendo giù dal muro	And as she took down from the wall
Del pacifico soggiorno	Of that quiet little place
Una pelle di somaro:	The hide of a donkey, she said:
«Prendi», disse, «o figlio caro!»	"Take this, my dear son!"
Poi disparve, e mi lasciò.	And then disappeared, and left me.

Mentre ancor, tacito,	While I was staring silently
Guardo quel dono,	At her gift,
Il ciel s'annuvola,	The sky had clouded over;
Rimbomba il tuono,	The thunder was crashing,
Mista alla grandine	And mixed with hail,
Scroscia la piova:	The rain was pouring down:
Ecco, le membra	So I managed
Coprir mi giova	To cover my limbs
Col manto d'asino	With the donkey's hide
Che mi donò.	She gave me.
Finisce il turbine,	The storm was over,
Né fo due passi,	And I had just set forth,
Che fiera orribile	When a horrible beast
Dianzi a me fassi:	Appeared in my path:
Già già mi tocca,	As its greedy jaws
L'ingorda bocca;	Reached out for me,
Già di difendermi	I lost all hope
Speme non ho.	Of defending myself.
Ma il fiuto ignobile	But the foul smell
Del mio vestito	Of my garment
Tolse alla belva	So robbed the beast
Sì l'appetito,	Of his appetite,
Che, disprezzandomi,	That in utter disgust
Si rinselvò.	He went back to the woods.
Così conoscere	And that's how
Mi fe' la sorte	Fate taught me
Ch'onte, pericoli,	That insults and danger
Vergogna e morte	And shame and death
Col cuoio d'asino	Can all be avoided
Fuggir si può.	Wearing the hide of an ass.

(They go off.)

Scene VIII

Figaro alone

Figaro

No. 26 Recitative and Aria
Recitative

Tutto è disposto: l'ora	Everything's ready: It must be
Dovrebbe esser vicina; io sento gente . . .	Nearly time; I hear someone coming . . .

È dessa . . . non è alcun . . . Buia è la
   notte . . .
Ed io comincio omai
A fare il scimunito
Mestiere di marito . . .
Ingrata! nel momento
Della mia cerimonia . . .
Ei godeva leggendo: e nel vederlo

Io rideva di me senza saperlo.

Oh, Susanna! Susanna!
Quanta pena mi costi!
Con quell'ingenua faccia,
Con quegli occhi innocenti . . .
Chi creduto l'avria! . . .
Ah, che il fidarsi a donna è ognor follia!

It's her . . . no, no one's there . . . The
   night is dark . . .
And I'm already beginning
To play the wretched part
Of the jealous husband . . .
That traitress! on the very day
Of our wedding . . .
He was enjoying her little note: and while
   I was watching
I didn't even know I was laughing at
   myself.
Oh, Susanna, Susanna!
You've caused me so much pain!
With that sweet little face
And those innocent eyes . . .
Who would ever believe it?
Ah, it's sheer madness to trust in a
   woman.

Aria

Aprite un po' quegli occhi
Uomini incauti e sciocchi,
Guardate queste femmine,
Guardate cosa son.

Queste chiamate Dee
Dagli ingannati sensi,
A cui tributa incensi
La debole ragion,
Son streghe che incantano

Per farci penar,
Sirene che cantano
Per farci affogar,

Civette che allettano
Per trarci le piume,
Comete che brillano
Per toglierci il lume;

Son rose spinose,
Son volpi vezzose,
Son orse benigne,
Colombe maligne,

Open up your eyes,
You rash and foolish men,
Just look at these women,
Just look what they are.

You call them all goddesses
When your senses are inflamed,
And with your feeble reasoning
You worship at their shrine.
They're just witches casting their
   spells
To cause us terrible pain,
They're sirens singing their songs
To drown us one and all,

They're screech-owls that lure us
To pluck out our feathers,
They're comets that flash
To take away our sight;

They're roses with thorns,
They're cunning little vixens,
They're gentle she-bears,
They're spiteful doves,

Maestre d'inganni,	They're masters of deceit,
Amiche d'affanni	They're friends of our troubles,
Che fingono, mentono,	They always lie and cheat,
Amore non senton,	They feel no love at all,
Non senton pietà.	Nor mercy will they show.
No, no, no, no!	No, no, no, no!
Il resto nol dico,	I won't even say the rest,
Già ognuno lo sa.	Because everyone already knows.

(He withdraws.)

SCENE IX

The Countess, Susanna, Marcellina, and Figaro apart

(Enter the Countess and Susanna, dressed in each other's clothes, and Marcellina.)

Recitative

SUSANNA

Signora, ella mi disse	My lady, Marcellina here says
Che Figaro verravvi.	Figaro is coming.

MARCELLINA

Anzi, è venuto:	He's already here:
Abbassa un po' la voce.	Lower your voice just a little.

SUSANNA

Dunque, un ci ascolta, e l'altro	So while one of them is listening, the other's
Dèe venir a cercarmi.	Due to meet me any moment.
Incominciam.	We might as well begin.

MARCELLINA

Io voglio qui celarmi.	And I'll just hide in here.

(She enters where Barbarina went.)

SCENE X

The Countess, Susanna and Figaro

SUSANNA

Madama, voi tremate: avreste freddo?	My lady, you're trembling: Are you cold?

COUNTESS

Parmi umida la notte ... lo mi ritiro.

The night air feels rather damp ... I think I'll go on in.

FIGARO (*aside*)

Eccoci della crisi al grande istante.

Here we all are at the height of the drama.

SUSANNA

Io sotto queste piante,
Se Madama il permette,
Resto a prendere il fresco una mezz'ora.

If your ladyship allows it,
I think I'll just stay here under the trees
And get some fresh air for half an hour.

FIGARO (*aside*)

Il fresco, il fresco!

And get some fresh air!

COUNTESS

Restaci, in buonora.

Stay as long as you want to.

(*She hides.*)

SUSANNA (*aside*)

Il birbo è in sentinella,
Divertiamci anche noi:
Diamogli la mercé de' dubbi suoi.

That rascal's watching,
But we'll have some fun, too:
Let's reward him for his doubts.

(*aloud*)

No. 27 Recitative and Aria
Recitative

Giunse alfin il momento
Che godrò senza affanno
In braccio all'idol mio! Timide cure,
Uscite dal mio petto,
A turbar non venite il mio diletto!
Oh, come par che all'amoroso foco
L'amenità del loco,
La terra e il ciel risponda!
Come la notte i furti miei seconda!

The moment's finally here
When I can freely rejoice
In the arms of my idol! I've done away
With all those silly scruples,
Which would only spoil my happiness!
Oh, how the beauty of this place,
And heaven and earth respond
To my burning passion!
How the night aids and abets my designs!

Aria

Deh, vieni, non tardar, o gioia bella,

Come now, my darling, no more delaying,

Vieni ove amore per goder t'appella,

Come and answer the call of love,

Finché non splende in ciel notturna
face
Finché l'aria è ancor bruna e il
mondo tace.

Qui mormora il ruscel, qui scherza
l'aura,
Che col dolce susurro il cor
ristaura;

Qui ridono i fioretti, e l'erba è
fresca:
Ai piaceri d'amor qui tutto adesca.

Vieni, ben mio: tra queste piante
ascose
Ti vo' la fronte incoronar di rose.

Before heaven's torch shines bright
in the sky,
While the night is still dark and the
world at rest.

Here the brook is babbling, and the
breezes are playing,
And their sweet sounds refresh my
heart;

Here the flowers are laughing, and
the grass is cool:
Here everything welcomes the
pleasures of love.

Come now, my dear one: and
among these sheltered trees
I'll crown your brow with roses.

Scene XI

*The Countess, Susanna, Figaro and Cherubino;
then the Count*

Recitative

FIGARO (*aside*)

Perfida! e in quella forma
Meco mentia? Non so s'io vegli o dorma.

That traitress! so this is how
She lied to me? I don't know whether I'm
awake or sleeping.

CHERUBINO (*He enters humming.*)

La la la, la la la, la lera.

La la la, la la la, la lera.

COUNTESS (*aside, from her hiding place*)

Il picciol paggio!

It's the little page!

CHERUBINO

Io sento gente: entriamo
Ove entrò Barbarina.

I heard someone: I'll just go in
Where Barbarina is.

(*noticing the Countess*)

Oh, vedo qui una donna!

Oh, there's a woman in there!

COUNTESS (*aside*)

Ahi, me meschina!

And now what'll I do?

CHERUBINO

M'inganno! A quel cappello

No, I'm wrong! From what I can see of that hat

Che nell'ombra vegg'io, parmi Susanna.

In the dark, it's got to be Susanna in there.

COUNTESS (*aside*)

E se il Conte ora vien? Sorte tiranna!

And what if the Count should show up? Oh, how cruel fate really is!

No. 28 Finale

CHERUBINO (*aside*)

Pian pianin le andrò più presso:
Tempo perso non sarà.

Little by little I'll get closer to her:
It won't be wasted time.

COUNTESS (*aside*)

Ah, se il Conte arriva adesso,

Oh, if the Count gets here right now,

Qualche imbroglio accaderà!

What a disaster it will be!

CHERUBINO (*to the Countess*)

Susannetta . . .

My dearest Susanna . . .

(*aside*)

Non risponde:
Colla mano il volto asconde . . .

She won't answer:
And she's hiding her face in her hands . . .

Or la burlo, in verità.

Now I can really tease her, I think.

(*He takes her hand and caresses it; the Countess tries to free herself.*)

COUNTESS (*disguising her voice*)

Arditello! sfacciatello!
Ite presto via di qua.

You fresh little brat!
Get out of here at once!

CHERUBINO

Smorfiosa, maliziosa,
Io già so perché sei qua.

Don't be coy and cruel to me:
I already know why you're here.

COUNT

(*peering at them from a distance*)

Ecco qui la mia Susanna.

There she is, my own Susanna.

FIGARO and SUSANNA (*far apart from each other*)

Ecco qui l'uccellatore.

And here comes the skirt-chaser himself.

CHERUBINO (*once again to the Countess*)

Non far meco la tiranna!

Don't play these games with me!

SUSANNA, COUNT and FIGARO (*aside*)

Ah, nel sen mi batte il core!

Oh, my heart's pounding in my breast!

Un altr'uom con lei si sta.

There's another man with her.

COUNTESS (*sottovoce to Cherubino*)

Via, partite, o chiamo gente.

Get out, or I'll call for help.

CHERUBINO (*still holding her hand*)

Dammi un bacio, o non fai niente.

Just give me one little kiss, it won't cost you a thing.

SUSANNA, COUNT and FIGARO (*aside*)

Alla voce, è quegli il paggio.

I can tell from his voice it's the page.

COUNTESS (*as before*)

Anche un bacio! che coraggio!

Just one little kiss! What nerve!

CHERUBINO

E perché far io non posso
Quel che il Conte or or farà?

And why shouldn't I get
What the Count gets every day?

COUNTESS, SUSANNA, COUNT and FIGARO (*all aside*)

Temerario!

Oh, that foolhardy boy!

CHERUBINO

Oh, ve' che smorfie!
Sai ch'io fui dietro il sofà.

And just look at those faces
You're making! You know I was behind the chair.

COUNTESS, SUSANNA, COUNT and FIGARO (*still aside*)

Se il ribaldo ancor sta saldo,
La faccenda guasterà.

If that rascal keeps on insisting,
He'll ruin all our plans.

CHERUBINO

Prendi intanto . . .

For a starter, how about this . . .

(*The page tries to kiss the Countess; the Count steps between them, and receives the kiss himself.*)

COUNTESS and CHERUBINO

Oh, ciel! il Conte.	Good heavens! It's the Count.

(The page goes and hides with Barbarina.)

FIGARO *(aside)*

Vo' veder cosa fan là.	I wonder what they're doing in there.

COUNT

Perché voi nol ripetete,	Just so you won't try that again,
Ricevete questo qua.	Why don't you take this instead.

(The Count goes to slap Cherubino; Figaro comes up at that moment, and receives the slap himself.)

FIGARO *(aside)*

Ah! ci ho fatto un bel guadagno,	Ah! It serves me right,
Colla mia curiosità!	For being so nosy!

(Susanna hears the slap, and laughs.)

COUNTESS and COUNT

Ah! ci ha fatto un bel guadagno,	Ah! It serves him right,
Colla sua temerità!	For being so bold!

SUSANNA

Ah! ci ha fatto un bel guadagno,	Ah! It serves him right,
Colla sua curiosità!	For being so nosy!

(Figaro withdraws.)

COUNT *(to the Countess)*

Partito è alfin l'audace:	Now that the little fool's finally gone,
Accòstati, ben mio!	Come closer to me, my dear!

COUNTESS

Giacché così vi piace,	If that's what you want,
Eccomi qui, signor.	Then here I am, my lord.

FIGARO *(aside)*

Che compiacente femmina!	What an obedient little miss!
Che sposa di buon cor!	And such a willing bride!

COUNT

Porgimi la manina.	Now give me your hand.

COUNTESS

Io ve la dò.   Here it is.

COUNT and FIGARO

Carina!   Oh, my dear!

COUNT

Che dita tenerelle!   What sweet little fingers you've got!
Che delicata pelle!   And such lovely delicate skin!
Mi pizzica, mi stuzzica,   It makes me tingle all over,
M'empie di un nuovo ardor.   And sets me on fire again.

SUSANNA, COUNTESS and FIGARO

La cieca prevenzione   This blind infatuation of his
Delude la ragione,   Has completely clouded his
Inganna i sensi ognor.   judgment,
                                                And tricked every one of his senses.

(Then all four, with the Count repeating his verses.)

COUNT

Oltre la dote, o cara,   Besides your dowry, my darling,
Ricevi anche un brillante,   Accept this diamond ring,
Che a te porge un amante   It's just a little token
In pegno del suo amor.   Of my undying love.

(He gives her a ring.)

COUNTESS

Tutto Susanna piglia   Susanna can't thank you enough
Dal suo benefattor.   For everything you've done.

SUSANNA, COUNT and FIGARO *(aside)*

Va tutto a maraviglia!   Everything's going so perfectly!
Ma il meglio manca ancor.   But the best is yet to come.

COUNTESS *(to the Count)*

Signor, d'accese fiaccole   My Lord, I can see the glow
Io veggio il balenar.   Of lighted torches fast approaching.

COUNT

Entriam, mia bella Venere.   Let's go on in, my pretty Venus,
Andiamoci a celar.   Let's go right now and hide.

SUSANNA and FIGARO *(aside)*

Mariti scimuniti,   Come, all you wretched husbands,
Venite ad imparar.   And learn your lesson well.

Countess

Al buio, signor mio?	In the dark, my lord?

Count

È quello che vogl'io:	That's the way I want it:
Tu sai che là per leggere	And you know I'm not going in
Io non desio d'entrar.	there
	Just so we can read.

Figaro (aside)

La perfida lo séguita:	That traitress is following him:
È vano il dubitar.	There's no doubt at all.

Countess and Susanna (aside)

I furbi sono in trappola,	The rogues are in the trap,
Cammina ben l'affar.	Our plans are going well.

(Figaro passes by.)

Count (disguising his voice)

Chi passa?	Who's there?

Figaro (angrily)

Passa gente!	Just someone going by.

Countess (sottovoce to the Count)

È Figaro: men vò.	It's Figaro: I'm leaving.

Count

Andate: io poi verrò.	Go ahead: I'll join you very soon.

(The Count disappears among the trees, and the Countess enters the arbor on the right.)

Figaro

Tutto è tranquillo e placido:	Everything's peaceful and quiet:
Entrò la bella Venere.	Our pretty Venus has gone in
Col vago Marte prendere,	To find her handsome Mars,
Nuovo Vulcan del secolo,	But like a modern-day Vulcan,
In rete la potrò.	I'll catch them in my net.

Susanna (disguising her voice)

Ehi, Figaro, tacete!	Hey, Figaro, be quiet!

Figaro

Oh, questa è la Contessa . . .	Oh, that must be the Countess . . .

(*to Susanna*)

A tempo qui giungete . . .	You've come just in time . . .
Vedrete là voi stessa . . .	You'll see it for yourself . . .
Il Conte e la mia sposa . . .	The Count's in there with my bride . . .
Di propria man la cosa	And they're so close to us
Toccar io vi farò.	You can touch them with your hand.

SUSANNA (*forgetting to disguise her voice*)

Parlate un po' più basso.	Just speak a little lower.
Di qua non muovo passo,	I'm not moving from this spot
Ma vendicar mi vo'.	Until I get revenge.

FIGARO (*aside*)

Susanna!	Susanna!

(*to Susanna*)

Vendicarsi?	Revenge?

SUSANNA

Sì.	Oh, yes.

FIGARO

Come potria farsi?	And how can that be done?

(*aside*)

La volpe vuol sorprendermi,	If the little vixen's trying to catch me,
E secondar la vo'.	I'll help her with her plan.

SUSANNA (*aside*)

L'iniquo io vo' sorprendere;	I'm trying to catch the villain,
Poi so quel che farò.	And I know just what to do.

FIGARO (*with comic exaggeration*)

Ah, se Madama il vuole!	Well, if that's what my lady wants!

SUSANNA

Su via, manco parole.	Come on, let's get going, and not another word.

FIGARO (*as before*)

Eccomi ai vostri piedi . . .	I'm kneeling here before you . . .
Ho pieno il cor di fuoco.	And my heart is full of fire.

Esaminate il loco . . .　　　　　　　Just take a look around you . . .
Pensate al traditor.　　　　　　　　And remember who betrayed you.

SUSANNA (*aside*)

Come la man mi pizzica!　　　　　　How my hand is itching!
Che smania! che furor!　　　　　　How mad I am! I'm furious!

FIGARO (*aside*)

Come il polmon mi si altera!　　　　How my bosom swells with love!
Che smania! che calor!　　　　　　How mad she is! She's feverish!

SUSANNA (*disguising her voice a little*)

E senza alcun affetto? . . .　　　　　Isn't there any affection at all
　　　　　　　　　　　　　　　　between us? . . .

FIGARO

Suppliscavi il dispetto.　　　　　　My respect for you forbade it.
Non perdiam tempo invano,　　　　But we mustn't waste any time,
Datemi un po' la mano . . .　　　　Give me your hand for just a
　　　　　　　　　　　　　　　　moment.

SUSANNA

(*She slaps his face as she speaks in her own voice.*)

Servitevi, signor!　　　　　　　　Help yourself, fine sir!

FIGARO

Che schiaffo!　　　　　　　　　　Oh, what a slap!

SUSANNA (*still slapping in time*)

E questo, e questo　　　　　　　　And take this, and this
E ancora questo, e questo, e poi　　And this one, too, and here's
　　quest'altro!　　　　　　　　　　another one!

FIGARO

Non batter così presto.　　　　　　I beg you, not so hard.

SUSANNA (*still slapping him*)

E questo, signor scaltro,　　　　　And this, you rascal,
E questo, e poi quest'altro ancor!　And this, and this one, too!

FIGARO

Oh, schiaffi graziosissimi!　　　　　Oh, those precious little slaps!
Oh, mio felice amor!　　　　　　　How happy is my love!

SUSANNA

| Impara, impara, o perfido, | I'll teach you, you faithless wretch, |
| A fare il seduttor. | To play the seducer with me. |

FIGARO (*falling on his knees*)

Pace, pace, mio dolce tesoro:	Forgive me, my dearest treasure:
Io conobbi la voce che adoro,	I recognized the voice I adore,
E che impressa ognor serbo nel cor.	Which is always engraved in my heart.

SUSANNA (*laughing in surprise*)

| La mia voce? | My voice? |

FIGARO

| La voce che adoro. | The voice I adore. |

FIGARO and SUSANNA

| Pace, pace, mio dolce tesoro, | Forgive me, my dearest treasure, |
| Pace, pace, mio tenero amor. | Forgive me, my sweet love. |

COUNT (*aside, returning*)

| Non la trovo, e girai tutto il bosco. | I've combed the woods, and I can't find her anywhere. |

SUSANNA and FIGARO

| Questi è il Conte, alla voce il conosco. | Here comes the Count, I can tell by his voice. |

COUNT

(*in the direction of the arbor which the Countess entered*)

| Ehi, Susanna . . . sei sorda . . . sei muta? | Hey, Susanna . . . are you deaf . . . and dumb? |

SUSANNA (*sottovoce to Figaro*)

| Bella! bella! non l'ha conosciuta! | Oh, that's perfect! He still hasn't recognized her! |

FIGARO (*sottovoce to Susanna*)

| Chi? | Who? |

SUSANNA (*as before*)

| Madama. | My lady. |

FIGARO (*as before*)

| Madama? | My lady? |

SUSANNA (*as before*)

Madama. Yes, my lady.

SUSANNA and FIGARO (*sottovoce*)

La commedia, idol mio, terminiamo: Let's end this farce, my dearest:
Consoliamo il bizzarro amator. And console this poor lover at last.

FIGARO

(*aloud, throwing himself at Susanna's feet*)

Sì, Madama, voi siete il ben mio. Yes, my lady, you're all I'm living
for.

COUNT (*aside*)

La mia sposa! Ah, senz'arme son io! My wife! Ah, and I'm not even
armed!

FIGARO (*still kneeling*)

Un ristoro al mio cor concedete. Won't you grant some solace to this
heart of mine?

SUSANNA (*disguising her voice*)

Io son qui, faccio quel che volete. Here I am, and I'll do whatever you
want.

COUNT (*aside*)

Ah, ribaldi! They're just shameless!

SUSANNA and FIGARO

Ah, corriamo, mio bene, Ah, let's make haste, my love,
E le pene compensi il piacer. And let pleasure make up for our
pain.

(*Figaro rises, and they both go towards the arbor on the left.*)

SCENE XII

The Count, the Countess, Susanna, Figaro, Marcellina, Bartolo, Cherubino, Barbarina, Antonio,
Basilio, Don Curzio and servants

COUNT (*stopping Figaro*)

Gente, gente! All'armi, all'armi! Hey there, my men! Bring your
weapons!

(*Susanna enters the arbor.*)

Le Nozze di Figaro

FIGARO (*pretending to be terrified*)

Il padrone!

It's the master!

COUNT

Gente, gente, aiuto, aiuto!

Help me, my men! Help me! Help me!

FIGARO (*as before*)

Son perduto!

Now I'm ruined!

(*Antonio, Basilio, Bartolo, Don Curzio and servants with lighted torches come running.*)

BASILIO, DON CURZIO, ANTONIO and BARTOLO

Cosa avvenne?

What's happened?

COUNT

Il scellerato!
M'ha tradito, m'ha infamato!

That villain!
He's betrayed me, and insulted my honor!

E con chi, state a veder.

And wait 'till you see who he's with.

BASILIO, DON CURZIO, ANTONIO and BARTOLO (*aside*)

Son stordito, sbalordito.
Non mi par che ciò sia ver.

I'm amazed and bewildered,
And I can't believe it's true.

FIGARO

Son storditi, sbalorditi:
Oh, che scena, che piacer!

They're all amazed and bewildered.
Oh, what a farce, what fun!

COUNT

Invan resistete,
Uscite, Madama!
Il premio or avrete
Di vostra onestà.
Il paggio!

It's useless to resist,
Madam, come on out!
And you'll be justly rewarded
For all your honesty.
The page!

(*The Count tugs on Cherubino's arm, who struggles not to come out, and can only be half seen; after the page come Barbarina, Marcellina and Susanna, dressed in the Countess' clothes: she holds a handkerchief to her face, and kneels down in front of the Count.*)

ANTONIO

Mia figlia!

My daughter!

FIGARO

Mia madre!

My mother!

283

BASILIO, DON CURZIO, ANTONIO
BARTOLO and FIGARO

Madama!   My lady!

COUNT

Scoperta è la trama,   The plot is now uncovered,
La perfida è qua.   And the traitress is right here.

(*One after the other they all kneel down.*)

SUSANNA

Perdono, perdono!   Forgive me, I beseech you!

COUNT

No, no, non sperarlo!   Oh no, don't even hope for it.

FIGARO

Perdono, perdono!   Forgive me, I beseech you!

COUNT

No, no, non vo' darlo!   Oh no, I never will.

SUSANNA, CHERUBINO, BARBARINA, MARCELLINA,
BASILIO, DON CURZIO, ANTONIO, BARTOLO and FIGARO

Perdono, perdono!   Forgive us, we beseech you!

COUNT (*louder*)

No, no, no, no, no!   No, no, no, no, no!

COUNTESS (*coming out of the other arbor*)

Almeno io per loro   At least I can try
Perdono otterrò.   To plead their case.

(*She tries to kneel but the Count will not let her.*)

COUNT, BASILIO, DON CURZIO, ANTONIO and BARTOLO

Oh cielo! che veggio!   Oh, my heavens! What do I see?
Deliro! vaneggio!   I'm raving! I've gone mad!
Che creder non so.   And I can't believe my eyes.

COUNT (*begging her*)

Contessa, perdono.   My Countess, please forgive me.

COUNTESS

Più docile io sono,   I'm more indulgent now,
E dico di sì.   And I really can say yes.

ALL

Ah! tutti contenti	Ah! And so we'll
Saremo così.	All be content at last.
Questo giorno di tormenti,	This day of torment,
Di capricci e di follia,	Whims and folly,
In contenti e in allegria	Love alone can crown
Solo amor può terminar.	With happiness and joy.
Sposi, amici, al ballo! al gioco!	Come, lovers and friends, let's dance and play!
Alle mine date fuoco,	Come, light the fireworks,
Ed al suon di lieta marcia	And to the sounds of a lively march
Corriam tutti a festeggiar.	Let's make haste to celebrate.

The End

DON GIOVANNI

WORLD PREMIERE: *Prague, National Theater, October 29, 1787*

UNITED STATES PREMIERE: *New York, Park Theater, November 7, 1817*

METROPOLITAN OPERA PREMIERE: *November 28, 1883*

IL DISSOLUTO PUNITO
(THE PROFLIGATE PUNISHED)
OR
DON GIOVANNI

Dramma giocoso in two acts

Libretto: Lorenzo da Ponte

English Translation: David Stivender
and Susan Webb

Music: Wolfgang Amadeus Mozart

DON GIOVANNI

CHARACTERS

DON GIOVANNI, *an extremely licentious young cavalier*	Bass
DONNA ANNA, *promised bride of Don Ottavio*	Soprano
THE COMMENDATORE, *father to Donna Anna*	Bass
DON OTTAVIO	Tenor
DONNA ELVIRA, *lady of Burgos, abandoned by Don Giovanni*	Soprano
LEPORELLO, *servant to Don Giovanni*	Bass
ZERLINA, *peasant girl, promised bride of Masetto*	Soprano
MASETTO, *peasant lad*	Bass

Peasants of both sexes. Servants and Musicians.

The action takes place in a Spanish city.

DON GIOVANNI

SYNOPSIS

Act I

At night, in front of the palace of the Commendatore (Commander), Leporello grumbles about his fatiguing duties as servant to Don Giovanni, a dissolute nobleman ("Notte e giorno faticar"). Suddenly the Commendatore's daughter, Donna Anna, appears, struggling with the masked Giovanni, who has entered her chamber and tried to seduce her ("Non sperar, se non m'uccidi"). When the lady's father comes out in answer to her cries, Giovanni kills the old man in a duel. Anna, having fled to get aid, returns with her fiancé, Don Ottavio, only to discover her father's body. Anna makes Ottavio swear vengeance ("Fuggi, crudele").

Giovanni accidentally encounters Donna Elvira, whom he abandoned in Burgos. She is still lamenting her loss ("Ah! chi mi dice mai"). As Leporello tries to discourage and distract her by reciting his master's catalog of lady loves ("Madamina! Il catalogo è questo"), Giovanni escapes.

Peasants celebrate the wedding of Masetto and Zerlina. Giovanni is attracted by the bride-to-be, bidding Leporello get rid of the groom, who departs under protest. Alone with Zerlina, the nobleman suavely persuades her to come with him to his little house ("Là ci darem la mano"). Elvira steps forth, warns the girl about her new suitor and leads her away. Momentarily thwarted, Giovanni greets Anna, now dressed in mourning, and Ottavio, only to be embarrassed by the persistent Elvira, who denounces him as a seducer (quartet: "Non ti fidar, o misera!"). Trying to dismiss her as a madwoman, he ushers Elvira off. Anna, in horror, recognizes his voice as that of her father's murderer. She calls on Ottavio to avenge her honor ("Or sai chi l'onore"), leaving him to thoughts of love ("Dalla sua pace").

At his palace, Giovanni prepares for a feast he has arranged, toasting the revelry to come ("Finch' han dal vino").

As Zerlina and the jealous Masetto approach the palace gate, she begs him to forgive her apparent infidelity ("Batti, batti, o bel Masetto"). Anna, Elvira and Ottavio arrive, masked and cloaked (trio: "Protegga il giusto cielo"); after Giovanni tells Leporello to invite them in, they vow to punish the libertine.

Guests crowd the ballroom, dancing to three different ensembles. While Leporello distracts Masetto, the host dances with Zerlina, enticing her to a nearby chamber. When the girl cries for help, Anna, Elvira and Ottavio unmask, and confront Giovanni, who escapes with Leporello.

Act II

Under Elvira's balcony, Leporello exchanges cloaks with Giovanni in order to woo the lady in his master's stead. Leporello and Elvira go off, leaving Giovanni free to serenade Elvira's maid ("Deh, vieni alla finestra"). When Masetto leads in a band of peasants bent on punishing Giovanni, the disguised rake gives them false directions, then beats up Masetto. Zerlina tenderly consoles the victim ("Vedrai, carino").

Elvira follows the disguised Leporello to Donna Anna's house, where they are surprised by Anna and Ottavio. Zerlina and Masetto also arrive and, mistaking servant for master, join in denouncing the supposed Don, despite Elvira's protests. Frightened, Leporello unmasks, and escapes. Ottavio reaffirms his love for Anna and leaves in search of the culprit ("Il mio tesoro"). Elvira can only add fury at her betrayal by Giovanni ("Mi tradì").

Leporello finds Giovanni in a deserted cemetery, where a statue of the slain Commendatore warns Giovanni of his doom. The Don forces the terrified Leporello to invite the statue to dinner ("O statua gentilissima"). The statue nods acceptance.

In Anna's house, Ottavio urges his fiancée to stop grieving and accept his love, but she implores him to wait until her father is avenged ("Non mi dir").

In his banquet hall, Giovanni orders Leporello to serve supper, as a stage orchestra provides music. Elvira begs Giovanni to reform, but he waves her aside. Leaving, she screams in terror: the stone guest has arrived. Refusing to open the door, Leporello hides. Giovanni bravely greets the statue, which bids him repent ("Don Giovanni, a cenar teco"). When he refuses, flames engulf his palace and he is dragged down to hell.

(As day breaks over the city) Elvira, Anna, Ottavio, Zerlina, Masetto and Leporello gather to plan their futures and state the moral: sad is a libertine's fate ("Questo è il fin di chi fa mal").

Opera News

TRANSLATOR'S NOTE

David Stivender was working on his translation of *Don Giovanni* when his health failed; his sudden and untimely death in February 1990 stunned us all. Since what he had already accomplished—a draft of nearly the whole libretto—was so valuable, we set about to bring it to completion. I agreed to play Alfano to David's Puccini—a humbling and enriching experience.

David turned to Fabrizio Melano, the distinguished Met stage director, for advice about

Italian language questions; I was fortunate enough to have him at my elbow, and we had some hilarious moments trying to invent English phrases ambiguous enough to allow for the double meanings of which librettist—and composer—were so fond. (A few inventions are my own, and Fabrizio is not to blame.) I am also indebted to Leslie Koenig for her valuable suggestions.

The Met uses the Bärenreiter edition of the score: this translation is based on that text, and on the photocopied libretto which David was using, for which no original has yet been found. (It is not the Lecaldano edition of Da Ponte's *Tre Libretti per Mozart*, Rizzoli, 1956; David was well on his way into the *Don Giovanni* translation before he acquired a copy of that in the summer of 1989.) The stage directions are quite brief in this version, and no numbers or instrumentation appear.

The entire libretto is printed, including text that was added after the Prague premiere on October 29, 1787. The tenor aria "Dalla sua pace," composed for the 1788 Vienna production, follows after Donna Anna's dramatic aria describing Don Giovanni's attempted seduction; Don Ottavio's second aria "Il mio tesoro," which was cut from this same production, remains in its second act position. Four other changes were made for Vienna: the addition of a low-comedy scene for Zerlina and Leporello, a solo recitative for Leporello, a recitative for Zerlina, Donna Elvira and Masetto (printed here in full) and finally, Elvira's great *scena* "In qual eccessi . . . Mi tradi," the only one of the four new scenes which was integrated into performances of the opera. Since the Met includes Elvira's aria in its production, it is printed in sequence after "Il mio tesoro"; the other three changes appear as an appendix.

A note about spellings: two or more spellings of words appear in the various versions of the libretto, both acceptable in the infant days of the "Italian" language: giovinetti/giovinotti; cade/cadde; prosciutti/presciutti; miele/mele; piccolo/picciolo; marchesine/marchesane; Almagna/Lamagna; meraviglia/maraviglia; cioccolate/cioccolata/cioccolatte; and alberi/albori/arbori, to name a few.

In the stage directions, both Donna Anna and Donna Elvira are listed as Donna; in the sung text, "Donn'Anna" and "Donn'Elvira" usually appear instead.

SUSAN WEBB

The vertical black lines to the left of the text indicate portions of the libretto not performed at the Metropolitan Opera.

DON GIOVANNI

ACT ONE

SCENE I

Garden. Night.

*Leporello, cloaked, who walks in front of Donna Anna's house;
later, Don Giovanni and Donna Anna, and finally the Commendatore.*

LEPORELLO

Notte e giorno faticar	To work hard night and day
per chi nulla sa gradir;	for one whom nothing can please;
piova e vento sopportar,	to endure rain and wind,
mangiar male e mal dormir!	to eat badly and not to sleep!
Voglio far il gentiluomo,	I wish to play the gentleman,
e non voglio più servir.	and don't want to serve any longer.
Oh che caro galantuomo!	Oh, what a precious man of honor!
Voi star dentro col la bella,	You stay inside with the lovely lady,
ed io far la sentinella!	and I play the sentinel!
Voglio far il gentiluomo,	I wish to play the gentleman,
e non voglio più servir.	and don't want to serve any longer.
Ma mi par che venga gente . . .	But it seems to me that people are coming . . .
Non mi voglio far sentir.	I don't want to be heard.

(He withdraws.)
(Don Giovanni from the Commendatore's palace followed by Donna Anna; he tries to cover his face and is wrapped in a long cloak.)

ANNA *(holding Don Giovanni back)*

Non sperar, se non m'uccidi	Unless you kill me, do not hope
ch'io ti lasci fuggir mai.	that I will ever let you escape.

GIOVANNI *(always trying to conceal himself)*

Donna folle! indarno gridi;	Foolish woman! in vain you scream;
chi son io tu non saprai.	You will not learn who I am.

LEPORELLO (*coming forward*)

(Che tumulto! . . . Oh ciel; che gridi!	(What a tumult! . . . Oh heaven; what screams!
Il padron in nuovi guai! . . .)	The master in new troubles! . . .)

ANNA

Gente! . . . servi! al traditore! . . .	People! . . . servants! At the traitor! . . .

GIOVANNI

Taci, e trema al mio furore.	Be silent, and tremble at my fury.

ANNA

Scellerato!	Scoundrel!

GIOVANNI

Sconsigliata!	Rash woman!
(Questa furia disperata	(This desperate Fury wants
mi vuol far precipitar.)	to make me do something rash.)

ANNA

Come furia disperata	Like a desperate Fury
ti saprò perseguitar.	I shall pursue you.

LEPORELLO

(Sta' a veder che il libertino	(One can see that the libertine
mi farà precipitar.)	will make me do something rash.)

COMMENDATORE (*with sword and torch*)

Lasciala, indegno!	Let her go, base man!

(*Donna Anna, hearing the voice of her father, lets go of Don Giovanni and enters the house.*)

Battiti meco.	Fight with me.

GIOVANNI

Va': non mi degno	Go: I do not deign
di pugnar teco.	to fight with you.

COMMENDATORE

Cosi pretendi	You wish thus
da me fuggir?	to escape me?

LEPORELLO

(Potessi almeno	(At least if I were able
di qua partir!)	to get away from here!)

GIOVANNI

Misero! attendi	Miserable man! Stay then
si vuoi morir.	if you wish to die.

(They fight. The Commendatore is wounded.)

COMMENDATORE

Ah soccorso! . . . son tradito . . .	Ah, help! . . . I am betrayed . . .
L'assassino . . . m'ha ferito . . .	The assassin . . . has wounded me . . .
E dal seno palpitante . . .	And from my throbbing breast . . .
Sento . . . l'anima partir . . .	I feel . . . my soul depart . . .

(The Commendatore dies.)

GIOVANNI

(Ah! già cade il sciagurato . . .	(Ah! the wretch already falls . . .
Affannosa e agonizzante	Already from his throbbing breast
già dal seno palpitante	I see his anguished and agonizing
veggo l'anima partir.)	soul depart.)

LEPORELLO

(Qual misfatto! qual eccesso!	(What a misdeed! what excess!
Entro il sen, dallo spavento,	In my breast, I feel my heart
palpitar il cor mi sento.	throbbing from terror.
Io non so che far, che dir.)	I don't know what to do, what to say.)

SCENE II

GIOVANNI *(still under his breath)*

Leporello, ove sei?	Leporello, where are you?

LEPORELLO *(still under his breath)*

Son qui, per mia disgrazia. E voi?	I'm here, to my misfortune. And you?

GIOVANNI

Son qui.	I'm here.

LEPORELLO

Chi è morto? voi o il vecchio?	Who is dead? you or the old man?

GIOVANNI

Che domanda da bestia! Il vecchio.	What a stupid question! The old man.

LEPORELLO

Bravo!	Bravo!
Due imprese leggiadre;	Two charming enterprises;

sforzar la figlia, ed ammazzar il padre.	Violating the daughter and killing the father.

GIOVANNI

L'ha voluto: suo danno.	He wanted it: so much the worse for him.

LEPORELLO

Ma Donn' Anna . . .	But Donn' Anna . . .
Cosa ha voluto?	What did she want?

GIOVANNI

Taci,	Quiet,
non mi seccar. Vien meco, se non vuoi	don't annoy me. Come with me, if you don't want
qualche cosa ancor tu.	something yourself.

LEPORELLO

Non vo' nulla, signor; non parlo più.	I don't want anything, sir; I say nothing more.

(Leporello picks up the lantern and cloak from the ground, and they leave.)

SCENE III

Don Ottavio, Donna Anna and Servants with lights

ANNA

Ah! del padre in periglio	Ah! let us fly to the aid
in soccorso voliam.	of my father in danger.

OTTAVIO *(with a naked sword in his hand)*

Tutto il mio sangue	All my blood
verserò, se bisogna:	shall I shed, if need be:
ma dov'è il scellerato?	but where is the scoundrel?

ANNA

In questo loco . . .	In this place.

(sees the body)

Ma qual mai s'offre, o Dei,	But what tragic spectacle, oh Gods!
spettacolo funesto agli occhi miei!	is offered to my eyes!
Il padre! . . . padre mio! . . . mio caro padre! . . .	Father! . . . my father! . . . my dear father! . . .

Don Giovanni

OTTAVIO

Signore . . .

Signore . . .

ANNA

Ah! l'assassino
mel trucidò . . . Quel sangue . . .
quella piaga . . . quel volto
tinto e coperto dei color di morte . . .

Ei non respira più . . . fredde ha le
  membra . . .
Padre mio! . . . caro padre! . . . padre
  amato! . . .
Io manco . . . io moro . . .

Ah! the assassin has
murdered him . . . That blood . . .
that wound . . . that face
Tinged and covered with the colors of
  death . . .
He is no longer breathing . . . his limbs
  are cold . . .
My father! . . . dear father! . . . beloved
  father!
I am fainting . . . I am dying . . .

(*She swoons.*)

OTTAVIO

Ah! soccorrete, amici, il mio tesoro.
Cercatemi, recatemi
Qualche odor, qualche spirto . . . Ah! non
  tardate!
Donn' Anna! . . . sposa! . . . amica! . . . il
  duolo estremo
la meschinella uccide!

Ah! friends, help my treasured one.
Find me, bring me
some salts, some spirits . . . Ah! do not
  delay!
Donn' Anna! . . . bride! . . . friend! . . . her
  extreme sorrow
is killing the poor lady!

ANNA

Ahi!

Ah!

OTTAVIO

Già rinviene.
Datele nuovi aiuti.

She is already recovering.
Renew your assistance to her.

ANNA

Padre mio!

My father!

OTTAVIO

Celate, allontanate agli occhi suoi
quell'oggetto d'orrore.

Hide, and take from her sight
that object of horror.

(*the corpse is carried away.*)

Anima mia, . . . consolati, . . . fa core! . . .

My soul, . . . console yourself, . . . take
  heart! . . .

301

ANNA (*desperately*)

Fuggi, crudele, fuggi!	Flee, cruel man, flee!
Lascia ch'io mora anch'io	Let me die also
ora ch'è morto, oh Dio!	now that he who gave me life, oh God!
chi a me la vita die'.	is dead.

OTTAVIO

Senti, cor mio, deh! senti:	Listen, my heart, ah! listen:
guardami un solo istante;	look at me for one moment;
ti parla il caro amante	a loving heart is speaking
che vive sol per te.	that lives only for you.

ANNA

Tu sei . . . perdon, mio bene . . .	You are . . . pardon, my beloved . . .
L'affanno mio . . . le pene . . .	My anguish . . . my afflictions . . .
Ah! il padre mio dov'è?	Ah! where is my father?

OTTAVIO

Il padre . . . lascia, o cara,	Your father . . . forget, oh dear one,
la rimembranza amara:	the bitter remembrance:
hai sposo e padre in me.	you have husband and father in me.

ANNA

Ah! vendicar, se il puoi,	Ah! swear always to avenge,
giura quel sangue ognor.	if you can, that blood.

OTTAVIO

Lo giuro agl' occhi tuoi,	I swear it by your eyes,
lo giuro al nostro amor.	I swear it by our love.

BOTH

Che giuramento, oh Dei!	What an oath, oh Gods!
Che barbaro momento!	What a barbarous moment!
Fra cento affetti e cento	My heart is wavering among
vammi ondeggiando il cor.	hundreds upon hundreds of emotions.

(*They leave.*)

SCENE IV

A street. Dawn.

Don Giovanni and Leporello, later Donna Elvira in travelling dress.

GIOVANNI

Orsù, spicciati presto. Cosa vuoi?	Come on, be quick. What do you want?

LEPORELLO

L'affar di cui si tratta è importante.	The matter in question is important.

GIOVANNI

Lo credo.	I believe it.

LEPORELLO

È importantissimo.	It's very important.

GIOVANNI

Meglio ancora! Finiscila:	Even better! Finish it.

LEPORELLO

Giurate di non andar in collera.	Swear not to get angry.

GIOVANNI

Lo giuro sul mio onore, purchè non parli del Commendatore.	I swear it on my honor, provided you don't speak about the Commendatore.

LEPORELLO

Siamo soli?	Are we alone?

GIOVANNI

Lo vedo.	As far as I can see.

LEPORELLO

Nessun ci sente?	No one is listening to us?

GIOVANNI

Via.	Come on.

LEPORELLO

Vi posso dire tutto liberamente? . . .	Can I freely tell you everything? . . .

GIOVANNI

Sì.	Yes.

LEPORELLO

Dunque, quando è così, caro signor padrone, la vita che menate	Well, when it's like that, dear Signor Padrone, the life you are leading

(in his ear, but loudly)

è da briccone.   is that of a rogue.

GIOVANNI

Temerario! in tal guisa . . .   Reckless man! in such a manner . . .

LEPORELLO

E il giuramento?   And the oath?

GIOVANNI

Non so di giuramenti. Taci, o ch'io . . .   I know nothing about oaths. Quiet, or
                                                  I'll . . .

LEPORELLO

Non parlo più, non fiato, o padron mio.   I won't speak any more, not a breath,
                                                  master mine.

GIOVANNI

Così saremo amici. Or odi un poco: Thus we shall be friends. Now listen a
                                                  bit:

sai tu perchè son qui?   do you know why I am here?

LEPORELLO

Non ne so nulla.   I don't know anything about it.
Ma, essendo l'alba chiara, non sarebbe   But, since it's dawn, would it not be
qualche nuova conquista?   Some new conquest?
Io lo devo saper per porla in lista.   I must know about it to put it on the list.

GIOVANNI

Va' là, che se' il grand'uom! Sappi ch'io   Well, aren't you the great man! Know
    sono   that I am
innamorato d'una bella dama,   enamored of a lovely lady,
e son certo che m'ama.   and am certain that she loves me.
La vidi, le parlai, meco al casino   I saw her, I spoke to her, she will come
                                                      with me
questa notte verrà . . .   tonight to my little house . . .
Zitto: mi pare   Silence: I seem
sentir odor di femmina . . .   to scent the odor of a woman . . .

LEPORELLO

(Cospetto!   (Good God!
Che odorato perfetto!)   What a perfect sense of smell!)

GIOVANNI

All'aria mi par bella.   By her air she seems beautiful to me.

LEPORELLO

(E che occhio, dico!)   (And what an eye, I say!)

GIOVANNI

Ritiriamoci un poco,	Let's withdraw a bit,
e scopriamo terren.	and study the lie of the land.

LEPORELLO

(Già prese foco.)   (He's catching fire already.)

(They go to one side.)

SCENE V

Donna Elvira and the abovementioned

ELVIRA

Ah! chi mi dice mai	Ah, who can tell me
quel barbaro dov'è,	where that barbarous man is,
che per mio scorno amai,	who to my shame I loved,
che mi mancò di fè?	who betrayed his faith to me?
Ah! se ritrovo l'empio,	Ah! if I find the impious man again,
e a me non torna ancor,	and he still does not return to me,
vo' farne orrendo scempio,	I'd like to butcher him horribly.
gli vo' cavare il cor.	I'd like to tear out his heart.

GIOVANNI *(softly to Leporello)*

Udisti? qualche bella	Did you hear? some lovely lady
dal vago abbandonata . . . Poverina!	abandoned by her charmer . . . poor little thing!
Cerchiam di consolare il suo tormento.	Let us try to console her in her torment.

LEPORELLO

(Così ne consolò mille e ottocento.)	(Thus he has consoled a thousand eight hundred of them.)

GIOVANNI

Signorina . . .   Signorina . . .

ELVIRA

Chi è là?   Who is there?

GIOVANNI

Stelle! che vedo!   Stars! what do I see!

LEPORELLO

Oh bella! Donna Elvira!   Oh splendid! Donna Elvira!

ELVIRA

Don Giovanni! . . .   Don Giovanni!

Sei qui, mostro, fellon, nido   Are you here, monster, treacherous man,
   d'inganni? . . .   nest of deceits? . . .

LEPORELLO

(Che titoli cruscanti! Manco male   (Such academic titles!* All the better that
che lo conosce bene!)   she knows him so well!)

GIOVANNI

Via, cara Donn' Elvira,   Come, dear Donn' Elvira,
calmate quella collera . . . sentite . . .   calm that anger . . . listen . . .
lasciatemi parlar . . .   let me speak . . .

ELVIRA

Cosa puoi dire,   What can you say,
dopo azion sì nera? In casa mia   after such a dark deed? Furtively you
                                      enter

entri furtivamente. A forza d'arte,   my house. With the aid of cunning,
di giuramenti e di lusinghe, arrivi   of oaths and of flattery, you succeed
a sedurre il cor mio: in seducing my heart:
m'innamori, o crudele!.   You make me fall in love, oh cruel man!
Mi dichiari tua sposa. E poi, mancando   You declare me your wife. And then,
                                      flaunting

della terra e del ciel al santo dritto,   the holy law of earth and heaven
con enorme delitto   with your monstrous crime
dopo tre dì da Burgos t'allontani.   after three days you leave Burgos.
M'abbandoni, mi fuggi, e lasci in preda   You abandon me, you flee from me, and
                                      leave me prey

al rimorso ed al pianto   to remorse and to weeping
per pena forse che t'amai cotanto!   As a punishment perhaps for loving you
                                      too much!

LEPORELLO

(Pare un libro stampato!)   (She seems like a printed book!)

GIOVANNI

Oh! In quanto a questo   Oh! As to all that
ebbi le mie ragioni!   I had my reasons!

(to Leporello)

È vero?   Isn't it true?

* The Accademia della Crusca, founded in Florence in 1583, was relentlessly dedicated to separating good
linguistic usage from bad: hence "crusca" or "chaff".

Don Giovanni

LEPORELLO (*ironically*)

È vero.   It's true.
E che ragioni forti!   And what strong reasons!

ELVIRA

E quali sono,   And what are they,
se non la tua perfidia,   apart from your perfidy,
la leggerezza tua? Ma il giusto cielo   your fickleness? But righteous heaven
volle ch'io ti trovassi   wished that I find you
per far le sue, le mie vendette.   to wreak its vengeance and mine.

GIOVANNI

Eh, via!   Come, come!
Siate più ragionevole . . . (Mi pone   Be more reasonable . . . (She's putting
a cimento costei.) Se non credete   me to the test.) If you don't believe
al labbro mio, credete   me, believe
a questo galantuomo.   this man of honor.

LEPORELLO

(Salvo il vero.)   (I tell everything except the truth.)

GIOVANNI

Via, dille un poco . . .   Come on, say something . . .

LEPORELLO (*under his breath to Don Giovanni*)

E cosa devo dirle?   And what must I tell her?

GIOVANNI

Sì, sì, dille pur tutto.   Yes, yes, tell her everything.

(*He leaves unseen by Donna Elvira*)

ELVIRA

Ebben, fa presto.   Well, be quick.

LEPORELLO

Madama . . . veramente . . . in questo   Madame . . . truly . . . in this world
   mondo
conciossiacosaquandofosseché   withthatmaybewhenwereitso
il quadro non è tondo . . .   the square is not round . . .

ELVIRA

Sciagurato!   Wretch!
Così del mio dolor gioco ti prendi?   Are you thus making sport of my sorrow?
Ah, voi . . .   Ah you . . .

(towards Don Giovanni who she thinks has not left)

Stelle! l'iniquo fuggì . . . misera me! . . . Dove? in qual parte? . . .	Stars! the wicked man has fled! . . . poor me! . . . Where is he? Where has he gone? . . .

LEPORELLO

Eh! lasciate che vada. Egli non merta che di lui ci pensiate.	Eh! let him go. He is not worthy of your thinking about him.

ELVIRA

Il scellerato m'ingannò, mi tradì . . .	The scoundrel has deceived me, betrayed me . . .

LEPORELLO

Eh! consolatevi; non siete voi, non foste e non sarete nè la prima, nè l'ultima. Guardate questo non picciol libro; è tutto pieno dei nomi di sue belle; ogni villa, ogni borgo, ogni paese è testimon di sue donnesche imprese. Madamina, il catalogo è questo delle belle che amò il padron mio: un catalogo egli è che ho fatt'io; osservate, leggete con me. In Italia seicento e quaranta, in Lamagna duecento e trentuna, cento in Francia, in Turchia novantuna, ma in Ispagna son già mille e tre. V'han fra queste contadine, cameriere e cittadine, v'han contesse, baronesse, marchesane, principesse, e v'han donne d'ogni grado, d'ogni forma, d'ogni età. Nella bionda egli ha l'usanza di lodar la gentilezza; nella bruna, la costanza; nella bianca, la dolcezza; vuol d'inverno la grassotta, vuol d'estate la magrotta;	Eh! console yourself; you are not, were not and will not be either the first or the last. Look at this not small book; it's completely full of the names of his beauties; every villa, every town, every country is witness to his womanizing enterprises. Dear madame, this is the catalogue of the beauties my master has loved: a catalogue that I have made; observe, read along with me. In Italy six hundred and forty, In Germany two hundred and thirty-one, a hundred in France, in Turkey ninety- one, but in Spain there are already one thousand and three. Among these are country girls, maids and city women. There are countesses, baronesses, marchionesses, princesses, there are women of every rank, of every shape, of every age. He habitually praises the gentleness of a blond one; of a dark one, her constancy; of a pale one, her sweetness; in the winter he wants a plump one, in the summer he wants a lean one;

è la grande maestosa,	the large one is imposing,
la piccina è ognor vezzosa;	the small one is always charming;
delle vecchie fa conquista	he makes conquest of the old ladies
pel piacer di porle in lista;	for the pleasure of putting them on the list;
sua passion predominante	but his predominant passion
è la giovin principiante;	is the young beginner;
non si picca se sia ricca,	he doesn't care if she is rich
se sia brutta, se sia bella;	if she is ugly, if she is lovely;
purché porti la gonnella,	as long as she wears a skirt,
voi sapete quel che fa.	you know what he does.

(He leaves.)

SCENE VI

Donna Elvira alone

ELVIRA

In questa forma dunque	So in this way
mi tradì il scellerato! È questo il premio	the scoundrel has betrayed me! Is this the reward
che quel barbaro rende all'amor mio?	that the barbarous man gives for my love?
Ah! vendicar vogl'io	Ah! I must avenge
l'ingannato mio cor. Pria ch'ei mi fugga	my deceived heart. Before he flees me
si ricorra . . . si vada . . . Io sento in petto	let me run after . . . let me go . . . I feel only vengeance,
sol vendetta parlar, rabbia e dispetto.	rage and contempt contending in my bosom.

(leaves)

SCENE VII

Zerlina, Masetto and Chorus of Peasants of both sexes, who sing, play and dance.

ZERLINA

Giovinette, che fate all'amore,	Young ladies, who play at love,
non lasciate che passi l'età;	do not let time pass you by;
se nel seno vi bulica il core,	if your heart boils in your breast,
il rimedio vedetelo qua.	look there for the remedy.
La ra la, la ra la, la ra la.	La ra la, la ra la, la ra la.
Che piacer! che piacer che sarà!	What pleasure! what pleasure it will be!

CHORUS (*of peasant girls*)

La ra la, etc.	La ra la, etc.

MASETTO

Giovinetti, leggeri di testa,	Young men, frivolous and fickle,
non andate girando qua e là;	don't turn from here to there;
poco dura de' matti la festa,	the party doesn't last long for crazy fools,
ma per me cominciato non ha.	for me it hasn't yet begun.
La ra la, la ra la, la ra la.	La ra la, la ra la, la ra la.
Che piacer! che piacer che sarà!	What pleasure! what pleasure it will be!

CHORUS (*of peasant girls*)

La ra la, etc.	La ra la, etc.

ZERLINA and MASETTO

Vieni, vieni, carin {o a,} e godiamo,	Come, come, dear one, let us revel,
e cantiamo e balliamo e saltiamo,	and sing and dance and skip,
Vieni, vieni, carin {o a,} e godiamo,	Come, come, dear one, let us revel,
che piacer! che piacer che sarà!	what pleasure! what pleasure it will be!

SCENE VIII

Don Giovanni, Leporello and the above mentioned

GIOVANNI

Manco male, è partita . . . Oh guarda, guarda	Thank Heaven she's gone . . . Oh, look, look
che bella gioventù, che belle donne!	what attractive young people, what lovely women!

LEPORELLO

(Fra tante, per mia fe',	(Among so many, by my faith,
vi sarà qualche cosa anche per me.)	there will be something for me too.)

GIOVANNI

Cari amici, buon giorno. Seguitate	Dear friends, good day. Continue
a stare allegramente,	to enjoy yourselves,
seguitate a suonar, o buona gente.	go on playing the music, good people.
C'è qualche sposalizio?	Is there some sort of marriage?

ZERLINA

Si, signore,	Yes, sir,
e la sposa son io.	and I am the bride.

GIOVANNI

Me ne consolo.

Lo sposo?

I'm terribly glad to hear it.

The bridegroom?

MASETTO

Io, per servirla.

I, at your service.

GIOVANNI

Oh, bravo! per servirmi; questo è vero
parlar da galantuomo.

Oh, bravo! at my service; this is truly the
speech of a man of honor.

LEPORELLO

Basta che sia marito!

It's enough that he be a husband!

ZERLINA

Oh! il mio Masetto
è un uom d'ottimo core.

Oh! my Masetto
is a man of the very best heart.

GIOVANNI

Oh, anch'io, vedete!
Voglio che siamo amici. Il vostro nome?

Oh, so am I, as you can see!
I want us to be friends. Your name?

ZERLINA

Zerlina.

Zerlina.

GIOVANNI

E il tuo?

And yours?

MASETTO

Masetto!

Masetto!

GIOVANNI

Oh! caro il mio Masetto!
Cara la mia Zerlina! v'esibisco
la mia protezïone . . . Leporello? . . .

Oh! my dear Masetto!
My dear Zerlina! I offer you
my protection . . . Leporello? . . .

(to Leporello who is dallying with the other peasant girls)

Cosa fai lì, birbone?

What are you doing there, rascal?

LEPORELLO

Anch'io, caro padrone,
esibisco la mia protezione.

I too, dear master,
am offering my protection.

GIOVANNI

Presto; va con costor: nel mio palazzo

Quick; go with them: take them
    immediately

311

conducili sul fatto: ordina che abbiano

cioccolata, caffè, vini, prosciutti:
cerca divertir tutti,
mostra loro il giardino,
la galleria, le camere; in effetto

(In passing near Zerlina he takes her by the waist.)

fa' che resti contento il mio Masetto.
Hai capito?

to my palazzo: give orders that they be given

chocolate, coffee, wine, ham:
try to amuse everyone,
show them the garden,
the gallery, the bedrooms: in fact

make sure that my Masetto stays content.
Have you understood?

LEPORELLO

Ho capito.

I've understood.

(to the peasants)

Andiam.

Let's go.

MASETTO

Signore . . .

Signore . . .

GIOVANNI

Cosa c'è?

What is it?

MASETTO

La Zerlina
Senza me non può star.

Zerlina
Cannot stay without me.

LEPORELLO

In vostro loco
ci sarà sua eccellenza, e saprà bene
fare le vostre parti.

His Excellency
will be here, and he will know very well
how to stand in your stead.

GIOVANNI

Oh! la Zerlina
è in man d'un cavalier. Va' pur; fra poco

ella meco verrà.

Oh! Zerlina
is in the hands of a cavalier. Just go; shortly
she will come with me.

ZERLINA

Va', non temere;
nelle mani son io d'un cavaliere.

Go, do not fear;
I am in the hands of a cavalier.

MASETTO

E per questo? . . .

And so? . . .

Don Giovanni

ZERLINA

E per questo	And so, there
Non c'è da dubitar . . .	is no reason for suspicion . . .

MASETTO

Ed io, cospetto! . . .   And I, by God! . . .

GIOVANNI

Olà, finiam le dispute; se subito,	Ho, let's end these arguments; if you do not go
senz'altro replicar, non te ne vai,	immediately without further objections,
Masetto, guarda ben, ti pentirai.	Masetto, look out, you will regret it.

(showing him his sword)

MASETTO (to Don Giovanni)

Ho capito, signor sì!	I've understood, yes, sir!
Chino il capo e me ne vo;	I bow my head and go;
giacchè piace a voi così,	since that is what pleases you
altre repliche non fo.	I make no further objections.
Cavalier voi siete già,	You are indeed a cavalier,
dubitar non posso, affè;	I cannot doubt it, in faith;
me lo dice la bontà	I can tell by the consideration
che volete aver per me.	you have for me.

(aside, to Zerlina)

Bricconaccia, malandrina,	Little rogue, little rascal,
fosti ognor la mia ruina.	You always were my downfall.

(to Leporello who wants to lead him off)

Vengo, vengo!   I am coming, I am coming!

(to Zerlina)

Resta, resta!	Stay, stay!
È una cosa molto onesta;	It is a very upright business;
faccia il nostro cavaliere	let our cavalier make
cavaliera ancora te.	a "cavaliera" of you too.

(Masetto leaves with Leporello and the Peasants.)

Scene IX

Don Giovanni and Zerlina

GIOVANNI

Alfin siam liberati,
Zerlinetta gentil, da quel scioccone.
Che ne dite, mio ben, so far pulito?

At last we are freed,
gentle Zerlinetta, from that great fool.
What do you say, my beloved, wasn't it
neatly done?

ZERLINA

Signore, è mio marito . . .

Sir, he is my husband . . .

GIOVANNI

Chi! colui?

Who! that one?

Vi par che un onest'uomo,
un nobil cavalier, com'io mi vanto,
possa soffrir, che quel visetto d'oro,
quel viso inzuccherato
da un bifolcaccio vil sia strapazzato?

Does it seem to you that an honest man,
a noble cavalier, as I pride myself to be,
could suffer that little golden face,
that delicious sweet face
be ill-treated by that rough ploughman?

ZERLINA

Ma, signor, io gli diedi
parola di sposarlo.

But, sir, I gave
my word to marry him.

GIOVANNI

Tal parola
non vale un zero. Voi non siete fatta
per esser paesana; un'altra sorte
vi procuran quegli occhi bricconcelli,
quei labbretti sì belli,

Such a promise
is worth nothing. You are not made
to be a peasant; those roguish eyes,
those little lips so lovely,
those little fingers, pale and sweet-
smelling,

quelle ditucce candide e odorose:
parmi toccar giuncata e fiutar rose.

are going to procure another fate for you:
I seem to touch cream* and to smell
roses.

ZERLINA

Ah! . . . non vorrei . . .

Ah! . . . I wouldn't want . . .

GIOVANNI

Che non vorreste?

What wouldn't you want?

* "Giuncata" has no English equivalent—certainly not "junket"! It was a delicacy made of milk curds which was served on a little mat of woven reeds ("giunchi").

314

ZERLINA

Alfine	To be left

ingannata restar. Io so che raro
colle donne voi altri cavalieri
siete onesti e sinceri.

deceived in the end. I know how rarely
you cavaliers are honest and sincere
with women.

GIOVANNI

È un'impostura
della gente plebea. La nobiltà
ha dipinta negli occhi l'onestà.
Orsù, non perdiam tempo; in questo
    istante
io ti voglio sposar.

The common people are
deceived in this. In the eyes of the
nobility you can read its honesty.
Come, let us not lose time; this very
    moment
I wish to marry you.

ZERLINA

Voi!

You!

GIOVANNI

Certo, io.
Quel casinetto è mio: soli saremo,

e là, gioiello mio, ci sposeremo.
Là ci darem la mano,
là mi dirai di sì.
Vedi, non è lontano:
partiam, ben mio, da qui.

Certainly, I.
That little house is mine: we shall be
    alone,
and there, my jewel, we shall be married.
There we shall give each other our hands,
there you will tell me "yes."
See, it is not far:
let us leave here, my beloved.

ZERLINA

(Vorrei, e non verrei . . .
Mi trema un poco il cor . . .
Felice, è ver, sarei:
ma può burlarmi ancor.)

(I would like to, and not like to . . .
My heart trembles a little . . .
I would be happy, it's true:
but he could still make light of me.)

GIOVANNI

Vieni, mio bel diletto!

Come, my lovely delight!

ZERLINA

(Mi fa pietà Masetto.)

(I feel sorry for Masetto.)

GIOVANNI

Io cangerò tua sorte.

I shall change your fate.

ZERLINA

Presto non son più forte.

Suddenly I am no longer strong.

BOTH

Andiam, andiam, mio bene,	Let us go, let us go, my beloved,
a ristorar le pene	to renew the pangs
d'un innocente amor!	of an innocent love!

(Entwined, they go toward the country-house)

SCENE X

Donna Elvira and the abovementioned

ELVIRA

(who stops Don Giovanni with desperate gestures)

Fermati, scellerato! Il ciel mi fece	Stop, scoundrel! Heaven has granted that
udir le tue perfidie. Io sono a tempo	I hear your treacheries. I am in time
di salvar questa misera innocente	to save this poor innocent girl
dal tuo barbaro artiglio.	from your barbarous clutches.

ZERLINA

Meschina! cosa sento!	Poor me! what do I hear!

GIOVANNI

(Amor, consiglio.)	(Love, advise me.)

(softly, to Donna Elvira)

Idol mio, non vedete	My idol, do you not see
ch'io voglio divertirmi?	that I wish to amuse myself?

ELVIRA *(loudly)*

Divertirti?	Amuse yourself?
è vero! divertirti . . . Io so, crudele,	It is true! amuse yourself . . . I know, cruel man,
come tu ti diverti.	how you amuse yourself.

ZERLINA

Ma, signor cavaliere,	But, signor cavalier,
è ver quel ch'ella dice?	is it true what she is saying?

GIOVANNI *(softly to Zerlina)*

La povera infelice	The poor, unhappy woman
è di me innamorata,	is in love with me,
e per pietà degg'io fingere amore,	and out of pity I must pretend love,
ch'io son, per mia disgrazia, uom di buon cuore.	since I am, to my misfortune, a man of good heart.

316

ELVIRA

Ah, fuggi il traditor,	Ah, flee the traitor,
non lo lasciar più dir:	do not let him say any more:
il labbro è mentitor,	his lips are liars,
fallace il ciglio.	false his face.
Da' miei tormenti impara	Learn from my torments
a creder a quel cor,	how best to believe that heart,
e nasca il tuo timor.	and let your fear be born
dal mio periglio.	from my danger.

(She leaves leading off Zerlina)

SCENE XI

Don Giovanni, later Don Ottavio and Donna Anna, who is dressed in mourning

GIOVANNI

Mi par ch'oggi il demonio si diverta	I think that today the devil is amusing himself
d'opporsi a' miei piacevoli progressi;	by opposing my pleasing proceedings;
vanno mal tutti quanti.	they are all going badly.

OTTAVIO (*to Donna Anna*)

Ah! ch'ora, idolo mio, son vani i pianti,	Ah! now that, my idol, tears are useless,
di vendetta si parli . . . Ah, Don Giovanni!	let us speak of vengeance . . . Oh, Don Giovanni!

GIOVANNI

(Mancava questo inver!)	(Only this was lacking!)

ANNA

Signore, a tempo	Signore, we have found
vi ritroviam, avete core, avete	you in time: do you have a heart? do you have
anima generosa?	a generous soul?

GIOVANNI

(Sta'a vedere	(One can see
Che il diavolo le ha detto qualche cosa.)	That the devil has told her something.)
Che domanda! perchè?	What a question! why?

OTTAVIO

Bisogno abbiamo	We have need
Della vostra amicizia.	Of your friendship.

GIOVANNI

(Mi torna il fiato in corpo.)
  Comandate . . .
I congiunti, i parenti,
questa man, questo ferro, i beni, il sangue
spenderò per servirvi.
Ma voi, bella Donn'Anna,
perchè così piangete?
Il crudele chi fù che osò la calma

turbar del viver vostro . . .

(The breath returns to my body.)
  Command me . . .
Relations, kindred,
this hand, this sword, goods, blood
shall I expend to serve you.
But you, lovely Donn' Anna,
why do you weep so?
Who was the cruel man who dared
  disturb
the calm of your life . . .

SCENE XII

Donna Elvira and the abovementioned

ELVIRA (*to Don Giovanni*)

Ah! ti ritrovo ancor, perfido mostro!

Ah! I find you again, perfidious monster!

(*to Donna Anna*)

Non ti fidar, o misera,
di quel ribaldo cor;
me già tradì quel barbaro,

te vuol tradire ancor.

Do not trust, oh unhappy woman,
in that villainous heart;
that barbarous man has already betrayed
  me,
he wishes to betray you as well.

ANNA and OTTAVIO

(Cieli, che aspetto nobile!
Che dolce maestà!
Il suo pallor, le lagrime,
m'empiono di pietà.)

(Heavens, what a noble appearance!
What gentle bearing!
Her pallor, her tears
fill me with pity.)

GIOVANNI

(*aside; Donna Elvira listens.*)

La povera ragazza
è pazza, amici miei;
Lasciatemi con lei,
forse si calmerà.

The poor girl
is crazy, my friends;
Leave me with her,
perhaps she will calm down.

ELVIRA

Ah! non credete al perfido!
restate ancor, restate . . .

Ah, do not believe the treacherous man!
yet stay, stay . . .

318

Don Giovanni

GIOVANNI

È pazza, non badate . . .   She is crazy, pay no mind . . .

ANNA and OTTAVIO

A chi si crederà?   Who is to be believed?
(Certo moto d'ignoto tormento   (I feel a certain unknown torment
dentro l'alma girare mi sento,   disturbing my soul,
che mi dice per quella infelice   and telling me a hundred things about
                                         that unhappy woman
cento cose che intender non sa.)   which my soul cannot understand.)

ELVIRA

(Sdegno, rabbia, dispetto, tormento (Indignation, rage, contempt, torment
dentro l'alma girare mi sento,   Disturb my soul
che mi dice di quel traditore   and tell me a hundred things
cento cose che intender non sa.)   about that traitor, which my soul cannot
                                         understand.)

OTTAVIO (*to Donna Anna*)

Io di qua non vado via   I am not leaving here
se non scopro quest'affar.   until I discover how this matter stands.

ANNA (*to Ottavio*)

Non ha l'aria di pazzia   Her face, her manner of speaking
il suo volto, il suo parlar.   do not have the air of madness.

GIOVANNI

(Se men vado, si potria   (If I leave, one could
qualche cosa sospettar.)   suspect something.)

ELVIRA

Da quel ceffo si dovria   From that cruel face one should
la ner'alma giudicar.   pass judgement on that black soul.

OTTAVIO (*to Don Giovanni*)

Dunque quella? . . .   Then that woman? . . .

GIOVANNI

È pazzerella.   Is a little crazy.

ANNA (*to Donna Elvira*)

Dunque quegli? . . .   Then that man? . . .

ELVIRA

È un traditore.   Is a traitor.

319

GIOVANNI

Infelice!   Unhappy woman!

ELVIRA

Mentitore!   Liar!

ANNA and OTTAVIO

Incomincio a dubitar.   I am beginning to doubt.

(*Some peasants pass by.*)

GIOVANNI

(*softly to Donna Elvira*)

Zitto, zitto, chè la gente   Quiet, quiet, since people
si raduna a noi d'intorno: are gathering around us:
siate un poco più prudente,   be a little more prudent,
vi farete criticar.   you will bring criticism on yourself.

ELVIRA

(*strongly to Don Giovanni*)

Non sperarlo, o scellerato: Do not hope for that, oh scoundrel:
ho perduto la prudenza.   I have lost all caution.
Le tue colpe ed il mio stato   I wish to reveal to everyone
voglio a tutti palesar.   your guilt and my state.

ANNA and OTTAVIO

(*aside, looking at Don Giovanni*)

Quegli accenti sì sommessi,   His words so subdued,
quel cangiarsi di colore,   that change of color,
sono indizi troppo espressi   are such explicit indications
che mi fan determinar.   that they are helping me decide.

(*Donna Elvira leaves.*)

GIOVANNI

Povera sventurata! i passi suoi   Poor unfortunate lady! I want
voglio seguir, non voglio   to follow her, I do not want her
che faccia un precipizio: to do something rash: pardon me,
perdonate, bellissima Donn'Anna: loveliest Donn' Anna:
se servirvi poss'io,   If I can serve you,
in mia casa v'aspetto, amici, addio! I await you at my home; friends, farewell!

(*He leaves hurriedly.*)

SCENE XIII

Donna Anna and Don Ottavio

ANNA

Don Ottavio . . . son morta!   Don Ottavio . . . I am dying!

OTTAVIO

Cos'è stato?   What has happened?

ANNA

Per pietà, soccorretemi.   For pity's sake, help me.

OTTAVIO

Mio bene,   My beloved,
fate coraggio.   take courage.

ANNA

Oh Dei! quegli è il carnefice   Oh Gods! that man is the murderer
del padre mio . . .   of my father . . .

OTTAVIO

Che dite?   What are you saying?

ANNA

Non dubitate più. Gli ultimi accenti,   Doubt it no longer. The last words
che l'empio proferì, tutta la voce   that the impious man proffered,
                                                  everything about his voice
richiamar nel cor mio di quell'indegno   recalled in my heart that base man
che nel mio appartamento . . .   who in my apartment . . .

OTTAVIO

Oh ciel! possibile   Oh heaven! is it possible
che sotto il sacro manto d'amicizia . . .   that under the sacred mantle of
                                                  friendship . . .
Ma come fu, narratemi   But how did it happen, relate
lo strano avvenimento.   the strange event to me.

ANNA

Era già alquanto   The night
avanzata la notte,   was already somewhat advanced,
quando nelle mie stanze, ove soletta   when into my rooms, where to my
                                                  misfortune
mi trovai per sventura, entrar io vidi   I found myself all alone, I saw enter,
in un mantello avvolto   wrapped in a cloak,

un uom che al primo istante
avea preso per voi;
ma riconobbi poi
che un inganno era il mio . . .

a man who at the first moment
I had taken for you;
but then I recognized
that I had been mistaken . . .

OTTAVIO (*with anxiety*)

Stelle! seguite.

Stars! continue.

ANNA

Tacito a me s'appressa,
e mi vuole abbracciar; sciogliermi cerco,

ei più mi stringe; grido:
non viene alcun: con una mano cerca
d'impedire la voce,
e coll'altra m'afferra
stretta così, che già mi credo vinta.

Silently he approaches me,
and wishes to embrace me; I try to free
	myself,
he grasps me tighter; I cry out:
no one comes: with one hand he tries
to stifle my voice,
with the other he seizes me
so tightly that I already believe myself
	vanquished.

OTTAVIO

Perfido! . . . e alfin? . . .

Treacherous man! . . . and finally? . . .

ANNA

Alfine il duol, l'orrore
dell'infame attentato
accrebbe sì la lena mia che, a forza
di svincolarmi, torcermi e piegarmi,

da lui mi sciolsi.

Finally the sorrow, the horror
of the infamous attack
so increased my energy
that by disengaging myself, twisting
	myself and bending myself,
I loosed myself from him.

OTTAVIO

Ohimè! respiro.

Ah! I breath again.

ANNA

Allora
rinforzo i stridi miei, chiamo soccorso,
fugge il fellon: arditamente il seguo
fin nella strada per fermarlo, e sono
assalitrice ed assalita: il padre
v'accorre, vuol conoscerlo, e l'iniquo,

che del povero vecchio era più forte,
compie il misfatto suo col dargli morte.

Then
I redouble my cries, I call for help,
the traitor flees: I boldly follow him
even into the street to stop him, and I am
assailant and assailed: my father
runs out, tries to identify him, and the
	wicked man
who was stronger than the poor old one
crowns his misdeed by giving him death.

Don Giovanni

Or sai chi l'onore	Now you know who wanted
rapire a me volse:	to ravish my honor:
chi fu il traditore,	who was the traitor,
che il padre mi tolse:	who took my father from me:
vendetta ti chieggo,	I ask you for vengeance,
la chiede il tuo cor.	your own heart asks for it.
Rammenta la piaga	Remember the wound
del misero seno:	in the poor breast:
rimira di sangue	see again the ground
coperto il terreno,	covered with blood,
se l'ira in te langue	if the anger of a righteous fury
d'un giusto furor.	languishes in you.

(She leaves.)

SCENE XIV

Ottavio alone

OTTAVIO

Come mai creder deggio	How can I ever believe
di sì nero delitto	a cavalier capable
capace un cavaliero!	of such a black crime!
Ah, di scoprire il vero	Ah, let every means of discovering the
ogni mezzo si cerchi. Io sento in petto	truth be sought. I feel in my breast,
e di sposo e d'amico	both as betrothed and as friend
il dover che mi parla:	the duty that speaks to me:
disingannarla voglio, o vendicarla.	I must undeceive her or avenge her.
Dalla sua pace la mia dipende,	On her peace of mind mine depends,
quel che a lei piace vita mi rende,	that which pleases her gives me life,
quel che le incresce morte mi dà.	that which wearies her gives me death.
S'ella sospira, sospiro anch'io,	If she sighs, I sigh also,
è mia quell'ira, quel pianto è mio	her anger is mine, her weeping is mine
e non ho bene s'ella non l'ha.	and I have no happiness if she has none.

(He leaves.)

SCENE XV

Leporello alone, then Don Giovanni

LEPORELLO

Io deggio, ad ogni patto,	I must, on any terms,
per sempre abbandonar questo bel matto . . .	abandon this arch-madman for ever . . .

Eccolo qui: guardate
con qual indifferenza se ne viene!

Here he is now: see
with what indifference he comes along!

GIOVANNI

Oh Leporello mio! va tutto bene.

Oh, my Leporello! everything is going
well.

LEPORELLO

Don Giovannino mio! va tutto male.

My Don Giovannino! everything is going
badly.

GIOVANNI

Come va tutto male?

How is everything going badly?

LEPORELLO

Vado a casa,
come voi l'ordinaste,
con tutta quella gente.

I go home
as you ordered,
with all those people.

GIOVANNI

Bravo!

Bravo!

LEPORELLO

A forza
di chiacchiere, di vezzi e di bugie,
ch'ho imparato sì bene a star con voi,

cerco d'intrattenerli . . .

By means of
chatter, endearments and lies,
which I have learned so well by being
with you,
I try to keep them amused . . .

GIOVANNI

Bravo!

Bravo!

LEPORELLO

Dico
mille cose a Masetto per placarlo,

per trargli dal pensier la gelosia . . .

I say
a thousand things to Masetto to placate
him,
to draw the jealousy out of his
thoughts . . .

GIOVANNI

Bravo, in coscienza mia!

Bravo, on my conscience!

LEPORELLO

Faccio che bevano
e gli uomini e le donne;

I get both
the men and women to drink;

son già mezzo ubbriachi,
altri canta, altri scherza,
altri seguita a ber . . . In sul più bello,

chi credete che capiti?

they are already half drunk,
some sing, some dally,
others continue to drink . . . And best of
    all,
who do you think arrives?

GIOVANNI

Zerlina!

Zerlina!

LEPORELLO

Bravo! e con lei chi venne?

Bravo! and who comes with her?

GIOVANNI

Donn' Elvira!

Donn' Elvira!

LEPORELLO

Bravo! e disse di voi?

Bravo! and she said about you?

GIOVANNI

Tutto quel mal che in bocca le venia?

Everything vile that came to her mouth?

LEPORELLO

Bravo, in coscienza mia!

Bravo, on my conscience!

GIOVANNI

E tu cosa facesti?

And what did you do?

LEPORELLO

Tacqui.

I was silent.

GIOVANNI

Ed ella?

And she?

LEPORELLO

Seguì a gridar.

She continued to scream.

GIOVANNI

E tu?

And you?

LEPORELLO

Quando mi parve
che già fosse sfogata, dolcemente
fuor dell'orto la trassi, e con bell'arte

chiusa la porta a chiave,
io mi cavai,
e sulla via soletta la lasciai.

When it seemed to me
that she had exhausted herself, gently
I drew her out of the garden, and with
    great cunning,
locking the door,
I escaped,
and left her all by herself in the street.

Giovanni

Bravo! bravo! arcibravo!	Bravo! bravo! triple bravo!
L'affar non può andar meglio.	The affair cannot go better. What you
Incominciasti,	began,
io saprò terminar; troppo mi premono	I know how to finish; I prize these
queste contadinotte:	lusty country girls too much:
le voglio divertir finchè vien notte.	I'd like to amuse them until night arrives.
Fin ch'han dal vino	While they still have heads
calda la testa,	hot from the wine,
una gran festa	have a grand celebration
fa'preparar.	prepared.
Se trovi in piazza	If you find some girl
qualche ragazza,	in the piazza,
teco ancor quella	try to carry her along
cerca menar.	with you too.
Senza alcun ordine	Let the dancing
la danza sia:	be without any order:
ch'il minuetto,	let whoever wants
chi la follia,	dance the minuet,
chi l'alemanna	the follia,
farai ballar.	the alemanna.
Ed io frattanto	And meanwhile I
dall'altro canto	on the other hand
con questa e quella	am going to make love to
vo' amoreggiar.	this or that girl.
Ah! la mia lista	Ah!
doman mattina	by tomorrow morning
d'una decina	will have to add ten or so
devi aumentar.	to my list.

(*They leave.*)

Scene XVI

Garden with two doors locked from the outside. Two niches.
Zerlina, Masetto and Peasants

Zerlina

Masetto . . . senti un po' . . . Masetto,	Masetto . . . listen a moment . . . Masetto,
dico . . .	I say . . .

Masetto

Non mi toccar!	Don't touch me!

326

ZERLINA

Perché?   Why?

MASETTO

　　　　Perché mi chiedi?   You ask me why?
Perfida! il tatto sopportar dovrei   Treacherous girl! must I bear the touch
d'una mano infedele?   of a faithless hand?

ZERLINA

Ah! no: taci, crudele!   Ah! no: be silent, cruel man!
Io non merto da te tal trattamento.   I do not deserve such treatment from
                                                              you.

MASETTO

Come! ed hai l'ardimento di scusarti?   What! and you have the boldness to
                                                              excuse yourself?
Star sola con un uom! abbandonarmi   To be alone with a man! to abandon me
                                                              on
il dì delle mie nozze! porre in fronte   the day of my wedding! to put this mark
                                                              of infamy
a un villano d'onore   on the forehead
questa marca d'infamia! Ah! se non fosse,   of an honorable villager! Ah! if it weren't,
se non fosse lo scandalo, vorrei . . .   if it weren't for the scandal, I would
                                                              like . . .

ZERLINA

Ma se colpa io non ho: ma se da lui   But what if I am not guilty: what if I
                                                              ended up
ingannata rimasi; e poi, che temi?   tricked by him; then, what do you fear?
Tranquillati, mia vita,   Calm yourself, my life.
non mi toccò la punta delle dita.   He didn't touch the tip of my finger.
Non me lo credi? Ingrato!   Don't you believe me? Ungrateful man!
Vien qui, sfogati, ammazzami, fa' tutto   Come here, give vent to your feelings, kill
                                                              me,
di me quel che ti piace,   do whatever you like to me,
ma poi, Masetto mio, ma poi fa pace.   but then, my Masetto, but then make
                                                              peace.

Batti, batti, o bel Masetto,   Beat, beat your poor Zerlina,
la tua povera Zerlina: oh handsome Masetto;
starò qui come agnellina   I shall stand here like a little lamb
le tue botte ad aspettar.   waiting for your blows.
Lascerò straziarmi il crine,   I shall let you pull out my hair,

lascerò cavarmi gli occhi;	I shall let you tear out my eyes;
e le care tue manine	and then, happy, I shall be able
lieta poi saprò baciar.	to kiss your dear little hands.
Ah! Io vedo, non hai core:	Ah! I see it, you have no heart for it:
pace, pace, o vita mia!	peace, peace, oh my life!
In contenti ed allegria	In delights and gladness
notte e dì vogliam passar.	let us pass the night and day.

SCENE XVII

Masetto, then Don Giovanni within and Zerlina again

MASETTO

Guarda un po' come seppe	Just look how this witch
questa strega sedurmi! Siamo pure	was able to seduce me! We are really
i deboli di testa!	weak in the head!

GIOVANNI (*from within*)

Sia preparato tutto a una gran festa.	Let all be prepared for a grand celebration.

ZERLINA

Ah! Masetto, Masetto, odi la voce	Ah! Masetto, Masetto, listen. The voice
del monsù cavaliero!	of Monsieur Cavalier!

MASETTO

Ebben, che c'è?   Well, what of it?

ZERLINA

Verra ...   He will come ...

MASETTO

Lascia che venga.   Let him come.

ZERLINA

Ah! se vi fosse   Ah! if there were
un buco da fuggir ...   a hole to climb into ...

MASETTO

Di cosa temi?   What are you afraid of?

Perchè diventi pallida? ... Ah! capisco:	Why are you becoming pale? ... Ah! I understand:
capisco, bricconcella,	I understand, little rogue,
hai timor ch' io comprenda	you are afraid I might understand

com'è tra voi passata la faccenda.
Presto, presto . . . pria che venga.
por mi vo' da qualche lato . . .
C'è una nicchia . . . qui celato
cheto, cheto mi vo' star.

how the business between you two went.
Quick, quick . . . before he comes,
I must place myself off to this side . . .
Here is a niche . . . I will stay here
quietly hidden.

ZERLINA

Senti, senti . . . dove vai?
Ah non l'asconder, O Masetto.
Se ti trova, poveretto!
tu non sai quel che può far.

Listen, listen . . . where are you going?
Don't hide yourself, Masetto.
If he finds you, poor boy!
You don't know what he can do.

MASETTO

Faccia, dica quel che vuole.

Let him do and say what he wants to.

ZERLINA (*under her breath*)

Ah, non giovan le parole . . .

Ah, words are useless . . .

MASETTO

Parla forte, e qui ti arresta.

Speak up, and stay here.

ZERLINA

Che capricco ha nella testa!

What a whim he has in his head!

MASETTO

(Capirò se m'è fedele,
e in qual modo andò l'affar.)

(I shall learn if she is faithful to me,
and how the matter went.)

(*He enters the niche.*)

ZERLINA

(Quell'ingrato, quel crudele
oggi vuol precipitar.)

(That ungrateful, cruel man
wants to act rashly today.)

SCENE XVIII

Don Giovanni, Peasants and Servants, Zerlina and Masetto, hidden.

GIOVANNI

Su, svegliatevi; da bravi!

Up, wake yourselves up; like good
fellows!

Su, coraggio, o buona gente;
vogliam stare allegramente,
vogliam rider e scherzar.

Up, have courage, oh good people;
Let us be cheerful,
Let us laugh and flirt.

(*to the servants*)

Alla stanza della danza	Lead the whole lot
conducete tutti quantì	to the ballroom
ed a tutti in abbondanza	and let refreshments in abundance
gran rifreschi fate dar.	be given to everyone.

CHORUS (*leaving with the servants*)

Su, svegliatevi; ecc.	Up, wake yourselves up; etc.

SCENE XIX

Don Giovanni, Zerlina and Masetto, hidden

ZERLINA

Tra quest' arbori celata	Maybe he won't see me
si può dar che non mi veda.	hidden among these trees.

(*tries to hide*)

GIOVANNI

Zerlinetta mia garbata,	My graceful little Zerlina,
ti ho già visto, non scappar.	I have already seen you, don't run away.

(*He catches hold of her*)

ZERLINA

Ah! lasciatemi andar via . . .	Ah! let me go . . .

GIOVANNI

No, no, resta, gioia mia!	No, no, stay, my joy!

ZERLINA

Se pietade avete in core!	If you have pity in your heart!

GIOVANNI

Sì, ben mio, son tutto amore . . .	Yes, my beloved! I am all love . . .
Vieni un poco in questo loco,	Come here for a moment,
fortunata io ti vo' far.	I want to make you happy.

ZERLINA

(Ah! s'ei vede il sposo mio,	(Ah! if he sees my betrothed
so ben io quel che può far.)	I know well what he can do.)

(*Don Giovanni, in opening the niche, discovers Masetto.*)

GIOVANNI

Masetto!	Masetto!

MASETTO

Sì, Masetto.   Yes, Masetto.

GIOVANNI (*somewhat confused*)

E chiuso là, perchè?   And why hidden in there?
La bella tua Zerlina   Your lovely Zerlina,
non può, la poverina,   poor little girl,
più star senza di te.   cannot be without you.

MASETTO

(*somewhat ironic*)

Capisco, sì, signore.   I understand, yes, sir.

GIOVANNI (*to Zerlina*)

Adesso fate core.   Now take heart.

(*An orchestra is heard in the distance.*)

I suonatori udite: Listen to the players:
venite omai con me.   come now with me.

MASETTO and ZERLINA

Sì, sì, facciamo core,   Yes, yes, let us take heart,
ed a ballar cogli altri   and let us all three go
andiamo tutti e tre.   to dance with the others.

(*They leave.*)

SCENE XX

Don Ottavio, Donna Anna and Donna Elvira in masks; later
Leporello and Don Giovanni at the window.

ELVIRA

Bisogna aver coraggio,   We must have courage,
o cari amici miei,   oh my dear friends,
e i suoi misfatti rei   and then we will be able to uncover
scoprir potremo allor.   his guilty crimes.

OTTAVIO

L'amica dice bene;   Our friend speaks well;
coraggio aver conviene.   it is necessary to have courage.

(*to Donna Anna*)

Discaccia, o vita mia,
l'affanno ed il timor.

Dismiss, oh my life,
anguish and fear.

ANNA

Il passo è perioglioso,
può nascer qualche imbroglio;
temo pel caro sposo
E per noi temo ancor.

It is a dangerous step,
some trouble could come of it;
I fear for my dear betrothed.
And I fear for us as well.

LEPORELLO (*opening the window*)

Signor, guardate un poco
che maschere galanti!

Signor, just look,
what elegant maskers!

GIOVANNI (*at the window*)

Falle passar avanti,
di' che ci fanno onor.

Have them come forward,
say that they do us honor.

ANNA, ELVIRA and OTTAVIO

(Al volto ed alla voce
si scopre il traditor.)

(By his face and his voice
the traitor reveals himself.)

LEPORELLO

Zì, zì, signore maschere;
Zì, zì . . .

Pst, pst, lady maskers,
Pst, pst . . .

ANNA and ELVIRA (*softly to Don Ottavio*)

Via rispondete.

Come, answer.

LEPORELLO

Zì, zì . . .

Pst, pst . . .

OTTAVIO

Cosa chiedete?

What do you ask?

LEPORELLO

Al ballo, se vi piace,
v'invita il mio signore.

If it please you, my lord
invites you to the ball.

OTTAVIO

Grazie di tanto onore.
Andiam, compagne belle.

Thank you for such an honor.
Let us go, lovely companions.

LEPORELLO

(L'amico anche su quelle
prova farà d'amor.)

(My friend will test his love
on these ladies as well.)

Don Giovanni

(*goes in, closing the window*)

ANNA and OTTAVIO

Protegga il giusto cielo
il zelo del mio cor.

May righteous heaven protect
the zeal of my heart.

ELVIRA

Vendichi il giusto cielo
il mio tradito amor.

May righteous heaven protect
my betrayed heart.

(*They enter.*)

SCENE XXI

Hall in Don Giovanni's house, illuminated and prepared for a grand ball.

Don Giovanni, Leporello, Zerlina, Masetto, Peasants of both sexes, servants with refreshments; later Don Ottavio, Donna Anna and Donna Elvira, masked.

Don Giovanni seats the girls and Leporello the boys who have just finished dancing.

GIOVANNI

Riposate, vezzose ragazze.

Rest, charming girls.

LEPORELLO

Rinfrescatevi, bei giovinotti.

Refresh yourselves, handsome fellows.

GIOVANNI and LEPORELLO

Tornerete a far presto le pazze,
tornerete a scherzare, a ballar.

Soon you will again be behaving madly,
you will again be flirting, dancing.

GIOVANNI

Ehi! caffè.

Hey! coffee.

LEPORELLO

Cioccolata.

Chocolate.

MASETTO (*softly to Zerlina*)

Ah! Zerlina, giudizio!

Ah! Zerlina, be careful!

GIOVANNI

Sorbetti.

Sherbets.

LEPORELLO

Confetti.

Sweets.

ZERLINA and MASETTO (*aside*)

(Troppo dolce comincia la scena.   (The scene begins too mildly.
In amaro potria terminar.)   It could end in bitterness.)

(*Refreshments are brought and distributed.*)

GIOVANNI (*caressing Zerlina*)

Sei pur vaga, brillante Zerlina!   You are truly beautiful, radiant Zerlina!

ZERLINA

Sua bontà.   You are kind.

MASETTO (*trembling with rage*)

(La briccona fa festa.)   (The roguish girl is having a good time.)

LEPORELLO (*imitating his master with the other girls*)

Sei pur cara, Giannotta, Sandrina!   You are truly dear, Giannotta, Sandrina!

MASETTO (*observing Don Giovanni*)

(Tocca pur, che ti cada la testa.)   (Just touch her, your head will fall.)

ZERLINA

(Quel Masetto mi par stralunato.   (It looks like Masetto is beside himself.
Brutto, brutto si fa quest'affar.)   This affair is becoming really ugly.)

GIOVANNI and LEPORELLO

(Quel Masetto mi par stralunato.   (It looks like Masetto is beside himself.
Qui bisogna cervello adoprar.)   Now one must put one's brain to use.)

MASETTO

Tocca, tocca!   Just touch her!
Ah, briccona!   Ah, little rogue!
mi vuoi disperar.   You want to drive me to despair.

SCENE XXII

Don Ottavio, Donna Anna, Donna Elvira and the abovementioned

LEPORELLO

Venite pur avanti,   Just come forward,
vezzose mascherette.   Charming maskers.

GIOVANNI

È aperto a tutti quanti.   It is open to everyone.

ALL

Viva la libertà!   Long live liberty!

ANNA, ELVIRA and OTTAVIO

Siam grati a tanti segni
di generosità.

We are grateful for so many signs
of generosity.

GIOVANNI

Ricominiciate il suono.

Let the playing begin again.

(*to Leporello*)

Tu accoppia i ballerini.

Couple the dancers.

(*Don Ottavio dances the minuet with Donna Anna.*)

LEPORELLO

Da bravi, via, ballate.

Come, dance, like good fellows.

(*They dance.*)

ELVIRA (*to Donna Anna*)

Quella è la contadina.

That is the peasant girl.

ANNA (*to Ottavio*)

Io moro!

I am dying!

OTTAVIO

Simulate.

Keep up appearances.

LEPORELLO and DON GIOVANNI

Va bene, in verità!

It's going well, truly!

MASETTO (*ironically*)

Va bene, in verità!

It's going well, truly!

GIOVANNI (*to Leporello*)

A bada tien Masetto.

Keep Masetto at bay.

(*to Zerlina*)

Il tuo compagno io sono,
Zerlina, vien pur qua . . .

I am your partner,
Zerlina, just come here . . .

(*He begins to dance a contredance with Zerlina.*)

LEPORELLO (*to Masetto*)

Non balli, poveretto?
Vien qua, Masetto caro,
facciam quel ch'altri fa.

You're not dancing, poor fellow?
Come here, dear Masetto,
let's do what the others are doing.

(*He forces Masetto to dance.*)

MASETTO

No, no, ballar non voglio.   No, no, I don't want to dance.

LEPORELLO

Eh! balla, amico mio.   Hey! dance, my friend.

ANNA (*to Donna Elvira*)

Resister non poss'io!   I cannot endure it!

ELVIRA and OTTAVIO (*to Donna Anna*)

Fingete, per pietà.   Pretend, for pity's sake.

(*Leporello dances the Deutsch with Masetto.*)

GIOVANNI

Vieni con me, mia vita . . .   Come with me, my life . . .

(*Dancing, he leads Zerlina off.*)

MASETTO

Lasciami . . . Ah . . . no . . . Zerlina!   Let me go . . . Ah . . . no . . . Zerlina!

(*He goes in shaking himself loose from Leporello.*)

ZERLINA

Oh Numi! son tradita! . . .   Oh Gods! I am betrayed! . . .

LEPORELLO

(Qui nasce una ruina.)   (Here disaster is born.)

(*He goes in.*)

ANNA, ELVIRA and OTTAVIO (*among themselves*)

L'iniquo da se stesso   The wicked man, on his own initiative,
nel laccio se ne va.   goes into the snare.

ZERLINA

Gente! . . . aiuto! . . . aiuto! gente!   People! . . . help! . . . help! people!

ANNA, ELVIRA and OTTAVIO

Soccorriamo l'innocente . . .   Let us help the innocent girl . . .

(*The musicians leave.*)

MASETTO

Ah! Zerlina! . . .   Ah! Zerlina! . . .

Don Giovanni

ZERLINA (*from within*)

Scellerato!   Scoundrel!

ANNA, ELVIRA and OTTAVIO

Ora grida da quel lato . . .   Now she is crying out from that side . . .
Ah! gettiamo giù la porta . . .   Ah! let us break down the door . . .

ZERLINA

Soccorretemi o son morta! . . .   Help me, or I am done for! . . .

ANNA, ELVIRA, OTTAVIO and MASETTO

Siam qui noi per tua difesa.   We are here in your defense.

(*Giovanni comes out with sword in hand, leading Leporello by an arm, and pretends to be unable to
unsheathe his sword so as to wound Leporello.*)

GIOVANNI

Ecco il birbo che t'ha offesa,   Here is the rascal who has offended you,
ma da me la pena avrà.   but he will have punishment from me.
Mori, iniquo!   Die, wicked fellow!

LEPORELLO

Ah! cosa fate? . . .   Ah, what are you doing? . . .

GIOVANNI

Mori, dico! . . .   Die, I say! . . .

OTTAVIO (*pulling out a pistol*)

Nol sperate . . .   Do not hope for that . . .

ANNA, ELVIRA and OTTAVIO

(L'empio crede con tal frode   (The impious man believes with such a
                                          fraud
di nasconder l'empietà.)   to hide his wickedness.)

(*They pull off their masks.*)

GIOVANNI

Donn' Elvira!   Donn' Elvira!

ELVIRA

Sì, malvagio!   Yes, wicked man!

GIOVANNI

Don Ottavio!   Don Ottavio!

337

OTTAVIO

Sì, signore!   Yes, signore!

GIOVANNI (*to Donna Anna*)

Ah! credete . . .   Ah! believe . . .

ANNA, ELVIRA, ZERLINA, OTTAVIO, MASETTO

Traditore!   Traitor!

Tutto, tutto già si sa.   Everything is known now, everything.

ALL (*except Giovanni and Leporello*)

Trema, tremo, o scellerato,	Tremble, tremble, scoundrel,
saprà tosto il mondo intero	soon the whole world will know of
il misfatto orrendo e nero,	the horrible and black deed,
la tua fiera crudeltà.	of your fierce cruelty.
Odi il tuon della vendetta	Hear the thundering of the vengeance
che ti fischia intorno, intorno;	that whistles all round you;
sul tuo capo in questo giorno	on your head today
il suo fulmine cadrà.	its bolt will fall.

GIOVANNI and LEPORELLO

È confusa la $\begin{cases} \text{mia} \\ \text{sua} \end{cases}$ testa,

$\text{Non} \begin{cases} \text{so} \\ \text{sa} \end{cases}$ più quel ch' $\begin{cases} \text{io mi} \\ \text{ei si} \end{cases}$ faccia,

E un'orribile tempesta

Minacciando, oh Dio, $\begin{cases} \text{mi} \\ \text{lo} \end{cases}$ va!

Ma non manca in $\begin{cases} \text{me} \\ \text{lui} \end{cases}$ coraggio,

$\text{Non} \begin{cases} \text{mi perdo} \\ \text{si perdo} \end{cases} \text{o} \begin{cases} \text{mi confondo:} \\ \text{si confonde:} \end{cases}$

Se cadesse ancora il mondo

nulla mai temer $\begin{cases} \text{mi} \\ \text{lo} \end{cases}$ fa.

$\begin{rcases} \text{My} \\ \text{His} \end{rcases}$ head is confused,

$\begin{rcases} \text{I don't know} \\ \text{He doesn't know} \end{rcases}$ any longer what $\begin{cases} \text{I am} \\ \text{he is} \end{cases}$ doing,

And a horrible tempest,

Oh God, menaces $\begin{cases} \text{me!} \\ \text{him!} \end{cases}$

But courage is not lacking in $\begin{cases} \text{me,} \\ \text{him,} \end{cases}$

$\begin{rcases} \text{I} \\ \text{He} \end{rcases}$ will neither lose $\begin{cases} \text{my} \\ \text{his} \end{cases}$ way nor become confused:

Even though the world may fall

nothing frightens $\begin{cases} \text{me.} \\ \text{him.} \end{cases}$

End of Act One

ACT TWO

SCENE I

Street.

Don Giovanni with a mandolin in his hand and Leporello

GIOVANNI

Eh via, buffone, non mi seccar.

Come on, buffoon, don't annoy me.

LEPORELLO

No, no, padrone, non vo' restar.

No, no, master, I don't want to stay.

GIOVANNI

Sentimi, amico . . .

Listen to me, friend . . .

LEPORELLO

Vo' andar, vi dico.

I must go, I tell you.

GIOVANNI

Ma che ti ho fatto, che vuoi lasciarmi?

But what have I done to you, that you want to leave me?

LEPORELLO

Oh, niente affatto, quasi ammazzarmi.

Oh, nothing at all, almost killed me.

GIOVANNI

Va', che sei matto, fu per burlar.

Go on, you're crazy, it was meant as a joke.

LEPORELLO

Ed io non burlo, ma voglio andar.

And I'm not joking, I want to go.

GIOVANNI

Leporello.

Leporello.

LEPORELLO

Signore.

Signor.

GIOVANNI

Vien qui, facciamo pace. Prendi . . .

Come here, let's make peace. Take this . . .

LEPORELLO

Cosa?   What?

GIOVANNI (*gives him some money*)

Quattro doppie.   Four doubloons.

LEPORELLO

Oh! sentite: Oh! listen:
per questa volta   This one time
la cerimonia accetto;   I agree to the ceremony;
ma non vi ci avvezzate: non credete   but don't accustom yourself to it: don't
                                                      think
di sedurre i miei pari,   to seduce my sort

(*taking the purse*)

come le donne, a forza di denari.   as you do the women, by means of
                                                      money.

GIOVANNI

Non parliam più di ciò. Ti basta l'animo   Let's not speak of that anymore. Do you
                                                      have enough courage
di far quel ch'io ti dico?   to do what I tell you?

LEPORELLO

Purchè lasciam le donne.   As long as we leave the women alone.

GIOVANNI

Lasciar le donne? Pazzo!   Leave the women alone? Crazy fellow!
Sai ch'elle per me   Don't you know that they are more
son necessarie più del pan che mangio,   necessary for me than the bread I eat,
più dell'aria che spiro?   more than the air I breathe?

LEPORELLO

E avete core   And do you have the heart
d'ingannarle poi tutte?   to deceive them all then?

GIOVANNI

É tutto amore.   It's entirely love.
Chi a una sola è fedele,   Whoever is faithful to one alone
verso l'altre è crudele.   is cruel to the others.
Io, che in me sento   I, who sense in myself
sì esteso sentimento,   such expansive feelings,
vo' bene a tutte quante.   love all of them.

Le donne poi, che calcolar non sanno,

il mio buon natural chiamano inganno.

So that women who are unable to grasp
the distinction

call my natural instinct deceit.

LEPORELLO

Non ho veduto mai
naturale più vasto e più benigno.

I have never seen
a greater or more generous natural
instinct.

Orsù, cosa vorreste?

All right, what do you want?

GIOVANNI

Odi. Vedesti tu la cameriera
di Donn' Elvira?

Listen. Did you see the chambermaid
of Donn' Elvira?

LEPORELLO

Io? No!

I? No!

GIOVANNI

Non hai veduto
qualche cosa di bello,
caro il mio Leporello! Ora io con lei
vo' tentar la mia sorte, ed ho pensato
giacché siam verso sera,
per aguzzarle meglio l'appetito,
di presentarmi a lei col tuo vestito.

You have never seen
such a thing of beauty,
my dear Leporello! Now I wish to try
my luck with her, and since it's getting
on towards evening, I thought
to better whet her appetite,
by presenting myself to her in your
clothes.

LEPORELLO

E perché non potreste
presentarvi col vostro?

And why could you not
present yourself in your own?

GIOVANNI

Han poco credito
Con gente di tal rango
Gli abiti signorili.

Aristocratic clothing
Has little credit
With people of that class.

(He pulls off his cloak.)

Sbrigati, via!

Make haste, come!

LEPORELLO

Signor, per più ragioni . . .

Sir, for more reasons . . .

GIOVANNI *(with anger)*

Finiscila; non soffro opposizioni.

Stop it; I will not suffer opposition.

(They exchange cloaks and hats.)

SCENE II

(Don Giovanni, Leporello and Donna Elvira at the window. It gradually becomes night.)

ELVIRA

Ah! taci, ingiusto core,	Ah! be silent, unfair heart,
non palpitarmi in seno;	do not throb in my breast;
è un empio, un traditore,	he is an impious man, a traitor,
è colpa aver pietà.	It is a sin to have pity.

LEPORELLO (*under his breath*)

Zitto . . . di Donna Elvira,	Silence . . . I hear the voice, signor,
signor, la voce io sento.	of Donna Elvira.

GIOVANNI

Cogliere io vo' il momento.	I must seize the moment.
Tu fermati un po' là.	You stay there for a bit.

(He places himself behind Leporello.)

Elvira, idolo mio! . . .	Elvira, my idol! . . .

ELVIRA

Non è costui l'ingrato?	Is that not the ungrateful man?

GIOVANNI

Sì, vita mia, son io.	Yes, my life, it is I.
E chiedo carità.	And I beg your forgiveness.

ELVIRA

(Numi, che strano affetto	(Gods, what strange passion
mi si risveglia in petto!)	Is reawakened in my heart!)

LEPORELLO

(State a veder la pazza,	(Just look at the crazy woman,
che ancor gli crederà!)	who still will believe him!)

GIOVANNI

Discendi, o gioia bella!	Come down, oh lovely jewel!
Vedrai che tu sei quella	You will see that you are the one
che adora l'alma mia:	whom my soul adores:
pentito io sono già.	I am already repentant.

ELVIRA

No, non ti credo, o barbaro.	No, I don't believe you, oh barbarous man.

Don Giovanni

GIOVANNI

(with rapture and almost weeping)

Ah, credimi, o m'uccido.	Ah, believe me, or I will kill myself.

LEPORELLO

(under his breath to Don Giovanni)

Se seguitate, io rido.	If you continue, I'll laugh.

GIOVANNI

Idolo mio, vien qua.	My idol, come here.

ELVIRA

(Dei, che cimento è questo,	(Gods, what a trial this is,
non so s'io vado o resto . . .	I don't know if I am going or staying . . .
Ah! proteggete voi	Ah, protect, ye Gods,
la mia credulità.)	my credulity.)

(She goes in.)

GIOVANNI

(Spero che cada presto;	(I hope she falls quickly;
che bel colpetto è questo!	what a lovely little stroke this is!
Più fertile talento	A more fertile talent
del mio, no, non si dà.)	than mine, no, is not granted.)

LEPORELLO

(Già quel mendace labbro	(Those lying lips are
torna a sedur costei;	returning to seduce that woman again;
deh, proteggete, o Dei,	ah, protect, oh Gods,
la sua credulità.)	her credulity.)

GIOVANNI *(very cheerful)*

Amico, che ti par?	Friend, how does it seem to you?

LEPORELLO

Mi par che abbiate	It seems to me that you have
Un'anima di bronzo.	A soul of bronze.

GIOVANNI

Va là, che se' il gran gonzo. Ascolta bene:	Go on, you're a great simpleton. Listen well:
quando costei qui viene,	when that woman comes here,
tu corri ad abbracciarla,	you run to embrace her,
falle quattro carezze,	give her a few caresses,

fingi la voce mia; poi con bell'arte
cerca teco condurla in altra parte.

use my voice; then with great cunning
try to lead her somewhere else.

LEPORELLO

Ma signore . . .

But signore . . .

GIOVANNI

Non più repliche.

No more objections.

LEPORELLO

Ma se poi mi conosce?

But what if she recognizes me?

GIOVANNI

Non ti conoscerà, se tu non vuoi.

She won't recognize you, if you don't
want her to.

Zitto: ell'apre; ehi, giudizio.

Silence: she is opening the door; be
careful.

(*He goes to one side.*)

SCENE III

Donna Elvira and the abovementioned

ELVIRA

Eccomi a voi.

Here I am for you.

GIOVANNI

(Veggiamo che farà.)

(Let's see what he will do.)

LEPORELLO

(Che imbroglio!)

(What a mess!)

ELVIRA

Dunque creder potrò che i pianti miei
abbian vinto quel cor? Dunque pentito

l'amato Don Giovanni al suo dovere
e all'amor mio ritorna?

Then can I believe that my tears
have vanquished that heart? That
repentant
my beloved Don Giovanni returns
to his duty and my love?

LEPORELLO (*always changing his voice*)

Si, carina!

Yes, dear!

ELVIRA

Crudele! se sapeste
quante lagrime e quanti
sospir voi mi costate!

Cruel man! if you knew
how many tears and how many
sighs you cost me!

344

LEPORELLO

Io, vita mia?   I, my life?

ELVIRA

Voi.   You.

LEPORELLO

Poverina! quanto mi dispiace!   Poor little girl! how sorry I am!

ELVIRA

Mi fuggirete più?   You will not flee from me again?

LEPORELLO

No, muso bello.   No, sweet face.

ELVIRA

Sarete sempre mio?   You will always be mine?

LEPORELLO

Sempre.   Always.

ELVIRA

Carissimo!   Dearest!

LEPORELLO

Carissima! (La burla mi dà gusto.)   Dearest! (The prank gives me pleasure.)

ELVIRA

Mio tesoro!   My treasure!

LEPORELLO

Mia Venere!   My Venus!

ELVIRA

Son per voi tutta foco.   For you I am all fire.

LEPORELLO

Io tutto cenere.   I, all ash.

GIOVANNI

(Il birbo si riscalda.)   (The rascal is warming up.)

ELVIRA

E non m'ingannerete?   And you will not deceive me?

LEPORELLO

No, sicuro.   No, of course not.

Elvira

Giuratemi.   Swear to me.

Leporello

Lo giuro a questa mano,   I swear it by this hand,
che bacio con trasporto, a quei bei   that I kiss with rapture, by those
  lumi . . .   beautiful eyes . . .

Giovanni

(*pretending to kill someone*)

Ah! eh! ih! ah! ih! ah! sei morto . . .   Ah! hey! hee! ah! hee! ah! you are
                                                 dead . . .

Elvira and Leporello

Oh Numi!   Oh Gods!

(*They flee together.*)

Giovanni (*laughing*)

Ih! oh! par che la sorte   Ha! ha! it seems that fate
mi secondi. Veggiamo;   is assisting me. Let's see:
le finestre son queste. Ora cantiamo.   these are the windows. Now let us sing.

(*He sings, accompanying himself on the mandolin.*)

Deh! vieni alla finestra, o mio tesoro.   Ah! come to the window, oh my treasure.
Deh, vieni a consolar il pianto mio.   Ah, come to console my weeping.
Se neghi a me di dar qualche ristoro,   If you refuse to give me some comfort,
davanti agli occhi tuoi morir vogl'io.   I wish to die before your eyes.
Tu ch'hai la bocca dolce più che il miele,   You who have a mouth sweeter than
                                                  honey
tu che il zucchero porti in mezzo il core,   you who have sugar at the core of your
                                                  heart,
non esser, gioia mia, con me crudele,   my joy, do not be cruel to me,
lasciati almen veder, mio bell'amore!   at least let yourself be seen, my beautiful
                                                  love!

Scene IV

Masetto, armed with an musket and a pistol, Peasants and the abovementioned

Giovanni

V'è gente alla finestra: There's someone at the window:
sarà dessa.   it must be she.

(*calling*)

Zi zi . . .   Pst, pst . . .

MASETTO

Non ci stanchiamo. Il cor mi dice
che trovarlo dobbiam.

Let's not tire ourselves. My heart tells me
that we must find him.

GIOVANNI

(Qualcuno parla.)

(Someone's speaking.)

MASETTO (*to the Peasants*)

Fermatevi; mi pare
che alcuno qui si muova.

Stop; it seems to me
that someone is moving about.

GIOVANNI

(Se non fallo è Masetto.)

(If I'm not mistaken, it's Masetto.)

MASETTO

Chi va là? . . . non risponde.

Who goes there? He doesn't answer.

(*to his men*)

Animo, schioppo al muso:

Courage, musket at the ready.

(*louder*)

chi va là?

Who goes there?

GIOVANNI

(Non è solo:
ci vuol giudizio.)

(He's not alone:
I'd best be careful.)

(*He attempts to imitate Leporello's voice*)

Amici . . .
(Non mi voglio scoprir.) Sei tu, Masetto?

Friends . . .
(I don't want to reveal myself.) Is it you,
Masetto?

MASETTO (*angrily*)

Appunto quello. E tu?

It just happens to be. And you?

GIOVANNI

Non mi conosci? Il servo
son io di Don Giovanni.

You don't recognize me? I am
Don Giovanni's servant.

MASETTO

Leporello!
Servo di quell'indegno cavaliere!

Leporello!
Servant of that base cavalier!

347

GIOVANNI

Certo, di quel briccone.	Certainly, of that rogue.

MASETTO

Di quell'uom senza onore! Ah, dimmi un poco,	Of that man without honor! Ah, tell me,
dove possiam trovarlo?	where can we find him?
Lo cerco con costor per trucidarlo.	I am looking for him with these fellows, to murder him.

GIOVANNI

(Bagattelle!) Bravissimo, Masetto,	(A mere trifle!) Bravissimo, Masetto,
anch'io con voi m'unisco,	I too, will join you,
per fargliela a quel birbo di padrone.	to do the same to that rascal of a master.
Or senti un po' qual'è la mia intenzione.	Now listen a bit to what my intention is.

(indicating to the right)

Metà di voi qua vadano,	Half of you go there,

(indicating to the left)

e gli altri vadan là,	and the others go there
e pian pianin lo cerchino,	and very quietly look for him,
lontan non fia di qua.	he won't be far from here.
Se un uom e una ragazza	If a man and a girl
passeggian per la piazza,	stroll through the piazza,
se sotto a una finestra	if under a window
fare all'amor sentite,	you hear someone making love,
ferite pur, ferite,	strike, just strike,
il mio padron sarà!	it will be my master!
In testa egli ha un cappello	On his head he has a large hat
con candidi pennacchi.	with white plumes.
Addosso un gran mantello	On his back he has a great cloak
e spada al fianco egli ha.	and he has a sword at his side.

(to the Peasants)

Andate, fate presto!	Go, do it quickly!

(to Masetto)

Tu sol verrai con me.	You'll go with me alone.
Noi far dobbiamo il resto,	We have to do the rest,
E già vedrai cos'è.	and now you'll see what it is.

(The Peasants leave in opposite directions.)

SCENE V

Don Giovanni, Masetto

GIOVANNI

Zitto . . . Lascia ch'io senta . . .   Silence . . . Let me listen . . . Very good.
  Ottimamente.

(being assured that the peasants are already far away)

Dunque dobbiam ucciderlo?   Then we must kill him?

MASETTO

       Sicuro.   Of course.

GIOVANNI

E non ti basteria rompergli l'ossa,   And it wouldn't be enough for you to
                                      break his bones,

fracassargli le spalle? . . .   to smash his shoulders? . . .

MASETTO

No, no; voglio ammazzarlo,   No, no; I want to kill him,
vo' farlo in cento brani.   I want to tear him into a hundred pieces.

GIOVANNI

Hai buon' arme?   Have you good weapons?

MASETTO

       Cospetto!   By God!
Ho pria questo moschetto,   I have this musket,
e poi questa pistola.   and this pistol.

(He gives the musket and pistol to Don Giovanni)

GIOVANNI

     E poi?   And?

MASETTO

     Non basta?   It's not enough?

GIOVANNI

Oh! basta certo. Or prendi: Oh! certainly it's enough. Now take:

(He beats Masetto with the flat of his sword.)

Questa, per la pistola, . . .   This, for the pistol, . . .
questa, per il moschetto . . .   this, for the musket . . .

MASETTO

Ahi, ahi! . . . soccorso! Ahi, ahi!	Ahi, ahi! . . . help! Ahi, ahi!

GIOVANNI

Taci, o sei morto . . .	Quiet, or you're dead . . .
Questa, per ammazzarlo.	This, for killing him.
Questa, per farlo in brani.	This, for tearing him to pieces.
Villano! mascalzon! ceffo da cani!	Peasant! ruffian! dog snout!

(Masetto falls and Don Giovanni leaves.)

SCENE VI

Masetto, then Zerlina with a lantern.

MASETTO

Ahi! ahi! la testa mia!	Ahi! ahi! my head!
Ahi! ahi! le spalle, e il petto!	Ahi! ahi! my shoulders and chest!

ZERLINA

Di sentire mi parve	I think I hear
la voce di Masetto.	Masetto's voice.

MASETTO

Oh Dio! Zerlina mia,	Oh God! My Zerlina,
soccorso.	help.

ZERLINA

Cosa è stato?	What happened?

MASETTO

L'iniquo, il scellerato	The wicked man, the scoundrel
mi ruppe l'ossa e i nervi.	has broken my bones and sinews.

ZERLINA

Oh poveretta me! Chi?	Oh, poor me! Who?

MASETTO

Leporello,	Leporello,
o qualche diavol che somiglia a lui.	or some devil that resembles him.

ZERLINA

Crudel! non tel diss'io	Cruel man! did I not tell you
che con questa tua pazza gelosia	that with this crazy jealousy of yours
ti ridurresti a qualche brutto passo?	you would be reduced to such a state?
Dove ti duole?	Where does it hurt you?

Don Giovanni

MASETTO

Qui.   Here.

ZERLINA

E poi?   And?

MASETTO

Qui . . . e ancora . . . qui.   Here . . . and also . . . here.

ZERLINA

E poi non ti duol altro?   And then does anything else hurt you?

MASETTO

        Duolmi un poco   This foot
Questo piè', questo braccio e questa   Hurts me a bit, this arm and this hand.
   mano.

ZERLINA

Via, via, non è gran mal, se il resto è   Come, come, that's not so very bad, if the
   sano.   rest is healthy.
Vientene meco a casa: Come home with me:
purché tu mi prometta   provided that you promise me
d'essere men geloso,   to be less jealous,
io, io ti guarirò, caro il mio sposo.   I will heal you, my dear betrothed.

Vedrai, carino,   You will see, dear one,
se sei buonino,   if you are really good,
che bel rimedio   what a lovely remedy
ti voglio dar.   I want to give you.
È naturale,   It's natural,
non dà disgusto,   it isn't distasteful,
e lo speziale   and the apothecary
non lo sa far.   doesn't know how to make it.
È un certo balsamo   It is a certain balm
che porto addosso,   that I carry about me.
dare tel posso   I can give it to you
se il vuoi provar.   if you want to try it.
Saper vorresti   If you would like to know
dove mi sta;   where it is on me;
sentilo battere,   feel it beat,
toccami qua.   touch me here.

(She has him touch her heart, then they leave.)

SCENE VII

A dark atrium with three doors, in Donna Anna's house. Donna Elvira and Leporello.

LEPORELLO (*mimicking the voice of his master*)

Di molte faci il lume
s'avvicina, o mio ben; stiamci qui ascosi

finché da noi si scosta.

The light of many torches
is approaching, oh my beloved; let us stay hidden here

until they move away from us.

ELVIRA

Ma che temi,
adorato mio sposo?

But what do you fear,
my adored husband?

LEPORELLO

Nulla, nulla . . .
Certi riguardi . . . Io vo' veder se il lume

è già lontano. (Ah, come
da costei liberarmi?)
Rimanti, anima bella . . .

Nothing, nothing . . .
Certain precautions . . . I want to see if the light

is far enough away. (Ah, how
to free myself from this woman?)
Remain, lovely soul . . .

ELVIRA

Ah! non lasciarmi.
Sola, sola, in buio loco,
palpitar il cor mi sento,
e m'assale un tal spavento
che mi sembra di morir.

Ah! do not leave me.
All alone, in this dark place,
I feel my heart throbbing,
and such terror assails me
that I seem to be dying.

LEPORELLO (*feeling his way*)

(Più che cerco, men ritrovo
questa porta sciagurata . . .
Piano, piano, l'ho trovata:
ecco il tempo di fuggir.)

(The more I search, the less I find
this wretched door . . .
Gently now, I've found it:
now is the time to flee.)

(*He mistakes the exit.*)

SCENE VIII

Donna Anna, Don Ottavio, both dressed in mourning. Servants with lights, and the abovementioned.

(*Donna Elvira, at the arrival of the lights, hides in one corner, Leporello in another.*)

OTTAVIO

Tergi il ciglio, o vita mia!
e da' calma al tuo dolore;

Dry your eyes, oh my life!
and calm your sorrow;

l'ombra omai del genitore / or the shade of your father
pena avrà de' tuoi martir. / will be distressed by your anguish.

ANNA

Lascia almeno alla mia pena / At least allow me this
questo picciolo ristoro; / small comfort in my pain;
sol la morte, o mio tesoro, / only death, oh my treasure,
il mio pianto può finir. / can end my weeping.

ELVIRA (*without being seen*)

(Ah! dov'è lo sposo mio?) / (Ah! where is my husband?)

LEPORELLO (*at the door, without being seen*)

(Se mi trova, son perduto.) / (If she finds me, I'm lost.)

ELVIRA and LEPORELLO

Una porta là vegg'io. / I see a door there.
Chet $\left\{ {a \atop o} \right.$ chet $\left\{ {a \atop o} \right.$ io vo' partir. / I must leave very quietly.

(*Leporello, in leaving, meets Masetto and Zerlina.*)

SCENE IX

Masetto with a stick, Zerlina and the above mentioned

ZERLINA and MASETTO

Ferma, briccone! Dove ten vai? / Stop, rogue! Where are you going?

(*Leporello hides his face.*)

ANNA and OTTAVIO

Ecco il fellone . . . Com'era qua? / Here is the traitor . . . How did he get here?

ANNA, ZERLINA, OTTAVIO and MASETTO

Ah! mora il perfido che m'ha tradito. / Ah! let the treacherous man die who has betrayed me.

ELVIRA

È mio marito . . . Pietà! pietà! / He is my husband . . . Mercy! Have mercy!

ANNA, ZERLINA, OTTAVIO and MASETTO

È Donna Elvira, quella ch'io vedo? / Is that Donna Elvira I see?
Appena il credo . . . / I scarcely believe it . . .

353

ELVIRA

Pietà! pietà!	Have mercy! have mercy!

ANNA, ZERLINA, OTTAVIO and MASETTO

No, morrà.	No he will die.

(As Don Ottavio is about to kill him, Leporello reveals himself and kneels.)

LEPORELLO

Perdon, perdono, signori miei:	Pardon, pardon, your lordships:
quello io non sono, sbaglia costei . . .	I am not he, she is mistaken . . .
Viver lasciatemi, per carità!	Let me live, please!

THE OTHERS

Dei! Leporello! . . . Che inganno è questo!	Gods! Leporello! . . . What deceit is this!
Stupid $\begin{cases} a \\ o \end{cases}$ resto!—che mai sarà?	I am thunderstruck!—what will happen?

LEPORELLO

(Mille torbidi pensieri	(A thousand troubled thoughts
mi s'aggiran per la testa;	are whirling in my head;
se mi salvo in tal tempesta	if I save myself in such a storm
è un prodigo in verità.)	it will truly be a marvel.)

THE OTHERS

(Mille torbidi pensieri	(A thousand troubled thoughts
mi s'aggiran per la testa . . .	are whirling in my head . . .
Che giornata, o stelle, è questa!	What a day, oh stars, is this!
Che impensata novità!)	What an unexpected new event!)

(Donna Anna leaves)

ZERLINA *(to Leporello, furiously)*

Dunque quello sei tu che il mio Masetto	Then you are the one who a short while ago
poco fa crudelmente maltrattasti.	cruelly mistreated my Masetto.

ELVIRA

Dunque tu m'ingannasti, o scellerato,	Then you deceived me, oh scoundrel, by
spacciandoti con me da Don Giovanni?	passing yourself off with me as Don Giovanni?

OTTAVIO

Dunque tu in questi panni	Then you came here in these
venisti qui per qualche tradimento.	clothes to carry out some betrayal.

ZERLINA

A me tocca punirlo.   It falls to me to punish him.

ELVIRA

Anzi a me.   Rather to me.

OTTAVIO

No, no, a me.   No, no, to me.

MASETTO

Accoppatelo meco tutti e tre.   All three beat him to death with me.

LEPORELLO

Ah! pietà, signori miei!   Ah! have mercy, my Lords!
Dò ragione a voi ... a lei ... ,   You are right ... so is she ...
Ma il delitto mio non è.   But the crime is not mine.
Il padron con prepotenza   My master arrogantly
l'innocenza mi rubò.   robbed me of my innocence.

(*softly to Donna Elvira*)

Donna Elvira! compatite: Donna Elvira! take pity:
già capite come andò.   you already understand how it went.
Di Masetto non so nulla,   I don't know anything about Masetto,

(*indicating Donna Elvira*)

vel dirà questa fanciulla;   This young lady will tell you that; I have
è un'oretta circumcirca   been wandering around with her for
che con lei girando vo.   an hour, more or less.

(*to Don Ottavio, in confusion*)

A voi, signore, non dico niente ...   To you, sir, I don't say anything ...
Certo timore ... certo accidente ...   A certain fear ... or certain
                                         misfortune ...

Di fuori chiaro ... di dentro scuro ... Outside clear ... dark within ...
Non c'è riparo ... la porta, il muro ... There's no shelter ... the door, the
                                           wall ...

(*indicating the door where he concealed himself by mistake*)

Lo ... il ... la ... vo da quel lato ...   I'm going towards that side ...
Poi qui celato, l'affar si sa ...   Then hidden here, one understands the
                                             matter ...

Ma s'io sapeva, fuggìa per qua! ...   But if I knew, I could have fled through
                                         there! ...

(*He flees hastily.*)

Scene X

Don Ottavio, Donna Elvira, Zerlina and Masetto

Elvira

Ferma, perfido; ferma . . .	Stop, treacherous man; stop . . .

Masetto

Il birbo ha l'ali ai piedi . . .	The rogue has wings on his feet . . .

Zerlina

Con qual arte	With what cunning
si sottrasse l'iniquo!	the wicked man rescued himself!

Ottavio

Amici miei!	My friends!
Dopo eccessi sì enormi,	After such monstrous excesses,
dubitar non possiam che Don Giovanni	we cannot doubt that Don Giovanni
non sia l'empio uccisore	is the impious killer
del padre di Donn'Anna. In questa casa	of Donn' Anna's father. Stay for a few hours
per poche ore fermatevi: un ricorso	in this house: I wish to make a complaint
vo' far a chi si deve, e in pochi istanti	to whomever one should, and in a few
vendicarvi prometto;	moments, I promise to avenge you.
così vuole dover, pietade, affetto.	Thus duty, compassion, love demand.
Il mio tesoro intanto	Meanwhile, go
andate a consolar:	and console my treasure
e del bel ciglio il pianto	and seek to dry
cercate d'asciugar.	the tears from her lovely eyes.
Ditele che i suoi torti	Tell her that I am going
a vendicar io vado;	to avenge her wrongs;
che sol di stragi e morti	that I wish to return only
nunzio vogl'io tornar.	as herald of slaughter and death.

(They leave.)

Scene XI

Donna Elvira alone

Elvira

In quali eccessi, o Numi! in quai misfatti	In what excesses, oh Gods! in what horrible,
orribili, tremendi,	tremendous misdeeds,
è avvolto il sciagurato!	is the wretch entangled!

Ah no, non puote tardar l'ira del cielo,

la giustizia tardar. Sentir già parmi
la fatale saetta,
che gli piomba sul capo! Aperto veggio
il baratro mortal . . . Misera Elvira!
Che contrasto d'affetti in sen ti nasce!

Perché questi sospiri e queste ambasce?
Mi tradì quell'alma ingrata,
infelice, oh Dio! mi fa.
Ma tradita, e abbandonata,
provo ancor per lui pietà.
Quando sento il mio tormento
di vendetta il cor favella,
ma se guardo il suo cimento
palpitando il cor mi va.

Ah no, the anger of heaven cannot be
    delayed, nor
justice held back. It seems I already hear
the fatal lightning bolt
that falls on his head! I see the deadly
abyss open . . . Miserable Elvira!
What a conflict of affections is born in
   your breast!

Why these sighs and these griefs?
That ungrateful soul betrayed me,
makes me, oh God! unhappy.
Yet betrayed and abandoned,
I still feel pity for him.
When I feel my torment
my heart speaks of vengeance
but when I see his danger
my heart begins to throb.

(Leaves)

SCENE XII

*An enclosed place in the shape of a cemetery, with several equestrian statues, among them that of the
Commendatore. Don Giovanni, later Leporello.*

GIOVANNI

(laughing, enters over the low wall)

Ah! ah! ah! ah! questa è buona!
Or lasciala cercar! Che bella notte!

È più chiara del giorno; sembra fatta
per gir a zonzo a caccia di ragazze.
È tardi?

Ah! ah! ah! ah! this is good!
Now let her search! What a beautiful
   night!

It's brighter than day; it seems made
for sauntering about, hunting for girls.
Is it late?

(looking at the clock)

   Oh, ancor non sono
due della notte. Avrei
voglia un po' di saper com'è finito
l'affar tra Leporello e Donn'Elvira,

s'egli ha avuto giudizio . . .

   Oh, it's not yet
two o'clock at night. I'd like to know
something of how the affair
between Leporello and Donn'Elvira
   ended,
if he had the judgement . . .

LEPORELLO

Alfin vuole ch'io faccia un precipizio.   At last he wants me to act rashly.

GIOVANNI

(È desso.) Oh, Leporello!   (It's he.) Oh, Leporello!

LEPORELLO (*from the low wall*)

Chi mi chiama?   Who is calling me?

GIOVANNI

Non conosci il padron?   Don't you know your master?

LEPORELLO

Così nol conoscessi!   If only I didn't know him!

GIOVANNI

Come, birbo?   What, rascal?

LEPORELLO

Ah, siete voi? Scusate!   Ah, is it you? Excuse me!

GIOVANNI

Cosa è stato?   What happened?

LEPORELLO

Per cagion vostra io fui quasi accoppato.   Because of you I was almost beaten to death.

GIOVANNI

Ebben, non era questo   Well, wasn't it
un onore per te?   an honor for you?

LEPORELLO

Signor, vel dono.   Signor, I give it to you.

GIOVANNI

Via, via; vien qua. Che belle   Listen, come here. What lovely
cose ti deggio dir!   things I must tell you!

LEPORELLO

Ma cosa fate qui?   But what are you doing here?

GIOVANNI

Vien dentro e lo saprai.   Come inside and you'll know what.
Diverse istorielle   Another time I'll tell you about various
che accadute mi son da che partisti,   adventures which happened to me

ti dirò un'altra volta; or la più bella	since you left; now I only want
ti vo' solo narrar.	to tell you the best one.

LEPORELLO

Donnesca al certo.	Concerning women of course.

*(He gives the hat and cloak back to his master, and takes back those
that he had exchanged with him.)*

GIOVANNI

C'è dubbio? una fanciulla	Is there any doubt? I met
bella, giovin, galante	a lovely, young, fetching girl
per la strada incontrai; le vado appresso,	on the street. I draw near her,
la prendo per la mano; fuggir mi vuole;	I take her by the hand; she wants to escape me;
dico poche parole; ella mi piglia . . .	I say a few words; do you know who she takes me for?
sai per chi?	

LEPORELLO

Non lo so.	I don't know.

GIOVANNI

Per Leporello.	For Leporello.

LEPORELLO

Per me?	For me?

GIOVANNI

Per te.	For you.

LEPORELLO

Va bene.	Very well.

GIOVANNI

Per la mano	Then she takes me
essa allora mi prende.	by the hand.

LEPORELLO

Ancora meglio.	Even better.

GIOVANNI

M'accarezza, mi abbraccia.	She caresses me, she embraces me.
«Caro il mio Leporello! . . .	"My dear Leporello!
Leporello mio caro!» . . . Allor m'accorsi	Leporello my dear!" . . . Then I realized
ch'era qualche tua bella.	she was some lovely thing of yours.

LEPORELLO

(Oh maledetto!)   (Oh curse him!)

GIOVANNI

Dell'inganno approfitto; non so come	I take advantage of the deception; I don't know how
mi riconosce: grida: sento gente,	she recognizes me: she screams: I hear people,
a fuggire mi metto, e, pronto, pronto,	I set about escaping, and, very quickly,
per quel muretto in questo loco io monto.	I climb over that low wall into this place.

LEPORELLO

E mi dite la cosa	And you tell me this
con tale indifferenza?	with such indifference?

GIOVANNI

Perché no?   Why not?

LEPORELLO

Ma se fosse	But what if she
costei stata mia moglie?	had been my wife?

GIOVANNI (*laughing loudly*)

Meglio ancora!   Even better!

COMMENDATORE

Di rider finirai pria dell'aurora.   You will cease laughing before dawn.

GIOVANNI

Chi ha parlato?   Who spoke?

LEPORELLO (*extremely frightened*)

Ah! qualche anima	Ah, it must be some soul
sarà dell'altro mondo,	from another world,
che vi conosce a fondo.	who knows you thoroughly.

GIOVANNI

Taci, sciocco!	Quiet, fool!
Chi va là? chi va là?	Who goes there? who goes there?

(*He places his hand on his sword, searches here and there in the cemetery, giving several blows to the statues.*)

COMMENDATORE

Ribaldo audace!	Audacious scoundrel!
Lascia a' morti la pace.	Leave the dead in peace.

LEPORELLO (*trembling*)

Ve l'ho detto? . . .   Didn't I tell you? . . .

GIOVANNI

Sarà qualcun di fuori   It must be someone outside
che si burla di noi . . .   who is mocking us . . .

(*with indifference and disdain.*)

Ehi! del Commendatore   Ah! isn't this the statue
non è questa la statua? Leggi un poco   of the Commendatore? Read out
quella iscrizion.   that inscription.

LEPORELLO

Scusate . . .   Excuse me . . .
Non ho imparato a leggere   I've not learned how to read
a' raggi della luna.   by the rays of the moon.

GIOVANNI

Leggi, dico.   Read, I say.

LEPORELLO (*reading*)

«Dell'empio, che mi trasse al passo   "Upon the impious man who drove me
  estremo   to the extreme step
Qui attendo la vendetta» . . . Udiste? . . .   Here I wait for vengeance" . . . Do you
  Io tremo!   hear? . . . I tremble!

GIOVANNI

Oh, vecchio beffonissimo!   Oh, most foolish old man!
Digli che questa sera   Tell him that this evening
l'attendo a cena meco.   I wait for him to have supper with me.

LEPORELLO

Che pazzia! Ma vi par? . . . Oh Dei!   What madness! But does it seem to
  mirate   you? . . . O Gods! see
che terribili occhiate egli ci dà . . .   what terrible intense looks he gives us . . .
Par vivo . . . par che senta . . .   He seems alive . . . it seems that he
                                                    hears . . .
E che voglia parlar . . .   And that he wants to speak . . .

GIOVANNI

Orsù, va là.   Come on, get on with it.
O qui t'ammazzo e poi ti seppellisco.   Or I will kill you and bury you right
                                                    here.

LEPORELLO

Piano . . . piano . . . , signore . . . ora
   ubbidisco.
O statua gentilissima
del gran Commendatore . . .
Padron . . . mi trema il core . . .
Non pos . . . so . . . ter . . . mi . . . nar . . .

Softly . . . softly . . . sir . . . now I obey.
O most noble statue
of the great Commendatore . . .
Master . . . my heart is trembling . . .
I can . . . not . . . end . .

GIOVANNI

Finiscila, o nel petto
ti metto quest'acciar.
(Che gusto! che spassetto!
Lo voglio far tremar.)

Finish it, or in your breast
I will put this sword.
(What pleasure! what amusement!
I want to make him tremble.)

LEPORELLO

(Che impiccio! che capriccio!
Io sentomi gelar!)
O statua gentilissima,
benché di marmo siate . . .
Ah! padron mio . . . mirate . . .
che seguita . . . a guardar . . .

(What a nuisance.! what a caprice!
I feel myself freezing!)
Oh most noble statue,
although you are of marble . . .
Ah, master . . . look . . .
how he continues . . . to look at . . .

GIOVANNI

Mori . . .

Die . . .

LEPORELLO

No, no . . . attendete . . .

No, no . . . wait . . .

(*to the statue*)

Signor, il padron mio . . .
Badate ben . . . non io . . .
Vorria con voi cenar . . .

Signor, my master . . .
Listen carefully, not I . . .
Would like to have supper with you . . .

(*The statue bows its head in assent.*)

Ah! ah! ah! che scena è questa! . . .
Oh ciel! . . . chinò la testa . . .

Ah! ah! ah! what a scene this is! . . .
O heavens! . . . he bowed his head . . .

GIOVANNI

Va là, che se' un buffone.

Go on, what a fool you are.

LEPORELLO

Guardate ancor . . . padrone . . .

Look again . . . master . . .

GIOVANNI

E che degg'io guardar?

And what should I look at?

LEPORELLO

Colla marmorea testa   With his marble head

(imitating the statue)

ei fa . . . così . . . così . . .   he does . . . like that . . . like that . . .

GIOVANNI

(Colla marmorea testa   (With his marble head
ei fa così . . . così!)   he does . . . like that . . . like that!)

(towards the statue)

Parlate, se potete: Speak, if you can:
verrete a cena?   will you come to supper?

COMMENDATORE

Sì.   Yes.

LEPORELLO

Mover . . . mi . . . posso appena . . .   I . . . can . . . scarcely . . . move . . .
Mi manca, oh Dei! . . . la lena . . .   I lack, oh Gods! . . . the energy . . .
Per carità . . . partiamo . . .   For heaven's sake . . . let's leave . . .
Andiamo—via di qui.   Let's go—away from here.

GIOVANNI

Bizzarra è inver la scena!   The scene is truly bizarre!
Verrà il buon vecchio a cena!   The good old man will come to supper!
A prepararla andiamo: Let us go to prepare it:
partiamo—via di qui.   Let us go—away from here.

(They leave.)

SCENE XIII

*Dark room in Donna Anna's house
Don Ottavio and Donna Anna*

OTTAVIO

Calmatevi, idol mio; di quel ribaldo   Calm yourself, my idol; we shall soon see
vedrem puniti in breve i gravi eccessi: the grave excesses of this scoundrel
                                                    punished:
vendicati sarem.   we shall be avenged.

ANNA

Ma il padre, oh Dio! . . .   But my father, oh God! . . .

OTTAVIO

Convien chinare il ciglio	It is necessary to bow one's head
ai voleri del ciel. Respira, o cara!	to the will of heaven. Breathe, oh dear one!
Di tua perdita amara	Tomorrow, if you wish,
fia domani, se vuoi, dolce compenso	For your bitter loss will be sweet reward:
questo cor, questa mano,	this heart, this hand,
che il mio tenero amor . . .	which my tender love . . .

ANNA

Oh Dei! che dite!	Oh Gods! what are you saying!
In sì tristi momenti . . .	In such sad moments . . .

OTTAVIO

E che! vorresti,	What! would you wish,
con indugi novelli,	with new delays,
accrescer le mie pene?	to increase my afflictions?
Crudele!	Cruel!

ANNA

Crudele?	Cruel?
Ah no, mio ben! troppo mi spiace	Ah no, my beloved! it displeases
allontanarti un ben che lungamente	me too much to withdraw from you a
la nostr'alma desìa . . . Ma il mondo, oh Dio!	blessing which for a long time our souls have
Non sedur la costanza	desired . . . But the world, oh God!
	Do not tempt the faithfulness of
del sensibil mio core:	my sensitive heart:
abbastanza per te mi parla amore.	love speaks to me sufficiently in your favor.
Non mi dir, bell'idol mio,	Do not tell me, my beautiful idol,
che son io crudel con te:	that I am cruel to you;
tu ben sai quant'io t'amai,	you know well how much I loved you,
tu conosci la mia fè'.	you know my loyalty.
Calma, calma il tuo tormento,	Calm, calm your torment,
se di duol non vuoi ch'io mora;	if you do not wish me to die of grief;
forse un giorno il cielo ancora	perhaps one day heaven will again
sentirà pietà di me.	feel compassion for me.

(She leaves.)

OTTAVIO

Ah, si segua il suo passo; io vo' con lei	Oh, let me follow her; I wish
dividere i martiri.	to share the torture with her.

Saran meco men gravi i suoi sospiri.	With me there, her sighs will be less grievous.

(He leaves.)

SCENE XIV

Hall in Don Giovanni's house, with a table prepared. Don Giovanni and Leporello. Servants, some musicians. A table laid for a banquet

GIOVANNI

Già la mensa è preparata:	Already the table is laid:
voi suonate, amici cari;	Play, dear friends;
giacché spendo i miei denari	Since I am spending my wealth
io mi voglio divertir.	I want to amuse myself.

(Sits down to table.)

Leporello, presto in tavola.	Leporello, quickly to the table.

LEPORELLO

Son prontissimo a servir.	I am most ready to serve.

(The musicians begin.)

Bravi! *Cosa rara.*	Bravi! *A Rare Thing.*

(alluding to a piece of music from the opera La Cosa Rara)*

GIOVANNI

Che ti par del bel concerto?	How does the beautiful concert seem to you?

LEPORELLO

È conforme al vostro merto.	It is in accordance with your worth.

GIOVANNI

(eating)

Ah, che piatto saporito!	Ah, what a tasty dish!

LEPORELLO

(Ah, che barbaro appetito!	(Ah, what a barbarous appetite!
Che bocconi da gigante!	What gigantic mouthfuls!
Mi par proprio di svenir.)	I am about to faint.)

* *Una Cosa Rara* is a opera written in Vienna in 1786 by the Spanish composer Vicenta Martin y Soler, with a libretto by Da Ponte.

GIOVANNI

(Nel veder i miei bocconi
gli par proprio di svenir.)
Piatto.

(Seeing my mouthfuls
he seems about to faint.)
Next course.

LEPORELLO

(changing the plate)

Servo.

Your servant.

(The musicians change the music.)

LEPORELLO

Evvivano i *Litiganti*.*

Long live the *Litigants*.*

(Alluding to another opera of this title)

GIOVANNI

Versa il vino.
Eccellente marzimino!

Pour the wine.
Excellent marzimino wine!

LEPORELLO

(eating and drinking stealthily)

(Questo pezzo di fagiano
piano, piano vo' inghiottir.)

(Very quietly I am going to swallow
this piece of pheasant.)

GIOVANNI

(Sta mangiando quel marrano;
fingerò di non capir.)

(That lout is eating; I will
pretend not to understand.)

LEPORELLO

(to the musicians who again change the tune)

Questa poi la conosco pur troppo.

This one I know only too well.

GIOVANNI

(without looking at him)

Leporello!

Leporello!

* *Fre I Due Litiganti il Terzo Gode* (*In a Quarrel Between Two, a Third Party Benefits*) is an opera written in Venice in 1782 by the Italian composer Giuseppe Sarti with a libretto by Carlo Goldoni. The third "tune" which Leporello "knows only too well" is from Mozart's own *Le Nozze di Figaro*, Act I: Figaro's "Non più andrai." At the Prague premiere, Giovanni was played by Luigi Bassi and Leporello by Felice Ponziani, the singers who had played the Count and Figaro in Prague a year earlier.

Don Giovanni

LEPORELLO

(*with his mouth full*)

Padron mio,   Master?

GIOVANNI

Parla schietto, mascalzone.   Speak clearly, rascal.

LEPORELLO

Non mi lascia una flussione   A bad cold doesn't allow me
le parole proferir.   to utter a word.

GIOVANNI

Mentre io mangio fischia un poco.   While I am eating, whistle a bit.

LEPORELLO

Non so far.   I don't know how to.

GIOVANNI

(*aware that he is eating*)

Cos'è?   What?

LEPORELLO

(*eating*)

            Scusate.   Excuse me.
Sì eccellente è il vostro cuoco   Your cook is so excellent
che lo volli anch'io provar.   that I also wanted to try him out.

GIOVANNI

(Sì eccellente è il cuoco mio   (My cook is so excellent
che lo volle anch'ei provar.)   that he also wanted to try him out.)

SCENE XV

Donna Elvira and the above mentioned

ELVIRA (*entering in desperation*)

L'ultima prova   I wish to make
dell'amor mio   the ultimate test
ancor vogl'io   of my love
fare con te.   for you.
Più non rammento   I recall your
gl'inganni tuoi;   deceits no more;
pietade io sento . . .   I feel only compassion . . .

367

Don Giovanni and Leporello

Cos'è, cos'è?	What is it? What's the matter?

Elvira (*kneels*)

Da te non chiede	This oppressed soul
quest'alma oppressa	does not ask for any
della sua fede	reward from you
qualche mercè'.	for her loyalty.

Giovanni

Mi maraviglio!	I am amazed!
Cosa volete?	What do you want?

(*To mock her, he kneels.*)

Se non sorgete	If you do not rise
non resto in pie'.	I will not remain standing.

Elvira

Ah, non deridere	Ah, do not deride
gli affanni miei.	my anguish.

Leporello

(Quasi da piangere mi fa costei.)	(She almost makes me weep.)

Giovanni

(*standing up and helping Donna Elvira stand*)

Io te deridere!	I deride you!
Cieli! perché?	Heavens! Why?

(*with affected tenderness*)

Che vuoi, mio bene!	What do you want, my beloved!

Elvira

Che vita cangi.	For you to change your life.

Giovanni (*mocking her*)

Brava!	Brava!

Elvira

Cor perfido!	Perfidious heart!

Giovanni

Lascia ch'io mangi;	Let me eat;

(*Returns to sit and eat*)

E, se ti piace,	And if you would like,
mangia con me.	eat with me.

ELVIRA

Restati, barbaro,	Stay then, barbarous man,
nel lezzo immondo,	in foul filth,
esempi orribile	horrible example
d'iniquità.	of wickedness.

(*Leaves*)

LEPORELLO

(Se non si muove	(If he is not moved
del suo dolore,	by her sorrow,
di sasso ha il core,	he has a heart of stone
o cor non ha.)	or no heart at all.)

GIOVANNI

Vivan le femmine!	Long live the ladies!
Viva il buon vino!	Hurrah for good wine!
Sostegno e gloria	Sustenance and glory
d'umanità!	of mankind!

ELVIRA

Ah!	Ah!

(*From within; then she re-enters, crosses the stage in flight, goes out on the other side.*)

GIOVANNI and LEPORELLO

Che grido è questo mai?	What is this screaming?

GIOVANNI

Va a veder che cos'è stato.	Go see what has happened.

(*Leporello goes out.*)

LEPORELLO (*from within*)

Ah!	Ah!

GIOVANNI

Che grido indiavolato!	What a diabolical scream!
Leporello, che cos'è?	Leporello, what is the matter?

LEPORELLO (*Enters terrified and closes the door.*)

Ah! . . . signor . . . per carità . . .	Ah! . . . sir . . . for heaven's sake . . .
Non an . . . da . . . te fuor . . . di qua . . .	Don't go out of here . . .

L'uom . . . di . . . sasso . . . l'uomo . . . bianco . . .	The stone . . . man . . . the white . . . man . . .
Ah, padron . . . io gelo . . . io manco . . .	Ah, master . . . I'm freezing . . . I'm fainting . . .
Se vedeste . . . che . . . figura . . .	If you were to see . . . what a . . . figure . . .
Se . . . sentiste . . . come . . . fa . . .	If you were to hear . . . how . . . he . . . walks . . .
Ta ta ta ta ta ta ta ta.	Ta ta ta ta ta ta ta ta

(imitating the walk of the Commendatore)

GIOVANNI

Non capisco niente affatto: tu sei matto in verità.	I understand absolutely nothing: You are truly insane.

(Knocking is heard at the door.)

LEPORELLO

Ah! sentite!	Ah! Listen!

GIOVANNI

Qualcun batte. Apri.	Someone is knocking. Open.

LEPORELLO

Io tremo . . .	I am trembling . . .

GIOVANNI

Apri, dico.	Open it, I tell you.

LEPORELLO

Ah! . . .	Ah!

GIOVANNI

Matto! Per togliermi d'intrico ad aprir io stesso andrò.	Madman! To get out of this tangle I myself will go to open the door.

(Takes the light and the unsheathed sword and goes to open the door.)

LEPORELLO

(Non vo' più veder l'amico; pian pianin m'asconderò.)	(I'm not going to see my friend again; very quietly I'll hide myself.)

(Conceals himself under the table)

SCENE XVI

(The Commendatore and the abovementioned)

COMMENDATORE

Don Giovanni, a cenar teco
m'invitasti, e son venuto.

Don Giovanni, you invited me to have
supper with you, and I have come.

GIOVANNI

Non l'avrei giammai creduto:
ma farò quel che potrò.
Leporello, un'altra cena
fa che subito si porti.

I never would have believed it:
but I will do what I can.
Leporello, let another supper
be quickly brought.

LEPORELLO

(peeping out from under the table)

Ah! padron . . . siam tutti morti . . .

Ah! master . . . we are all dead . . .

GIOVANNI

(pulling him out)

Vanne, dico.

Go do it, I tell you.

COMMENDATORE

(to Leporello, who is in the act of leaving)

Ferma un po'.
Non si pasce di cibo mortale
chi si pasce di cibo celeste;
altre cure più gravi di queste,
altra brama quaggiù mi guidò.

Wait a moment.
He is not nourished by mortal food
who is nourished by celestial food;
other cares more grave than these,
other desires guided me here below.

LEPORELLO

(La terzana d'avere mi sembra . . .
E le membra fermar più non so.)

(I feel as if I have a fever . . .
and my limbs—I don't know how to
stop them from shaking.)

GIOVANNI

Parla dunque: che chiedi? che vuoi?

Speak then: what are you asking? what do
you want?

COMMENDATORE

Parlo, ascolta: più tempo non ho.

I will speak, you listen: I have time for no
more than that.

GIOVANNI

Parla, parla: ascoltando ti sto.

Speak, speak: I am listening to you.

COMMENDATORE

Tu m'invitasti a cena:	You invited me to supper:
il tuo dover or sai.	now learn your obligation.
Rispondimi: verrai	Answer me: will you come to
tu a cenar meco?	supper with me?

LEPORELLO

(from a distance, still trembling)

Oibo!	Alas!
Tempo non ha . . . scusate.	He doesn't have time . . . pardon.

GIOVANNI

A torto di viltate,	I will never be wrongfully
tacciato mai sarò.	charged with cowardice.

COMMENDATORE

Risolvi.	Decide.

GIOVANNI

Ho già risolto.	I have already decided.

COMMENDATORE

Verrai?	Will you come?

LEPORELLO (*to Don Giovanni*)

Dite di no, dite di no!	Say no, say no.

GIOVANNI

Ho fermo il core in petto:	My heart is steady in my breast:
non ho timor, verrò.	I am not afraid, I will come.

COMMENDATORE

Dammi la mano in pegno.	Give me your hand in pledge.

GIOVANNI

(offering him his hand)

Eccola . . . Ohimé! . . .	Here it is . . . Ah! . . .

COMMENDATORE

Cos'hai?	What is the matter with you?

GIOVANNI

Che gelo è questo mai!	What is this chill!

COMMENDATORE

Pèntiti, cangia vita:	Repent, change your life:
è l'ultimo momento.	it is the last opportunity.

GIOVANNI (*wants to tear himself away, but in vain*)

No, no, ch'io non mi pento;	No, no, I don't repent;
vanne lontan da me.	get away from me.

COMMENDATORE

Pentiti, scellerato.	Repent, scoundrel.

GIOVANNI

No, vecchio infatuato.	No, silly old man.

COMMENDATORE

Pentiti.	Repent.

GIOVANNI

No.	No.

COMMENDATORE and LEPORELLO

Si.	Yes.

GIOVANNI

No.	No.

COMMENDATORE

Ah! tempo più non v'è.	Ah! there is no more time left to you.

(*Fire from various locations, the Commendatore disappears and a chasm opens.*)

GIOVANNI

Da qual tremore insolito . . .	By what extraordinary tremor
Sento . . . assalir . . . gli spiriti . . .	Do I feel . . . my spirits . . . assailed . . .
Donde escono quei vortici	Where do these fiery whirlwinds
di foco pien d'orror! . . .	full of horror come from . . . !

CHORUS (*from under the earth, with dark voices*)

Tutto a tue colpe è poco:	These are not enough, considering all your sins:
vieni; c'è un mal peggior.	come; there is worse pain.

GIOVANNI

Chi l'anima mi lacera! . . .	Who rends my spirit! . . .
Chi m'agita le viscere! . . .	Who tears my bowels! . . .

Che strazio! ohimè! che smania!	What torment! ah! what frenzy!
Che inferno! . . . che terror! . . .	What hell! . . . what terror! . . .

LEPORELLO

(Che ceffo disperato! . . .	(What a desperate grimace! . . .
Che gesti da dannato! . . .	What gestures of a damned man! . . .
Che gridi! che lamenti! . . .	What screams! what cries of pain! . . .
Come mi fa terror! . . .)	How it terrifies me! . . .)

CHORUS

Tutto a tue colpe è poco:	These are not enough, considering all your sins:
vieni; c'è un mal peggior.	come; there is worse pain.

(*The fire mounts, several Furies appear, take possession of Don Giovanni, and sink down with him.*)

LAST SCENE

Leporello, Donna Elvira, Donna Anna, Zerlina, Don Ottavio, Masetto, with ministers of justice

ALL

(except for Leporello)

Ah! dov'è il perfido?	Ah! where is the perfidious man?
Dov'è l'indegno?	Where is the base man?
Tutto il mio sdegno	I must give vent to
sfogar io vo'.	all my indignation.

ANNA

Solo mirandolo	Only seeing him
stretto in catene	tightly in chains
alle mie pene	would calm
calma darò.	my afflictions.

LEPORELLO

Più non sperate	Do not hope to find him any more . . .
di ritrovarlo . . .	do not search any further . . .
Più non cercate . . .	He has gone
Lontano andò.	far away.

ALL

Cos'è? Favella!	What? tell us!

LEPORELLO

Venne un colosso . . .	A colossus came . . .

ALL

Via, presto, sbrigati!	Come on, quickly, hurry!

LEPORELLO

Ma, se non posso . . .	But if I can't . . .

ALL

Presto! Favella! Sbrigati!	Quickly! tell us! hurry!

LEPORELLO

Tra fumo e fuoco . . . badate un poco . . .	Through smoke and fire . . . heed a little . . .
L'uomo di sasso . . . fermate il passo . . .	The man of stone . . . stop where you are . . .
Giusto là sotto . . . diede il gran botto . . .	Right there below . . . he struck a great blow . . .
Giusto là il diavolo se'l trangugiò.	Right there the devil gulped him down.

ALL

Stelle! che sento!	Stars! what do I hear!

LEPORELLO

Vero è l'evento.	True is the outcome.

ALL

Ah, certo è l'ombra che $\begin{cases} \text{l'} \\ \text{m'} \end{cases}$, incontrò. Ah, certainly it is the shade that $\begin{cases} \text{he} \\ \text{I} \end{cases}$ met.

OTTAVIO

Or che tutti, o mio tesoro,	Now that we are completely avenged by heaven,
vendicati siam dal cielo,	oh my treasure,
porgi, porgi a me un ristoro,	pour, pour for me a restorative;
non mi far languire ancor.	do not cause me to languish any longer.

ANNA

Lascia, o caro, un anno ancora	Allow, oh dear one, another year
allo sfogo del mio cor.	for the relief of my heart.

ANNA and OTTAVIO

Al desio di chi $\begin{cases} \text{t'} \\ \text{m'} \end{cases}$, adora To the desire of the one who loves $\begin{cases} \text{you} \\ \text{me} \end{cases}$

ceder deve un fido amor.	A faithful love must yield.

ELVIRA

Io men vado in un ritiro	I will go into a convent
a finir la vita mia!	to finish out my life!

ZERLINA and MASETTO

Noi, {Zerlina, Masetto,} a casa andiamo. A cenar in compagnia.	We, {Zerlina Masetto} will go home To have supper together.

LEPORELLO

Ed io vado all'osteria
a trovar padron miglior.

And I will go to the inn
to find a better master.

ZERLINA, MASETTO and LEPORELLO

Resti dunque quel birbon
con Proserpina e Pluton;
e noi tutti, o buona gente,
ripetiam allegramente
l'antichissima canzon:

Let this knave remain
with Proserpina and Pluto;
and let us all, oh good people,
repeat cheerfully
the oldest of songs:

ALL

Questo è il fin di chi fa mal!
E de' perfidi la morte
alla vita è sempre ugual.

This is the end of evildoers!
And the death of the wicked
is no better than the life.

The End

SCENE XI APPENDIX

(At the Vienna premiere, these scenes appeared after Act II, Scene X.)

Zerlina, with a lantern in her hand, leads Leporello out by the hair.

ZERLINA

Restati qua.

Stop here.

LEPORELLO

Per carità, Zerlina!

For pity's sake, Zerlina!

ZERLINA

Eh! non c'è carità pei pari tuoi.

Eh! there is no pity for the likes of you.

LEPORELLO

Dunque cavarmi vuoi? . . .

So you want to tear from me? . . .

ZERLINA

I capelli, la testa, il core e gli occhi!

Your hair, your head, your heart and your
eyes!

LEPORELLO

Senti, carina mia!   Listen, my dear one!

(Tries to make advances to her.)

ZERLINA *(repulses him)*

Guai se mi tocchi!   Beware if you touch me!
Vedrai, schiuma de' birbi,   You will see, scum of rascals,
qual premio n'ha chi le ragazze ingiuria.   what reward he has who wrongs young
women.

LEPORELLO

(Liberatemi, o Dei, da questa furia!)   (Liberate me, O Gods, from this Fury!)

ZERLINA

(calling towards the wings)

Masetto, olà, Masetto!   Masetto, hey, Masetto!
dove diavolo è ito . . . servi, gente!   Where the devil has he gone . . .
Servants, people!

Nessun vien . . . nessun sente.   No one comes . . . no one hears.

(She drags Leporello behind her all around the stage.)

LEPORELLO

Fa' piano, per pietà, non trascinarmi   Take it easy, please, don't drag me
a coda di cavallo.   by the ponytail.

ZERLINA

Vedrai, vedrai come finisce il ballo!   You will see, you will see how the
Presto qua quella sedia.   dance will end. Bring that chair, quickly.

LEPORELLO

Eccola!   Here it is!

ZERLINA

Siedi!   Sit down!

LEPORELLO

Stanco non son.   I am not tired.

ZERLINA

(draws a razor out of her pocket)

Siedi, o con queste mani   Sit down, or with these hands I
ti strappo il cor e poi lo getto ai cani.   will tear out your heart and throw it to
the dogs.

LEPORELLO

Siedo, ma tu, di grazia,
metti giù quel rasoio:
mi vuol forse sbarbar?

I will sit, but please,
put that razor away:
or maybe you just want to shave me?

ZERLINA

Sì, mascalzone!
Io sbarbare ti vo' senza sapone.

Yes, scoundrel! I want to shave you
without soap.

LEPORELLO

Eterni Dei!

Eternal Gods!

ZERLINA

Dammi la man!

Give me your hand!

LEPORELLO

(hesitates)

La mano?

My hand?

ZERLINA

(threatening him)

L'altra.

The other one.

LEPORELLO

Ma che vuoi farmi?

But what do you want to do to me?

ZERLINA

Voglio far . . . voglio far quello che parmi!

I want to do . . . I want to do what suits
me!

(Ties up Leporello's hands with a handkerchief)

LEPORELLO

Per queste tue manine
candide e tenerelle,
per questa fresca pelle,
abbi pietà di me!

By these your hands
white and tender,
by this fresh skin,
have mercy on me!

ZERLINA

Non v'è pietà, briccone;
son una tigre irata,
un aspide, un leone,
no, no, pietà non v'è.

There is no mercy, rogue;
I am an angry tiger,
an asp, a lion,
no, no, there is no mercy.

LEPORELLO

Ah! di fuggir si provi . . .   Ah, if I tried to flee . . .

ZERLINA

Sei morto se ti muovi.   You are dead if you move.

LEPORELLO

Barbari, ingiusti Dei!   Barbarous, unjust Gods!
In mano di costei   Who caused me to fall
chi capitar mi fe'?   into her hands?

ZERLINA

Barbaro, traditore!   Barbarous man, traitor!

(She ties him to the chair with a rope, and ties the rope to the window.)

Del tuo padrone il core   If only I had the heart
avessi qui con te.   of your master here with you.

LEPORELLO

Deh! non mi stringer tanto,   Oof! don't bind me so tightly,
l'anima mia sen va.   my spirit is going out of me.

ZERLINA

Sen vada o resti, intanto   Let it go or stay, but you will not
non partirai de qua!   be leaving here.

LEPORELLO

Che strette, o Dei, che botte!   What straits, o Gods, what blows!
È giorno, ovvero è notte?   Is it day, or is it night?
Che scosse di tremuoto!   What shaking of earth!
Che buia oscurità!   What murky darkness!

ZERLINA

Di gioia, e di diletto   I feel joy and delight
sento brillarmi il petto.   sparkling within my breast.
Così, così, cogli uomini,   Thus, thus, with men,
così, così si fa.   this is how it's done.

(She leaves.)

379

SCENE XII

Leporello seated and bound

LEPORELLO

(to a peasant man who is passing at the back of the stage)

Amico, per pietà,	Friend, for pity's sake,
un poco d'acqua fresca o ch'io mi moro!	a little fresh water or I will die!
Guarda un po' come stretto	See how tightly
mi legò l'assassina! Se potessi	the assassin tied me!
liberarmi coi denti . . . Oh, venga il diavolo	If I could free myself with my teeth . . .
	Oh, if only the devil would come to untie
a disfar questi gruppi!	these knots!
Io vo' vedere di rompere la corda . . .	I must try to break the rope . . .
Come è forte! Paura della morte,	how strong it is! Fear of death,
e tu, Mercurio, protettor de' ladri,	and you, Mercury, patron of thieves,
proteggi un galantuom. Coraggio . . .	Protect a man of honor. Courage . . .
Bravo!	Bravo!

(Makes an effort to untie himself; the window to which the end of the rope is tied falls out.)

Ciel, che	Heavens!
veggio! . . . non serve;	What do I see . . . It's no use;
Pria che costei ritorni	Before she returns
bisogna dar di sprone alle calcagna,	I had better set spurs to my heels,
e strascinar, se occorre, una montagna.	dragging an entire mountain if I have to.

(Runs away dragging chair and window with him.)

SCENE XIII

Donna Elvira and Zerlina, then Masetto with two peasant boys

ZERLINA

Andiam, andiam, signora. Vedrete in qual maniera	My lady, let's go. You will see how
ho concio il scellerato.	I have trussed up the rogue.

ELVIRA

Ah! sopra lui si sfoghi il mio furor.	Ah! let my fury be vented upon him.

ZERLINA

Stelle! in qual modo si salvò il briccone?	Stars! how did the rogue save himself?

ELVIRA

L'avrà sottratto l'empio suo padrone.	His impious master has taken him away.

Don Giovanni

MASETTO

No, non si trova un'anima più nera.   No, a blacker soul is not to be found.

ZERLINA

Ah, Masetto, Masetto,   Ah, Masetto, Masetto,
dove fosti finor?   where were you until now?

MASETTO

Un' infelice   Heaven wanted me to save
Volle il ciel ch'io salvassi.   an unfortunate.
Era io sol pochi passi   I was only a few steps away from
lontan da te, quando gridare io sento   you when I hear screaming in the
nell' opposto sentiero;   opposite direction;
Con lor v'accorro, veggio   With these fellows I run, I see
una donna che piange,   a woman who is crying,
ed un uomo che fugge; vo' inseguirlo;   and a man fleeing; I try to follow him;
mi sparisce dagli occhi   He disappears from my view,
ma da quel che mi disse la fancuilla,   but from what the girl tells me,
ai tratti, alle sembianze, alle maniere,   about his gestures, his features, his
                                                           behavior,

Io credo quel briccon del Cavaliere.   I believe it was that rogue of a cavalier.

ZERLINA

È desso senza fallo: anche di questo   It was he, without fail: let's inform
informiam Don Ottavio; a lui si aspetta   Don Ottavio about this too; it is his
far per noi tutti, o domandar   responsibility to act for all of us
vendetta.   himself, or to demand vengeance.

(*They leave.*)

381

COSÌ FAN TUTTE

WORLD PREMIERE: *Vienna, Burgtheater, January 26, 1790*

UNITED STATES PREMIERE: *New York, Metropolitan Opera, March 24, 1922*

LA SCUOLA DEGLI AMANTI
(THE SCHOOL FOR LOVERS)
OR
COSÌ FAN TUTTE
(ALL WOMEN ARE THE SAME)

Comic Opera in Two Acts

Libretto: Lorenzo Da Ponte

English Translation: Judyth Schaubhut Smith

Music: Wolfgang Amadeus Mozart

COSÌ FAN TUTTE

CHARACTERS

FIORDILIGI	Soprano
sisters from	
Ferrara living in Naples	
DORABELLA	Mezzo-Soprano
GUGLIELMO, *Fiordiligi's fiancé*	Baritone
officers	
FERRANDO, *Dorabella's fiancé*	Tenor
DESPINA, *a chamber maid*	Soprano
DON ALFONSO, *an old philospher*	Bass
CHORUS OF SOLDIERS AND TOWNSPEOPLE	
CHORUS OF SAILORS	
CHORUS OF SERVANTS	

The action takes place in Naples.

COSÌ FAN TUTTE

SYNOPSIS

ACT I

In eighteenth-century Naples, the elderly cynic Don Alfonso discusses women with two young officers, Ferrando and Guglielmo. The two gallants insist their sweethearts are paragons of virtue ("La mia Dorabella") and accept Alfonso's bet that he can prove the girls fickle.

In their garden, the sisters Fiordiligi and Dorabella revel in their love for Guglielmo and Ferrando, respectively, showing pictures they carry in their lockets ("Ah, guarda, sorella"). Alfonso comes in with sad news: the young men have been called to their regiment. They appear, and the five make elaborate farewells ("Sento, o Dio"). As soldiers march by, Ferrando and Guglielmo fall in, lamented in a trio ("Soave sia il vento"). Alfonso, alone, delivers one last jeer at women's inconstancy.

The maid, Despina, offers the girls morning chocolate and advice about forgetting old lovers with the help of new ones ("In uomini, in soldati"), but her mistresses, hysterical with grief, resent her capricious approach to love. Dorabella in fact is outraged ("Smanie implacabili"). When they leave, Alfonso comes to bribe Despina to help introduce two foreign friends of his to the ladies. When they arrive, the ladies are scandalized to see the strangers, whom they do not recognize as their lovers in disguise. The "Albanians" declare their admiration for the sisters, but both repulse them, and Fiordiligi likens her fidelity to an immovable rock ("Come scoglio"). The men are thrilled, but Alfonso warns the bet isn't won yet; Ferrando blissfully reiterates his passion for Dorabella ("Un'aura amorosa").

Alone in their garden, the sisters unite in despair. Suddenly the men stagger in, pretending to have poisoned themselves. Alfonso and Despina run for a doctor while the ladies begin to waiver: their pity for the newcomers will be their undoing. Now Despina returns, disguised as a doctor, using Dr. Mesmer's invention, the magnet, to draw out the poison. The men revive ("Dove son?"), but the girls angrily refuse to grant them a kiss.

Act II

Attending the ladies in their boudoir, Despina urges them to relent and give in to their suitors ("Una donna a quindici anni"). Dorabella thinks they ought to, the reluctant Fiordiligi gives way, and they decide who will pair off with whom ("Prenderò quel brunettino").

The young men have arranged a serenade in the garden. Seeing the wager through, Guglielmo pairs off with Dorabella while Ferrando woos Fiordiligi ("Ah, lo veggio quell'anima bella"), who admits to herself that he has touched her heart ("Per pietà"), hoping her absent lover will forgive her. When the men compare notes, Guglielmo is glad to see Fiordiligi standing fast—or so he thinks—but Ferrando is dismayed that Dorabella has given Guglielmo a locket. His anger amuses Guglielmo, who comments on the waywardness of the fair sex ("Donne mie, la fate a tanti!"). Left alone, Ferrando expresses his love for Dorabella, though he feels betrayed ("Tradito, schernito").

On the terrace, the sisters tell Despina they have lost their hearts—Fiordiligi with misgivings, Dorabella with enthusiasm. Love is a thief, the maid replies, and people get robbed every day ("È amore un ladroncello"). Alone, the troubled Fiordiligi decides to drag Dorabella off to join their sweethearts at the front. Eavesdropping, Guglielmo is in ecstasy until Ferrando pursues the wager by threatening suicide, and Fiordiligi gives in to him. Now Guglielmo is furious, but Alfonso counsels forgiveness: that's just the way women are, he claims ("Tutti accusan le donne").

Now for a double wedding between the sisters and the "Albanians." Servants, musicians and guests salute the two couples as Alfonso brings in a notary—Despina in another disguise. Just as the ladies have signed the marriage contract, familiar martial strains outside draw Alfonso to a window: the girls' former lovers are returning with their regiment. In panic, Fiordiligi and Dorabella push their intended husbands from the room and go more or less to pieces when the men reappear without their "Albanian" mufti. Ferrando and Guglielmo play their true identities to the hilt, storming at the ladies when the contract is discovered. But Alfonso reveals the disguises and hails the triumph of reason over unrealistic expectations, as forgiveness prevails.

Opera News

PREFACE

The fifteenth of Mozart's operas, Così Fan Tutte dates from the final period of his life. With Le Nozze di Figaro and Don Giovanni behind him and his last three symphonies recently completed, the composer was yet to undertake Die Zauberflöte and La Clemenza di Tito. Introduced in Vienna on the eve of Mozart's thirty-fourth birthday, Così Fan Tutte is a quintessential example of Italian-style opera buffa. It was written at the request of Emperor Joseph II, who is believed to have suggested to the librettist, Lorenzo da Ponte, a subject drawn from current gossip in the city: disguised lovers court each other's sweethearts to test the girls' fidelity. The nineteenth century tended to reject this out of hand, finding the subject trivial and scandalous, degrading to the romantic idealization of women. Until modern times *Così Fan Tutte* remained, therefore, the least known or performed of Mozart's major operas.

"Perhaps the modern public does not fully appreciate the parodistic style," gently remarked Richard Strauss, a champion of the work and one of its legendary conductors. According to the eminent critic Edward J. Dent, modern listeners "cannot bear to feel that it [the sheer beauty of the music itself] is a deliberate expression of sham feeling and sometimes of comically exaggerated passion." But as he points out, "The artificiality of the comedy makes its charm."

Commentators today are more likely to dwell on the warmth and humanity found in *Così Fan Tutte*. Alfred Einstein writes, "There is an evening glow over this whole score. Mozart is full of sympathy for his two victims, the representatives of frail femininity. . . . There is a touch of melancholy in the moral of the burlesque incident, and we can hear it already in the *andante* of the overture." Virgil Thomson commends the opera "for tenderness, for human compassion and philosophic toleration of human weakness." Mozart lived in what afterward was soon considered a period of appalling moral laxity, and perhaps it helps to know that shortly before composing *Così* he wrote to his wife, Constanze, gently remonstrating with her for behaving flirtatiously while away on vacation. He himself was no stranger to flirtation, and in his comic operas he knew whereof he wrote. The dramatic crux of *Così* had special meaning for him, because he had been in love with Constanze's sister before marrying her.

People still argue about which lover ends up with which at the opera's end, and productions often leave it up to the audience by simply having all the characters hold hands. Eighteenth-century symmetry, plus a few clues in the libretto, make it seem that Mozart and Da Ponte took for granted a return to the original pairing. Yet the moral of the opera—and it is certainly no immoral work, as the nineteenth century assumed—can be read differently for our own time, when priorities, assumptions and conventions have changed.

The truth about *Così*, as with Mozart's other comedies, is that on one level it is artificial, on another absolutely real. The sense of emotional rightness and verisimilitude is conveyed by the music, which treats situations seriously even when exaggerating or spoofing them. This split-level approach, particularly in *Don Giovanni* and *Così*, has always worried the literal-minded while delighting those who sense universality in Mozart's art. There are plenty of moments in real life when one is torn between tears and laughter, between thought and sensuality, between practical considerations and inmost wishes. Mozart, unlike other purveyors of opera buffa, did not narrow his vision to create an unreal world of comedy: he insisted on giving it all, rendering the artifice in terms of the full range of feelings everyone has.

When Mozart received the libretto, in early November 1789, his fortunes were at a low ebb. The middle of that month, one of his children died shortly after birth. The Mozarts had been obliged to leave their suburban apartment for a less expensive one in the city. It helped him in the work to focus his attention on the performers destined for the premiere. Mme. Ferrarese del Bene, for example, the current mistress of Da Ponte, was a type of singer the composer did not particularly like, using several different registers of her voice for display effects. He treated her somewhat ironically, exploiting the tricks she could do while infusing them with expressive depth beyond her usual range. The result is the role of Fiordiligi (Italian for Fleur-de-lis), one of the paragons of flexibility and endurance for a soprano with spinto or dramatic overtones and an absolute command of coloratura technique.

Emperor Joseph II never lived to hear *Così Fan Tutte*. He died at forty-eight, a month after the opera's premiere at the Burgtheater on January 26, 1790. His death in fact interrupted the run of performances. *Così* had seven repetitions that season and was not revived in what little remained of Mozart's lifetime.

A true ensemble opera, with more ensembles than solos, *Così* continued to attract the serious-minded Romantic Era with its music but not with its libretto, which was heavily adapted by many translators, especially in Germany. It was in France, however, that impresario Léon Carvalho hatched the scheme of fitting an entirely new libretto, based on Shakespeare's *Love's Labours Lost*, a somewhat comparable plot, to the music. Though his librettists were Barbier and Carré, who provided the texts for *Carmen* and *Les Contes d'Hoffmann*, their efforts went for naught. That was in 1863. As late as 1909, after German-language *Così* revivals under Hermann Levi and Gustav Mahler, the singer Karl Scheidemantel concocted a version based on Calderón's *Dame Kobold*. The breakthrough did not come until 1920, when Strauss led a revival in Vienna, quickly if briefly followed by the first Metropolitan Opera production—a dozen performances between 1922 and 1928. During the 1930's *Così* became a favorite at the Glyndebourne Festival. The Rudolf Bing management scored a great success with its production at the Met in 1951.

Thirty seasons later, the company took a fresh look at *Così* through the eyes of two designers new to the Met, Hayden Griffin (sets) and Deirdre Clancy (costumes), who chose a stage-within-a-stage concept. Having been seen from different perspectives in various modern productions, *Così Fan Tutte* seems to be the Mozart comedy for today, dealing in an intimate way with the ambiguities, perplexities and joys of life.

JOHN W. FREEMAN

COSÌ FAN TUTTE

ACT I

SCENE I

A coffee-house.

Ferrando, Guglielmo and Don Alfonso

No. 1 Trio

FERRANDO

La mia Dorabella	My Dorabella
Capace non è:	Couldn't do such a thing:
Fedel quanto bella	Heaven made her as faithful
Il cielo la fe'.	As she is beautiful.

GUGLIELMO

La mia Fiordiligi	My Fiordiligi
Tradirmi non sa:	Would never betray me:
Uguale in lei credo	I'm sure her loyalty
Costanza e beltà.	Equals her beauty.

DON ALFONSO

Ho i crini già grigi,	My hair's already gray,
Ex cathedra parlo;	And I speak from years of experience;
Ma tali litigi	But let's stop this bickering
Finiscano qua.	Right here and now.

FERRANDO and GUGLIELMO

No, detto ci avete	Oh no, you've told us
Che infide esser ponno:	They could be untrue:

Provar ce 'l dovete,	Now you've got to prove it,
Se avete onestà.	If you're as good as your word.

Don Alfonso

Tai prove lasciamo . . .	Let's just forget about the proof . . .

Ferrando and Guglielmo

(putting their hands on their swords)

No, no, le vogliamo:	No, no, we insist on having it:
O, fuori la spada,	Or else you can take out your sword,
Rompiam l'amistà.	And we'll put an end to this friendship.

Don Alfonso (*aside*)

O pazzo desire!	Oh, what an insane idea!
Cercar di scoprire	To try to root out
Quel mal che, trovato,	The worm in the apple
Meschini ci fa.	That's the bane of our existence.

Ferrando and Guglielmo (*aside*)

Sul vivo mi tocca	Anybody who dares
Chi lascia di bocca	Say one word
Sortire un accento	Against her
Che torto le fa.	Cuts me to the quick.

Secco Recitative

Guglielmo

Fuor la spada! Scegliete	Now out with your sword! And choose
Qual di noi più vi piace.	Which one of us you like.

Don Alfonso (*calmly*)

Io son uomo di pace,	I'm just a peace-loving fellow,
E duelli non fo, se non a mensa.	And the only duels I fight are at table.

Ferrando

O battervi, o dir subito	Either you'll fight, or you'll tell us right now
Perché d'infedeltà le nostre amanti	How you could possibly suspect our sweethearts
Sospettate capaci!	Of any infidelity at all!

DON ALFONSO

Cara semplicità, quanto mi piaci!	Oh, how innocent you are! It really makes me laugh!

FERRANDO

Cessate di scherzar, o giuro al cielo! . . .	And if you don't stop joking, I swear by heaven! . . .

DON ALFONSO

Ed io, giuro alla terra,	And I swear by this earth,
Non scherzo, amici miei.	I'm not joking, my friends.
Solo saper vorrei	I'd just like to know
Che razza d'animali	What breed of beast
Son queste vostre belle,	These beauties of yours really are,
Se han come tutti noi carne, ossa e pelle,	If they're made of flesh and blood like everyone else,
Se mangian come noi, se veston gonne,	If they eat like us, if they wear long skirts,
Alfin, se Dee, se donne son . . .	In fact, if they're goddesses, or women . . .

FERRANDO and GUGLIELMO

Son donne,	They're women,
Ma . . . son tali . . . son tali . . .	But . . . the likes . . . of them . . .

DON ALFONSO

E in donne pretendete	And you really expect
Di trovar fedeltà?	Women to be faithful?
Quanto mi piaci mai, semplicità!	Oh, how I love your innocence!

No. 2 Trio

(jokingly)

È la fede delle femmine	Women's faithfulness
Come l'araba fenice:	Is like the Arabian phoenix:
Che vi sia, ciascun lo dice;	Everyone says it exists;
Dove sia, nessun lo sa.	But no one knows where it is.

FERRANDO *(eagerly)*

La fenice è Dorabella!	Dorabella's the Phoenix!

GUGLIELMO *(eagerly)*

La fenice è Fiordiligi!	Fiordiligi's the Phoenix!

DON ALFONSO

Non è questa, non è quella:	No, it's not one or the other, I'm afraid:
Non fu mai, non vi sarà.	It never existed, and it never will.

Secco Recitative

FERRANDO

Scioccherie di poeti!	Oh, what poetic nonsense!

GUGLIELMO

Scempiaggini di vecchi!	Oh, what senile foolishness!

DON ALFONSO

Orbene, udite,	Just hear me out,
Ma senza andar in collera:	And don't fly off the handle:
Qual prova avete voi che ognor costanti	What proof have you got
Vi sien le vostri amanti;	That your sweethearts are faithful;
Chi vi fe' sicurtà che invariabili	What makes you so sure
Sono i lor cori?	They aren't fickle instead?

FERRANDO

Lunga esperienza . . .	We've known them so long . . .

GUGLIELMO

Nobil educazion . . .	They're so well brought up . . .

FERRANDO

Pensar sublime . . .	Their thoughts are sublime . . .

GUGLIELMO

Analogia d'umor . . .	They're ever so compatible . . .

FERRANDO

Disinteresse . . .	They're generous to a fault . . .

GUGLIELMO

Immutabil carattere . . .	Their attitudes never change . . .

FERRANDO

Promesse . . .	The promises they've made . . .

GUGLIELMO

Proteste . . .	And all their protests, too . . .

FERRANDO

Giuramenti . . .	And their vows of love . . .

Così Fan Tutte

DON ALFONSO

Pianti, sospir, carezze, svenimenti.

Lasciatemi un po' ridere . . .

And their tears, their sighs, their caresses,
and their fainting-fits.

I'm sorry, but I can't help laughing . . .

FERRANDO

Cospetto!

Finite di deriderci?

Confound it!

Are you through making fun of us?

DON ALFONSO

Pian piano:
E se toccar con mano
Oggi vi fo che come l'altre sono?

Hold on just a moment:
What if I could show you right now
That they're exactly like the others?

GUGLIELMO

Non si può dar!

That's ridiculous!

FERRANDO

Non è!

That's impossible!

DON ALFONSO

Giochiam!

Let's bet on it then!

FERRANDO

Giochiamo!

You're on!

DON ALFONSO

Cento zecchini.

A hundred gold pieces.

GUGLIELMO

E mille, se volete.

A thousand, if you like.

DON ALFONSO

Parola . . .

Your word . . .

FERRANDO

Parolissima.

Our solemn word.

DON ALFONSO

E un cenno, un motto, un gesto
Giurate di non far di tutto questo
Alle vostre Penelopi.

And you swear you won't give
The slightest sign, or whisper, or hint
Of all this to your Penelopes?

FERRANDO

Giuriamo.

We swear it.

397

DON ALFONSO

Da soldati d'onore.   On your honor as soldiers.

GUGLIELMO

Da soldati d'onore.   On our honor as soldiers.

DON ALFONSO

E tutto quel farete   And you'll do everything
Ch'io vi dirò di far.   I tell you to do.

FERRANDO

          Tutto!   Everything!

GUGLIELMO

        Tuttissimo!   Anything at all!

DON ALFONSO

Bravissimi!   Good for you!

FERRANDO and GUGLIELMO

      Bravissimo,   And good for you, too,
Signor Don Alfonsetto!   My dear Don Alfonso!

FERRANDO

        A spese vostre   Now we'll have a little fun
Or ci divertiremo.   At your expense.

GUGLIELMO (to Ferrando)

E de' cento zecchini, che faremo?   And what'll we do with the hundred gold
                                         pieces?

No. 3 Trio

FERRANDO

Una bella serenata   I'm going to have
Far io voglio alla mia Dea.   My goddess serenaded in style.

GUGLIELMO

In onor di Citerea   I'm going to give a banquet
Un convito io voglio far.   In honor of my Venus.

DON ALFONSO

Sarò anch'io de' convitati?   Will I be one of the guests?

FERRANDO and GUGLIELMO

Ci sarete, sì signor.   Yes sir, of course you will.

398

FERRANDO, GUGLIELMO and DON ALFONSO

E che brindis replicati	And many a toast we'll propose
Far vogliamo al Dio d'amor!	To the god of love!

(They go off.)

SCENE II

A garden by the seashore.

Fiordiligi and Dorabella

(The two girls are each gazing at miniature portraits hanging at their waists.)

No. 4 Duet

FIORDILIGI

Ah, guarda, sorella,	Ah, tell me, my sister,
Se bocca più bella,	If you could ever find
Se aspetto più nobile	A sweeter mouth,
Si può ritrovar.	Or a nobler face.

DORABELLA

Osserva tu un poco	And just look at
Che fuoco ha ne' sguardi!	That fiery glance!
Se fiamma, se dardi	Doesn't it seem like it's
Non sembran scoccar.	Shooting off darts and flames?

FIORDILIGI

Si vede un sembiante	He's got the face
Guerriero ed amante.	Of a fighter and a lover.

DORABELLA

Si vede una faccia	He's got a look
Che alletta e minaccia.	That fascinates and scares me, too.

FIORDILIGI and DORABELLA

Io sono felice!	Oh, how happy I am!
Se questo mio core	If my feelings for him
Mai cangia desio,	Should ever change,
Amore mi faccia	May love make me
Vivendo penar!	Live in misery!

Secco Recitative

FIORDILIGI

Mi par che stamattina volentieri	This morning I really feel like
Farei la pazzarella: ho un certo fuoco,	Getting into mischief: I've got a kind of fever,
Un certo pizzicor entro le vene . . .	A tingling in my veins . . .
Quando Guglielmo viene, se sapessi	If you only knew the joke I'm going to play
Che burla gli vo' far.	On Guglielmo when he gets here.

DORABELLA

Per dirti il vero,	To tell you the truth,
Qualche cosa di nuovo	I feel a little peculiar myself:
Anch'io nell'alma provo: io giurerei	I'd swear that our wedding
Che lontane non siam dagli imenei.	Isn't very far away.

FIORDILIGI

Dammi la mano, io voglio astrologarti.	Just let me see your hand a moment, I want to tell your fortune.
Uh, che bell' *Emme*! E questo	Oh, what a nice M! And here's
È un *Pi*! Va bene: *matrimonio presto*.	A P, too! So that's it: *matrimony presently*.

DORABELLA

Affè, che ci avrei gusto!	Oh, I'd like that a lot!

FIORDILIGI

Ed io non ci avrei rabbia.	And I wouldn't mind a bit.

DORABELLA

Ma che diavol vuol dir che i nostri sposi	But why on earth are our fiancés
Ritardano a venir? Son già le sei . . .	So late? It's already six o'clock . . .

FIORDILIGI

Eccoli.	There they are now.

SCENE III

Fiordiligi, Dorabella and Don Alfonso

DORABELLA

Non son essi: è Don Alfonso,	No, it's not them: It's their friend
L'amico lor.	Don Alfonso.

FIORDILIGI

Ben venga	Good morning,
Il signor Don Alfonso!	Don Alfonso!

DON ALFONSO

Riverisco.	Young ladies, good morning to you!

DORABELLA

Cos'è? perché qui solo? Voi piangete?	What's the matter? Where are the others? You're crying?
Parlate, per pietà: che cosa è nato?	Speak up, for pity's sake: What's happened?
L'amante . . .	My lover . . .

FIORDILIGI

L'idol mio . . .	My darling . . .

DON ALFONSO

Barbaro fato!	Oh, how cruel fate can be!

No. 5 Aria

Vorrei dir, e cor non ho,	I'd like to tell you, but I just don't dare,
Balbettando il labbro va;	All I can do is stammer and stutter;
Fuor la voce uscir non può,	I just can't get the words out,
Ma mi resta mezza qua.	They seem to be stuck in my throat.
Che farete? che farò?	What'll you do? What'll I do?
Oh, che gran fatalità!	Oh, what a horrible mess!
Dar di peggio non si può:	Nothing worse could happen,
Ho di voi, di lor pietà!	How I grieve for you and them both!

Secco Recitative

FIORDILIGI

Stelle! Per carità, signor Alfonso,	Oh, heavens! For pity's sake, Don Alfonso,
Non ci fate morir.	Don't keep us in suspense.

DON ALFONSO

Convien armarvi,	Now's the time, my dear girls,
Figlie mie, di costanza.	To muster all the strength you've got.

DORABELLA

O Dei! Qual male
È addivenuto mai, qual caso rio?

Forse è morto il mio bene?

Oh, God! What terrible thing
Has happened, what disaster has there
been?

Are you saying my lover is dead?

FIORDILIGI

È morto il mio?

And is mine dead, too?

DON ALFONSO

Morti . . . non son; ma poco men che
morti.

They're . . . not dead; but they might as
well be.

DORABELLA

Feriti?

Are they wounded?

DON ALFONSO

No.

No, they're not.

FIORDILIGI

Ammalati?

Are they sick?

DON ALFONSO

Neppur.

No, it's not that either.

FIORDILIGI

Che cosa, dunque?

Just what is it then?

DON ALFONSO

Al marzial campo
Ordin regio li chiama.

They've been called
To battle by a royal command.

FIORDILIGI and DORABELLA

Ohimè, che sento!

Good heavens! What am I hearing?

FIORDILIGI

E partiran?

When will they have to leave?

DON ALFONSO

Sul fatto.

They've got to leave at once.

DORABELLA

E non v'è modo
D'impedirlo?

And there's
No way to stop them?

Così Fan Tutte

DON ALFONSO

Non v'è.   No, there's not.

FIORDILIGI

Né un solo addio? . . .   Can't we even say good-bye? . . .

DON ALFONSO

Gli infelici non hanno   The poor wretches
Coraggio di vedervi.   Don't dare to see you.
Ma se voi lo bramate,   But if you really want to,
Son pronti . . .   They're ready . . .

DORABELLA

Dove son?   Where are they?

DON ALFONSO

Amici, entrate.   Come on ahead, my friends.

SCENE IV

Fiordiligi, Dorabella, Don Alfonso;
Ferrando and Guglielmo in travelling clothes, etc.

No. 6 Quintet

GUGLIELMO

Sento, oddio, che questo piede   My God, I'm dragging my feet,
È restio nel girle avante.   I can hardly show my face.

FERRANDO

Il mio labbro palpitante   My lips are trembling so badly
Non può detto pronunziar.   That I can hardly say a word.

DON ALFONSO

Nei momenti i più terribili   When things are at their worst,
Sua virtù l'eroe palesa.   A hero shows his stuff.

FIORDILIGI and DORABELLA

Or che abbiam la nuova intesa,   And now that we've heard the
                                                          news,

A voi resta a fare il meno.   There's one more thing you must
                                                          do.

Fate core: a entrambe in seno   Be brave: and plunge your swords
Immergeteci l'acciar.   Right through our hearts.

Ferrando and Guglielmo

Idol mio, la sorte incolpa,
Se ti deggio abbandonar.

My darling, it's not my fault
If I've got to leave you.

Dorabella

Ah, no, no, non partirai!

Oh, no, no, you can't leave!

Fiordiligi

No, crudel, non te ne andrai!

Oh no, you're so cruel, you can't go
away!

Dorabella

Voglio pria cavarmi il core!

I'd sooner tear my heart out!

Fiordiligi

Pria ti vo' morire ai piedi!

I'd rather die at your feet!

Ferrando (*sottovoce to Don Alfonso*)

Cosa dici?

What do you think?

Guglielmo (*sottovoce to Don Alfonso*)

Te n'avvedi?

Do you realize?

Don Alfonso (*sottovoce to the two young men*)

Saldo, amico: *finem lauda*.

Hold on, my friends: It's not over
yet.

Fiordiligi, Dorabella, Ferrando, Guglielmo and Don Alfonso

Il destin così defrauda
Le speranze de' mortali.
Ah, chi mai fra tanti mali,
Chi mai può la vita amar?

That's how fate plays havoc
With the hopes of mortal men.
Ah, who could still love life
When there's so much pain and
grief?

Secco Recitative

Guglielmo

Non piangere, idol mio!

Oh, please don't cry, my dearest!

Ferrando

Non disperarti,
Adorata mia sposa!

Don't give in to despair,
My sweetheart!

Don Alfonso

Lasciate lor tal sfogo: è troppo giusta
La cagion di quel pianto.

Let them have a good cry: They've got
Plenty to cry about.

Così Fan Tutte

(The lovers embrace each other tenderly.)

FIORDILIGI

Chi sa s'io più ti veggio!	Who knows if I'll ever see you again!

DORABELLA

Chi sa se più ritorni!	Who knows if you'll ever come back!

FIORDILIGI

Lasciami questo ferro: ei mi dia morte,	Leave your dagger with me: I'll take my own life
Se mai barbara sorte	If a cruel fate should ever pierce
In quel seno a me caro . . .	That breast so dear to me . . .

DORABELLA

Morrei di duol; d'uopo non ho d'acciaro.	And I would die of grief; I wouldn't need a dagger.

FERRANDO and GUGLIELMO

Non farmi, anima mia,	Oh, my love, please don't make
Questi infausti presagi.	Such dire predictions to me.
Proteggeran gli Dei	As long as I live, I promise you,
La pace del tuo cor ne' giorni miei.	The gods will protect your peace of mind.

No. 7 Duet

Al fato dàn legge	Those precious little eyes
Quegli occhi vezzosi:	Will alone decide our fate:
Amor li protegge,	Love will surely protect them,
Né i loro riposi	And even the cruelest stars
Le barbare stelle	Won't dare disturb
Ardiscon turbar.	Their rest.
Il ciglio sereno,	Now give me a sweet smile,
Mio bene, a me gira:	My darling,
Felice al tuo seno	And in no time at all
Io spero tornar.	I'll be back in your arms again.

Secco Recitative

DON ALFONSO *(aside)*

La commedia è graziosa, e tutti e due	This farce is most amusing, and they're both
Fan ben la loro parte.	Playing their parts well.

(A drum is heard in the distance.)

FERRANDO

O cielo! questo   God help me! There's
È il tamburo funesto   The fatal drum
Che a divider mi vien dal mio tesoro.   That's come to take me away from my
                                                   love.

DON ALFONSO

Ecco, amici, la barca.   The boat's arrived, my friends.

FIORDILIGI

Io manco.   I'm fainting.

DORABELLA

Io moro.   And I'm dying.

SCENE V

Fiordiligi, Dorabella, Don Alfonso, Ferrando, Guglielmo, soldiers and townspeople

No. 8 Chorus

*(A military march in the distance. A boat arrives at the shore; then a troop of
soldiers enters, accompanied by men and women.)*

CHORUS (*soldiers and people*)

Bella vita militar!   A soldier's life for me!
Ogni dì si cangia loco,   Every day a change of scene,
Oggi molto, doman poco,   Today a lot, tomorrow a little,
Ora in terra ed or sul mar.   First on land and then at sea.

Il fragor di trombe e pifferi,   The sound of trumpets and fifes,
Lo sparar di schioppi e bombe   While shells and bombs explode
Forza accresce al braccio e   Makes your body and soul much
   all'anima,   stronger,
Vaga sol di trionfar.   You who only fight to win!

Bella vita militar!   A soldier's life for me!

Secco Recitative

DON ALFONSO

Non v'è più tempo, amici: andar conviene   There's no more time, my friends: Duty
                                                      calls,
Ove il destino, anzi il dover v'invita.   And you've got to meet your fate.

406

FIORDILIGI

Mio cor . . .   My dearest . . .

DORABELLA

Idolo mio . . .   My darling . . .

FERRANDO

Mio ben . . .   My love . . .

GUGLIELMO

Mia vita . . .   My life . . .

FIORDILIGI

Ah, per un sol momento . . .   Ah, for just one moment . . .

DON ALFONSO

Del vostro reggimento   Your regiment's ship
Già è partita la barca.   Has already left.
Raggiungerla convien coi pochi amici   Now you'll have to join it with a few
                                         friends
Che su legno più lieve   Who're waiting for you
Attendendo vi stanno.   In a smaller boat.

FERRANDO and GUGLIELMO

Abbracciami, idol mio!   Embrace me, my love!

FIORDILIGI and DORABELLA

Muoio d'affanno.   I'm dying of grief.

No. 9 Quintet

FIORDILIGI (*in tears*)

Di scrivermi ogni giorno   My darling, promise me
Giurami, vita mia!   You'll write every day!

DORABELLA (*in tears*)

Due volte ancora   Write me twice as often,
Tu scrivimi, se puoi.   If you can.

FERRANDO

Sii certa, o cara.   Of course I will, my dearest.

GUGLIELMO

Non dubitar, mio bene.   I swear I will, my love.

Don Alfonso

(aside, together with the other four, who repeat the preceding verses)

Io crepo, se non rido!	If I don't laugh, I'll bust!

Fiordiligi

Sii costante a me sol . . .	Be faithful only to me . . .

Dorabella

Sèrbati fido.	Don't ever be untrue.

Ferrando

Addio!	Good-bye!

Guglielmo

Addio!	Good-bye!

Fiordiligi and Dorabella

Addio!	Good-bye!

Fiordiligi, Dorabella, Ferrando and Guglielmo

Mi si divide il cor, bell'idol mio!	You're breaking my heart, my darling!

Addio, addio, addio!	Good-bye, good-bye, good-bye!

Don Alfonso *(aside)*

Io crepo, se non rido!	If I don't laugh, I'll bust!

Chorus

Bella vita militar!	A soldier's life for me!
Ogni dì si cangia loco,	Every day a change of scene,
Oggi molto, doman poco,	Today a lot, tomorrow a little,
Ora in terra ed or sul mar.	First on land and then at sea.
Il fragor di trombe e pifferi,	The sound of trumpets and fifes,
Lo sparar di schioppi e bombe	While shells and bombs explode
Forza accresce al braccio e all'anima,	Makes your body and soul much stronger,
Vaga sol di trionfar.	You who only fight to win!
Bella vita militar!	A soldier's life for me!

(While the chorus is repeated, Ferrando and Guglielmo get into the boat, which then sails away amid the sound of drums, etc. The soldiers go off, followed by the townspeople. The sisters remain standing on the shore.)

SCENE VI

Fiordiligi, Dorabella and Don Alfonso

Secco Recitative

DORABELLA (*as if coming out of a trance*)

Dove son?	Where are they?

DON ALFONSO

Son partiti.	They've already gone, I'm afraid.

FIORDILIGI

Oh, dipartenza	Oh, that was
Crudelissima! amara!	The cruelest, most bitter good-bye!

DON ALFONSO

Fate core,	Now you've got to be brave,
Carissime figliuole.	My darling girls.

(*A handkerchief is seen waving in the distance.*)

Guardate, da lontano	Look at that: Your sweethearts
Vi fan cenno con mano i cari sposi.	Are waving at you from so far away.

FIORDILIGI (*waving back*)

Buon viaggio, mia vita!	God bless you, my love!

DORABELLA (*waving back*)

Buon viaggio!	God bless you!

FIORDILIGI

O Dei, come veloce	Good gracious, look how fast
Se ne va quella barca! Già sparisce,	Their boat's moving away! It's almost disappeared,
Già non si vede più. Deh, faccia il cielo	It's already out of sight. May heaven
Ch'abbia prospero corso.	Guide them on their way.

DORABELLA

Faccia che al campo giunga	And may they reach the battlefield
Con fortunati auspici.	Safe and sound.

DON ALFONSO

E a voi salvi gli amanti, a me gli amici.	May it preserve your sweethearts for you, and my good friends for me.

409

Fiordiligi, Dorabella and Don Alfonso
No. 10 Terzettino

Soave sia il vento,	May the breezes blow gently,
Tranquilla sia l'onda,	May the waves be calm;
Ed ogni elemento	And may all the elements
Benigno risponda	Be as kind as they can
Ai nostri desir.	In answer to our prayers.

(The two sisters go off.)

Scene VII

Don Alfonso alone

Secco Recitative

Don Alfonso

Non son cattivo comico! Va bene . . .	I'm not such a bad actor after all! Now then . . .
Al concertato loco i due campioni	Those two champions of Venus and Mars
Di Ciprigna e di Marte	Are already waiting for me
Mi staranno attendendo: or senza indugio	Where we said: I'd better go and meet them
Raggiungerli conviene. Quante smorfie,	Without any further delay. Pulling all those faces,
Quante buffonerie!	And all that carrying on!
Tanto meglio per me . . .	So much the better for me . . .
Cadran più facilmente:	They'll give in far more easily:
Questa razza di gente è la più presta	People like that are always so quick
A cangiarsi d'umore. Oh, poverini!	To change their minds. Oh, those poor boys!
Per femmina giocar cento zecchini?	Who'd bother to bet a hundred gold pieces on a couple of fickle girls?

Accompanied Recitative

Nel mare solca e nell'arena semina	Basing your hopes on a woman's heart
E il vago vento spera in rete accogliere	Is like trying to plow the seas and sow the sands
Chi fonda sue speranze in cor di femmina.	Or catch the wild wind in your net.

(He goes off.)

SCENE VIII

A pleasant room with several chairs, a little table, etc.;
three doors, two at the sides, and one at the back.

Despina alone

Secco Recitative

DESPINA (*stirring her chocolate*)

Che vita maledetta	There's nothing more miserable
È il far la cameriera!	Than being a maid!
Dal mattino alla sera	From morning till night
Si fa, si suda, si lavora, e poi	You're busy, you're sweating and slaving, and then
Di tanto che si fa nulla è per noi.	When you're done, there's nothing left for you.
È mezz'ora che sbatto;	I've been stirring this for half an hour:
Il cioccolatte è fatto, ed a me tocca	The chocolate's ready, and all I can do
Restar ad odorarlo a secca bocca?	Is stand here with my tongue hanging out?
Non è forse la mia come la vostra,	Isn't my taste the same as yours,
O garbate signore,	My dear young ladies,
Che a voi dessi l'essenza e a me l'odore?	But you get the substance and I get the smell?
Perbacco, vo' assaggiarlo!	By God, I'm going to try it!
Com'è buono!	Oh, how delicious it is!

(*She wipes her mouth.*)

Viene gente.	Someone's coming.
O ciel, son le padrone!	Egad, it's my mistresses!

SCENE IX

Despina, Fiordiligi and Dorabella

(*Fiordiligi and Dorabella enter in despair.*)

DESPINA
(*serving the chocolate on a tray*)

Madame, ecco la vostra colazione.	My ladies, here's your breakfast.

(*Dorabella throws everything on the floor.*)

Diamine! Cosa fate?	Goodness! What're you doing?

411

FIORDILIGI

Ah!   Ah!

DORABELLA

Ah!   Ah!

(*Both of them tear off their jewelry.*)

DESPINA

Che cosa è nato?   What's happened?

FIORDILIGI

Ov'è un acciaro?   Is there a dagger around?

Un veleno dov'è?   Have we got any poison at all?

DESPINA

Padrone, dico! . . .   My ladies, I beg you! . . .

DORABELLA

Accompanied Recitative

Ah, scòstati! Paventa il triste effetto   Oh, just get away from me! I'm afraid I'm going

D'un disperato affetto!   To do something really desperate!
Chiudi quelle finestre! Odio la luce,   Hurry up and close those windows! I hate the light of day,

Odio l'aria che spiro, odio me stessa.   I hate the air I'm breathing, and I even hate myself.
Chi schernisce il mio duol, chi mi consola? . . .   Who could soothe my pain, who could possibly console me? . . .
Deh, fuggi, per pietà: lasciami sola!   Get out of here, for pity's sake! Just leave me alone!

No. 11 Aria

Smanie implacabili   May those terrible pangs
Che m'agitate,   That torment me so,
Entro quest'anima   Not subside
Più non cessate   Within my breast
Finché l'angoscia   Until my anguish
Mi fa morir!   Brings me death!

Esempio misero   And if I'm still alive,
D'amor funesto   I'll show the Furies

Darò all'Eumenidi,	How wretched is
Se viva resto,	This tragic love
Col suono orribile	With the horrible sound
De' miei sospir!	Of my sighs!

(The two girls collapse in their chairs in utter despair.)

Secco Recitative

DESPINA

Signora Dorabella,	Miss Dorabella,
Signora Fiordiligi,	Miss Fiordiligi,
Ditemi: che cosa è stato?	Just tell me: What's happened now?

DORABELLA

Oh, terribil disgrazia!	Oh, what a disaster!

DESPINA

Sbrigatevi, in buonora!	Hurry up, I can't wait any longer!

FIORDILIGI

Da Napoli partiti	Our fiancés
Sono gli amanti nostri.	Have both left Naples.

DESPINA *(laughing)*

Non c'è altro?	That's all?
Ritorneran.	They'll be coming back, I'm sure.

DORABELLA

Chi sa!	Who knows!

DESPINA *(as before)*

Come, chi sa?	What do you mean,
Dove son iti?	Who knows? Where have they gone off to?

DORABELLA

Al campo di battaglia.	They're off to the battlefield.

DESPINA

Tanto meglio per loro:	So much the better for them:
Li vedrete tornar carchi d'alloro.	When they come back they'll be covered with medals.

FIORDILIGI

Ma ponno anche perir.	But they could also be killed.

DESPINA

Allora, poi,   In that case,
Tanto meglio per voi.   So much the better for you.

FIORDILIGI (*rising angrily*)

Sciocca! che dici?   You silly girl! What're you trying to say?

DESPINA

La pura verità: due ne perdete,   I'm telling you the truth: Even if you lose
                                  those two,

Vi restan tutti gli altri.   There are lots more fish in the sea.

FIORDILIGI

Ah, perdendo Guglielmo   Ah, I think I'd die
Mi pare ch'io morrei!   If I ever lost Guglielmo!

DORABELLA

Ah, Ferrando perdendo   Ah, I think I'd bury myself alive
Mi par che viva a seppellirmi andrei!   If I ever lost Ferrando!

DESPINA

Brave, «vi par», ma non è ver: ancora   Good for you! "You think," but it's just
                                  not so:

Non vi fu donna che d'amor sia morta.   There's never been a woman yet who
                                  actually died of love.

Per un uomo morir! . . . Altri ve n'hanno   Die for a man! . . . There're plenty of
                                  others

Che compensano il danno.   Who'll be more than happy to console
                                  you.

DORABELLA

E credi che potria   And you think we could love
Altr'uomo amar chi s'ebbe per amante   Anyone else after we've been loved by
Un Guglielmo, un Ferrando?   The likes of Guglielmo and Ferrando?

DESPINA

Han gli altri ancora   But all the others
Tutto quello ch'han essi.   Have just what they've got.
Un uomo adesso amate,   Right now you're in love with them,
Un altro n'amerete: uno val l'altro,   And tomorrow you'll love someone else:
                                  One's as good as the other,

Perché nessun val nulla.   Because none of them's worth a rap.
Ma non parliam di ciò: sono ancor vivi,   But let's not talk about that: They're still
                                  alive and kicking,

E vivi torneran; ma son lontani,

E, piuttosto che in vani
Pianti perdere il tempo,
Pensate a divertirvi.

And they'll both be back safe and sound;
　　but they're far away,
And instead of wasting your time
Crying useless tears,
Why don't you go and amuse yourselves?

FIORDILIGI (*in a rage*)

Divertirci?　　　　　　　　　　　Go and amuse ourselves?

DESPINA

Sicuro! E, quel ch'è meglio,
Far all'amor come assassine e come
Faranno al campo i vostri cari amanti.

Of course! And what's even better,
Make love for all you're worth, which is
Just what your sweethearts are doing in
　　the field.

DORABELLA

Non offender così quelle alme belle,
Di fedeltà, d'intatto amore esempî!

Don't insult those pure souls like that,
Those shining examples of love and
　　devotion.

DESPINA

Via, via! Passaro i tempi

Da spacciar queste favole ai bambini!

Oh, come on now! The time for fairy-
　　tales
Has long since passed!

No. 12 Aria

In uomini, in soldati
Sperare fedeltà?

So you really hold out hopes
That men and soldiers can be
　　faithful?

(*laughing*)

Non vi fate sentir, per carità!

Don't let anyone hear you, for
　　goodness sake!

Di pasta·simile
Son tutti quanti:
Le fronde mobili,
L'aure incostanti
Han più degli uomini
Stabilità.
Mentite lagrime,
Fallaci sguardi,
Voci ingannevoli,

Every one of them's made
Of the same old stuff:
Even the quivering leaves
And the fickle breezes
Have more stability
Than men.
Those crocodile tears,
Those longing looks,
Those deceitful words,

Vezzi bugiardi	Those charming lies
Son le primarie	Are all their outstanding
Lor qualità.	Qualities.

In noi non amano	All they want from us
Che 'l lor diletto;	Is to take their own pleasure;
Poi ci dispregiano,	And then they despise us,
Neganci affetto,	And deny their affection,
Né val da' barbari	You might as well ask
Chieder pietà.	A barbarian for mercy.

Paghiam, o femmine,	My ladies, let's pay back
D'ugual moneta	In kind
Questa malefica	This evil,
Razza indiscreta:	Impudent breed:
Amiam per comodo,	Let's love for our own good,
Per vanità!	And for our vanity!
La ra la, la ra la, la ra la, la.	Tra la la, la la la, la la la, la.

(They all go off.)

SCENE X

Don Alfonso alone; then Despina

Secco Recitative

DON ALFONSO

Che silenzio! che aspetto di tristezza	How quiet it is! And what a
Spirano queste stanze! Poverette!	Gloomy atmosphere I can feel in these rooms! Those poor girls!
Non han già tutto il torto:	It's certainly not all their fault:
Bisogna consolarle. Infin che vanno	I really should comfort them a bit. Now while
I due creduli sposi,	Those two naive young fools
Com'io loro commisi, a mascherarsi,	Are going to get their disguises, as I told them to,
Pensiam cosa può farsi.	Let's think for a moment about what to do next.
Temo un po' per Despina: quella furba	I'm a little worried about Despina: that sly little minx
Potrebbe riconoscerli, potrebbe	Could recognize them, and then she'd
Rovesciarmi le macchine. Vedremo . . .	Upset my whole scheme. We'll just see . . .
Se mai farà bisogno,	Maybe a nice little bribe at the right time

Un regaletto a tempo: un zecchinetto
Per una cameriera è un gran scongiuro.
Ma, per esser sicuro, si potria
Metterla in parte a parte del segreto . . .
Eccellente è il progetto . . .
La sua camera è questa:

Would come in handy: A gold piece
For a maid is always good insurance.
But just to be sure, I could
Let her in on the secret . . .
That's an excellent idea . . .
Her room's this one here, I think:

(*He knocks.*)

Despinetta!

Despinetta!

DESPINA

Chi batte?

Who's there?

DON ALFONSO

Oh!

Oh!

DESPINA

Ih!

Eeh!

DON ALFONSO

Despina mia,
Di te bisogno avrei.

My dear Despina,
I need your help.

DESPINA

Ed io niente di lei.

And I don't need anything from you.

DON ALFONSO

Ti vo' fare del ben.

But I want to do you a favor.

DESPINA

A una fanciulla
Un vecchio come lei non può far nulla.

An old geezer like you
Can't do much for a girl like me.

DON ALFONSO

Parla piano, ed osserva.

Keep your voice down, and look at this.

(*He shows her a gold piece.*)

DESPINA

Me la dona?

Is that for me?

DON ALFONSO

Sì, se meco sei buona.

Yes it is, if you'll be a good girl and do
what I say.

417

DESPINA

E che vorrebbe?
È l'oro il mio giulebbe.

What is it you want?
Gold's always been a weakness of mine.

DON ALFONSO

Ed oro avrai;
Ma ci vuol fedeltà.

And gold you shall have.
But I need your support.

DESPINA

Non c'è altro? Son qua.

Is that all there is to it? Well then, here I am.

DON ALFONSO

Prendi, ed ascolta:
Sai che le tue padrone
Han perduto gli amanti.

Now take this, and listen:
You know your mistresses
Have lost their lovers.

DESPINA

Lo so.

Yes, I do.

DON ALFONSO

Tutti i lor pianti
Tutti i deliri loro anco tu sai.

And you've heard
All their weeping and wailing.

DESPINA

So tutto.

I've heard everything.

DON ALFONSO

Orben, se mai,
Per consolarle un poco
E trar, come diciam, chiodo per chiodo,

Tu ritrovassi il modo
Da metter in lor grazia
Due soggetti di garbo
Che vorrieno provar . . . già mi
    capisci . . .
C'è una mancia per te di venti scudi,

Se li fai riuscir.

All right then, if you could
Give them a little consolation,
Or, as they say, make the best of a bad
    situation;
If you could just find the way
To make them accept
Two nice young men
Who'd like to try . . . I'm sure you get
    what I mean . . .
There'll be a tip of twenty crowns for
    you,
If you can help them pull it off.

DESPINA

Non mi dispiace
Questa proposizione.

Well, your suggestion
Sounds pretty good to me.

Ma con quelle buffone . . . Basta, udite:

But with those two silly girls . . . Never mind, just listen to this:

Son giovani? Son belli? E, sopra tutto,

Are these admirers of yours young? Are they handsome? And above all,

Hanno una buona borsa
I vostri concorrenti?

Have they got
A big fat purse?

DON ALFONSO

Han tutto quello
Che piacer può alle donne di giudizio.
Li vuoi veder?

They've got everything
A sensible girl could ever want.
Now would you like to see them?

DESPINA

E dove son?

Where are they?

DON ALFONSO

Son lì.
Li posso far entrar?

They're right here.
Is it all right to bring them in?

DESPINA

Direi di sì.

I don't see why not.

(Don Alfonso brings in the young men, who are in disguise.)

SCENE XI

Don Alfonso, Despina, Ferrando, Guglielmo; then Fiordiligi and Dorabella

No. 13 Sextet

DON ALFONSO

Alla bella Despinetta
Vi presento, amici miei;
Non dipende che da lei
Consolar il vostro cor.

My friends, may I present you
To my pretty Despinetta;
The consolation of your hearts
Depends entirely on her.

FERRANDO and GUGLIELMO

(with affected tenderness)

Per la man che lieto io bacio,
Per quei rai di grazie pieni,
Fa' che volga a me sereni
I begli occhi il mio tesor.

By this hand I gladly kiss,
By this smile so full of grace,
Make my darling look at me
With her sweet and gentle eyes.

DESPINA *(aside, laughing)*

Che sembianze! che vestiti!
Che figure! che mustacchi!

What faces! What clothes!
What get-ups! What beards!

Io non so se son valacchi,
O se turchi son costor.

I can't even tell
If they're Wallachians or Turks.

DON ALFONSO (*sottovoce to Despina*)

Che ti par di quell'aspetto?

What do you think of their looks?

DESPINA (*sottovoce to Don Alfonso*)

Per parlarvi schietto schietto,
Hanno un muso fuor dell'uso,
Vero antidoto d'amor.

To be perfectly frank about it,
Their mugs are so peculiar
They'd make me give up love for
good.

DON ALFONSO, FERRANDO and GUGLIELMO (*aside*)

Ora la cosa è appien decisa:
Se costei non { li ravvisa / ci
Non c'è più nessun timor.

Now we're really on our way:
And if she doesn't recognize { them / us
There's nothing more to fear.

DESPINA (*aside, laughing*)

Che figure! che mustacchi!
Io non so se son valacchi,
O se turchi son costor.

What get-ups! What beards!
I can't even tell
If they're Wallachians or Turks.

FIORDILIGI and DORABELLA
(*from within*)

Ehi, Despina! Olà, Despina!

Oh, Despina, Despina!

DESPINA

Le padrone!

It's my mistresses!

DON ALFONSO (*to Despina*)

Ecco l'istante!
Fa' con arte: io qui m'ascondo.

The moment's arrived!
Now use your wits: I'll hide over
here.

(*He retires.*)

FIORDILIGI and DORABELLA (*entering*)

Ragazzaccia tracotante,
Che fai, lì, con simil gente?

Fàlli uscire immantinente,
O ti fo pentir con lor.

You obnoxious little gutter-snipe,
What're you doing with those
people?

Get them out of here at once,
Or I'll make you regret it along
with them.

DESPINA, FERRANDO and GUGLIELMO

Ah, madame, perdonate!	Oh, my ladies, please forgive us!
Al bel piè languir mirate	Look at these two poor wretches
Due meschin, di vostro merto	Who've thrown themselves at your feet,
Spasimanti adorator.	They can't help it, they absolutely adore you.

FIORDILIGI and DORABELLA

Giusti Numi! cosa sento?	Good heavens! What am I hearing?
Dell'enorme tradimento	Who on earth was the fiend behind
Chi fu mai l'indegno autor?	Such a terrible betrayal?

DESPINA, FERRANDO and GUGLIELMO

Deh, calmate quello sdegno . . .	Please don't be so indignant . . .

FIORDILIGI and DORABELLA

Ah, che più non ho ritegno!	Oh, I can't contain myself anymore!
Tutta piena ho l'alma in petto	My heart's bursting in my breast
Di dispetto e di furor!	With outrage and disgust!
Ah, perdon, mio bel diletto!	Oh, forgive me, my dearest darling!
Innocente è questo cor.	This heart of mine is innocent.

FERRANDO and GUGLIELMO

(aside)

Qual diletto è a questo petto	All this ranting and raving
Quella rabbia e quel furor!	Is music to my ears.

DESPINA and DON ALFONSO

(aside; Don Alfonso from the door)

Mi dà un poco di sospetto	All this ranting and raving
Quella rabbia e quel furor.	Makes me a little suspicious.

Secco Recitative

DON ALFONSO (*as though entering*)

Che sussurro! che strepito!	What an uproar! What a commotion!
Che scompiglio è mai questo! Siete pazze,	And what's all this confusion? My dear young ladies,
Care le mie ragazze?	Have you both gone berserk?
Volete sollevar il vicinato?	Do you want to rouse the whole neighborhood?

421

Cosa avete? che è nato?	What's the matter? What's happened now?

DORABELLA (*furiously*)

Oh, ciel! Mirate:	Oh, God! Just look at this:
Uomini in casa nostra!	There are men in our house!

DON ALFONSO (*without looking at the young men*)

Che male c'è?	So what's wrong with that?

FIORDILIGI (*excitedly*)

Che male? In questo giorno! . . .	What's wrong? And especially today! . . .
Dopo il caso funesto! . . .	After everything we've been through! . . .

DON ALFONSO

Accompanied Recitative

Stelle! Sogno o son desto? Amici miei,	Ye Gods! Am I awake or dreaming? My friends,
Miei dolcissimi amici!	My dearest friends!
Voi qui? Come? perché? quando? in qual modo?	You here? How? Why? When? By what means?
Numi! Quanto ne godo!	Goodness gracious! How delighted I am!

Secco Recitative

(*sottovoce to the two young men*)

Secondatemi.	Now play along with me.

FERRANDO

Amico Don Alfonso!	It's my dear friend Don Alfonso!

GUGLIELMO

Amico caro!	It's my good old friend!

(*They embrace one another warmly.*)

DON ALFONSO

Oh, che bella improvvisata!	Oh, what an unexpected pleasure!

DESPINA (*to Don Alfonso*)

Li conoscete, voi?	Do you really know these two?

DON ALFONSO

Se li conosco! Questi	Do I know them! These
Sono i più dolci amici	Are the dearest friends

Ch'io m'abbia in questo mondo,	I've got in the whole wide world,
E vostri ancor saranno.	And they'll soon be yours as well.

FIORDILIGI

E in casa mia che fanno?	And what're they doing in my house?

GUGLIELMO

Ai vostri piedi	My dear ladies, we're just
Due rei, due delinquenti, ecco, madame!	A couple of culprits and criminals who've thrown themselves at your feet!

Accompanied Recitative

Amor . . .	It was love . . .

FIORDILIGI

Numi! Che sento!	My God! What am I hearing?

FERRANDO

Amor, il Nume	It was Almighty
Sì possente, per voi qui ci conduce.	Love that brought us here to you.

(The girls retreat, pursued by the young men.)

GUGLIELMO

. . . Vista appena la luce	. . . As soon as we saw that light
Di vostre fulgidissime pupille . . .	Gleaming in your eyes . . .

FERRANDO

. . . Che alle vive faville . . .	. . . With all those bright little sparks . . .

GUGLIELMO

. . . Farfallette amorose e agonizzanti . . .	. . . Like moths dying of love . . .

FERRANDO

. . . Vi voliamo davanti . . .	. . . We fluttered here before you . . .

GUGLIELMO

. . . Ed ai lati, ed a retro . . .	. . . And around you, and behind you . . .

FERRANDO and GUGLIELMO

. . . Per implorar pietade in flebil metro!	. . . To beg for mercy in a pitiful voice!

FIORDILIGI

Stelle! Che ardir!   Good heavens! How dare you!

DORABELLA

Sorella, che facciamo?   Dear sister, what do we do now?

(Despina goes off in a fright.)

FIORDILIGI

Temerari! sortite	Have you ever seen such nerve! Now just get out
Fuori di questo loco! E non profani	Of this house! We won't let you corrupt
L'alito infausto degl'infami detti	Our hearts and minds and senses
Nostro cor, nostro orecchio e nostri affetti!	With your terrible, vile words!
Invan per voi, per gli altri invan si cerca	It's useless for you, and all the others
Le nostre alme sedur: l'intatta fede	To try to win our trust: We'll keep the faith
Che per noi già si diede ai cari amanti	We've pledged to our sweethearts
Saprem loro serbar infino a morte,	Until the day we die,
A dispetto del mondo e della sorte.	In spite of the rest of world and our fate.

No. 14 Aria

Come scoglio immoto resta	Like a rocky fortress
Contro i venti e la tempesta,	Against the winds and storms,
Così ognor quest'alma è forte	This heart stands ever strong
Nella fede e nell'amore.	In its faith and love.
Con noi nacque quella face	Together we've kindled the flame
Che ci piace e ci consola;	That warms us and consoles us;
E potrà la morte sola	And only death itself
Far che cangi affetto il cor.	Could bring a change of heart.
Rispettate, anime ingrate,	Show some respect for our vows,
Questo esempio di costanza;	You two miserable souls,
E una barbara speranza	And don't ever let such outrageous hopes
Non vi renda audaci ancor.	Make you so reckless again.

(She starts to leave. Ferrando calls her back; Guglielmo calls back her sister.)

Così Fan Tutte

Secco Recitative

FERRANDO (*to Fiordiligi*)

Ah, non partite!   Oh, please don't go!

GUGLIELMO (*to Dorabella*)

Ah, barbara, restate!   Oh, you mean, cruel girl, just stay!

(*sottovoce to Don Alfonso*)

Che vi pare?   What do you think of all this?

DON ALFONSO (*sottovoce to Guglielmo*)

Aspettate.   Hold on for just a moment.

(*to the two sisters*)

Per carità, ragazze,   For pity's sake, my girls,
Non mi fate più far trista figura!   Don't make me look any worse!

DORABELLA (*angrily*)

E che pretendereste?   Just what did you expect?

DON ALFONSO

Eh, nulla . . . Ma mi pare . . .   Oh, nothing . . . But it seems to me . . .
Che un pochin di dolcezza . . .   With a little bit of kindness . . .
Alfn, son galantuomini   After all, they're gentlemen,
E sono amici miei.   And they're both good friends of mine.

FIORDILIGI

Come! E udire dovrei . . .   What! I'm supposed to stand here and
                    listen . . .

GUGLIELMO
            Le nostre pene,   To our suffering,
E sentirne pietà!   And take pity on us!
La celeste beltà degli occhi vostri   The heavenly beauty of your eyes
La piaga aprì nei nostri   Opened up a wound in our own
Cui rimediar può solo   That only the salve of love
Il balsamo d'amore: Could ever hope to heal:
Un solo istante il core aprite, o belle,   My beautiful girls, open up your hearts to
                    its sweet words

A sue dolci facelle, o a voi davanti   For just one moment, or you'll see the
                    most faithful of lovers

Spirar vedrete i più fedeli amanti.   Die right before your eyes.

No. 15 Aria

Non siate ritrosi,	Don't be so reluctant,
Occhietti vezzosi:	You charming little eyes;
Due lampi amorosi	Just flash two bolts of lightning
Vibrate un po' qua.	Lovingly at us.
Felici rendeteci,	If you choose to make us happy,
Amate con noi,	And love us as we do you,
E noi felicissime	We'll make you very happy,
Faremo anche voi.	As much as we are, too.
Guardate, toccate,	Just look at us, reach out and touch,
Il tutto osservate:	Look us over well:
Siam forti e ben fatti,	We're big strapping men,
E, come ognun vede,	And, as anyone can see,
Sia merito o caso,	Whether or not it's our own doing,
Abbiamo bel piede,	We've got good feet,
Bell'occhio, bel naso;	Good eyes, and good noses;
E questi mustacchi	And as for these moustaches,
Chiamare si possono	You might even call them
Trionfi degli uomini,	The triumph of all men,
Pennacchi d'amor.	The fancy feathers of love.

(The two girls go off angrily.)

SCENE XII

Ferrando, Guglielmo and Don Alfonso

(The two young men are laughing heartily as they make fun of Don Alfonso.)

No. 16 Trio

DON ALFONSO

E voi ridete?   And you're laughing at all this?

FERRANDO and GUGLIELMO
(laughing more loudly)

Certo, ridiamo.   Of course we're laughing.

DON ALFONSO

Ma cosa avete?   But what's the matter with you?

FERRANDO and GUGLIELMO

Già lo sappiamo.   Why should we tell you?

DON ALFONSO

Ridete piano!   Just don't laugh so loudly!

FERRANDO and GUGLIELMO

Parlate invano!   It's useless to insist!

DON ALFONSO

Se vi sentissero,   If they should ever hear you,
Se vi scoprissero,   If they ever found you out,
Si guasterebbe   The whole thing
Tutto l'affar.   Would be ruined for good.

(aside)

Mi fa da ridere   It makes me laugh
Questo lor ridere,   To see them laughing,
Ma so che in piangere   But I know they'll both
Dèe terminar.   End up in tears.

FERRANDO and GUGLIELMO

(aside, trying not to laugh)

Ah, che dal ridere   Oh, I'm laughing
L'alma dividere,   Myself sick,
Ah, che le viscere   Oh, my sides
Sento scoppiar!   Are ready to split!

Secco Recitative

DON ALFONSO

Si può sapere un poco   Would you mind telling me
La cagion di quel riso?   Just what's so funny?

GUGLIELMO

Oh, cospettaccio!   Well, I'll be damned!
Non vi pare che abbiam giusta ragione,   Don't you think we've got every right to laugh,
Il mio caro padrone?   My good old friend?

FERRANDO (*playfully*)

Quanto pagar volete,   So how much are you willing to pay,
E a monte è la scommessa?   Now that you've lost the bet?

GUGLIELMO (*playfully*)

Pagate la metà!   How about paying half!

427

FERRANDO (*as before*)

Pagate solo	How about paying
Ventiquattro zecchini!	Twenty-four gold pieces!

DON ALFONSO

Poveri innocentini!	Oh, you two are such babes in the woods!
Venite qua: vi voglio	Come over here a moment, and let me stick
Porre il ditino in bocca!	My thumb in your mouth!

GUGLIELMO

E avete ancora	And you still have
Coraggio di fiatar?	The nerve to go on?

DON ALFONSO

Avanti sera	Before this evening
Ci parlerem.	We'll talk some more about this.

FERRANDO

Quando volete!	Whenever you wish!

DON ALFONSO

Intanto,	In the meantime,
Silenzio e ubbidienza	Keep quiet and do what I say
Fino a doman mattina.	Until tomorrow morning.

GUGLIELMO

Siamo soldati, e amiam la disciplina.	We're soldiers, and we like all this discipline.

DON ALFONSO

Orbene, andate un poco	Now then, both of you go ahead
Ad attendermi entrambi in giardinetto:	And wait for me in the garden:
Colà vi manderò gli ordini miei.	I'll give your orders to you there.

GUGLIELMO

Ed oggi non si mangia?	And we're not getting anything to eat today?

FERRANDO

Cosa serve?	Why bother?
A battaglia finita	When the battle's over
Fia la cena per noi più saporita.	Our supper'll taste even better.

No. 17 Aria

Un'aura amorosa	A breath of love
Del nostro tesoro	From our sweethearts
Un dolce ristoro	Is nourishment enough
Al cor porgerà;	For our hearts.
Al cor che, nudrito	Our hearts are so full
Da speme, da amore,	Of hope and love
Di un'esca migliore	That we'd do without
Bisogno non ha.	Our daily bread.

(Ferrando and Guglielmo go off.)

Scene XIII

Don Alfonso alone; then Despina

Secco Recitative

DON ALFONSO

Oh, la saria da ridere: sì poche	Oh, that would be just too ridiculous:
	When there're so few
Son le donne costanti, in questo mondo,	Faithful women in this world,
E qui ve ne son due! Non sarà nulla . . .	We've got to have two of them here!
	I don't believe it one bit . . .

(Despina enters.)

Vieni, vieni, fanciulla, e dimmi un poco	Come on over here, my child, and tell me
Dove sono e che fan le tue padrone.	Where your mistresses are and what
	they're up to now.

DESPINA

Le povere buffone	The poor silly girls
Stanno nel giardinetto	Are out in the garden
A lagnarsi coll'aria e colle mosche	Squawking at the birds and the bees
D'aver perso gli amanti.	Because they've lost their loves.

DON ALFONSO

E come credi	And how do you think
Che l'affar finirà? vogliam sperare	This whole thing's going to end? Is there
	any chance
Che faranno giudizio?	That they'll come to their senses?

DESPINA

Io lo farei;
E dove piangon esse io riderei.

Disperarsi, strozzarsi
Perché parte un amante?
Guardate che pazzia!
Se ne pigliano due, s'uno va via.

Well, I know I would;
And what they're crying about would
only make me laugh.

Moaning and groaning
Because your lover's gone away?
Think how foolish that is!
If one of them went off, I'd take two of
them instead.

DON ALFONSO

Brava, questa è prudenza!

Good for you, my girl, that's what I call
common sense!

(aside)

Bisogna impuntigliarla.

I've got to egg her on.

DESPINA

È legge di natura,
E non prudenza sola. Amor cos'è?

Piacer, comodo, gusto,
Gioia, divertimento,
Passatempo, allegria: non è più amore,

Se incomodo diventa,
Se invece di piacer nuoce e tormenta.

It's a law of nature,
And not just common sense. What is love
after all?

It's passion, it's diversion, it's indulgence,
It's romance and entertainment,
It's a way to pass the time: It's not love
anymore,
When it stops being fun,
When it only means torment and pain.

DON ALFONSO

Ma intanto queste pazze . . .

And meanwhile those silly girls . . .

DESPINA

Quelle pazze
Faranno a modo nostro. È buon che
sappiano
D'esser amate da color.

Those foolish girls
Will do whatever we say. It's about time
they realized
Those two are in love with them.

DON ALFONSO

Lo sanno.

But they do.

DESPINA

Dunque riameranno.
«Diglielo», si suol dire,
«E lascia far al diavolo».

So then they'll learn to love them, too.
"Just tell them," as they say,
"And let the devil have his due."

Così Fan Tutte

DON ALFONSO

Ma come	But how
Far vuoi perché ritornino,	Do you plan to bring them back,
Or che partiti sono, e che li sentano	When they've already gone away,
E tentare si lascino,	And get those little brats of yours to
	listen to them,
Queste tue bestioline?	And finally give in to temptation?

DESPINA

A me lasciate	Just leave
La briga di condur tutta la macchina.	The whole business to me.
Quando Despina macchina una cosa,	When Despina puts her mind to
	something,
Non può mancar d'effetto: ho già menati	It can't possibly go wrong: I've already
	led
Mill'uomini pel naso,	A thousand men around by the nose,
Saprò menar due femmine. Son ricchi	And I can certainly handle two girls. Are
	those two
I due monsù mustacchi?	Bearded monsters loaded with dough?

DON ALFONSO

Son ricchissimi.	Oh yes, they are, and more.

DESPINA

Dove son?	And just where are they now?

DON ALFONSO

Sulla strada	They're waiting for me
Attendendo mi stanno.	Outside in the street.

DESPINA

Ite, e sul fatto	Well, go on out,
Per la picciola porta	And bring them in to me
A me riconduceteli; v'aspetto	Through the little garden door: I'll be
	waiting for you
Nella camera mia.	In my room.
Purché tutto facciate	And if you do everything
Quel ch'io v'ordinerò, pria di domani	I tell you to, by tomorrow
I vostri amici canteran vittoria;	Your friends'll be toasting their victory;
Ed essi avranno il gusto, ed io la gloria.	They'll have their fun, and I'll get the
	glory.

(They go off.)

Scene XIV

A pleasant little garden; grassy banks on each side.

Fiordiligi and Dorabella

No. 18 Finale
Fiordiligi and Dorabella

Ah, che tutta in un momento	Oh, how my future has changed
Si cangiò la sorte mia . . .	From one moment to the next . . .
Ah, che un mar pien di tormento	Oh, what a sea of troubles
È la vita omai per me!	My life has come to be!
Finché meco il caro bene	So long as the cruel stars above
Mi lasciar le ingrate stelle,	Left my darling here with me,
Non sapea cos'eran pene,	I knew not what suffering was,
Non sapea languir cos'è.	I knew not what it meant to pine.
Ah, che tutta in un momento	Oh, how my future has changed
Si cangiò la sorte mia . . .	From one moment to the next . . .
Ah, che un mar pien di tormento	Oh, what a sea of troubles
È la vita omai per me!	My life has come to be!

Scene XV

Fiordiligi and Dorbella; Ferrando, Guglielmo and Don Alfonso; then Despina

Ferrando and Guglielmo (*off-stage*)

Si mora, sì, si mora	Just let me die, yes, let me die,
Onde appagar le ingrate!	If that's what it takes to melt her heart!

Don Alfonso (*off-stage*)

C'è una speranza ancora:	There's still a ray of hope:
Non fate, o Dei, non fate!	Oh God, don't do it, I beg you, don't do it!

Fiordiligi and Dorabella

Stelle, che grida orribili!	Good heavens, what horrible screams!

Ferrando and Guglielmo (*as before*)

Lasciatemi!	Just leave me alone!

Don Alfonso (*as before*)

Aspettate!	No, wait!

(*Ferrando and Guglielmo, each carrying a small bottle, enter followed by Don Alfonso.*)

FERRANDO and GUGLIELMO

L'arsenico mi liberi	Let this arsenic set me free
Di tanta crudeltà!	From so much cruelty!

(*They drink from the bottles and throw them away. As they turn around they notice the two girls.*)

FIORDILIGI and DORABELLA

Stelle! Un velen fu quello?	Good God! Was that poison they drank?

DON ALFONSO

Veleno buono e bello	It's poison all right,
Che ad essi in pochi istanti	And in just a few seconds
La vita toglierà.	It's going to take their life.

FIORDILIGI and DORABELLA

Il tragico spettacolo	What a tragic sight,
Gelare il cor mi fa.	It makes my blood run cold.

FERRANDO and GUGLIELMO

Barbare, avvicinatevi:	You heartless girls, come closer:
D'un disperato affetto	See the disastrous effect
Mirate il tristo effetto	Of a desperate love
E abbiate almen pietà.	And at least take pity on us.

FIORDILIGI and DORABELLA

Il tragico spettacolo	What a tragic sight,
Gelare il cor mi fa.	It makes my blood run cold.

FIORDILIGI, DORABELLA, FERRANDO, GUGLIELMO and DON ALFONSO

Ah, che del sole il raggio	Ah, the sun's rays
Fosco per me diventa.	Are getting darker.
Tremo le fibre, e l'anima	I'm trembling in every limb,
Par che mancar si senta,	My head feels like it's reeling,
Né può la lingua o il labbro	And my tongue and lips
Accenti articolar!	Can't make a single sound!

(*Ferrando and Guglielmo fall down on the grassy banks.*)

DON ALFONSO

Giacché a morir vicini	Since these poor souls
Sono quei meschinelli,	Are so near to death,

Pietade almeno a quelli
Cercate di mostrar.

The least you can do for them
Is try to show a little mercy.

FIORDILIGI and DORABELLA

Gente, accorrete, gente!
Nessuno, oddio, ci sente!
Despina!

Somebody help us, please!
Oh God, nobody can hear us!
Despina!

DESPINA (*off-stage*)

Chi mi chiama?

Who's that calling me?

FIORDILIGI and DORABELLA

Despina!

Despina!

DESPINA (*entering*)

Cosa vedo!
Morti i meschini io credo,
O prossimi a spirar.

What am I seeing?
Those two poor wretches are dead,
Or pretty close to it, I think.

DON ALFONSO

Ah, che purtroppo è vero!
Furenti, disperati,
Si sono avvelenati.

Ah, I'm afraid you're right!
In a fit of desperation,
They've gone and poisoned
    themselves.

Oh, amore singolar!

Oh, what love indeed!

DESPINA

Abbandonar i miseri
Saria per voi vergogna:
Soccorrerli bisogna.

It would be shameful of you
To abandon these poor souls:
You've got to try and help.

FIORDILIGI, DORABELLA and DON ALFONSO

Cosa possiam mai far?

Whatever can we do?

DESPINA

Di vita ancor dàn segno:
Colle pietose mani
Fate un po' lor sostegno.

They still show signs of life:
Hold out your tender hands,
And see if you can give them some
    comfort.

(*to Don Alfonso*)

E voi con me correte:

And you hurry up and come with
    me:

Un medico, un antidoto
Voliamo a ricercar.

We've got to get
A doctor, or at least an antidote.

434

Così Fan Tutte

(*Despina and Don Alfonso go off.*)

FIORDILIGI and DORABELLA

Dei, che cimento è questo!   My God, what a disaster this is!

Evento più funesto   A more awful situation
Non si potea trovar!   Could never be imagined!

FERRANDO and GUGLIELMO (*aside*)

Più bella commediola   A sillier little farce
Non si potea trovar!   Could never be imagined!

(*aloud*)

Ah!   Ah!

FIORDILIGI and DORABELLA

(*standing at a distance from the young men*)

Sospiran gli infelici!   The wretched things are sighing!

FIORDILIGI

Che facciamo?   Now what do we do next?

DORABELLA

Tu che dici?   What do you think we should do?

FIORDILIGI

In momenti sì dolenti,   At such a painful moment,
Chi potriali abbandonar?   Who could possibly forsake them?

DORABELLA (*approaching a little*)

Che figure interessanti!   What interesting looks they've got!

FIORDILIGI (*approaching a little*)

Possiam farci un poco avanti.   I think we can move a little closer.

DORABELLA

Ha freddissima la testa.   His head's as cold as ice.

FIORDILIGI

Fredda fredda è ancora questa.   This one's cold as well.

DORABELLA

Ed il polso?   And what about his pulse?

FIORDILIGI

Io non gliel sento.   I can't feel it at all.

DORABELLA

Questo batte lento lento.   This one's beating awfully slowly.

FIORDILIGI and DORABELLA

Ah, se tarda ancor l'aita,   Ah, if help is late in coming,
Speme più non v'è di vita.   There's no hope that they'll survive.

FERRANDO and GUGLIELMO (aside)

Più domestiche e trattabili   Both of them are getting
Sono entrambe diventate.   Tamer by the minute.

Sta' a veder che lor pietate   I'll just bet their pity
Va in amore a terminar.   Will soon turn into love.

FIORDILIGI and DORABELLA

Poverini! La lor morte   Poor souls! Their death
Mi farebbe lagrimar.   Would make me cry.

SCENE XVI

Fiordiligi, Dorabella, Ferrando, Guglielmo; Despina disguised as a doctor, and Don Alfonso

DON ALFONSO

Eccovi il medico,   My dear girls,
Signore belle.   The doctor's here at last.

FERRANDO and GUGLIELMO (aside)

Despina in maschera!   It's Despina in disguise!
Che trista pelle!   Oh, what a ghastly sight!

DESPINA

Salvete, amabiles   *Salvate, amabiles*
Bonae puellae!   *Bonae puellae!*

FIORDILIGI and DORABELLA

Parla un linguaggio   He's speaking a language
Che non sappiamo.   We don't understand.

DESPINA

Come comandano,   Whatever you decide,
Dunque, parliamo: That's what we can speak:
So il greco e l'arabo,   I know Greek and Arabic,
So il turco e il vandalo;   I know Turkish and Vandalic;
Lo svevo e il tartaro   I can also speak
So ancor parlar.   Swabian and Tartar.

Don Alfonso

Tanti linguaggi	Save all these languages
Per sé conservi.	For yourself.
Quei miserabili	Right now you should look at
Per ora osservi:	These miserable souls:
Preso hanno il tossico,	They've taken some poison,
Che si può far?	Just what can be done?

Fiordiligi and Dorabella

Signor dottore,	Oh, doctor,
Che si può far?	Just what can be done?

Despina

(She feels the pulse and the forehead of first one and then the other.)

Saper bisognami	First I've got to know
Pria la cagione,	The reason why,
E quinci l'indole	And then the type
Della pozione:	Of poison:
Se calda o frigida,	Was it hot or cold,
Se poca o molta,	A little or a lot,
Se in una volta	In just one dose,
Ovvero in più.	Or several.

Fiordiligi, Dorabella and Don Alfonso

Preso han l'arsenico,	They took arsenic,
Signor dottore:	My good doctor:
Qui dentro il bevvero,	They drank it on the spot,
La causa è amore,	The cause of it all was love,
Ed in un sorso	And they swallowed it
Se 'l mandar giù.	In just one gulp.

Despina

Non vi affannate,	Don't get so excited,
Non vi turbate:	Don't be so upset:
Ecco una prova	Now you'll really see
Di mia virtù.	How talented I am.

Fiordiligi, Dorabella and Don Alfonso

Egli ha di un ferro	He's got some kind
La man fornita.	Of metal instrument in his hand.

DESPINA

(She touches each of the would-be invalids on the head with a magnet and draws it slowly over their bodies.)

Questo è quel pezzo	This is that piece
Di calamita,	Of magnet known as
Pietra mesmerica,	Mesmer's stone,
Ch'ebbe l'origine	Which they originally
Nell'Alemagna,	Found in Germany,
Che poi sì celebre	And which was then
Là in Francia fu.	So famous in France.

FIORDILIGI, DORABELLA and DON ALFONSO

Come si muovono,	Look how they're writhing,
Torcono, scuotono!	They're squirming and wriggling!
In terra il cranio	Before you know it,
Presto percuotono.	They'll crack open their skulls.

DESPINA

Ah, lor la fronte	Ah, now help me
Tenete su.	To hold up their heads.

FIORDILIGI and DORABELLA

Eccoci pronte.	We're ready to do what we can.

(They place their hands on the young men's foreheads.)

DESPINA

Tenete forte.	Hang on, my men,
Coraggio! Or liberi	Be brave! And now
Siete da morte.	You're safe from death.

FIORDILIGI, DORABELLA and DON ALFONSO

Attorno guardano,	They're looking around,
Forze riprendono . . .	They're getting their strength . . .
Ah, questo medico	Oh, this doctor
Vale un Perù!	Is worth his weight in gold!

FERRANDO and GUGLIELMO (*getting to their feet*)

Dove son? che loco è questo?	Where am I? What is this place?
Chi è colui? color chi sono?	Who's he? And who're they?
Son di Giove innanzi al trono?	Am I standing in front of Jove's throne?

(Ferrando to Fiordiligi, Guglielmo to Dorabella)

Così Fan Tutte

Sei tu Palla o Citerea?
No . . . tu sei l'alma mia Dea:
Ti ravviso al dolce viso
E alla man ch'or ben conosco
E che sola è il mio tesor.

Are you Pallas or Venus?
No . . . you're the goddess I adore:
I recognize your own sweet face
And the hand I know so well:
It's my only treasure on earth.

(They embrace the sisters tenderly and kiss their hands.)

DESPINA and DON ALFONSO *(to the girls)*

Son effetti ancor del tosco:

Non abbiate alcun timor.

Those are still the effects of the poison:

There's nothing for you to fear.

FIORDILIGI and DORABELLA

Sarà ver, ma tante smorfie

Fanno torto al nostro onor.

Maybe so, but when they get carried away like that

It insults our reputation.

FERRANDO and GUGLIELMO

(aside, together with the other four, who repeat their verses)

Dalla voglia ch'ho di ridere
Il polmon mi scoppia or or.

I'm trying so hard not to laugh
That my lungs are ready to burst.

(Ferrando to Fiordiligi, Guglielmo to Dorabella)

Per pietà, bell'idol mio . . .

I beg you, my adorable girl . . .

FIORDILIGI and DORABELLA

Più resister non poss'io.

I can't hold out any longer.

FERRANDO and GUGLIELMO *(as before)*

Volgi a me le luci liete!

Just shine those bright little eyes on me!

DESPINA and DON ALFONSO *(to the girls)*

In poch'ore, lo vedrete,
Per virtù del magnetismo
Finirà quel parossismo,
Torneranno al primo umor.

In a couple of hours, you'll see,
Thanks to the magnet's effect
These spasms will come to an end,
And they'll be themselves again.

(The six characters repeat together part of their last lines.)

FERRANDO and GUGLIELMO *(as before)*

Dammi un bacio, o mio tesoro;
Un sol bacio, o qui mi moro!

Give me a kiss, my darling;
Just one little kiss, or I'll die right here!

FIORDILIGI and DORABELLA

Stelle! Un bacio? Good God! A kiss?

DESPINA and DON ALFONSO (*to the girls*)

Secondate Try to be kind
Per effetto di bontate. And humor them a little.

FIORDILIGI and DORABELLA

Ah, che troppo si richiede Ah, now you're asking too much
Da una fida, onesta amante. From such an honest girl.
Oltraggiata è la mia fede, It's an insult to my devotion,
Oltraggiato è questo cor! It's an insult to my love!

DESPINA and DON ALFONSO (*aside*)

Un quadretto più giocondo A more amusing little picture
Non si vide in tutto il mondo. You couldn't find in all the world.
Quel che più mi fa da ridere What makes me laugh the most
È quell'ira e quel furor. Is all this ranting and raving.

FERRANDO and GUGLIELMO (*aside*)

Un quadretto più giocondo A more amusing little picture
Non s'è visto, in questo mondo. You couldn't find in all the world.
Ma non so se finta o vera But I don't know if this ranting and
raving
Sia quell'ira e quel furor. Is a sham, or if it's real.

FIORDILIGI and DORABELLA

Disperati, attossicati, I don't care if you're desperate, or
poisoned,
Ite al diavol quanti siete! Go to the devil the lot of you!
Tardi inver vi pentirete, It'll be too late to be sorry,
Se più cresce il mio furor! If my anger gets any worse!

DESPINA and DON ALFONSO

(*aside, together with Fiordiligi and Dorabella, who repeat their quartina*)

Un quadretto più giocondo A more amusing little picture
Non si vide in tutto il mondo. You couldn't find in all the world.
Quel che più mi fa da ridere What makes me laugh the most
È quell'ira e quel furor, Is all this ranting and raving,
Ch'io ben so che tanto fuoco Because I'm sure that so much
passion
Cangerassi in quel d'amor. Can only turn into love.

FERRANDO and GUGLIELMO

(aside, together with Fiordiligi and Dorabella, who repeat their quartina)

Un quadretto più giocondo	A more amusing little picture
Non s'è visto, in questo mondo.	You couldn't find in all the world.
Ma non so se finta o vera	But I don't know if this ranting and raving
Sia quell'ira e quel furor.	Is a sham, or if it's real.
Né vorrei che tanto fuoco	And I wouldn't want so much passion
Terminasse in quel d'amor.	To end up being love.

End of Act One

ACT TWO

SCENE I

A room.
Fiordiligi, Dorabella and Despina

Secco Recitative

DESPINA

Andate là, che siete	Well, I must say, you girls
Due bizzarre ragazze!	Are the strangest creatures!

FIORDILIGI

Oh, cospettaccio!	Oh, for heaven's sake!
Cosa pretenderesti?	What're you after now?

DESPINA

Per me nulla.	Nothing for me.

FIORDILIGI

Per chi, dunque?	For who then?

DESPINA

Per voi.	For you.

DORABELLA

Per noi?   For us?

DESPINA

Per voi: Yes, for you:
Siete voi donne, o no?   Are you two supposed to be women or
                               not?

FIORDILIGI

E per questo?   And just what do you mean by that?

DESPINA

E per questo   What I'm trying to say is
Dovete far da donne.   You should both start acting like women.

DORABELLA

Cioè?   How's that?

DESPINA

Trattar l'amore *en bagatelle:*   Take love ever so lightly:
Le occasioni belle   And never miss
Non negliger giammai; cangiar a tempo,   Your golden opportunities: Be fickle when
                               you want to,
A tempo esser costanti;   And when you feel like it, be faithful;
Coquettizzar con grazia;   Flirt as gracefully as you can;
Prevenir la disgrazia, sì comune   Try to avoid disaster: That's what happens
A chi si fida in uomo;   When you trust in men;
Mangiar il fico e non gittare il pomo.   And above all, have your cake and eat it,
                               too.

FIORDILIGI (*aside*)

Che diavolo!   Good gracious!

(*to Despina*)

Tai cose   Go ahead and do those things yourself,
Fàlle tu, se n'hai voglia.   If that's your attitude.

DESPINA

Io già le faccio.   I'm already doing them.
Ma vorrei che anche voi,   But I wish both of you
Per gloria del bel sesso,   Would follow in my footsteps,
Faceste un po' lo stesso. Per esempio: For the sake of the fairer sex. For
                               example:
I vostri ganimedi   Your young Romeos

Son andati alla guerra? Infin che tornano,	Have gone off to war? Until they come back,
Fate alla militare: reclutate.	You can be soldiers, too: Enlist everyone you can.

DORABELLA

Il cielo ce ne guardi!	Heaven forbid!

DESPINA

Eh, che noi siamo in terra, e non in cielo!	But we're not in heaven, we're here on earth!
Fidatevi al mio zelo: giacché questi	Just trust me, I won't let you down: Since these
Forastieri v'adorano,	Foreigners adore you,
Lasciatevi adorar. Son ricchi, belli,	Why not let them have their way? They're rich and handsome,
Nobili, generosi, come fede	And noble and generous, Don Alfonso
Fece a voi Don Alfonso; avean coraggio	Swears it; they were brave enough
Di morire per voi: questi son merti	To die for you: These are qualities
Che sprezzar non si denno	Not to be sneezed at
Da giovani qual voi belle e galanti,	By charming, beautiful girls like you,
Che pon star senza amor, non senza amanti.	Who can live without love, but not without lovers.

(*aside*)

Par che ci trovin gusto.	Maybe I'm making some headway.

FIORDILIGI

Perbacco, ci faresti	My God, you're asking us to do
Far delle belle cose!	Some pretty awful things!
Credi tu che vogliamo	Do you really think we want
Favola diventar degli oziosi?	To be the talk of idle gossips?
Ai nostri cari sposi	Do you really think we want
Credi tu che vogliam dar tal tormento?	To torment our fiancés like that?

DESPINA

E chi dice che abbiate	And who says you'd be
A far loro alcun torto?	Doing them any harm?

DORABELLA

Non ti pare che sia torto bastante,	Don't you think it's harm enough
Se noto si facesse	If anybody sees
Che trattiamo costor?	We're entertaining the others?

443

DESPINA

Anche per questo   Ah, for that
C'è un mezzo sicurissimo: I've got a perfectly safe method:
Io voglio sparger fama   I'll just spread it around
Che vengono da me.   That they're really after me.

DORABELLA

Chi vuoi che il creda?   Do you really expect anybody
To believe that?

DESPINA

Oh, bella! Non ha forse   Oh, come on now! Hasn't a maid got the
right

Merto una cameriera   To have a couple of lovers?
D'aver due cicisbei? Di me fidatevi.   Just trust me for a change.

FIORDILIGI

No, nò: son troppo audaci,   Oh, no: Those foreigners of yours
Questi tuoi forastieri.   Are just too bold.
Non ebber la baldanza   Didn't they already try
Fin di chieder dei baci?   To steal kisses from us?

DESPINA (*aside*)

Che disgrazia!   Oh, how shocking!

(*to her mistresses*)

Io posso assicurarvi   I can assure you both
Che le cose che han fatto   That everything they did
Furo effetti del tossico che han preso: Was because of the poison they took:
Convulsioni, deliri,   Their fits, their frenzy,
Follie, vaneggiamenti.   Their outbursts and explosions.
Ma or vedrete come son discreti,   But now you'll see how discreet they are,
Manierosi, modesti e mansueti.   How polite and modest and mild.
Lasciateli venir.   Just let them come back again.

DORABELLA

E poi?   And then what?

DESPINA

E poi . . .   And then . . .
Caspita! Fate voi!   Blast it all! It's up to you!

(*aside*)

L'ho detto che cadrebbero.   I said they'd cave in.

FIORDILIGI

Cosa dobbiamo far?   But what're we supposed to do?

DESPINA

                Quel che volete: Anything you want:
Siete d'ossa e di carne, o cosa siete?   Are you made of flesh and blood, or
                                                                    aren't you?

No. 19 Aria

Una donna a quindici anni   By the time she's reached fifteen,
Dèe saper ogni gran moda,   A girl should be worldly wise,
Dove il diavolo ha la coda,   She should know where the devil
                                                                    hides his tail,

Cosa è bene e mal cos'è;   And be able to tell right from
                                                                    wrong;

Dèe saper le maliziette   She should know all the little tricks
Che innamorano gli amanti: That make lovers fall in love:
Finger riso, finger pianti,   How to feign laughter or tears,
Inventar i bei perché;   And come up with good excuses;

Dèe in un momento   She should listen to a hundred men
Dar retta a cento;   All at the same time,
Colle pupille   And speak with her eyes
Parlar con mille;   To a thousand of them;
Dar speme a tutti,   She should give everyone hope,
Sien belli o brutti;   Whether handsome or ugly;
Saper nascondersi   She should know how to hide
                                                                    things

Senza confondersi;   Without getting flustered,
Senza arrossire   And without ever blushing
Saper mentire;   She should know how to lie;
E, qual regina   And like a queen
Dall'alto soglio,   On her lofty throne,
Col «posso e voglio»   With "I can and I will"
Farsi ubbidir.   She should get her own way.

                                    (*aside*)

Par ch'abbian gusto   It looks like my message
Di tal dottrina.   Is getting through.
Viva Despina   Hurray for Despina,
Che sa servir!   Who's serving them well!

(*She goes off.*)

SCENE II

Fiordiligi and Dorabella

Secco Recitative

FIORDILIGI

Sorella, cosa dici?	Sister, what do you say?

DORABELLA

Io son stordita	I'm amazed
Dallo spirto infernal di tal ragazza.	At how fiendish that girl can be.

FIORDILIGI

Ma, credimi: è una pazza.	Believe me, she's a little crazy.
Ti par che siamo in caso	But do you think it makes any sense
Di seguir suoi consigli?	To follow her advice?

DORABELLA

Oh, certo, se tu pigli	Oh, of course, if you turn
Pel rovescio il negozio.	Everything upside down.

FIORDILIGI

Anzi, io lo piglio	No, I'd rather
Per il suo verso dritto:	Take it rightside up.
Non credi tu delitto,	Don't you think it's a crime
Per due giovani omai promesse spose,	For two young girls who're already engaged,
Il far di queste cose?	To be doing things like that?

DORABELLA

Ella non dice	But she says
Che facciamo alcun mal.	We wouldn't be doing anything wrong.

FIORDILIGI

È mal che basta,	It would be bad enough
Il far parlar di noi.	To have people talking about us.

DORABELLA

Quando si dice	But what if we said
Che vengon per Despina! . . .	They were after Despina? . . .

FIORDILIGI

Oh, tu sei troppo	Oh, you're just
Larga di coscienza! E che diranno,	Too broad-minded! And what will
Gli sposi nostri?	Our sweethearts say?

DORABELLA

Nulla:	Nothing:
O non sapran l'affare,	Either they won't know anything about it,
Ed è tutto finito;	And it'll all be over and done with;
O sapran qualche cosa, e allor diremo	Or they'll find something out, and then we'll say
Che vennero per lei.	It was her they were after.

FIORDILIGI

Ma i nostri cori?	But what about our feelings?

DORABELLA

Restano quel che sono:	They don't have to change at all:
Per divertirsi un poco e non morire	If we kick up our heels
Dalla malinconia,	Instead of moping around
Non si manca di fè, sorella mia.	We can still be faithful, dear sister.

FIORDILIGI

Questo è ver.	I guess you're right.

DORABELLA

Dunque?	Well then?

FIORDILIGI

Dunque,	Well then,
Fa' un po' tu; ma non voglio	You decide what to do; but I don't want
Aver colpa, se poi nasce un imbroglio.	To be blamed if it causes a scandal.

DORABELLA

Che imbroglio nascer deve,	How could there be any scandal,
Con tanta precauzion? Per altro, ascolta:	When we're being so careful? But hear me out:
Per intenderci bene,	Just to make sure we understand each other,
Qual vuoi sceglier per te de' due narcisi?	Which of the two Narcissuses do you want for yourself?

FIORDILIGI

Decidi tu, sorella.	It's up to you, my sister.

DORABELLA

Io già decisi:	I've already made my choice:

447

No. 20 Duet

Prenderò quel brunettino,	I think I'll take the dark one,
Che più lepido mi par.	He looks like more fun to me.

FIORDILIGI

Ed intanto io col biondino	And I guess I'll take the blond one,
Vo' un po' ridere e burlar.	Maybe he'll be good for a couple of laughs.

DORABELLA

Scherzosetta, ai dolci detti	I'll answer him ever so coyly
Io di quel risponderò.	When he whispers sweet nothings in my ear.

FIORDILIGI

Sospirando, i sospiretti	And every time he moans and sighs,
Io dell'altro imiterò.	I'll just sigh gently back.

DORABELLA

Mi dirà: «Ben mio, mi moro!»	He'll say: "My love, I'm dying!"

FIORDILIGI

Mi dirà: «Mio bel tesoro!»	He'll say: "My precious one!"

FIORDILIGI and DORABELLA

Ed intanto, che diletto,	And meanwhile, I'll be having
Che spassetto io proverò!	The time of my life!

(*They start to leave, and run into Don Alfonso.*)

SCENE III

Fiordiligi, Dorabella and Don Alfonso

Secco Recitative

DON ALFONSO

Ah, correte al giardino,	Ah, hurry up and go out to the garden,
Le mie care ragazze! Che allegria!	My dear girls! What fun!
Che musica! che canto!	What music! What singing!
Che brillante spettacolo! che incanto!	What a spectacular show! It's just like magic!
Fate presto, correte!	Hurry up now, go on out!

DORABELLA

Che diamine esser può?	What in the world is going on?

DON ALFONSO

Tosto vedrete.   You'll soon see for yourselves.

(They go off.)

SCENE IV

*A garden by the seashore, with grass seats and two little
stone tables. At the dock a boat decorated with flowers.*

Ferrando, Guglielmo, Despina, Fiordiligi, Dorabella, Don Alfonso, sailors and servants

*(Ferrando and Guglielmo are in the boat with a band of singers and musicians; Despina is in the
garden; Fiordiligi and Dorabella, accompanied by Don Alfonso, enter from one side; attendants in rich
liveries are standing by to receive them.)*

No. 21 Duet and Chorus

FERRANDO and GUGLIELMO

Secondate, aurette amiche,	Oh, friendly breezes, help me,
Secondate i miei desiri,	Help me make my dreams come true,
E portate i miei sospiri	And carry the sound of my sighs
Alla Dea di questo cor.	To the goddess I adore.
Voi che udiste mille volte	Oh, you who have heard a thousand times
Il tenor delle mie pene,	The strains of my laments,
Ripetete al caro bene	Repeat to the one I love
Tutto quel che udiste allor.	All that you heard then.

CHORUS

Secondate, aurette amiche,	Oh, friendly breezes, help them,
Il desir di sì bei cor.	Help them make their dreams come true.

*(During the chorus, Ferrando and Guglielmo come off the boat carrying garlands of flowers. Don
Alfonso and Despina lead them over to the two sisters, who are stunned into silence.)*

Secco Recitative

DON ALFONSO

(to the servants, who are carrying baskets of flowers)

Il tutto deponete	Just leave everything
Sopra quei tavolini, e nella barca	On those tables, my friends,
Ritiratevi, amici.	And then go back to your boat.

FIORDILIGI and DORABELLA

Cos'è tal mascherata? | What's this charade all about?

DESPINA (*to Ferrando and Guglielmo*)

Animo, via, coraggio! Avete perso | Come on now, show your stuff! Speak up for yourselves!

L'uso della favella? | Has the cat got your tongue?

(*The boat moves away from the shore.*)

FERRANDO

Io tremo e palpito | I'm trembling and shaking
Dalla testa alle piante. | From head to toe.

GUGLIELMO

Amor lega le membra a vero amante. | I'm so much in love that I can't move at all.

DON ALFONSO (*to the girls*)

Da brave, incoraggiateli! | Be good now, and give them a little encouragement!

FIORDILIGI (*to the two young men*)

Parlate. | Speak up, then.

DORABELLA (*to the two young men*)

Liberi dite pur quel che bramate. | You can say whatever you want.

FERRANDO

Madama . . . | My lady . . .

GUGLIELMO

Anzi, madame . . . | Or rather, my ladies . . .

FERRANDO (*to Guglielmo*)

Parla pur tu. | You go ahead and say something first.

GUGLIELMO (*to Ferrando*)

No, no, parla pur tu. | Oh no, you should do the talking.

DON ALFONSO

Oh, cospetto del diavolo! | Oh, the devil take you both!
Lasciate tali smorfie | Just stop acting like a couple
Del secolo passato. Despinetta, | Of old fogies. Despinetta,
Terminiam questa festa: | Let's get this business over with:
Fa' tu con lei quel ch'io farò con questa. | You handle that one and I'll handle this one.

No. 22 Quartet

(He takes Dorabella by the hand; Despina takes Fiordiligi's.)

La mano a me date,	Now give me your hand,
Movetevi un po'.	And come over here with me.

(to the two young men)

Se voi non parlate,	If you won't speak for yourselves,
Per voi parlerò.	Then I'll speak for you instead.

(to the two girls)

Perdono vi chiede	A trembling slave
Un schiavo tremante:	Is asking your forgiveness:
V'offese, lo vede,	He's offended you, he knows it,
Ma solo un istante.	But only for a moment,
Or pena, ma tace . . .	And now he's suffering in
	silence . . .

FERRANDO and GUGLIELMO

(repeating the last two words in the same tone)

. . . Tace . . .	. . . In silence . . .

DON ALFONSO

. . . Or lasciavi in pace . . .	. . . He's left you in peace . . .

FERRANDO and GUGLIELMO *(as before)*

. . . In pace . . .	. . . In peace . . .

DON ALFONSO

. . . Non può quel che vuole,	. . . And since he can't do what he
	wants,
Vorrà quel che può.	He'll do whatever he can.

FERRANDO and GUGLIELMO

(repeating the last two lines, with a sigh)

. . . Non può quel che vuole,	. . . And since he can't do what he
	wants,
Vorrà quel che può.	He'll do whatever he can.

DON ALFONSO *(to the two girls)*

Su, via, rispondete!	Come on now, give them an answer!
Guardate . . . e ridete?	You're standing there gawking . . .
	and giggling?

DESPINA

(moving in front of the two girls)

Per voi la risposta	I'll give them an answer
A loro darò.	For you.

Recitative

Quello ch'è state è stato.	What's done is done,
Scordiamci del passato:	And the less said, the better.
Rompasi omai quel laccio,	Let's break all ties to the past,
Segno di servitù.	As a symbol of servitude.

(Despina takes Dorabella's hand and Don Alfonso takes Fiordiligi's; they have them break their garlands and then lace them around the arms of the two young men.)

(to the two young men)

A me porgete il braccio,	Now give me your arm,
Né sospirate più.	And stop all that sighing.

DESPINA and DON ALFONSO *(aside, sottovoce)*

Per carità, partiamo;	For heaven's sake, let's get out of here;
Quel che san far veggiamo.	Then we'll see what they can do.
Le stimo più del diavolo,	I'll think more of them than the devil,
S'ora non cascan giù.	If they don't give in this time.

(They go off.)

SCENE V

Fiordiligi, Dorabella, Ferrando and Guglielmo

(Dorabella on Guglielmo's arm; Fiordiligi with Ferrando, without giving him her arm. They perform a brief pantomime, gazing at each other, sighing, laughing, etc.)

Secco Recitative

FIORDILIGI

Oh, che bella giornata!	Oh, what a beautiful day!

FERRANDO

Caldetta anziché no.	I think it's a little too warm.

DORABELLA

Che vezzosi arboscelli!   Oh, look how pretty those trees are!

GUGLIELMO

Certo, certo, son belli: Yes, of course they're pretty:
Han più foglie che frutti.   They've got more leaves than fruit.

FIORDILIGI

          Quei viali   Oh, those paths
Come sono leggiadri!   Look so inviting!
Volete passeggiar?   Would you like to go for a walk?

FERRANDO

        Son pronto, o cara,   Your every wish
Ad ogni vostro cenno.   Is my command.

FIORDILIGI

      Troppa grazia!   You're really much too kind!

FERRANDO

(sottovoce, as he goes by Guglielmo)

Eccoci alla gran crisi.   This is our big moment.

FIORDILIGI

Cosa gli avete detto?   What did you just say to him?

FERRANDO

Eh, gli raccomandai   Oh, I only told him to make sure
Di divertirla bene.   She's having a good time.

DORABELLA (*to Guglielmo*)

Passeggiamo anche noi.   Let's take a little walk ourselves.

GUGLIELMO

        Come vi piace.   Whatever you like.

(They stroll around. Then after a moment of silence)

Ahimè!   Oh, my God!

DORABELLA

      Che cosa avete?   What's the matter now?

GUGLIELMO

Io mi sento sì male,   Sweetheart, I feel so bad,
Sì male, anima mia,   So absolutely awful,
Che mi par di morire.   That I think I'm going to die.

(The other two can be seen pantomiming in the distance.)

DORABELLA *(aside)*

Non otterà nientissimo.

He'll get nothing out of this from me.

(to Guglielmo)

Saranno rimasugli
Del velen che beveste.

It's probably just the after-effects
Of the poison that you drank.

GUGLIELMO *(extremely agitated)*

Ah, che un veleno assai più forte io bevo
In que' crudi e focosi
Mongibelli amorosi!

Ah, those fiery eyes,
Those volcanoes of love,
Are a much deadlier poison for me!

(Fiordiligi and Ferrando stroll off-stage.)

DORABELLA

Sarà veleno càlido:
Fatevi un poco fresco.

You're probably feverish from the poison:
Just fan yourself a little.

GUGLIELMO

Ingrata, voi burlate,

You're making fun of me, you heartless
creature,

Ed intanto io mi moro!

And all the while I'm dying!

(aside)

Son spariti:
Dove diamin son iti?

They've disappeared from sight:
Where the devil have they gone off to?

DORABELLA

Eh, via, non fate . . .

Oh, come on now, don't be so . . .

GUGLIELMO

Io mi moro, crudele, e voi burlate?

You mean, cruel girl, how can you make
fun of me
When I'm dying right in front of your
eyes?

DORABELLA

Io burlo? io burlo?

What do you mean? Making fun of you?

GUGLIELMO

Dunque,
Datemi qualche segno, anima bella,
Della vostra pietà.

Well then,
My darling, give me some little sign
That you really feel sorry for me.

DORABELLA

Due, se volete:
Dite quel che far deggio, e lo vedrete.

I'll give you a couple if you like;
Tell me what you want, and then you'll
see for sure.

GUGLIELMO (*aside*)

Scherza, o dice davvero?

Is she joking, or telling the truth?

(*to Dorabella, showing her a charm*)

Questa picciola offerta
D'accettare degnatevi.

Here's a little token from me,
Will you please just take it now?

DORABELLA

Un core?

A heart for me?

GUGLIELMO

Un core: è simbolo di quello

Yes, it's a heart: It's to remind you of the
one

Ch'arde, languisce e spasima per voi.

That's aching and breaking for you.

DORABELLA (*aside*)

Che dono prezioso.

Oh, what a wonderful present.

GUGLIELMO

L'accettate?

Now will you just take it?

DORABELLA

Crudele!
Di sedur non tentate un cor fedele.

How cruel you are!
Stop trying to tempt an honest girl.

GUGLIELMO (*aside*)

La montagna vacilla.
Mi spiace; ma impegnato
È l'onor di soldato.

The mountain's beginning to move.
I don't like this business one bit; but my
Soldier's honor is at stake.

(*to Dorabella*)

V'adoro!

I adore you!

DORABELLA

Per pietà . . .

For heaven's sake . . .

GUGLIELMO

Son tutto vostro!

I'm yours alone!

DORABELLA

Oh, Dei!

Oh, God!

GUGLIELMO

Cedete, o cara!   Give in to me, my darling!

DORABELLA

Mi farete morir . . .   You're killing me, you know . . .

GUGLIELMO

Morremo insieme,   Well then, we'll die together:
Amorosa mia speme.   You're all my hopes and dreams come true.

L'accettate?   Now will you take my present?

DORABELLA (*after a moment, with a sigh*)

L'accetto.   Yes, I'll take it.

GUGLIELMO (*aside*)

Infelice Ferrando!   Oh, that poor Ferrando!

(*to Dorabella*)

Oh, che diletto!   Oh, you've made me so very happy!

No. 23 Duet

Il core vi dono,   I'm giving you my heart,
Bell'idolo mio.   My adorable girl,
Ma il vostro vo' anch'io: But I want yours in return:
Via, datelo a me.   Come on now, give it to me.

DORABELLA

Mel date, lo prendo;   If you're giving it to me, I'll take it;
Ma il mio non vi rendo.   But I won't give you mine in return.
Invan mel chiedete: It's useless to ask me for it:
Più meco ei non è.   It no longer belongs to me.

GUGLIELMO

Se teco non l'hai,   If it's not yours anymore,
Perché batte qui?   Why is it beating in here?

DORABELLA

Se a me tu lo dài,   If you're giving it to me,
Che mai balza lí?   Why is it beating in there?

DORABELLA and GUGLIELMO

È il mio coricino   It's just my own little heart
Che più non è meco: That no longer belongs to me:

Ei venne a star teco,   It went to stay with you,
Ei batte così.   And that's why it's beating so fast.

GUGLIELMO

(*He tries to put the heart where she keeps the portrait of Ferrando.*)
Qui lascia che il metta.   Now let me put it right here.

DORABELLA

Ei qui non può star.   No, it can't go there.

GUGLIELMO

T'intendo, furbetta.   I understand, you naughty girl.

DORABELLA

Che fai?   What're you doing now?

GUGLIELMO

Non guardar.   You're not supposed to look.

(*He gently turns her face away, and takes out the portrait and puts the heart in its place.*)

DORABELLA (*aside*)

Nel petto un Vesuvio   I feel like Vesuvius
D'avere mi par.   Is erupting in my breast.

GUGLIELMO (*aside*)

Ferrando meschino!   I feel so sorry for Ferrando!
Possibil non par.   I can't believe it's true.

(*to Dorabella*)

L'occhietto a me gira.   Now turn your head towards me.

DORABELLA

Che brami?   What is it that you want?

GUGLIELMO

Rimira   Just tell me
Se meglio può andar.   It could look any better.

DORABELLA and GUGLIELMO

Oh, cambio felice   Oh, what a happy exchange
Di cori e d'affetti!   Of hearts and affections!
Che nuovi diletti,   What new delights,
Che dolce penar!   And what sweet pain!

(*They go off with their arms around each other.*)

Scene VI

Fiordiligi and Ferrando

Accompanied Recitative

(Fiordiligi enters in agitation, followed by Ferrando.)

FERRANDO

Barbara, perché fuggi?

You hard-hearted girl, why are you running away?

FIORDILIGI

Ho visto un aspide,
Un'idra, un basilisco!

I thought
I saw a serpent, and a dragon, and a two-headed monster!

FERRANDO

Ah, crudel, ti capisco!

Ah, you mean, cruel girl, I know what you're trying to say!

L'aspide, l'idra, il basilisco, e quanto

A serpent, a dragon, a two-headed monster,

I libici deserti han di più fiero,

And the most ferocious beasts in the Libyan desert

In me solo tu vedi.

Are all you can see in me.

FIORDILIGI

È vero, è vero.
Tu vuoi tormi la pace.

Yes, I'm afraid it's true,
Because you're trying to rob me of my peace of mind.

FERRANDO

Ma per farti felice.

I'm only trying to make you happy.

FIORDILIGI

Cessa di molestarmi!

Just stop bothering me!

FERRANDO

Non ti chiedo che un guardo.

All I'm asking is just one glance.

FIORDILIGI

Pàrtiti!

Leave me alone, I beg of you!

FERRANDO

Non sperarlo,
Se pria gli occhi men fieri a me non giri.

There's no hope for that,
Unless you first show me a little more tenderness.

O ciel, ma tu mi guardi e poi sospiri?	My God, why are you sighing when you look at me?

No. 24 Aria

(overjoyed)

Ah, lo veggio: quell'anima bella	Ah, now I see it all: Your sweet soul
Al mio pianto resister non sa;	Just can't resist my tears:
Non è fatta per esser rubella	It's not capable of rebelling
Agli affetti di amica pietà.	Against such merciful feelings.
In quel guardo, in quei cari sospiri	By that glance, and those dear sighs,
Dolce raggio lampeggia al mio cor:	A sweet ray of hope lights up my heart:
Già rispondi a' miei caldi desiri,	You're yielding to my passionate desires,
Già tu cedi al più tenero amor.	You're giving in to the tenderest love.

(sad and melancholy)

Ma tu fuggi, spietata, tu taci,	But you flee from me, without saying why,
Ed invano mi senti languir?	And you hear my laments, and show me no pity?
Ah, cessate, speranze fallaci:	Ah, away with such false hopes:
La crudel mi condanna a morir.	You have cruelly condemned me to die.

(He goes off.)

SCENE VII

Fiordiligi alone

FIORDILIGI

Accompanied Recitative

Ei parte . . . Senti! . . . Ah, no: partir si lasci,	He's leaving . . . Listen! . . . Oh, no: Let him go,
Si tolga ai sguardi miei l'infausto oggetto	At least the fatal object of my attraction
Della mia debolezza. A qual cimento	Will finally be out of my sight. Look what anguish

Il barbaro mi pose . . . Un premio è
    questo
Ben dovuto a mie colpe! In tale
    istante
Dovea di nuovo amante
I sospiri ascoltar? l'altrui querele

Dovea volger in gioco? Ah, questo
    core
A ragione condanni, o giusto amore!

Io ardo; e l'ardor mio non è più
    effetto
D'un amor virtuoso: è smania,
    affanno,
Rimorso, pentimento,
Leggerezza, perfidia e tradimento!

That cruel man has caused me . . .
    This is a just
Reward for my sins! At a time like
    this
How could I ever listen to the sighs
Of another man? Should I have
    treated

His proposal more lightly? Ah, love
    that judges all,
You're right in condemning this
    heart of mine! But I feel
Like I'm burning up; and this fire
    inside me's no longer
The effect of a virtuous love: It's
    madness and weakness,
Remorse and repentance,
It's fickleness and falseness and
    treason!

No. 25 Rondo

Per pietà, ben mio, perdona

All'error d'un'alma amante:

Fra quest'ombre e queste piante
Sempre ascoso, oh, Dio, sarà!
Svenerà quest'empia voglia
L'ardir mio, la mia costanza.
Perderà la rimembranza
Che vergogna e orror mi fa.

A chi mai mancò di fede

Questo vano, ingrato cor!
Si dovea miglior mercede,
Caro bene, al tuo candor.

Have pity on me, my darling, and
    forgive
The wrong this wayward heart has
    done:
Oh God, let it be hidden forever
Among these shady groves!
I'll rid myself of this terrible desire
With my devotion and my love,
And I'll blot out the memory
That makes me cringe with shame.

Could ever this vain, ungrateful
    heart
Have betrayed a more worthy soul?
Your faithfulness, my darling,
Deserved a far better reward.

(She goes off.)

SCENE VIII

Ferrando and Guglielmo

Secco Recitative

FERRANDO (*overjoyed*)

Amico, abbiamo vinto!   My friend, we've won!

GUGLIELMO

Un ambo, o un terno?   A double or a triple?

FERRANDO

Una cinquina, amico: Fiordiligi   We've won the jackpot, my boy: Fiordiligi
È la modestia in carne.   Is honesty itself.

GUGLIELMO

Niente meno?   And nothing less?

FERRANDO

Nientissimo. Sta' attento   Absolutely nothing. Now listen carefully,
E ascolta come fu.   And I'll tell you how it went.

GUGLIELMO

T'ascolto: di' pur su.   I'm all ears: Tell me everything.

FERRANDO

        Pel giardinetto,   In the garden,
Come eravam d'accordo,   Where we all agreed to meet,
A passeggiar mi metto;   I started walking up and down;
Le dò il braccio; si parla   And then I gave her my arm; we talked
Di mille cose indifferenti; alfine   For awhile about this and that; and finally
Viensi all'amor.   We got to the subject of love.

GUGLIELMO

        Avanti.   I'm listening. Go ahead.

FERRANDO

Fingo labbra tremanti,   I made my lips start trembling,
Fingo di pianger, fingo   I cried a few real tears, and I even
Di morir al suo piè.   Threatened to die right there at her feet.

GUGLIELMO

Bravo assai, per mia fé.   Good for you, I must say.
Ed ella?   And what about her?

461

FERRANDO

Ella da prima
Ride, scherza, mi burla.

At the beginning
She was laughing, and joking, and making
fun of me.

GUGLIELMO

E poi?

And then?

FERRANDO

E poi
Finge d'impietosirsi.

And then
She let down her defenses a little.

GUGLIELMO

Oh, cospettaccio!

Dammit all, go on!

FERRANDO

Alfin scoppia la bomba.
Pura come colomba
Al suo caro Guglielmo ella si serba:

Mi discaccia superba,

Mi maltratta, mi fugge,
Testimonio rendendomi e messaggio

Che una femmina ell'è senza paraggio.

And finally the bomb exploded.
She's pure as the driven snow,
And she's saving herself for her darling
Guglielmo:

She was outraged when she turned me
away,

She called me names and left me flat,
And she proved beyond a reasonable
doubt

That she's in a class all by herself.

GUGLIELMO

Bravo tu, bravo io,
Brava la mia Penelope!
Lascia un po' ch'io ti abbracci
Per sì felice augurio,
O mio fido Mercurio!

Well, good for you, and good for me,
And good for my Penelope!
Now let me embrace you
For such happy tidings,
My trusty Mercury!

(*They embrace.*)

FERRANDO

E la mia Dorabella?
Come s'è diportata?

And what about my Dorabella?
How did she behave?

(*enthusiastically*)

Oh, non ci ho neppur dubbio! assai
conosco
Quella sensibil alma.

Oh, about her I've got no doubts! I think
I know that sensitive soul
As well as I possibly could.

Così Fan Tutte

GUGLIELMO

Eppur, un dubbio,	Well,
Parlandoti a quattr'occhi,	Just between us, it wouldn't hurt
Non saria mal, se tu l'avessi!	If you did have a couple of doubts!

FERRANDO

Come?	What's that?

GUGLIELMO

Dico così per dir.	It was only a manner of speaking.

(aside)

Avrei piacere	How I wish I could
D'indorargli la pillola.	Soften the blow.

FERRANDO

Stelle! Cesse ella forse	My God! So she actually
Alle lusinghe tue? Ah, s'io potessi	Fell for your flattery? Ah, if I even
Sospettarlo soltanto!	Suspected such a thing!

GUGLIELMO

È sempre bene	It's always a good idea
Il sospettare un poco, in questo mondo.	To be a little suspicious, in this world of
	ours.

FERRANDO

Eterni Dei, favella! A fuoco lento	For God's sake, tell me! Don't let me
Non mi far qui morir . . . Ma no, tu vuoi	Twist slowly in the wind . . . But no,
	you're just trying
Prenderti meco spasso: ella non ama,	To tease me: I'm the only one
Non adora che me.	She's ever loved and adored.

GUGLIELMO

Certo! Anzi, in prova	Of course! In fact, as proof
Di suo amor, di sua fede,	Of her love and devotion,
Questo bel ritrattino ella mi diede.	She gave me this sweet little portrait.

(He shows him the portrait that Dorabella gave him.)

FERRANDO (*furiously*)

Il mio ritratto!	She gave you my portrait!

Accompanied Recitative

Ah, perfida!	Oh, that traitress!

(He starts to leave.)

GUGLIELMO

Ove vai?   Where are you going?

FERRANDO

A trarle il cor dal scellerato petto   I'm going to tear the heart out of
                                                                    her wicked breast

(furiously)

E a vendicar il mio tradito affetto.   And avenge the love she betrayed.

GUGLIELMO

Férmati!   Stop!

FERRANDO *(determined)*

No, mi lascia!   No, let me go!

GUGLIELMO

          Sei tu pazzo?   Have you completely lost your mind?
Vuoi tu precipitarti   Do you really want to ruin yourself
Per una donna che non val due   For a girl who's not worth two
    soldi?   cents?

(aside)

Non vorrei che facesse   I wouldn't want him to do
Qualche corbelleria.   Something foolish.

FERRANDO

Numi! Tante promesse,   My God! How could she forget
E lagrime, e sospiri, e giuramenti,   All those promises,
In sì pochi momenti   And tears, and sighs, and vows,
Come l'empia obliò?   From one moment to the next?

GUGLIELMO

Perbacco, io non lo so.   By God, I just don't know.

FERRANDO

          Che fare or deggio?   And what am I supposed to do now?
A qual partito, a qual idea   Which way should I turn, what
    m'appiglio?   should I hold on to?
Abbi di me pietà: dammi consiglio.   Take pity on me, please: Give me
                                                                    your advice.

GUGLIELMO

Amico, non saprei	My friend, I simply don't know
Qual consiglio a te dar.	What advice I could possibly give you.

FERRANDO

Barbara! ingrata!	How cruel she is! How heartless!
In un giorno! . . . in poche ore! . . .	And after only a day! . . . In a couple of hours! . . .

GUGLIELMO

Certo, un caso quest'è da far stupore.	I must say, a situation like this is really quite amazing.

No. 26 Aria

Donne mie, la fate a tanti,	Dear ladies, to tell you the truth,
Che, se il ver vi deggio dir,	You've cheated on so many,
Se si lagnano gli amanti,	That when I hear all your lovers complain,
Li comincio a compatir.	I'm beginning to feel sympathetic.
Io vo' bene al sesso vostro,	I'm more than fond of your sex,
Lo sapete, ognun lo sa:	You know it, and so does everyone else:
Ogni giorno ve lo mostro,	I prove it to you every day,
Vi dò segno d'amistà;	When I always take your side;
Ma quel farla a tanti e tanti	But when you cheat on so many like that
M'avvilisce, in verità.	It depresses me, in fact.
Mille volte il brando presi	A thousand times I've drawn my sword
Per salvar il vostro onor,	To try to save your honor,
Mille volte vi difesi	A thousand times I've defended you
Colla bocca e più col cor;	With my tongue and still more with my heart;
Ma quel farla a tanti e tanti	But when you cheat on so many like that
È un vizietto seccator.	It's an annoying little vice.
Siete vaghe, siete amabili,	You're all charming, you're adorable,
Più tesori il ciel vi diè,	Heaven has given you many gifts,

E le grazie vi circondano	And an aura of beauty surrounds you
Dalla testa sino ai piè;	From your head to the soles of your feet;
Ma la fate a tanti e tanti,	But when you cheat on so many like that
Che credibile non è.	I can hardly believe what I see.
Ma la fate a tanti e tanti,	But when you cheat on so many like that,
Che, se gridano gli amanti,	And all your lovers cry and shout,
Hanno certo un gran perché.	I think they've got every right.

(He goes off.)

Scene IX

Ferrando alone; then Guglielmo and Don Alfonso

Ferrando

Accompanied Recitative

In qual fiero contrasto, in qual disordine	What an awful predicament, and what a
Di pensieri e di affetti io mi ritrovo?	Tormented state my heart and mind are in!
Tanto insolito e novo è il caso mio,	My dilemma's so unusual, so unheard of,
Che non altri, non io	That there's no one, not even me
Basto per consigliarmi . . . Alfonso, Alfonso,	Who can give me any advice . . . Alfonso, Alfonso,
Quanto rider vorrai	How you'll laugh
Della mia stupidezza!	At my stupidity!
Ma mi vendicherò: saprò dal seno	But I'll take my revenge: I'll erase
Cancellar quell'iniqua . . .	That wicked girl from my thoughts . . .
Cancellarla?	Erase her?
Troppo, oddio, questo cor per lei mi parla.	Oh God, this heart of mine won't ever let me forget her.

(Don Alfonso meets Guglielmo, and listens in.)

No. 27 Cavatina

Traditio, schernito	Betrayed and scorned
Dal perfido cor,	By her treacherous heart,

Io sento che ancora	This soul of mine
Quest'alma l'adora,	Still adores her,
Io sento per essa	And hears only
Le voci d'amor.	The voices of love.

Secco Recitative

DON ALFONSO

(as he approaches Ferrando)

Bravo! Questa è costanza!	Good for you! Now that's what I call loyalty!

FERRANDO

Andate, o barbaro!	Oh, leave me alone, you fiend!
Per voi misero sono.	It's your fault that I'm so miserable.

DON ALFONSO

Via, se sarete buono	Come on now, if you behave yourself
Vi tornerò l'antica calma. Udite:	I'll help you get back your peace of mind. Just listen to this:

(indicating Guglielmo)

Fiordiligi a Guglielmo	Fiordiligi was faithful
Si conserva fedel, e Dorabella	To Guglielmo, and Dorabella
Infedel a voi fu.	Was unfaithful to you.

FERRANDO

Per mia vergogna.	She's disgraced me.

GUGLIELMO

Caro amico, bisogna	My dear friend, one must
Far delle differenze in ogni cosa:	Differentiate in everything:
Ti pare che una sposa	Do you really think that any girl
Mancar possa a un Guglielmo? Un picciol calcolo,	Could fail someone like Guglielmo? I don't want to boast,
Non parlo per lodarmi,	But if we make
Se facciamo tra noi . . . Tu vedi, amico,	A comparison between us . . . you can see, my friend,
Che un poco più di merto . . .	That I've got a slight advantage . . .

DON ALFONSO

Eh, anch'io lo dico.	Yes, I think you've got a point there.

GUGLIELMO

Intanto mi darete	And meanwhile you'll pay me
Cinquanta zecchinetti.	The fifty gold pieces you owe me.

DON ALFONSO

Volontieri.	I'd be glad to.
Pria però di pagar, vo' che facciamo	But before I pay up, I want us to try
Qualche altra esperienza.	One more little experiment.

GUGLIELMO

Come?	How's that?

DON ALFONSO

Abbiate pazienza; infin domani	Just be patient: Till tomorrow
Siete entrambi miei schiavi: a me voi deste	You're both my slaves: and you gave me
Parola da soldati	Your word as soldiers
Di far quel ch'io dirò. Venite: io spero	That you'd do everything I say. Now come with me: I plan
Mostrarvi ben che folle è quel cervello	To convince you that only a madman
Che sulla frasca ancor vende l'uccello.	Would count his chickens before they're hatched.

(They go off.)

SCENE X

A room with several doors, little tables and a mirror.

Dorabella and Despina; then Fiordiligi

DESPINA

Ora vedo che siete	Now I can see you're
Una donna di garbo.	A woman of the world.

DORABELLA

Invan, Despina,	Despina, I tried
Di resister tentai: quel demonietto	But I couldn't resist temptation: That little devil
Ha un artifizio, un'eloquenza, un tratto	Is so clever, and eloquent, and flattering
Che ti fa cader giù se sei di sasso.	That I fell like a ton of bricks.

DESPINA

Corpo di satanasso,	Well, I'll be darned!
Questo vuol dir saper! Tanto di raro	That's what I call being smart! We poor girls

Noi povere ragazze
Abbiamo un po' di bene,
Che bisogna pigliarlo, allor ch'ei viene.

So rarely
Get any affection,
That we've got to take it when it comes.

(Fiordiligi enters.)

Ma ecco la sorella.
Che ceffo!

But here comes your sister.
What a puss she's pulling!

FIORDILIGI

Sciagurate!
Ecco per colpa vostra
In che stato mi trovo!

You're both outrageous!
It's all your fault
That I'm in such a state!

DESPINA

Cosa è nato,
Cara madamigella?

What's the matter,
My dear young lady?

DORABELLA

Hai qualche mal, sorella?

Is something wrong with you, my sister?

FIORDILIGI

Ho il diavolo, che porti

The devil's in me, that's all, and he can take

Me, te, lei, Don Alfonso, i forastieri

You, and me, and her, and Don Alfonso, and those foreigners,

E quanti pazzi ha il mondo!

And every other fool in the world!

DORABELLA

Hai perduto il giudizio?

Have you gone stark-raving mad?

FIORDILIGI

Peggio, peggio . . .
Inorridisci: io amo! e l'amor mio

It's much worse than that . . .
You'll be horrified: I'm in love! And my love

Non è sol per Guglielmo.

Isn't just for Guglielmo.

DESPINA

Meglio, meglio!

It's much better than I thought!

DORABELLA

E che sì, che anche tu se' innamorata

Oh, yes it is, and by any chance are you in love

Del galante biondino?

With that dashing blond fellow, too?

FIORDILIGI (*sighing*)

Ah, purtroppo per noi!   So much the worse for us!

DESPINA

Ma brava!   Well, good for you!

DORABELLA

Tieni   I feel like giving you
Settantamila baci.   Seventy thousand kisses.
Tu il biondino, io 'l brunetto: You've got the blond one, I've got the
         dark one:
Eccoci entrambe spose!   And here we are both engaged!

FIORDILIGI

Cosa dici?   What're you saying?
Non pensi agli infelici   Aren't you thinking about that unhappy
         pair
Che stamane partir? Ai loro pianti,   Who left here just this morning? Have
         you forgotten
Alla lor fedeltà tu più non pensi?   All about their tears and vows of love?
Così barbari sensi   Where, oh where did you ever learn
Dove, dove apprendesti?   To be so hard-hearted?
Sì diversa da te come ti festi?   How did you ever get to be so unlike
         yourself?

DORABELLA

Odimi: sei tu certa   Listen to me for a moment: Are you so
         sure
Che non muoiano in guerra,   That our old flames
I nostri vecchi amanti? E allora entrambe   Won't be killed in battle? And then we'd
         both
Resterem colle man piene di mosche.   End up disappointed.
Tra un ben certo e un incerto   A bird in hand is worth
C'è sempre un gran divario!   Two in the bush!

FIORDILIGI

E se poi torneranno?   And what happens if they come back?

DORABELLA

Se torneran, lor danno!   If they do come back, so much the worse
         for them!
Noi saremo allor mogli, noi saremo   We'll both be married already, and we'll
         be
Lontane mille miglia.   A thousand miles away.

FIORDILIGI

Ma non so come mai	But I don't understand how anyone's heart
Si può cangiar in un sol giorno un core.	Can change so much in just a single day.

DORABELLA

Che domanda ridicola! Siam donne!	What a ridiculous question! We're women after all!
E poi, tu com'hai fatto?	And as for that, what were you up to yourself?

FIORDILIGI

Io saprò vincermi.	I know how to control myself.

DESPINA

Voi non saprete nulla.	You don't know anything at all.

FIORDILIGI

Farò che tu lo veda.	And I'll just show you yet.

DORABELLA

Credi, sorella, è meglio che tu ceda.	Believe me, my sister, you might as well give in.

No. 28 Aria

È amore un ladroncello,	Love's like a little thief,
Un serpentello è amor.	Love's a vicious little viper,
Ei toglie e dà la pace,	He brings us peace of mind,
Come gli piace, ai cor.	And takes it away when he likes.
Per gli occhi al seno appena	As soon as he's opened up a path
Un varco aprir si fa,	Through our eyes right to our hearts,
Che l'anima incatena	He wraps his chains around our souls
E toglie libertà.	And deprives us of our freedom.
Porta dolcezza e gusto,	He'll bring you sweet contentment,
Se tu lo lasci far;	If you let him have his way,
Ma t'empie di disgusto,	But he'll fill you with disgust,
Se tenti di pugnar.	If you try to fight him back.
Se nel tuo petto ei siede,	If he's settled in your heart,
S'egli ti becca qui,	If he's already bitten you here,

Fa' tutto quel ch'ei chiede,	Do everything he asks you to,
Che anch'io farò così.	And I will do the same.

(Dorabella and Despina go off.)

SCENE XI

Fiordiligi alone; then Ferrando, Guglielmo, and Don Alfonso in another room; later Despina

Secco Recitative

FIORDILIGI

Come tutto congiura	How everything's conspiring
A sedurre il mio cor! Ma no! Si mora	To make me break my word! But no! I'll die
E non si ceda! Errai, quando alla suora	Before I give in! I was wrong to confide
Io mi scopersi ed alla serva mia:	In my sister and my maid:
Esse a lui diran tutto, ed ei, più audace,	They'll go and tell him the whole story, and he'll be even bolder,
Fia di tutto capace . . . Agli occhi miei	He'll be capable of anything . . . May he never show
Mai più non comparisca! A tutti i servi	His face again! I'll threaten

(Ferrando, Guglielmo and Don Alfonso can be seen through the open door, watching Fiordiligi from the next room.)

Minaccerò il congedo,	To dismiss all the servants,
Se lo lascian passar: veder nol voglio,	If they dare to let him in: I don't want to see him,
Quel seduttor.	That little Casanova.

GUGLIELMO *(to his friends)*

Bravissima,	Bravissima,
La mia casta Artemisia! La sentite?	My chaste Diana! Did you both hear what she said?

FIORDILIGI

Ma potria Dorabella,	But behind my back
Senza saputa mia . . . Piano! un pensiero	Could Dorabella . . . Wait a minute! I just had
Per la mente mi passa: in casa mia	A thought: There are lots of uniforms
Restar molte uniformi	From Guglielmo and Ferrando
Di Guglielmo e di Ferrando . . . Ardir! Despina!	Still in the house . . . Now's the time for action! Despina!
Despina!	Despina!

DESPINA (*entering*)

Cosa c'è?   What is it?

FIORDILIGI

Tieni un po' questa chiave, e senza   Take this key, and without talking back,
   replica,
Senza replica alcuna,   Without talking back even once,
Prendi nel guardaroba e qui mi porta   Go to the closet and get
Due spade, due cappelli e due vestiti   Two swords, two hats and two uniforms
De' nostri sposi.   From our fiancés, and bring them here to
                             me.

DESPINA

E che volete fare?   What for?

FIORDILIGI

Vanne, non replicare!   Just go, and don't bother talking back!

DESPINA (*aside*)

Comanda in *abrégé,* Donna Arroganza!   Whatever you say, Miss Hoity-toity!

(*She goes off.*)

FIORDILIGI

Non c'è altro: ho speranza   There's nothing else to do: I only hope
Che Dorabella stessa   That Dorabella herself
Seguirà il bell'esempio. Al campo! al   Will follow my good example. Off we go
   campo!   to the battlefield!
Altra strada non resta,   There's no other way left
Per serbarci innocenti.   To keep us innocent.

DON ALFONSO (*aside*)

Ho capito abbastanza.   I think I've got the picture.

(*to Despina, as she re-enters the room*)

Vanne pur, non temer.   Go ahead and do it, and don't be so
                             afraid.

DESPINA (*to Fiordiligi*)

Eccomi.   Here I am.

FIORDILIGI

          Vanne.   Now go on out,
Sei cavalli di posta   And send a servant at once
Voli un servo a ordinar. Di' a Dorabella   To order six post horses. And tell
                             Dorabella
Che parlar le vorrei.   I need to speak to her.

DESPINA

Sarà servita.   Very good, my lady.

(aside)

Questa donna mi par di senno uscita.   I think that girl's off her rocker.

(She goes off.)

SCENE XII

Fiordiligi, then Ferrando;
Guglielmo and Don Alfonso in the other room

FIORDILIGI

L'abito di Ferrando	Ferrando's uniform
Sarà buono per me; può Dorabella	Will do just fine for me; Dorabella can
Prender quel di Guglielmo. In questi arnesi	Take Guglielmo's. In these outfits
Raggiungerem gli sposi nostri: al loro	We'll join our fiancés: We can
Fianco pugnar potremo,	Fight beside them,
E morir, se fa d'uopo.	And die, if we have to.

(tearing off her head-dress)

Ite in malora,   The devil take
Ornamenti fatali! Io vi detesto.   All these hideous frills! Oh, how I've
                                                                    come to hate them.

GUGLIELMO *(to his friends)*

Si può dar un amor simile a questo?   Have you ever seen a love like this?

FIORDILIGI

Di tornar non sperate alla mia fronte	Don't expect me to wear you again
Pria ch'io qui torni col mio ben; in vostro	Until I'm back home with my love; I'll put on
Loco porrò questo cappello. Oh, come	This hat in your place. Oh, how
Ei mi trasforma le sembianze e il viso!	It changes my looks and my features!
Come appena io medesma or mi ravviso!	I can hardly recognize myself!

No. 29 Duet

Tra gli amplessi in pochi istanti	In no time at all I'll be back
Giungerò del fido sposo;	In the arms of my own true love;
Sconosciuta, a lui davanti	I'll come before him in disguise,
In quest'abito verrò.	Dressed in this uniform.

Oh, che gioia il suo bel core	Oh, how his noble heart will rejoice
Proverà nel ravvisarmi!	When he finally sees me again!

FERRANDO (*to Fiordiligi, as he enters*)

Ed intanto di dolore,	And meanwhile, wretched me,
Meschinello, io mi morrò.	I'll die of misery.

FIORDILIGI

Cosa veggio! Son tradita.	What am I seeing? I've been betrayed.
Deh, partite!	Just leave me, I implore you!

FERRANDO

Ah, no, mia vita!	Ah, no, my life!

(*He takes his sword from the table, and unsheathes it, etc.*)

Con quel ferro di tua mano	Take this sword of mine in your hand
Questo cor tu ferirai;	And plunge it through my heart;
E se forza, oddio, non hai,	And if you can't find the strength,
Io la man ti reggerò.	I'll guide your hand myself.

(*He falls on his knees.*)

FIORDILIGI

Taci, ahimè! Son abbastanza	Oh God, just keep quiet! I'm already
Tormentata ed infelice!	So miserable and unhappy!

FIORDILIGI and FERRANDO (*aside*)

Ah, che omai la ⎰ mia ⎱ costanza, ⎱ sua ⎰	Ah, judging by these looks and words,
A quei sguardi, a quel che dice,	By now it's all too clear,
Incomincia a vacillar.	My ⎱ loyalty's beginning to waver. Her ⎰

FIORDILIGI

Sorgi, sorgi!	Get up, I beg you!

FERRANDO

Invan lo credi.	It's useless to insist.

FIORDILIGI

Per pietà, da me che chiedi?	For pity's sake, what do you want from me?

FERRANDO

Il tuo cor, o la mia morte.   Your heart or my own death.

FIORDILIGI

Ah, non son, non son più forte . . .   Ah, I can't hold out much
                                          longer . . .

FERRANDO

Cedi, cara!   Just give in, my love!

(He takes her hand and kisses it.)

FIORDILIGI

Dei, consiglio!   God help me!

FERRANDO

Volgi a me pietoso il ciglio: Just show me a little compassion:
In me sol trovar tu puoi   In me alone can you find
Sposo, amante . . . e più, se vuoi.   A husband, a lover . . . and more, if
                                          you like.

(most tenderly)

Idol mio, più non tardar.   My adorable girl, don't make me
                                          wait any longer.

FIORDILIGI *(trembling)*

Giusto ciel! Crudel, hai vinto: Oh, God! You mean, cruel man,
                                          you've won:

Fa' di me quel che ti par.   Do with me what you will.

(Don Alfonso restrains Guglielmo from bursting in.)

FIORDILIGI and FERRANDO

Abbracciamci, o caro bene,   Embrace me, my own darling,
E un conforto a tante pene   And to make up for all our pain
Sia languir di dolce affetto,   May we moan with pleasure,
Di diletto sospirar.   And sigh with sheer delight.

(They go off.)

SCENE XIII

Guglielmo and Don Alfonso; then Ferrando

Secco Recitative

GUGLIELMO (*entering with Don Alfonso*)

Oh, poveretto me! Cosa ho veduto,	Oh, my God! I can't believe what I've just seen and heard,
Cosa ho sentito mai!	This can't be happening!

DON ALFONSO

Per carità, silenzio!	For pity's sake, be quiet!

GUGLIELMO

Mi pelerei la barba,	I feel like plucking out my beard,
Mi graffierei la pelle,	And tearing off my skin,
E darei colle corna entro le stelle!	And butting my horns at the sky!
Fu quella, Fiordiligi! La Penelope,	So that was Fiordiligi! The modern-day Penelope,
L'Artemisia del secolo! Briccona,	The Diana of our time! That little cheat,
Assassina, furfante, ladra, cagna!	That minx, that murderess, that thief, that bitch!

DON ALFONSO (*happily, aside*)

Lasciamolo sfogar.	Let's let him blow off steam.

FERRANDO (*entering*)

Ebben!	Well, then!

GUGLIELMO

Dov'è?	Where is she?

FERRANDO

Chi? la tua Fiordiligi?	Who do you mean? Your Fiordiligi?

GUGLIELMO

La mia Fior . . . fior di diavolo, che strozzi	My Fior . . . the devil can take her, and strangle
Lei prima e dopo me!	Her first, and then he can strangle me!

FERRANDO (*sarcastically*)

Tu vedi bene:	So now you see:
V'han delle differenze in ogni cosa.	There are differences in everything.
Un poco più di merto . . .	I'm worth a little more . . .

GUGLIELMO

Ah, cessa, cessa	Oh, will you just stop
Di tormentarmi; ed una via piuttosto	Torturing me; and let's find a way instead
Studiam di castigarle	Of punishing them
Sonoramente.	Soundly.

DON ALFONSO

Io so qual è: sposarle.	I know what to do: You should marry them.

GUGLIELMO

Vorrei sposar piuttosto	I'd rather marry
La barca di Caronte.	Charon's boat.

FERRANDO

La grotta di Vulcano.	Or Vulcan's forge.

GUGLIELMO

La porta dell'inferno.	Or the gates of hell.

DON ALFONSO

Dunque, restate celibi in eterno.	So you'd rather be bachelors forever.

FERRANDO

Mancheran forse donne	Do you think men like us
Ad uomin come noi?	Could ever lack for women?

DON ALFONSO

Non c'è abbondanza d'altro.	There's plenty more where they came from.
Ma l'altre che faran, se ciò fer queste?	But what'll the others do, if these two did what they did?
In fondo, voi le amate	Deep down inside you love them,
Queste vostre cornacchie spennacchiate.	These little plucked chickens of yours.

GUGLIELMO

Ah, purtroppo!	Ah, so much the worse for us!

FERRANDO

Purtroppo!	So much the worse!

DON ALFONSO

Ebben, pigliatele	Well then, take them
Com'elle son. Natura non potea	As they are. Nature
Fare l'eccezione, il privilegio	Can't make any exceptions,

Di creare due donne d'altra pasta	Or create two women of a different stuff
Per i vostri bei musi; in ogni cosa	Just to suit your tastes; in situations like this
Ci vuol filosofia. Venite meco:	It can't hurt to be a bit philosophical. Now come along with me:
Di combinar le cose	We'll find a way
Studierem la maniera.	To work things out,
Vo' che ancor questa sera	And before the day is done
Doppie nozze si facciano. Frattanto,	We'll have a double wedding. Meanwhile,
Un'ottava ascoltate:	I'll tell you an old adage:
Felicissimi voi, se la imparate.	It's to your advantage to take it to heart.

No. 30 Aria

Tutti accusan le donne, ed io le scuso	Everyone blames women, everyone but me,
Se mille volte al dì cangiano amore;	If they change their lovers a thousand times a day;
Altri un vizio lo chiama ed altri un uso:	Some call it a vice, and others a habit:
Ed a me par necessità del core.	But to me it's the way their hearts work.
L'amante che si trova alfin deluso	The lover who's deceived in the end
Non condanni l'altrui, ma il proprio errore;	Can't condemn anyone but himself;
Giacchè, giovani, vecchie, e belle e brutte,	Whether they're young or old, or beautiful or ugly,
Ripetete con me: «Così fan tutte!»	Now repeat along with me: "All women are the same!"

FERRANDO, GUGLIELMO and DON ALFONSO

Così fan tutte!	All women are the same!

SCENE XIV

Ferrando, Guglielmo, Don Alfonso and Despina

Secco Recitative

DESPINA (*entering*)

Vittoria, padroncini!	Well, gentlemen, you've won!
A sposarvi disposte	The dear ladies are
Son le care madame; a nome vostro	Willing to marry you; and for your sake

Loro io promisi che in tre giorni circa	I promised them that in about three days' time
Partiranno con voi; l'ordin mi diero	They'd be going away with you; they ordered me
Di trovar un notaio	To find a notary
Che stipuli il contratto; alla lor camera	To draw up the contract, and they're waiting for you
Attendendo vi stanno.	In their room.
Siete così contenti?	Are you satisfied with that?

FERRANDO, GUGLIELMO and DON ALFONSO

Contentissimi.   We're more than satisfied.

DESPINA

Non è mai senza effetto,	When Despina's involved in a scheme,
Quand'entra la Despina in un progetto.	She always gets results.

(They go off.)

SCENE XV

A hall, richly decorated and illuminated. An orchestra at the back.
A table set for four people, with silver candlesticks, etc.

Despina, servants and musicians; then Don Alfonso

No. 31 Finale

DESPINA *(to the servants)*

Fate presto, o cari amici,	Dear friends, go ahead
Alle faci il fuoco date	And light the candles,
E la mensa preparate	And make the table
Con ricchezza e nobiltà.	As fancy as you can.
Delle nostre padroncine	Our mistresses' wedding
Gl'imenei son già disposti.	Is already arranged.

(to the musicians)

E voi gite ai vostri posti,	And you should take your places,
Finché i sposi vengon qua.	As soon as the bridal couples come in.

CHORUS *(servants)*

Facciam presto, o cari amici,	Dear friends, let's go ahead
Alle faci il fuoco diamo	And light the candles,

E la mensa prepariamo	And make the table
Con ricchezza e nobiltà.	As fancy as we can.

DON ALFONSO (*entering*)

Bravi, bravi! Ottimamente!	Good for all of you! You've done an excellent job!
Che abbondanza! che eleganza!	Such abundance! And such elegance!
Una mancia conveniente	You'll be given a suitable reward
L'un e l'altro a voi darà.	By each of the two young men.

(While Don Alfonso sings, the musicians are tuning their instruments.)

Le due coppie omai si avanzano.	The two couples are on their way.
Fate plauso al loro arrivo:	Let's applaud them when they arrive;
Lieto canto e suon giulivo	And let joyful songs and happy tunes
Empia il ciel d'ilarità.	Fill the air with the sounds of celebration.

DESPINA and DON ALFONSO

(sottovoce, as they leave by separate doors)

La più bella commediola	A more amusing little farce
Non s'è vista o si vedrà!	There never was, nor ever will be!

SCENE XVI

Fiordiligi, Dorabella, Ferrando, Guglielmo, servants and musicians
(As the two couples move forward, the chorus sings, and the orchestra starts playing a march.)

CHORUS

Benedetti i doppi coniugi	Blessed by the bridegrooms,
E le amabili sposine!	And their lovely brides!
Splenda lor il ciel benefico,	May heaven look down on them kindly,
Ed a guisa di galline	And like two mother hens
Sien di figli ognor prolifiche,	May they both have many children
Che le agguaglino in beltà.	Who are as beautiful as they are.

FIORDILIGI, DORABELLA,
FERRANDO and GUGLIELMO

Come par che qui prometta	How everything seems to promise
Tutto gioia e tutto amore!	So much love and joy!
Della cara Despinetta	And we can all give thanks

Certo il merito sarà.	To our darling Despinetta!
Raddoppiate il lieto suono,	Play again those happy tunes,
Replicate il dolce canto,	Repeat those joyful songs,
E noi qui seggiamo intanto	And while we're sitting here
In maggior giovialità. ·	We'll enjoy ourselves much more.

CHORUS

Benedetti i doppi coniugi	Blessed be the bridegrooms,
E le amabili sposine!	And their lovely brides!
Splenda loro il ciel benefico,	May heaven look down on them kindly,
Ed a guisa di galline	And like two mother hens
Sien di figli ognor prolifiche,	May they both have many children
Che le agguaglino in beltà.	Who are as beautiful as they are.

(The chorus goes off; four servants remain
to wait on the bridal couples, who seat themselves at the table.)

FERRANDO and GUGLIELMO

Tutto, tutto, o vita mia,	My happiness is complete, my dear,
Al mio fuoco or ben risponde.	It's like a dream come true.

FIORDILIGI and DORABELLA

Pel mio sangue l'allegria	My happiness is overflowing,
Cresce, cresce e si diffonde.	It's coursing through my veins.

FERRANDO and GUGLIELMO

Sei pur bella!	You're so beautiful!

FIORDILIGI and DORABELLA

Sei pur vago!	And you're so handsome!

FERRANDO and GUGLIELMO

Che bei rai!	What bewitching eyes you've got!

FIORDILIGI and DORABELLA

Che bella bocca!	And what a tempting mouth!

FERRANDO, GUGLIELMO,
FIORDILIGI and DORABELLA
(clinking their glasses)

Tocca e bevi! Bevi e tocca!	Let's drink a toast to us! Let's drink a toast to love!

FIORDILIGI, DORABELLA and FERRANDO

E nel tuo, nel mio bicchiero	And let all our cares be drowned
Si sommerga ogni pensiero.	In your glass and in mine.

(The two sisters drink.)

E non resti più memoria	And let all memories of the past
Del passato, ai nostri cor.	Be banished from our hearts.

GUGLIELMO (*aside*)

Ah, bevessero del tossico,	Ah, I wish their drinks were poisoned,
Queste volpi senza onor!	Those shameless little hussies.

SCENE XVII

Fiordiligi, Dorabella, Ferrando, Guglielmo and Don Alfonso; then Despina disguised as a notary

DON ALFONSO (*entering*)

Miei signori, tutto è fatto:	Everything's ready, my friends:
Col contratto nuziale	The notary's on the stairs;
Il notaio è sulle scale,	He's got the marriage contract,
E, *ipso facto*, qui verrà.	And he'll be here *ipso facto*.

FIORDILIGI, DORABELLA, FERRANDO and GUGLIELMO

Bravo, bravo! Passi subito!	Bravo, bravo! Let him come in right away!

DON ALFONSO

Vò a chiamarlo. Eccolo qua.	I'll go and call him. And here he is right now.

DESPINA (*entering, and in a nasal voice*)

Augurandovi ogni bene,	Wishing you every happiness,
Il notaio Beccavivi	Notary Beccavivi
Coll'usata a voi sen viene	Stands here before you
Notarile dignità.	With his usual notarial dignity.
E il contratto stipulato	First coughing, and then sitting down,
Colle regole ordinarie	In a clear voice he'll begin to read
Nelle forme giudiziarie,	The stipulated contract,
Pria tossendo, poi sedendo,	With the normal provisions
Clara voce leggerà.	And the right legal forms.

FIORDILIGI, DORABELLA, FERRANDO,
GUGLIELMO and DON ALFONSO

Bravo, bravo, in verità!	Bravo, bravo, yes indeed!

DESPINA

Per contratto da me fatto,	By this contract drawn up by me,
Si congiunge in matrimonio	The following are joined in wedlock:
Fiordiligi con Sempronio	Fiordiligi and Sempronio
E con Tizio Dorabella,	And Tizio and Dorabella,
Sua legittima sorella:	Her own legitimate sister:
Quelle, dame ferraresi;	The former are ladies from Ferrara;
Questi, nobili albanesi.	The latter are Albanian nobles.
E, per dote e controdote . . .	And as for a dowry and a settlement . . .

FIORDILIGI, DORABELLA,
FERRANDO and GUGLIELMO

Cose note, cose note!	We already know all that!
Vi crediamo, ci fidiamo,	We believe you, we trust you,
Soscriviam: date pur qua.	Give it here and we'll sign it.

(Only the two girls sign.)

DESPINA and DON ALFONSO

Bravo, bravo, in verità!	Bravo, bravo, yes indeed!

(Don Alfonso is still holding the marriage contract,
when the sound of loud drums and singing is heard in the distance.)

CHORUS (off-stage)

Bella vita militar!	A soldier's life for me!
Ogni dì si cangia loco,	Every day a change of scene,
Oggi molto e doman poco,	Today a lot, tomorrow a little,
Ora in terra ed or sul mar.	First on land and then at sea.

FIORDILIGI, DORABELLA, DESPINA,
FERRANDO and GUGLIELMO

Che rumor, che canto è questo?	What's all this noise, all this singing about?

DON ALFONSO

State cheti; io vò a guardar.	Wait a moment: I'll go and look.

(He goes to the window.)

Misericordia!	God help us!
Numi del cielo!	By all the saints above!
Che caso orribile!	What an awful situation!
Io tremo! io gelo!	I'm trembling! My blood's running cold!
Gli sposi vostri . . .	Your old sweethearts . . .

FIORDILIGI and DORABELLA

Lo sposo mio . . .	My old sweetheart . . .

DON ALFONSO

In questo istante	Oh God, they've come back
Tornaro, oddio;	Just this instant;
Ed alla riva	And they're already landing
Sbarcano già!	On the shore!

FIORDILIGI, DORABELLA,
FERRANDO and GUGLIELMO

Cosa mai sento!	What's this I'm hearing?
Barbare stelle!	What a twist of fate!
In tal momento	At a time like this
Che si farà?	Just what can we do?

(The servants remove the table, and the musicians go off hurriedly.)

FIORDILIGI and DORABELLA *(to the young men)*

Presto, partite!	Get out of here at once!

FERRANDO, GUGLIELMO,
DESPINA and DON ALFONSO

Ma se $\begin{cases} \text{ci} \\ \text{li} \end{cases}$ veggono?	But what if they should see $\begin{cases} \text{us?} \\ \text{them?} \end{cases}$

FIORDILIGI and DORABELLA

Presto, fuggite!	Get away from here right now!

FERRANDO, GUGLIELMO,
DESPINA and DON ALFONSO

Ma se $\begin{cases} \text{ci} \\ \text{li} \end{cases}$ incontrano?	But what if they should run into $\begin{cases} \text{us?} \\ \text{them?} \end{cases}$

(Don Alfonso leads Despina to another room.)

FIORDILIGI and DORABELLA

Là, là; celatevi,	Go and hide in there,
Per carità.	For pity's sake.

(They lead their lovers to another room. The young men slip out, unseen, and leave.)

Numi, soccorso!	Heaven help us!

DON ALFONSO

Rasserenatevi . . .	Just keep calm . . .

FIORDILIGI and DORABELLA

Numi, consiglio!	Heaven guide us!

DON ALFONSO

Ritranquillatevi . . .	Just don't get ruffled . . .

FIORDILIGI and DORABELLA *(almost frantically)*

Chi dal periglio	Who's going to save us
Ci salverà?	From a disaster like this?

DON ALFONSO

In me fidatevi:	Have faith in me,
Ben tutto andrà.	And all will be well.

FIORDILIGI and DORABELLA

Mille barbari pensieri	A thousand terrible thoughts
Tormentando il cor mi vanno:	Are racing through my head:
Se discoprono l'inganno,	If they find out we've betrayed them,
Ah, di noi che mai sarà.	Whatever will become of us!

SCENE XVIII

Fiordiligi and Dorabella; Ferrando and Guglielmo with military capes and hats; Despina in the room next door; Don Alfonso

FERRANDO and GUGLIELMO

Sani e salvi, agli amplessi amorosi	With our hearts full of joy, we've come back
Delle nostre fidissime amanti	Safe and sound to the loving arms
Ritorniamo, di gioia esultanti,	Of our faithful sweethearts,
Per dar premio alla lor fedeltà.	To reward them for all their devotion.

DON ALFONSO

Giusti Numi! Guglielmo, Ferrando!	Good God! It's Guglielmo, Ferrando!

Oh, che giubilo! Qui? Come, e quando?	Oh, what a pleasant surprise! You here! How, and when?

FERRANDO and GUGLIELMO

Richiamati da regio contrordine,	We've been recalled by a royal command,
Pieno il cor di contento e di gaudio,	And our hearts are brimming over with joy;
Ritorniamo alle spose adorabili,	We've come back to our adorable sweethearts,
Ritorniamo alla vostra amistà.	We've come back to our good old friend.

GUGLIELMO (*to Fiordiligi*)

Ma cos'è quel pallor, quel silenzio?	But why're you so pale, and so quiet?

FERRANDO (*to Dorabella*)

L'idol mio perché mesto si sta?	Why's my darling looking so sad?

DON ALFONSO

Dal diletto confuse ed attonite,	They're so happy they're stunned and stupified,
Mute mute si restano là.	They're speechless and they're tongue-tied.

FIORDILIGI and DORABELLA (*aside*)

Ah, che al labbro le voci mi mancano:	Ah, I can't get the words out of my mouth:
Se non moro, un prodigio sarà.	It'll be a miracle if I don't die on the spot.

(The servants bring in a trunk.)

GUGLIELMO

Permettete che sia posto Quel baul in quella stanza . . .	Would you mind if we leave Our trunk in that room . . .

(He goes out of the door through which Despina went, and returns immediately.)

Dei, che veggio! Un uom nascosto?	Oh God, what am I seeing? There's a man hiding in there?
Un notaio! Qui che fa?	He's a notary! Now what's he doing here?

DESPINA (*entering hatless*)

Nossignor, non è un notaio:	No sirree, it's not a notary:
È Despina mascherata	It's Despina in disguise;
Che dal ballo or è tornata,	She's just returned from the ball,
E a spogliarsi venne qua.	And she's come in here to change.

(*aside*)

Una furba che m'agguagli	Could you ever find
Dove mai si troverà?	A more cunning little vixen than me?

FERRANDO and GUGLIELMO (*aside*)

Una furba uguale a questa	Could you ever find
Dove mai si troverà?	A more cunning little vixen than her?

(*Don Alfonso lets the contract signed by the two sisters fall to the floor.*)

FIORDILIGI and DORABELLA

La Despina! La Despina!	Despina! Despina!
Non capisco come va.	I don't understand what's happening.

DON ALFONSO

(*sottovoce to the young men, together with the two girls, who repeat their verses*)

Già cader lasciai le carte:	I've just dropped the papers:
Raccoglietele con arte.	Now pick them up by chance.

FERRANDO (*recovering the contract*)

Ma che carte sono queste?	But what are all these papers?

GUGLIELMO

Un contratto nuziale?	Is this a marriage contract?

FERRANDO and GUGLIELMO (*to the girls*)

Giusto ciel! Voi qui scriveste;	Good heavens! You've signed right here:
Contraddirci omai non vale!	Don't bother to deny it!
Tradimento, tradimento!	We've been double-crossed!
Ah, si faccia il scoprimento,	Ah, let's expose the plot,
E a torrenti, a fiumi, a mari	And then the blood will flow,
Indi il sangue scorrerà!	A torrent, a river, a flood!

(*They start to go into the other room; the girls hold them back.*)

FIORDILIGI and DORABELLA

Ah, signor, son rea di morte,	Oh, my love, I've committed a mortal sin,
E la morte io sol vi chiedo.	And all I ask from you is death.
Il mio fallo tardi vedo:	I'm seeing my error too late:
Con quel ferro un sen ferite	Plunge your sword right through this heart
Che non merita pietà.	With no feelings of pity at all.

FERRANDO and GUGLIELMO

Cosa fu?	What's all this about?

FIORDILIGI and DORABELLA

(*pointing at Don Alfonso and Despina*)

Per noi favelli	Let them speak for us,
Il crudel, la seduttrice . . .	That mean, cruel man, and that cheap little vamp . . .

DON ALFONSO

Troppo vero è quel che dice,	What you're saying is all too true,
E la prova è chiusa lì.	And the proof is locked in there.

(*He indicates the room which the young men had previously entered,
and Ferrando and Guglielmo go in.*)

FIORDILIGI and DORABELLA (*aside*)

Dal timor io gelo, io palpito:	I'm so scared that I'm shivering and shaking,
Perché mai li discopri!	Why did he ever turn against them?

(*Ferrando and Guglielmo come out of the room without their hats, capes and beards, but in Albanian
costume; they start clowning with their sweethearts and Despina.*)

FERRANDO

(*paying exaggerated compliments to Fiordiligi*)

A voi s'inchina,	Lovely lady,
Bella damina,	Bowing down before you
Il cavaliere	Is your knight in shining armor,
Dell'Albania!	Your admirer from Albania!

GUGLIELMO (*to Dorabella, returning the miniature*)

Il ritrattino	My lady,
Pel coricino,	As for the portrait

Ecco, io le rendo,	Exchanged for the little heart,
Signora mia.	Here it is, I'm giving it back.

FERRANDO and GUGLIELMO (*to Despina*)

Ed al magnetico	And as for the doctor
Signor dottore	With the magnetic personality,
Rendo l'onore	I'm giving him
Che meritò.	The respect he deserves.

FIORDILIGI, DORABELLA and DESPINA

Stelle! Che veggo!	Good heavens! What am I seeing?

FERRANDO, GUGLIELMO and DON ALFONSO

Son stupefatte!	They're stupified!

FIORDILIGI, DORABELLA and DESPINA

Al duol non reggo!	I'm overcome with grief!

FERRANDO, GUGLIELMO and DON ALFONSO

Son mezze matte!	They're half crazed!

FIORDILIGI and DORABELLA
(*indicating Don Alfonso*)

Ecco là il barbaro	And there's the culprit
Che c'ingannò!	Who deceived us!

DON ALFONSO

V'ingannai, ma fu l'inganno	I deceived you, but my deception
Disinganno ai vostri amanti,	Was to undeceive your lovers;
Che più saggi omai saranno,	From now on they'll both be wiser,
Che faran quel ch'io vorrò.	And they'll do just what I say.

(He brings them together and makes them embrace.)

Qua le destre: siete sposi.	Give me your hands, you're bride and groom,
Abbracciatevi e tacete.	Embrace each other and say no more,
Tutti quattro ora ridete,	Now all four of you can have a good laugh,
Ch'io già risi e riderò.	Even though I've been laughing all along.

FIORDILIGI and DORABELLA

Idol mio, se questo è vero,	My darling, if this is true,
Colla fede e coll'amore	With my love and devotion

Compensar saprò il tuo core,	I'll find the way to console you,
Adorarti ognor saprò.	And adore you forever more.

FERRANDO and GUGLIELMO

Te lo credo, gioia bella,	I believe you, my beautiful girl,
Ma la prova io far non vo'.	But I won't put you to the test.

DESPINA

(together with the other four, who repeat their verses)

Io non so se questo è sogno:	I don't know if I'm awake or dreaming:
Mi confondo, mi vergogno.	I'm confused, and I'm so ashamed.
Manco mal, se a me l'han fatta,	At least if they've bamboozled me,
Che a molt'altri anch'io la fo.	I can bamboozle plenty of others.

FIORDILIGI, DORABELLA, DESPINA,
FERRANDO, GUGLIELMO and DON ALFONSO

Fortunato l'uom che prende	Happy is the man who looks
Ogni cosa pel buon verso,	On the brighter side of life,
E tra i casi e le vicende	And through trials and tribulations
Da ragion guidar si fa.	Lets reason be his guide.
Quel che suole altrui far piangere	What makes others weep as a matter of course
Fia per lui cagion di riso;	Will do his heart good instead;
E del mondo in mezzo ai turbini	And amid all the upheavals in this world
Bella calma troverà.	He'll find his peace of mind.

The End

LA CLEMENZA DI TITO

WORLD PREMIERE:	*Prague, National Theater, September 6, 1791*
UNITED STATES PREMIERE:	*Mutual Broadcasting System, June 22 and 29, 1940 (radio performance); Lenox, Mass., Tanglewood, August 4, 1952*
METROPOLITAN OPERA PREMIERE:	*October 18, 1984*

LA CLEMENZA DI TITO
(THE CLEMENCY OF TITUS)

Opera seria in Two Acts

Libretto: Caterino Mazzolà (after Pietro Metastasio)
English translation and notes: David Stivender
Music: Wolfgang Amadeus Mozart

LA CLEMENZA DI TITO

CHARACTERS

TITO VESPASIANO (Titus Vespasian), *Emperor of Rome*	Tenor
VITELLIA, *daughter of the emperor Vitellius*	Soprano
SERVILLIA, *Sextus' sister, in love with Annio*	Soprano
SESTO (Sextus), *Titus' friend, in love with Vitellia*	Mezzo-soprano
ANNIO (Annius), *Sextus' friend, in love with Servilia*	Mezzo-soprano
PUBLIO (Publius), *prefect of the Praetorian Guard*	Bass

The action takes place in Rome.

LA CLEMENZA DI TITO

S Y N O P S I S

HISTORICAL BACKGROUND

The profligate Roman emperor Vitellius (reigned A.D. 69) was deposed by the sober and popular Vespasian who reigned for ten years (69–79). He was the first Roman emperor to die a natural death and to be succeeded by his son. This son, the Titus of the opera, while serving in the Jewish campaign (67–70) fell in love with Queen Berenice, the eldest daughter of Herod Agrippa, King of the Jews. Though married several times, she lived in incest with her brother, King Agrippa II. She followed Vespasian to Rome and lived openly there with Titus. Her liaison with her brother was well known (Juvenal refers to it in Satire VI), and was strongly resented by the Roman people. Titus sent her back to Jerusalem shortly after he succeeded his father as emperor in 79.

ACT I

Vitellia, the daughter of the emperor Vitellius, has enlisted the aid of two Roman patricians, Sextus and Lentulus, in a plot against Titus. Sextus, though a trusted friend of the emperor, is smitten by Vitellia and has become a pawn in her hands. Vitellia upbraids Sextus for vacillating in carrying out her orders when Annius, a close friend of Sextus, enters and informs them that Titus has just sent Berenice back to Jerusalem. He tells Sextus that the emperor is asking for him. Vitellia, now hoping that Titus will choose her as empress, tells Sextus to postpone carrying out the plot for the time being. She leaves. Annius requests that Sextus now ask Titus for permission for him to marry Servilia, Sextus' sister. Sextus promises to do so.

The scene changes to a part of the Roman Forum. Titus, accompanied by Publius, the prefect of the Praetorian Guard, is welcomed by the Roman populace. After they leave, Titus announces to Sextus that he has chosen his sister, Servilia, to be his consort. Annius, rather than see his friend embarrassed, interrupts and assures Titus that he could not make a better choice. Titus asks Annius to take the news to Servilia, and goes off with Sextus. Annius barely has time to assure himself that what he has done is the proper thing for a generous lover, when Servilia enters. Annius tells her that she is to be the new empress and that they must forget their love.

In the imperial gardens, Publius warns Titus of slander against the Crown, but the emperor chooses to ignore it. Servilia enters and tells Titus that her heart is already given to Annius, but that if he wishes she will still become his bride. Titus magnanimously refuses. No sooner have he and Publius gone off than Vitellia enters to offer ironically her congratulations to the new empress. Servilia says that perhaps the royal hand will be reserved for Vitellia and leaves. Sextus arrives and Vitellia again incites him to carry out the burning of the Capitol which will serve as an opportunity for the murder of Titus. Sextus, after much hesitation, goes off to do as she demands. Annius and Publius now enter and inform Vitellia that Titus has chosen her to be his empress. Vitellia, knowing that Sextus is at that moment setting the plot in motion, runs off to find him. Annius and Publius follow. Sextus is now discovered before the Capitol. He has just decided that he cannot allow Titus to be murdered when he sees flames spring up around the building. Annius enters just as Sextus rushes off to try and save the life of the emperor and friend. Servilia hurries in, soon followed by Publius, and it is learned that the fire may not have been started by chance and that Titus' life could well be in danger. Vitellia enters looking for Sextus. He soon arrives, announcing that he has seen Titus dead. He is about to confess that he instigated the plot, but Vitellia silences him. The act closes with a funeral dirge for Titus sung by the principal characters on stage and the chorus in the distance.

ACT II

On the Palatine Hill Annius informs Sextus that Titus did not die after all: someone else dressed in the imperial robes was struck down. Sextus does not believe him, whereupon Annius tells him to go to the emperor and see for himself. Sextus replies that he cannot do so since it was he that instigated the plot. As he is leaving, Annius advises Sextus to go immediately and confess to Titus. Vitellia now arrives and counsels Sextus to flee for his life. At this moment Publius comes in and arrests Sextus. He tells him that the man in the emperor's robes who was thought to be murdered was none other than Lentulus, Sextus' co-conspirator, who in the event was only wounded. Sextus is taken away to prison. The scene changes to a large hall where Titus is congratulated by the Roman people on his escape. After they leave, Publius informs Titus that Lentulus has admitted to his part in the plot and named Sextus as a member of the conspiracy. Even now the Senate is hearing Sextus' confession. Titus impatiently sends Publius to learn the outcome of the trial. Annius comes in and is about to plead for Sextus' life when Publius returns and says that Sextus has indeed confirmed all that Lentulus said and admits that he is guilty of all he has been charged with. The Senate has condemned him to be torn apart by wild beasts in the arena. Titus orders

Annius and Publius to go, but before he does so, Annius asks Titus to look in his heart and find mercy there. Left alone, Titus reflects on Sextus' betrayal and realizes he cannot condemn him without hearing him first. Sextus is brought in and rather than implicate Vitellia in the conspiracy refuses to explain why he attempted to kill his friend. Angered by Sextus' silence, Titus tells him that he will die, and returns Sextus to prison. Left alone a second time, Titus now signs Sextus' death warrant but then considers that he has already pardoned the man in his heart and that he will not have posterity say his clemency was only a sham. He tears up the warrant. Publius enters and Titus tells him to bring Sextus to the arena. He leaves. As Publius is about to follow him, Vitellia accosts him and asks news of Sextus. Publius replies that he is to be brought to the arena on Titus' orders. After he leaves, Vitellia muses that it is obvious Sextus has weakened and revealed her part in the conspiracy. Annius and Servilia rush in to request her help in pardoning Sextus: she, after all, will be the emperor's wife. She sends them both off, saying that she will do what she can. Alone, she realizes that she had best confess to Titus that she was the main perpetrator of the plot, thereby at least mitigating Sextus' involvement.

The scene changes to the entrance to the arena. Acclaimed by the crowd, Titus enters and commands that Sextus be brought before him. After Sextus' arrival Titus is about to pardon him when Vitellia rushes in and, throwing herself at the emperor's feet, confesses all. Titus claims that this is but another trial of his clemency and pardons Vitellia, Sextus and the conspirators. All join in praising the emperor's goodness of heart.

MOZART, METASTASIO AND MAZZOLÁ

Throughout his life Mozart was no stranger to the *opera seria*. This form of musical drama, with its libretto based on the heroes of antiquity acting in a noble and generous manner and the music written for virtuoso singers was what the serious composer of Mozart's youth wrote if he expected the patronage of royalty and the aristocracy. During his career Mozart was to write four of them. The first two, *Mitridate* (written at age 14) and *Lucio Silla* (at age 16), conform to the conventional rules of the day, always allowing, of course, for the extraordinary genius of the young man. The third, *Idomeneo* (written at age 25), is his first great opera. Though its exterior form is still that of the *opera seria*, musically it is something of a hybrid, with its dramatic choruses, trio and quartet. It inaugurates the series of great operas which was to begin the following year (1782) with *Die Entführung aus dem Serail* and continue with *Le Nozze di Figaro, Don Giovanni, Così Fan Tutte* and *Die Zauberflöte*. In these works he raised the old traditions of the *opera buffa* and Viennese pantomime to that species of musical drama which we today recognize as uniquely Mozartean.

It was in July of 1791, while he was at work on *Die Zauberflöte*, that Mozart received the commission for *La Clemenza di Tito* as part of the festivities for the coronation of Leopold II as King of Bohemia. Since we know from his letters how careful he was in his selection of libretti and how closely he oversaw his librettists' shaping of them, it is therefore reasonable to assume that not only did he agree to set *Tito* in spite of the short time available to him for its composition, but that he also felt that there was still something left for him to say in the *opera seria* form.

Mozart's first biographer, Franz Niemetschek, stated that he wrote the work in eighteen days, beginning its composition in the coach on the way from Vienna to Prague where it was to have its premiere. Though the premiere reportedly made a poor impression on Leopold and his Empress, the work was to remain popular throughout Europe for a number of years to come.

With the triumph of the romantic sensibility in the nineteenth century, *Tito* was all but forgotten, and it is only in the last few decades that it has been revived with any frequency. The myths that have accumulated around it stated that the music was that of a tired man who was about to die, that he had little interest in composing an opera in what was by then a dead form, and that in any case the work had to be composed so hurriedly that it could not merit any kind of serious attention. Yet in recent years, with the systematic and minute study of every fact of Mozart's life and work, it has gradually come to be realized that not only was it possible that Mozart had been considering a work on this very text for as long as two years, but that the *opera seria* was, in the 1780's, a far from dead form. Musicians and scholars alike saw that Mozart's score, when approached on its own merits, demonstrated a profound interest in, and a unique interpretation of, this famous text.

La Clemenza di Tito was one of the most celebrated and frequently composed libretti of the eminent Pietro Metastasio (1698–1782), the man who was the single most influential force in the history of the *opera seria*. He had written it in 1734 in Vienna at the command of Charles VI, whose Court Poet he was. It was destined to be set over forty times by composers, among them Hasse, Gluck and Jomelli, to name only three of the best known today. This libretto was greatly admired by the eighteenth century, especially the famous scene in Metastasio's Act III (Mozart's II), where Titus confronts Sextus. Voltaire himself said of this scene that it was "comparable, if not superior, to all that is most beautiful in Greek drama; . . . worthy of Corneille when he is not being rhetorical, and Racine when he is not weak; [it is] not based upon operatic love but on the noble sentiments of the heart." It is surely this last quality that appealed most to Mozart when he came to set it.

Metastasio's drama is in three acts, as are all of his twenty-six great *opera seria* texts. He based it very loosely on Roman history, prefacing his drama with the following words:

> Antiquity did not know a better or better loved prince than Titus Vespasian. His virtues made him so beloved by everyone that he was called "the delight of mankind." And yet two young patricians, one of whom was his favorite, conspired against him. Once the conspiracy was discovered, however, they were condemned by the Senate to death. But the most clement Caesar, content with having admonished them paternally, granted a generous pardon to them and their accomplices.

Among other sources he named Suetonius' *Lives of the Twelve Caesars*; a reading of this work's chapters on Vitellius, Vespasian and Titus will yield many scraps of information from which Metastasio built up his drama. To take a single example from many: one of the dominating themes of the work, in addition to the emperor's clemency, is friendship. In his dramas Metastasio wished to provide material for reflection as well as for entertainment and in *Tito* he examines the idea of friendship from many angles. That the historical Titus had a strong sense of this virtue was plain to him from his reading of Suetonius: "When Britannicus [Claudius' son] drank his fatal dose of poison [sent by Nero, who was said to be jealous of the boy's superior singing voice], Titus, who was reclining at the same table, is said to have emptied the glass in sympathy and to have been dangerous ill for some time." It is not too much to postulate that the close friendship of Titus and Sextus in Metastasio's drama had its origin in this passage. In any case, it makes Titus' sometimes too-clement actions seem more plausible.

The figure of Vitellia, though her name may be invented, comes from a remark by Suetonius that the emperor Vitellius had a daughter. She is without a doubt the strongest character in the work, though not the most sympathetic (that must surely be Sextus, in spite of his weakness and vacillation). Vitellia cast a long shadow over Italian opera: her prototype can be seen as late as Verdi's Abigaille (*Nabucco*). The character of Annius also plays a strong part in the friendship theme and his love for Sextus' sister Servilia seems natural and true to life.

It is curious that with all of the reverence Metastasio's contemporaries felt for him, this feeling did not extend to their fidelity to his text, since with the exception of the first composer of each of his dramas, those who came after almost never set the text as Metastasio published it. Cutting was inevitable, particularly in the dry recitative, and often new aria texts were substituted. The poet himself was, understandably, unhappy over the butchery his texts were subjected to.

On occasion, though, he consented to do it himself, if it was for a close friend. Consider the following letter written to his "dear twin," the famous *castrato* Farinelli: "I have already circumcised the first act of *Alessandro*: oh, what a slaughter! I have cut 266 verses and three arias. Dear *gemello*, this very ungrateful work could only be done for you. To make oneself a eunuch with one's own hand is a sacrifice that has few examples." In short, if it had to be done, do it oneself and do it right.

The text that Mozart finally set was quite different from the original and was arranged "à vera opera" ("into a real opera," as Mozart himself described it) by one Caterino Mazzolà, the Court Poet to the Elector of Saxony at Dresden. He reduced Metastasio's three acts of two, cut over 700 lines of recitative and more than 100 lines of aria texts. Of his own manufacture he added, usually taking his cue from the author, over 70 lines of recitative and some 60 lines for the various ensembles that he provided for Mozart. The most important addition is certainly his creation of the finale for Mozart's Act I, with the Capitol burning in the distance, the principals lamenting Titus' murder onstage and the chorus off.

But Metastasio's carefully plotted drama is no more and his text, in the words of a modern commentator, is "distorted out of recognition." Where the original poet's dramaturgy moved smoothly and with a clockwork precision, where each character acted within his own bounds as defined by his individual personality, in Mazzolà there is a feeling of breathlessness and inconsistency. To give a single example, Metastasio was interested in the moral situation, and his characters always earn their just rewards. Mazzolà, however, says nothing of the disposition of the two pairs of lovers at the end. It is obvious that Annius and Servilia will marry, but not a word is said as to the future of Sextus and Vitellia. Metastasio, however, with his keen and ironic sense of justice, has Titus announce at the very end of the drama:

TITUS

(to Vitellia)

I wish you to be content
At least partially. You will not see a rival
On the throne, that I promise you. I want
    no other
Wife than Rome: my children will be
The subject populace;
For them my affections will be kept
    undivided.
Have your wedding at the same time
As Annius and Servilia.
Princess, if you like. Only grant
Your hand to Sextus: this desired
    acquisition
Has already cost him enough.

VITELLIA

As long as I live
Your wish shall be my heart's command.

Sextus, with his weakness of character, and Vitellia, with her never-ending scorn for others who do not think or act according to her mind, certainly deserve one another, and the spectator takes pleasure in contemplating their future life together.

This pleasure is increased when we know that, according to Metastasio himself, Vitellia did not love Sextus. Writing to a friend who requested a duet text for the opera, Metastasio replied: "The duet cannot fall anywhere else than at the end of Act II, in place of the last two arias of Sesto and Vitellia. This lady not being in love with the aforesaid youth will make it difficult to create a tender duet between them. The best expedient which has occurred to me is to introduce in Vitellia, to the misfortune of a man blindly resigned to her, such a violent remorse and such a lively compassion that she can confuse it with love."

Mazzolà's versification is as weak as his dramaturgy. Metastasio was justly famous for his mellifluous and smooth verse, and his style came to be widely imitated. That the imitators seldom rose to the level of the imitated can easily be seen by anyone who takes a glance at the

Italian libretti of Mozart's three earlier *opera serie* by Cigna-Santi (*Mitridate*), Gamerra (*Lucio Silla*)—who at least had the sense to ask Metastasio to make alterations in his verse—and Varesco (*Idomeneo*), and then compare them with *La Clemenza di Tito*. A prime example of Mazzolà's fumbling in the midst of Metastasian verse is Publius' speech in Act II when he comes to arrest Sextus. Here he has to convey a good deal of information (it was Lentulus, dressed in Titus' robes, who was mistakenly struck down) in as short a time as possible. This information, though not the words, is a reduction of fourteen lines of Servilia in the original Act II, which Mazzolà attempts to scale down to six. Mazzolà's maze of subordinate clauses and welter of the letter "c" cannot be called a success on any level. It sits very uneasily among Metastasio's lines.

But however unsuccessful the details of Mazzolà's revision for Mozart may be, the basic framework of this opera in two acts containing ensembles—surely the qualities which made it a "vera opera" for Mozart—served the composer's purpose. Though he was required to write it in a short time (even assigning the composition of the dry recitative to a pupil, probably Süssmayer), Mozart' score is a faithful realization of the climate of Metastasio's drama. Mozart had composed this poet's words since the age of nine—sixteen concert arias, *Betulia Liberata, Il Sogno di Scipione, Il Re Pastore*—and as a child of fourteen was presented with the nine volumes of the Turin edition of the complete works, so the composer knew and understood his poet well. As stated earlier, it is probable that Mozart discussed the shape of his *Tito* libretto with Mazzolà and we can assume that in its general outlines it answered his demands for a modern opera text. Certainly the music in which he clothed it reflects his response to Metastasio's vision of antique Rome, and the characters' "noble sentiments of heart" were not far from the climate of *Die Zauberflöte*, the opera he was writing concurrently. Indeed, it has long been noticed that *La Clemenza di Tito* breathes the same spirit of humanism, if not Masonry, that that opera does.

From the first bars of the *Tito* overture we know we are in the world of the *opera seria*, but with a marked difference. The surprising *fermate* in the fourth and sixth bars serve to call attention to the "imperial" theme which is hammered out by the full orchestra. Whenever Titus and his concerns are center stage in the opera the musical atmosphere of this familiar rhythm will not be far away. A detail unique in Mozart's operatic overtures is to be noted in the last three unison C's at the close of the overture: these same notes, in the same rhythm, will bring down the final curtain.

The remainder of the opera is no less surprising. Metastasio's words and situations are familiar, Mozart's musical forms (especially in the large scale arias) retain vestiges of their old *opera seria* outlines, but the content, the music itself, now inhabits a new world, the world of late Mozart. For *La Clemenza di Tito* is written in that style which has all too few examples: *Die Zauberflöte*, the clarinet concerto, the "Ave verum corpus" motet, the *Requiem*. Our world is not so rich in these late works that it can afford to ignore a single one of them. Surely the time has come for *La Clemenza di Tito*, the one outstanding omission in that list, to take its rightful place as a repertory piece. The combination of Mozart's last music and the words of the poet of his earliest years yields one of opera's most fascinating scores.

A Note on the Translation

This translation of Metastasio's text has been kept as literal as possible within rational bounds. More often than not, the inversion of the word order in the Italian text has been retained in the English. One or two felicitous phrases from the Hoole translation (2 volumes, 1767; an expanded edition in 3 volumes was issued later) are used. John Hoole (1727–1803) was a member of the Johnson-Boswell-Reynolds circle and a great admirer and translator (Tasso, Ariosto) of Italian literature.

The vertical black lines down the left hand sides of the Italian and English texts indicate omissions in the dry recitative made at the Metropolitan Opera during the season of its premiere there, 1984–85. It is well known that Mozart did not compose the music for these recitatives.

DAVID STIVENDER

LA CLEMENZA DI TITO

ACT ONE

SCENE I

Vitellia's apartments.

Vitellia and Sextus

VITELLIA

Ma che! sempre l'istesso,
Sesto, a dirmi verrai? So che sedotto

Fu Lentulo da te; che i suoi seguaci
Son pronti già; che il Campidoglio acceso
Darà moto a un tumulto. Io tutto questo

Già mille volte udii: la mia vendetta
Mai non veggo però. S'aspetta forse
Che Tito a Berenice in faccia mia
Offra, d'amore insano,
L'usurpato mio soglio e la sua mano?
Parla! di'! che s'attende?

What? always the same thing,
Sextus, will you come to tell me? I know
that Lentulus
Was won over by you; that his followers
Are now ready; that the burning Capitol
Will signal an uproar. I've already heard
all this
A thousand times; yet I still don't see
My revenge. Perhaps you are waiting
For Titus, mad with love for Berenice,
To offer her, in my presence,
My usurped throne and his hand?
Speak! tell me! what are you waiting for?

SEXTUS

Oh Dio!

O God!

VITELLIA

Sospiri?

You sigh?

SEXTUS

Pensaci meglio, o cara,
Pensaci meglio. Ah! non togliamo, in Tito,

Let us think more carefully, dearest,
Let us think more carefully. Ah, let us
not deprive,

507

La sua delizia al mondo, il padre a Roma,

L'amico a noi. Fra le memorie antiche
Trova l'egual, se puoi. Fingiti in mente

Eroe più generoso o più clemente.
Parlagli di premiar: poveri a lui
Sembran gli erari sui.
Parlagli di punir: scuse al delitto

Cerca in ognun. Chi all'inesperta ei dona,

Chi alla canuta età. Risparmia in uno

L'onor del sangue illustre; il basso stato

Compatisce nell'altro. Inutil chiama,
Perduto il giorno ei dice,
In cui fatto non ha qualcun felice.

In Titus, the world of its delight, Rome of
  its father,
And us of our friend. Find, if you can,
His equal in the records of antiquity. Let
  your mind imagine
A more generous or more clement hero.
Speak to him of reward: his treasury
Is not large enough.
Speak to him of punishing: he attempts to
  excuse
Each man's crime. He forgives some for
  inexperience,
Others for extreme old age. In one he
  spares
The honor of an illustrious lineage; in
  another
He pities the man's lowly condition.
He calls that day useless and lost
In which he has not made someone
  happy.

VITELLIA

Dunque a vantarmi in faccia
Venisti il mio nemico; e più non pensi
Che questo eroe clemente un soglio
  usurpa
Dal suo tolto al mio padre?
Che m'ingannò, che mi riddusse (e questo

È il suo fallo maggior) quasi ad amarlo?
E poi, perfido! e poi di nuovo al Tebro

Richiamar Berenice! Una rivale
Avesse scelta almeno
Degna di me fra le beltà di Roma:

Ma una barbara, o Sesto,
Un'esule antepormi! una regina!

So you come to boast of my enemy
In my presence; and you no longer think
That this clement hero fraudently
  occupies
A throne stolen from my father?
That he cheated me, that he reduced me
  (and this
Is his greatest fault) almost to loving him?
And then, false man! and then to recall
  Berenice
Back to the Tiber! At least
He could have chosen a rival
Worthy of me from among the beauties
  of Rome:
But a barbarian, Sextus,
To prefer an exile to me! a queen!

SEXTUS

Sai pur che Berenice
Volontaria tornò.

Yet you know that Berenice
Came back voluntarily.

VITELLIA

Narra a' fanciulli	Tell such nonsense
Codeste fole. Io so gli antichi amori;	To the children. I know about his old love;
So le lagrime sparse allor che quindi	I know about the tears shed when she left
L'altra volta partì; so come adesso	Once before; I know that this time
L'accolse e l'onorò. Chi non lo vede?	He received and honored her. Who cannot see it?
Il perfido l'adora.	The treacherous man adores her.

SEXTUS

Ah! principessa,	Ah! princess,
Tu sei gelosa.	You are jealous.

VITELLIA

Io!	I!

SEXTUS

Sì.	Yes.

VITELLIA

Gelosa io sono,	I am jealous
Se non soffro un disprezzo?	If I do not suffer to be despised?

SEXTUS

E pur . . .	And yet . . .

VITELLIA

E pure	And yet
Non hai cor d'acquistarmi.	You don't have the heart to win me.

SEXTUS

Io son . . .	I am . . .

VITELLIA

Tu sei	You are
Sciolto d'ogni promessa. A me non manca	Released from your every promise. I am not lacking
Più degno esecutor dell'odio mio.	An even worthier executor of my hate.

SEXTUS

Sentimi!	Listen to me!

VITELLIA

Intesi assai.	I've listened enough.

SEXTUS

Fermati!   Stop!

VITELLIA

Addio.   Farewell.

SEXTUS

Ah, Vitellia! ah, mio nume!   Ah, Vitellia! ah, my goddess!
Non partir. Dove vai!   Do not leave. Where are you going?
Perdonami, ti credo: io m'ingannai.   Forgive me, I believe you: I was mistaken.

No. 1 Duet

SEXTUS

Come ti piace, imponi: Command me as you please:
Regola i moti miei;   Control my comings and goings;
Il mio destin tu sei,   You are my destiny,
Tutto farò per te.   I will do everything for you.

VITELLIA

Prima che il sol tramonti,   Before the sun sets,
Estinto io vo' l'indegno;   I want the worthless man dead;
Sai ch'egli usurpa un regno,   You know he stole a kingdom
Che in sorte il ciel mi diè.   That heaven gave me as my destiny.

SEXTUS

Già il tuo furor m'accende.   Already your fury is igniting me.

VITELLIA

Ebben, che più s'attende?   Well, what more are you waiting for?

SEXTUS

Un dolce sguardo almeno   Let at least one sweet glance
Sia premio alla mia fè!   Be the reward of my faith!

BOTH

Fan mille affetti insieme   A thousand emotions
Battaglia in me spietata;   Are ruthlessly warring within me;
Un'alma lacerata   There is no soul
Più della mia non v'è.   More wounded than mine.

(*Enter Annius.*)

ANNIUS

Amico, il passo affretta,   My friend, hurry,
Cesare a se ti chiama.   Caesar is calling for you.

VITELLIA

Ah! non perdete
Questi brevi momenti. A Berenice

Tito gli usurpa.

ANNIUS

Ingiustamente oltraggi,
Vitellia, il nostro eroe: Tito ha l'impero

E del mondo e di se. Già per suo cenno
Berenice partì.

SEXTUS

Come!

VITELLIA

Che dici!

ANNIUS

Voi stupite a ragion. Roma ne piange

Di meraviglia e di piacere. Io stesso
Quasi nol credo; ed io
Fui presente, o Vitellia, al grande addio.

VITELLIA

(Oh speranze!)

SEXTUS

Oh virtù!

VITELLIA

Quella superba
Oh, come volentieri udita avrei

Esclamar contro Tito!

ANNIUS

Anzi giammai
Più tenera non fu. Partì; ma vide

Che adorata partiva, e che al suo caro

VITELLIA

Ah! do not lose
These few moments! Titus is stealing
  them
From Berenice.

ANNIUS

Vitellia, you insult
Our hero unjustly: Titus controls the
  empire,
The world and himself. At his bidding
Berenice has already left.

SEXTUS

What?

VITELLIA

What are you saying?

ANNIUS

You are surprised with good reason.
  Rome is weeping
With wonder and pleasure. I myself
Almost do not believe it; and I
Was present, Vitellia, at the grand
  farewell.

VITELLIA

(My hopes!)

SEXTUS

What virtue!

VITELLIA

Oh, how gladly
Would I have listened to that proud
  woman
Inveigh against Titus!

ANNIUS

Indeed, never
Was she more tender. She left; but one
  saw
That she left adored, and that the bitter
  blow

Men che a lei non costava il colpo amaro.

Did not cost his feelings any less than hers.

VITELLIA

Ognun può lusingarsi.

Anyone can be mistaken.

ANNIUS

Eh! si conobbe
Che bisognava a Tito
Tutto l'eroe per superar l'amante.

Vinse, ma combattè. Non era oppresso,

Ma tranquillo non era; ed in quel volto,

Dicasi per sua gloria,
Si vedea la battaglia e la vittoria.

Oh! one understood
That it was necessary
For all the hero in Titus to conquer the lover.

He won, but had to fight. He was not weighed down,

But neither was he tranquil; and in his face,

Let it be said to his credit,
One saw the battlefield and the victory.

VITELLIA

(E pur forse con me, quanto credei,

Tito ingrato non è.

(So in spite of what I believed, perhaps Titus

Is not unmindful of me.)

(aside to Sextus)

Sesto, sospendi
D'eseguire i miei cenni. Il colpo ancora

Non è maturo.

Sextus, put off
Doing my bidding. The time is not ready yet

For the blow.

SEXTUS *(angrily)*

E tu non vuoi ch'io vegga . . .
Ch'io mi lagni, o crudele . . .

You don't want me to see . . .
To complain, cruel woman . . .

VITELLIA *(angrily)*

Or che vedesti?
Di che ti puoi lagnar?

Now what do you see?
What are you complaining about?

SEXTUS *(submissively)*

Di nulla. (Oh Dio!
Chi provò mai tormento eguale al mio?)

Nothing. (Oh God!
Who has ever suffered torment equal to mine?)

No. 2 Aria

VITELLIA

Deh! se piacer mi vuoi,	Ah! if you wish to please me,
Lascia i sospetti tuoi;	Give up your suspicions.
Non mi stancar con questo	Don't weary me with this
Molesto dubitar.	Tiresome doubting.
Chi ciecamente crede,	Whoever believes blindly,
Impegna a serbar fede;	Pledges to keep faith;
Chi sempre inganni aspetta,	Whoever always expects deceit
Alletta ad ingannar.	Delights in being deceived.

(She leaves.)

ANNIUS

Amico, ecco il momento	My friend, now is the moment
Di rendermi felice. All'amor mio	In which to make me happy. You promised
Servilia promettesti. Altro non manca	Servilia to my love. Only the assent
Che d'Augusto l'assenso. Ora da lui	Of the Emperor is lacking. Now
Impetrar lo potresti.	You could ask him for it.

SEXTUS

Ogni tua brama,	Annius,
Annio, m'è legge. Impaziente anch'io	Your every wish is my command. I, too,
Questo nuovo legame, Annio, desio.	Impatiently desire this new bond, Annius.

No. 3 Duet

BOTH

Deh prendi un dolce amplesso,	Ah, receive this warm embrace,
Amico mio fedel;	My faithful friend;
E ognor per me lo stesso	And may heaven always
Ti serbi amico il ciel.	Keep you the same friend to me.

(They leave.)

SCENE II

A part of the Roman Forum, magnificently adorned with arches, obelisks and trophies; facing the spectator, the exterior of the Capitol, and a magnificent avenue by which one may climb to it.

(Publius, the Roman senators and the legates of the subject provinces, who will present to the Senate the yearly tributes. As Titus, preceded by lictors, followed by Praetorian Guards, accompanied by Sextus and Annius, and surrounded by the numerous populace, descends from the Capitol, the following is sung.)

No. 4 March
No. 5 Chorus

CHORUS

Serbate, o dèi custodi	Preserve, oh custodian gods
Della romana sorte,	Of the Roman destiny,
In Tito, il giusto, il forte,	The honor of our age
L'onor di nostra età.	In the just and strong Titus.

(At the end of the chorus, Annius and Sextus enter from different sides.)

PUBLIUS (*to Titus*)

Te "della patria il padre"	"The father of your country"
Oggi appella il Senato; e mai più giusto	The Senate names you today; and never
Non fu ne' suoi decreti, o invitto	Has it been more just in its decrees, oh
Augusto.	mighty Emperor.

ANNIUS

Nè padre sol, ma sei	Not only father, but you are
Suo nume tutelar. Più che mortale	Its tutelary god. Since you prove yourself
Giacchè altrui ti dimostri, a' voti altrui	More a god than a mortal, so must you begin
Cominicia ad avvezzarti. Eccelso tempio	To accustom yourself to prayers for a god. The Senate
Ti destina il Senato; e là si vuole	Has destined a high temple for you; and there it is wished
Che fra divini onori	That Tiber may adore also the name of Titus
Anche il nume di Tito il Tebro adori.	Among the gods' divine honors.

PUBLIUS

Quei tesori che vedi,	These treasures that you see,
Delle serve province annui tributi,	The annual tribute of the subject provinces,
All'opra consacriam. Tito non sdegni	We sanction for this work. Let not Titus disdain
Questi del nostro amor pubblici segni.	These public signs of our love.

TITUS

Romani, unico oggetto	Romans, your love
È dei voti di Tito il vostro amore;	Is the single object of Titus' prayers;
Ma il vostro amor non passi	But let not your love pass
Tanto i confini suoi,	So far beyond its limits
Che debbano arrossirne e Tito e voi.	That it embarrasses both Titus and you.

Quegli offerti tesori	These proffered treasures
Non ricuso però: cambiarne solo	I do not refuse, however: only change
L'uso pretendo. Udite. Oltre l'usato	Their expected use. Listen. Beyond its accustomed
Terribile il Vesevo ardenti fiumi	Dread Vesuvius has belched forth burning rivers
Dalle fauci eruttò; scosse le rupi,	From its vents; shaken cliffs,
Riempiè di ruine	Filled with ruins
I campi intorno e le città vicine.	The surrounding fields and nearby cities.
Le desolate genti	The disconsolate people
Fuggendo van; ma la miseria opprime	Flee; but misfortune overwhelms
Quei che al fuoco avanzar. Serva quell'oro	Those who escape the fire. Let that gold serve
Di tanti afflitti a riparar lo scempio.	To alleviate the slaughter of many afflicted people.
Questo, o Romani, è fabbricarmi il tempio.	This, oh Romans, is the way to build a temple for me.

ANNIUS

Oh vero croe!	Oh, true hero!

PUBLIUS

Quanto di te minori	How much less than you
Tutti i premi son mai, tutte le lodi!	Are all rewards, all praise!

TITUS

Basta, basta, o miei fidi.	Enough, enough, my faithful people.
Sesto a me s'avvicini; Annio non parta;	Let Sextus approach; and Annius not leave;
Ogni altro si allontani.	All others depart.

(All retire from the atrium. Titus, Sextus and Annius remain.)

ANNIUS

(Adesso, o Sesto,	(Speak for me
Parla per me.)	Now, Sextus.)

SEXTUS

Come. signor, potesti	How, my lord, could you allow
La tua bella regina . . .	Your lovely queen . . .

TITUS

Ah, Sesto, amico,	Ah, Sextus, my friend,
Che terribil momento! Io non credei . . .	What a terrible moment! I did not believe . . .

Basta, ho vinto: partì.
Tolgasi adesso a Roma ogni sospetto
Di vederla mia sposa. Una sua figlia
Vuol veder sul mio soglio;
E appagarla convien. Giacchè l'amore
Scelse in vano i miei lacci, io vuo' che almeno
L'amicizia gli scelga. Al tuo s'unisca,

Sesto, il cesareo sangue. Oggi mia sposa

Sarà la tua germana.

Enough, I conquered: she left.
May Rome have no suspicion now
Of seeing her my wife. I desire to see
One of Rome's daughters on my throne;
It is necessary to placate her. Since love
Chose my bonds in vain, I desire that at least
Friendship shall choose them. Let the royal blood
Be joined to yours, Sextus. Today your sister
Shall be my wife.

SEXTUS

Servilia?

Servilia?

TITUS

Appunto.

Precisely.

ANNIUS

(Oh me infelice!)

(Unhappy Annius!)

SEXTUS

(Oh, dèi!
Annio è perduto.)

(Oh gods!
Annius is lost!)

TITUS

Udisti?
Che dici? Non rispondi?

Did you hear?
What do you say? You don't answer?

SEXTUS

E chi potrebbe
Risponderti, signor? M'opprime a segno
La tua bontà, che non ho cor . . .
Vorrei . . .

And who could
Answer you, my lord? Your goodness overwhelms me
So that I haven't the heart . . . I would like . . .

ANNIUS

(Sesto è in pena per me.)

(Sextus is in torment for me.)

TITUS

Spiegati. Io tutto
Farò per tuo vantaggio.

Explain yourself. I shall do
Everything to your advantage.

516

SEXTUS

(Ah! si serva l'amico.) | (Ah! let me help my friend.)

ANNIUS

(Annio, coraggio!) | (Annius, courage!)

SEXTUS (*resolutely*)

Tito! . . . | Titus! . . .

ANNIUS (*resolutely*)

Augusto, io conosco	Emperor, I understand
Di Sesto il cor. Fin dalla cuna insieme	Sextus' heart. Since the cradle, tender love
Tenero amor ne strinse. Ei, di se stesso	Has bound us together. He, a modest estimator
Modesto estimator, teme che sembri	Of himself, fears that this gift
Sproporzionato il dono; e non s'avvede	May seem out of proportion; and he doesn't notice that
Ch'ogni distanza eguaglia	The favor of Caesar
D'un Cesare il favor. Ma tu consiglio	Makes all distances equal. But you must not
Da lui prender non dei. Come potresti	Take advice from him. How could you
Sposa elegger più degna	Choose a wife more worthy
Dell'impero e di te? Virtù, bellezza,	Of the empire and of yourself? Virtue, beauty,
Tutto è in Servilia. Io le conobbi in volto	Servilia has everything. I knew by her face
Ch'era nata a regnar. De' miei presagi	That she was born to rule. This is the realization
L'adempimento è questo.	Of my premonitions.

SEXTUS

(Annio parla così! Sogno o son desto?) | (Annius speaking like this! Am I dreaming or awake?)

TITUS

E ben! recane a lei,	Well! you take her the news,
Annio, tu la novella; e tu mi segui,	Annius; and you, beloved Sextus,
Amato Sesto, e queste	Follow me, and put aside
Tue dubbiezze deponi. Avrai tal parte	Your doubts. You shall yet
Tu ancor nel soglio, e tanto	Have a part in the throne, and I shall raise you
T'innalzerò, che resterà ben poco	So high, that very little shall remain Of that tiny space

Dello spazio infinito,
Che frapposer gli dèi fra Sesto e Tito.

Which the gods placed between Sextus and Titus.

SEXTUS

Questo è troppo, o signor. Modera almeno,
Se ingrati non ci vuoi,
Modera, Augusto, i benefizi tuoi.

This is too much, my lord. At least moderate
Your gifts, Emperor,
Lest you wish us ungrateful.

TITUS

Ma che! se mi negate
Che benefico io sia, che mi lasciate?

What! if you deny my being
Beneficial, what do you leave me?

No. 6 Aria

TITUS

Del più sublime soglio
L'unico frutto è questo:
Tutto è tormento il resto,
E tutto è servitù.
    Che avrei, se ancor perdessi

Of the most subline throne
This is the single fruit:
All the rest is torment,
And all is slavery.
    What would I have, if I were yet to lose

Le sole ore felici
Che ho nel giovar gli oppressi,
Nel sollevar gli amici,
Nel dispensar tesori,
Al merto e alla virtù?

The only happy hours
That I have in helping the oppressed,
In elevating my friends,
In dispensing treasures
According to worth and virtue?

(He leaves with Sextus.)

ANNIUS

Non ci pentiam. D'un generoso amante
Era questo il dover. Mio cor, deponi
Le tenerezze antiche. È tua sovrana
Chi fu l'idolo tuo. Cambiar conviene

Let us not be sorry. This was the duty
Of a generous lover. My heart, lay aside
Your former love. She is your sovereign
Who once was your idol. It is necessary to change

In rispetto l'amore. Eccola. Oh dèi!
Mai non parve sì bella agli occhi miei.

Love into respect. Here she is. Oh gods!
She never looked so lovely to my eyes.

SERVILIA

Mio ben . . .

My love . . .

ANNIUS

    Taci, Servilia. Ora è delitto
Il chiamarmi così.

    Silence, Servilia. It is now a crime
To call me thus.

SERVILIA

Perchè?	Why?

ANNIUS

Ti scelse	Caesar
Cesare (che martir!) per sua consorte.	Has chosen you (what martyrdom!) as his consort.
A te (morir mi sento!), a te m'impose	To bring (I feel I am dying!), to bring you the news
Di recarne l'avviso (oh pena!), ed io . . .	He commanded me (what pain!), and I . . .
Io fui . . . (parlar non posso) . . . Augusta, addio!	I was . . . (I cannot speak) . . . Empress, farewell!

SERVILIA

Come! Fermati! Io sposa	What? Stop! I the wife
Di Cesare! E perchè?	Of Caesar! And why?

ANNIUS

Perchè non trova	Because such
Beltà, virtù che sia	Beauty and virtue cannot be found which
Più degna d'un impero, anima . . . Oh stelle!	Are more worthy of an empire; my soul . . . Oh heavens!
Che dirò? Lascia, Augusta,	What shall I say? Allow me, Empress,
Deh! lasciami partir.	Ah! allow me to leave.

SERVILIA

Così confusa	In such a confused state
Abbandonar mi vuoi? Spiegati, dimmi:	Do you wish to leave me? Explain to me, tell me:
Come fu? per qual via? . . .	How did it come about? by what means? . . .

ANNIUS

Mi perdo s'io non parto, anima mia.	I am lost if I do not go, my soul.

No. 7 Duet

ANNIUS

Ah! perdona al primo affetto	Ah! forgive that former love
Questo accento sconsigliato:	This ill-advised word:
Colpa fu del labbro, usato	It was the fault of my lips, accustomed
A così chiamarti ognor.	Always to call you thus.

SERVILIA

Ah! tu fosti il primo oggetto	Ah! you were the first man
Che sinor fedel amai,	That I loved faithfully till now,
E tu l'ultimo sarai	And you shall be the last
Ch'abbia nido in questo cor.	That will have a nest in my heart.

ANNIUS

Cari accenti del mio bene!	Dear words of my beloved!

SERVILIA

Oh, mia dolce, cara speme!	Oh, my sweet, dear hope!

BOTH

Più che ascolto i sensi tuoi,	The more I listen to what you say,
In me cresce più l'ardor.	The more my ardor increases.
Quando un'alma è all'altra unita,	When one soul is united to another
Qual piacer un cor risente!	What pleasures a heart feels!
Ah, si tolga dalla vita	Ah, let every thing that is not love
Tutto quel che non è amor.	Be taken from life.

(*They leave.*)

SCENE III

A delightful retreat in the imperial residence on the Palatine Hill.

Titus and Publius with a sheet of paper

TITUS

Che mi rechi in quel foglio?	What are you bringing me in that paper?

PUBLIUS

I nomi ei chiude	It holds the names
De' rei che osar con temerari accenti	Of the guilty ones who dare with reckless words
De' Cesari già spenti	Insult the memory
La memoria oltraggiar.	Of those Caesars already dead.

TITUS

Barbara inchiesta,	A barbarous investigation,
Che agli estinti non giova e somministra	Which is useless to the dead and provides
Mille strade alla frode	A thousand avenues for fraud
D'insidiar gl'innocenti!	To lay a trap for the innocent!

PUBLIUS

Ma v'è, signor, chi lacerare ardisce	But there is one, lord, who dares slander
Anche il tuo nome.	Even your name.

TITUS

E che perciò? Se il mosse
Leggerezza, nol curo;
Se follia, lo compiango;
Se ragion, gli son grato; e se in lui sono

Impeti di malizia, io gli perdono.

So what? If it causes
Mirth, I don't care;
If foolishness, I pity him;
If he is right, I am grateful; and if there are

Outbursts of malice I pardon him.

PUBLIUS

Almen . . .

At least . . .

(*Enter Servilia.*)

SERVILIA

Di Tito al piè . . .

At Titus' feet . . .

TITUS

Servilia! Augusta!

Servilia! Empress!

SERVILIA

Ah! signor, sì gran nome
Non darmi ancora: odimi prima. Io deggio
Palesarti un arcan.

Ah! my lord, do not yet bestow on me
Such a great name: hear me first. I must
Reveal a secret to you.

TITUS

Publio, ti scosta,
Ma non partir.

Publius, stand back,
But do not leave.

(*Publius withdraws.*)

SERVILIA

Che del cesareo alloro
Me, fra tante più degne,

Generoso monarca, inviti a parte,
E dono tal, che desteria tumulto
Nel più stupido cor . . .

That a generous monarch
Would urge me, from among others more worthy,
To the imperial laurel,
Is a gift such as would awaken tumult
In the most unconscious heart . . .

TITUS

Parla . . .

Speak . . .

521

SERVILIA

Il core,	My heart,
Signor, non è più mio: già da gran tempo	Lord, is no longer mine: for a long time now
Annio me lo rapì. Valor che basti,	Annius has stolen it from me. I have not the boldness
Non ho per obbliarlo. Anche dal trono	To forget him. Even from the throne
Il solito sentiero	My thought would take its usual course
Farebbe a mio dispetto il mio pensiero.	In spite of myself.
So che oppormi è delitto	I know that for me to oppose the will of Caesar
D'un Cesare al voler; ma tutto almeno	Is a crime; but at least everything
Sia noto al mio sovrano:	Is known to my sovereign:
Poi se mi vuol sua sposa, ecco la mano.	So if he wants me as his wife, here is my hand.

TITUS

Grazie, o numi del ciel! Pur si ritrova	Thanks, oh heavenly gods! at last one is found
Chi s'avventuri a dispiacer col vero.	Who ventures to displease with the truth.
Alla grandezza tua la propria pace	Annius defers his own peace
Annio propose! Tu ricusi un trono	To your glory! You refuse a throne
Per essergli fedele! Ed io dovrei	To remain faithful to him! And should I
Turbar fiamme sì belle? Ah! non produce	Disturb such noble passions? Ah! Titus' heart
Sentimenti sì rei di Tito il core.	Cannot produce such unworthy sentiments.
Sgombra ogni tema. Io voglio	Banish all your fears. I wish
Stringer nodo sì degno e n'abbia poi	To tie such a worthy knot, and ever may
Cittadini la patria eguali a voi.	Our country have citizens equal to you.

SERVILIA

O Tito! o Augusto! o vera	Oh Titus! oh Emperor! oh true
Delizia de' mortali! io non saprei	Delight of men! I wouldn't know
Come il grato mio cor . . .	How my grateful heart . . .

TITUS

Se grata appieno	If you would wish me
Esser mi vuoi, Servilia, agli altri inspira	Full of gratitude, Servilia, let your honesty
Il tuo candor. Di pubblicar procura	Inspire others. Let it be proclaimed
Che grato a me si rende,	That the truth that offends makes me more grateful
Più del falso che piace, il ver che offende.	Than the lie which pleases.

No. 8 Aria

Titus

Ah! se fosse intorno al trono	Ah! if every heart around the throne
Ogni cor così sincero,	Were as sincere as this,
Non tormento un vasto impero,	A vast empire would not be torment
Ma saria felicità.	But happiness.
Non dovrebbero i regnanti	Rulers should not
Tollerar sì grave affanno,	Tolerate such deep sorrow
Per distinguer dall'inganno	In distinguishing between lies
l'insidiata verità.	And deceptive truth.

(*He leaves.*)

Servilia

Felice me!	Happy Servilia!

Vitellia (*entering*)

Posso alla mia sovrana	May I offer the first tokens
Offrir del mio rispetto i primi omaggi?	Of respect to my sovereign?
Posso adorar quel volto,	May I adore that face,
Per cui, d'amor ferito,	On account of which Titus' heart,
Ha perduto il riposo il cor di Tito?	Wounded by love, has lost its repose?

Servilia

Non esser meco irata;	Do not be angry with me;
Forse la regia destra è a te serbata.	Perhaps the royal hand is reserved for you.

(*She leaves.*)

Vitellia

Ancora mi schernisce? Questo soffrir degg'io	She still scorns me? Must I suffer this
Vergognoso disprezzo? Ah, con qual fasto	Shameful contempt? Ah, how ostentatiously
Qui mi lascia costei! Barbaro Tito!	Did she leave me here! Cruel Titus!
Ti parea dunque poco	Did it seem such a small thing to you
Berenice antepormi? Io dunque sono	To prefer Berenice to me? Am I thus
L'ultima de' viventi? Ah, trema, ingrato!	The last of the living? Ah, tremble, ungrateful man!
Trema d'avermi offesa! Oggi il tuo sangue . . .	Tremble for having offended me! Today your blood . . .

SEXTUS

Mia vita.	My life.

VITELLIA

E ben, che rechi? Il Campidoglio
È acceso? è incenerito?
Lentulo dove sta? Tito è punito?

Well, what news do you bring?
Is the Capitol burning? in ashes?
Where is Lentulus? Has Titus been
 punished?

SEXTUS

Nulla intrapresi ancor.

I've begun nothing yet.

VITELLIA

Nulla! E sì franco
Mi torni innanzi? e con qual merto ardisci

Di chiamarmi tua vita?

Nothing? And you can return
To me so unconcerned? and on what basis
 do you dare
Call me your life?

SEXTUS

È tuo comando
Il sospendere il colpo.

It was your command
To put off the blow.

VITELLIA

E non udisti
I miei novelli oltraggi? Un altro cenno
Aspetti ancor? Ma ch'io ti creda amante,

Dimmi, come pretendi,
Se così poco i miei pensieri intendi?

And have you not heard about
The latest insults to me? Are you waiting
For a second bidding? Tell me, how can
 you expect
That I consider you my lover
If you understand my thoughts so little?

SEXTUS

Se una ragion potesse
Almen giustificarmi . . .

If one reason at least
Were able to justify me . . .

VITELLIA

Una ragione!
Mille ne avrai, qualunque sia l'affetto

Da cui prenda il tuo cor regola e moto.

È la gloria il tuo voto? Io ti propongo
La patria a liberar. Sei d'un'illustre
Ambizion capace? Eccoti aperta

One reason!
You shall have a thousand of them, no
 matter what the emotion may be
From which your heart takes its laws and
 pulses.
Is glory your wish? I propose that
You free your country. Are you capable
Of great ambition? Here is a way to the
 throne

Una strada all'impero. Renderti fortunato
Può la mia mano? Corri,
Mi vendica, e son tua.
D'altri stimoli hai d'uopo?
Sappi che Tito amai, che del mio cor
   l'acquisto
Ei t'impedì; che, se rimane in vita,

Si può pentir; ch'io ritornar potrei,
Non mi fido di me, forse ad amarlo.

Or va: se non ti muove
Desio di gloria, ambizione, amore;

Se tolleri un rivale,
Che usurpò, che contrasta,
Che involarti potrà gli affetti miei,
Degli uomini il più vil dirò che sei.

Open to you. Can my hand in marriage
Make you happy? Run,
Avenge me, and I am yours.
Do you need other incentives?
Then know that I loved Titus, that he
   prevented
The winning of my heart; that if he
   remains alive
He will be sorry; that I could go back,
Perhaps, to loving him: I don't trust
   myself.
Now go: if desire for
Glory, ambition and love do not move
   you;
If you can tolerate a rival
Who stole, who resists,
Who will steal my affections from you,
Then I say you are the most cowardly of
   men.

SEXTUS

Quante vie d'assalirmi!
Basta, basta, non più! Già m'inspirasti,
Vitellia, il tuo furore. Arder vedrai

Fra poco il Campidoglio; e questo acciaro
Nel sen di Tito . . . (Ah! sommi dèi, qual
   gelo
Mi ricerca le vene!)

How many ways am I beset!
Enough, enough, no more! Your fury,
Vitellia, has already inspired me. Shortly
   you will
See the Capitol burning, and this sword
In Titus' breast . . . (Ah, great gods, what
   ice
Touches my heart!)

VITELLIA

Ed or che pensi?
And now what are you thinking?

SEXTUS

Ah, Vitellia!
Ah, Vitellia!

VITELLIA

Il previdi:
Tu pentito già sei . . .
I knew it:
You are already sorry . . .

SEXTUS

Non son pentito;
Ma . . .
I am not sorry;
But . . .

525

Vitellia

Non stancarmi più. Conosco,
    ingrato,
Che amor non hai per me. Folle ch'io fui!
	Weary me no longer. I know,
	    ungrateful man,
	That you have no love for me. Foolish
	    woman that I was!

Già ti credea, già mi piacevi, e quasi	I already believed you, I already liked you, and almost
Cominciavo ad amarti. Agli occhi miei Involati per sempre, E scordati di me.	Was beginning to love you. Hide yourself From my sight forever, And forget me.

Sextus

Fermati! io cedo; Io già volo a servirti.	Stop! I yield; Already I fly to serve you.

Vitellia

Eh! non ti credo. M'ingannerai di nuovo. In mezzo all'opra Ricorderai . . .	Oh! I don't believe you. You will deceive me once more. In the midst of the work You will remember . . .

Sextus

No: mi punisca Amore, Se penso ad ingannarti.	No: may Love punish me If I think of deceiving you.

Vitellia

Dunque, corri! Che fai? Perchè non parti?	Run then! What are you doing? Why don't you leave?

No. 9 Aria

Sextus

Parto; ma tu, ben mio, Meco ritorna in pace. Sarò qual piu ti piace; Quel che vorrai farò. Guardami, e tutto obblio, E a vendicarti io volo. A questo sguardo solo Da me si penserà. Ah, qual poter, oh dèi! Donaste alla beltà!	I am leaving; but you, my dearest, Must make peace with me again. I shall be whatever you like; Whatever you wish I shall do. Look at me, and I forget everything, And I fly to avenge you. I shall think only Of that glance. Ah, what power, oh gods! Did you give to beauty!

(*He leaves.*)

VITELLIA

Vedrai, Tito, vedrai che al fin sì vile	One day you will see, Titus, that my face
Questo volto non è. Basta a sedurti	Is not so wretched. At least it suffices
Gli amici almen, se ad invaghirti è poco.	To seduce your friends, though it cannot charm you.
Ti pentirai . . .	You will be sorry . . .

(Enter Publius and Annius.)

PUBLIUS

Tu qui, Vitellia? Ah! corri:	You here, Vitellia? Ah! run,
Va Tito alle tue stanze.	Titus is going to your chambers.

ANNIUS

Vitellia, il passo affretta,	Vitellia, hurry,
Cesare di te cerca.	Caesar is looking for you.

VITELLIA

Cesare!	Caesar!

PUBLIUS

Ancor nol sai? sua consorte t'elesse.	You don't know yet? he has chosen you as his consort.

ANNIUS

Tu sei la nostra Augusta;	You are our Empress;
E il primo omaggio già da noi ti si rende.	And already he makes you his first obeisance through us.

PUBLIUS

Ah, principessa, andiam: Cesare attende.	Ah, princess, let us go: Caesar is waiting.

No. 10 Trio

VITELLIA

Vengo! Aspettate! Sesto!	I am coming! Wait! Sextus!
Ahimè! Sesto! È partito?	Alas! Sextus! Has he gone?
O sdegno mio funesto!	Oh my fatal scorn!
O insano mio furor!	Oh my insane fury!
Che angustia! che tormento!	What anxiety! what torment!
Io gelo, o Dio! d'orror.	Oh God! I freeze with horror.

ANNIUS and PUBLIUS

O come un gran contento,	Oh, how a great happiness
Come confonde un cor!	Confuses a heart!

(They leave.)

SCENE IV

The Capitol.

No. 11 Accompanied Recitative

SEXTUS (*alone*)

Oh dèi, che smania è questa!	Oh gods, what is this frenzy?
Che tumulto ho nel cor! Palpito, agghiaccio:	What tumult do I have in my heart! I tremble, I freeze:
M'incammino, m'arresto: ogni aura, Ogni ombra	I make a start, I stop: every breeze, Every shadow
Mi fa tremare. Io non credea che fosse	Makes me shiver. I didn't believe that it was
Sì difficile impresa esser malvagio.	Such a difficult undertaking to be evil.
Ma compirla convien. Almen si vada	But I have to accomplish it. At least one may
Con valore a perir. Valore? E come	Die with courage. Courage? And how
Può averne un traditor? Sesto infelice,	Can a traitor have any? Unhappy Sextus,
Tu traditor! Che orribil nome! E pure	You a traitor! What a horrible name. And yet
T'affretti a meritarlo. E chi tradisci?	You are rushing off to earn it. And who are you betraying?
Il più grande, il più giusto, il più clemente	The greatest, most just, most clement
Principe della terra, a cui tu devi	Prince of the earth, to whom you owe
Quanto puoi, quanto sei. Bella mercede	All you are able to do, all that you are. Truly,
Gli rendi in vero! Ei t'innalzò per farti	You repay him handsomely! He has raised you up
Il carnefice suo. M'inghiotta il suolo	So you can be his executioner. May the ground swallow me
Prima ch'io tal divenga. Ah! non ho core,	Before I become such a thing. Ah! I haven't the heart,
Vitellia, a secondar gli sdegni tuoi.	Vitellia, to support your scorn.
Morrei, prima del colpo, in faccia a lui.	I would die, before the blow, in his presence.
S'impedisca . . . Ma come,	It must be prevented . . . What,
Arde già il Campidoglio?	Is the Capitol already burning?
Un gran tumulto io sento	I hear a great noise
D'armi, e d'armati:	Of weapons and armed men:
Ahi! tardo è il pentimento.	Ah! my regret is too late.

No. 12 Quintet and Chorus

Deh conservate, o dèi!	Ah preserve, oh gods!
A Roma il suo splendor;	His glory for the sake of Rome;
O almeno i giorni miei	Or at least cut short
Coi suoi troncate ancor!	My days with his!

(*Annius enters.*)

ANNIUS

Amico, dove vai?	My friend, where are you going?

SEXTUS

Io vado,	I am going,
Io vado . . . lo saprai	I am going . . . Oh God,
O Dio, per mio rossor.	You will know by my shame.

(*He leaves.*)

ANNIUS

Io Sesto non intendo;	I don't understand Sextus;
Ma qui Servilia viene.	But Servilia is coming here.

SERVILIA (*entering*)

Ah! che tumulto orrendo!	Ah! what a dreadful uproar!

ANNIUS

Fuggi di qua, mio bene!	Fly from here, my dearest!

SERVILIA

Si teme che l'incendio	It is feared that the fire
Non sia dal caso nato,	May not be born of chance,
Ma con peggior disegno	But deliberately provoked
Ad arte suscitato.	With the worst intent.

CHORUS (*in the distance*)

Ah!	Ah!

PUBLIUS

V'è in Roma una congiura;	There is a conspiracy in Rome;
Per Tito, ahimè, pavento.	Alas, I fear for Titus.
Di questo tradimento	Whoever could be the perpetrator
Chi mai sarà l'autor?	Of this betrayal?

CHORUS

Ah!   Ah!

SERVILIA, ANNIUS and PUBLIUS

Le grida, ahimè! ch'io sento   Alas! the screams that I hear
Mi fan gelar d'orror!   Make me freeze with horror!

CHORUS

Ah!   Ah!

(Enter Vitellia.)

VITELLIA

Chi, per pietade, o Dio!   Oh God! who, for pity's sake,
M'addita dov'è Sesto?   Will show me where Sextus is?
(In odio a me son io,   (I hate myself,
Ed ho di me terror.)   And am afraid of myself.)

SERVILIA, ANNIUS and PUBLIUS

Di questo tradimento   Whoever could be the perpetrator
Chi mai sarà l'autor?   Of this betrayal?

CHORUS

Ah!   Ah!

SERVILIA, ANNIUS, PUBLIUS and VITELLIA

Le grida, ahimè! ch'io sento   Alas! the screams that I hear
Mi fan gelar d'orror!   Make me freeze with horror!

SEXTUS *(entering)*

(Ah, dove mai m'ascondo?   (Ah, where can I hide myself?
Apriti, o terra, inghiottimi!   Open, oh earth, swallow me!
E nel tuo sen profondo   And in your fathomless breast
Rinserra un traditor!)   Conceal a traitor!)

VITELLIA

Sesto!   Sextus!

SEXTUS

Da me che vuoi?   What do you want of me?

VITELLIA

Quai sguardi vibri intorno?   Why are your eyes flashing?

SEXTUS

Mi fa terror il giorno.   The day terrifies me.

VITELLIA

Tito? ...   Titus? ...

SEXTUS

   La nobil alma   His noble soul
Versò dal sen trafitto!   Poured forth from his wounded breast!

SERVILIA, ANNIUS and PUBLIUS

Qual destra rea macchiarsi   What guilty hand was able
Potè d'un tal delitto?   To stain itself with such a crime?

SEXTUS

Fu l'uom più scellerato,   It was a man most evil,
L'orror della natura.   The horror of nature.
Fu ... fu ...   It was ... it was ...

VITELLIA (*to Sextus*)

   Taci, forsennato,   Quiet, madman,
Deh! non ti palesar.   Do not reveal yourself.

ALL

Ah! dunque l'astro è spento,   Ah! then our star is gone,
È spento di pace apportator.   The bringer of peace is gone.

CHORUS

O nero tradimento!   Oh, black betrayal!
O giorno di dolor!   Oh, day of sorrow!

End of Act One

ACT TWO

SCENE I

A delightful retreat in the imperial residence on the Palatine Hill.

Annius and Sextus

ANNIUS

Sesto, come tu credi, Augusto non perì.   Sextus, the Emperor did not die as you
                                     thought.

| Calma il tuo duolo; | Calm your grief;

531

In questo punto ei torna
Illeso dal tumulto.

Just now he returned
Unharmed from the uproar.

SEXTUS

Eh! tu m'inganni:
Io stesso lo mirai cader trafitto
Da scellerato acciaro.

Ah! you are deceiving me:
I myself saw him fall wounded
By the evil sword.

ANNIUS

Dove?

Where?

SEXTUS

Nel varco angusto, ove si ascende

Quinci presso al Tarpeo.

In the narrow passage, where
from here
You climb up to the Tarpeian Rock.

ANNIUS

No, travedesti:
Tra il fumo e tra il tumulto,
Altri Tito ti parve.

No, you were mistaken:
Between the smoke and the uproar,
You mistook someone else for Titus.

SEXTUS

Altri? E chi mai
Delle cesaree vesti
Ardirebbe adornarsi? Il sacro alloro,
L'augusto ammanto . . .

Someone else? And whoever
Would dare put on
The imperial robes? The sacred laurel,
The royal mantle . . .

ANNIUS

Ogni argomento è vano:
Vive Tito ed è illeso. In questo istante

Io da lui mi divido.

All arguments are useless:
Titus is alive and unharmed. A moment
ago
I left him.

SEXTUS

Oh dèi pietosi!
Oh caro prence! oh dolce amico! Ah!
lascia
Che a questo sen . . . Ma non m'inganni?

Oh merciful gods!
Oh dear prince! oh sweet friend! Ah!
permit me,
That to my breast . . . But you are not
deceiving me?

ANNIUS

Io merto
Sì poca fè! Dunque tu stesso a lui

Corri e 'l vedrai.

Am I worthy
Of so little faith? Run to him yourself,
then,
And you will see.

SEXTUS

Ch'io mi presenti a Tito
Dopo averlo tradito?

Can I come before Titus
After having betrayed him?

ANNIUS

Tu lo tradisti?

You betrayed him?

SEXTUS

Io del tumulto, io sono
Il primo autor.

I was the original perpetrator
Of the uproar.

ANNIUS

Come! Perchè!

How? Why?

SEXTUS

Non posso
Dirti di più.

I cannot
Tell you more.

ANNIUS

Sesto è infedele!

Sextus faithless!

SEXTUS

Amico,
M'ha perduto un istante. Addio. M'involo

Alla patria per sempre.
Ricordati di me. Tito difendi
Da nuove insidie. Io vo ramingo, afflitto

A pianger fra le selve il mio delitto.

My friend,
A single moment was my downfall.
Farewell. I am leaving
My country forever.
Remember me. Defend Titus
From new dangers. I go a wanderer,
cursed
To bewail my crime in the forests.

ANNIUS

Fermati! Oh dèi! Pensiamo . . .
Incolpan molti di questo incendio il caso;

E la congiura non è certa finora . . .

Stop! Oh gods! Let us think . . .
Many people are blaming chance for the
fire;
And the conspiracy is still not proved . . .

SEXTUS

E ben, che vuoi?.

Well, what do you want?

ANNIUS

Che tu non parta ancora.

That you not leave yet.

533

No. 13 Aria

ANNIUS

Torna di Tito a lato,	Return to Titus' side,
E l'error passato	And make amends
Con replicate emenda	For your past mistake
Prove di fedeltà.	With repeated proofs of fidelity.
L'acerbo tuo dolore	Your bitter sorrow
È segno manifesto,	Is an obvious sign
Che di virtù nel core	That the image of virtue
L'immagine ti sta.	Is in your heart.

(He leaves.)

SEXTUS

Partir deggio, o restar?	Must I go or stay?
Io non ho mente per distinguer consigli.	I have no mind for making distinctions.

VITELLIA (entering)

Sesto, fuggi, conserva	Sextus, flee, save
La tua vita, e il mio onor. Tu sei perduto,	Your life and my honor. You are lost
Se alcun ti scopre, e, se scoperto sei,	If anyone discovers you, and if you are discovered
Pubblico è il mio segreto.	My secret is known.

SEXTUS

In questo seno	It will remain buried
Sepolto resterà. Nessuno il seppe:	In my breast. No one knew about it:
Tacendolo morrò.	I shall die keeping it quiet.

VITELLIA

Mi fiderei,	I would trust you
Se minor tenerezza	If I saw you felt
Per Tito in te vedessi. Il suo rigore	Less tenderness for Titus. I no longer fear
Non temo già; la sua clemenza io temo:	His severity; I fear his clemency:
Questa ti vincerà.	This will conquer you.

(Enter Publius with guards.)

PUBLIUS

Sesto!	Sextus!

SEXTUS

Che chiedi?	What do you want?

PUBLIUS

La tua spada.   Your sword.

SEXTUS

E perchè?   And why?

PUBLIUS

Colui, che cinto   The man
Delle spoglie regali agli occhi tuoi,   Who to your eyes was dressed in royal
                                                  robes,

Cadde trafitto al suolo,   Who fell wounded to the ground,
Ed ingannato dall'apparenza   And, deceived by his appearance,
Tu credesti Tito, era Lentulo;   Whom you thought was Titus, was
                                                  Lentulus;

Il colpo la vita a lui non tolse;   The blow did not deprive him of life;
Il resto intendi.   You understand the rest.
Vieni.   Come.

VITELLIA

(Oh colpo fatale!)   (Oh fatal blow!)

(Sextus gives up his sword.)

SEXTUS

Al fin, tiranna . . .   So at last, tyrannical woman . . .

PUBLIUS

Sesto, partir conviene. È già raccolto   Sextus, you must go. The Senate has
                                                  already assembled
Per udirti il Senato, e non poss'io   To hear you, and I am unable
Differir di condurti.   To delay escorting you.

SEXTUS

Ingrata, addio!   Ungrateful woman, farewell!

No. 14 Trio

SEXTUS

Se al volto mai ti senti   If ever you feel a light breeze
Lieve aura che s'aggiri,   Play around your face,
Gli estremi miei sospiri   That breath will be
Quell'alito sarà.   My last sighs.

VITELLIA

(Per me vien tratto a morte: (On account of me he is led to
                                                  death:

535

Ah, dove mai m'ascondo?
Fra poco noto al mondo
Il fallo mio sarà.)

Ah, wherever can I hide?
Soon my crime
Will be known to the world.)

PUBLIUS

Vieni . . .

Come . . .

SEXTUS (*to Publius*)

Ti seguo . . .

I am following you . . .

(*to Vitellia*)

Addio.

Farewell.

VITELLIA (*to Sextus*)

Senti . . . mi perdo . . . oh Dio!

Listen . . . I am lost . . . oh God!

(*to Publius*)

Che crudeltà!

What cruelty!

SEXTUS (*to Vitellia*)

Rammenta chi t'adora
In questo stato ancora.
Mercede al mio dolore
Sia almen la tua pietà.

Remember the one who still
Adores you in this condition.
At least let your pity
Be a recompense for my sorrow.

VITELLIA

(Mi laceran il core,
Rimorso, orror, spavento!
Quel che nell'alma io sento
Di duol morir mi fa.)

(Remorse, horror and terror
Rend my heart!
That which I feel in my soul
Will make me die of sorrow.)

PUBLIUS

(L'acerbo amaro pianto,
Che da' suoi lumi piove,
L'anima mi commove,
Ma vana è la pieta.)

(The bitter and harsh tears
Which fall from his eyes,
Move my spirit,
But pity is useless.)

(*Sextus leaves with Publius and the guards.*)

SCENE II

A large hall designed for public hearings. A throne, chair and
table. Titus, Publius, patricians, Praetorian Guards and people.

No. 15 Chorus

CHORUS

Ah grazie si rendano
Al sommo fattor,
Che in Tito del trono
Salvò lo splendor.

Ah let us give thanks
To the almighty Creator,
Who in Titus has kept
The glory of the throne safe.

TITUS

Ah no, sventurato
Non sono cotanto,
Se in Roma il mio fato
Si trova compianto,
Se voti per Tito
Si formano ancor.

Ah no, I am not
So unfortunate,
If my fate finds
Condolence in Rome,
If prayers for Titus
Are still offered.

CHORUS

Ah grazie si rendano, *ecc.*

Ah let us give thanks, *etc.*

(*They leave.*)

PUBLIUS

Già de' pubblici giuochi,
Signor, l'ora trascorre. Il dì solenne

Sai che non soffre il trascurarli. È tutto

Colà, d'intorno alla festiva arena,
Il popolo raccolto, e non si attende
Che la presenza tua. Ciascun sospira,
Dopo il noto periglio,
Di rivederti salvo. Alla tua Roma

Non differir sì bel contento.

Lord, the hour of the public games
Already hastens on. You know that this
solemn day
Does not suffer them to be neglected.
The public
Is all gathered there, around the festive
Arena, and only your presence
Is wanting. Everyone longs
To see you safe,
After your well-known danger. Do not
deny
Your Rome such satisfaction.

TITUS

Andremo,
Publio, fra poco. Io non avrei riposo,

We shall go
In a moment, Publius. I would have no
rest

Se di Sesto il destino	If I did not know Sextus' fate
Pria non sapessi. Avrà il Senato ormai	First. By now the Senate will have heard
Le sue discolpe udite; avrà scoperto,	His defense: it will have discovered,
Vedrai, ch'egli è innocente; e non dovrebbe	You'll see, that he is innocent; and it should not
Tardar molto l'avviso.	Delay its verdict too long.

PUBLIUS

Ah! troppo chiaro	Ah! Lentulus
Lentulo favellò.	Spoke all too clearly.

TITUS

Lentulo forse	Lentulus is perhaps
Cerca al fallo un compagno,	Looking for a companion in crime,
Per averlo al perdono. Ei non ignora	So as to be pardoned with him. He is not ignorant
Quanto Sesto m'è caro. Arte comune	Of how dear Sextus is to me. This is the usual
Questa è de' rei. Pur dal Senato ancora	Cunning of the guilty. Yet no one has returned
Non torna alcun! Che mai sarà? Va, chiedi	From the Senate! What can this mean? Go, ask
Che si fa, che s'attende. Io tutto voglio	What they are doing, what they are waiting for. I want
Saper pria di partir.	To know everything before leaving.

PUBLIUS

Vado: ma temo	I am going: but I fear
Di non tornar nunzio felice.	That I shall not return a herald of felicity.

TITUS

E puoi	Can you
Creder Sesto infedele? Io dal mio core	Believe Sextus faithless? I measure his heart
Il suo misuro; e un impossibil parmi	By my own: and it seems impossible to me
Ch'egli m'abbia tradito.	That he has betrayed me.

PUBLIUS

Ma, signor, non han tutti il cor di Tito.	But lord, not all have the heart of Titus.

No. 16 Aria

PUBLIUS

Tardi s'avvede	He becomes aware
D'un tradimento	Of betrayal too late
Chi mai di fede	Who has never been
Mancar non sa.	Faithless.
Un cor verace,	It is no miracle
Pieno d'onore,	If a true heart,
Non è portento,	Full of honor,
Se ogni altro core	Believes every other heart
Crede incapace	Incapable
D'infedeltà.	Of faithlessness.

(He leaves.)

TITUS

No, così scellerato	No, I do not believe
Il mio Sesto non credo. Io l'ho veduto	My Sextus to be so evil. I have seen him
Non sol fido ed amico,	Not only loyal and friendly to me,
Ma tenero per me. Tanto cambiarsi	But also tender. A soul
Un'alma non potrebbe. Annio, che rechi?	Could not change so much. Annius, what are you bringing?
L'innocenza di Sesto?	Sextus' innocence?
Consolami.	Comfort me.

ANNIUS *(entering)*

Ah! signor, pietà per lui	My lord, I come
Ad implorar io vengo.	To beg pity for him.

(Enter Publius with a sheet of paper.)

PUBLIUS

Cesare, nol diss'io? Sesto è l'autore	Caesar, did I not say it? Sextus is the perpetrator
Della trama crudel.	Of the cruel plot.

TITUS

Publio, ed è vero?	Is it true, Publius?

PUBLIUS

Pur troppo ei di sua bocca	Unfortunately, he confirmed everything
Tutto affermò. Coi complici il Senato	With his own lips. The Senate has condemned

Alle fiere il condanna. Ecco il decreto	Him and his accomplices to the wild beasts. Here
Terribile, ma giusto;	Is the harsh, but just, decree;

(giving the paper to Titus)

Nè vi manca, o signor, che il nome augusto.	Only your royal name, lord, is lacking.

TITUS

Onnipotenti dèi!	All powerful gods!

(He throws himself into a chair.)

ANNIUS

Ah! pietoso monarca . . .	Ah! merciful monarch . . .

(kneeling)

TITUS

Annio, per ora		Annius, leave me
Lasciami in pace.	In peace for now.	

(Annius rises.)

PUBLIUS

Alla gran pompa unite		You know that by now
Sai che le genti ormai . . .	The people are gathered at the solemnities . . .	

TITUS

Lo so. Partite.	I know. Leave.

(Publius withdraws.)

ANNIUS

Deh, perdona, s'io parlo in favor d'un insano.	Pardon if I speak in a madman's favor.
Della mia cara sposa egli è germano.	He is the brother of my dear bride.

No. 17 Aria

ANNIUS

Tu fosti tradito:	You were betrayed:
Ei degno è di morte,	He is worthy of death,
Ma il core di Tito	Yet the heart of Titus
Pur lascia sperar.	Still allows for hope.

Deh prendi consiglio,	Take counsel,
Signor, dal tuo core:	Lord, from your heart:
Il nostro dolore	Deign to look
Ti degna mirar.	On our grief.

(*He leaves.*)

Accompanied Recitative

TITUS

Che orror! che tradimento!	What horror! what betrayal!
Che nera infedeltà! Fingersi amico,	What black infidelity! To pretend to be my friend,
Essermi sempre al fianco, ogni momento	Be always at my side, every moment
Esiger dal mio core	Exact proofs of love
Qualche prova d'amore; e starmi intanto	From my heart; and all the while
Preparando la morte! Ed io sospendo	Be preparing my death! And yet I
Ancor la pena? e la sentenza ancora	Am to withhold punishment? and yet not sign
Non segno? . . . Ah! sì, lo scellerato mora.	The sentence? . . . Ah yes, let the evil man die.

(*He takes up the pen to sign, but then stops.*)

Mora! . . . Ma senza udirlo	Die! . . . Yet send Sextus to death
Mando Sesto a morir? . . . Sì, già l'intese	Without hearing him? . . . Yes, the Senate
Abbastanza il Senato. E s'egli avesse	Heard enough already. But what if he had
Qualche arcano a svelarmi? Olà!	Some secret to reveal to me? Ho!

(*He puts down the pen as a guard appears.*)

(S'ascolti,	(I'll hear him,
E poi vada al supplizio.) A me si guidi	Then let him go to the scaffold.) Bring
Sesto.	Sextus to me.

(*The guard leaves.*)

È pur di chi regna	The fate of a ruler
Infelice il destino!	Is truly unhappy!

(*He rises.*)

A noi si nega	We are denied that
Ciò che a' più bassi è dato. In mezzo al bosco	Which is given to the lowliest. In the depths of the forest
Quel villanel mendico, a ciu circonda	That mendicant peasant, whose rough side

Ruvida lana il rozzo fianco, a cui	Is encircled with coarse wool, whose
È mal fido riparo	Squalid hovel is
Dall'ingiurie del ciel tugurio informe,	An untrustworthy shelter from the injuries of heaven,
Placido i sonni dorme,	Placidly and soundly sleeps,
Pass tranquillo i dì, molto non brama,	Passes the days tranquilly, does not long for much,
Sa chi l'odia e chi l'ama, unito o solo	Knows who hates and who loves him, in company or alone
Torna sicuro alla foresta, al monte,	He returns safely to his forest, to his mountain,
E vede il core a ciascheduno in fronte.	And sees each one's heart mirrored in his face.
Noi fra tante grandezze	We always live uncertainly
Sempre incerti viviam; chè in faccia a noi	Amid such splendor; since in our presence
La speranza o il timore	Hope or fear
Sulla fronte d'ognun trasforma il core.	Transforms the heart on the face.
Chi dall'infido amico ... Olà! ... chi mai	Who from a faithless friend ... Ho! ... whoever
Questo temer dovea?	Had to fear this?

(*Publius enters.*)

TITUS

Ma, Publio, ancora Sesto non viene.	But Publius, Sextus Has still not come.

PUBLIUS

Ad eseguir il cenno Già volaro i custodi.	The guards are already Hurrying to do your bidding.

TITUS

Io non comprendo Un sì lungo tardar.	I don't understand Such a long delay.

PUBLIUS

Pochi momenti Sono scorsi, o signor.	Only a few moments Have passed, lord.

TITUS

Vanne tu stesso; Affrettalo.	Go yourself; Hurry it along.

PUBLIUS

Ubbidisco.	I obey.

La Clemenza di Tito

(*about to go*)

I tuoi littori Veggonsi comparir: Sesto dovrebbe Non molto esser lontano. Eccolo.	Your lictors Can be seen appearing: Sextus should Not be too far off. Here he is.

TITUS

Ingrato!	Ungrateful man!

All'udir che s'appressa,
Già mi parla a suo pro l'affetto antico.
 	
Ma no; trovi il suo prence e non l'amico.
	Yet hearing that he approaches,
	My old affection for him speaks on his
	   behalf.
	But no; let him find his prince and not
	   his friend.

(*He sits and assumes an air of majesty.*)

(*Sextus and guards enter. Sextus, barely in the room, stops.*)

No. 18 Trio

SEXTUS

(Quello di Tito è il volto! Ah! dove, o stelle! è andata La sua dolcezza usata! Or ei mi fa tremar!)	(Such is Titus' face! Ah where, oh stars, has Its accustomed sweetness gone! Now it makes me tremble!)

TITUS

(Eterni dèi! di Sesto Dunque il sembiante è questo! Oh come può un delitto Un volto trasformar!)	(Eternal gods! this then Is Sextus' aspect! Oh how a crime can Transform a face!)

PUBLIUS

(Mille diversi affetti In Tito guerra fanno, S'ei prova un tale affanno, Lo seguita ad amar.)	(A thousand different emotions Are at war within Titus. If he experiences such sorrow He will follow it with love.)

TITUS (*to Sextus*)

Avvicinati!	Come near!

SEXTUS

(Oh voce che piombami sul core.)	(Oh voice that falls heavily on my heart.)

TITUS

Non odi?	Don't you hear?

SEXTUS

(Di sudore
Mi sento, oh Dio! bagnar!)

(Oh God! I feel
Bathed in sweat!)

TITUS

Avvicinati.

Come near.

SEXTUS

(Oh voce!)

(That voice!)

TITUS

Non odi?

Don't you hear?

SEXTUS

(Oh Dio! Non può chi muore di più
penar.)

(Oh God! One who is dying couldn't
suffer more.)

TITUS and PUBLIUS

(Palpita il traditore, nè gli occhi ardisce
alzar.)

(The traitor trembles, nor does he dare
raise his eyes.)

TITUS

(E pur mi fa pietà.) Publio, custodi,

Lasciatemi con lui.

(And yet he stirs my pity.) Publius,
guards,
Leave me with him.

(Publius and the guards leave.)

SEXTUS

(No, di quel volto
Non ho costanza a sostener l'impero.)

(No, I don't have the persistence
To withstand the command of that face.)

TITUS

(Now alone with Sextus, he lays aside his air of majesty.)

Ah! Sesto, dunque è vero?
Dunque vuoi la mia morte! E in che
t'offese
Il tuo prence, il tuo padre,
Il tuo benefattor? Se Tito Augusto

Hai potuto obbliar, di Tito amico

Come non ti sovvenne? Il premio è
questo

Ah, Sextus! then it is true?
Then you wish for my death! And in
what
Did your prince, your father,
Your benefactor offend you? If you have
been able
To forget the Emperor Titus, why did you
not remember
Titus your friend? Is this the reward

Della tenera cura	Of the tender care
Ch'ebbe sempre di te? Di chi fidarmi	I have always taken of you? Who can I trust
In avvenir potrò, se giunse, oh dèi!	In the future, if even Sextus, oh Gods!
Anche Sesto a tradirmi? E lo potesti?	Came to betray me? And were you able to?
E il cor te lo sofferse?	And did your heart allow it?

SEXTUS

(bursting into tears and throwing himself at Titus' feet)

Ah, Tito! ah, mio	Ah, Titus! ah my
Clementissimo prence!	Most clement prince!
Non più, non più. Se tu veder potessi	No more, no more. If you could see
Questo misero cor, spergiuro, ingrato,	Into this unhappy heart, perjured, ungrateful,
Pur ti farei pietà. Tutte ho su gli occhi,	Yet would it stir your pity. I have it all before my eyes,
Tutte le colpe mie; tutti rammento	All my guilt; I remember
I benefizi tuoi: soffrir non posso	All your kindnesses: I cannot bear
Nè l'idea di me stesso,	Either the idea of myself,
Nè la presenza tua. Quel sacro volto,	Or your presence. That sacred face,
La voce tua, la tua clemenza istessa	Your voice, your clemency itself
Diventò mio supplizio. Affretta almeno,	Become my punishment. At least hurry,
Affretta il mio morir. Toglimi presto	Hurry my death. Take from me quickly
Questa vita infedel; lascia ch'io versi,	This faithless life; let me pour out,
Se pietoso esser vuoi,	If you wish to be merciful,
Questo perfido sangue a' piedi tuoi.	This perfidious blood at your feet.

TITUS

Sorgi, infelice!	Rise, unhappy man!

(Sextus rises.)

(Il contenersi è pena	(It is difficult to contain oneself
A quel tenero pianto.) Or vedi a quale	At that tender weeping.) Now see to what
Lagrimevole stato	A pathetic state
Un delitto riduce, una sfrenata	A crime can reduce one, an unchecked
Avidità d'impero! E che sperasti	Greed for empire! And what did you
Di trovar mai nel trono? Il sommo forse	Ever hope for in the throne? The summit, perhaps,
D'ogni contento? Ah! sconsigliato, osserva	Of every contentment? Ah, rash man, look at

Quai frutti io ne raccolgo;
E bramalo, se puoi.

The fruits I gather from it,
And desire it if you can.

SEXTUS

No, questa brama
Non fu che mi sedusse.

No, this was
Not the desire that seduced me.

TITUS

Dunque che fu?

Then what was?

SEXTUS

La debolezza mia,
La mia fatalità.

My weakness,
My destiny.

TITUS

Più chiaro almeno
Spiegati.

Explain yourself
More clearly.

SEXTUS

Oh Dio! non posso.

Oh God! I cannot.

TITUS

Odimi, o Sesto:
Siam soli; il tuo sovrano
Non è presente. Apri il tuo core a Tito,
Confidati all'amico; io ti prometto
Che Augusto nol saprà. Del tuo delitto

Di' la prima cagion. Cerchiamo insieme

Una via di scusarti. Io ne sarei

Forse di te più lieto.

Hear me, Sextus:
We are alone; your sovereign
Is not present. Open your heart to Titus,
Confide in your friend; I promise you
That the Emperor will not know of it.
  Tell me
The prime reason for your crime. Let us
  search together
For a way to pardon you. Perhaps I
  would be
Even happier than you to find it.

SEXTUS

Ah! la mia colpa
Non ha difesa.

Ah! my guilt
Has no defense.

TITUS

In contraccambio almeno
D'amicizia lo chiedo. Io non celai
Alla tua fede i più gelosi arcani;
Merita ben che Sesto
Mi fidi un suo segreto.

At least I ask it
In exchange of friendship. I never hid
From your trust my most jealous secrets;
It well behooves Sextus
To trust me with one of his secrets.

SEXTUS

(Ecco una nuova   (Here is a new
Specie di pena! o dispiacere a Tito,   Kind of punishment! either displease Titus

O Vitellia accusar.)   Or accuse Vitellia.)

TITUS

Dubiti ancora?   You still doubt?

(beginning to be uneasy)

Ma, Sesto, mi ferisci   Sextus, you wound me
Nel più vivo del cor. Vedi che troppo To the bottom of my heart. You see that
Tu l'amicizia oltraggi   With this lack of confidence
Con questo diffidar. Pensaci.   You offend our friendship. Think about it.

(impatiently)

Appaga   Grant
Il mio giusto desio.   My just request.

SEXTUS *(desperately)*

(Ma qual astro splendeva al nascer mio!) (What star blazed at my birth?)

TITUS

E taci? e non rispondi? Ah! già che puoi You are silent? and do not answer? Ah! since you are able

Tanto abusar di mia pietà . . .   To abuse my mercy so much . . .

SEXTUS

Signore . . .   My lord . . .
Sappi dunque . . . (Che fo?)   You must know then . . . (What am I doing?)

TITUS

Siegui.   Continue.

SEXTUS

(Ma quando   (When
Finirò di penar?)   Shall I stop suffering?)

TITUS

Parla una volta: Speak only once:
Che mi volevi dir?   What did you want to tell me?

547

SEXTUS

Ch'io son l'oggetto	That I am the object
Dell'ira degli dèi; che la mia sorte	Of the gods' anger; that I no longer have the strength
Non ho più forza a tollerar; ch'io stesso	To tolerate my fate; that I myself
Traditor mi confesso, empio mi chiamo;	Confess I am a traitor, I call myself evil;
Ch'io merito la morte e ch'io la bramo.	That I am worthy of death and that I desire it.

TITUS (*resuming his air of majesty*)

Sconoscente! e l'avrai!	Thankless man, you shall have it!

(*to the guards who have entered*)

Custodi! il reo Toglietemi dinanzi.	Guards! take The guilty man from my sight.

SEXTUS

Il bacio estremo Su quella invitta man . . .	One last kiss On that invincible hand . . .

TITUS (*not granting it*)

Parti. Non è più tempo; or tuo giudice sono.	Go. There is no more time; I am now your judge.

SEXTUS

Ah, sia questo, Signor, l'ultimo dono.	Ah, Lord, let this be your last gift.

No. 19 Rondo

SEXTUS

Deh, per questo istante solo	Ah, for this moment only
Ti ricorda il primo amor.	Remember our first love.
Che morir mi fa di duolo	Since your scorn, your severity
Il tuo sdegno, il tuo rigor.	Make me die of grief.
Di pietade indegno, è vero,	Unworthy of pity, it is true,
Sol spirar io deggio orror.	I should only inspire horror.
Pur saresti men severo,	Yet you would be less severe
Se vedessi questo cor.	If you could see into my heart.
Disperato vado a morte;	Desperate I go to death;
Ma il morir non mi spaventa.	But dying does not frighten me.
Il pensiero mi tormenta	The thought that I was a traitor
Che fui teco un traditor!	To you torments me.

(Tanto affanno soffre un core,
Nè si more di dolor!)

(A heart can undergo such suffering,
And not die of sorrow!)

(*He leaves with the guards.*)

TITUS

Ove s'intese mai
Più contumace infedeltà!
Deggio alla mia negletta
Disprezzata clemenza una vendetta.

When was there ever heard
Such obstinate faithlessness!
I owe revenge to my
Negligent, despised clemency.

(*He goes scornfully to the table, and stops.*)

Vendetta! Il cor di Tito
Tali sensi produce? Eh! viva . . . In vano

Parlan dunque le leggi? Io lor custode
Le eseguisco così? Di Sesto amico
Non sa Tito scordarsi?

Revenge! Can the heart of Titus
Yield such sentiments? Ah! let him
 live . . . So

Laws speak uselessly? I, their custodian,
Carry them out like this? Is Titus unable
To forget his friend Sextus?

(*sitting*)

Ogni altro affetto
D'amicizia e pietà taccia per ora.

Sesto è reo: Sesto mora! . . .

For now
Let every sentiment of friendship and
 mercy be silent.

Sextus is guilty: let Sextus die! . . .

(*signing the paper*)

Eccoci aspersi
Di cittadino sangue, e s'incomincia
Dal sangue d'un amico. Or che diranno

I posteri di noi? Diran che in Tito

Si stancò la clemenza,
Come in Silla e in Augusto
La crudeltà; che Tito
Era l'offeso, e che le proprie offese,

Senza ingiuria del giusto,
Ben poteva obbliar . . . Ma dunque faccio

Sì gran forza al mio cor? Nè almen sicuro

Behold us sprinkled
With a citizen's blood, and beginning
With the blood of a friend. Now what
 will

Posterity say about us? It will say that
 Titus

Wearied of clemency,
Just as Augustus and Sulla wearied
Of cruelty; that Titus
Was the offended one, and yet he could
 have forgotten,

Without injury to the law,
The offenses against him . . . Then shall I
 do

Such great violence to my heart? Nor
 even be sure

Sarò ch'altri m'approvi? Ah! non si lasci

Il solito cammin.

That others will commend me? Ah, let us not leave

Our usual path.

(tearing up the paper)

Viva l'amico,
Benchè infedele; e, se accusarmi il mondo
Vuol pur di qualche errore,
M'accusi di pietà, non di rigore.

Let our friend live,
Even faithless; and if the world wishes
To accuse me of any mistakes,
Let them accuse me of mercy, not severity.

(He throws the torn-up paper aside.)

Publio!

Publius!

PUBLIUS *(entering)*

Cesare.

Caesar.

TITUS

Andiamo
Al popolo che attende.

Let us go
To the awaiting people.

PUBLIUS

E Sesto?

And Sextus?

TITUS

E Sesto
Venga all'arena ancor.

Let Sextus
Still come to the arena.

PUBLIUS

Dunque il suo fato . . .

Then his fate . . .

TITUS

Sì, Publio, è già deciso.

Yes, Publius, it is already decided.

PUBLIUS

(Oh sventurato!)

(Poor wretch!)

No. 20 Aria

TITUS

Se all'impero, amici dèi,
Necessario è un cor severo,
O togliete a me l'impero,
O a me date un altro cor.

If a severe heart, friendly gods,
Is necessary for the empire,
Either take the empire from me,
Or give me another heart.

La Clemenza di Tito

Se la fè de' regni miei	If I cannot insure the faith
Con l'amor non assicuro,	Of my realms with love,
D'una fede io non mi curo	I will pay no attention to a faith
Che sia frutto del timor.	That is the fruit of terror.

(He leaves.)

VITELLIA

(Coming from an opposite door, she calls back Publius, who had followed Titus.)

VITELLIA

Publio, ascolta.	Publius, listen.

PUBLIUS *(about to leave)*

Perdona;	Pardon me,
Deggio a Cesare appresso	But I must follow
Andar . . .	Caesar closely . . .

VITELLIA

Dove?	Where?

PUBLIUS *(idem)*

All'arena.	To the arena.

VITELLIA

E Sesto?	And Sextus?

PUBLIUS

Anch'esso.	He also.

VITELLIA

Dunque morrà?	Then he is to die?

PUBLIUS

Pur troppo.	Unfortunately.

VITELLIA

(Aimè!) Con Tito	(Alas!) Did Sextus
Sesto ha parlato?	Speak with Titus?

PUBLIUS

E lungamente.	At length.

VITELLIA

E sai	Do you know
Quel ch'ei dicesse?	What he said?

PUBLIUS

No. Solo con lui
Restar Cesare volle: escluso io fui.

No. Caesar wished to remain
Alone with him: I was excluded.

(*He leaves.*)

VITELLIA

Non giova lusingarsi;
Sesto già mi scoperse: a Publio istesso

Si conosce sul volto. Ei non fu mai
Con me sì ritenuto; ei fugge; ei teme

Di restar meco. Ah! secondato avessi

Gl'impulsi del mio cor. Per tempo a Tito

Dovea svelarmi e confessar l'errore.

Sempre in bocca d'un reo, che la detesta,

Scema d'orror la colpa. Or questo ancora

Tardi saria. Seppe il delitto Augusto,

E non da me. Questa ragione istessa
Fa più grave . . .

It is no use deluding myself:
Sextus has already exposed me: I knew it
already
By Publius' own face. He was never
So restrained with me; he shuns me; he is
afraid
To remain with me. Ah! If I had only
followed
The impulses of my heart. For sometime
now I should have
Revealed myself to Titus and confessed
my mistake.
When a crime is confessed and detested
by the guilty one,
The horror of it is lessened. Now even
this
Would be too late. The Emperor knows
my crime,
And not from me. This reason alone
Makes even more serious . . .

(*Annius and Servilia enter from different sides.*)

SERVILIA

Ah, Vitellia!

Ah, Vitellia!

ANNIUS

Ah, principessa!

Ah, princess!

SERVILIA

Il misero germano . . .

My poor brother . . .

ANNIUS

Il caro amico . . .

My dear friend . . .

SERVILIA

È condotto a morir.

Is condemned to death.

ANNIUS

Fra poco, in faccia
Di Roma spettatrice,
Delle fiere sarà pasto infelice.

Soon, in the presence
Of an onlooking Rome,
He will be made a wretched meal for the
wild beasts.

VITELLIA

Ma che posso per lui?

But what can I do for him?

SERVILIA

Tutto. A' tuoi prieghi
Tito lo donerà.

Everything. Titus will
Grant your request.

ANNIUS

Non può negarlo
Alla novella Augusta.

He cannot deny it
To his new Empress.

VITELLIA

Annio, non sono
Augusta ancor.

My friend, I am not
The Empress yet.

ANNIUS

Pria che tramonti il sole
Tito sarà tuo sposo. Or, me presente,

Per le pompe festive il cenno ei diede.

Before the sun goes down
Titus will be your husband. Just now,
while I was there,
He gave the order for the solemn
festivities.

VITELLIA

(Dunque Sesto ha taciuto! Oh amore! oh
fede!)
Annio, Servilia, andiam. (Ma dove corro

Così, senza pensar?) Partite, amici:
Vi seguirò.

(Then Sextus has remained silent! what
love! what faith!)
Annius, Servilia, let us go. (But where am
I running to
So thoughtlessly?) You go, my friends:
I will follow you.

ANNIUS

Ma, se d'un tardo aiuto
Sesto fidar si dee, Sesto è perduto.

But if Sextus has to rely upon
Such tardy help, Sextus is lost.

(*He leaves.*)

SERVILIA

Andiam. Quell'infelice	Let us go. That unhappy man
T'ama più di se stesso; avea fra' labbri	Loves you more than himself; he always had your name
Sempre il tuo nome; impallidia qualora	On his lips; he turned pale whenever
Si parlava di te. Tu piangi!	You were spoken of. You weep!

VITELLIA

Ah! parti.	Ah! go.

SERVILIA

Ma tu perchè restar? Vitellia, ah! parmi ...	But why are you staying here? Vitellia! it seems to me ...

VITELLIA

Oh dèi! parti, verrò: non tormentari!	Oh gods! go, I shall come: do not torment me!

No. 21 Aria

SERVILIA

S'altro che lagrime	If only tears
Per lui non tenti,	You attempt for him,
Tutto il tuo piangere	All of your weeping
Non gioverà.	Will be of little moment.
A questa inutile	To this useless
Pietà che senti,	Pity which you feel,
Oh, quanto è simile	Oh, how similar
La crudeltà!	Is cruelty!

(She leaves.)

No. 22 Accompanied Recitative

VITELLIA

Ecco il punto, o Vitellia,	Now is the time, Vitellia,
D'esaminar la tua costanza. Avrai	To examine your steadfastness. Will you have
Valor che basti a rimirare esangue	The courage to look upon your faithful Sextus
Il tuo Sesto fedel? Sesto, che t'ama	Dead? Sextus, who loves you
Più della vita sua? che per tua colpa	More than his own life? who through your crime
Divenne reo? che t'ubbidì crudele?	Became guilty? who obeyed you even when you were cruel?

Che ingiusta t'adorò?	Who adored you even when you were unfair?
Che in faccia a morte	Who in the presence of death
Sì gran fede ti serba? E tu frattanto,	Keeps such great faith with you? And in the meantime you,
Non ignota a te stessa, andrai tranquilla	Not ignorant of all this, will tranquilly go
Al talamo d'Augusto? Ah! mi vedrei	To the Emperor's nuptial couch? Ah! I would always see
Sempre Sesto d'intorno; e l'aure e i sassi	Sextus before me; and I would be afraid that
Temerei che loquaci	The breezes and stones
Mi scoprissero a Tito. A' piedi suoi	Would reveal me to Titus. Let me go and disclose
Vadasi il tutto a palesar. Si scemi	Everything at his feet. Let me lessen
Il delitto di Sesto,	Sextus' crime
Se scusar non si può col fallo mio.	With my guilt, even if I can't excuse it.
D'impero e d'imenei, speranze, addio.	Farewell, hopes of empire and marriage.

No. 23 Rondo

VITELLIA

Non più di fiori	No more will Hymen
Vaghe catene	Descend to weave
Discenda Imene	Lovely chains
Ad intrecciar.	Of flowers.
Stretta fra barbare	Bound in barbarous
Aspre ritorte	Harsh chains
Veggo la morte	I see death
Ver me avanzar.	Advance toward me.
Infelice! qual orrore!	Unhappy woman! what horror!
Ah, di me che si dirà?	Ah, what will be said of me?
Chi vedesse il mio dolore,	Yet whoever could see my suffering
Pur avria di me pietà.	Would take pity on me.

(She leaves.)

SCENE III

A magnificent entrance to a spacious amphitheater, the inside of which can be seen through various arches. The members of the conspiracy, condemned to the wild beasts, can be seen in the arena already.

(During the singing of the chorus Titus enters, preceded by lictors, surrounded by Roman senators and patricians, and followed by the Praetorian Guard; later Annius and Servilia from different sides.)

No. 24 Chorus

Che del Ciel, che degli dèi	That you have the attention,
Tu il pensier, l'amor tu sei,	The love of Heaven,
Grand'eroe, nel giro angusto	Great hero, has been shown
Si mostrò di questo dì.	In the brief duration of this single day.
Ma cagion di meraviglia	But there is indeed no reason
Non è già, felice Augusto,	To marvel, happy Emperor,
Che gli dèi chi lor somiglia	Since the gods in this manner
Custodiscano così.	Look after those who resemble them.

TITUS

Pria che principio a' lieti	Before the signal for the festive
Spettacoli si dia, custodi, innanzi	Entertainment is given, guards, lead
Conducetemi il reo. (Più di perdono	The guilty man before me. (He has no more
Speme non ha: quanto aspettato meno,	Hope of pardon: the less looked for,
Più caro esser gli dee.)	The more welcome will it be to him.)

ANNIUS

Pietà, signore!	Mercy, lord!

SERVILIA

Signor, pietà!	My lord, have mercy!

TITUS

Se a chiederla venite	If you come to sue
Per Sesto, è tardi. È il suo destin deciso.	For Sextus, it is too late. His fate has been decided.

ANNIUS

E sì tranquillo in viso	And with such a tranquil mien
Lo condanni a morir?	You can condemn him to death?

SERVILIA

Di Tito il core	How can
Come il dolce perdè costume antico?	Titus' heart lose its former generous habit?

TITUS

Ei s'appressa: tacete!	He is approaching: be silent!

SERVILIA

Oh Sesto!	Sextus!

La Clemenza di Tito

ANNIUS

Oh amico!   My friend!

(Enter Publius, Sextus guarded by lictors, then Vitellia.)

TITUS

Sesto, de' tuoi delitti	Sextus, you know the extent
Tu sai la serie, e sai	Of your crimes, and you know what punishment
Qual pena ti si dee. Roma sconvolta,	Must be exacted from you. Rome in confusion,
L'offesa maestà, le leggi offese,	Offended majesty, offended laws,
L'amicizia tradita, il mondo, il Cielo	Betrayed friendship, the world and Heaven:
Voglion la morte tua. De' tradimenti	All demand your death. You know further
Sai pur ch'io son l'unico oggetto. Or senti.	That I was the one object of your betrayal. Now listen.

VITELLIA

Eccoti, eccelso Augusto.   Here, exalted Emperor.

(She kneels.)

Eccoti al piè la più confusa . . .   Here at your feet the most ashamed . . .

TITUS

               Ah! sorgi: Ah, rise!

Che fai? che brami?   What are you doing? what do you wish?

VITELLIA

            Io ti conduco innanzi   I lead before you

L'autor dell'empia trama.   The perpetrator of the evil plot.

TITUS

            Ov'è? chi mai   Where is he? whoever

Preparò tante insidie al viver mio?   Laid so many snares for my life?

VITELLIA

Nol crederai.   You will not believe it.

TITUS

          Perchè?   Why?

VITELLIA

        Perchè son io.   Because it is I.

TITUS

Tu ancora!   Even you!

SEXTUS and SERVILIA

Oh stelle!   Oh stars!

ANNIUS and PUBLIUS

Oh numi!   Oh gods!

TITUS

E quanti mai,   How many,
Quanti siete a tradirmi?   How many are there to betray me?

VITELLIA

Io la più rea   I am the guiltiest
Son di ciascuno; io meditai la trama;   Of all; I designed the plot;
Il più fedele amico   I seduced
Io ti sedussi; io del suo cieco amore   Your most faithful friend; I took
                                                   advantage
A tuo danno abusai.   Of his blind love to harm you.

TITUS

Ma del tuo sdegno   But what was the reason
Chi fu cagion?   For your scorn?

VITELLIA

La tua bontà. Credei   Your goodness, I mistook it
Che questa fosse amor. La destra e il   For love. Your hand and your throne
  trono
Da te speravo in dono; e poi negletta   I hoped for as a gift; and then I was
Restai due volte, e procurai vendetta.   Passed over twice, and sought revenge.

No. 25 Accompanied Recitative

TITUS

Ma che giorno è mai questo! Al punto   But what a day this is! In the very
  istesso   moment in which
Che assolvo un reo, ne scopro un altro! I pardon one guilty person, I discover
                                             another!

E quando   And when,
Troverò, giusti numi!   Just gods! shall I find
Un'anima fedel? Congiuran gli astri,   A faithful soul? The stars are conspiring,
Cred'io, per obbligarmi, a mio dispetto, I believe, to obligate me, against my
                                             wishes,

A diventar crudel. No! non avranno	To become cruel. No! They will not have
Questo trionfo. A sostener la gara	This victory. My virtue has already pledged itself
Già s'impegnò la mia virtù. Vediamo	To continue the struggle. Let us see
Se più costante sia	Whether the treachery of others or my clemency
L'altrui perfidia o la clemenza mia.	Be the more constant.
Olà! Sesto si sciolga: abbian di nuovo	Ho! Free Sextus; let Lentulus
Lentulo e i suoi seguaci	And his accomplices have again both
E vita e libertà. Sia noto a Roma	Life and liberty. Let it be known in Rome
Ch'io son l'istesso, e ch'io	That I am still the same, that I
Tutto so, tutti assolvo e tutto obblio.	Know all, pardon everyone and forget everything.

No. 26 Sextet and Chorus

SEXTUS

Tu, è ver, m'assolvi, Augusto:	Emperor, it is true that you pardon me:
Ma non m'assolve il core,	But my heart does not pardon me;
Che piangerà l'errore,	It will bewail my mistake
Fin che memoria avrà.	As long as it can remember.

TITUS

Il vero pentimento,	True repentance,
Di cui tu sei capace,	Of which you are capable,
Val più d'una verace	Is worth more than true
Costante fedeltà.	Constant fidelity.

VITELLIA, SERVILIA and ANNIUS

Oh generoso! oh grande!	Generous one! great one!
E chi mai giunse a tanto?	Who has ever attained so much?
Mi trae dagli occhi il pianto	His lofty goodness
L'eccelsa sua bontà.	Draws tears from my eyes.

ALL (*less Titus*)

Eterni dèi, vegliate	Eternal Gods, watch over
Sui sacri giorni suoi,	His sacred life,
A Roma in lui serbate	In him preserve
La sua felicità.	Rome's happiness.

TITUS

Troncate, eterni dèi,	Cut short, eternal Gods,
Troncate i giorni miei,	Cut short my life,
Quel dì che il ben di Roma	On that day in which
Mia cura non sarà.	The good of Rome shall not be my care.

The End

DIE ZAUBERFLÖTE

WORLD PREMIERE: *Vienna, Theater auf der Wieden, September 30, 1791*

UNITED STATES PREMIERE: *New York, Park Theatre, April 17, 1833*

METROPOLITAN OPERA PREMIERE: *March 30, 1900*

DIE ZAUBERFLÖTE
(THE MAGIC FLUTE)

Opera in Two Acts

Libretto: Emanuel Schikaneder

English Translation: Susan Webb

Music: Wolfgang Amadeus Mozart

DIE ZAUBERFLÖTE

CHARACTERS

SARASTRO	Bass
TAMINO	Tenor
SPEAKER	Bass
FIRST PRIEST	Bass*
SECOND PRIEST	Tenor
THIRD PRIEST	Speaking Part
QUEEN OF THE NIGHT	Soprano
PAMINA, *her daughter*	Soprano
FIRST LADY	Soprano
SECOND LADY	Soprano
THIRD LADY	Soprano
FIRST BOY	Soprano
SECOND BOY	Soprano
THIRD BOY	Soprano
PAPAGENO	Bass
AN OLD WOMAN (PAPAGENA)	Soprano
MONOSTATOS, *a Moor*	Tenor
FIRST ARMORED MAN	Tenor
SECOND ARMORED MAN	Bass
FIRST SLAVE	Speaking Part
SECOND SLAVE	Speaking Part
THIRD SLAVE	Speaking Part

PRIESTS, SLAVES AND FOLLOWERS

The action takes place in an eastern country, in legendary times.

* See Notes on the Translation

In memoriam
Max Epstein
1951–1990

ACKNOWLEDGMENTS

New York Public Library for the Performing Arts at Lincoln Center, Dr. Irene Spiegelman, Walter Taussig.

Cosí Fan Tutte

TOP: *Joseph Urban set for the 1922 production (Metropolitan Opera Archives)*

LEFT: *Florence Easton as Fiordiligi in the 1922 production (Robert Tuggle Collection)*

BOTTOM RIGHT: *Lucrezia Bori as Despina (dressed as the doctor) in the 1922 production (Robert Tuggle Collection)*

COSÍ FAN TUTTE

TOP: *Eleanor Steber as Fiordiligi,*
Blanche Thebom as Dorabella, and
Patrice Munsel as Despina in the 1951
production, designed by Rolf Gérard
(Opera News)

CENTER: *Richard Tucker as Ferrando*
and Leontyne Price as Fiordiligi (Frank
Dunand/Metropolitan Opera Guild
Education Department)

BOTTOM: *Kiri Te Kanawa as Fiordiligi,*
Maria Ewing as Dorabella, and Kathleen
Battle as Despina in the 1982
production, designed by Hayden Griffen
(© Beth Bergman 1991)

LA CLEMENZA DI TITO

TOP: *Renata Scotto as Vitellia and Tatiana Troyanos as Sesto in the 1985 production, designed by Jean-Pierre Ponnelle (© Beth Bergman 1991)*

BOTTOM: *Renata Scotto and Tatiana Troyanos (© Beth Bergman 1991)*

LA CLEMENZA DI TITO

TOP: *John Cheek as Publio and Kenneth Riegel as Tito* (© *Beth Bergman 1991*)

BOTTOM: *Tatiana Troyanos and Kenneth Riegel* (© *Beth Bergman 1991*)

DIE ZAUBERFLÖTE

ABOVE: *Frieda Hempel as the Queen of the Night (Opera News)*

RIGHT: *Emmy Destinn as Pamina, Edward Lankow as Sarastro, and Leo Slezak as Tamino in the 1912 production, designed by Hans Kautsky (Metropolitan Opera Archives)*

BOTTOM: *Hans Kautsky set for the 1912 production (Opera News)*

DIE ZAUBERFLÖTE

TOP: *Jerome Hines as Sarastro in the 1956 production, designed by Harry Horner (Opera News)*

BOTTOM: *Edda Moser as the Queen of the Night in the 1967 production, designed by Marc Chagall (E. Fred Sher/Opera News)*

DIE ZAUBERFLÖTE

TOP: *David Rendall as Tamino* (© *Beth Bergman 1991*)

BOTTOM: *Patricia Welting as Papagena and Theodor Uppman as Papageno* (*Gary Renaud/Opera News*)

DIE ZAUBERFLÖTE

TOP: *Nicolai Gedda as Tamino,
Hermann Prey as Papageno, Jerome
Hines as Sarastro, Paul Franke as
Monostatos, and Pilar Lorengar as
Pamina (Opera News)*

BOTTOM: *Francisco Araiza as Tamino
and the three boys, Ted Huffman,
Benjamin Schott and Per-Christian
Brevig in the 1991 production, designed
by David Hockney (© Beth Bergman
1991)*

DIE ZAUBERFLÖTE

SYNOPSIS

ACT I

Three Ladies, attendants of the Queen of the Night, save the fainting Prince Tamino from a huge serpent. After they have killed the beast ("Triumph! Triumph!"), the Ladies linger to admire the unconscious youth. Deciding to leave together rather than allowing any one of them the treat of staying to protect him, they exit to inform the Queen of his arrival. The birdcatcher Papageno bounces in and introduces himself, pining for a pretty wife ("Der Vogelfänger bin ich ja"), then boasts to Tamino that he himself slew the monster. The Ladies return to give Tamino a portrait of the Queen's daughter Pamina, who they say is enslaved by the evil Sarastro, and they padlock Papageno's mouth for lying. Tamino falls in love at first sight ("Dies Bildniß"). The Queen appears in a burst of thunder and, lamenting the loss of her daughter ("Zum Leiden bin ich auserkoren"), charges Tamino with Pamina's rescue. Papageno is delighted when the Three Ladies unclasp his mouth but not so pleased when they order him to accompany Tamino on his dangerous mission. The Ladies hand a magic flute to Tamino and magic silver bells to Papageno to ensure their safety, appointing Three Boys to guide them on their way (quintet: "Hm hm hm hm hm").

Sarastro's Moorish slave Monostatos pursues and catches Pamina but is frightened away by the outlandish, feather-covered Papageno, who tells Pamina that Tamino loves her and intends to save her. The two join voices in praise of love ("Bei Männern").

Led by the Boys to the Temple of Sarastro, Tamino tries three gates before a High Priest appears and advises him that it is the Queen, not Sarastro, who is evil. When voices within proclaim Pamina safe, Tamino charms the animals with his flute, then runs off in search of her. No sooner is he gone than Pamina and Papageno rush in, chased by Monostatos and his retainers, who are rendered helpless by Papageno's magic bells. Sarastro, entering in ceremony, promises Pamina eventual freedom but warns against her proud mother. When Monostatos enters with the captured Tamino, he is punished rather than rewarded by Sarastro, who upbraids him for tormenting Pamina. The latter is enchanted by a glimpse of Tamino, who is led into the temple with Papageno.

ACT II

The priests file in to hear Sarastro announce Tamino's candidacy for initiation; he prays that the gods may bless the youth ("O Isis und Osiris"). Warned of the trials ahead and sworn to silence, Tamino is impervious to the temptations of the Three Ladies, who have no trouble derailing the cheerful Papageno from his course of virtue (quintet: "Wie? Wie? Wie?").

Monostatos, finding Pamina asleep in the temple garden, tries to steal a kiss ("Alles fühlt der Liebe Freuden") but is frightened by the arrival of the wrathful Queen of the Night, who gives her daughter a dagger with which to murder Sarastro ("Der Hölle Rache"). Monostatos returns when the Queen vanishes, but Pamina is rescued by Sarastro, who consoles her ("In diesen heil'gen Hallen").

The gourmand Papageno is quick to break a new oath of fasting, and he jokes with an old lady who vanishes when asked her name. The Boys reassure the two initiates and bring them food, but Tamino maintains his vow, breaking Pamina's heart: she cannot understand his silence ("Ach, ich fühl's"). When she leaves, the prince drags off gluttonous Papageno.

The priests laud Tamino's virtue and inform him that he has only two more trials to complete his initiation. Pamina is relieved when Tamino speaks to her but upset when she hears of his further ordeals; Sarastro says the lovers will meet again and separates them ("Soll ich dich Teurer! nicht mehr seh'n?").

Papageno is eliminated from further trials, still wishing for a pretty girl ("Ein Mädchen oder Weibchen"), but he settles for the old lady, who turns into Papagena when the resigned Papageno promises to be faithful. However, a priest tells the birdman he is still not worthy of a wife.

Pamina, on the verge of suicide, is saved by the Boys and led to Tamino. Later, at the caverns of fire and water, two armored Guards proclaim that Tamino must pass the test of the elements (chorale: "Der welcher wandert"). Pamina walks with him through fire and water, protected by the magic flute.

Papageno is also saved from attempted suicide (by hanging) by the Boys, who remind him to use his magic bellls, which summon Papagena. The two plan for the future.

The Queen of the Night, her Three Ladies and Monostatos intend to attack the temple but are repulsed as the throng hails Sarastro, Pamina and Tamino.

OPERA NEWS

PREFACE

During a visit to Vienna in the summer of 1985, I went several times to the Museum der Stadt Wien (Museum of the City of Vienna). Among the Biedermeier furniture and the captured Turkish battle flags from the siege of 1683 is an anonymous oil painting of a long windowless hall filled with groups of men in eighteenth-century dress. The viewer sees the room as if it were a stage set, in perspective, the walls lined with benches receding toward a raised platform at the back; on this dais are three men, one with a raised gavel, one reading a scroll, one addressing the assembly. In the center is a group greeting a man with bandaged eyes. The wall benches are occupied by men holding ceremonial swords, in attitudes of waiting, or in conversation with each other. Suddenly the viewer looks closer: surely that slim figure with head inclined and eyes rolled toward the man next to him is familiar . . . It looks like Mozart!

Reading the painting's inscription dispels any doubt: depicted so remarkably is a meeting, traditionally secret, of a Viennese Masonic lodge. According to H.C. Robbins Landon, who has devoted his book *Mozart and the Masons* to unravelling the secrets of the painting, it is the "Neugekrönte Hoffnung" (Newly Crowned Hope) Lodge, one of the three which was left in Vienna after royal displeasure forced the original eight to consolidate their memberships late in 1785; the lodge "Zur Wohltätigkeit" (Beneficence) into which Mozart was initiated on December 14, 1784, was its sub-lodge.

Wolfgang's father Leopold, Ignaz Alberti (publisher of the original text of *Die Zauberflöte*), Ignaz von Born (probably the model for Sarastro) and Emanuel Schikaneder (librettist of *Die Zauberflöte*) were all Masons in Viennese lodges, Schikaneder a rather Papagenoesque member who, according to Paul Nettl in *Mozart and Masonry*, was reprimanded for bringing scandal upon his lodge, and banished from meetings for six months! Among the three major authors of books on the subject—the third is Jacques Chailley, writer of *The Magic Flute: A Masonic Opera*—there is agreement that Mozart embraced Freemasonry (he attained the Third Degree), found it to be of great comfort in his own life, and a healing factor in his sometimes difficult relationship with his father.

In the eighteenth century, Freemasons were considered suspect by political and religious authorities—they concerned themselves with the rights of the individual and freedom of expression. But even for supposedly enlightened humanists, there are areas of shadow: they apparently didn't see the contradiction in excluding women and slaves from their list of individuals whose rights were to be upheld. In the libretto of *Die Zauberflöte*, remarks which we might consider sexist or racist are put into the mouth of the assembly's noble leader, Sarastro. However, this High Priest of the order, whose name probably derives from Zoroaster, a Persian god whose adherents thought him to be the embodiment of light, also sings the "credo" of Freemasonry: "In Diesen Heil'gen Hallen."

Throughout the libretto, references to masonry, walls, temples and foundations can be taken to have double meanings. The number three certainly has Masonic significance. The *Zauberflöte* libretto abounds in trinities: three ladies bearing three spears cutting a serpent into three pieces (!), three boys (appearing in Alberti's cast list for the 1791 premiere as *Drey Genien*, in the sense of "sprites" or "spirits of the place"), three priests, three slaves. Three sets of chords in that most Masonic key—E flat, with three flats in the signature—begin the opera's overture, and are interspersed throughout, usually for ritual purposes. (Harmonic relationships which have Masonic possibilities are thoroughly explored by Jacques Chailley.)

Bandaged eyes, ritual handshakes, trials by water and fire—all are part of Masonic initiation proceedings.

The balance to this noble and spiritual side of the work is provided by Emanuel Schikaneder's imperishable creation, Papageno, who has endeared himself to countless opera-goers by providing a more down-to-earth perspective on all these trials and tests and things. How we love a character who can say, "Actually, I don't need much wisdom," and "If the gods already intend Papagena for me, why do I have to go through all this trouble to win her?" (Schikaneder was as "many-colored" as his feathered friend: violinist, singer, actor and manager of his own theater company, whose home was the Theater an der Wien.)

Though the serious and comic elements of *Die Zauberflöte* are less subtly handled and more polarized than in Mozart's previous operas, their fantastic, larger-than-life qualities have captured our imaginations.

NOTES ON THE TRANSLATION

This is a translation from a facsimile-reproduction of Ignaz Alberti's original 1791 text published by the Wiener Bibliophilengesellschaft in 1942, edited by Michael Maria Rabenlechner. The text has been put into modern type, and some spellings and word combinations have been modernized to concur with the more recent Bärenreiter edition.

The Met currently uses the Schirmer edition, which in a few instances differs from both of the above. In addition, the Met normally cuts much of the spoken dialogue, as do other theaters in English-speaking countries. The dialogue here, however, is presented complete.

The confusion about who sang or spoke the priests' text began early in the opera's history. At the premiere, Schikaneder's elder brother Urban, an actor, performed the role of the First Priest; Mr. Kistler, a tenor, was listed as Second Priest, Mr. Moll, a bass, as Third Priest and Mr. Winter, the stage manager, was listed as the Speaker! In the Met's current production, the Speaker who converses with Tamino in the First Act Finale is a principal singer; in the Second Act the First and Second Priests, bass and tenor, who sing the Duet (#11) and provide guidance for Tamino and Papageno are supporting singers, but they also speak the lines of text assigned to the Speaker and the Second Priest.

DIE ZAUBERFLÖTE

ACT ONE

SCENE I

The stage set shows a rocky landscape overgrown here and there with trees; on both sides are mountains, which can be walked on; there is also a circular temple.

(Tamino comes in from the right, down from a rock, dressed in a splendid Javanese hunting outfit, armed with a bow but without arrows; A serpent pursues him.)

No. 1 Introduction

TAMINO

Zu Hülfe! Zu Hülfe! sonst bin ich verloren,	Help! Help! Or else I am lost,
Der listigen Schlange zum Opfer erkoren.	Intended as a sacrifice to the cunning serpent.
Barmherzige Götter! Schon nahet sie sich!	Merciful gods! It is already coming nearer!
Ach rettet mich! Ach schützet mich!	Oh rescue me! Oh protect me!

(He loses consciousness; immediately the door of the temple is opened and three veiled ladies come out, each with a silver javelin.)

THE THREE LADIES

Stirb, Ungeheu'r, durch unsre Macht!	Die, monster, by our might!
Triumph! Triumph! Sie ist vollbracht,	Triumph! Triumph! The heroic deed
Die Heldentat. Er ist befreit	Has been carried out. He has been delivered
Durch unsres Armes Tapferkeit.	By our valor.

FIRST LADY *(inspecting him)*

Ein holder Jüngling, sanft und schön.	A sweet youth, gentle and handsome.

SECOND LADY

So schön, als ich noch nie gesehn.

I've never seen anyone so handsome.

THIRD LADY

Ja, ja, gewiß zum Malen schön.

Yes, yes, certainly, handsome enough to be painted.

ALL THREE

Würd' ich mein Herz der Liebe weih'n,
So müßt' es dieser Jüngling sein.
Laßt uns zu unsrer Fürstin eilen,
Ihr diese Nachricht zu erteilen.
Vielleicht, daß dieser schöne Mann
Die vor'ge Ruh' ihr geben kann.

Were I to dedicate my heart to love
It would be for this youth.
Let us hurry to our sovereign
To give her this news.
Perhaps this handsome man
Can give her back her former peace of mind.

FIRST LADY

So geht und sagt es ihr!
Ich bleib' indessen hier.

You two go and tell her!
I'll stay here meanwhile.

SECOND LADY

Nein, nein, geht ihr nur hin,
Ich wache hier für ihn!

No, no, you just go along;
I'll watch over him here.

THIRD LADY

Nein, nein, das kann nicht sein!
Ich schütze ihn allein.

No, no, that cannot be!
I alone will protect him.

FIRST LADY

Ich bleib' indessen hier!

I'll stay here meanwhile!

SECOND LADY

Ich wache hier für ihn!

I'll watch over him here!

THIRD LADY

Ich schütze ihn allein!

I alone will protect him!

FIRST LADY

Ich bleibe!

I'll stay!

SECOND LADY

Ich wache!

I'll watch!

THIRD LADY

Ich schütze!

I'll protect!

ALL THREE

Ich! Ich! Ich!

I! I! I!

(each to herself)

Ich sollte fort? Ei, ei, wie fein!	I am to go away? Well, well, how splendid!
Sie wären gern bei ihm allein.	They would happily be alone with him.
Nein, nein! Das kann nicht sein.	No, no! That cannot be.
Was wollte ich darum nicht geben,	What would I not give,
Könnt' ich mit diesem Jüngling leben!	If I could live with this youth!
Hätt' ich ihn doch so ganz allein!	If only I had him completely alone!
Doch keine geht; es kann nicht sein.	But no one is leaving; it cannot be.
Am besten ist es nun, ich geh'.	It would be best if I were to go now.
Du, Jüngling, schön und liebevoll!	You, handsome and loving youth!
Du trauter Jüngling, lebe wohl,	You dear youth, farewell,
Bis ich dich wieder seh.	Until I see you again.

(All three leave through the temple door, which opens and closes by itself.)

Spoken monologue

TAMINO *(awakens, looking fearfully around)*

Wo bin ich? Ist's Phantasie, daß ich noch lebe? Oder hat eine höhere Macht mich gerettet?	Where am I? Is it my imagination that I am still alive? Or has a higher power rescued me?

(stands up, looks around)

Wie?—Die bösartige Schlange liegt tot zu meinen Füßen?—	What? The vicious serpent is lying dead at my feet?

(In the distance, panpipes are heard, which are lightly accompanied by the orchestra. Tamino speaks over the introduction.)

Was hör' ich? Wo bin ich? Welch' unbekannter Ort?—Ha, eine männliche Figur nähert sich dem Tal.	What do I hear? Where am I? In what unfamiliar place? Ah, some sort of man is approaching the valley.

(Hides behind a tree)

SCENE II

(Papageno comes down the footpath, on his back a large birdcage, which reaches high above his head, in which there are different kinds of birds; in addition, he holds panpipes with both hands; pipes and sings.)

No. 2 Aria

PAPAGENO

Der Vogelfänger bin ich ja,	I am the birdcatcher,
Stets lustig, heisa, hopsassa!	Always merry, tra, la, la!
Ich Vogelfänger bin bekannt	I the birdcatcher am well-known
Bei Alt und Jung im ganzen Land.	By old and young throughout the countryside.
Weiß mit dem Locken umzugehn	I know how to deal with nets and snares
Und mich aufs Pfeifen zu verstehn.	And how to make myself understood by piping.
Drum kann ich froh und lustig sein,	Thus I can be cheerful and merry
Denn alle Vögel sind ja mein.	Since all the birds are surely mine.

(*pipes*)

Ein Netz für Mädchen möchte ich,	A net for maidens would I like,
Ich fing' sie dutzendweis für mich,	I would catch them by the dozen for myself.
Dann sperrte ich sie bei mir ein,	Then I would lock them up at home,
Und alle Mädchen wären mein.	And all the maidens would be mine.

(*pipes*)

Wenn alle Mädchen wären mein,	If all the maidens were mine*
So tauschte ich brav Zucker ein,	Then I would barter for sugar,
Die, welche mir am liebsten wär',	She, who was dearest to me,
Der gäb' ich gleich den Zucker her.	To her would I give all the sugar.
Und küßte sie mich zärtlich dann,	And if she would kiss me sweetly,
Wär' sie mein Weib und ich ihr Mann.	Then she would be my wife, and I her husband.
Sie schlief' an meiner Seite ein,	She would fall asleep at my side,
Ich wiegte wie ein Kind sie ein.	I would rock her like a child.

(*pipes; after the aria, is about to go toward the doors*)

Spoken dialogue

TAMINO (*takes him by the hand*)

Heda!	Hey there!

PAPAGENO

Was da!	What there!

*The third verse of Papageno's aria is neither in the urtext of the libretto nor in the manuscript of the full score.

TAMINO

Sag mir, du lustiger Freund, wer du seist.	Tell me, you merry fellow, who you may be.

PAPAGENO

Wer ich bin?	Who I am?

(*to himself*)

Dumme Frage!	Silly question!

(*aloud*)

Ein Mensch wie du.——Wenn ich dich nun fragte, wer du bist?	A human being like you. What if I asked you who you are?

TAMINO

So würde ich dir antworten, daß ich aus fürstlichem Geblüte bin.	Then I would answer you that I am of princely lineage.

PAPAGENO

Das ist mir zu hoch.——Mußt dich deutlicher erklären, wenn ich dich verstehen soll!	That's beyond me.——You must explain yourself more clearly if I'm to understand you!

TAMINO

Mein Vater ist Fürst, der über viele Länder und Menschen herrscht; darum nennt man mich Prinz.	My father is a sovereign, who rules over many lands and people; that is why they call me prince.

PAPAGENO

Länder?——Menschen?——Prinz?——	Lands?——People?——Prince?——

TAMINO

Daher frag' ich dich——	Therefore I am asking you . . .

PAPAGENO

Langsam! Laß mich fragen.——Sag du mir zuvor: gibt's außer diesen Bergen auch noch Länder und Menschen?	Slowly! Let me do the asking. Tell me first of all: are there more lands and people beyond these mountains?

TAMINO

Viele Tausende!	Many thousands!

PAPAGENO

Da ließ sich eine Spekulation mit meinen Vögeln machen.	So then maybe a deal could be made for my birds.

TAMINO

Nun sag du mir, in welcher Gegend wir
sind.

Now you tell me what sort of country we
are in.

PAPAGENO

In welcher Gegend?

In what sort of country?

(looks around)

Zwischen Tälern und Bergen.

Between valleys and mountains.

TAMINO

Schon recht! aber wie nennt man
eigentlich diese Gegend?—Wer
beherrscht sie?—

Absolutely right! But what exactly is this
country called? Who rules it?

PAPAGENO

Das kann ich dir ebensowenig
beantworten, als ich weiß, wie ich auf die
Welt gekommen bin.

I know the answer to that as little as I
know how I came into the world.

TAMINO *(laughs)*

Wie? Du wüßtest nicht, wo du geboren,
oder wer deine Eltern waren?

What? You don't know where you were
born or who your parents were?

PAPAGENO

Kein Wort!—Ich weiß nicht mehr und
nicht weniger, als daß mich ein alter, aber
sehr lustiger Mann auferzogen und
ernährt hat.

Not a clue! I know that an old, very
cheerful man bred me and fed me—no
more and no less.

TAMINO

Das war vermutlich dein Vater?

Presumably that was your father?

PAPAGENO

Das weiß ich nicht.

I don't know.

TAMINO

Hattest du denn deine Mutter nicht
gekannt?

Have you never known your mother?

PAPAGENO

Gekannt hab'ich sie nicht; erzählen ließ
ich mir's einige Mal, daß meine Mutter
einst da in diesem verschlossenen

I didn't know her. It was explained to me
several times that my mother once served
the star-blazing Queen of the Night in

Gebäude bei der nächtlich
sternflammenden Königin gedient hätte.
Ob sie noch lebt oder was aus ihr
geworden ist, weiß ich nicht.—Ich weiß
nur so viel, daß nicht weit von hier meine
Strohhütte steht, die mich vor Regen und
Kälte schützt.

this locked building. I don't know
whether she still lives or what has
become of her. I only know this much:
that not far from here stands my straw
hut, which protects me from rain and
cold.

TAMINO

Aber wie lebst du?

But how do you live?

PAPAGENO

Von Essen und Trinken, wie alle
Menschen.

On food and drink, like all human beings.

TAMINO

Wodurch erhältst du das?

How do you come by that?

PAPAGENO

Durch Tausch.—Ich fange für die
sternflammende Königin und ihre
Jungfrauen verschiedene Vögel; dafür
erhalt' ich täglich Speis' und Trank von
ihr.

Through barter. I catch different kinds of
birds for the star-blazing queen and her
maidens; for that every day I receive food
and drink from her.

TAMINO (*to himself*)

Sternflammende Königin? Wenn es etwa
gar die mächtige Herrscherin der Nacht
wäre!—

Star-blazing queen? What if that were the
mighty majesty of the night?—

(*aloud*)

Sag mir, gute Freund, warst du schon so
glücklich, diese Göttin der Nacht zu
sehen?

Tell me, good friend! Have you ever been
so fortunate as to see this goddess of the
night?

PAPAGENO

(*who has played his pipes several times until now*)

Deine letzte alberne Frage überzeugt
mich, daß du in einem fremden Lande
geboren bist.

Your last crazy question convinces me
that you were born in a foreign country.

TAMINO

Sei darüber nicht ungehalten, lieber
Freund! Ich dachte nur—

Do not be annoyed by that, dear friend! I
was only thinking . . .

PAPAGENO

Sehen?—Die sternflammende Königin sehen?—Wenn du noch mit einer solchen albernen Frage an mich kommst, so sperr' ich dich, so wahr ich Papageno heiße, wie einen Gimpel in mein Vogelhaus, verhandle dich dann mit meinen übrigen Vögeln an die nächtliche Königin und ihre Jungfrauen; dann mögen sie dich meinetwegen sieden oder braten.

See her? See the star-blazing queen? If you ask me one more crazy question like that, as sure as my name is Papageno, I will shut you up like a bullfinch in my birdhouse, and then trade you with my other birds to the Queen of the Night and her maidens; then they may boil you or roast you, I don't care which.

TAMINO (*to himself*)

Ein wunderlicher Mann!

What a strange man!

PAPAGENO

Sehen? Die sternflammende Königin sehen? Welcher Sterbliche kann sich rühmen, sie je gesehen zu haben?— Welches Menschen Auge würde durch ihren schwarz durchwebten Schleier blicken können?

See? See the star-blazing queen? What mortal can boast of ever having seen her? What human eye would be able to see through her black woven veil?

TAMINO (*to himself*)

Nun ist's klar; es ist eben diese nächtliche Königin, von der mein Vater mir so oft erzählte.—Aber zu fassen, wie ich mich hierher verirrte, ist außer meiner Macht.—Unfehlbar ist auch dieser Mann kein gewöhnlicher Mensch—Vielleicht einer ihrer dienstbaren Geister.

Now it is clear; this is the very same Queen of the Night of whom my father has spoken so often. But to understand how I strayed here is beyond my power. Just as certainly, this man is no ordinary human being—perhaps one of her servants.

PAPAGENO (*to himself*)

Wie er mich so starr anblickt! Bald fang' ich an, mich vor ihm zu fürchten.—

How fixedly he looks at me! Soon I will begin to be frightened of him.

(*to Tamino*)

Warum siehst du so verdächtig und schelmisch nach mir?

Why do you look so suspiciously and so mischievously at me?

TAMINO

Weil—weil ich zweifle, ob du Mensch bist.

Because . . . because I doubt that you are a human being.

PAPAGENO

Wie war das?	What did you say?

TAMINO

Nach deinen Federn, die dich bedecken, halt' ich dich—	By the feathers that cover you, I take you for . . .

(*goes up to him*)

PAPAGENO

Doch für keinen Vogel? Bleib zurück, sag' ich, und traue mir nicht, denn ich habe Riesenkraft, wenn ich jemand packe.	Surely not for a bird? Stay back, I tell you, and don't trust me, because I have a giant's strength if I grab someone.

(*to himself*)

Wenn er sich nicht bald von mir schrecken läßt, so lauf' ich davon.	If he isn't going to be afraid of me soon, I will run away.

TAMINO

Riesenkraft?	A giant's strength?

(*He looks at the serpent.*)

Also warst du wohl gar mein Erretter, der diese giftige Schlange bekämpfte?	So it was you who was my rescuer, who fought against this poisonous serpent?

PAPAGENO

Schlange?	Serpent?

(*looks around him, takes a few steps back, trembling*)

Was da! Ist sie tot oder lebendig?	What's that! Is it dead or alive?

TAMINO

Du willst durch deine bescheidene Frage meinen Dank ablehnen—aber ich muß dir sagen, daß ich ewig für deine so tapfere Handlung dankbar sein werde.	You are trying by your modest question to refuse my thanks—but I must tell you I will be forever grateful to you for such a brave deed.

PAPAGENO

Schweigen wir davon still.—Freuen wir uns, daß sie so glücklich überwunden ist.	Let's not say anything more about it. Let's be glad that fortunately it has been vanquished.

TAMINO

Aber um alles in der Welt, Freund, wie hast du dieses Ungeheuer bekämpft?— Du bist ohne Waffen.	But how in the world, friend, did you fight the monster? You are without weapons.

PAPAGENO

Brauch' keine!—Bei mir ist ein starker Druck mit der Hand mehr als Waffen.

Don't need any! The strength of my hands is better than weapons.

TAMINO

Du hast sie also erdrosselt?

So you strangled it?

PAPAGENO

Erdrosselt!

Strangled it!

(*to himself*)

Bin in meinem Leben nicht so stark gewesen als heute.

In my life I have never been as strong as I am today.

SCENE III

The Three Ladies. The above.

THE THREE LADIES (*calling threateningly*)

Papageno!

Papageno!

PAPAGENO

Aha! das geht mich an.—Sieh dich um, Freund!

Aha! That's for me. Look around, friend!

TAMINO

Wer sind diese Damen?

Who are these ladies?

PAPAGENO

Wer sie eigentlich sind, weiß ich selbst nicht.—Ich weiß nur so viel, daß sie mir täglich meine Vögel abnehmen, und mir dafür Wein, Zuckerbrot und süße Feigen bringen.

Who they actually are, I don't know myself. I know only this much: that daily they collect my birds from me and in exchange they bring me wine, sugar-bread and sweet figs.

TAMINO

Sie sind vermutlich sehr schön?

They are presumably very beautiful?

PAPAGENO

Ich denke nicht.—denn wenn sie schön wären, würden sie ihre Gesichter nicht bedecken.

I don't think so—if they were beautiful, they wouldn't cover their faces.

THE THREE LADIES (*threateningly*)

Papageno!

Papageno!

PAPAGENO

Sei still! Sie drohen mir schon.—Du fragst, ob sie schön sind, und ich kann dir darauf nichts antworten, als daß ich in meinem Leben nichts Reizenderes sah.— Jetzt werden sie bald wieder gut werden.—

Quiet! They are already threatening me as it is. You ask whether they are beautiful, and I can only reply to you that I have never seen anyone more charming in my life. Now they will be friendly again.

THE THREE LADIES (*threateningly*)

Papageno!

Papageno!

PAPAGENO

Was muß ich denn heute verbrochen haben, daß sie gar so aufgebracht wider mich sind?—Hier, meine Schönen, übergeb' ich meine Vögel.

How could I have offended them today, that they are so infuriated with me? Here, my beauties, I am delivering my birds.

FIRST LADY (*hands him a lovely bottle of water*)

Dafür schickt dir unsre Fürstin heute zum ersten mal statt Wein reines, helles Wasser.

For them our sovereign sends you today for the first time, instead of wine, pure, clear water.

SECOND LADY

Und mir befahl sie, daß ich, statt Zuckerbrot, diesen Stein dir überbringen soll. Ich wünsche, daß er dir wohlbekommen möge.

And she ordered me to deliver to you, instead of sugar-bread, this stone. I hope that it will agree with you.

PAPAGENO

Was? Steine soll ich fressen?

What? I am to feed on stones?

THIRD LADY

Und statt der süßen Feigen hab' ich die Ehre, dir dies goldene Schloß vor den Mund zu schlagen.

And instead of sweet figs, I have the honor to place this golden lock on your mouth.

(*She places the lock on him.*)
(*Papageno shows his pain* through mimicry.*)

FIRST LADY

Du willst vermutlich wissen, warum die Fürstin dich heute so wunderbar bestraft?

You probably want to know why the sovereign punishes you today in this unusual way?

---

*The new Mozart edition shows here "Scherz" (joy/fun) instead of "Schmerz" (pain).

(Papageno nods)

SECOND LADY

Damit du künftig nie mehr Fremde belügst.

So that in the future, you will never lie to strangers again.

THIRD LADY

Und daß du nie dich der Heldentaten rühmst, die andre vollzogen.

And so that you will never boast of the heroic deeds performed by others.

FIRST LADY

Sag an! Hast du diese Schlange bekämpft?

Tell us! Did you fight with this serpent?

(Papageno shakes his head)

SECOND LADY

Wer denn also?

So who did then?

(Papageno indicates that he does not know.)

THIRD LADY

Wir waren's, Jüngling, die dich befreiten. Zittre nicht, dich erwartet Freude und Entzücken.—Hier, dies Gemälde schickt dir die große Fürstin, es ist das Bildniß ihrer Tochter—findest du, sagte sie, daß diese Züge dir nicht gleichgültig sind, dann ist Glück, Ehr' und Ruhm dein Los.—Auf Wiedersehen!

Youth, we were the ones who freed you. Do not be afraid; joy and delight await you. Here, the great sovereign sends you this portrait; it is the likeness of her daughter. She says, if you find that you are not indifferent to these features, then good fortune, honor and fame will be your lot. Farewell!

(She leaves.)

SECOND LADY

Adieu, Monsieur Papageno!

Adieu, Monsieur Papageno!

(She leaves.)

FIRST LADY

Fein nicht zu hastig getrunken!

Be sure not to drink too quickly!

(She leaves, laughing.)

(All this time, Papageno has been silently gesticulating. Tamino, after receiving the portrait, has become attentive to it; his loving feelings so increase that throughout all these speeches he appears to be deaf.)

SCENE IV

Tamino, Papageno

No. 3 Aria

TAMINO

Dies Bildniß ist bezaubernd schön,	This likeness is bewitchingly beautiful,
Wie noch keine Auge je geseh'n!	Like none the eye has ever seen!
Ich fühl' es, wie dies Götterbild	I feel it, I feel it, how this divine image
Mein Herz mit neuer Regung füllt.	Fills my heart with new emotion.
Dies Etwas kann ich zwar nicht nennen,	I can scarcely give a name to this something,
Doch fühl' ich's hier wie Feuer brennen.	Yet I feel it here, burning like fire.
Soll die Empfindung Liebe sein?	Could this sensation be love?
Ja, ja, die Liebe ist's allein.—	Yes, yes, it is love alone.
O wenn ich sie nur finden könnte!	Oh, if only I could find her!
O wenn sie doch schon vor mir stände!	Oh, if she already stood before me!
Ich würde—würde—warm und rein—	I would . . . would . . . warmly and purely—
Was würde ich?—ich würde sie voll Entzücken	What would I?—Completely captivated
An diesen heißen Busen drücken,	I would press her to this ardent breast,
Und ewig wäre sie dann mein.	And then she would be forever mine.

(He is about to leave.)

SCENE V

The Three Ladies. The above.

Spoken dialogue

FIRST LADY

Rüste dich mit Mut und Standhaftigkeit, schöner Jüngling! Die Fürstin—	Prepare yourself with courage and steadfastness, handsome youth! The sovereign . . .

SECOND LADY

Hat mir aufgetragen, dir zu sagen—	Has instructed me to tell you . . .

THIRD LADY

Daß der Weg zu deinem künftigen Glücke nunmehr gebahnt sei.	That the way to your future good fortune is now clear.

583

FIRST LADY

Sie hat jedes deiner Worte gehört, so du sprachst; sie hat—

She has heard every word that you have said; she has . . .

SECOND LADY

Jeden Zug in deinem Gesichte gelesen. Ja noch mehr, ihr mütterliches Herz—

Read every feature in your face. Even more, her maternal heart . . .

THIRD LADY

Hat beschlossen, dich ganz glücklich zu machen. Hat dieser Jüngling, sprach sie, auch so viel Mut und Tapferkeit, als er zärtlich ist, so ist meine Tochter ganz gewiß gerettet.

Has decided to make you completely happy. If this youth has, she said, as much courage and valor as he is tender, then my daughter is surely rescued.

TAMINO

Gerettet? O ewige Dunkelheit! Was hör' ich? Das Original—

Rescued? Oh eternal darkness! What do I hear? The model for the portrait . . .

FIRST LADY

Hat ein mächtiger, böser Dämon ihr entrissen.

Has been torn away from her by a powerful, evil demon.

TAMINO

Entrissen? O ihr Götter!—sagt, wie konnte das geschehen?

Torn away? Oh ye gods! Tell me, how could it have happened?

FIRST LADY

Sie saß an einem schönen Maientag ganz allein in dem alles belebenden Zypressenwäldchen, welches immer ihr Lieblingsaufenthalt war. Der Bösewicht schlich unbemerkt hinein—

On a beautiful May day, she sat all alone in the refreshing little cypress wood which was always her favorite place. The villain slipped in unnoticed . . .

SECOND LADY

Belauschte sie und—

Eavesdropped on her, and . . .

THIRD LADY

Er hat nebst seinem bösen Herzen auch noch die Macht, sich in jede erdenkliche Gestalt zu verwandeln; auf solche Weise hat er auch Pamina—

He also has, besides his evil heart, the power to change himself into every imaginable guise; by such means he abducted Pamina . . .

FIRST LADY

Dies ist der Name der königlichen Tochter, so Ihr anbetet.

This is the name of the royal daughter whom you worship.

TAMINO

O Pamina! du mir entrissen—du in der Gewalt eines üppigen Bösewichts! Bist vielleicht in diesem Augenblicke— schrecklicher Gedanke!

Oh Pamina! You torn from me—you in the power of a presumptuous villain! You are perhaps at this very moment— horrible thought!

THE THREE LADIES

Schweig, Jüngling!

Silence, youth!

FIRST LADY

Lästere der holden Schönheit Tugend nicht. Trotz aller Pein, so die Unschuld duldet, ist sie sich immer gleich. Weder Zwang noch Schmeichelei ist vermögend, sie zum Wege des Lasters zu verführen.

Do not slander the virtue of the lovely beauty! Despite all the pain the innocent one has suffered, she remains the same. Neither force nor flattery is able to tempt her down the pathway of vice.

TAMINO

O sagt, Mädchen, sagt! wo ist des Tyrannen Aufenthalt?

Oh tell me, maidens! Tell me, where is the tyrant's dwelling?

SECOND LADY

Sehr nahe an unsern Bergen lebt er in einem angenehmen und reizenden Tal. Seine Burg ist prachtvoll, und sorgsam bewacht.

He lives very near our mountains in a pleasant and lovely valley. His castle is magnificent, and carefully guarded.

TAMINO

Kommt, Mädchen! führt mich! Pamina sei gerettet! Der Bösewicht falle von meinem Arm; das schwör' ich bei meiner Liebe, bei meinem Herzen!

Come, maidens! Lead me there! Let Pamina be rescued! The villain will fall by my arm; I swear it by my love, by my heart!

(Immediately a heavy percussive musical chord is heard.)

Ihr Götter! Was ist das?

Ye gods! What is that?

THE THREE LADIES

Fasse dich!

Compose yourself!

FIRST LADY

Es verkündet die Ankunft unserer Königin.

It proclaims the arrival of our queen.

(thunder)

585

THE THREE LADIES

Sie kommt!	She comes!

(thunder)

Sie kommt!	She comes!

(thunder)

Sie kommt!	She comes!

SCENE VI

The mountains divide, and the stage set is changed into a splendid chamber. The queen is seated upon a throne ornamented with transparent stars.

No. 4 Recitative
and Aria

QUEEN

O zittre nicht, mein lieber Sohn!	Oh do not be afraid, my dear son!
Du bist unschuldig, weise, fromm;	You are innocent, wise, pious;
Ein Jüngling, so wie du, vermag am besten	A youth like you can best comfort
Dies tiefbetrübte Mutterherz zu trösten.	The deeply afflicted heart of a mother.
Zum Leiden bin ich auserkoren;	For suffering am I fated;
Denn meine Tochter fehlet mir,	Because I miss my daughter.
Durch sie ging all mein Glück verloren—	All my happiness was lost with her—
Ein Bösewicht entfloh mit ihr.	A villain fled with her.
Noch seh' ich ihr Zittern	I still see her trembling
Mit bangem Erschüttern,	With anxious emotion,
Ihr ängstliches Beben,	Her nervous shivering,
Ihr schüchternes Streben.	Her timid struggles.
Ich mußte sie mir rauben sehen,	I had to watch her being stolen from me,
Ach helft! war alles, was sie sprach;	"Ah help!" was all that she said;
Allein vergebens war ihr Flehen,	But her pleading was in vain,
Denn meine Hülfe war zu schwach.	Since my means of helping her were too weak.
Du wirst sie zu befreien gehen,	You will go to free her,
Du wirst der Tochter Retter sein!—ja!	You will be my daughter's rescuer! Yes!
Und werd ich dich als Sieger sehen,	And when I behold you the victor,
So sei sie dann auf ewig dein.	Then will she be forever yours.

(leaves with The Three Ladies)

SCENE VII

Tamino. Papageno.
(The stage set is changed back to what it was before.)

Spoken monologue

TAMINO *(after a pause)*

Ist's denn auch Wirklichkeit, was ich sah? oder betäuben mich meine Sinnen? Oh ihr guten Götter, täuscht mich nicht! oder ich unterliege eurer Prüfung.—Schützet meinen Arm, stählt meinen Mut, und Taminos Herz wird ewigen Dank euch entgegenschlagen.

Was it real then, what I saw? Or have my senses been stunned? Oh you good gods, do not deceive me! Or else I will not be able to stand up to your testing. Protect my arm, steel my courage and Tamino's heart will beat for you in eternal gratitude.

(He is about to go. Papageno steps in his way.)

No. 5 Quintet

PAPAGENO

(with the lock on his mouth, gestures sadly at it)

Hm! hm! hm! hm! hm! hm! hm!

Hm! hm! hm! hm! hm! hm! hm!

TAMINO

Der Arme kann von Strafe sagen,

Denn seine Sprache ist dahin.

The poor fellow can really talk about punishment

Because his speech is taken from him.

PAPAGENO

Hm! hm! hm! hm! hm! hm! hm!

Hm! hm! hm! hm! hm! hm! hm!

TAMINO

Ich kann nichts tun, als dich beklagen,
Weil ich zu schwach zu helfen bin.

I can do no more than pity you,
Since I am too weak to help.

PAPAGENO

Hm! hm! hm! hm! hm! hm! hm!

Hm! hm! hm! hm! hm! hm! hm!

SCENE VIII

The Three Ladies. The above.

FIRST LADY

Die Königin begnadigt dich,

The queen pardons you,

(takes the lock away from his mouth)

Erläßt die Strafe dir durch mich.	And remits your punishment through me.

PAPAGENO

Nun plaudert Papageno wieder?	Now can Papageno chatter again?

SECOND LADY

Ja, plaudre!—Lüge nur nicht wieder.	Yes, chatter—just don't lie anymore.

PAPAGENO

Ich lüge nimmermehr! Nein! Nein!	I'll never lie again! No! No!

THE THREE LADIES

Dies Schloß soll deine Warnung sein.	This lock shall be your warning.

PAPAGENO

Dies Schloß soll meine Warnung sein!	This lock shall be my warning!

ALL

Bekämen doch die Lügner alle	If only all liars were given
Ein solches Schloß vor ihren Mund;	Such a lock on their mouths;
Statt Haß, Verleumdung, schwarzer Galle,	Instead of hate, defamation and black bile,
Bestünde Lieb und Bruderbund.	Love and brotherhood would endure.

FIRST LADY

O Prinz, nimm dies Geschenk von mir!	Oh Prince, take this gift from me!
Dies sendet unsre Fürstin dir!	Our sovereign sends it to you!

(gives him a golden flute)

Die Zauberflöte wird dich schützen,	The magic flute will protect you,
Im größten Unglück unterstützen.	In the greatest misfortune, sustain you.

THE THREE LADIES

Hiemit kannst du allmächtig handeln,	With it you can act as if omnipotent,
Der Menschen Leidenschaft verwandeln.	Transform the passions of human beings.
Der Traurige wird freudig sein,	The sad will be joyful,
Den Hagestolz nimmt Liebe ein.	The bachelor will be filled with love.

ALL

O so eine Flöte ist mehr als Gold und Kronen wert,	Oh such a flute is worth more than gold and crowns,
Denn durch sie wird Menschenglück und	Since through it, humanity's happiness and
Zufriedenheit vermehrt.	Contentment will increase.

Die Zauberflöte

PAPAGENO

Nun, ihr schönen Frauenzimmer,	Now you beautiful ladies,
Darf ich—so empfehl ich mich.	May I take my leave?

THE THREE LADIES

Dich empfehlen kannst du immer,	You can always take your leave,
Doch bestimmt die Fürstin dich	However the sovereign has decided
Mit dem Prinzen ohn' Verweilen	That without delay you should hasten
Nach Sarastros Burg zu eilen.	With the prince to Sarastro's castle.

PAPAGENO

Nein, dafür bedank' ich mich!	No, I thank you for that!
Von euch selbsten hörte ich,	I have heard from you yourselves
Daß er wie ein Tigertier	That he is like a tiger.
Sicher ließ ohn' alle Gnaden	Surely Sarastro without mercy
Mich Sarastro rupfen, braten,	Would have me plucked and roasted,
Setzte mich den Hunden für.	He would set me before the dogs.

THE THREE LADIES

Dich schützt der Prinz, trau ihm allein!	The prince will protect you—trust only him!
Dafür sollst du sein Diener sein.	For that reason you are to be his servant.

PAPAGENO (*to himself*)

Daß doch der Prinz beim Teufel wäre!	Let the prince go to the devil!
Mein Leben ist mir lieb;	My life is dear to me;
Am Ende schleicht, bei meiner Ehre,	By my honor, in the end he will creep away
Er von mir wie ein Dieb.	From me like a thief.

FIRST LADY

(*gives him a little wooden box with bells* inside*)

Hier nimm dies Kleinod, es ist dein.	Here take this treasure, it is yours.

PAPAGENO

Ei, ei! Was mag darinnen sein?	Well, well! What could be inside there?

THE THREE LADIES

Darinnen hörst du Glöckchen tönen.	You hear little bells sounding inside.

*The bells are described in Alberti as "eine Maschine wie ein holzernes Gelächter"—a machine like wooden laughter! Pictures of the period show a little, closed box worn at Papageno's hip, and secured by a shoulder strap. Later librettos have "stahlnes Gelächter" or steel laughter, hence Glockenspiel. In the premiere performance, November 30, 1791, a Kapellmeister of the company played the magic bells on a keyboard glockenspiel.

PAPAGENO

| Werd ich sie auch wohl spielen können? | Would I be able to play them? |

THE THREE LADIES

O ganz gewiß! Ja, ja! gewiß!	Oh absolutely! Yes indeed!
Silberglöckchen, Zauberflöten,	Little silver bells, magic flute
Sind zu eurem Schutz vonnöten.	Are necessary for your protection.
Lebet wohl! Wir wollen gehn,	Farewell! We intend to go!
Lebet wohl! Auf Wiedersehn!	Farewell! Until we meet again!

TAMINO and PAPAGENO

Silberglöckchen, Zauberflöten,	Little silver bells, magic flute
Sind zu unserm Schutz vonnöten.	Are necessary for our protection.
Lebet wohl! Wir wollen gehn,	Farewell! We intend to go.
Lebet wohl! Auf Wiedersehn!	Farewell! Until we meet again.

(all are about to leave)

TAMINO

| Doch schöne Damen, saget an! | But, beautiful ladies, tell us! |

PAPAGENO

| Wie man die Burg wohl finden kann? | How one may find the castle? |

BOTH

| Wie man die Burg wohl finden kann? | How one may find the castle? |

THE THREE LADIES

Drei Knäblein, jung, schön, hold und weise,	Three little boys, young, handsome, sweet and wise,
Umschweben euch auf eurer Reise.	Will hover above you on your journey.
Sie werden eure Führer sein,	They will be your guides,
Folgt ihrem Rate ganz allein.	Follow only their advice.

TAMINO and PAPAGENO

| Drei Knäblein, jung, schön, hold und weise, | Three little boys, young, handsome, sweet and wise, |
| Umschweben uns auf unsrer Reise. | Will hover above us on our journey. |

ALL

| So lebet wohl! Wir wollen gehn, | So farewell! We intend to go, |
| Lebt wohl, lebt wohl! Auf Wiedersehn! | Farewell, farewell! Until we meet again! |

(All leave.)

SCENE IX

(As soon as the stage set is changed into a magnificent Egyptian room, two slaves drag out beautiful cushions along with a splendid Turkish table, and spread out rugs; then the third slave appears.)

Spoken dialogue

THIRD SLAVE

Hahaha! Ha, ha, ha!

FIRST SLAVE

Pst, pst! Pst, pst!

SECOND SLAVE

Was soll denn das Lachen?— Why the laughter?

THIRD SLAVE

Unser Peiniger, der alles belauschende Our tormenter, the all-overhearing Moor,
Mohr, wird morgen sicherlich gehangen will surely be hanged or spitted
oder gespießt.—Pamina!—Hahaha! tomorrow—Pamina—ha, ha, ha!

FIRST SLAVE

Nun? Yes?

THIRD SLAVE

Das reizende Mädchen!—Hahaha! The charming maiden! Ha, ha, ha!

SECOND SLAVE

Nun? Yes?

THIRD SLAVE

Ist entsprungen. Has escaped.

FIRST and SECOND SLAVE

Entsprungen?— Escaped?

FIRST SLAVE

Und sie entkam? And she got away?

THIRD SLAVE

Unfehlbar!—Wenigstens ist's mein Without fail! At least it is my sincere
wahrer Wunsch. wish.

FIRST SLAVE

O Dank euch, ihr guten Götter! ihr habt Oh thank you, you good gods! You have
meine Bitte erhört. heard my entreaty.

Third Slave

Sagt ich euch nicht immer, es wird doch ein Tag für uns scheinen, wo wir gerochen und der schwarze Monostatos bestraft werden wird.

Have I not always told you that a day would dawn for us when we shall be avenged, and the black Monostatos will be punished.

Second Slave

Was spricht nun der Mohr zu der Geschichte?

What does the Moor say now about the situation?

First Slave

Er weiß doch davon?

Does he know about it then?

Third Slave

Natürlich! Sie entlief vor seinen Augen.— Wie mir einige Brüder erzählten, die im Garten arbeiteten, und von weitem sahen und hörten, so ist der Mohr nicht mehr zu retten; auch wenn Pamina von Sarastros Gefolge wieder eingebracht würde.

Naturally! She ran away under his very eyes. As some of the brothers told me who work in the garden, and who saw and heard from a distance, the Moor can no longer be saved; even if Pamina were to be brought back by Sarastro's followers.

First and Second Slave

Wieso?

Why is that?

Third Slave

Du kennst ja den üppigen Wanst und seine Weise; das Mädchen aber war klüger als ich dachte.—In dem Augenblicke, als er zu siegen glaubte, rief sie Sarastros Namen: das erschütterte den Mohren; er blieb stumm und unbeweglich stehen—indes lief Pamina nach dem Kanal, und schiffte von selbst in einer Gondel dem Palmenwäldchen zu.

You know the presumptuous potbelly and his ways; but the maiden was cleverer than I thought. At the moment when he believed himself victorious, she called out Sarastro's name; that shocked the Moor; he remained dumb and motionless, while Pamina ran toward the canal, and all by herself sailed a boat to the palm grove.

First Slave

O wie wird das schüchterne Reh mit Todesangst dem Palaste ihrer zärtlichen Mutter zueilen.

How the timid doe must be hurrying in deadly fear to the palace of her tender mother.

SCENE X

The above. Monostatos from within.

MONOSTATOS

He Sklaven!   Hey, slaves!

FIRST SLAVE

Monostatos' Stimme!   Monostatos' voice!

MONOSTATOS

He Sklaven! Schafft Fesseln herbei.—   Hey, slaves! Bring chains here.

ALL THREE SLAVES

Fesseln?   Chains?

FIRST SLAVE (*runs to the side door*)

Doch nicht für Pamina? O ihr Götter! Da   But not for Pamina? Oh, ye gods! See
seht, Brüder, das Mädchen ist gefangen.   there, brothers, the maiden has been
                                          captured.

SECOND and THIRD SLAVE

Pamina?—Schrecklicher Anblick!   Pamina? Terrible sight!

FIRST SLAVE

Seht, wie der unbarmherzige Teufel sie   See how the merciless devil grasps her by
bei ihren zarten Händchen faßt—das halt   her soft little hand. I cannot bear it.
ich nicht aus.

(*goes out the other side*)

SECOND SLAVE

Ich noch weniger.   I even less.

(*also goes out that way*)

THIRD SLAVE

So was sehen zu müssen, ist   To have to see such a thing is hellish
    Höllenmarter.   torment.

(*leaves*)

593

SCENE XI

Monostatos. Pamina, who is led in by slaves.

No. 6 Trio

MONOSTATOS

Du feines Täubchen, nur herein. | You delicate little dove, in here.

PAMINA

O welche Marter! welche Pein! | Oh what torment! What pain!

MONOSTATOS

Verloren ist dein Leben! | Your life is forfeit!

PAMINA

Der Tod macht mich nicht beben. | Death doesn't make me tremble,
Nur meine Mutter dauert mich; | I feel sorry only for my mother;
Sie stirbt vor Gram ganz sicherlich. | She will certainly die of grief.

MONOSTATOS

He Sklaven! Legt ihr Fesseln an; | Hey, slaves, put chains on her;
Mein Haß soll dich verderben. | My hatred will destroy you.

(They put chains on her.)

PAMINA

O laßt mich lieber sterben, | Oh rather let me die,
Weil nichts, Barbar! dich rühren kann. | Since nothing can move you, barbarian!

(sinks down in a faint on a sofa)

MONOSTATOS

Nun fort! Laßt mich bei ihr allein. | Away with you! Leave me alone with her.

(The slaves leave.)

SCENE XII

Papageno. The above.

PAPAGENO

(outside the window, without at first being seen)

Wo bin ich wohl! Wo mag ich sein? | Where am I? Where could I be?
Aha! da find ich Leute; | Aha! There are people;
Gewagt! ich geh' herein. | I'll dare! I'll go in.

(goes inside)

Schön Mädchen, jung und fein,	Beautiful maiden, young and delicate,
Viel weißer noch als Kreide!	Much whiter than chalk!

MONOSTATOS and PAPAGENO

(see each other—each frightened by the other)

Hu! Das ist—der Teu-fel si-cherlich!	Hoo! that is—surely—the devil!
Hab Mitleid—verschone mich!	Have pity—spare me!
Hu! Hu! Hu!	Hoo! Hoo! Hoo!

(Both run off.)

SCENE XIII

Pamina alone.

Spoken monologue

PAMINA *(speaks as if in a dream)*

Mutter—Mutter—Mutter!	Mother . . . mother . . . mother!

(She revives, looks around.)

Wie?—Noch schlägt dieses Herz?—	What? This heart is still beating? Not yet
Noch nicht vernichtet?—Zu neuen	destroyed? Awakened to new agonies? Oh
Qualen erwacht?—O das ist hart, sehr	that is cruel, very cruel! More bitter to
hart!—Mir bitterer als der Tod.	me than death.

SCENE XIV

Papageno. Pamina.

Spoken dialogue

PAPAGENO

Bin ich nicht ein Narr, daß ich mich	Am I not a fool, to let myself be terrified?
schrecken ließ?—Es gibt ja schwarze	There certainly are black birds in the
Vögel in der Welt, warum denn nicht	world, so why not black people? Ah,
auch schwarze Menschen?—Ah, sieh da!	look! The beautiful young woman is still
Hier ist das schöne Fräuleinbild noch.—	here. You, daughter of the Queen of the
Du Tochter der nächtlichen Königin!	Night!

PAMINA

Nächtliche Königin?—Wer bist du?	Queen of the Night? Who are you?

PAPAGENO

Ein Abgesandter der sternflammenden Königin.	A messenger from the star-blazing queen.

PAMINA (*joyfully*)

Meiner Mutter?—O Wonne!—Dein Name!	From my mother? Oh joy! Your name!

PAPAGENO

Papageno.	Papageno.

PAMINA

Papageno?—Papageno—Ich erinnere mich den Namen oft gehört zu haben, dich selbst aber sah ich nie.—	Papageno? Papageno—I remember having heard the name often, but you yourself I never saw.

PAPAGENO

Ich dich ebensowenig.	I saw you just as little.

PAMINA

Du kennst also meine gute, zärtliche Mutter?	So you know my good, gentle mother?

PAPAGENO

Wenn du die Tochter der nächtlichen Königin bist—ja!	If you are the daughter of the Queen of the Night—yes!

PAMINA

Oh, ich bin es.	Oh, I am she.

PAPAGENO

Das will ich gleich erkennen.	I will verify that right now.

(*He looks at the portrait which the prince had received previously, and which Papageno now wears on a ribbon around his neck.*)

Die Augen schwarz—richtig, schwarz.— Die Lippen rot—richtig, rot.—Blonde Haare—blonde Haare.—Alles trifft ein, bis auf Händ' und Füße.—Nach dem Gemälde zu schließen, sollst du weder Hände noch Füße haben; denn hier sind keine angezeigt.	Eyes black—correct, black. Lips red— correct, red. Blond hair—blond hair. Everything agrees except for the hands and feet. Judging from the painting, you shouldn't have hands or feet, since none are shown here.

PAMINA

Erlaube mir—Ja, ich bin's—Wie kam es in deine Hände?	Allow me—yes, that is me. How did it come into your hands?

PAPAGENO

Dir das zu erzählen, wäre zu weitläufig; es kam von Hand zu Hand.	To tell you that would be too long-winded; it was passed from hand to hand.

PAMINA

Wie aber es in die deinige?	How did it come into yours?

PAPAGENO

Auf eine wunderbare Art.—Ich habe es gefangen.	In a strange way—I captured it.

PAMINA

Gefangen?	Captured it?

PAPAGENO

Ich muß dir das umständlicher erzählen.—Ich kam heute früh wie gewöhnlich zu deiner Mutter Palast mit meiner Lieferung—	I must tell you the circumstances. This morning, I came as usual to your mother's palace with my delivery . . .

PAMINA

Lieferung?	Delivery?

PAPAGENO

Ja, ich liefere deiner Mutter und ihren Jungfrauen schon seit vielen Jahren alle die schönen Vögel in den Palast. Eben als ich im Begriff war, meine Vögel abzugeben, sah ich einen Menschen vor mir, der sich Prinz nennen läßt.—Dieser Prinz hat deine Mutter so eingenommen, daß sie ihm dein Bildniß schenkte und ihm befahl, dich zu befreien.—Sein Entschluß war so schnell als seine Liebe zu dir.	Yes, for many years now I have been delivering all kinds of beautiful birds to your mother and her maidens at the palace. Just as I was about to hand over my birds, I saw a man before me who was called "Prince." This prince had so charmed your mother that she made him a present of your portrait, and commanded him to free you. His decision was as sudden as his love for you.

PAMINA

Liebe?	Love?

(*joyfully*)

Er liebt mich also? O sage mir das noch einmal, ich höre das Wort Liebe gar zu gerne.

So he loves me? Oh tell me that once more. I enjoy hearing the word "love" so much.

PAPAGENO

Das glaub' ich dir ohne zu schwören; du bist ja ein Fräuleinbild.—Wo blieb ich denn?

I believe you without your swearing to it; after all, you are a lovely woman. Where was I?

PAMINA

Bei der Liebe.

You were talking about love.

PAPAGENO

Richtig, bei der Liebe.—Das nenn' ich ein Gedächtniß haben. Kurz also, diese große Liebe zu dir war der Peitschenstreich, um unsere Füße in schnellen Gang zu bringen; nun sind wir hier, dir tausend schöne und angenehme Sachen zu sagen; dich in unsere Arme zu nehmen, und wenn es möglich ist, ebenso schnell, wo nicht schneller als hierher, in den Palast deiner Mutter zu eilen.

Right, about love—I call that having a good memory—in short, this great love for you was the whiplash that set our feet quickly in motion. Now we are here, to say a thousand beautiful and pleasant things to you; to take you into our arms, and if it be possible, just as quickly, if not quicker than before, to hurry to your mother's palace.

PAMINA

Das ist alles sehr schön gesagt; aber lieber Freund! wenn der unbekannte Jüngling oder Prinz, wie er sich nennt, Liebe für mich fühlt, warum säumt er so lange, mich von meinen Fesseln zu befreien?—

That is all beautifully said; but dear friend! If the unknown youth or prince as he calls himself feels love for me, why does he delay so long in freeing me from my chains?

PAPAGENO

Da steckt eben der Haken.—Wie wir von den Jungfrauen Abschied nehmen, so sagten sie uns, drei holde Knaben würden unsere Wegweiser sein, sie würden uns belehren, wie und auf was Art wir handeln sollen.

That's the hitch—as we said farewell to the maidens, they told us that three sweet boys would be our guides, that they would instruct us how and in what way we should proceed.

PAMINA

Sie lehrten euch?

They instructed you?

PAPAGENO

Nichts lehrten sie uns, denn wir haben keinen gesehen.—Zur Sicherheit also war

They instructed us about nothing, since we have not seen them. For safety's sake,

der Prinz so fein, mich vorauszuschicken, um dir unsere Ankunft anzukündigen.—

the prince was good enough to send me ahead to announce our arrival to you.

PAMINA

Freund, du hast viel gewagt!—Wenn Sarastro dich hier erblicken sollte—

Friend, you have dared much! If Sarastro were to catch sight of you here . . .

PAPAGENO

So wird mir meine Rückreise erspart— das kann ich mir denken.

Then I can well imagine I would be spared my return trip.

PAMINA

Dein martervoller Tod würde ohne Grenzen sein.

You would suffer death by unending torture.

PAPAGENO

Um diesem auszuweichen so gehen wir lieber beizeiten.

To avoid this, let's go in quick time.

PAMINA

Wie hoch mag wohl die Sonne sein?

How high do you think the sun is?

PAPAGENO

Bald gegen Mittag.

It will soon be midday.

PAMINA

So haben wir keine Minute zu versäumen.—Um diese Zeit kommt Sarastro gewöhnlich von der Jagd zurück.

Then we have not a moment to lose— usually Sarastro comes back from hunting about this time.

PAPAGENO

Sarastro ist also nicht zu Hause?—Pah! da haben wir gewonnenes Spiel!— Komm, schönes Fräuleinbild! du wirst Augen machen, wenn du den schönen Jüngling erblickst.

Then Sarastro is not at home? Ha! Then we're ahead of the game. Come, lovely young woman. You will get an eyeful when you catch sight of the handsome youth.

PAMINA

Wohl denn! es sei gewagt!

Well then! Let's dare it!

(They go. Pamina turns back.)

Aber wenn dies ein Fallstrick wäre?— Wenn dieser nun ein böser Geist von Sarastros Gefolge wäre?—

But what if this is a trap? What if this man is an evil spirit from Sarastro's following?

(looks at him doubtfully)

PAPAGENO

Ich ein böser Geist?—Wo denkt Ihr hin, Fräuleinbild?—Ich bin der beste Geist von der Welt.

Me, an evil spirit? What are you thinking of, young lady? I am the best spirit in the world!

PAMINA

Doch nein; das Bild hier überzeugt mich, daß ich nicht getäuscht bin; es kommt aus den Händen meiner zärtlichsten Mutter.

But no, this picture here convinces me that I am not being deceived; it comes from the hands of my most gentle mother.

PAPAGENO

Schön's Fräuleinbild, wenn dir wieder ein so böser Verdacht aufsteigen sollte, daß ich dich betrügen wollte, so denke nur fleißig an die Liebe, und jeder böse Argwohn wird schwinden.

Pretty young lady, if such a nasty thought were to strike you again —that I would want to deceive you—you should think quickly about love, and every evil suspicion would disappear.

PAMINA

Freund, vergib! vergib! wenn ich dich beleidigte. Du hast ein gefühlvolles Herz, das sehe ich in jedem deiner Züge.

Friend, forgive! Forgive if I've offended you. You have a heart full of emotion, I see that in your every feature.

PAPAGENO

Ach freilich hab' ich ein gefühlvolles Herz.—Aber was nützt mir das alles?— Ich möchte mir oft alle meine Federn ausrupfen, wenn ich bedenke, daß Papageno noch keine Papagena hat.

Yes, certainly I have a heart full of emotion. But what good is all that to me? Often I could pull out all my feathers when I consider that Papageno has no Papagena yet.

PAMINA

Armer Mann! du hast also noch kein Weib?

Poor man! You do not have a wife yet?

PAPAGENO

Nicht einmal ein Mädchen, viel weniger ein Weib!—Ja, das ist betrübt!—Und unsereiner hat doch auch bisweilen seine lustigen Stunden, wo man gern gesellschaftliche Unterhaltung haben möcht'.

Not even a girlfriend, much less a wife. Now that is sad! And our kind also has its cheerful hours sometimes, when one would very much like to have some entertaining company.

PAMINA

Geduld, Freund! Der Himmel wird auch für dich sorgen; er wird dir eine Freundin schicken, ehe du dir's vermutest.	Patience, friend! Heaven will take care of you too; it will send you a friend before you know it.

PAPAGENO

Wenn er's nur bald schickte.	If only it would send her soon!

No. 7 Duet

PAMINA

Bei Männern, welche Liebe fühlen, Fehlt auch ein gutes Herze nicht.	With men who feel love A good heart is also not amiss.

PAPAGENO

Die süßen Triebe mitzufühlen, Ist dann der Weiber erste Pflicht.	Then it is the woman's first obligation To feel those sweet urges along with him.

BOTH

Wir wollen uns der Liebe freu'n, Wir leben durch die Lieb' allein.	We want to enjoy love; We live through love alone.

PAMINA

Die Lieb' versüßet jede Plage, Ihr opfert jede Kreatur.	Love sweetens every pain; Every creature makes sacrifices for it.

PAPAGENO

Sie würzet unsre Lebenstage, Sie wirkt im Kreise der Natur.	It flavors our daily life; It works throughout the cycle of nature.

BOTH

Ihr hoher Zweck zeigt deutlich an, Nichts edlers sei, als Weib und Mann.	Its high purpose shows clearly, That nothing is more noble than woman and man.
Mann und Weib, und Weib und Mann, Reichen an die Gottheit an.	Man and woman, and woman and man, Aspire to godliness.

(Both leave.)

Scene XV

The stage set is changed to a grove. All the way at the back of the stage is a beautiful temple, upon which these words appear: "Temple of Wisdom". Columns lead from this temple to two others; on the right-handed one appears: "Temple of Reason". On the left one: "Temple of Nature".

(Three boys lead Tamino in; each boy has a silver palm frond in his hand.)

No. 8 Finale

The Three Boys

Zum Ziele führt dich diese Bahn,	This path leads you to your goal,
Doch mußt du Jüngling! männlich siegen.	Youth! But you must achieve it in manly fashion.
Drum höre unsre Lehre an:	Therefore listen to our advice:
Sei standhaft, duldsam und verschwiegen!	Be steadfast, tolerant and discreet!

Tamino

Ihr holden Knaben sagt mir an,	Tell me, you sweet boys,
Ob ich Paminen retten kann.	Whether I will be able to rescue Pamina.

The Three Boys

Dies kundzutun steht uns nicht an.—	It is not appropriate for us to tell you.
Sei standhaft, duldsam und verschwiegen.	Be steadfast, tolerant and discreet!
Bedenke dies: kurz, sei ein Mann,	Consider this: in short, be a man.
Dann, Jüngling, wirst du männlich siegen.	Then, youth, you will conquer in manly fashion.

(They leave.)

Tamino

Die Weisheitslehre dieser Knaben	The wise counsel of these boys
Sei ewig mir ins Herz gegraben.	Be forever engraved in my heart.
Wo bin ich nun?—Was wird mit mir?	Where am I now? What will become of me?
Ist dies der Sitz der Götter hier?	Is this the seat of the gods?
Es zeigen die Pforten, es zeigen die Säulen,	The doors and columns show,
Daß Klugheit und Arbeit und Künste hier weilen.	That intelligence and work and arts dwell here.
Wo Tätigkeit thronet und Müßiggang weicht,	Where activity is enthroned and idleness yields,
Erhält seine Herrschaft das Laster nicht leicht.	Vice does not easily maintain its dominion.
Ich wage mich mutig zur Pforte hinein,	With courage I will try to enter this door.
Die Absicht ist edel, und lauter und rein.	My purpose is noble, and sincere and pure.
Erzittre feiger Bösewicht!	Tremble, cowardly villain!
Paminen retten ist mir Pflicht.	To save Pamina is my obligation.

(He goes to the right-hand door, opens it, and as he is about to go in, a distant Voice is heard.)

Voice

Zurück!	Stay back!

TAMINO

| Zurück? So wag' ich hier mein Glück! | Stay back? So I will try my luck here. |

(He goes to the left-hand door.)

VOICE *(from within)*

| Zurück! | Stay back! |

TAMINO

| Auch hier ruft man: zurück! | Here too someone calls out: stay back! |

(looks around him)

| Da seh'ich noch eine Tür, | I see still another door. |
| Vielleicht find' ich den Eingang hier! | Perhaps I shall find entry here! |

(He knocks, an old Priest appears.)

PRIEST

| Wo willst du kühner Fremdling hin? | Where do you want to go, bold stranger? |
| Was suchst du hier im Heiligtum? | What do you seek here in the sanctuary? |

TAMINO

| Der Lieb' und Tugend Eigentum. | The qualities of love and virtue. |

PRIEST

Die Worte sind von hohem Sinn!	The words are those of a high mind!
Allein, wie willst du diese finden?	But how will you find these?
Dich leitet Lieb' und Tugend nicht,	Love and virtue do not lead you,
Weil Tod und Rache dich entzünden.	Because death and vengeance inflame you.

TAMINO

| Nur Rache für den Bösewicht. | Only vengeance on an villain. |

PRIEST

| Den wirst du wohl bei uns nicht finden. | You will definitely not find such a one among us. |

TAMINO

| Sarastro herrscht in diesen Gründen? | Sarastro rules in these lands? |

PRIEST

| Ja, ja! Sarastro herrschet hier! | Yes, yes, Sarastro rules here. |

TAMINO

| Doch in dem Weisheitstempel nicht? | Though not in Wisdom's temple? |

PRIEST

Er herrscht im Weisheitstempel hier.   He rules here in Wisdom's temple.

TAMINO

So ist denn alles Heuchelei!   Then everything is a sham!

(is about to leave)

PRIEST

Willst du schon wieder gehn?   Do you already want to leave?

TAMINO

Ja, ich will geh'n, froh und frei,   Yes, I want to leave happy and free,
Nie euren Tempel seh'n.   Never to see your temple.

PRIEST

Erklär dich näher mir,   Make yourself clearer to me,
Dich täuschet ein Betrug.   A deceit is misleading you.

TAMINO

Sarastro wohnet hier,   Sarastro lives here,
Das ist mir schon genug.   That is already enough for me.

PRIEST

Wenn du dein Leben liebst,   If you love your life,
So rede, bleibe da!   Speak out, remain here.
Sarastro hassest du?   You hate Sarastro?

TAMINO

Ich haß' ihn ewig! Ja!   I will always hate him! Yes!

PRIEST

Nun gib mir deine Gründe an.   Now state your reasons to me.

TAMINO

Er ist ein Unmensch, ein Tyrann.   He is a monster, a tyrant.

PRIEST

Ist das, was du gesagt, erwiesen?   Has what you have said been proven?

TAMINO

Durch ein unglücklich Weib bewiesen,   Attested to by an unfortunate woman
Das Gram und Jammer niederdrückt.   Who is weighed down by grief and
    misery.

PRIEST

Ein Weib hat also dich berückt?   Has a woman beguiled you so?
Ein Weib tut wenig, plaudert viel.   A woman does little, chatters a lot.

Du Jüngling glaubst dem Zungenspiel?
O legte doch Sarastro dir
Die Absicht seiner Handlung für.

Youth, do you believe the tongue's game?
Oh were Sarastro only to lay before you
The purpose of his action.

TAMINO

Die Absicht ist nur allzu klar;
Riß nicht der Räuber ohn' Erbarmen
Paminen aus der Mutter Armen?

The purpose is only all too clear;
Did the robber not mercilessly tear
Pamina from her mother's arms?

PRIEST

Ja, Jüngling! Was du sagst, ist wahr.

Yes, youth! What you say is true.

TAMINO

Wo ist sie, die er uns geraubt?
Man opferte vielleicht sie schon?

Where is she, whom he stole from us?
Has she perhaps been sacrificed?

PRIEST

Dir dies zu sagen, teurer Sohn,
Ist jetztund mir noch nicht erlaubt.

I am not allowed, at present,
To tell you this, dear son.

TAMINO

Erklär dies Rätsel, täusch mich nicht.

Explain this riddle, do not deceive me.

PRIEST

Die Zunge bindet Eid und Pflicht.

Oath and duty bind my tongue.

TAMINO

Wann also wird die Decke schwinden?

When will the veil of secrecy be lifted?

PRIEST

Sobald dich führt der Freundschaft Hand,
Ins Heiligtum zum ew'gen Band.

As soon as friendship's hand leads you
Into the sanctuary to the eternal
assembly.

(*goes out*)

TAMINO (*alone*)

O ew'ge Nacht! wann wirst du
schwinden?
Wann wird das Licht mein Auge finden?

Oh eternal night! When will you
disappear?
When will my eyes find the light?

SEVERAL VOICES

Bald, Jüngling, oder nie!

Soon, youth, or never!

TAMINO

Bald, sagt ihr, oder nie?	Soon, you say, or never?
Ihr Unsichtbaren, saget mir!	You invisible ones, tell me!
Lebt denn Pamina noch?	Does Pamina still live?

THE VOICES

Pamina lebet noch!	Pamina still lives!

TAMINO (*joyfully*)

Sie lebt!	She lives!
Ich danke euch dafür.	I thank you for that.

(He takes out his flute.)

O wenn ich doch im Stande wäre,	Oh if only I were able,
Allmächtige, zu eurer Ehre	Almighty ones, in your honor
Mit jedem Tone meinen Dank	To express my thanks,
Zu schildern, wie er hier, hier entsprang!	To describe with every tone how they sprang from here!

(He indicates his heart. He plays; at once, wild animals of all species come out to listen to him. He stops, and they all flee. The birds twitter along with his playing.)

Wie stark ist nicht dein Zauberton,	How powerful is your magic tone,
Weil, holde Flöte, durch dein Spielen	Sweet flute; for through your playing
Selbst wilde Tiere Freude fühlen.	Even wild beasts feel joy.
Doch nur Pamina bleibt davon.	Yet only Pamina stays away.

(He plays.)

Pamina! höre, höre mich!	Pamina! Hear me! Listen to me!
Umsonst!	In vain!

(He plays.)

Wo? ach, wo find ich dich?	Where! Oh, where will I find you?

(He plays; Papageno answers from within on his panpipes.)

Ha, das ist Papagenos Ton!	Aha, that is Papageno's sound!

(He plays. Papageno answers several times.)

Vielleicht sah er Paminen schon,	Perhaps he has seen Pamina already,
Vielleicht eilt sie mit ihm zu mir!	Perhaps she is hurrying with him to me!
Vielleicht führt mich der Ton zu ihr.	Perhaps the sound is leading me to her!

(hurries off)

SCENE XVI

Papageno. Pamina without chains.

PAPAGENO and PAMINA

Schnelle Füße, rascher Mut,	Quick feet, swift courage,
Schützt vor Feindes List und Wut;	Protect from enemy's cunning and fury;
Fänden wir Tamino doch!	If we could only find Tamino!
Sonst erwischen sie uns noch.	Otherwise, they may yet catch us.

PAMINA

Holder Jüngling!	Sweet youth!

PAPAGENO

Stille, stille! ich kann's besser!	Quiet! I know a better way!

(He pipes.)
(Tamino, from outside, answers on his flute.)

BOTH

Welche Freude ist wohl größer,	What joy could be greater?
Freund Tamino hört uns schon;	Our friend Tamino has already heard us;
Hieher kam der Flötenton.	From here came the flute sound.
Welch ein Glück, wenn ich ihn finde!	What good fortune, if I find him!
Nur geschwinde! Nur geschwinde!	Only, swiftly, swiftly!

(They are about to go in.)

SCENE XVII

The above. Monostatos.

MONOSTATOS (*mocking them*)

Nur geschwinde! Nur geschwinde!	Only, swiftly, swiftly!
Ha, hab' ich euch noch erwischt!	Ha, I have caught you just in time!
Nur herbei mit Stahl und Eisen;	Come here with steel and iron;
Wart, man wird euch Mores weisen.	Just wait, you will be taught an unforgettable lesson.
Den Monostatos berücken!	To fool Monostatos!
Nur herbei mit Band und Stricken,	Here with bonds and ropes,
He, ihr Sklaven, kommt herbei!	Hey, you slaves, come here.

(The slaves come with chains.)

PAMINA and PAPAGENO

Ach, nun ist's mit uns vorbei!	Ah, now it's all over for us!

PAPAGENO

Wer viel wagt, gewinnt oft viel!	He who risks much, often wins much!
Komm du schönes Glockenspiel!	Come, you beautiful bells!
Laß die Glöckchen klingen, klingen,	So that their ears may sing,
Daß die Ohren ihnen singen.	Let the little bells ring, ring.

(He strikes his bell-instrument.)

MONOSTATOS and SLAVES

Das klinget so herrlich, das klinget so schön!	That rings so marvelously, that rings so prettily!
Larala, larala!	La ra la! La ra la!
Nie hab' ich so etwas gehört und geseh'n!	Never have I heard or seen anything like it!
Larala, larala!	La ra la! La ra la!

(They go marching off.)

PAPAGENO and PAMINA *(laughing)*

Könnte jeder brave Mann	If every brave man
Solche Glöckchen finden,	Could find such little bells,
Seine Feinde würden dann	Without effort he could
Ohne Mühe schwinden,	Make his enemies disappear,
Und er lebte ohne sie	And he would live without them
In der besten Harmonie.	In the best of harmony.
Nur der Freundschaft Harmonie	Only friendship's harmony
Mildert die Beschwerden;	Relieves troubles;
Ohne diese Sympathie	Without this sympathy
Ist kein Glück auf Erden!	There is no happiness on earth!

(A loud march with trumpets and kettle-drums breaks in.)

CHORUS *(from within)*

Es lebe Sarastro! Sarastro lebe!	Long live Sarastro!

PAPAGENO

Was soll das bedeuten? Ich zittre, ich bebe.	What does that mean? I tremble, I shiver.

PAMINA

O Freund, nun ist's um uns getan!	Oh friend, now we are done for!
Dies kündigt den Sarastro an.	This announces Sarastro.

PAPAGENO

O wär' ich eine Maus,	Oh if I were a mouse.
Wie wollt' ich mich verstecken,	How quickly I would hide myself,

Wär' ich so klein wie Schnecken,
So kröch' ich in mein Haus.
Mein Kind, was werden wir nun
    sprechen?

If I were as small as a snail,
Then I would crawl into my house.
My child, now what shall we tell him?

PAMINA

Die Wahrheit! Die Wahrheit,
sei sie auch Verbrechen.

The truth! The truth,
Even if it should be a crime.

SCENE XVIII

A procession of followers; lastly Sarastro in a triumphal chariot drawn by six lions. The above.

CHORUS

Es lebe Sarastro! Sarastro soll leben!
Er ist es, dem wir uns mit Freuden
    ergeben!
Stets mög' er des Lebens als Weiser sich
    freun.
Er ist unser Abgott, dem alle sich weihn.

Long live Sarastro! May Sarastro live long!
He is the one to whom we joyfully devote
    ourselves!
May he always enjoy the life of a Wise
    One.
He is our idol, to whom we all consecrate
    ourselves.

(The chorus is sung until Sarastro has come down from the chariot.)

PAMINA (*kneels*)

Herr, ich bin zwar Verbrecherin!
Ich wollte deiner Macht entfliehn.
Allein die Schuld ist nicht an mir—
Der böse Mohr verlangte Liebe;
Darum, o Herr! entfloh ich dir.

Lord, I am indeed a criminal!
I wanted to flee from your power.
But the blame doesn't lie with me . . .
The evil Moor demanded my love;
For that reason, oh lord! I fled from you.

SARASTRO

Steh auf, erheitre dich, o Liebe!
Denn ohne erst in dich zu dringen,
Weiß ich von deinem Herzen mehr:
Du liebest einen andern sehr.
Zur Liebe will ich dich nicht zwingen,
Doch geb' ich dir die Freiheit nicht.

Stand up, be cheered, beloved one!
For without first requiring it from you
I know more about your heart:
You love another deeply.
I shall neither compel you to love,
Nor shall I give you your freedom.

PAMINA

Mich rufet ja die Kindespflicht,
Denn meine Mutter—

A child's duty called me,
for my mother . . .

609

SARASTRO

Steht in meiner Macht.
Du würdest um dein Glück gebracht,
Wenn ich dich ihren Händen ließe.

Is in my power.
Your good fortune would have ended,
If I had left you in her hands.

PAMINA

Mir klingt der Muttername süße;
Sie ist es—

My mother's name sounds sweet to me;
She is that . . .

SARASTRO

Und ein stolzes Weib.
Ein Mann muß Eure Herzen leiten,
Denn ohne ihn pflegt jedes Weib
Aus ihrem Wirkungskreis zu schreiten.

And a proud woman.
A man must guide your hearts,
For without him, every woman
Steps beyond her customary domain.

SCENE XIX

Monostatos, Tamino. The above.

MONOSTATOS

Nun, stolzer Jüngling, nur hieher!
Hier ist Sarastro, unser Herr.

Now, proud youth, this way!
Here is Sarastro, our lord.

PAMINA

Er ist's.

It's he.

TAMINO

Sie ist's!

It's she!

PAMINA

Ich glaub' es kaum!

I can scarcely believe it.

TAMINO

Sie ist's!

It's she!

PAMINA

Er ist's.

It's he!

TAMINO

Es ist kein Traum!

It is no dream!

PAMINA

Es schlingt mein Arm sich um ihn her,

To put my arms around him!

TAMINO

Es schlingt mein Arm sich um sie her,

To put my arms around her!

610

BOTH

Und wenn es auch mein Ende wär'!	Even if it be the end of me!

ALL

Was soll das heißen?	What does that mean?

MONOSTATOS

Welch eine Dreistigkeit!	What impudence!
Gleich auseinander, das geht zu weit!	Apart, immediately, that goes too far!

(He separates them, kneels.)

Dein Sklave liegt zu deinen Füßen,	Your slave lies at your feet,
Laß den verweg'nen Frevler büßen.	Let the audacious offender do penance,
Bedenk, wie frech der Knabe ist!	Consider how insolent the boy is!
Durch dieses seltnen Vogels List	Through this rare bird's cunning
Wollt' er Paminen dir entführen,	He tried to carry Pamina off from you,
Allein, ich wußt' ihn auszuspüren!	I alone knew to track him down.
Du kennst mich!—Meine	You know me—my vigilance . . .
Wachsamkeit—	

SARASTRO

Verdient, daß man ihr Lorbeer streut.	Deserves that laurel-leaves be strewn before you.
He! Gebt dem Ehrenmann sogleich—	Ho! Give that honorable man at once . . .

MONOSTATOS

Schon deine Gnade macht mich reich.	Your favor already makes me rich.

SARASTRO

Nur siebenundsiebzig Sohlenstreich'.	Only seventy-seven lashes on the soles of his feet.

MONOSTATOS

Ach, Herr, den Lohn verhofft' ich nicht!	Ah, lord, I did not hope for this reward!

SARASTRO

Nicht Dank! es ist ja meine Pflicht!	Do not thank me! It is only my duty!

(Monostatos is led away.)

ALL

Es lebe Sarastro, der göttliche Weise,	Long live Sarastro, the god-like sage,
Er lohnet und strafet in ähnlichem Kreise.	He rewards and punishes in turn.

SARASTRO

Führt diese beiden Fremdlinge	Lead both of these strangers
In unsern Prüfungstempel ein;	Into our temple to be tested;
Bedecket ihre Häupter dann,—	Cover their heads—
Sie müssen erst gereinigt sein.	They must first be purified.

(Two priests bring a sort of sack, and cover the heads of the two strangers.)

FINAL CHORUS

Wenn Tugend und Gerechtigkeit	If virtue and justice
Der Großen Pfad mit Ruhm bestreut,	Bestrew the pathway of the great ones with glory;
Dann ist die Erd' ein Himmelreich,	Then is the earth a heavenly kingdom,
Und Sterbliche den Göttern gleich.	And mortals are like the gods.

End of Act One

ACT TWO

SCENE I

The stage set is a palm grove, all the trees appear to be made of silver, the leaves, of gold. There are eighteen chairs made of leaves, on each seat stands a pyramid and a large black horn in a golden setting. In the middle are the largest pyramid, and also the largest trees.

(Sarastro comes in solemn procession with the other priests, each with a palm frond in his hand.)

No. 9 March
Spoken dialogue

SARASTRO *(after a pause)*

Ihr, in dem Weisheitstempel eingeweihten	You, in the temple of Wisdom,
Diener der großen Götter Osiris und	consecrated servants of the great gods
Isis!—Mit reiner Seele erklär' ich euch,	Osiris and Isis! With pure soul I declare
daß unsre heutige Versammlung eine der	to you that today our gathering is one of
wichtigsten unsrer Zeit ist.—Tamino, ein	the most important of our time. Tamino,
Königssohn, zwanzig Jahre seines Alters,	a king's son, twenty years old, has come
wandelt an der nördlichen Pforte unsers	to the northern door of our temple, and
Tempels und seufzt mit tugendvollem	sighs with virtuous heart after something
Herzen nach einem Gegenstande, den wir	which we all with effort and diligence

alle mit Mühe und Fleiß erringen müssen.—Kurz, dieser Jüngling will seinen nächtlichen Schleier von sich reißen und ins Heiligtum des größten Lichtes blicken.—Diesen Tugendhaften zu bewachen, ihm freundschaftlich die Hand zu bieten, sei heute eine unsrer wichtigsten Pflichten.

must obtain. In short, the youth wishes to tear his dark veil from himself and to gaze into the sanctuary of the greatest light. To guard this virtuous one, to offer him the hand of friendship, these are our most important duties today.

FIRST PRIEST (*stands up*)

Er besitzt Tugend?

He possesses virtue?

SARASTRO

Tugend!

Virtue!

SECOND PRIEST

Auch Verschwiegenheit?

Also discretion?

SARASTRO

Verschwiegenheit!

Discretion!

THIRD PRIEST

Ist wohltätig?

Is he charitable?

SARASTRO

Wohltätig!—Haltet ihr ihn für würdig, so folgt meinem Beispiele.

Charitable! If you take him to be worthy, then follow my example.

(*They blow three times on the horns*)

Gerührt über die Einigkeit eurer Herzen, dankt Sarastro euch im Namen der Menschheit.—Mag immer das Vorurteil seinen Tadel über uns Eingeweihte auslassen!—Weisheit und Vernunft zerstückt es gleich dem Spinnengewebe.—Unsere Säulen erschüttern sie nie. Jedoch, das böse Vorurteil soll schwinden, und es wird schwinden sobald Tamino selbst die Größe unserer schweren Kunst besitzen wird.—Pamina, das sanfte, tugendhafte Mädchen, haben die Götter dem holden Jünglinge bestimmt; dies ist der Grundstein warum ich sie der stolzen

Moved by the unity of your hearts, Sarastro thanks you in the name of mankind. Let prejudice unleash its censure of us Initiated Ones—wisdom and reason will pluck it apart like a spiderweb. Our columns will not be shaken. But evil prejudice must disappear, as soon as Tamino himself comes into possession of the greatness of our difficult craft.—The gods have intended Pamina, the gentle, virtuous maiden, for the sweet youth; this is the basis for my wrenching her away from her proud mother. The woman thinks herself great; hopes through tricks and superstition to fool

Mutter entriß. Das Weib dünkt sich groß zu sein, hofft durch Blendwerk und Aberglauben das Volk zu berücken, und unsern festen Tempelbau zu zerstören. Allein, das soll sie nicht; Tamino, der holde Jüngling selbst, soll ihn mit uns befestigen und als Eingeweihter der Tugend Lohn, dem Laster aber Strafe sein.

the people, and to destroy our strong temple foundation! However, she is not to accomplish it; Tamino, the sweet youth himself, is to ally himself with us, and as initiate, be the reward of virtue and the scourge of vice.

(The chord on the horns is repeated three times by all.)

SPEAKER *(stands up)*

Großer Sarastro, deine weisheitsvollen Reden erkennen und bewundern wir; allein, wird Tamino auch die harten Prüfungen, so seiner warten, bekämpfen?—Verzeih, daß ich so frei bin, dir meinen Zweifel zu eröffnen! mich bangt es um den Jüngling. Wenn nun im Schmerz dahingesunken sein Geist ihn verließe, und er dem harten Kampf unterläge?—Er ist Prinz!—

Great Sarastro, we acknowledge and admire the wisdom of your speech; but will Tamino take upon himself the difficult trials which await him? Forgive me for being so free to reveal my doubt to you. I am worried about the youth. What if, sunk in suffering, his spirit deserts him, and he is defeated in the difficult battle? He is a prince!—

SARASTRO

Noch mehr—Er ist Mensch!

Even more, he is a human being!

SPEAKER

Wenn er nun aber in seiner frühen Jugend leblos erblaßte?

What if, now still in his early youth, he were to die?

SARASTRO

Dann ist er Osiris und Isis gegeben, und wird der Götter Freuden früher fühlen als wir.

Then he would be given to Osiris and Isis, and would experience the joy of the gods earlier than we.

(The chord is repeated three times.)

Man führe Tamino mit seinem Reisegefährten in den Vorhof des Tempels ein.

Let Tamino with his travelling companion be led into the forecourt of the temple.

(To the Speaker, who kneels before him)

Und du, Freund! den die Götter durch uns zum Verteidiger der Wahrheit

And you, friend! Whom the gods through us appointed as defender of the truth—

bestimmten—vollziehe dein heiliges Amt, und lehre durch deine Weisheit beide, was Pflicht der Menschheit sei, lehre sie die Macht der Götter erkennen.

perform your holy office, and teach them both by your wisdom what the duty of humanity is, teach them to acknowledge the might of the gods.

(The Speaker goes out with another priest, and all the priests with their palm fronds join together.)

No. 10 Aria with Chorus

SARASTRO and CHORUS

O Isis und Osiris, schenket
Der Weisheit Geist dem neuen Paar!
Die ihr der Wandrer Schritte lenket,
Stärkt mit Geduld sie in Gefahr.
Laßt sie der Prüfung Früchte sehen.
Doch sollten sie zu Grabe gehen,
So lohnt der Tugend kühnen Lauf,
Nehmt sie in euren Wohnsitz auf.

Oh Isis and Osiris, bestow
The spirit of wisdom upon the new pair!
Guide the wanderers' steps,
Strengthen them with patience in danger.
Let them behold the fruits of their trials.
But should they go to their graves,
Then reward virtue's bold run,
Take them to your dwelling.

(Sarastro goes first, then all follow out after him.)

SCENE II

Night. Thunder rumbles in the distance. The stage set is changed into a small forecourt of the temple where vestiges of fallen columns and pyramids and some thorn bushes can be seen. On both sides stand tall ancient Egyptian doors which open, and which represent flanking buildings.

(Tamino and Papageno are led in by the Speaker and the other priest; they remove the head-coverings from them; then the priests go out.)

Spoken dialogue

TAMINO

Eine schreckliche Nacht!—Papageno, bist du noch bei mir?

A terrible night! Papageno, are you still with me?

PAPAGENO

I, freilich!

Of course!

TAMINO

Wo denkst du, daß wir uns nun befinden?

Where do you think we are now?

PAPAGENO

Wo? Ja, wenn's nicht finster wäre, wollt' ich dir's schon sagen—aber so—

Where? Well, if it was dark, I could tell you, but as it is—

(thunderclap)

O weh! | Alas!

TAMINO

Was ist's? | What is it?

PAPAGENO

Mir wird nicht wohl bei der Sache. | I'm not very happy with all this.

TAMINO

Du hast Furcht, wie ich höre. | I can hear that you are frightened.

PAPAGENO

Furcht eben nicht, nur eiskalt läuft's mir über den Rücken. | Not frightened so much, only there is this ice-cold feeling running down my back.

(strong thunderclap)

O weh! | Alas!

TAMINO

Was soll's? | What is it?

PAPAGENO

Ich glaube, ich bekomme ein kleines Fieber. | I think I'm getting a little fever.

TAMINO

Pfui, Papageno! Sei ein Mann! | For shame, Papageno. Be a man!

PAPAGENO

Ich wollt', ich wär' ein Mädchen! | I wish I was a girl!

(a very strong thunderclap)

O! O! O! Das ist mein letzter Augenblick. | Oh! Oh! Oh! It is my last moment.

SCENE III

Speaker and the other priest with torches. The above.

SPEAKER

Ihr Fremdlinge, was sucht oder fordert ihr von uns? Was treibt euch an, in unsere Mauern zu dringen? | You strangers, what do you seek or require from us? What drives you to penetrate within our walls?

TAMINO

Freundschaft und Liebe. | Friendship and love.

SPEAKER

Bist du bereit, es mit deinem Leben zu erkämpfen?	Are you ready to battle for them with your life?

TAMINO

Ja!	Yes!

SPEAKER

Auch wenn Tod dein Los wäre?	Even if death be your destiny?

TAMINO

Ja!	Yes!

SPEAKER

Prinz! Noch ist's Zeit zu weichen—einen Schritt weiter, und es ist zu spät.	Prince, there is still time to retreat—one step farther and it will be too late.

TAMINO

Weisheitslehre sei mein Sieg; Pamina, das holde Mädchen, mein Lohn.	The teachings of wisdom be my victory; Pamina, the sweet maiden, my reward.

SPEAKER

Du unterziehst jeder Prüfung dich?	You will undergo every trial?

TAMINO

Jeder!	Every one.

SPEAKER

Reiche deine Hand mir!—	Give me your hand.

(They clasp hands.)

So!	Agreed!

SECOND PRIEST

Ehe du weiter sprichst, erlaube mir ein paar Worte mit diesem Fremdling zu sprechen.—Willst auch du dir Weisheitsliebe erkämpfen?	Before you say anything further, allow me to speak a few words with this stranger.—Will you also fight for the love of wisdom for yourself?

PAPAGENO

Kämpfen ist meine Sache nicht.—Ich verlang' auch im Grund gar keine Weisheit. Ich bin so ein Naturmensch,	Fighting is not in my line. Actually, I don't require any wisdom. I am a sort of child of nature, who is satisfied with

der sich mit Schlaf, Speise und Trank begnügt;—und wenn es ja sein könnte, daß ich mir einmal ein schönes Weibchen fange—

sleep, food and drink—and if I could capture a beautiful little wife for myself . . .

SECOND PRIEST

Die wirst du nie erhalten, wenn du dich nicht unsern Prüfungen unterziehst.

You will never obtain her, if you do not undergo our trials.

PAPAGENO

Worin besteht diese Prüfung?—

What do these trials consist of?

SECOND PRIEST

Dich allen unsern Gesetzen unterwerfen, selbst den Tod nicht scheuen.

Submitting yourself to all of our laws, not even shrinking from death.

PAPAGENO

Ich bleibe ledig!

I'll stay single!

SPEAKER

Aber wenn du dir ein tugendhaftes schönes Mädchen erwerben könntest?

But if you could win a virtuous, beautiful maiden for yourself?

PAPAGENO

Ich bleibe ledig!

I'll stay single!

SECOND PRIEST

Wenn nun aber Sarastro dir ein Mädchen aufbewahrt hätte, das an Farbe und Kleidung dir ganz gleich wäre?—

If, however, Sarastro had a maiden kept safe for you who was exactly like you are in color and garb?

PAPAGENO

Mir gleich! Ist sie jung?

Like me? Is she young?

SECOND PRIEST

Jung und schön.

Young and beautiful.

PAPAGENO

Und heißt?

And is named?

SECOND PRIEST

Papagena.

Papagena!

PAPAGENO

Wie? Pa—?

What? Pa . . . ?

SECOND PRIEST

Papagena!

Papagena.

PAPAGENO

Papagena?—Die möcht' ich aus bloßer Neugierde sehen.

Papagena? I'd like to see her, just out of pure curiosity.

SECOND PRIEST

Sehen kannst du sie!—

You may see her!

PAPAGENO

Aber wenn ich sie gesehen habe, hernach muß ich sterben?

But once I've seen her, must I die afterwards?

(Second Priest makes an ambiguous gesture.)

Ja?—Ich bleibe ledig!

Yes? I'll stay single!

SECOND PRIEST

Sehen kannst du sie, aber bis zur verlaufenen Zeit kein Wort mit ihr sprechen; wird dein Geist so viel Standhaftigkeit besitzen, deine Zunge in Schranken zu halten?

You may see her, but until the allotted time, you may not speak a word with her. Will your spirit possess sufficient steadfastness to restrain your tongue?

PAPAGENO

O ja!

Oh yes!

SECOND PRIEST

Deine Hand! du sollst sie sehen.

Your hand! You shall see her.

SPEAKER

Auch dir, Prinz, legen die Götter ein heilsames Stillschweigen auf; ohne dieses seid ihr beide verloren. Du wirst Pamina sehen, aber nie sie sprechen dürfen; dies ist der Anfang eurer Prüfungszeit.

Also on you, Prince, the gods lay a beneficial ban on speech; without it, both of you are lost. You will see Pamina, but you must never speak to her; this is the beginning of the time of testing.

No. 11 Duet

SPEAKER and SECOND PRIEST

Bewahret euch vor Weibertücken:

Be on your guard against the guile of women:

Dies ist des Bundes erste Pflicht!
Manch weiser Mann ließ sich berücken,

This is the first obligation of the Craft!
Many a wise man has let himself be captivated,

Er fehlte, und versah sich's nicht.
Verlassen sah er sich am Ende,

He erred, and was not aware of it!
At the end he found himself abandoned,

Vergolten seine Treu mit Hohn!	His loyalty repaid with scorn.
Vergebens rang er seine Hände,	In vain he wrung his hands,
Tod und Verzweiflung war sein Lohn.	Death and despair were his reward.

(Both priests leave.)

SCENE IV

Tamino. Papageno.

Spoken dialogue

PAPAGENO

He, Lichter her! Lichter her!—Das ist doch wunderlich, so oft einen die Herrn verlassen, so sieht man mit offenen Augen nichts.	Hey, lights here! Lights here! It is really strange, whenever these men leave, you can't see anything even with your eyes open.

TAMINO

Ertrag es mit Geduld, und denke, es ist der Götter Wille.	Endure it with patience, and consider it the will of the gods.

SCENE V

The three Ladies (out of the trap-door) The above.

No. 12 Quintet

THE THREE LADIES

Wie? Wie? Wie?	What? What? What?
Ihr an diesem Schreckensort?	You in this horrible place?
Nie! Nie! Nie!	Never! Never! Never!
Kommt ihr wieder glücklich fort!	Will you escape unharmed!
Tamino, dir ist Tod geschworen!	Tamino, to you death is sworn!
Du, Papageno! bist verloren!	You, Papageno, are lost!

PAPAGENO

Nein! nein! nein! Das wär' zu viel.	No, no, no! That would be too much.

TAMINO

Papageno, schweige still!	Papageno, be still!
Willst du dein Gelübde brechen,	Do you want to break your vow,
Nichts mit Weibern hier zu sprechen?	Not to talk to women here?

PAPAGENO

Du hörst ja, wir sind beide hin.	You heard, we are both done for.

TAMINO

Stille, sag' ich!—Schweige still!	Quiet, I tell you! Be quiet!

PAPAGENO

Immer still und immer still!	Always quiet and always quiet!

THE THREE LADIES

Ganz nah ist euch die Königin!	The queen is very near to you!
Sie drang in Tempel heimlich ein.	She has secretly gotten into the temple.

PAPAGENO

Wie? Was? Sie soll im Tempel sein?	How? What? She is in the temple?

TAMINO

Stille, sag' ich!—Schweige still!—	Quiet, I tell you! Be quiet!
Wirst du immer so vermessen	Will you impudently forget
Deiner Eidespflicht vergessen?	The obligation of your oath?

THE THREE LADIES

Tamino, hör! Du bist verloren!	Tamino, listen! You are lost!
Gedenke an die Königin!	Think about the queen!
Man zischelt viel sich in die Ohren	A great deal is being whispered
Von dieser Priester falschem Sinn.	About the treacherous minds of these priests.

TAMINO (*to himself*)

Ein Weiser prüft und achtet nicht,	A wise man considers and disregards
Was der gemeine Pöbel spricht.	What the common rabble says.

THE THREE LADIES

Man sagt, wer ihrem Bunde schwört,	It is said that whoever is initiated into their Craft
Der fährt zur Höll' mit Haut und Haar.	Goes straight to hell.

PAPAGENO

Das wär' der Teufel unerhört!	The devil! That would be outrageous!
Sag an, Tamino, ist das wahr?	Tell me, Tamino, is that so?

TAMINO

Geschwätz von Weibern nachgesagt,	Prattle repeated by women,
Von Heuchlern aber ausgedacht.	But invented by hypocrites.

PAPAGENO

Doch sagt es auch die Königin.	But the queen says it too!

TAMINO

Sie ist ein Weib, hat Weibersinn.	She is a woman, has a woman's mind.
Sei still, mein Wort sei dir genug.	Be quiet, let my word be good enough for you.
Denk deiner Pflicht und handle klug.	Think about your oath and act prudently.

THE THREE LADIES (*to Tamino*)

Warum bist du mit uns so spröde?	Why are you so reserved with us?

(Tamino indicates modestly that he is not allowed to speak.)

Auch Papageno schweigt—so rede!	Papageno also is silent—tell us!

PAPAGENO (*to the Ladies, furtively*)

Ich möchte gerne—woll—	I would like to very much . . .

TAMINO

Still!	Quiet!

PAPAGENO (*furtively*)

Ihr seht, daß ich nicht soll—	You see, that I shouldn't . . .

TAMINO

Still!	Quiet!
Daß du nicht kannst das Plaudern lassen,	That you cannot give up chattering
Ist wahrlich eine Schand' für dich!	Is really a disgrace!

PAPAGENO

Daß ich nicht kann das Plaudern lassen,	That I cannot give up chattering
Ist wahrlich eine Schand' für mich!	Is really a disgrace.

THE THREE LADIES

Wir müssen sie mit Scham verlassen,	We must abandon them in shame.
Es plaudert keiner sicherlich!	It is certain that no one will chatter.
Von festem Geiste ist ein Mann,	A man is of firm spirit;
Er denket, was er sprechen kann.	He thinks about what he may say.

TAMINO and PAPAGENO

Sie müssen uns mit Scham verlassen,	They must abandon us in shame,
Es plaudert keiner sicherlich!	It is certain that no one will chatter.
Von festen Geiste ist ein Mann,	A man is of firm spirit.
Er denket, was er sprechen kann.	He thinks about what he may say.

(The Ladies are about to go. The Initiated Ones shout from within.)

CHORUS

Entweiht ist die heilige Schwelle!	Profaned is the holy threshold!
Hinab mit den Weibern zur Hölle!	Down to hell with the women!

(A terrifying chord on all instruments. Thunder, lightning and crashing, two strong thunderclaps at the same time.)

THE THREE LADIES

O weh! O weh! O weh!   Alas! Alas! Alas!

(They fall into the trap opening.)

PAPAGENO

(falls terrified to the ground.)

O wch! O weh! O weh!   Alas! Alas! Alas!

(Then the chord is heard three times.)

SCENE VI

Tamino, Papageno, Speaker and Second Priest with torches.

Spoken dialogue

SPEAKER

Heil dir, Jüngling! Dein standhaft männliches Betragen hat gesiegt. Zwar hast du noch manch rauhen und gefährlichen Weg zu wandern, den du aber durch Hülfe der Götter glücklich endigen wirst.—Wir wollen also mit reinem Herzen unsere Wanderschaft weiter fortsetzen.—

Hail to thee, youth! Your steadfast, manly conduct has been victorious. You still have many rough and dangerous paths to travel, which however with the help of the gods will end in happiness. Therefore, with pure hearts we shall continue our travels.

(He covers Tamino's head.)

So! Nun komm!   There! Now come!

(They leave.)

SECOND PRIEST

Was seh'ich! Freund, stehe auf! Wie ist dir?

What do I see! Friend, stand up! What is the matter with you?

PAPAGENO

Ich lieg' in einer Ohnmacht.   I am lying in a faint.

SECOND PRIEST

Auf! Sammle dich, und sei ein Mann!   Up! Pull yourself together and be a man!

PAPAGENO (*stands up*)

Aber sagt mir nur, meine Lieben Herren, warum muß ich denn alle diese Qualen und Schrecken empfinden?—Wenn mir ja die Götter eine Papagena bestimmten, warum denn mit so viel Gefahren sie erringen?

But just tell me this, my dear sirs, why must I experience all these ordeals and terrors? If the gods have indeed designated a Papagena for me, why then must I go through so many dangers to win her?

SECOND PRIEST

Diese neugierige Frage mag deine Vernunft dir beantworten. Komm! meine Pflicht heischt dich weiterzuführen.

May your reason answer this prying question for you. Come! My duty is to lead you further.

(*He puts the covering over Papageno's head.*)

PAPAGENO

Bei so einer ewigen Wanderschaft möcht' einem wohl die Liebe auf immer vergehen.

With such eternal wandering one may as well give up love forever!

(*leaves*)

SCENE VII

The stage set is changed into a pleasant garden. Trees are set out in a sort of horseshoe pattern; in the middle stands an arbor of blossoms and roses in which Pamina sleeps. The moon illuminates her face. Downstage stands a bench.

(*Monostatos appears, and after a pause sits down.*)

Spoken monologue

MONOSTATOS

Ha, da find' ich ja die spröde Schöne!— Und um so einer geringen Pflanze wegen wollte man meine Fußsohlen behämmern?—Also bloß dem heutigen Tag hab' ich's zu verdanken, daß ich noch mit heiler Haut auf die Erde trete. Hm!—Was war denn eigentlich mein Verbrechen? daß ich mich in eine Blume vergaffte, die auf fremdem Boden versetzt war?—Und welcher Mensch, wenn er auch von gelinderm Himmelsstrich

Ha, here I find the coy beauty! And on behalf of such an inferior plant, they wanted to beat the soles of my feet? I owe it only to this eventful day that I still walk the earth with a whole skin! Hm! Then what was my offense exactly? That I fell in love with a flower that had been transplanted into foreign soil? And what man, if he had also travelled here from a milder climate, would at such a sight remain cold and unfeeling? By all the

daherwanderte, würde bei so einem
Anblick kalt und unempfindlich
bleiben?—Bei allen Sternen! das
Mädchen wird noch um meinen Verstand
mich bringen! Das Feuer, das in mir
glimmt, wird mich noch verzehren.

stars, the maiden still drives me mad! The
fire which glows in me will finally
consume me.

(He looks all around him.)

Wenn ich wüßte—daß ich so ganz allein
und unbelauscht wäre,—ich wagte es
noch einmal.

If I knew that I was completely alone and
could not be overheard, I would dare it
once more.

(He fans himself with both hands.)

Es ist doch eine verdammt närrische
Sache um die Liebe!—Ein Küßchen,
dächte ich, ließe sich entschuldigen.

It is a damned foolish thing—love!—a
little kiss, I would think, would be
excused.

No. 13 Aria

Alles fühlt der Liebe Freuden,
Schnäbelt, tändelt, herzet, küßt;
Und ich soll die Liebe meiden,
Weil ein Schwarzer häßlich ist.
Ist mir denn kein Herz gegeben?
Bin ich nicht von Fleisch und Blut?
Immer ohne Weibchen leben,
Wäre wahrlich Höllenglut.

Everyone feels the joys of love,
Bills and coos, flirts, cuddles, kisses;
And I am to avoid love,
Since a black man is considered ugly.
Didn't I receive a heart as well?
Am I not of flesh and blood?
To always live without a little wife
Would truly be hellfire.

Drum so will ich, weil ich lebe,
Schnäbeln, küssen, zärtlich sein!
Lieber guter Mond—vergebe,
Eine Weiße nahm mich ein.
Weiß ist schön!—Ich muß sie küssen;
Mond! verstecke dich dazu!—
Sollt' es dich zu sehr verdrießen,
O so mach die Augen zu!

Therefore, because I am alive, I want to
Bill and coo, kiss, be tender!
Dear, good moon, forgive me,
A white woman has charmed me.
White is beautiful! I must kiss her;
Moon! Hide yourself from it!
If it should annoy you too much,
Oh then, shut your eyes!

(He creeps slowly and softly within.)

SCENE VIII

(Accompanied by thunder, the queen comes from the middle trap door, and in such a way that she comes to stand directly in front of Pamina.)

Spoken dialogue

QUEEN

Zurück!   Stand back!

PAMINA *(awakes)*

Ihr Götter!   Ye gods!

MONOSTATOS *(recoils)*

O weh!—Das ist—wo ich nicht irre, die Göttin der Nacht.	Alas!—that is—if I am not mistaken, the goddess of the night.

(stands very still)

PAMINA

Mutter! Mutter! meine Mutter!   Mother! Mother! My mother!

(She falls into her arms.)

MONOSTATOS

Mutter? Hm! Das muß man von weitem belauschen.	Mother? Hm! I must listen to this—at a distance.

(creeps out)

QUEEN

Verdank es der Gewalt, mit der man dich mir entriß, daß ich noch deine Mutter mich nenne.—Wo ist der Jüngling, den ich an dich sandte?	You should thank the force by which you were torn from me, that I still call myself your mother. Where is the youth whom I sent to you?

PAMINA

Ach, Mutter, der ist der Welt und den Menschen auf ewig entzogen.—Er hat sich den Eingeweihten gewidmet.	Ah, Mother, he is beyond the world and men forever. He has dedicated himself to the Initiated Ones.

QUEEN

Den Eingeweihten?—Unglückliche Tochter, nun bist du auf ewig mir entrissen.—	The Initiated Ones? Unhappy daughter, now you are torn from me forever.

PAMINA

Entrissen?—O fliehen wir, liebe Mutter! Unter deinem Schutz trotz ich jeder Gefahr.

Torn from you? Oh let us flee, dear mother! Under your protection I will defy every danger.

QUEEN

Schutz? Liebes Kind, deine Mutter kann dich nicht mehr schützen. —Mit deines Vaters Tod ging meine Macht zu Grabe.

Protection? Dear child, your mother can no longer protect you. My power ended with your father's death.

PAMINA

Mein Vater—

My father—

QUEEN

Übergab freiwillig den siebenfachen Sonnenkreis den Eingeweihten; diesen mächtigen Sonnenkreis trägt Sarastro auf seiner Brust.—Als ich ihn darüber beredete, so sprach er mit gefalteter Stirne: «Weib! meine letzte Stunde ist da—alle Schätze, so ich allein besaß, sind dein und deiner Tochter.»—«Der alles verzehrende Sonnenkreis» —fiel ich ihm hastig in die Rede—«Ist den Geweihten bestimmt», antwortete er. «Sarastro wird ihn so männlich verwalten, wie ich bisher. Und nun kein Wort weiter; forsche nicht nach Wesen, die dem weiblichen Geist unbegreiflich sind.—Deine Pflicht ist, dich und deine Tochter, der Führung weiser Männer zu überlassen.»

Surrendered voluntarily the Sevenfold Suncircle to the Initiated Ones; Sarastro wears this powerful suncircle on his breast. When I spoke to your father about it, he said with furrowed brow, "Wife! My last hour is at hand—all the treasure which I alone possessed is yours and your daughter's." "The all-consuming suncircle," I quickly interrupted him. "Is intended for the initiates," he answered. "Sarastro will manfully hold it in trust, as I did. And not one word more; inquire not about matters which are incomprehensible to the female mind. Your obligation is to surrender yourself and your daughter to the leadership of wise men."

PAMINA

Liebe Mutter, nach allem dem zu schließen, ist wohl auch der Jüngling auf immer für mich verloren.

Dear Mother, apparently, the youth is lost to me forever.

QUEEN

Verloren, wenn du nicht, eh' die Sonne die Erde färbt, ihn durch diese unterirdischen Gewölber zu fliehen beredest.—Der erste Schimmer des Tages entscheidet, ob er ganz dir oder den Eingeweihten gegeben sei.

Lost, if before day dawns, you don't persuade him to flee these underground vaults. The first glimmer of day decides whether he be given wholly to you or to the Initiated Ones.

PAMINA

Liebe Mutter, dürft' ich den Jüngling als Eingeweihten denn nicht auch ebenso zärtlich lieben, wie ich ihn jetzt liebe?— Mein Vater selbst war ja mit diesen weisen Männern verbunden; er sprach jederzeit mit Entzücken von ihnen, preiste ihre Güte—ihren Verstand—ihre Tugend.—Sarastro ist nicht weniger tugendhaft.—

Dear Mother, could I not love the youth just as tenderly as an Initiated One as I love him now? My father himself was associated with these wise men; he always spoke with enthusiasm about them, praised their goodness—their intelligence—their virtue. Sarastro is no less virtuous.

QUEEN

Was hör' ich!—Du, meine Tochter, könntest die schändlichen Gründe dieser Barbaren verteidigen?—So einen Mann lieben, der, mit meinem Todfeind verbunden, mit jedem Augenblick mir meinen Sturz bereiten würde?—Siehst du hier diesen Stahl?—Er ist für Sarastro geschliffen.—Du wirst ihn töten und den mächtigen Sonnenkreis mir überliefern.

What do I hear! You, my daughter, could defend the shameful cause of these barbarians—to love such a man, who, allied with my arch-enemy, would be preparing my overthrow with every moment? Do you see this blade? It has been sharpened for Sarastro. You will kill him, and deliver the powerful suncircle to me.

PAMINA

Aber liebste Mutter!—

But dearest Mother!

QUEEN

Kein Wort!

Not a word!

No. 14 Aria

Der Hölle Rache kocht in meinem Herzen,
Tod und Verzweiflung flammet um mich her!
Fühlt nicht durch dich Sarastro Todesschmerzen,
So bist du meine Tochter nimmermehr.
Verstoßen sei auf ewig, verlassen sei auf ewig,
Zertrümmert sei'n auf ewig alle Bande der Natur,
Wenn nicht durch dich Sarastro wird erblassen!
Hört, Rachegötter! Hört der Mutter Schwur!

Hell's revenge boils in my heart,

Death and desperation blaze all around me!
If, through you, Sarastro does not feel the pains of death,
Then you are no longer my daughter.
Be cast out forever, be forsaken forever,

Be crushed forever all natural bonds,

If Sarastro be not destroyed by you!

Heed, gods of vengeance. Heed a mother's oath!

(*She sinks down.*)

SCENE IX

Pamina alone

Spoken monologue

PAMINA (*with the dagger in her hand*)

Morden soll ich?—Götter! Das kann ich nicht—das kann ich nicht!

I am to commit murder? Gods! That I cannot do—that I cannot do!

(*stands lost in thought*)

SCENE X

The above. Monostatos.

Spoken dialogue

MONOSTATOS

(*comes forward swiftly, stealthily and very joyfully*)

Sarastros Sonnenkreis hat also auch seine Wirkung?—Und diesen zu erhalten, soll das schöne Mädchen ihn morden?—Das ist Salz in meine Suppe.

Then Sarastro's suncircle also has its influence? And in order to obtain it, the beautiful maiden is to commit murder? That is salt in my soup.

PAMINA

Aber schwur sie nicht bei allen Göttern, mich zu verstoßen, wenn ich den Dolch nicht gegen Sarastro kehre?—Götter!— Was soll ich tun?

But did she not swear by all the gods to cast me out, if I didn't turn the dagger on Sarastro? Gods! What am I to do now?

MONOSTATOS

Dich mir anvertraun!

Entrust yourself to me!

(*takes the dagger from her*)

PAMINA (*startled, cries out*)

Ha!

Ah!

MONOSTATOS

Warum zitterst du? Vor meiner schwarzen Farbe oder vor dem ausgedachten Mord?

Why do you tremble? Because of my black color, or because of the murder that is planned?

PAMINA (*timidly*)

Du weißt also?

Then you know?

MONOSTATOS

Alles.—Ich weiß sogar, daß nicht nur dein, sondern auch deiner Mutter Leben in meiner Hand steht.—Ein einziges Wort sprech' ich zu Sarastro, und deine Mutter wird in diesem Gewölbe, in eben dem Wasser, das die Eingeweihten reinigen soll, wie man sagt, ersäuft.—Aus diesem Gewölbe kommt sie nun sicher nicht mehr mit heiler Haut, wenn ich es will.—Du hast also nur einen Weg, dich und deine Mutter zu retten.

Everything. I even know that not only your life but also that of your mother is in my hands. I speak a single word to Sarastro and your mother drowns in this cavern, in the very water in which the Initiated are to be purified. If I choose, it is certain that she will never come out of this vault again with a whole skin. So you have only one way to save yourself and your mother.

PAMINA

Der wäre?

That is?

MONOSTATOS

Mich zu lieben!

To love me!

PAMINA (*trembling, to herself*)

Götter!

Gods!

MONOSTATOS (*joyfully*)

Das junge Bäumchen jagt der Sturm auf meine Seite.—Nun, Mädchen!—ja oder nein!

The storm chases the uprooted sapling to my side. Now, maiden! Yes or no!

PAMINA (*resolutely*)

Nein!

No!

MONOSTATOS (*full of rage*)

Nein? Und warum? Weil ich die Farbe eines schwarzen Gespensts trage?— Nicht?—Ha! so stirb!

No? And why not? Because I wear the color of a black specter? Isn't that it? Ha! Then die!

(*He grasps her by the hand.*)

PAMINA

Monostatos, sieh mich hier auf meinen Knien—schone meiner!

Monostatos, see me here on my knees! Spare me!

MONOSTATOS

Liebe oder Tod!—Sprich! Dein Leben steht auf der Spitze.

Love or death! Speak! Your life stands at the point of this dagger.

PAMINA

Mein Herz hab ich dem Jüngling geopfert.	I have pledged my heart to the youth.

MONOSTATOS

Was kümmert mich dein Opfer— sprich!—	What do I care about your pledge— speak!

PAMINA (*resolute*)

Nie!	Never!

SCENE XI

The above. Sarastro.

MONOSTATOS

So fahr denn hin!	Then farewell.

(*Sarastro quickly restrains him.*)

Herr, mein Unternehmen ist nicht strafbar; man hat deinen Tod geschworen, darum wollt' ich dich rächen.	Lord, my action is not criminal; they have sworn your death, therefore I wished to avenge you.

SARASTRO

Ich weiß nur allzuviel. Weiß, daß deine Seele ebenso schwarz als dein Gesicht ist.—Auch würde ich dies schwarze Unternehmen mit höchster Strenge an dir bestrafen, wenn nicht ein böses Weib, das zwar eine sehr gute Tochter hat, den Dolch dazu geschmiedet hätte. — Verdank es der bösen Handlung des Weibes, daß du ungestraft davonziehst.— Geh!—	I understand all too well. I know that your soul is as black as your face. I would surely punish you for this black deed with the utmost severity, had not an evil woman, who has a very good daughter, had the dagger forged. It is thanks to the evil doings of that woman that you get away unpunished. Go!

MONOSTATOS (*as he is leaving*)

Jetzt such' ich die Mutter auf, weil die Tochter mir nicht beschieden ist.	Now I will seek out the mother, since the daughter is not granted to me.

(*leaves*)

Scene XII

The above, without Monostatos.

PAMINA

Herr, strafe meine Mutter nicht, der
Schmerz über meine Abwesenheit—

Lord, do not punish my mother; the pain
of my absence—

SARASTRO

Ich weiß alles.—Weiß, daß sie in
unterirdischen Gemächern des Tempels
herumirrt und Rache über mich und die
Menschheit kocht; —Allein, du sollst
sehen, wie ich mich an deiner Mutter
räche.—Der Himmel schenke nur dem
holden Jüngling Mut und Standhaftigkeit
in seinem frommen Vorsatz, dann bist du
mit ihm glücklich, und deine Mutter soll
beschämt nach ihrer Burg zurückkehren.

I know everything. I know that she
wanders about in the underground
chambers of the temple and plans revenge
on me and all of mankind; but, you will
see how I avenge myself on your mother.
If only heaven grant to the sweet youth
courage and steadfastness in his pious
purpose, then you will be happy with
him, and your mother, humiliated, will
return to her castle.

No. 15 Aria

In diesen heil'gen Hallen
Kennt man die Rache nicht.—
Und ist ein Mensch gefallen,
Führt Liebe hin zur Pflicht.
Dann wandelt er an Freundes Hand
Vergnügt und froh ins beß're Land.

Within these sacred halls,
Vengeance is unknown.
And should a man err,
Love leads him to his duty.
Then he travels, guided by a friend
Delighted and cheerful in a better land.

In diesen heil'gen Mauern,
Wo Mensch den Menschen liebt,
Kann kein Verräter lauern,
Weil man dem Feind vergibt.
Wen solche Lehren nicht erfreu'n,
Verdienet nicht, ein Mensch zu sein.

Within these sacred walls,
Where human beings love one another,
No traitor can lie in wait,
Since everyone forgives his enemy.
He who doesn't rejoice in such teachings
Doesn't deserve to be called a human
being.

(They both go out.)

Scene XIII

*The stage set is changed into a hall, where an aerial gondola can
fly. The gondola is covered with roses and other flowers, and it
has a door that opens. In the foreground are two benches.*

(Tamino and Papageno, without headcovering, are being led in by the two priests.)

Spoken dialogue

SPEAKER

Hier seid ihr euch beide allein überlassen.—Sobald die röchelnde Posaune tönt, dann nehmt ihr euren Weg dahin.—Prinz, lebt wohl! Wir sehen uns, eh' ihr ganz am Ziele seid.—Noch einmal, vergeßt das Wort nicht: Schweigen!—

Here you will be left to yourselves. As soon as the roaring trombones sound, then make your way in that direction. Prince, farewell! We will see each other again before you have quite attained your goal. Once again, do not forget the word "silence."

(leaves)

SECOND PRIEST

Papageno, wer an diesem Ort sein Stillschweigen bricht, den strafen die Götter durch Donner und Blitz. Leb wohl!

Papageno, he who breaks his vow of silence in this place, will be punished by the gods with thunder and lightning. Farewell!

(leaves)

SCENE XIV

Tamino. Papageno.

(Tamino sits down on a bench.)

PAPAGENO *(after a pause)*

Tamino!

Tamino!

TAMINO *(disapproving)*

St!

Sh!

PAPAGENO

Das ist ein lustiges Leben!—Wär' ich lieber in meiner Strohhütte oder im Walde, so hört' ich doch manchmal einen Vogel pfeifen.

This is a merry life! I would rather be in my straw hut or in the woods; at least then I might hear a bird chirping sometimes.

TAMINO *(disapproving)*

St!

Sh!

PAPAGENO

Mit mir selbst werd' ich wohl sprechen dürfen; und auch wir zwei können zusammen sprechen, wir sind ja Männer.

I should be able to talk to myself. And we two could talk together; after all, we are men.

TAMINO (*disapproving*)

St!	Sh!

PAPAGENO (*sings*)

Lalala—lalala!—Nicht einmal einen Tropfen Wasser bekommt man bei diesen Leuten; viel weniger sonst was.—	La la la—la la la!. Not so much as a drop of water do you get from these people, much less anything else.

SCENE XV

(*An ugly old woman comes out of the trap, carrying a large glass of water on a tray.*)

PAPAGENO (*looks at her for a long time*)

Ist das für mich?	Is that for me?

WOMAN

Ja, mein Engel!	Yes, my angel!

PAPAGENO (*looks at her again, drinks*)

Nicht mehr und nicht weniger als Wasser.—Sag du mir, du unbekannte Schöne! werden alle fremde Gäste auf diese Art bewirtet?	No more and no less than water. Tell me, you unknown beauty! Are all foreign guests entertained in this way?

WOMAN

Freilich, mein Engel!	Of course, my angel!

PAPAGENO

So, so!—Auf die Art werden die Fremden auch nicht gar zu häufig kommen.—	I see! In that case, strangers must not come very frequently.

WOMAN

Sehr wenig.	Very few do.

PAPAGENO

Kann mir's denken.—Geh, Alte, setze dich her zu mir, mir ist die Zeit verdammt lange.—Sag du mir, wie alt bist du denn?	I can well imagine. Come, old woman, sit here beside me. I've got a lot of time to kill. Tell me, how old are you?

WOMAN

Wie alt?	How old?

PAPAGENO

Ja!	Yes.

WOMAN

Achtzehn Jahr und zwei Minuten.   Eighteen years and two minutes.

PAPAGENO

Achtzehn Jahr und zwei Minuten?   Eighteen years and two minutes?

WOMAN

Ja!   Yes.

PAPAGENO

Hahaha! Ei, du junger Engel! Hast du   Ha, ha, ha! Well, you young angel! Do
auch einen Geliebten?   you have a sweetheart too?

WOMAN

I, freilich!   Ooh, of course!

PAPAGENO

Ist er auch so jung wie du?   Is he also as young as you are?

WOMAN

Nicht gar, er ist um zehn Jahre älter.—   Not quite, he is ten years older.

PAPAGENO

Um zehn Jahre ist er älter als du?—Das   He is ten years older than you? That must
muß eine Liebe sein!—Wie nennt sich   be quite a romance. What is the name of
denn dein Liebhaber?   your lover?

WOMAN

Papageno!   Papageno!

PAPAGENO (*startled; pause*)

Papageno!—Wo ist er denn, dieser   Papageno? Where is he, this Papageno?
Papageno?

WOMAN

Da sitzt er, mein Engel.   He's sitting right here, my angel.

PAPAGENO

Ich wär' dein Geliebter?   I'm your sweetheart?

WOMAN

Ja, mein Engel!   Yes, my angel!

PAPAGENO
(*quickly takes the water, and sprinkles her in the face*)

Sag du mir, wie heißt du denn?   Tell me, what is your name?

WOMAN

Ich heiße—	My name is—

(Loud thunder. The old woman quickly limps off.)

PAPAGENO

O weh!	Alas!

(Tamino stands up, wags his finger at him.)

Nun sprech ich kein Wort mehr!	Now I won't say another word!

SCENE XVI

(The three boys come flying on in a gondola covered with roses. In the middle of it stands a table, beautifully set. One of the boys has the flute, another has the little box with the bells in it. The above.)

No. 16 Trio

THE THREE BOYS

Seid uns zum zweitenmal willkommen,	You men are welcome for the second time
Ihr Männer, in Sarastros Reich!	In Sarastro's kingdom!
Er schickt, was man euch abgenommen,	He sends what was taken from you,
Die Flöte und die Glöckchen euch.	Your flute and your bells.
Wollt ihr die Speisen nicht verschmähen,	Do not disdain the food,
So esset, trinket froh davon.	Eat and drink freely of it.
Wenn wir zum drittenmal uns sehen,	If we see each other for a third time,
Ist Freude eures Mutes Lohn!	Then joy will be the reward for your courage!
Tamino, Mut! Nah ist das Ziel!	Tamino, courage! Your goal is near!
Du, Papageno, schweige still!	You, Papageno, be silent!

(During the trio, they put the table in the middle of the stage, and then travel off.)

SCENE XVII

Tamino. Papageno.

Spoken monologue

PAPAGENO

Tamino, wollen wir nicht speisen?—	Tamino, aren't we going to eat?

(Tamino blows on his flute.)

Blase du nur fort auf deiner Flöte, ich will meine Brocken blasen.——Herr Sarastro führt eine gute Küche.——Auf die Art, ja da will ich schon schweigen, wenn ich immer solche gute Bissen bekomme. Nun ich will sehen, ob auch der Keller so gut bestellt ist.——

You go on blowing on your flute, I am going to play a different tune. Lord Sarastro runs a good kitchen. This way I'll gladly be silent, as long as I always get such goodies. Now I'll see if the cellar is as well stocked.

(He drinks.)

Ha!   das ist Götterwein!——

Ah! That is wine fit for the gods!

(The flute is silent.)

SCENE XVIII

Pamina. The above.

Spoken dialogue

PAMINA (*joyfully*)

Du hier?——Gütige Götter! Dank euch, daß ihr mich diesen Weg führtet.——Ich hörte deine Flöte, und so lief ich pfeilschnell dem Tone nach.——Aber du bist traurig?——Sprichst nicht eine Silbe mit deiner Pamina?

You here? Kindly gods, thank you for leading me this way. I heard your flute and ran as quickly as an arrow towards the sound. But you are sad? Won't you say even a syllable to your Pamina?

TAMINO (*sighs*)

Ah!

Ah!

(gestures for her to go away)

PAMINA

Wie? Ich soll dich meiden? Liebst du mich nicht mehr?

What? I am to stay away from you? Don't you love me any more?

TAMINO (*sighs*)

Ah!

Ah!

(waves her away again)

PAMINA

Ich soll fliehen, ohne zu wissen, warum?——Tamino, holder Jüngling! Hab' ich dich beleidigt?——O kränke mein Herz nicht noch mehr.——Bei dir such' ich

I am to flee without knowing why? Tamino, sweet youth! Have I offended you? Oh, do not wound my heart still more. I seek comfort——help——from you

Trost—Hülfe—und du kannst mein
liebevolles Herz noch mehr kränken?—
Liebst du mich nicht mehr?

and can you wound my loving heart even
more? Don't you love me any more?

(Tamino sighs.)

Papageno, sag du mir, sag, was ist
meinem Freund?

Papageno, you tell me, what is wrong
with my friend?

*(Papageno has some food in his mouth, covers the food on the
table with both hands, signals her to go away.)*

Wie? Auch du?—Erkläre mir wenigstens
die Ursache eures Stillschweigens.—

What? You too? At least explain to me
the reason for your keeping still.

PAPAGENO

St!

Sh!

(He shows her that she should go away.)

PAMINA

O das ist mehr als Kränkung—mehr als
Tod!

Oh that is worse than injury—worse
than death.

(pause)

Liebster, einziger Tamino!—

Beloved, one and only, Tamino!

No. 17 Aria

Ach ich fühl's, es ist verschwunden,—
Ewig hin der Liebe Glück!
Nimmer kommt ihr Wonnestunden
Meinem Herzen mehr zurück!
Sieh Tamino diese Tränen
Fließen Trauter dir allein.
Fühlst du nicht der Liebe Sehnen,
So wird Ruh' im Tode sein!

Ah, I feel it, it has vanished,
Forever gone is love's happiness!
Those hours of bliss will never
Return to my heart again!
Tamino, see these tears which are
Flowing, dear one, for you alone.
If you no longer feel the yearning of love,
Then I will find rest in death.

(leaves)

SCENE XIX

Tamino. Papageno.

Spoken dialogue

PAPAGENO (*eats hastily*)

Nicht wahr, Tamino, ich kann auch
schweigen, wenn's sein muß——Ja, bei so
einem Unternehmen, da bin ich Mann.

At the crucial moment, Tamino, I can also
be quiet, can't I? When it counts, I'm a
man.

(*He drinks.*)

Der Herr Koch und der Herr
Kellermeister sollen leben.——

Long live the cook and the wine cellar
master.

(*The trombone chord sounds three times.*)
(*Tamino gestures to Papageno that he is to go.*)

Gehe du nur voraus, ich komm schon
nach.

You go ahead, I'll come right after you.

(*Tamino tries to take him by force.*)

Der Stärkere bleibt da!

The stronger man stays here.

(*Tamino threatens him and goes off to the right, even though he came on from the left.*)

Jetzt will ich mir's erst recht wohl sein
lassen.——Da ich in meinem besten
Appetit bin, soll ich gehen?——Das laß' ich
wohl bleiben.——Ich ging' jetzt nicht fort,
und wenn Herr Sarastro seine sechs
Löwen an mich spannte.

Now at least I am going to have a good
time. I should leave when my appetite is
at its peak? I won't do that. I wouldn't
leave now if Lord Sarastro hitched his six
lions up to me.

(*The lions come out; he is terrified.*)

O Barmherzigkeit, ihr gütigen Götter!——
Tamino, rette mich! Die Herren Löwen
machen eine Mahlzeit aus mir.——

Have mercy, you kindly gods! Tamino,
save me! The lord's lions are making a
meal out of me!

(*Tamino blows on his flute; comes back quickly; the lions go back in; beckons to him.*)

Ich gehe schon! heiß du mich einen
Schelmen, wenn ich dir nicht in allem
folge.

I'm coming; you can call me a fool if I
don't follow you everywhere.

(*The trombone chord sounds three times.*)

Das geht uns an.—Wir kommen
schon.—Aber hör einmal, Tamino, was
wird denn noch alles mit uns werden?

That's for us. We're coming. But listen,
Tamino, what is to become of us now?

(Tamino gestures toward heaven.)

Die Götter soll ich fragen?

I should ask the gods?

(Tamino nods.)

Ja, die könnten uns freilich mehr sagen,
als wir wissen.

Yes, they could certainly tell us more
than we know now.

(The trombone chord sounds three times.)
(Tamino tugs him along by force.)

Eile nur nicht so, wir kommen noch
immer zeitig genug, um uns braten zu
lassen.

Don't hurry so, we'll be in plenty of time
to be roasted.

(They leave.)

SCENE XX

The stage set is changed into the pyramids' vaults. Speaker and several priests.

(Two priests carry an illuminated pyramid on their shoulders; each priest has a transparent pyramid the size of a lantern in his hand.)

No. 18 Chorus

CHORUS OF PRIESTS

O Isis und Osiris, welche Wonne!
Die düstre Nacht verscheucht der Glanz
   der Sonne.
Bald fühlt der edle Jüngling neues Leben:
Bald ist er unserm Dienste ganz gegeben.

Sein Geist ist kühn, sein Herz ist rein,
Bald wird er unser würdig sein.

Oh Isis and Osiris, what joy!
The brilliance of the sun banishes the
   gloomy night.
Soon the youth will feel new life,
Soon he will be wholly given to our
   service.

His spirit is bold, his heart is pure,
Soon he will be worthy to be one of us.

Scene XXI

Sarastro. Tamino, who is led in. The above. Then Pamina.

Spoken dialogue

SARASTRO

Prinz, dein Betragen war bis hierher männlich und gelassen; nun hast du noch zwei gefährliche Wege zu wandern. Schlägt dein Herz noch ebenso warm für Pamina und wünschest du einst als ein weiser Fürst zu regieren, so mögen die Götter dich ferner begleiten.—Deine Hand—Man bringe Paminen!

Prince, your conduct up to now has been manly and self-possessed; you still have two dangerous paths to travel. If your heart still beats as warmly for Pamina, and if you wish someday to reign as a wise ruler, then may the gods accompany you further. Your hand—let Pamina be brought!

(*A silence reigns over all the priests. Pamina, wearing the same head-covering previously worn by the initiates, is led on. Sarastro unties the binding of the sack.*)

PAMINA

Wo bin ich?—Welch eine fürchterliche Stille!—Saget, wo ist mein Jüngling?—

Where am I? What a frightful silence! Tell me where my young man is.

SARASTRO

Er wartet deiner, um dir das letzte Lebewohl zu sagen.

He awaits you in order to say his last farewell.

PAMINA

Das letzte Lebewohl?—Oh, wo ist er?— Führe mich zu ihm!—

His last farewell? Oh where is he? Lead me to him!

SARASTRO

Hier.—

Here—

PAMINA

Tamino!

Tamino!

TAMINO

Zurück!

Stand back!

No. 19 Trio

PAMINA

Soll ich dich, Teurer! nicht mehr seh'n?

Shall I, dear one, see you no more?

SARASTRO

Ihr werdet froh euch wiedersehn!

You will see each other again in joy!

PAMINA

Dein warten tödliche Gefahren!—	Deadly dangers await you!

TAMINO

Die Götter mögen mich bewahren!—	May the gods preserve me!

SARASTRO

Die Götter mögen ihn bewahren!	May the gods preserve him!

PAMINA

Du wirst dem Tode nicht entgehen;	The apprehension I feel suggests that you
Mir flüstert dieses Ahnung ein.	Will not escape from death.

TAMINO and SARASTRO

Der Götter Wille mag geschehen;	Let the will of the gods be fulfilled,
Ihr Wink soll {ihm / mir} Gesetze sein!—	Their sign shall be {my / his} law.

PAMINA

O liebtest du, wie ich dich liebe,	If you loved me as I love you
Du würdest nicht so ruhig sein.	You would not be so calm.

TAMINO and SARASTRO

Glaub mir, {er / ich} fühlet gleiche Triebe,	Believe me, {I feel / he feels} the same impulse,
	and will
Wird / Werd} ewig dein Getreuer sein.	Always be faithful to you.

SARASTRO

Die Stunde schlägt, nun müßt ihr scheiden.	The hour strikes, now you must depart.

TAMINO and PAMINA

Wie bitter sind der Trennung Leiden!	How sharp are the pangs of separation!

SARASTRO

Tamino muß nun wieder fort!	Tamino must now be on his way again!

TAMINO

Pamina, ich muß wirklich fort!	Pamina, I must really be gone!

PAMINA

Tamino muß nun wirklich fort?	Tamino must really be gone?

SARASTRO and TAMINO

Nun muß $\left\{\begin{array}{l} \text{er} \\ \text{ich} \end{array}\right.$ fort!

$\left.\begin{array}{l} \text{He} \\ \text{I} \end{array}\right\}$ must go now.

PAMINA

So mußt du fort!

Then you must go!

TAMINO

Pamina, lebe wohl!

Pamina, farewell!

PAMINA

Tamino, lebe wohl!

Tamino, farewell!

SARASTRO

Nun eile fort!
Dich ruft dein Wort.
Die Stunde schlägt, wir seh'n uns wieder!

Now hurry away!
Your promise summons you.
The hour strikes, we shall see each other
again!

TAMINO and PAMINA

Ach, goldne Ruhe, kehre wieder!
Lebe wohl! Lebe wohl!

Ah, golden calm, return!
Farewell! Farewell!

SARASTRO

Wir seh'n uns wieder!

We shall see each other again!

(*They withdraw.*)

SCENE XXII

Papageno.

Spoken dialogue

PAPAGENO (*from without*)

Tamino! Tamino! Willst du mich denn gänzlich verlassen?

Tamino! Tamino! Will you completely abandon me?

(*He looks for a way in.*)

Wenn ich nur wenigstens wüßte, wo ich wäre.—Tamino!—Tamino!—Solang ich lebe, bleib' ich nicht mehr von dir.—Nur diesmal verlaß mich armen Reisegefährten nicht!

If only I knew at least where I was . . . Tamino! Tamino! As long as I live, I will never budge from your side. Just this once, don't abandon your poor travelling companion!

(*He comes upon the door, out through which Tamino has been led.*)

A VOICE (*calls out*)

Zurück!   Stay back!

(*Then a thunderclap; flames shoot out from the door; a loud chord.*)

PAPAGENO

Barmherzige Götter!—Wo wend' ich   Merciful gods! Where do I turn back? If I
mich hin?—Wenn ich nur wüßte, wo ich   only knew where I came in.
hereinkam.

(*He comes to the door through which he came in.*)

THE VOICE

Zurück!   Go back!

(*Thunder, fire and chord as before.*)

PAPAGENO

Nun kann ich weder zurück noch   Now I can neither go backwards nor
vorwärts.   forwards.

(*weeps*)

Muß vielleicht am Ende gar verhungern.   In the end, maybe I'll have to starve to
Schon recht!—Warum bin ich mitgereist.   death. Fine thing! Why did I come along?

SCENE XXIII

Speaker with his pyramid. The above.

SPEAKER

Mensch! Du hättest verdient, auf immer   Mortal, you deserve to wander forever in
in finstern Klüften der Erde zu   the dark chasms of the earth; however,
wandern;—die gütigen Götter aber   the kindly gods do not resign you to your
entlassen der Strafe dich.—Dafür aber   punishment. But you will never
wirst du das himmlische Vergnügen der   experience the heavenly pleasures of the
Eingeweihten nie fühlen.   Initiated.

PAPAGENO

Je nun, es gibt ja noch mehr Leute   Oh well, there are plenty of other folks in
meinesgleichen. Mir wäre jetzt ein gut   my situation. Right now the greatest
Glas Wein das größte Vergnügen.   pleasure for me would be a good glass of
                                           wine.

SPEAKER

Sonst hast du keinen Wunsch in dieser   You have no other wish in this world?
Welt?

PAPAGENO

Bis jetzt nicht.

Not up to now.

SPEAKER

Man wird dich damit bedienen.—

You will be served with it.

(Leaves. Immediately a large glass filled with red wine appears from underground.)

PAPAGENO

Juchhe! da ist er schon!—

Hooray! There it is already.

(drinks)

Herrlich!—Himmlisch!—Göttlich!—Ha!
Ich bin jetzt so vergnügt, daß ich bis zur
Sonne fliegen wollte, wenn ich Flügel
hätte. Ha! mir wird ganz wunderlich ums
Herz. Ich möchte—ich wünschte—ja
was denn?

Wonderful! Heavenly! Divine! Ah! I am so
overjoyed that I would like to fly up to
the sun if I had wings. My heart is
suddenly feeling very strange. I would
like—I want—what?

(strikes the bells)

No. 20 Aria

Ein Mädchen oder Weibchen
Wünscht Papageno sich!
O so ein sanftes Täubchen
Wär' Seligkeit für mich!
Dann schmeckte mir Trinken und Essen,

Dann könnt' ich mit Fürsten mich
    messen,
Des Lebens als Weiser mich freu'n
Und wie im Elysium sein.

Ein Mädchen oder Weibchen
Wünscht Papageno sich!
O so ein sanftes Täubchen
Wär Seligkeit für mich!—
Ach kann ich denn keiner von allen
Den reizenden Mädchen gefallen?
Helf eine mir nur aus der Not,

Sonst gräm ich mich wahrlich zu Tod.

Papagena would like a girlfriend
Or a wife for himself!
Oh some gentle little dove
Would make me very happy!
Then food and drink would taste
    wonderful,
Then I could compare myself with
    princes,
Delight in life as a wise man does
And live as if I were in paradise.

Papageno would like a girlfriend
Or a wife for himself!
Oh some gentle little dove
Would make me very happy!
Oh can't I please any
Of the charming maidens?
If only one would help me out of my
    difficulty,
Otherwise I will worry myself to death.

Ein Mädchen oder Weibchen	Papageno would like a girlfriend
Wünscht Papageno sich!	Or a wife for himself!
O so ein sanftes Täubchen	Oh some gentle little dove
Wär' Seligkeit für mich!	Would make me very happy!
Wird keine mir Liebe gewähren,	If no one will grant me love,
So muß mich die Flamme verzehren!	Then I must be consumed by flames!
Doch küßt mich ein weiblicher Mund,	But as soon as I'm kissed by a woman's mouth,
So bin ich schon wieder gesund!	I will be healthy again.

SCENE XXIV

The old woman, dancing, all the time supported by her stick. The above.

Spoken Dialogue

WOMAN

Da bin ich schon, mein Engel!	Here I am again, my angel!

PAPAGENO

Du hast dich meiner erbarmt?	Have you taken pity on me?

WOMAN

Ja, mein Engel!	Yes, my angel!

PAPAGENO

Das ist ein Glück!	That's a piece of luck!

WOMAN

Und wenn du mir versprichst, mir ewig treu zu bleiben, dann sollst du sehen, wie zärtlich dein Weibchen dich lieben wird.	And if you promise to remain forever faithful to me, then you will see how tenderly your little wife will love you.

PAPAGENO

Ei du zärtliches Närrchen!	Oh, you sweet little fool!

WOMAN

Oh wie will ich dich umarmen, dich liebkosen, dich an mein Herz drücken!	Oh how I will embrace you, cuddle you, press you to my heart!

PAPAGENO

Auch ans Herz drücken?	Even press me to your heart?

WOMAN

Komm, reiche mir zum Pfand unsers Bundes deine Hand.	Come, give me your hand in pledge of our union.

PAPAGENO

Nur nicht so hastig, lieber Engel! So ein Bundniß braucht doch auch seine Überlegung.

Not quite so hasty, dear angel! Such an alliance needs some consideration.

WOMAN

Papageno, ich rate dir, zaudre nicht. Deine Hand, oder du bist auf immer hier eingekerkert!

Papageno, I advise you, don't hesitate. Your hand, or you will be imprisoned here forever.

PAPAGENO

Eingekerkert?

Imprisoned?

WOMAN

Wasser und Brot wird deine tägliche Kost sein.—Ohne Freund, ohne Freundin mußt du leben, und der Welt auf immer entsagen.—

Water and bread will be your daily diet. You will have to live without friends, male or female, and to renounce the world forever.

PAPAGENO

Wasser trinken?—Der Welt entsagen?— Nein, da will ich doch lieber eine Alte nehmen, als gar keine.—Nun, da hast du meine Hand mit der Versicherung, daß ich dir immer getreu bleibe,

Drink water? Renounce the world? No, then I would rather take an old woman than none at all. There, you have my hand with the assurance that I will remain forever true to you.

(to himself)

solang ich keine Schönere sehe.

as long as I don't see someone prettier.

WOMAN

Das schwörst du?

You swear it?

PAPAGENO

Ja, das schwör' ich!

Yes, I swear it!

(The Woman is changed into a young woman dressed just like Papageno.)

Pa—Pa—Papagena!

Pa—Pa—Papagena!

(He is about to embrace her.)

SCENE XXV

Speaker. The above.

SPEAKER *(takes her quickly by the hand)*

Fort mit dir, junges Weib! Er ist deiner noch nicht würdig.

Away with you, young woman! He is not yet worthy of you.

(He drags her inside, Papageno is about to follow.)

Zurück, sag ich! Oder zittre.——	Back, I say, or tremble!

PAPAGENO

Eh' ich mich zurückziehe, soll die Erde mich verschlingen.	Before I retreat, may the earth swallow me up.

(He sinks down.)

O ihr Götter!	Oh ye gods!

SCENE XXVI

The stage set is changed into a small garden.
(The three boys travel down in their gondola.)

No. 21 Finale

THE THREE BOYS

Bald prangt, den Morgen zu verkünden,	Soon the sun, shining along its golden pathway,
Die Sonn' auf goldner Bahn.——	Will proclaim the arrival of morning.
Bald soll der Aberglaube schwinden,	Soon superstition will vanish,
Bald siegt der weise Mann.——	Soon the wise man will conquer.
O holde Ruhe, steig hernieder,	Oh sweet calm, descend again
Kehr in der Menschen Herzen wieder;	Return to the hearts of mankind;
Dann ist die Erd' ein Himmelreich,	Then the earth will be a heavenly kingdom,
Und Sterbliche den Göttern gleich.——	And mortals will be like the gods.

FIRST BOY

Doch seht, Verzweiflung quält Paminen!	But look, desperation torments Pamina!

SECOND and THIRD BOYS

Wo ist sie denn?	Where is she?

FIRST BOY

Sie ist von Sinnen!	She is out of her senses!

THE THREE BOYS

Sie quält verschmähter Liebe Leiden.	She is tormented by the suffering of love scorned.
Laßt uns der Armen Trost bereiten!	Let us give the poor one comfort!
Fürwahr, ihr Schicksal geht uns nah!	In truth, her fate grieves us!
O wäre nur ihr Jüngling da!——	If only the youth were here!

Sie kommt, laßt uns beiseite geh'n,   She is coming! Let us go off to one side,
Damit wir, was sie mache, seh'n.   So that we can see what she is doing.

(They go off to one side.)

Scene XXVII

Pamina, half mad, with a dagger in her hand. The above.

PAMINA *(to the dagger)*

Du also bist mein Bräutigam?   So you will be my bridegroom?
Durch dich vollend' ich meinen Gram.—   Through you will I end my grief.

THE THREE BOYS *(aside)*

Welch dunkle Worte sprach sie da?   What dark words is she speaking?
Die Arme ist dem Wahnsinn nah.   The poor one is near to madness.

PAMINA

Geduld, mein Trauter! ich bin dein;   Patience, my faithful one, I am yours;
Bald werden wir vermählet sein.   Soon we shall be wed!

THE THREE BOYS *(aside)*

Wahnsinn tobt ihr im Gehirne;   Madness rages in her brain;
Selbstmord steht auf ihrer Stirne.   Suicide is written on her brow.

(to Pamina)

Holdes Mädchen, sieh uns an!   Sweet maiden, look at us!

PAMINA

Sterben will ich, weil der Mann,   I want to die, since the man
Den ich nimmermehr kann hassen,   Whom I can never hate, is able to
Seine Traute kann verlassen.   Forsake his faithful one.

(indicating the dagger)

Dies gab meine Mutter mir.   My mother gave this to me.

THE THREE BOYS

Selbstmord strafet Gott an dir.   God will punish you for committing
      suicide.

PAMINA

Lieber durch dies Eisen sterben,   I would rather die by this knife
Als durch Liebesgram verderben.   Than be destroyed by the sorrow of love!
Mutter, durch dich leide ich,   Mother! Through you I am suffering,
Und dein Fluch verfolget mich.   And your curse pursues me.

The Three Boys

Mädchen, willst du mit uns gehn?   Maiden, will you go with us?

Pamina

Ja des Jammers Maß ist voll!   The cup of my misery is full.
Falscher Jüngling, lebe wohl!   False youth, farewell!
Sieh, Pamina stirbt durch dich: See, Pamina dies because of you!
Dieses Eisen töte mich.   This knife will kill me.

(She raises it to stab herself.)

The Three Boys *(catching her arm)*

Ha, Unglückliche! Halt ein!   Ah! Unhappy one! Stop!
Sollte dies dein Jüngling sehen,   If your young man were to see this,
Würde er vor Gram vergehen,   He would die of sorrow,
Denn er liebet dich allein.   For he loves only you.

Pamina *(recovering herself)*

Was? Er fühlte Gegenliebe   What? He returned my love
Und verbarg mir seine Triebe,   Yet concealed his feelings from me,
Wandte sein Gesicht von mir?   Turned his face away from me?
Warum sprach er nicht mit mir?   Why didn't he speak to me?

The Three Boys

Dieses müssen wir verschweigen,   We must keep this hidden,
Doch, wir wollen dir ihn zeigen,   But we will show him to you,
Und du wirst mit Staunen seh'n,   And you will see with amazement,
Daß er dir sein Herz geweiht,   That he has consecrated his heart to you,
Und den Tod für dich nicht scheut.   And for your sake shrinks not from death.

Pamina

Führt mich hin, ich möcht ihn seh'n.   Lead me there, I want to see him.

The Three Boys

Komm, wir wollen zu ihm geh'n.   Come, we will go to him.

All Four

Zwei Herzen, die von Liebe brennen,   Two hearts which burn with love,
Kann Menschenohnmacht niemals trennen.   Can never be separated by human helplessness.
Verloren ist der Feinde Müh';   The enemy's efforts are futile;
Die Götter selbsten schützen sie.   The gods themselves are protecting you.

(They leave.)

SCENE XXVIII

The stage set is changed to two high mountains; inside one is a waterfall which is heard to rush and roar; the other spits out fire; each mountain has a grating through which the fire and water are visible. Where the fire is burning, the horizon must reflect the bright-red glow and where the water is, lies a black mist. The set-pieces are rocks; each set-piece is closed with an iron door. Tamino is lightly dressed, without sandals.

(*Two black-armored men lead Tamino in. Fire burns on their helms. They read him the transparent writing which appears on a pyramid. This pyramid stands in the middle, high up near the grating.*)

THE ARMORED MEN

Der, welcher wandert diese Straße voll Beschwerden,	He who travels these pathways full of difficulties,
Wird rein durch Feuer, Wasser, Luft und Erden;	Will pass through fire, water, air and earth;
Wenn er des Todes Schrecken überwinden kann,	If he can overcome the terror of death,
Schwingt er sich aus der Erde himmelan.	Then he will be raised from earth heavenward.
Erleuchtet wird er dann im Stande sein,	Then he will be able to be enlightened,
Sich den Mysterien der Isis ganz zu weih'n.	To dedicate himself wholly to the mysteries of Isis.

TAMINO

Mich schreckt kein Tod, als Mann zu handeln,—	Death doesn't make me afraid to act like a man,
Den Weg der Tugend fortzuwandeln.	To travel forth on the road of virtue.
Schließt mir des Schreckens Pforten auf,	Open the Gates of Terror to me,
Ich wage froh den kühnen Lauf.	I will gladly dare the bold course.

PAMINA (*from within*)

Tamino, halt! Ich muß dich seh'n.	Tamino, wait! I must see you!

TAMINO

Was hör'ich? Paminens Stimme?	What do I hear? Pamina's voice?

THE ARMORED MEN

Ja, ja, das ist Paminens Stimme!	Yes, yes, that is Pamina's voice!

TAMINO and THE ARMORED MEN

Wohl {mir / dir}, nun kann sie mit {mir / dir} gehn,

Nun trennet {uns / euch} kein Schicksal mehr,

Wenn auch der Tod beschieden wär'!

Then she can now go with {me / you,}

Now no fate separates {us / you} any longer.

Even if death were to be {our / your} lot!

TAMINO

Ist mir erlaubt, mit ihr zu sprechen?   Am I allowed to speak with her?

THE ARMORED MEN

Dir sei erlaubt, mit ihr zu sprechen!   You are allowed to speak with her.

TAMINO and THE ARMORED MEN

Welch Glück, wenn wir $\begin{cases} \text{uns} \\ \text{euch} \end{cases}$
wiederseh'n

What happiness, for $\begin{cases} \text{us} \\ \text{you} \end{cases}$ to see each
other again.

Froh Hand in Hand in Tempel geh'n.

Gladly, hand in hand, to go into the
temple.

Ein Weib, das Nacht und Tod nicht
scheut,
Ist würdig, und wird eingeweiht.

A woman who does not shrink from
night and death,
Is worthy, and will be initiated.

(The door is opened. Tamino & Pamina embrace each other.)

PAMINA

Tamino mein! O welch ein Glück!   My Tamino! Oh what happiness!

TAMINO

Pamina mein! O welch ein Glück!
Hier sind die Schreckenspforten,
Die Not und Tod mir dräun.

My Pamina! Oh what happiness!
Here are the Gates of Terror,
Where danger and death threaten me.

PAMINA

Ich werde aller Orten
An deiner Seite sein.
Ich selbsten führe dich,
Die Liebe leite mich!

Everywhere you go
I will be at your side.
I will lead you myself,
Love guides me!

(She takes him by the hand.)

Sie mag den Weg mit Rosen streu'n,
Weil Rosen stets bei Dornen sein.
Spiel du die Zauberflöte an;
Sie schütze uns auf unsrer Bahn.
Es schnitt in einer Zauberstunde
Mein Vater sie aus tiefstem Grunde
Der tausendjähr'gen Eiche aus
Bei Blitz und Donner, Sturm und Braus.

It may be—strew the path with roses,
Yet roses always have thorns.
You play on the magic flute;
It will protect us along our way.
During a magical hour my father
Carved it from the inner core of
A thousand-year-old oak tree
Amid lightning and thunder, storm and
bluster.

Nun komm und spiel die Flöte an,
Sie leite uns auf grauser Bahn.

Now come and play on the flute!
It will guide us along the grim pathway.

Die Zauberflöte

TAMINO, PAMINA and THE ARMORED MEN

Wir wandeln⎫
Ihr wandelt ⎬ durch des Tones Macht

We ⎫
You ⎬ travel by the power of sound

Froh durch des Todes düstre Nacht.

Gladly through death's gloomy night.

(The doors are slammed shut behind them; one sees Tamino and Pamina walking; one hears the crackling of the fire and the howling of the wind; sometimes also the dull sound of the thunder, and the rushing of water. Tamino blows on the flute. As soon as they come out of the fire they embrace, standing in the middle of the stage.)

TAMINO and PAMINA

Wir wandelten durch Feuergluten,
Bekämpften mutig die Gefahr.
Dein Ton sei Schutz in Wasserfluten,

So wie er es im Feuer war.

We traveled through the fire's glow,
Battled the danger courageously,
Let your sound be our protection in the
    waterfall,
As it was in the fire.

(Tamino blows; one sees them step down and after a little while come out again; immediately a door is opened; one sees the entrance to a brightly-lit temple. A solemn silence. This sight must be of the utmost brilliance. At once the chorus appears, accompanied by kettle drums and trumpets. Before this, however, Tamino and Pamina sing:)

Ihr Götter, welch ein Augenblick!
Gewähret ist uns Isis' Glück.

Ye gods! What a moment!
Isis' happiness is granted to us.

CHORUS

Triumph! Triumph! Du edles Paar!
Besieget hast du die Gefahr!
Der Isis Weihe ist nun dein!
Kommt, tretet in den Tempel ein!

Triumph! Triumph! You noble pair!
You have conquered the danger!
The consecration of Isis is now yours!
Come, enter the temple.

(All leave.)

SCENE XXIX

The stage set is changed back into the garden of the preceding scene.
Papageno. Then the three boys. Finally Papagena.

PAPAGENO *(calls with his panpipes)*

Papagena! Papagena! Papagena!
Weibchen! Täubchen! Meine Schöne!
Vergebens! Ach sie ist verloren!
Ich bin zum Unglück schon geboren.
Ich plauderte—und das war schlecht,

Papagena! Papagena! Papagena!
Little wife! Little dove! My beauty!
In vain! Ah, she is lost!
I was really born unlucky.
I chattered—and that was bad.

Darum geschieht es mir schon recht.	Therefore I got what I really deserved.
Seit ich gekostet diesen Wein—	Since I have tasted this wine—
Seit ich das schöne Weibchen sah—	Since I have seen the beautiful woman—
So brennt's im Herzenskämmerlein.	It burns in my heart's little chamber,
So zwickt es hier, so zwickt es da.	It pinches here, it pinches there!
Papagena! Herzensweibchen!	Papagena! My heart's true love!
Papagena! Liebes Täubchen!	Papagena! Dearest little dove!
'S ist umsonst! Es ist vergebens!	It's no use, it's all in vain,
Müde bin ich meines Lebens!	I am tired of my life!
Sterben macht der Lieb' ein End',	If love burns so fiercely in my heart,
Wenn's im Herzen noch so brennt.	I'll die, and put an end to it.

(Takes a rope from around his middle.)

Diesen Baum da will ich zieren,	I will decorate this tree,
Mir an ihm den Hals zuschnüren,	Hang myself up on it,
Weil das Leben mir mißfällt;	Since life is disagreeable to me;
Gute Nacht, du schwarze Welt!	Good night, you black world!
Weil du böse an mir handelst,	Since you treat me badly,
Mir kein schönes Kind zubandelst,	Bind no beautiful child to me,
So ist's aus, so sterbe ich.	So that's it, then I'll die.
Schöne Mädchen, denkt an mich.	Beautiful girls, think of me.
Will sich eine um mich Armen,	If anyone would take pity
Eh' ich hänge, noch erbarmen,	On poor me before I hang,
Wohl, so laß ich's diesmal sein!	Then just this once, I'd give up the idea.
Rufet nur—ja oder nein.—	Just call out "Yes" or "No".
Keine hört mich; alles stille!	No one hears me, everything is quiet!

(looks around)

Also ist es euer Wille?	So that is your will?
Papageno, frisch hinauf!	Papageno, lively up!
Ende deinen Lebenslauf.	End your life's run.

(Looks around)

Nun, ich warte noch, es sei,	But, I'll wait a bit, it will happen,
Bis man zählet: Eins, zwei, drei.	After I've counted: one, two, three.

(pipes)

Eins!	One!

(looks around, pipes)

Zwei!	Two!

(looks around)

Zwei ist schon vorbei.	Two is already past.

(pipes)

Drei!	Three!

(looks around)

Nun, wohlan, es bleibt dabei!	Well! That's it then!
Weil mich nichts zurücke hält,	Since nothing is holding me back,
Gute Nacht, du falsche Welt!	Good night, you false world!

(is about to hang himself)

THE THREE BOYS *(travel down)*

Halt ein, o Papageno! Und sei klug	Oh Papageno, stop and be smart;
Man lebt nur einmal, dies sei dir genug.	You only live once and that should be enough.

PAPAGENO

Ihr habt gut reden, habt gut scherzen;	You may very well talk and joke;
Doch brennt es euch, wie mich im Herzen,	Yet if you had a burning in your heart like I do,
Ihr würdet auch nach Mädchen geh'n.	You would also chase after girls.

THE THREE BOYS

So lasse deine Glöckchen klingen:	So let your little bells ring,
Dies wird dein Weibchen zu dir bringen.	These will bring your little wife to you.

PAPAGENO

Ich Narr vergaß der Zauberdinge.	Foolish me, I forgot the magic thing!

(Takes out his instrument)

Erklinge, Glockenspiel, erklinge!	Resound, bells, resound!
Ich muß mein liebes Mädchen sehn.	I must see my beloved maiden.
Klinget, Glöckchen, klinget,	Ring, little bells, ring.
Schafft mein Mädchen her!	Cause my maiden to be brought here!
Klinget, Glöckchen, klinget!	Ring, little bells, ring,
Bringt mein Weibchen her!	Bring my little wife here!

(While the bells are playing the three boys run to their gondola and bring the woman forward.)

THE THREE BOYS

Nun, Papageno, sieh dich um!	Now, Papageno, look around!

(They travel off.)

(Papageno looks around; during the introduction, comic by-play between the two.)

PAPAGENO

Pa—Pa—Pa—Pa—Pa—Pa—
Papagena!

Pa—Pa—Pa—Pa—Pa—Pa—
Papagena!

PAPAGENA

Pa—Pa—Pa—Pa—Pa—Pa—
Papageno!

Pa—Pa—Pa—Pa—Pa—Pa—
Papageno!

PAPAGENO

Bist du mir nun ganz gegeben?

Are you finally completely mine?

PAPAGENA

Nun bin ich dir ganz gegeben!

I am finally completely yours!

PAPAGENO

Nun so sei mein liebes Weibchen!

Now be my beloved wife!

PAPAGENA

Nun, so sei mein Herzenstäubchen!

Now be my heart's little dove!

BOTH

Welche Freude wird das sein,
Wenn die Götter uns bedenken,
Unsrer Liebe Kinder schenken.
So liebe, kleine Kinderlein.

What joy it will be,
If the gods remember us,
Give us dear children,
Dear, little children.

PAPAGENO

Erst einen kleinen Papageno!

First a little Papageno!

PAPAGENA

Dann eine kleine Papagena.

Then a little Papagena!

PAPAGENO

Dann wieder einen Papageno.

Then another Papageno!

PAPAGENA

Dann wieder eine Papagena.

Then another Papagena!

BOTH

Papagena! Papageno! Papagena!
Es ist das höchste der Gefühle,
Wenn viele, viele, viele, viele
Pa—Pa—Pa—Pa—geno,
Pa—Pa—Pa—Pa—gena,
Der Eltern Segen werden sein.

Papagena! Papageno! Papagena!
That would be the greatest feeling,
If many, many, many, many
Pa—Pa—Pa—Pa—genos,
Pa—Pa—Pa—Pa—genas,
Would be the blessing of their parents.

(Both leave.)

Scene XXX

(The Moor, the queen with all of her ladies, come out of both traps; they carry black torches in their hands.)

Monostatos

Nur stille! Stille! Stille! Stille!
Bald dringen wir in Tempel ein.

Be quiet! Quiet! Quiet! Quiet!
Soon we will be entering the temple.

Queen and the Three Ladies

Nur stille! Stille! Stille! Stille!
Bald dringen wir in Tempel ein.

Be quiet! Quiet! Quiet! Quiet!
Soon we will be entering the temple.

Monostatos

Doch, Fürstin, halte Wort!—Erfülle!

Dein Kind muß meine Gattin sein.

But Your Majesty! Keep your word! Fulfill it!

Your child must be my wife.

Queen

Ich halte Wort; es ist mein Wille.
Mein Kind soll deine Gattin sein.

I keep my word; it is my will;
My child is to be your wife.

The Three Ladies

Ihr Kind soll deine Gattin sein.

Her child is to be your wife.

(Dull thunder and rushing water are heard.)

Monostatos

Doch still, ich höre schrecklich Rauschen
Wie Donnerton und Wasserfall.

Be still, I hear a terrible roaring
Like the sounds of thunder and waterfall.

Queen and Ladies

Ja, fürchterlich ist dieses Rauschen
Wie fernen Donners Widerhall!

Yes, dreadful is this roaring
Like the echo of distant thunder.

Monostatos

Nun sind sie in des Tempels Hallen.

Now they are within the temple's halls.

All

Dort wollen wir sie überfallen,
Die Frömmler tilgen von der Erd'
Mit Feuersglut und mächt'gem Schwert.

We will attack them there,
Eradicate the bigots from the earth
With glowing fire and mighty sword.

The Three Ladies and Monostatos

(kneeling)

Dir, große Königin der Nacht,
Sei unsrer Rache Opfer gebracht.

To you, great Queen of the Night,
Be our offering of vengeance made.

(A very loud chord is heard, thunder, lightning, storm. Immediately the whole stage set is changed into a sun. Sarastro stands in an elevated position; Tamino, Pamina, both in priestly raiment. Beside them on both sides, the Egyptian priests. The three boys are holding flowers.)

MONOSTATOS, QUEEN and THE THREE LADIES

Zerschmettert, zernichtet ist unsere Macht,	Smashed, annihilated is our power,
Wir alle gestürzet in ewige Nacht.	We all plunge into eternal night.

(They sink down.)

SARASTRO

Die Strahlen der Sonne vertreiben die Nacht,	The rays of the sun drive out the night,
Zernichten der Heuchler erschlichene Macht.	Annihilate the illicit power of the hypocrite.

CHORUS OF PRIESTS

Heil sei euch Geweihten!	Hail to thee, initiates!
Ihr dranget durch Nacht.	You have penetrated the night!
Dank sei dir, Osiris,	Thanks be to you, Osiris,
Dank dir, Isis, gebracht!	Thanks given to you, Isis!
Es siegte die Stärke	The mighty have conquered
Und krönet zum Lohn	And been rewarded with
Die Schönheit und Weisheit	The everlasting crowns
Mit ewiger Kron'!	Of beauty and wisdom!

The End